Machine Learning Applications in Non-Conventional Machining Processes

Goutam Kumar Bose
Haldia Institute of Technology, India

Pritam Pain
Haldia Institute of Technology, India

IGI Global
PUBLISHER of TIMELY KNOWLEDGE

A volume in the Advances in Computational Intelligence and Robotics (ACIR) Book Series

Published in the United States of America by
IGI Global
Engineering Science Reference (an imprint of IGI Global)
701 E. Chocolate Avenue
Hershey PA, USA 17033
Tel: 717-533-8845
Fax: 717-533-8661
E-mail: cust@igi-global.com
Web site: http://www.igi-global.com

Library of Congress Cataloging-in-Publication Data

Names: Bose, Goutam Kumar, 1970- editor. | Pain, Pritam, 1993- editor.
Title: Machine learning applications in non-conventional machining processes / Goutam Kumar Bose and Pritam Pain, editors.
Description: Hershey, PA : Engineering Science Reference, an imprint of IGI Global, [2020] | Includes bibliographical references and index. | Summary: "This book is a collection of research on the advancement of intelligent technology in industrial environments and its applications within the manufacturing field"-- Provided by publisher.
Identifiers: LCCN 2019057523 (print) | LCCN 2019057524 (ebook) | ISBN 9781799836247 (hardcover) | ISBN 9781799836254 (paperback) | ISBN 9781799836261 (ebook)
Subjects: LCSH: Machining--Data processing. | Machine learning.
Classification: LCC TJ1189 .M234 2020 (print) | LCC TJ1189 (ebook) | DDC 671.3/50285631--dc23
LC record available at https://lccn.loc.gov/2019057523
LC ebook record available at https://lccn.loc.gov/2019057524

This book is published in the IGI Global book series Advances in Computational Intelligence and Robotics (ACIR) (ISSN: 2327-0411; eISSN: 2327-042X)

British Cataloguing in Publication Data
A Cataloguing in Publication record for this book is available from the British Library.

Advances in Computational Intelligence and Robotics (ACIR) Book Series

Ivan Giannoccaro
University of Salento, Italy

ISSN:2327-0411
EISSN:2327-042X

Mission

While intelligence is traditionally a term applied to humans and human cognition, technology has progressed in such a way to allow for the development of intelligent systems able to simulate many human traits. With this new era of simulated and artificial intelligence, much research is needed in order to continue to advance the field and also to evaluate the ethical and societal concerns of the existence of artificial life and machine learning.

The **Advances in Computational Intelligence and Robotics (ACIR) Book Series** encourages scholarly discourse on all topics pertaining to evolutionary computing, artificial life, computational intelligence, machine learning, and robotics. ACIR presents the latest research being conducted on diverse topics in intelligence technologies with the goal of advancing knowledge and applications in this rapidly evolving field.

Coverage

- Synthetic Emotions
- Pattern Recognition
- Artificial Life
- Computational Logic
- Brain Simulation
- Cognitive Informatics
- Machine Learning
- Fuzzy Systems
- Natural Language Processing
- Cyborgs

IGI Global is currently accepting manuscripts for publication within this series. To submit a proposal for a volume in this series, please contact our Acquisition Editors at Acquisitions@igi-global.com or visit: http://www.igi-global.com/publish/.

The Advances in Computational Intelligence and Robotics (ACIR) Book Series (ISSN 2327-0411) is published by IGI Global, 701 E. Chocolate Avenue, Hershey, PA 17033-1240, USA, www.igi-global.com. This series is composed of titles available for purchase individually; each title is edited to be contextually exclusive from any other title within the series. For pricing and ordering information please visit http://www.igi-global.com/book-series/advances-computational-intelligence-robotics/73674. Postmaster: Send all address changes to above address.

Titles in this Series

For a list of additional titles in this series, please visit:
http://www.igi-global.com/book-series/advances-computational-intelligence-robotics/73674

Artificial Neural Network Applications in Business and Engineering
Quang Hung Do (University of Transport Technology, Vietnam)
Engineering Science Reference • © 2021 • 275pp • H/C (ISBN: 9781799832386) • US $245.00

Multimedia and Sensory Input for Augmented, Mixed, and Virtual Reality
Amit Kumar Tyagi (Research Division of Advanced Data Science, Vellore Institute of Technolgy, Chennai, India)
Engineering Science Reference • © 2021 • 310pp • H/C (ISBN: 9781799847038) • US $225.00

Cases on Edge Computing and Analytics
Paranthaman Ambika (Kristu Jayanti College, India) A. Cecil Donald (Kristu Jayanti College, India) and A. Dalvin Vinoth Kumar (Kristu Jayanti College, India)
Engineering Science Reference • © 2021 • 320pp • H/C (ISBN: 9781799848738) • US $215.00

Handbook of Research on Deep Learning-Based Image Analysis Under Constrained and Unconstrained Environments
Alex Noel Joseph Raj (Shantou University, China) Vijayalakshmi G. V. Mahesh (BMS Institute of Technology and Management, India) and Ruban Nersisson (Vellore Institute of Technology, India)
Engineering Science Reference • © 2021 • 381pp • H/C (ISBN: 9781799866909) • US $295.00

AI Tools and Electronic Virtual Assistants for Improved Business Performance
Christian Graham (University of Maine, USA)
Business Science Reference • © 2021 • 300pp • H/C (ISBN: 9781799838418) • US $245.00

Advanced Concepts, Methods, and Applications in Semantic Computing
Olawande Daramola (Cape Peninsula University of Technology, South Africa) and Thomas Moser (St. Pölten University of Applied Sciences, Austria)
Engineering Science Reference • © 2021 • 305pp • H/C (ISBN: 9781799866978) • US $215.00

Applications of Artificial Intelligence for Smart Technology
P. Swarnalatha (Vellore Institute of Technology, Vellore, India) and S. Prabu (Vellore Institute of Technology, Vellore, India)
Engineering Science Reference • © 2021 • 330pp • H/C (ISBN: 9781799833352) • US $215.00

IGI Global
PUBLISHER of TIMELY KNOWLEDGE

701 East Chocolate Avenue, Hershey, PA 17033, USA
Tel: 717-533-8845 x100 • Fax: 717-533-8661
E-Mail: cust@igi-global.com • www.igi-global.com

Editorial Advisory Board

Table of Contents

Foreword xviii

Preface xix

Acknowledgment xxv

Chapter 1
Parametric Optimization of Dry Laser Cleaning Using Metaheuristics Processes: To Study the Effect of Laser Cleaning Parameters on Surface Temperature Rise and Thermo-Elastic Force 1
Pritam Pain, Haldia Institute of Technology, India
Goutam Kumar Bose, Haldia Institute of Technology, India
Sayantan Roy, Haldia Institute of Technology, India

Chapter 2
MCDM-Based Optimization of Performance Characteristics During µEDMing of SS 304 18
Premangshu Mukhopadhyay, Haldia Institute of Technology, India
Goutam Kumar Bose, Haldia Institute of Technology, India
Pritam Pain, Haldia Institute of Technology, India

Chapter 3
Multi-Objective Optimization of EDM Process on AISI P-20 Tool Steel Using Multi-Criteria Decision-Making Technique 33
Souvick Chakraborty, Bengal Institute of Technology and Management, India

Chapter 4
Analysis of Performance Characteristics by Firefly Algorithm-Based Electro Discharge Machining of SS 316 45
Premangshu Mukhopadhyay, Haldia Institute of Technology, India

Chapter 5
Programming for Machining in Electrical Discharge Machine: A Non-Conventional Machining Technique 55
Chikesh Ranjan, RTC Institute of Technology, India
Hridayjit Kalita, Birla Institute of Technology, Mesra, India
T. Vishnu Vardhan, CMR Institute of Technology, India
Kaushik Kumar, Birla Institute of Technology, Mesra, India

Chapter 6
Multi-Objective Optimization in WEDM of Al 7075 Alloy Using TOPSIS and GRA Method 76
K. Mandal, Jadavpur University, India
S. Sarkar, Jadavpur University, India
S. Mitra, Jadavpur University, India
Dipankar Bose, National Institute of Technical Teachers' Training and Research, Kolkata, India

Chapter 7
Experimental Evaluation on Corner Accuracy in WEDM for Aluminium 6061 Alloy 96
Debal Pramanik, Jadavpur University, India
Dipankar Bose, National Institute of Technical Teachers' Training and Research, Kolkata, India

Chapter 8
Evaluation of Surface Roughness in Wire Electrical Discharge Turning Process 114
Sibabrata Mondal, Society for Applied Microwave Electronics Engineering and Research (SAMEER), Kolkata, India
Dipankar Bose, National Institute of Technical Teachers' Training and Research (NITTTR), Kolkata, India

Chapter 9
Laser Trepan Drilling of Monel k-500 Superalloy in Low Power Laser Beam Machining 137
D. Pramanik, Jadavpur University, India
N. Roy, Jadavpur University, India
A. S. Kuar, Jadavpur University, India
S. Sarkar, Jadavpur University, India
S. Mitra, Jadavpur University, India
Dipankar Bose, National Institute of Technical Teachers' Training and Research (NITTTR), Kolkata, India

Chapter 10
Experimental Investigation on Laser Transmission Welding of Polycarbonate and Acrylic 160
Dhiraj Kumar, Jadavpur University, India
Sudipta Paitandi, Jadavpur University, India
Arunanshu Shekhar Kuar, Jadavpur University, India
Dipankar Bose, National Institute of Technical Teachers' Training and Research (NITTTR), Kolkata, India

Chapter 11
Application of Evolutionary Optimization Techniques Towards Non-Traditional Machining for Performance Enhancement 181
Chikesh Ranjan, RTC Institute of Technology, India
Hridayjit Kalita, Birla Institute of Technology, Mesra, India
B. Sridhar Babu, CMR Institute of Technology, India
Kaushik Kumar, Birla Institute of Technology, Mesra, India

Chapter 12
Analysis of Non-Traditional Machining Processes Using Machine Learning 195
Somnath Das, Swami Vivekananda Institute of Science and Technology, India

Chapter 13
Role of Non-Traditional Machining Equipment in Industry 4.0 203
Tarun Kanti Jana, Haldia Institute of Technology, India

Chapter 14
Finite Element-Based Optimization of Additive Manufacturing Process Using Statistical Modelling and League of Champion Algorithm 215
Anoop Kumar Sood, National Institute of Foundry and Forge Technology, India

Chapter 15
A Novel Approach Towards Selection of Role Model Cluster Head for Power Management in WSN 235
Ramkrishna Ghosh, KIIT University (Deemed), India
Suneeta Mohanty, KIIT University (Deemed), India
Prasant Kumar Pattnaik, KIIT University (Deemed), India
Sabyasachi Pramanik, Haldia Institute of Technology, India

Chapter 16
Synthesis and Characterization of Nanocomposites for the Application in Hybrid Solar Cell 250
Sakshi Tyagi, Haldia Institute of Technology, India
Pawan Kumar Singh, Indian Institute of Technology (Indian School of Mines), Dhanbad, India
Arun Kumar Tiwari, Institute of Engineering and Technology, Lucknow, India

Chapter 17
Intelligent Investment Approaches for Mutual Funds: An Evolutionary Model 267
Dipankar Majumdar, RCC Institute of Information Technology, India
Arup Kumar Bhattacharjee, RCC Institute of Information Technology, India
Soumen Mukherjee, RCC Institute of Information Technology, India

Compilation of References 282

About the Contributors 305

Index 311

Detailed Table of Contents

Foreword xviii

Preface xix

Acknowledgment xxv

Chapter 1
Parametric Optimization of Dry Laser Cleaning Using Metaheuristics Processes: To Study the Effect of Laser Cleaning Parameters on Surface Temperature Rise and Thermo-Elastic Force 1
Pritam Pain, Haldia Institute of Technology, India
Goutam Kumar Bose, Haldia Institute of Technology, India
Sayantan Roy, Haldia Institute of Technology, India

The workpiece sample which is a copper printed circuit board (PCB) is mounted on a micro-controlled assembly with double-faced adhesive tape. Here the primary objective is to study the effect of laser cleaning parameters on surface temperature rise and thermoelastic force. The variation of instantaneous temperature rise and thermoelastic force with time using different process parameters (e.g., type of power, focal length, and scanning speed) at a constant absorption coefficient is also investigated, and the best parametric combination have been found out in this experiment. After successful completion of the experimentation, it is observed that the surface temperature increases with the increase in laser power. The maximum temperature rise is observed when the laser power is maximum, and the focal length is minimum. It is further observed that the thermoelastic force increases with the increase in laser power. Maximum thermoelastic force is observed when the laser power is maximum, and the focal length is minimum.

Chapter 2
MCDM-Based Optimization of Performance Characteristics During μEDMing of SS 304 18
Premangshu Mukhopadhyay, Haldia Institute of Technology, India
Goutam Kumar Bose, Haldia Institute of Technology, India
Pritam Pain, Haldia Institute of Technology, India

Micro-EDM is most widely used for developing perfect drilled micro features/parts. Research was carried out to improve the material removal and tool wear of any conductive machined product by EDM and micro-EDM process. In this chapter, RSM was used for designing the experiments with 20 set of experiments. In this present research work, performance characteristics like MRR and Overcut have got a different level of importance. Here the stress was given on MRR rather than on OC. In this MCDM analysis, the weight of MRR is considered to be maximum (i.e., larger is better), and other weights of other responses are considered to be the minimum (i.e., smaller is better). Finally, in the midst of all the combinations of process parameters considered one that acquires the highest grey relational grade is the best parametric combination. The research findings in the area of machining of stainless steel 304 will be helpful to manufacturing engineers for selecting the optimized parametric combinations of micro-EDM process with stainless steel.

Chapter 3
Multi-Objective Optimization of EDM Process on AISI P-20 Tool Steel Using Multi-Criteria Decision-Making Technique 33
Souvick Chakraborty, Bengal Institute of Technology and Management, India

The optimization technique is introduced to overcome the problem. Here the author introduces multi-criteria decision-making technique to get the optimization value. Electrical discharge machining (EDM) in nontraditional machining process is applied for machining complicated or intricate geometries on raw materials. The present work attempts to optimize several responses of machining operation using multi-criteria decision making (MCDM) by employing different machining parameters like current, voltage, pulse. The Taguchi L9 orthogonal experimental design is followed during electrical discharge machining of AISI P20 tool steel. Four responses, namely metal removal rate, tool life, surface roughness, and over cut, are considered for optimization. The present work is aimed at multi-response optimization (i.e., higher MRR, higher tool life, lower surface roughness, and minimum overcut), which is conducted using MCDM technique.

Chapter 4
Analysis of Performance Characteristics by Firefly Algorithm-Based Electro Discharge Machining of SS 316 45
Premangshu Mukhopadhyay, Haldia Institute of Technology, India

The process of combining two or more non-conventional machining processes to obtain the required machining performance is known as hybridisation. Hybrid electro discharge machining came into the picture of macro machining due to the requirement of more rapid machining process with improved efficiency of non-conventional machining process. The technique of vibration assisted EDM process did not prove to be successful due to some disadvantages like increase in tool wear for low melting and comparatively softer tool material. Therefore, a need for more advanced hybridised process has been realized to improve the overall machining efficiency specially circularity and radial overcut. A permanent magnetic field force assisted EDM process was carried out on SS 316 plate with tungsten carbide tool of 5 mm diameter. MRR, TWR, and diametral overcut have been optimized by firefly algorithm technique which showed satisfactory results. It has been found that tool wear and diametral overcut has been found to be reduced with magnetic field-assisted EDM than conventional EDM processes.

Chapter 5
Programming for Machining in Electrical Discharge Machine: A Non-Conventional Machining Technique 55
Chikesh Ranjan, RTC Institute of Technology, India
Hridayjit Kalita, Birla Institute of Technology, Mesra, India
T. Vishnu Vardhan, CMR Institute of Technology, India
Kaushik Kumar, Birla Institute of Technology, Mesra, India

The correct selection of manufacturing conditions is one of the most important aspects to take into consideration in most manufacturing processes and, particularly, in processes related to electrical discharge machining (EDM). It is a capable of machining geometrically complex or hard material components that are precise and difficult-to-machine such as heat-treated tool steels, composites, super alloys, ceramics, carbides, heat resistant steels, etc. being widely used in die and mold making industries, aerospace, aeronautics, and nuclear industries. This chapter highlights the programming for machining in electrical discharge machine.

Chapter 6
Multi-Objective Optimization in WEDM of Al 7075 Alloy Using TOPSIS and GRA Method 76
K. Mandal, Jadavpur University, India
S. Sarkar, Jadavpur University, India
S. Mitra, Jadavpur University, India
Dipankar Bose, National Institute of Technical Teachers' Training and Research, Kolkata, India

In this research study, Taguchi grey relational analysis (GRA) has been coupled with the technique for order of preference by similarity to ideal solution (TOPSIS) to optimize the multi-performance characteristics in WEDM of Al 7075 alloy. The influence of process factors such as pulse duration (Ton), pulse interval (Toff), flushing pressure (Fp), and servo voltage (Sv) on output responses machining speed (Vc) and corner inaccuracy (Ce) have been considered. The analysis of variance (ANOVA) for the grey relational grade (GRG) and order of preference value generated by TOPSIS have been carried out to justify the optimal results. The recommended input factor settings are found to be Ton = 1.1 μs, Toff = 20 μs, Fp = 9 kg/cm2, and Sv = 20 volt from TOPSIS, and from GRA is Ton = 1.1 μs, Toff = 10 μs, Fp = 12 kg/cm2, and Sv = 40 volt. Finally, surface roughness and surface topography evaluation have been carried out in-depth understanding of influencing factors.

Chapter 7
Experimental Evaluation on Corner Accuracy in WEDM for Aluminium 6061 Alloy 96
Debal Pramanik, Jadavpur University, India
Dipankar Bose, National Institute of Technical Teachers' Training and Research, Kolkata, India

An important electro-thermal process known as wire electrical discharge machining (WEDM) is applied for machining of conductive materials to generate most precisely. All cutting inaccuracies of WEDM arise out of the major cause of wire bending. At the time of cutting a sharp corner or cut profile, bending of the wire leads to a geometrical error on the workpiece. Though this type of error may be of a few hundred microns, it is not suitable for micro applications. In this research study, an experimental investigation based on response surface methodology (RSM) has been done on wire EDM of Aluminium 6061 t6 alloy. This chapter studies the outcome of input process variables (i.e., wire feed rate, pulse on time, pulse off time, and gap voltage) on machining output responses (i.e., corner inaccuracy) extensively. Experimental validation of the proposed model shows that corner inaccuracy value may be reduced by modification of input parameters.

Chapter 8
Evaluation of Surface Roughness in Wire Electrical Discharge Turning Process............................ 114
Sibabrata Mondal, Society for Applied Microwave Electronics Engineering and Research (SAMEER), Kolkata, India
Dipankar Bose, National Institute of Technical Teachers' Training and Research (NITTTR), Kolkata, India

This investigation presents an experimental investigation in developing small cylindrical pins in electrolytic tough pitch copper (ETP Cu) material using wire electrical discharge turning (WEDT) to evaluate surface roughness of the cylindrical turning faces. The material ETP Cu is soft in nature and has growing range of application in the field of aerospace and electronics industries for advanced applications. In this process, a customized rotary spindle has been developed and added to five-axis CNC wire electrical discharge machine (WEDM) and straight turning of the cylindrical pin has been done up to a length of 15mm with 0.5mm diameter. Under this investigation, 31 experiments along with two confirmation tests have been carried out to study the influence of four design factors—pulse on time, pulse off time, spindle speed, and servo voltage—on the machining performance of surface roughness by means the technique of design of experiment (DOE).

Chapter 9
Laser Trepan Drilling of Monel k-500 Superalloy in Low Power Laser Beam Machining............... 137
D. Pramanik, Jadavpur University, India
N. Roy, Jadavpur University, India
A. S. Kuar, Jadavpur University, India
S. Sarkar, Jadavpur University, India
S. Mitra, Jadavpur University, India
Dipankar Bose, National Institute of Technical Teachers' Training and Research (NITTTR), Kolkata, India

In the field of micro processing of materials, laser has great importance as a source of heat and for its ability to deliver a coherent beam. The use of 50-watt average power for through-hole is impossible to achieve good quality drilling of the metal sheet upto 2 mm thickness. But the use of unique parameter sawing angle and constant focal point distance plays a significant role on hole diameter and circularity in laser trepan drilling. In the present research study, laser trepan drilling is investigated through multi diode pulsed fiber laser beam machining. Experimental analysis based on central composite design (CCD) of response surface methodology (RSM) has been fulfilled to find out the mathematical model. A study of the effect of sawing angle with other process parameters such as cutting speed, power, duty cycle, and pulse frequency on overcut bottom diameter and circularity at bottom for a monel k-500 has been conducted. Experimental validation of the proposed model shows that desired hole quality can be obtained by optimization of controllable of suitable process parameters.

Chapter 10
Experimental Investigation on Laser Transmission Welding of Polycarbonate and Acrylic............ 160
Dhiraj Kumar, Jadavpur University, India
Sudipta Paitandi, Jadavpur University, India
Arunanshu Shekhar Kuar, Jadavpur University, India
Dipankar Bose, National Institute of Technical Teachers' Training and Research (NITTTR), Kolkata, India

This chapter presents the effect of various process parameters, namely laser power, pulse frequency, and welding speed, on the weld shear strength and weld width using a diode laser system. Here, laser transmission welding of transparent polycarbonate and black carbon filled acrylic each of 2.8 mm thickness have been performed to create lap joint by using low power laser. Response surface methodology is applied to develop the mathematical model between the laser welding process parameters and the responses of weld joint. The developed mathematical model is tested for its adequacy using analysis of variance and other adequacy measures. It has been observed that laser power and welding speed are the dominant factor followed by frequency. A confirmation test has also been conducted to validate the experimental results at optimum parameter setting. Results show that weld strength of 34.3173 N/mm and weld width of 2.61547 mm have been achieved at optimum parameter setting using desirability function-based optimization technique.

Chapter 11
Application of Evolutionary Optimization Techniques Towards Non-Traditional Machining for Performance Enhancement 181
Chikesh Ranjan, RTC Institute of Technology, India
Hridayjit Kalita, Birla Institute of Technology, Mesra, India
B. Sridhar Babu, CMR Institute of Technology, India
Kaushik Kumar, Birla Institute of Technology, Mesra, India

Electro-chemical machining is a non-conventional machining method that is used for machining of very complicated shape. In this chapter an attempt has been made to carry out multi-objective optimization of the surface roughness (SR) and material removal rate (MRR) for the ECM process of EN 19 on a CNC ECM machine using copper electrode through evolutionary optimization techniques like teaching-learning-based optimization (TLBO) technique and biogeography-based optimization (BBO) technique. The input parameters considered are electrolyte concentration, voltage, feed rate, inter-electrode gap. TLBO and BBO techniques were used to obtain maximum MRR and minimum SR. In addition, obtained optimized values were validated for testing the significance of the TLBO and BBO techniques, and a very small error value of MRR and SR was found. BBO outperformed TLBO in every aspect like less percentage error and better-optimized values; however, TLBO took less computation time than the BBO.

Chapter 12
Analysis of Non-Traditional Machining Processes Using Machine Learning................................ 195
Somnath Das, Swami Vivekananda Institute of Science and Technology, India

The nature of manufacturing systems faces increasingly complex dynamics to meet the demand for high quality products efficiently. One area, which experienced rapid development in terms not only of promising results but also of usability, is machine learning. New developments in certain domains such as mathematics, computer science, and the availability of easy-to-use tools, often freely available, offer great potential to transform the non-traditional machining domain and its understanding of the increase in manufacturing data. However, the field is very broad and even confusing, which presents a challenge and a barrier that hinders wide application. Here, this chapter helps to present an overview of the available machine learning techniques for improving the non-traditional machining process area. It provides a basis for the subsequent argument that the machine learning is a suitable tool for manufacturers to face these challenges head-on in non-traditional machining processes.

Chapter 13
Role of Non-Traditional Machining Equipment in Industry 4.0 203
Tarun Kanti Jana, Haldia Institute of Technology, India

The manufacturing industry is undergoing drastic changes owing to a steep rise in business competition and growing complexities in other business perspectives. The highly turbulent market is characterized by ever-increasing mass customization, wide volume-mix, shorter lead time, and low cost, which along with varieties of internal disturbances have complicated the business stability. The multi-agent-based systems comprising of fundamental entities called agents and characterized by autonomy, cooperation, and self-organizing abilities have already made remarkable breakthrough to deal with the challenges through increased robustness, scalability, and enhanced adaptability through their dynamic capabilities. The decision-making ability of the agents can be augmented if equipped with cognitive abilities like that of human beings. The chapter discusses cyber-physical production system (CPPS) to realize cognitive manufacturing in non-conventional machining environments.

Chapter 14
Finite Element-Based Optimization of Additive Manufacturing Process Using Statistical Modelling and League of Champion Algorithm... 215
Anoop Kumar Sood, National Institute of Foundry and Forge Technology, India

The study develops a 2D (two-dimensional) finite element model with a Gaussian heat source to simulate powder bed-based laser additive manufacturing process of Ti6Al4V alloy. The modelling approach provides insight into the process by correlating laser power and scan speed with melt pool temperature distribution and size. To tackle the FEA result in optimization environment, statistical approach of data normalization and regression modelling is adopted. Statistical treatment is not only able to deduce the interdependence of various objectives consider but also make the representation of objectives and constraint computationally simple. Adoption of a new stochastic algorithm namely league of a champion algorithm (LCA) together with penalty function approach for non-linear constraint handling reduces the effort required and computational complexity involved in determining the optimum parameter setting.

Chapter 15
A Novel Approach Towards Selection of Role Model Cluster Head for Power Management in WSN... 235
Ramkrishna Ghosh, KIIT University (Deemed), India
Suneeta Mohanty, KIIT University (Deemed), India
Prasant Kumar Pattnaik, KIIT University (Deemed), India
Sabyasachi Pramanik, Haldia Institute of Technology, India

In this chapter, the authors present an innovative, smart controller to sustain mobility in wireless sensor networks (WSNs). Principally, the focal point is dependent on the arrangement of fuzzy input variables (i.e., remaining battery power [RBP], mobility, and centrality solution) to crucial usages, similar to personnel safety in an industrialized atmosphere. A mobility controller dependent upon type-1 fuzzy logic (T1FL) is planned to support sensor mobile nodes (MN). Here, a role model cluster head (RMCH) is picked out among the cluster heads (CHs) that may simply convey the message to the mobile base station (BS) by determining the appropriate type-1 fuzzy (T1F) descriptors such as RBP, mobility of the sink, and the centrality of the clusters. Type-1 fuzzy inference system (Mamdani's rule) is utilized to opt for the possibility to be RMCH. The validity of the introduced model is carried out by means of multiple linear regressions.

Chapter 16
Synthesis and Characterization of Nanocomposites for the Application in Hybrid Solar Cell 250
Sakshi Tyagi, Haldia Institute of Technology, India
Pawan Kumar Singh, Indian Institute of Technology (Indian School of Mines), Dhanbad, India
Arun Kumar Tiwari, Institute of Engineering and Technology, Lucknow, India

In today's era, a lot of interest is gained by solar cell formed by combination of organic and inorganic nano-particle semiconductors mainly because of its major features such as scalable solar power conversion and cost effectiveness, which makes the cell a desirable photovoltaic device. This piece of work is an attempt to make a solar cells by the combination of zinc oxide (ZnO) and graphite. ZnO is a good n-type material for the application in photovoltaic (PV) devices due to its better optical, electrical, structural, and environmentally friendly properties, and on the other hand, graphite, an organic semiconductor, enhances the rate of charge transfer in the device. These materials are so designed to help bring in more understanding in a wider range of the solar spectrum. This work focuses on developing solid-state polymer and hybrid solar cells.

Chapter 17
Intelligent Investment Approaches for Mutual Funds: An Evolutionary Model 267
Dipankar Majumdar, RCC Institute of Information Technology, India
Arup Kumar Bhattacharjee, RCC Institute of Information Technology, India
Soumen Mukherjee, RCC Institute of Information Technology, India

Investment in the right fund at the right time happens to be the key to success in the stock trading business. Therefore, for strategic investment, the selection of the right opportunity has to be executed crucially so as to reap the maximum returns from the market. Predicting the stock market has always been known to be very critical and needs years of experience as it involves lots of interleaving parameters and constraints. Intelligent investment in mutual funds (MF) can be done when various machine learning tools are used to predict future fund value using the past fund value. In this chapter, an elaborate discussion is presented on the different types of mutual funds and how these data can be used in prediction by machine learning in different literature. In this work, the NAV of a total of 17 different mutual funds have been extracted from the website of AMFI, and thereafter, ANFIS is used to forecast the time series of the NAV of the MF. They have been trained using ANFIS and thereafter tested for prediction with satisfactory results.

Compilation of References 282

About the Contributors 305

Index 311

Foreword

In the increasingly comparative environment of the day machine learning has become a key to industry 4.0. The rapid advancement in the field of optimization technique various nature-inspired algorithms/ metaheuristics have evolved aimed at developing highly sophisticated machine learning tools to enhance productivity. In such an environment a systematic program to train the machine resources to prepare them to competitive enough to face this challenge becomes a key issue. Many machine learning applications have been developed such as image processing in the manufacturing industry for automation in the assembly line, biometric recognition, pattern recognition, text retrieval, speech recognition and so on. In industry collecting huge volumes of historical data portraying their operations, products and customers take place regularly. The field of machine learning addresses the question of how best to use this historical data to discover the general patterns and improve the process of making decisions.

I'm pleased and proud to introduce this book. It will fulfill a much-needed niche in machine learning textbook under and postgraduate and also for those in engineering practice. There is a significant advancement in theory and algorithms that form the foundations of machine learning filed. This textbook presents the basic concept of the theory and a variety of algorithms that can be implemented in several non-traditional machining processes. It is now well established that the conventional machining methods are unable to mid the challenges posed by the demand for economics machining of ultra-hard and ultra-strength materials to close tolerances. Non-Traditional Machining has evolved as a game-changer in modern machining technology.

On account of the importance of these cutting-edge technologies in modern manufacturing systems, non-conventional machining methods are now included in the curriculum of most graduate and post-graduate courses in the country and abroad. Applications of machine learning toward non-conventional machining provide necessary ingrediency for understanding the concepts and techniques while solving real-life problems.

The coverage of this book establishes the strong desire of the authors to methodically link the concepts to the processes and display the complete subject in a logical sequence. I congratulate the authors for bringing out their experience and expertise in the form of this book for the benefits of practicing engineers and students. I understand that many technical institutions and universities have introduced machine learning and non-conventional machining in their curriculum. I'm sure that the industrial expertise and wealth of knowledge presented in this book will fulfill the long full need of the students and engineers in understanding and applications of this concept.

Asim Kumar Bose
Mechanical Engineering Department, IIST, Shibpur, India

Preface

AN OVERVIEW OF THE SUBJECT MATTER

To overcome the limitation of the Traditional machining, Non-Traditional machining has immersed as potential machining techniques. However, with the advent of new technologies related to machining and ignoramus development in the field of material science the evolution of hybrid technology came in to being. During the process of Non-Traditional machining huge amount of data gets generated. In order to satisfy the objective function during the process various optimization techniques are applied. Machine learning is one such growing technology which is used to mine knowledge from data. It is mend from automatic learning from various data set. Statistical Learning Algorithms are advanced tools and models which are currently used, rather than relying on classical and trial and error methods, in order to enhance quality of engineering processes and productivity. Optimization techniques are commonly used as a part of machine learning algorithm. Some learning algorithms are inspired from nature for the development of novel problem-solving techniques.

Artificial intelligence based random search algorithms, namely, Genetic Algorithm, Ant Colony Optimization and so forth have found their applicability in solving various Non-Traditional Machining problems of complex nature.

A DESCRIPTION OF WHERE YOUR TOPIC FITS IN THE WORLD TODAY

In the field of machine learning significant advancement is observed related to its theory and algorithm. The primary focus of this text book is to portray the application of the various algorithms of machine learning in the field of nontraditional machining. Machine learning is finding its application in all sphere in life.

A DESCRIPTION OF THE TARGET AUDIENCE

This book is ideally designed for manufacturing managers, engineers, researchers, and academicians seeking current research on non-conventional and technologically advanced machining processes and modern computing techniques.

A DESCRIPTION OF THE IMPORTANCE OF EACH OF THE CHAPTER SUBMISSIONS

Chapter 1 describes the parametric optimization of dry laser cleaning using metaheuristics processes. Here a copper PCB is taken as workpiece and then mounted on a micro controlled assembly with the help of an adhesive tape. In this research work a study is conducted to observe the effect of laser cleaning parameters on surface temperature rise and thermoelastic force. The variation of instantaneous temperature rise and thermoelastic force with respect to time are investigated. The various process parameters considered here are type of power, focal length and scanning speed at a constant absorption coefficient. The best parametric combination is determined. It is revealed that surface temperature increases with the increase in laser power.

The maximum temperature rise is observed when the laser power is maximum, and the focal length is minimum. It is further observed that the thermoelastic force increases with the increase in laser power. Maximum thermoelastic force is observed when the laser power is maximum, and the focal length is minimum.

Chapter 2 introduces MCDM based Optimization of Performance Characteristics during µEDMing of SS 304. µEDM has gained importance in recent times for drilling micro features / parts. Here research is carried out to increase the MRR and minimize the tool wear of any conductive machined product by EDM and micro-EDM process. In this chapter, RSM has been used for designing the experiments by performing 20 set of experiments. Here performance characteristics like MRR and Overcut have got a different level of importance. Here the priority has been given on MRR rather than on OC. In this MCDM analysis, the weight of MRR is considered to be maximum i.e. larger is better and other weights of other responses are considered to be the minimum, i.e. smaller is better. Finally, amongst all the combinations of process parameters considered one that attains the highest grey relational grade is considered to be the best parametric combination. The findings as obtained here in the area of machining of stainless steel 304 will be beneficial to manufacturing engineers for selecting the optimized parametric combinations of micro-EDM process with stainless steel.

Chapter 3 presents Multi-Objective Optimization of EDM process on AISI P-20 Tool Steel Using Multi Criteria Decision Making Technique. Today the manufacturing world is dependent on high production rate. In order to overcome this challenge optimization techniques in the form of multi criteria decision making are applied. Electrical Discharge Machining (EDM) in nontraditional machining process applied for machining complicated or intricate geometries on raw materials. The present research study several responses of machining operation using Multi Criteria Decision Making (MCDM) are optimized through different machining parameters like current, voltage, pulse. The Taguchi L9 orthogonal experimental design is followed during Electrical Discharge Machining of AISI P20 tool steel. Four responses namely Metal Removal Rate, Tool Life, Surface Roughness and Over Cut are considered for optimization. The present work is intended to determine the multi-response optimization of high MRR, high Tool life, low Surface roughness and minimum Overcut.

Chapter 4 discusses the analysis of performance characteristics by Firefly Algorithm based Electro Discharge Machining of SS 316. Hybridization is the process of combining two or more non-conventional machining processes in order to obtain the required machining. Hybrid electro discharge machining came into the limelight of macro machining due to its rapid machining capability with improved efficiency of non-conventional machining process. Earlier the technique of vibration assisted EDM process proved to be non-satisfactory due to some drawbacks like increase in tool wear for low melting and comparatively softer tool material. Therefore, the necessity for more advanced hybridized process has been appreciated to enhance the overall machining efficiency specially circularity and radial overcut. A permanent magnetic field force assisted EDM process is performed on SS 316 plate with tungsten carbide tool of 5 mm diameter. Responses like MRR, TWR and diametral overcut is optimized by applying firefly algorithm technique which exhibited satisfactory results. It is observed that tool wear and diametral overcut reduced with magnetic field assisted EDM as compared to the conventional EDM process.

Chapter 5 describes the Programming for Machining in Electrical Discharge Machine: A Non – Conventional Machining Technique. One of the most vital aspect of manufacturing is to identify its right condition. Electrical Discharge Machining (EDM) is one such non traditional machining process with which geometrically complex or hard material components, that are precise and difficult-to-machine such as heat-treated tool steels, composites, super alloys, ceramics, carbides, heat resistant steels etc. being widely used in die and mold making industries, aerospace, aeronautics and nuclear industries can be machined. In this chapter the programming techniques of EDM has been portrayed.

Chapter 6 presents the Taguchi grey relational analysis (GRA) along with the technique for order of preference by similarity to ideal solution (TOPSIS) for optimizing the multi-performance characteristics in WEDM of Al 7075 alloy. The effect of process parameters such as pulse duration (Ton), pulse interval (Toff), flushing pressure (Fp) and servo voltage (Sv) on output response machining speed (Vc) and corner inaccuracy (Ce) are considered. The analysis of variance (ANOVA) for the grey relational grade (GRG) and order of preference value generated by TOPSIS is conducted to validate the optimal results. Finally, surface roughness and surface topography estimation is performed thoroughly for identifying the influencing factors.

Chapter 7 discusses the experimental evaluation on corner accuracy in WEDM for aluminium 6061 alloy. Wire Electrical Discharge Machining (WEDM) is an electro-thermal process for accurate machining of conductive materials. In WEDM machining imprecisions result from wire bending. This generally happens during machining sharp corners or intricate profiles on the workpiece. Although this type of error apparently seems negligible but it cannot be accepted in micro machining. Here an experimental investigation based on response surface methodology (RSM) is done on wire EDM of Aluminium 6061 t6 alloy. To study the outcome of input process variables i.e. wire feed rate, pulse on time, pulse off time and gap voltage on machining output responses i.e. corner inaccuracy extensively. Experimental validation of the proposed models highlights that corner inaccuracy value can be reduced by modification of input parameters.

Chapter 8 introduces the evaluation of surface roughness in wire electrical discharge turning process. Here an experimental investigation in developing small cylindrical pins in electrolytic tough pitch copper (ETP Cu) material using wire electrical discharge turning (WEDT) to evaluate surface roughness of the cylindrical turning faces is done. Since the material ETP Cu is soft in nature hence it is widely applied in the field of aerospace and electronics industries. Here a customized rotary spindle is developed and added to five-axis CNC wire electrical discharge machine (WEDM) and straight turning of the cylindrical pin is performed up to a length of 15mm with 0.5mm diameter. Finally, 31 numbers of experiments along with 2 numbers of confirmation tests is conducted and the influence of four design factors pulse on time, pulse off time, spindle speed and servo voltage on surface roughness is done by applying design of experiment (DOE).

Chapter 9 presents Laser trepan drilling of monel k500 superalloy in low power laser beam machining: Low power laser beam machining. In the field of micro processing of materials, laser has got great importance as a source of heat and for its ability to deliver coherent beam. Use of 50-watt average power for through-hole is impossible to achieve good quality drilling of the metal sheet upto 2 mm thickness. But the use of unique parameter sawing angle and constant focal point distance play a significant role on hole diameter and circularity in laser trepan drilling. In the present research study laser trepan drilling is investigated through multi diode pulsed fiber laser beam machining. Experimental analysis based on Central Composite Design (CCD) of Response Surface Methodology (RSM) has been fulfilled to find out the mathematical model. Study of the effect of sawing angle with other process parameters such as cutting speed, power, duty cycle and pulse frequency on overcut bottom diameter and circularity at bottom for a monel k-500 has been conducted. Experimental validation of the proposed model shows that desired hole quality can be obtained by optimization of controllable of suitable process parameters.

Chapter 10 describes the experimental Investigation on Laser transmission welding of Polycarbonate and Acrylic. Here the effect of various process parameters, namely, laser power, pulse frequency and welding speed are studied on the weld shear strength and weld width using a diode laser system. The laser transmission welding of transparent polycarbonate and black carbon filled acrylic each of 2.8 mm thickness is performed to create lap joint by using low power laser. Response surface methodology is utilised to explain the mathematical model between the laser welding process parameters and the responses of weld joint. The developed mathematical model is tested for its adequacy using analysis of variance and other adequacy measures. It has been found that laser power and welding speed are the dominant factor followed by frequency. A confirmation test is also conducted to validate the experimental results at optimum parameter setting. Results show that weld strength of 34.3173 N/mm and weld width of 2.61547 mm is achieved at optimum parameter setting using Desirability function-based optimization technique.

Chapter 11 introduces the application of evolutionary optimization techniques towards non – traditional machining for performance enhancement. Electro-Chemical machining is a non-conventional machining method applied for machining of complex design. Here an effort is made to perform a multi-objective optimization of the surface roughness (SR) and material removal rate (MRR) for the ECM process of EN 19 on a CNC ECM machine using copper electrode through evolutionary optimization techniques like teaching Learning Based Optimization (TLBO) technique and biogeography-based optimization (BBO) technique. The input parameter considered are Electrolyte concentration, Voltage, Feed rate, Inter-electrode gap. TLBO and BBO technique is applied to achieve maximum MRR and minimum SR. further the optimized values are validated for testing the significance of the TLBO and BBO technique and a very small error value of MRR and SR is found. BBO outperformed TLBO in every aspect like less percentage error and better-optimized values, however, TLBO took less computation time as compared to the BBO.

Chapter 12 discusses the analysis of non-traditional machining processes using machine learning. The nature of manufacturing systems faces increasingly complex, dynamic to meet the demand for high quality products efficiently. One area, which experienced rapid development in terms not only of promising results but also of usability, is machine learning. New developments in certain domains such as mathematics, computer science and the availability of easy-to-use tools, often freely available, offer great potential to transform the non-traditional machining domain and its understanding of the increase in manufacturing data. However, the field is very broad and even confusing, which presents a challenge and a barrier that hinders wide application. Here, this research article helps to present an overview of the available machine learning techniques for improving the non-traditional machining process area. It provides a basis for the subsequent argument that machine learning is a suitable tool for manufacturers to face these challenges head-on in non-traditional machining process.

Chapter 13 describes the role of non-traditional machining equipment in industry 4.0. The manufacturing industries is undergoing drastic changes owing to steep rise in business competition and growing complexities in other business perspective. The highly turbulent market is characterized by ever-increasing mass customization, wide volume-mix, shorter lead time, and low cost, which along with varieties internal disturbances has complicated the business stability by many-fold. The multi agent-based systems comprising of fundamental entities called agents and characterized by autonomy, cooperation, and self-organizing abilities, have already made remarkable breakthrough to deal with the challenges through increased robustness, scalability, and enhanced adaptability through their dynamic capabilities. The decision-making ability of the agents can be augmented if equipped with cognitive abilities like that of human being. The present chapter discusses Cyber-Physical Production System (CPPS) to realize cognitive manufacturing in non-conventional machining environment.

Chapter 14 presents finite element-based optimization of additive manufacturing process using statistical modelling and league of champion algorithm. The study results in a 2D (two dimensional) finite element model with a Gaussian heat source to simulate powder bed-based laser additive manufacturing process of Ti6Al4V alloy. The modelling approach delivers insight into the process by correlating laser power and scan speed with melt pool temperature distribution and size. To tackle the FEA result in optimization environment statistical approach of data normalization and regression modelling is adopted. Statistical treatment not only able to deduce the interdependence of various objectives consider but also make the representation of objectives and constraint computationally simple. Adoption of a new stochastic algorithm namely league of a champion algorithm (LCA) together with penalty function approach for non-linear constraint handling reduces the effort required and computational complexity involved in determining the optimum parameter setting.

Chapter 15 describes a novel approach towards selection of role model cluster head for power management in WSN: selection of role model cluster head for power management in WSN. Here an innovative, smart controller to sustain mobility in wireless sensor networks (WSNs) is presented. Principally, the focal point is dependent on the arrangement of fuzzy input variables viz Remaining Battery Power (RBP), Mobility and Centrality solution to crucial usages, similar to personnel safety in an industrialized atmosphere. A mobility controller dependent upon Type-1 Fuzzy Logic (T1FL) is planned to support sensor Mobile Nodes (MN). Here, a Role Model Cluster Head (RMCH) is picked out among the cluster heads (CHs) that may simply convey the message to the mobile base station (BS) by determining the appropriate type-1 fuzzy (T1F) descriptors such as RBP, Mobility of the sink and the Centrality of the clusters. Type-1 Fuzzy inference system (Mamdani's rule) is utilized to opt for the possibility to be RMCH. The validity of the introduced model is carried out by means of multiple linear regressions.

Chapter 16 highlights a synthesis and characterization of nanocomposites for the application in hybrid solar cell. In today's era, a lot of interest is gained by solar cell formed by combination of organic and inorganic nano-particle semiconductors mainly because of its major features such as, scalable solar power conversion and cost effectiveness which makes the cell, a desirable photovoltaic device. Here an attempt to make a solar cell by the combination of Zinc Oxide (ZnO) and Graphite. ZnO is a good n-type material for the application in photovoltaic (PV) devices due to its better optical, electrical, structural and environment-friendly properties and on the other hand Graphite, an organic semiconductor enhances the rate of charge transfer in the device. These materials are so designed to help bring in more understanding in a wider range of the solar spectrum. This work focuses on developing solid-state polymer and hybrid solar cells.

Chapter 17 presents intelligent investment approaches for mutual funds - an evolutionary model. Investment on the right fund and at the right time happens to be the right key to success in stock trading business. Therefore for strategic investment, the selection of the right opportunity has to be executed crucially so as to reap the maximum returns from the market. Predicting the stock market has always been known to be very critical and needs years of experience as it involves lots of interleaving parameters and constraints. Intelligent investment in Mutual Fund (MF) can be done when various machine learning tools are used to predict future fund value using the past fund value. Here an elaborate discussion is presented on the different types of Mutual Funds and how these data can be used in prediction by machine learning in different literature. The authors have presented that the NAV of a total of 17 different mutual funds have been extracted from the website of AMFI and thereafter ANFIS is used to forecast the time series of the NAV of the MF. They have been trained using ANFIS and thereafter tested for prediction with satisfactory results.

CONCLUSION

From this book the reader will not only get the theoretical knowledge regarding the application of machine learning but also gain the practical know how needed to quickly and powerfully apply these techniques to the challenging practical problems. Through this they will learn how to conceptualized a problem, representation of data, selecting and tuning algorithms, interpreting the results correctly and finally analyzing the results in order to take strategies decisions

Acknowledgment

The editors wish to acknowledge the encouragement of some faculty members of the Production Engineering of Jadavpur University, Kolkata, especially, Prof. Souren Mitra for his advice on various topics of the book. We would like to express our appreciation to Dr. Kaushik Kumar, Dr. Dipankar Bose, Mr. Dhiraj Kumar, Mr. Debal Pramanik & Mr. Kingshuk Mandal for their support and roles played in preparing the manuscript.

We want to acknowledge our colleagues and authorities at the Haldia Institute of Technology for their help and well wishes. Our family members have been inspirational in their understanding, endurance, and encouragement during the long period that was devoted to completing this task.

We are deeply indebted to our parents for their constant love and blessings. Lastly, we would thank the almighty for giving us the strength to complete this work.

Goutam Kumar Bose
Haldia Institute of Technology, India

Pritam Pain
Haldia Institute of Technology, India

Chapter 1
Parametric Optimization of Dry Laser Cleaning Using Metaheuristics Processes:
To Study the Effect of Laser Cleaning Parameters on Surface Temperature Rise and Thermo-Elastic Force

Pritam Pain
https://orcid.org/0000-0001-5270-8439
Haldia Institute of Technology, India

Goutam Kumar Bose
https://orcid.org/0000-0002-4347-3508
Haldia Institute of Technology, India

Sayantan Roy
Haldia Institute of Technology, India

ABSTRACT

The workpiece sample which is a copper printed circuit board (PCB) is mounted on a micro-controlled assembly with double-faced adhesive tape. Here the primary objective is to study the effect of laser cleaning parameters on surface temperature rise and thermoelastic force. The variation of instantaneous temperature rise and thermoelastic force with time using different process parameters (e.g., type of power, focal length, and scanning speed) at a constant absorption coefficient is also investigated, and the best parametric combination have been found out in this experiment. After successful completion of the experimentation, it is observed that the surface temperature increases with the increase in laser power. The maximum temperature rise is observed when the laser power is maximum, and the focal length is minimum. It is further observed that the thermoelastic force increases with the increase in laser power. Maximum thermoelastic force is observed when the laser power is maximum, and the focal length is minimum.

DOI: 10.4018/978-1-7998-3624-7.ch001

INTRODUCTION

Laser cleaning is a method of laser ablation done on the laser milling system where an offset is created to decrease the laser fluence. Due to this the substrate is only heated to reach a temperature near the melting point of the particular material and thus to "flatten" any debris and other recast contaminants on the surface. Any variation from the accurate focal distance causes a decrease in the volume of material removed from the target and this harms the process performance. As this is an undesirable effect, therefore it should be avoided. Hence, an optical sensor system is combined to the machine to determine the distance to the target surface and to modify the laser power output when required, so that a constant material removal rate is sustained.

Chemical and abrasive processing which are traditional cleaning processes is getting near the end of their capability limit as they are both technically and environmentally useless for the severe cleaning requirements.

The dry laser cleaning efficiency for a certified spherical particle (SiO2, 5.0, 2.5, 1.0, and 0.5 μm) is experimentally analyzed from different substrates (Si, Ge, and NiP). The effect of various options (laser wavelength, incident angle, substrate properties, i.e., type of material, surface roughness, etc.) on the cleaning efficiency is presented along with commonly analyzed options (cleaning efficiency versus laser fluence and particle size). The laser cleaning efficiency demonstrates great sensitivity to some of these options (e.g., laser wavelength, angle of incidence, etc.). Partly these properties can be described within the frame of the microelectronics engineering (MIE) theory of scattering. Other effects (e.g., influence of roughness) can be explained along the more complex line, related to examination of the problem "particle on the surface" beyond the MIE theory. The theory of dry laser cleaning, grounded on one-dimensional thermal expansion of the substrate, validates a great sensitivity of the cleaning efficiency on laser pulse shape. For the realistic pulse shape, this theory produces the threshold fluence by the order of magnitude greater than the experimental one. At the same time, the theory which considers the near-field optical enhancement and three-dimensional thermal expansion effects produce the exact values for the threshold.

Particle removal utilizing dry laser cleaning (DLC) has grown in importance during the last decade. It is used, or consider for usage, in the fabrication of printed circuit boards (PCB), in the production of dynamic random-access memory (DRAM), in lithography and epitaxial growth for the removal of contaminations during via hole production for the cleaning of micro-optical and micromechanical components. In the case of damage-free DLC, the expansion of the substrate or the particle heads to particle removal. In some cases, other mechanisms related to field enhancement and local ablation may play a role. One more technique is steam laser cleaning (SLC) which is due to laser-induced explosive vaporization of an auxiliary liquid layer. "Ablative" cleaning is founded on the elimination of particles/contaminants by ablation. SLC, though more efficient, cannot be applied to hygroscopic materials, and is incompatible with many applications where high purity is required, as in small-scale optics and nanocluster technology. It is also a multiple-step process due to the required liquid delivery. With DLC it is observed that it is more difficult to remove smaller particles. This has been explained by higher specific adhesion forces. Though precise theoretical estimates for the necessity of the cleaning fluence on particle size have not been obtained, it is not completely clear which parameters should be optimized to enhance the cleaning efficiency and reduce the cleaning threshold, especially with smaller particles. Usually, cleaning forces acting on the particles are compared with measured adhesion forces. At the same time, nanosecond laser cleaning takes place over very short time scales, which as opposed to conventional adhesion measurements requires the consideration of dynamic effects. Several models of DLC exist. Accelerations and forces due to thermal expansion of the substrate and particles, elastic deformation of the particles which are compressed by the expanding substrate cleaning via generation of surface acoustic waves, the influence of hydrogen bonds have been considered. The behavior of the particles after the detachment and the redeposition has been studied. These models employ many inadequate assumptions. Among these are: Thermal expansion of the substrate and particle are often treated separately and incorrectly. The temporal profile of the laser pulse is not considered. This assumes infinite acceleration or deceleration of the substrate at the beginning or end of the laser pulse. Deformation of the substrate and particle, their interdependence and influence of the particle on the substrate expansion are not described properly. Adhesion forces are treated separately from the elastic forces, which can lead to erroneous results. Though the importance of force and energy criteria were mentioned, their regions of applicability are not clearly stated. The removal of absorbing particles and elasticity of the substrate is analyzed based on force balance only without considering particle movement. The particles are estimated in a very crude way there. Here the temperatures of dissipative processes are considered, but only in the post-detachment stage. Numerical calculations are unable to provide formulas concerning cleaning fluence to laser and material parameters.

Based on the past research work a brief literature survey is described here. Cavallaro et al. 2019 worked on emulsion gels based on halloysite nanotubes and described the properties and cleaning action on the marble surface of ionic biopolymers. Balakhnina et al. 2018 analyzed single-pulse two-threshold laser ablation of historical paper. Zanini et al. 2018 discussed the utilization of laser as a tool for the cleaning of cultural heritage. Sanz et al. 2017 defined the influence of wavelength on the laser removal of lichens colonizing heritage stone. Palomar et al. 2016 investigated about evaluation of laser cleaning for the restoration of tarnished silver artifacts. Voltolina et al. 2016 described the assessment of plasma torches as an innovative tool for the cleaning of historical stone materials. Striova et al. 2016 analyzed how the optical devices provide unprecedented insights into the laser cleaning of calcium oxalate layers. Ciofini et al. 2016 performed the spectroscopic assessment of the UV laser removal of varnishes from painted surfaces. Alves et al. 2015 described the conservation of stony materials in the built environment. Li et al. 2015 studied the thick plate ultra-narrow-gap multi-pass multi-layer laser welding technology combined with laser cleaning. Striova et al. 2015 utilized the optical and spectroscopic tools for evaluating Er: YAG laser removal of shellac varnish. Sansonetti et al. 2015 performed the laser cleaning of a nineteenth-century bronze sculpture. Vergès-Belmin et al. 2015 examined the Nd: YAG long Q-switched versus short free-running laser cleaning trials at Chartres cathedral, France. Mascalchi et al. 2015 performed a preliminary investigation of combined laser and microwave treatment for stone biodeterioration. Samolik et al. 2015 investigated the removal of graffiti on mineral supports and compared the nano-second Nd: YAG laser cleaning with traditional mechanical and chemical methods. Qiao et al. 2010 worked on the laser cleaning and its application on PCB. Song et al. 2005 described the typical application of laser cleaning comprising mainly on removal on rust and paint. Song et al. 2003 demonstrated that laser cleaning is a powerful tool to remove resin contaminants from printed circuit boards. Lee et al. 2000 monitored and characterized the laser cleaning of copper surfaces with an Nd: YAG Q-switched laser pulse for the improvement of solder quality on printed circuit boards (PCBs) by detecting the acoustic emission through the process and one-dimensional mathematical model analysis. Feng-Lu et al. 1994 worked on the mechanisms of laser cleaning that may include laser photodecomposition, laser ablation and surface vibration due to the impact of the laser pulse and its application on cleaning PCB.

Therefore, it is observed that very few, almost negligible work has been done with Ytterbium fiber laser IPG-YLR 100 on copper printed circuit board (PCB). The present research work involves the study on the effect of laser cleaning parameters on surface temperature rise and thermoelastic force. The different process parameters viz. type of power, focal length and scanning speed at a constant absorption coefficient are taken into consideration and the best parametric combination is found out through experimentation.

The responses are initially tested and trained by applying the Artificial Neural Network (ANN). During computation 55% of the data are considered for training, 25% of the data are considered for validation and 20% of the data are considered for testing. Next, multi-objective optimization of all the responses considered is carried out by applying the Firefly Algorithm.

EXPERIMENTAL SETUP

The working sample which is a copper printed circuit board (PCB) is mounted on the holder with embedded electric heater to allow sample preheating up to 700 K. For laser heating, an ytterbium fiber laser IPG YLR-100 is used and a pyrometer (Kleiber KGA 740-LO) is used for temperature measurements. To eliminate the influence of the reflected laser radiation on the detector, an optical filter is used and a fast photodiode (EG&G FND-100) with rise time of less than 1 ns into 50 ohms is mounted on a micro control assembly with a double-faced adhesive tape is used to control laser pulses shape and duration. The surface height profiles are measured with an optical profilometer of Maher Gmbh. The assembly can be precisely moved in the direction of the laser beam propagation and the analysis of the sample surface is performed with an optical microscope.

METHODOLOGY

Artificial Neural Network (ANN)

Artificial neural networks are one of the main tools which are used in machine learning. As the "neural" part of their name indicates, they are brain-inspired systems which are planned to duplicate the means that we humans learn. Neural networks comprise of input and output layers, as well as a hidden layer comprising of units that convert the input into something that the output layer can use. They are brilliant tools for acquiring patterns which are much composite or plentiful for a human programmer to separate and train the machine to recognize. Artificial neural network is a powerful data-driven, self-adaptive, flexible computational tool having the ability of apprehending nonlinear and complex underlying characteristics of any physical process (e.g. Damage detection) with a high degree of accuracy.

The main advantages of using Artificial Neural Networks (ANN) include: - it can handle large amount of data sets; it can implicitly detect complex nonlinear relationships between dependent and independent variables; it has ability to detect all possible interactions between predictor variables; etc.

Figure 1. Photograph of the temperature measurement setup

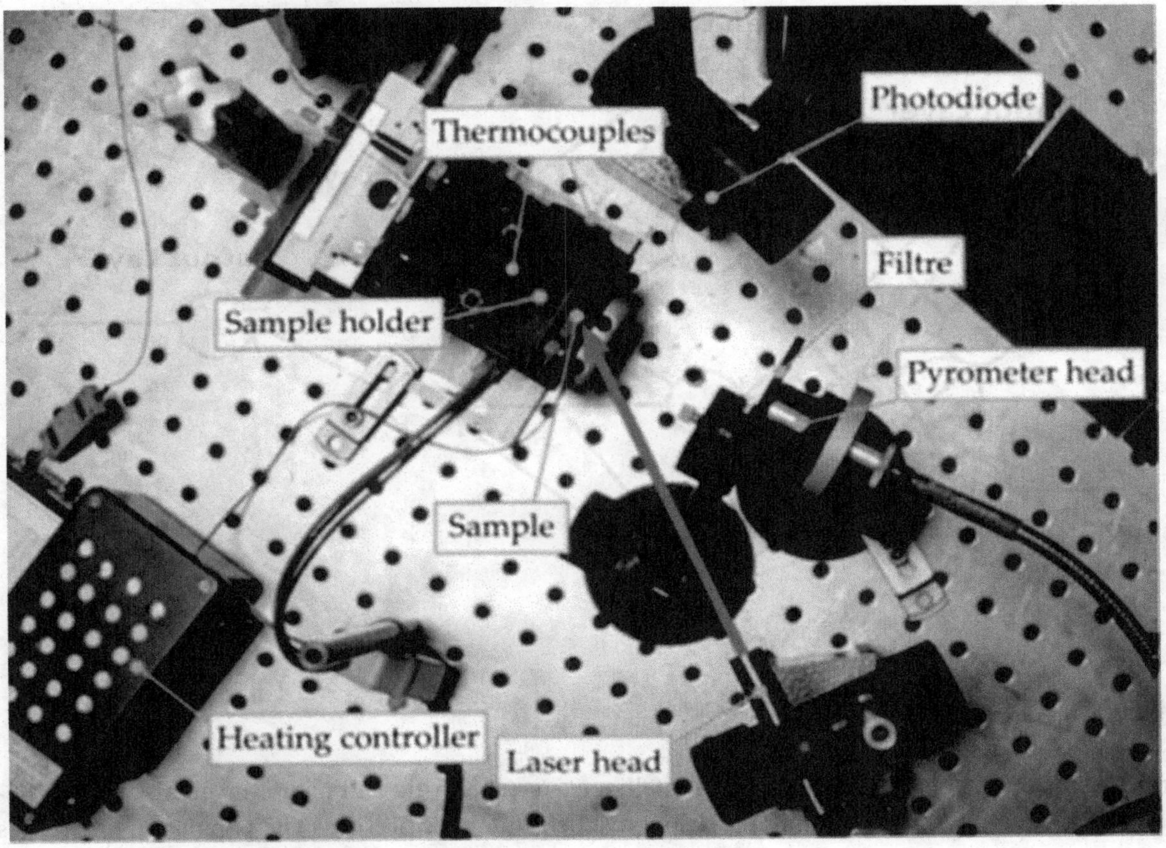

Types of ANN

Feed Forward ANN

Feedforward neural networks are artificial neural networks where the connections between units do not form a cycle. Feedforward neural networks are the first type of artificial neural network invented and are simpler than their counterpart, recurrent neural networks. They are called feedforward because information only travels forward in the network (no loops), first through the input nodes, then through the hidden nodes (if present), and finally through the output nodes.

Feed Backward ANN

In this type of ANN, the output returns to the network to attain the best-evolved results internally. The feedback network supplies information back into itself and is suitable to resolve optimization problems.

Figure 2. Feed forward

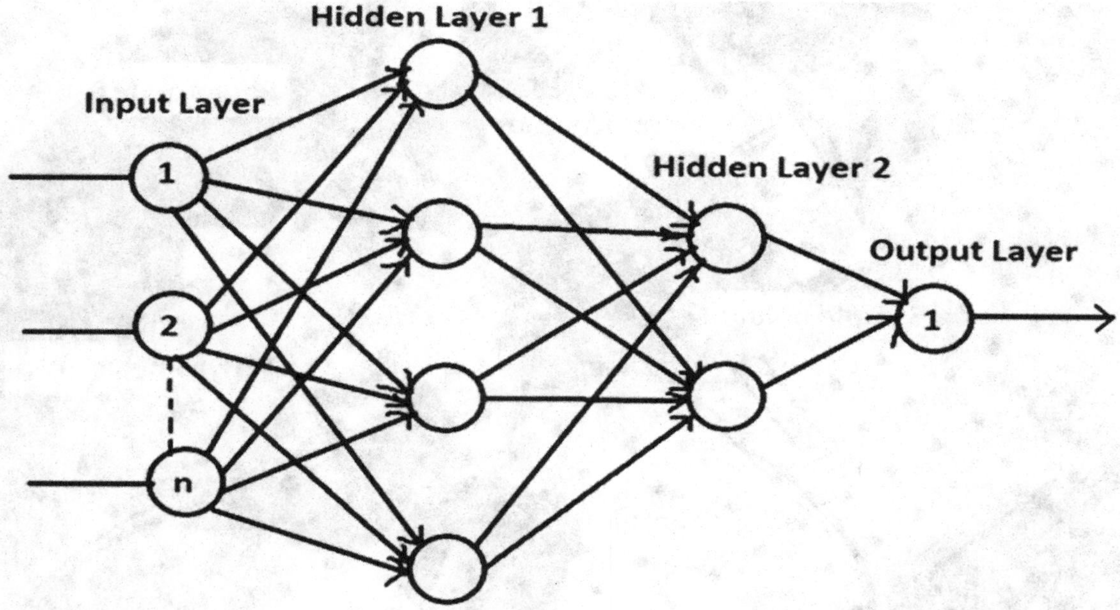

FIREFLY ALGORITHM (FA)

Firefly algorithm is categorized as swarm intelligent, metaheuristic and nature-inspired, and it is developed by Yang in 2008 by inciting the distinctive behaviours of fireflies. The population of fireflies

Figure 3. Feed backward

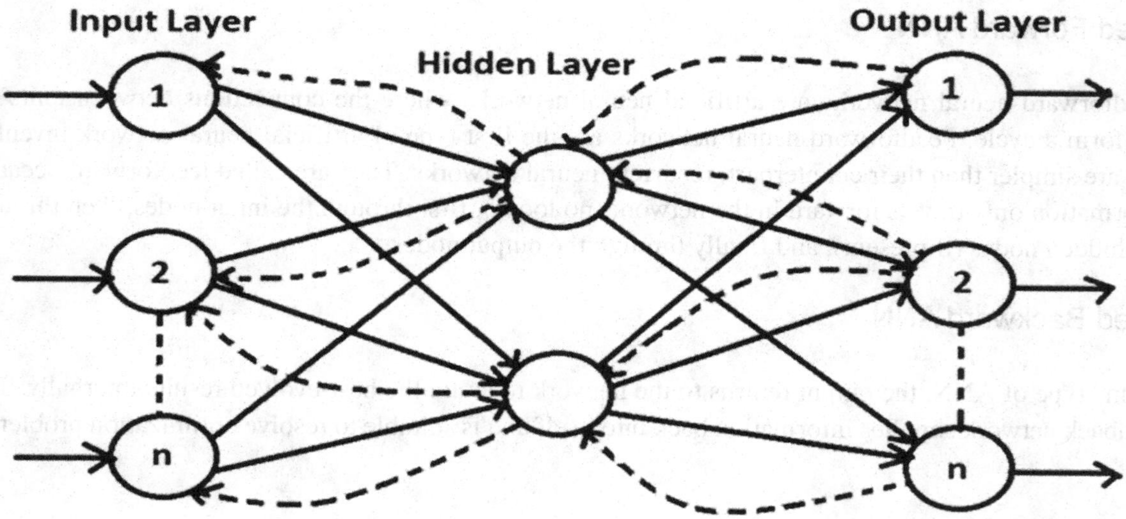

shows distinguishing luminary flashing activities to perform as appealing the partners, communication, and risk warning for predators. From those activities, Yang outlined this method under the assumption of all fireflies are unisexual so that all fireflies have attracted potential for each other and the attractiveness is directly proportional to the brightness level of the individuals. Hence, the brighter fireflies attract the less bright ones to move toward to them, besides that in the case of no fireflies brighter than a certain firefly then it moves randomly.

In the formulation of the firefly algorithm, the objective function is related to the flashing light characteristics of the firefly population. Seeing the physical principle of the light intensity, it is inversely quadratic proportional to the square of the area, this principle allows us to describe fitting function for the distance between any two fireflies. To optimization the fitting function, the individuals are required to have systematic or random moves in the population. Like this, it is confirmed that all the fireflies move toward the more attractive ones which have brighter flashing till the population meets the brightest one. In this procedure, the firefly algorithm is accomplished by three parameters namely attractiveness, randomization, and absorption. Attractiveness parameter is centred on light intensity between two fireflies and well-defined with exponential functions which when set to zero, causes the random walk corresponding to the randomization parameter determined by Gaussian distribution principle as producing the number from the [0,1] interval. Absorption parameters assume the value of attractiveness parameters as varying from zero to infinity. And, when converging to infinity, the move of fireflies seems like a random walk.

Firefly Algorithm is swarm-intelligence-based, so it has advantages like another swarm intelligence-based algorithm. However, FA has two main advantages over other algorithms: - automatic subdivision and the capability to deal with multimodality. Foremost, FA is founded on attraction and attractiveness declines with distance. This heads to the fact that the whole population can inevitably subdivide into subgroups and each group can group around each mode or local optimum. Amid all these modes, the best global solution can be found. Secondly, this subdivision lets the fireflies to be capable of finding optima concurrently if the population size is adequately higher than the number of modes.

Furthermore, the parameters in FA can be adjusted to control the randomness as iterations proceed, so that the convergence can also be raced up by tuning these parameters. These above advantages make it flexible to deal with continuous problems, clustering and classifications, and combinatorial optimization as well.

RESULT AND DISCUSSION

Based on the previous research works and introductory assessment, three parameters i.e., laser power (POW), Focal length (FL) and Scanning speed (SS) are selected as control factors. These are varied with three levels during experimentation. There are other factors such as type of absorption coefficient, number of passes etc. which may impact the measured performance, however, are kept constant during experimentation. The experimental information is composed and documented in term of means. Three factors with their three levels are shown in table 1.

The experimental data are now further trained and validated and finally tested in ANN and single objective optimization has been done by applying Firefly Algorithm.

Figure 4. Process flow of Genetic Algorithm

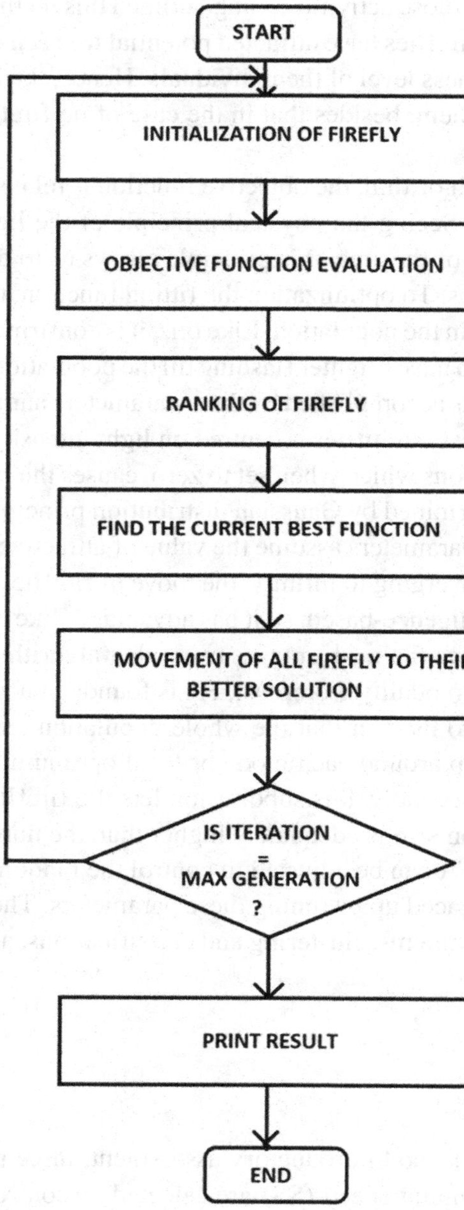

Result Analysis by Using ANN

In this current research paper 3 input parameters are analyzed through 10 hidden layer and finally gives the output. The neural structure is as below in figure 5.

Table 1. Control parameters with their different levels

Sl. No	Factors	Unit	Levels		
			L1	L2	L3
1.	Power (POW)	Watt	8	10	12
2.	Focal Length (FL)	cm	2.0	2.2	2.4
3.	Scanning Speed (SS)	mm/s	2	4	6

Result Analysis for Temperature Rise

Applying ANN, 45% of the data are used for training, 30% are used for testing, and 25% are used for validation in Temperature Rise. After 4 number of iterations, and 3 number of validations checks it is terminated since the Mean Square Error (MSE) is achieved. It is observed that the experimental run is terminated as the gradient is below 1.0 x 10^{-7}. If the validation reaches 6, the training will stop. Here the number of successive iterations performed for validation checks is 4. Figure 6 represents the neural network training performance progress.

Figure 5. Neural Structure

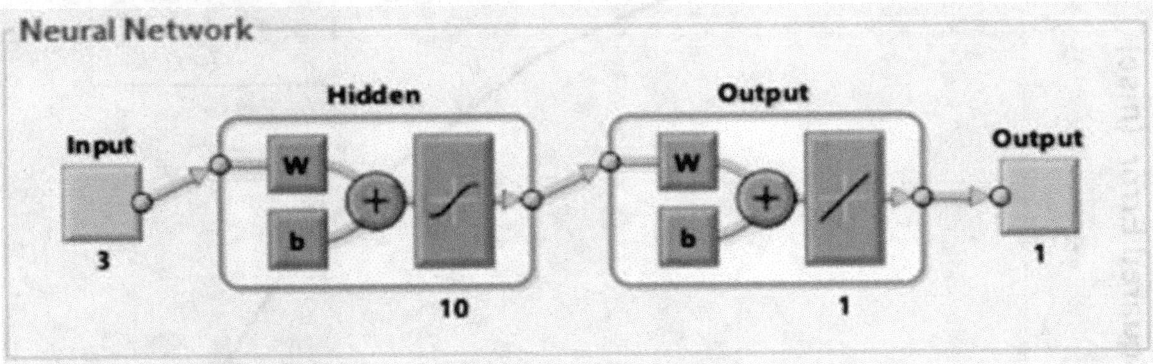

Best validation performance is about 28017.3657 at epoch 1, which is a low prediction error when it is measured with the help of MSE.

The figure 7 indicates the minimum level of the validation performance. Before the stoppage of the training, it sustained for about 4 iterations. No major complications are indicated in the figure. The validation and test curves are quite like each other. The regression plot during the training, validation, testing along with the overall are shown below.

From the regression plot as shown in figure 8, for Temperature Rise, the regression in case of training R=0.99512, in case of validation R=1 and in case of testing R=0.99777. Hence overall R=0.69086. Therefore, the training data indicates a good fit as the validation and test results both show R values that greater than 0.9.

Figure 6. Process output of Temperature Rise

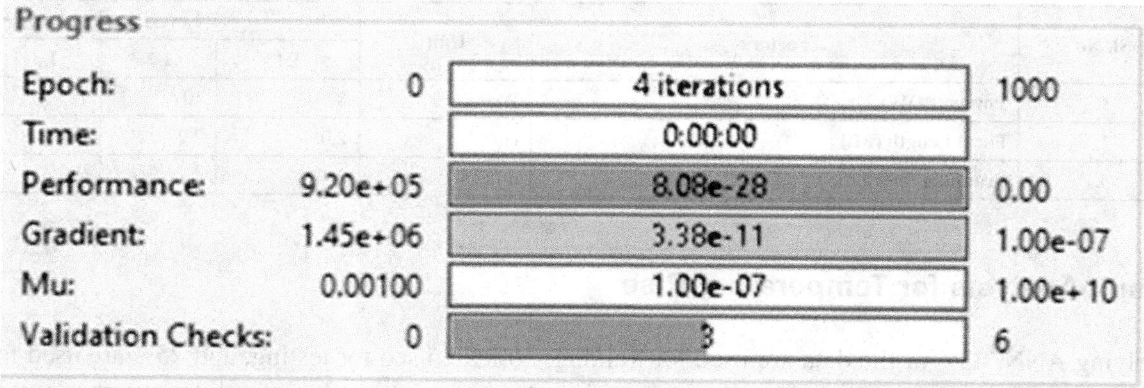

Figure 7. Performance plot of Temperature Rise

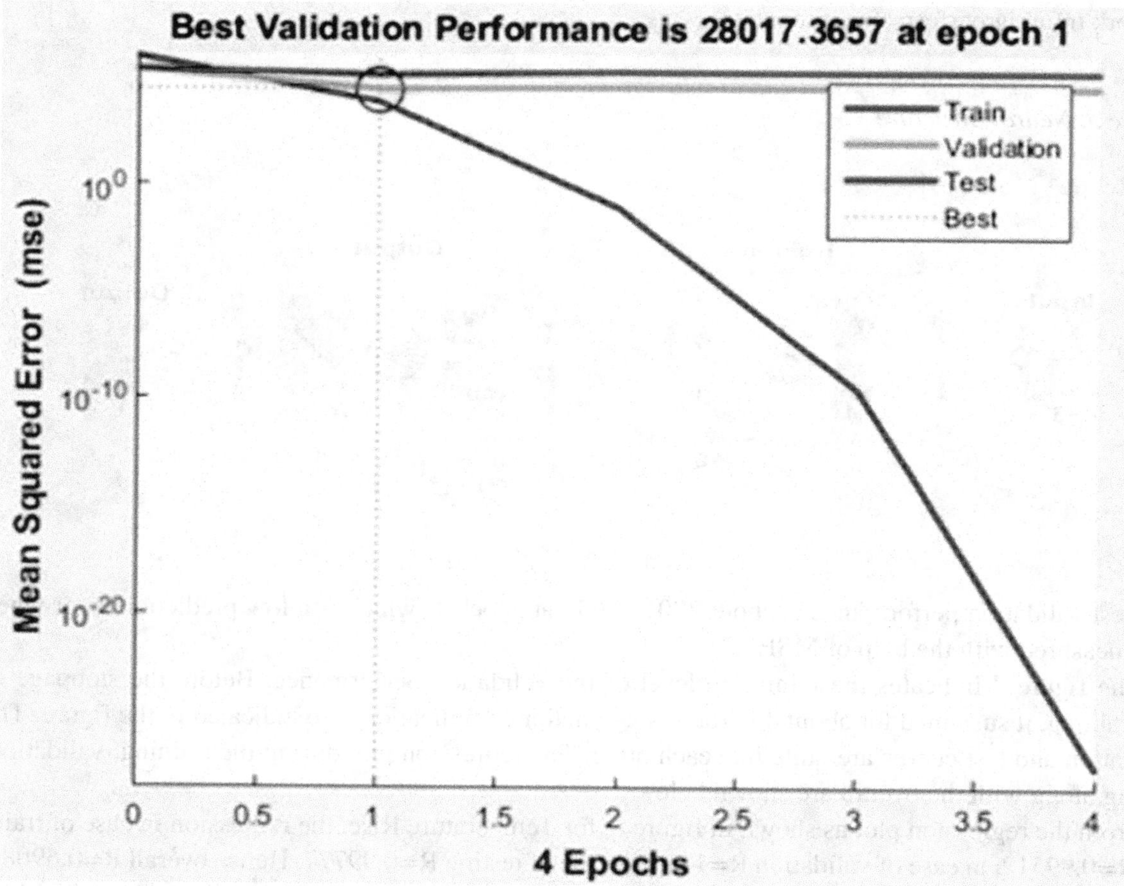

Figure 8. Regression plot of Temperature Rise

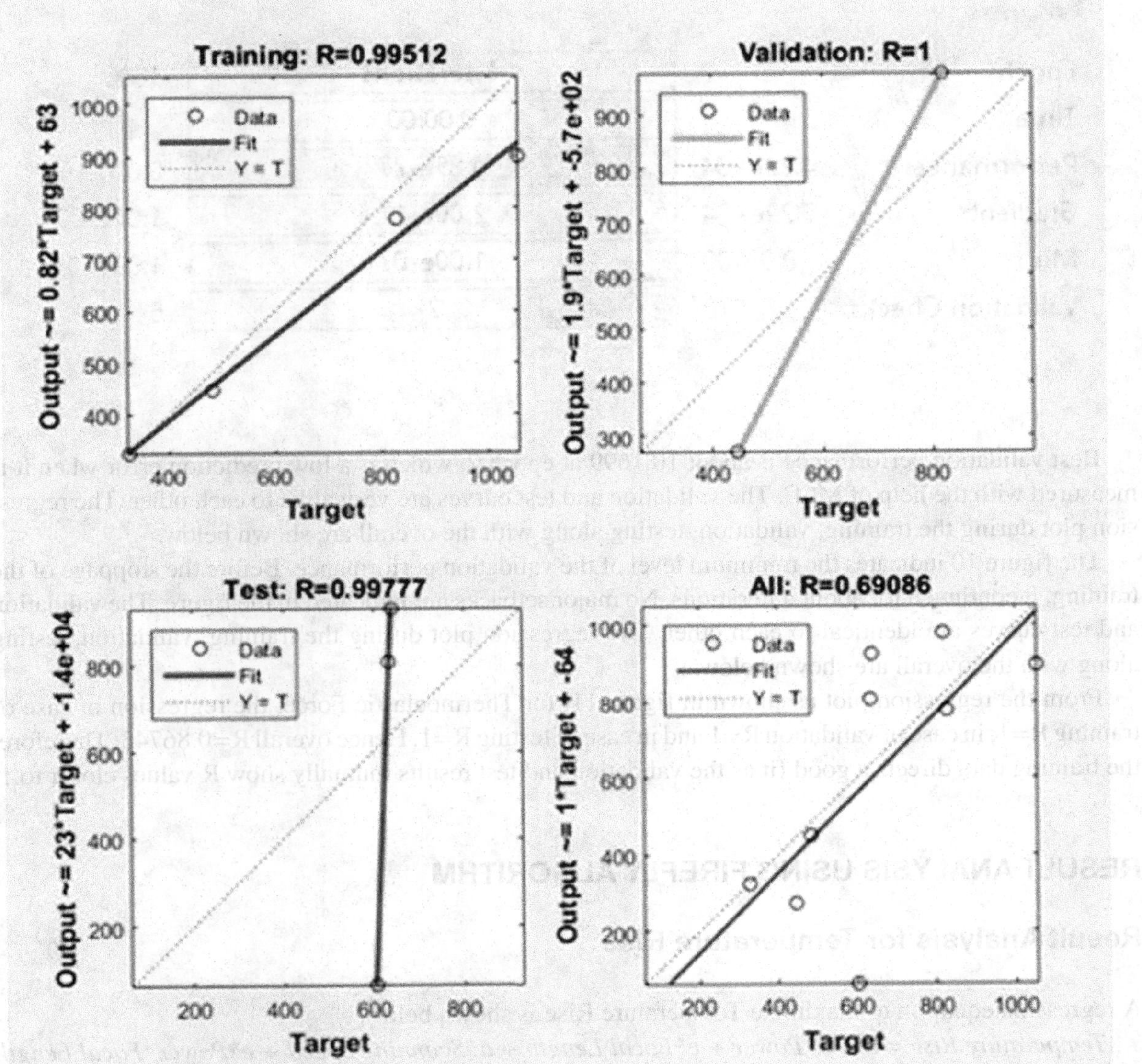

Result Analysis for Thermoelastic Force

Now in ANN, 55% of the data are used for training, 20% are used for testing, and 25% are used for validation in Thermoelastic Force. After 4 number of iterations, and 2 number of validations checks it is terminated as the MSE is achieved. It is seen that the experimental run ended as the gradient is below 1.0 X 10^{-7}. If the validation reaches 6, the training will stop. Here the number of successive iterations performed for validation checks is 4. Figure 9 represents the neural network training performance progress.

Figure 9. Process output of Thermoelastic Force

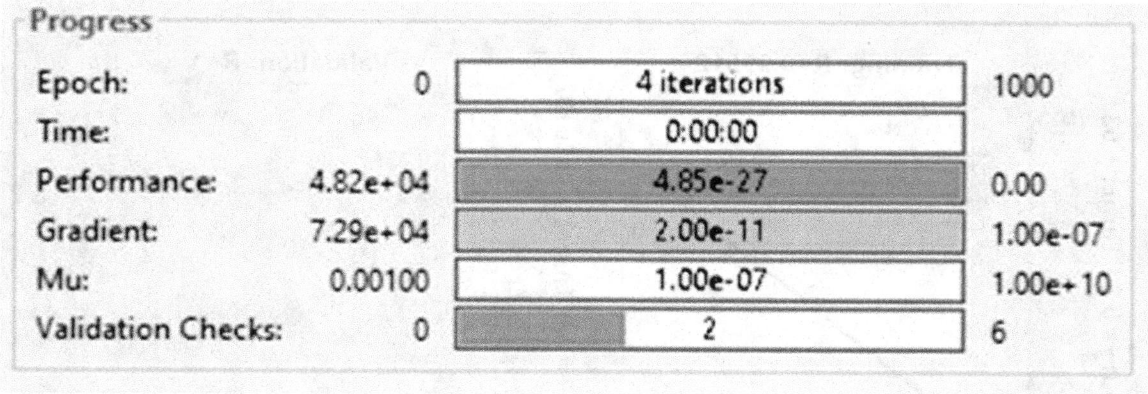

Best validation performance is about 10.1699 at epoch 2, which is a low prediction error when it is measured with the help of MSE. The validation and test curves are very alike to each other. The regression plot during the training, validation, testing along with the overall are shown below.

The figure 10 indicates the minimum level of the validation performance. Before the stoppage of the training, it continued for about 4 iterations. No major setbacks are indicated in the figure. The validation and test curves are identical to each other. The regression plot during the training, validation, testing along with the overall are shown below.

From the regression plot as shown in figure 11, for Thermoelastic Force, the regression in case of training R=1, in case of validation R=1 and in case of testing R=1. Hence overall R=0.86743. Therefore, the training data directs a good fit as the validation and test results mutually show R values closer to 1.

RESULT ANALYSIS USING FIREFLY ALGORITHM

Result Analysis for Temperature Rise

A regression equation to maximize Temperature Rise is shown below.

*Temperature Rise = a + b*Power + c*Focal Length + d*Scanning Speed + e*Power*Focal Length + f*Power*Scanning Speed + g*Focal Length*Scanning Speed + h*Power*Focal Length*Scanning Speed* (1)

In the above regression equation, a, b, c, d, etc. are constant.

By applying the Firefly Algorithm in the regression equation, the optimum solution of Temperature Rise is achieved as 1057.4 K when the values of Power = 12-Watt, Focal Length = 2 mm and Scanning Speed = 6 mm/s respectively.

Result Analysis for Thermoelastic Force

A regression equation to maximize Thermoelastic Force is shown below.

Figure 10. Performance plot of Thermoelastic Force

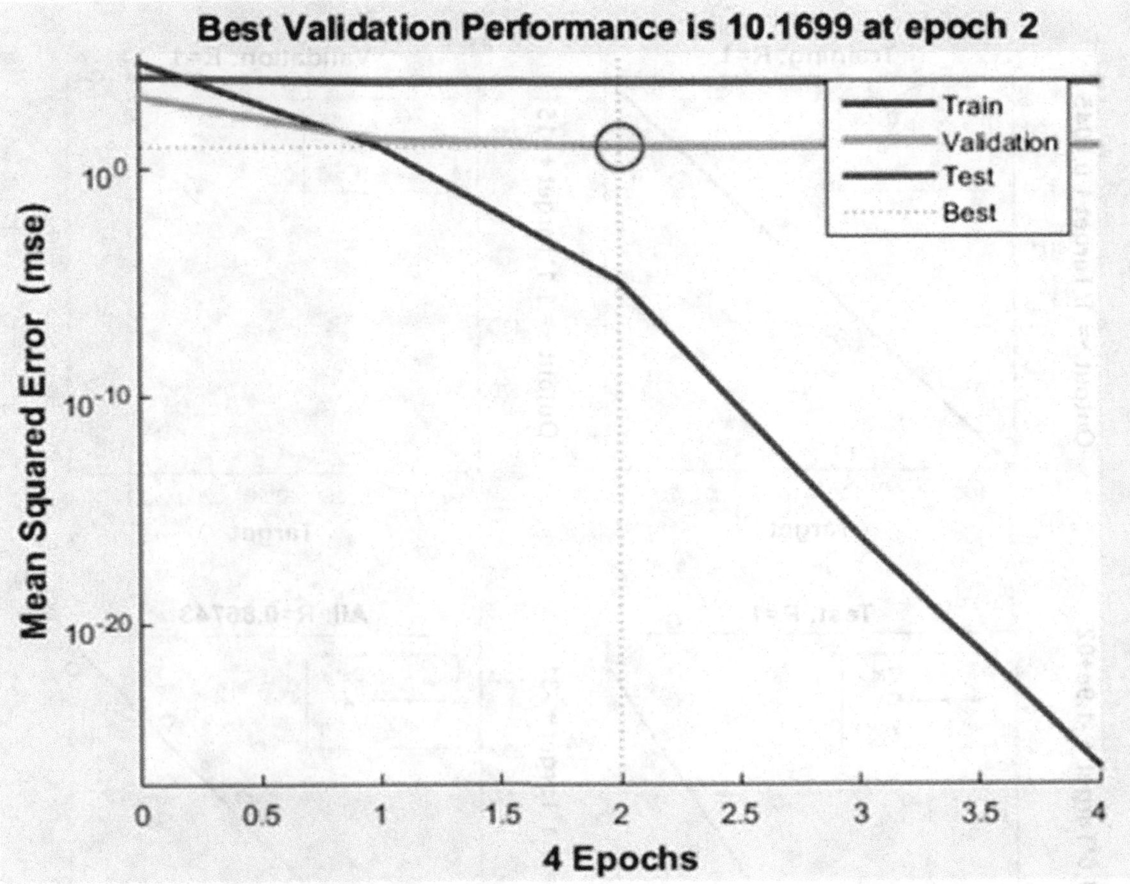

Thermoelastic Force = *p* + *q*Power* + *r*Focal Length* + *s*Scanning Speed* + *t*Power*Focal Length* +*u*Power*Scanning Speed*+ *v*Focal Length*Scanning Speed* + *w*Power*Focal Length*Scanning Speed* (2)

In the above regression equation, p, q, r, s, etc. are constant.

By applying the Firefly Algorithm on the regression equation (2), the optimum solution of Thermoelastic Force is obtained as 277.24 dyne when the values of Power = 12-Watt, Focal Length = 2 mm and Scanning Speed =6 mm/s respectively.

CONCLUSION

Here the primary objective is to study the effect of laser cleaning parameters on surface temperature rise and thermo elastic force. It is also investigated the variation of instantaneous temperature rise and thermo elastic force with time using different process parameters viz. type of power, focal length and scanning speed at a constant absorption coefficient and the best parametric combination has been found out in this experiment. Figure 12 illustrates the workpieces which has been Laser cleaned. While analyz-

Figure 11. Regression plot of Thermoelastic Force

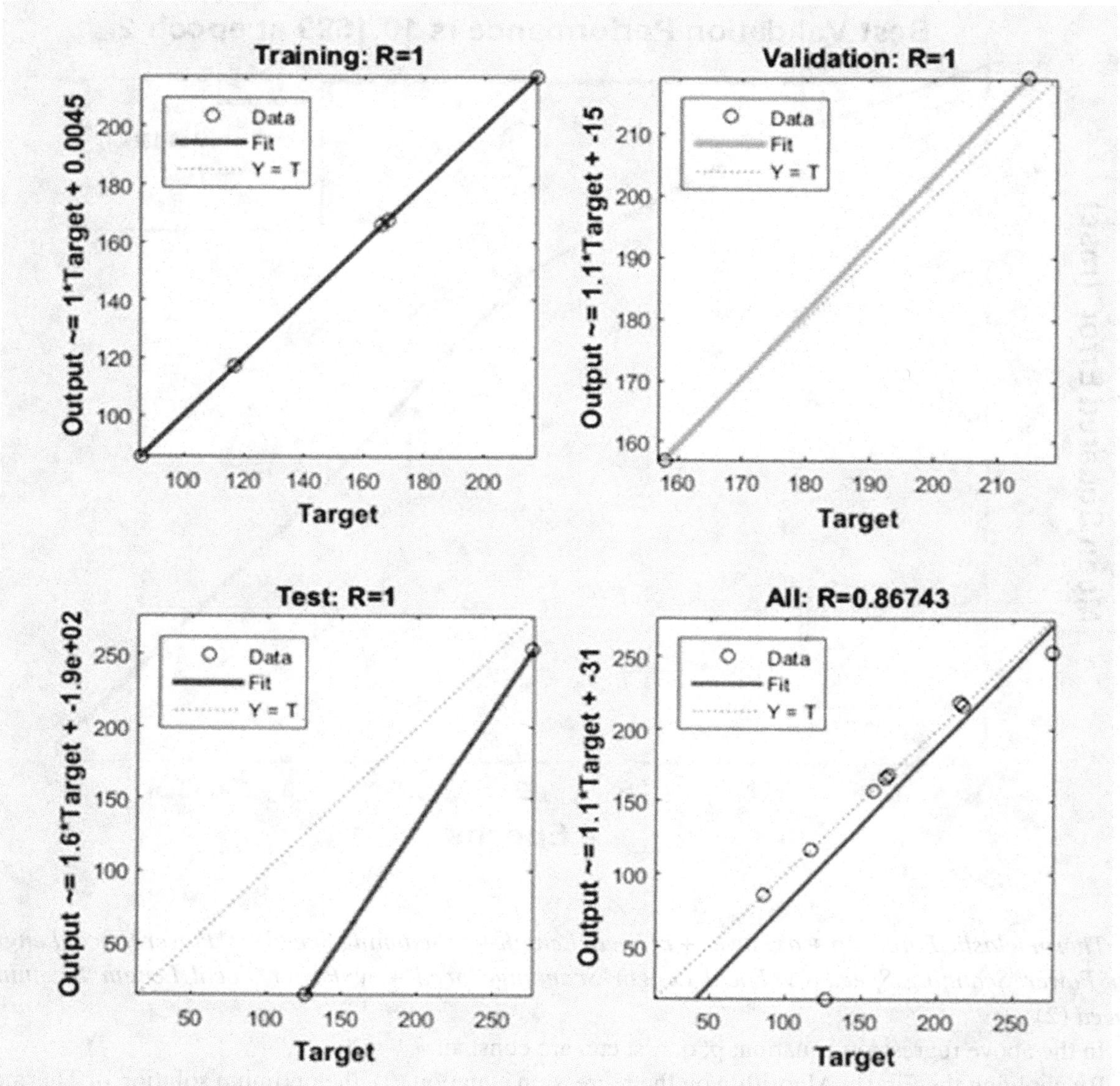

ing the data using an artificial neural network to achieve the optimum values of Temperature Rise and Thermoelastic Force the training, validation and testing data indicate that the values of 'R' tends to 1. This indicates that there is a precise relationship between outputs and targets.

Then the individual responses are optimized applying Firefly Algorithm where the following parametric combinations are found: Maximum Temperature Rise of 1057.4 K is obtained at Power = 12-Watt, Focal Length = 2 mm and Scanning Speed = 6 mm/s. Maximum Thermoelastic Force= 277.24 dyne is obtained at Power = 12-Watt, Focal Length = 2 mm and Scanning Speed = 6 mm/s.

Applying the same control parameter values a validation experiment is performed where the result obtained for Temperature Rise is 1054.53 K as shown in table 2. Similarly, applying the same control

Figure 12. Work piece after cleaning

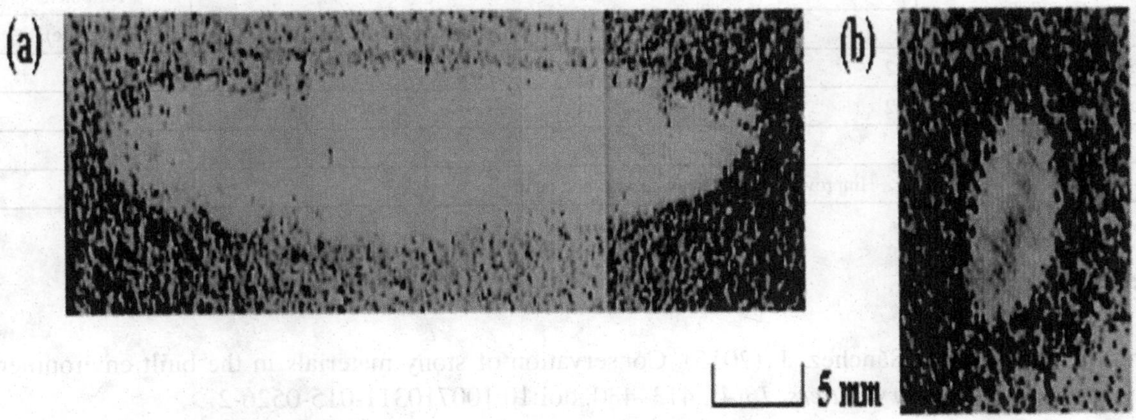

Table 2. Validation Experimental Results for Temperature Rise

Exp Type	Control Parameter			Response
	POW (Watt)	FL (mm)	SS (mm/s)	T (K)
From FA	12	2	6	1057.4
From Exp.	12	2	6	1054.53
Difference in the response				2.87
Improvement in the response in percentage				0.27142

parameter values a validation experiment is performed where the result obtained for Thermoelastic Force is 276.18 dyne as shown in table 3.

Thus, while cleaning PCB by means of dry laser cleaning, this experimental analysis can be used to regulate the cleaning condition. Future work in this emerging area can be considered with other parameter and different responses such as material removal rate, surface finish, etc. to capture the process in perspective.

Table 3. Validation Experimental Results for Thermoelastic Force

Exp Type	Control Parameter			Response
	POW (Watt)	FL (mm)	SS (mm/s)	F (dyne)
From FA	12	2	6	277.24
From Exp.	12	2	6	276.18
Difference in the response				1.06
Improvement in the response in percentage				0.38234

REFERENCES

Alves, C., & Sanjurjo-Sánchez, J. (2015). Conservation of stony materials in the built environment. *Environmental Chemistry Letters*, *13*(4), 413–430. doi:10.100710311-015-0526-2

Balakhnina, I. A., Brandt, N. N., Chikishev, A. Y., & Shpachenko, I. G. (2018). Single-pulse two-threshold laser ablation of historical paper. *Laser Physics Letters*, *15*(6), 065605. doi:10.1088/1612-202X/aab94e

Cavallaro, G., Milioto, S., Nigamatzyanova, L., Akhatova, F., Fakhrullin, R., & Lazzara, G. (2019). Pickering Emulsion Gels Based on Halloysite Nanotubes and Ionic Biopolymers: Properties and Cleaning Action on Marble Surface. *ACS Applied Nano Materials*, *2*(5), 3169–3176. doi:10.1021/acsanm.9b00487

Ciofini, D., Oujja, M., Cañamares, M. V., Siano, S., & Castillejo, M. (2016). Spectroscopic assessment of the UV laser removal of varnishes from painted surfaces. *Microchemical Journal*, *124*, 792–803. doi:10.1016/j.microc.2015.10.031

Li, R., Yue, J., Shao, X., Wang, C., Yan, F., & Hu, X. (2015). A study of thick plate ultra-narrow-gap multi-pass multi-layer laser welding technology combined with laser cleaning. *International Journal of Advanced Manufacturing Technology*, *81*(1-4), 113–127. doi:10.100700170-015-7193-0

Palomar, T., Oujja, M., Llorente, I., Ramírez Barat, B., Cañamares, M. V., Cano, E., & Castillejo, M. (2016). Evaluation of laser cleaning for the restoration of tarnished silver artifacts. *Applied Surface Science*, *387*, 118–127. doi:10.1016/j.apsusc.2016.06.017

Sansonetti, A., Colella, M., Letardi, P., Salvadori, B., & Striova, J. (2015). Laser cleaning of a nineteenth-century bronze sculpture: In situ multi-analytical evaluation. *Studies in Conservation*, *60*(sup1), S28–S33. doi:10.1179/0039363015Z.000000000204

Sanz, M., Oujja, M., Ascaso, C., Pérez-Ortega, S., Souza-Egipsy, V., Fort, R., de los Rios, A., Wierzchos, J., Cañamares, M. V., & Castillejo, M. (2017). Influence of wavelength on the laser removal of lichens colonizing heritage stone. *Applied Surface Science*, *399*, 758–768. doi:10.1016/j.apsusc.2016.12.032

Striova, J., Fontana, R., Barucci, M., Felici, A., Marconi, E., Pampaloni, E., Raffaelli, M., & Riminesi, C. (2016). Optical devices provide unprecedented insights into the laser cleaning of calcium oxalate layers. *Microchemical Journal*, *124*, 331–337. doi:10.1016/j.microc.2015.09.005

Striova, J., Salvadori, B., Fontana, R., Sansonetti, A., Barucci, M., Pampaloni, E., Marconi, E., Pezzati, L., & Colombini, M. P. (2015). Optical and spectroscopic tools for evaluating Er:YAG laser removal of shellac varnish. *Studies in Conservation*, *60*(sup1), S91–S96. doi:10.1179/0039363015Z.000000000213

Voltolina, S., Nodari, L., Aibéo, C., Egel, E., Pamplona, M., Simon, S., Falzacappa, E. V., Scopece, P., Gambirasi, A., Favaro, M., & Patelli, A. (2016). Assessment of plasma torches as innovative tool for cleaning of historical stone materials. *Journal of Cultural Heritage*, *22*, 940–950. doi:10.1016/j.culher.2016.05.001

Zanini, A., Trafeli, V., & Bartoli, L. (2018). The laser as a tool for the cleaning of Cultural Heritage. *IOP Conference Series. Materials Science and Engineering*, *364*, 012078. doi:10.1088/1757-899X/364/1/012078

Chapter 2
MCDM-Based Optimization of Performance Characteristics During μEDMing of SS 304

Premangshu Mukhopadhyay
https://orcid.org/0000-0001-8892-5443
Haldia Institute of Technology, India

Goutam Kumar Bose
Haldia Institute of Technology, India

Pritam Pain
https://orcid.org/0000-0001-5270-8439
Haldia Institute of Technology, India

ABSTRACT

Micro-EDM is most widely used for developing perfect drilled micro features/parts. Research was carried out to improve the material removal and tool wear of any conductive machined product by EDM and micro-EDM process. In this chapter, RSM was used for designing the experiments with 20 set of experiments. In this present research work, performance characteristics like MRR and Overcut have got a different level of importance. Here the stress was given on MRR rather than on OC. In this MCDM analysis, the weight of MRR is considered to be maximum (i.e., larger is better), and other weights of other responses are considered to be the minimum (i.e., smaller is better). Finally, in the midst of all the combinations of process parameters considered one that acquires the highest grey relational grade is the best parametric combination. The research findings in the area of machining of stainless steel 304 will be helpful to manufacturing engineers for selecting the optimized parametric combinations of micro-EDM process with stainless steel.

DOI: 10.4018/978-1-7998-3624-7.ch002

INTRODUCTION

In these recent times, demands of manufactured products are not only limited to high accuracy and better quality but also to obtain maximum quantity in a justified time period. Because of this, it is very important to gain the knowledge of optimum values of various input parameters to maximize or minimize ano utput. Genetic Algorithm (GA) is a robust optimized technique for getting optimum values in micro machining of engineering materials. Kiranet al. (2007) presented a model based on the configuration of a single spark cavity formed as a function of process parameters. Bhattacharyya et al. (2007) developed a mathematical model based on response surface methodology (RSM) for correlating the interactive and higher order influences of peak current and pulse on-duration on different aspects of surface integrity of M2 die steel machined through conventional EDM. Jahan et al. (2009) conducted investigations with intension of obtaining fine surface finish in the micro-EDM of WC using tungsten (W), copper tungsten (CuW) and silver tungsten (AgW) electrodes and showed that surface characteristics depend mostly on discharge energy during machining. Ekmekci et al. (2009) studied the variations of various pulse energies on surface profile of micro-hole diameter on plastic mold steel samples. Significant work efficiency and machining accuracy have been gained with the use of on machine measurement techniques. S/N ratios and AVOVA analysis have been done to investigate the effects of parameters on MRR and to find optimum cutting parameters. Surface defects such as in homogeneity, cracks, arc spots and black spots have been analyzed and reduced. Attention was given to process control methods to ensure high consistency accuracy in machining multi-nozzles. Dastagiri et al. (2014) conducted experiments on stainless steel and EN41b using full factorial design 23 with three central point in DOE techniques. Till now, very few experiments have been carried out to improve the performance features of micro-EDMing of stainless steel 304 taking dielectric flushing pressure as one of the process parameters. While optimizing a complex design which is an assortment of continuous discrete variables, irregular and nonconvex design space, by employing standard non-linear programming techniques, for these types of problems will be ineffective. Genetic algorithm (GA) on other hand is well designed for solving such problems, and it is efficient in finding the global optimum solution with maximum probability. GA is based on the theory of survival of the fittest by Darwin. Using the penalty function, the first transformation alters the original constrained function into an unconstraint function. Therefore, the objective of this research paper is to study the influence of various process parameters on performance characteristics using MCDM based approach during micro-electro-discharge machining of SS 304.

EXPERIMENTAL SET UP AND PROCEDURE

A cylindrical Pure Copper (Cu) rod of 430µm as tool electrode tip diameter with 30-40mm length and SS 304 sheet of 1cm×1cm size with 300µm thickness as workpiece material were taken during the micro-EDM process. A new tool electrode was used for each set of experiments. Tool tip diameter was measured by Mitituyo digital micrometer and circularity was examined by Leica Optical Microscope and corrected with fine emery paper. Machined micro holes on SS 304 were measured using Leica Optical Microscope. Hole diameter was calculated taking average diameters of all 3 micro holes for each set of experiments. Experiments were carried out on ELECTRONICA ZNC EDM machine with SZNC V5 control panel. A total of 20 sets of experiments have been done with 3 number of experiments in each set using central composite design based on Response Surface Methodology with coded values as -1.682

(-α), -1, 0, 1, +1.682 (α).Genetic Algorithm based optimization and regression analysis have been conducted to establish a mathematical relationship between MRR, TWR, Overcut and Peak current, Pulse on Time, Flushing pressure. Gap current, Pulse On-time and Flushing pressure have been selected from 1-10A, 1-10µs and 0.05-0.5 kg/cm2 respectively. Gap voltage and servo voltage have been kept fixed at 40V and 45V respectively. Pulse Off Time has been kept fixed at 5µsec. Analysis of experiments have been done based on contour plots where values are encoded in coded units where values coded as 0 represent the mid values. Negative coded values represent lower ranges from mid value and positive coded values represent higher ranges of values. Actual values of process parameters against coded values are as shown in Table 1.

Table 1. Experimental Conditions for micro-EDMing of SS

Process Parameters	-1.682 (α)	-1	0	1	1.682 (α)
Gap Current (A)	1	2	3	4	5
Pulse on Time (µs)	1	2	3	4	5
Flushing Pressure (kg/cm²)	0.06	0.12	0.18	0.24	0.30

REGRESSION ANALYSIS

Say, the dependent variable 'Y' in a multiple regression model with 'k' regressor variables (X_1, X_2, …,X_k), the intercept of that equation is B_0 and the partial regressor coefficients are β_0,β_1, β_2, …, β_k then theequation can be expressed with a small error ε as following equation 1.

$$Y = \beta_0 + \beta_1 X_1 + \beta_2 X_2 + ... + \varepsilon \quad (1)$$

Model Development by Using Regression Analysis

Thegenerated regression equationswith X, Y and Z as Gap Current, Pulse-On Time and Flushing Pressure respectivelyobtained are as follows:

$$MRR = 0.000442 + 0.000116 * X + 0.000031 * Y + 0.000002 * Z \quad (2)$$

$$TWR = 0.000666 + 0.000238 * X + 0.000132 * Y + 0.000028 * Z \quad (3)$$

$$OC = 143 + 9.66 * X - 3.04 * Y + 4.41 * Z \quad (4)$$

Response Surface Methodology (RSM)

In statistics, response surface methodology RSM explores the relationships between several explanatory variables and one or more response variables. The method was introduced by George E. P. Box and K. B. Wilson in 1951. The main idea of RSM is to use a sequence of designed experiments to obtain an optimal response. Box and Wilson suggest using a second-degree polynomial model to do this. They acknowledge that this model is only an approximation, but they use it because such a model is easy to estimate and apply, even when little is known about the process.

Statistical approaches such as RSM can be employed to maximize the production of a special substance by optimization of operational factors. In contrast to conventional methods, the interaction among process variables can be determined by statistical techniques. An easy way to estimate a first-degree polynomial model is to use a factorial experiment or a fractional factorial design. This is enough to determine which explanatory variables affect the response variable(s) of interest. Once it is suspected that only significant explanatory variables are left, then a more complicated design, such as a central composite design can be implemented to estimate a second-degree polynomial model, which is still only an approximation at best. However, the second-degree model can be used to optimize (maximize, minimize, or attain a specific target for) the response variable(s) of interest.

Analysis of the Result for Response Surface Methodology

Experiments were designed and analyzed based on Response Surface Methodology. A total of 60 experiments were conducted (20 × 3) number of experiments. The tabulation for micro-EDMing of SS 304 has been shown as below in Table 2.

It shows the measured values for MRR, TWR and Overcut for all 20 sets of experiments. Tool diameter was measured as 430μm. Overcut was measured as difference of average entry diameter of micro hole and tool tip diameter and TWR was measured as the ratio of difference in initial and final weights of electrodes to machining time. The values were analyzed by response surface methods using contour plots shown in Figure 2, Figure 3 and Figure 4. An equation has been obtained to formulate a link between MRR, TWR and Overcut with Gap Current, Pulse on Time and Flushing Pressure. The values of all the three machining parameters namely Pulse On time, Gap Current and Flushing pressure are given in coded values where -1.682 was taken as lowest value and +1.682 was taken as highest value. 0 was taken as mid value. -0.5, -1.0, -1.5 represent lower ranges of values and 0.5, 1.0, 1.5 represent higher ranges of values.

Pressure having nil effect

Figure 1 shows surface plot of MRR that has been analyzed assuming flushing pressure non effective. Similarly, Figure 2 shows the surface plot graph for TWR with Flushing Pressure and Pulse On-time by assuming null effects of Peak current. Figure 3 shows the surface plot graph for Overcut with Peak current and Flushing pressure by assuming Pulse On-time having nil effects. It is observed from Figure 1 that MRR increases with increase in peak current. So, material removal rate increases as the value of peak current increases and decreases to a certain extent then increases with rise in values of pulse on-time. This might be due to the increase in thermal energy at machining zone resulted in increase in rate of melting and vaporization of workpiece surface. From Figure 2 and Figure 3, it is concluded that

Table 2. Experimental values ofMRR, TWR and Overcut for micro-EDMing of SS 304

Experiment Set No.	MRR (in g/min)	TWR (in g/min)	Overcut, D_h - D_t (in µm)
1	0.00023	0.00028	140
2	0.00042	0.00066	158.5
3	0.0004	0.00057	167.5
4	0.00045	0.00108	150
5	0.00051	0.00046	110
6	0.00049	0.00026	131.5
7	0.00054	0.0007	124
8	0.00066	0.00093	197
9	0.00017	0.00079	141
10	0.00079	0.00092	168.5
11	0.00073	0.0009	145
12	0.00065	0.00116	170
13	0.00015	0.00021	127.5
14	0.00061	0.00096	159
15	0.00054	0.00083	150
16	0.00054	0.00049	105
17	0.00025	0.00055	118.5
18	0.00025	0.00059	129
19	0.00023	0.00027	127
20	0.00022	0.00071	130.5

Overcut increases rapidly with increase in peak current and decreases with rising flushing pressure of dielectric whereas TWR increases spontaneously with increase in flushing pressure. Due to increase in flushing pressure, debris have been removed at faster rate from the machining zone resulted in direct sparking energy between the workpiece surface and tool bottom surface and finally tool wear decreases. Also, reason for the increase in overcut might be due to increase in thermal energy with more sparking density in the machining zone. As a result, melting and vaporization of machining holes was quite irregular.*Figure 2. Surface Plot graph for TWR vs. Flushing Pressure and Pulse on Time by assuming Peak Current having nil effects*

GENETIC ALGORITHM

Genetic algorithm (GA) is a nature inspired technique which can find out the global best or near best solution from a set of contradictory objective function when the variables are discrete, non-linear and non-convex.This algorithm is developed on the basis of the theory of survival of the fittest by Darwin.

To find out the finest solution the function needs to make two modifications. Using the penalty function, the first alteration changed the original constrained function into a variable function, as:

Figure 1. Surface Plot graph for MRR vs. Pulse on Time and Peak Current by assuming Flushing

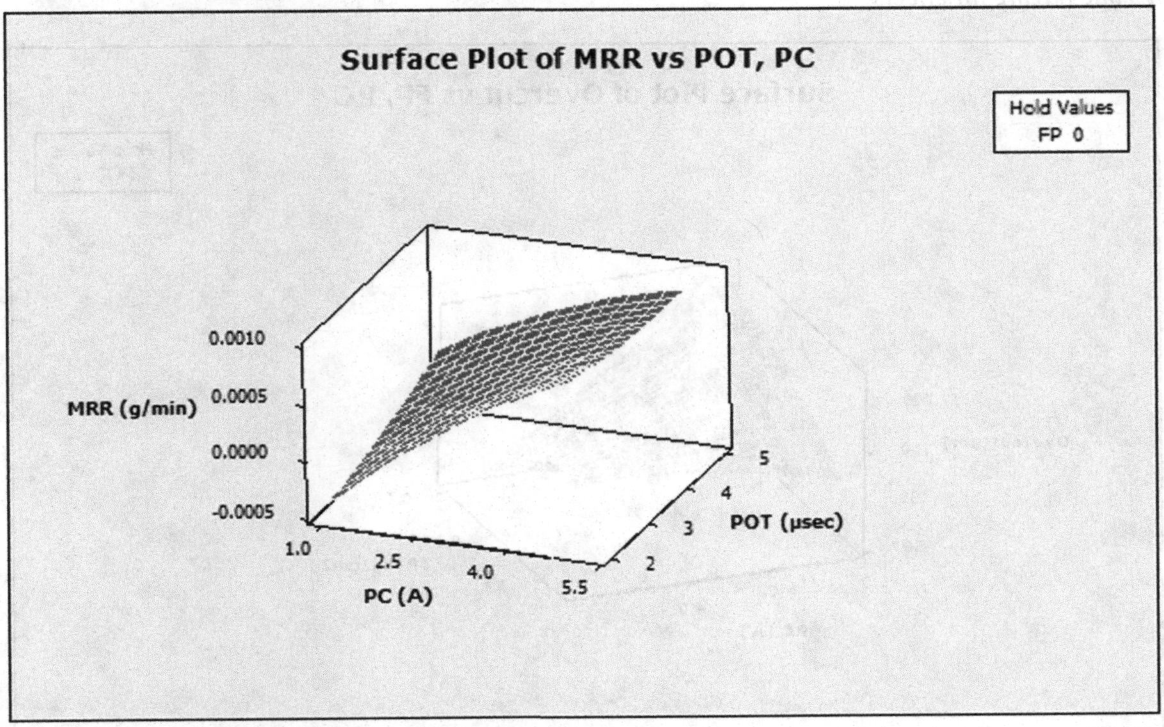

Figure 2. Surface Plot graph for TWR vs. Flushing Pressure and Pulse on Time by assuming Peak Current having nil effects

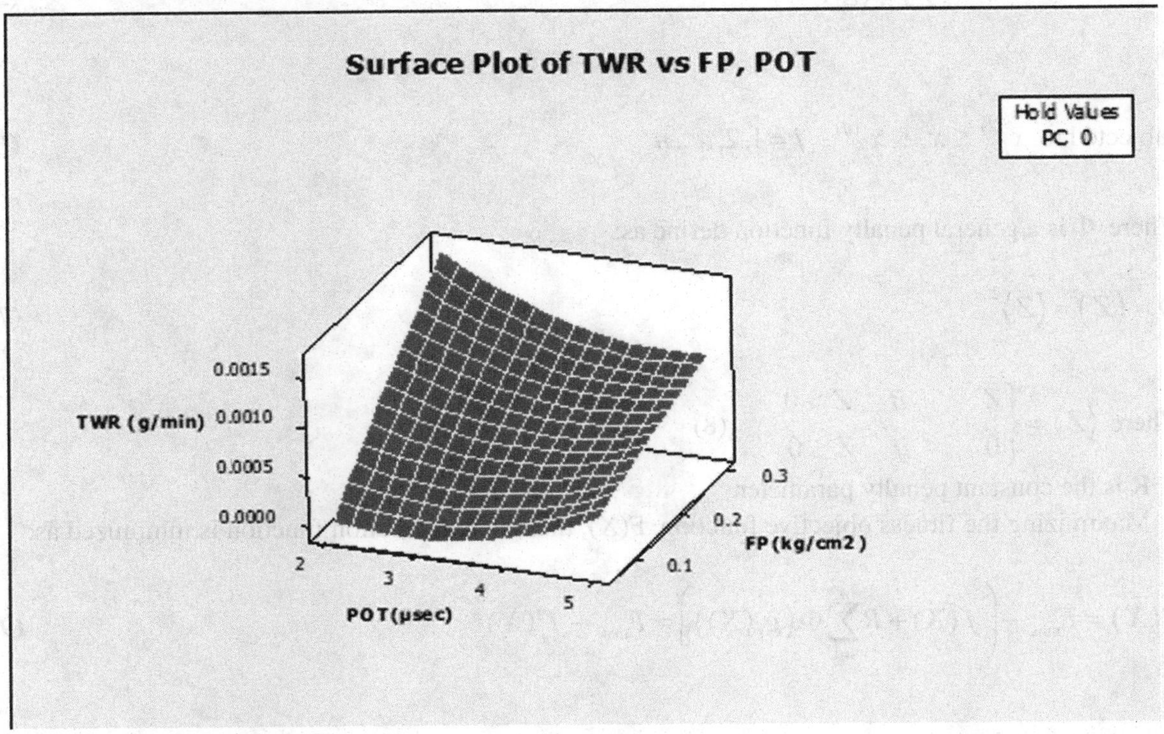

Figure 3. Surface Plot graph for Overcut vs. Peak Current and Flushing Pressure by assuming Pulse On-Time having nil effects

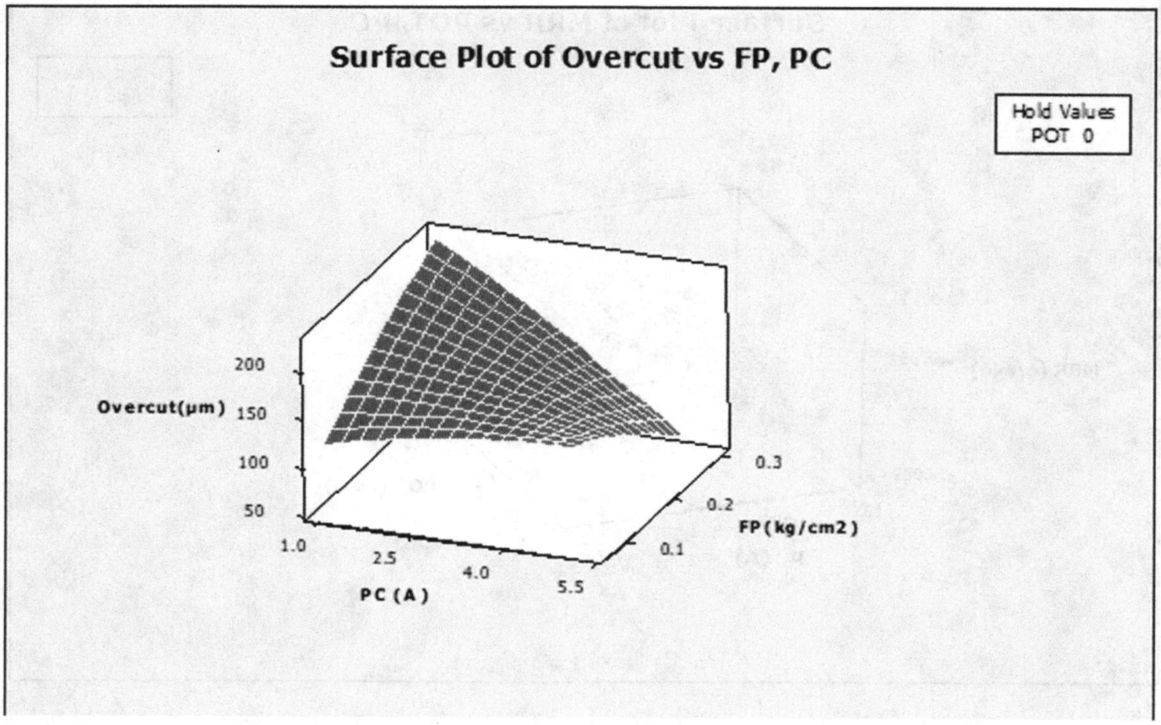

Minimize $f(\mathrm{X})+R\sum_{i=1}^{n}\Phi\left(g_i(\mathrm{X})\right)$ (5)

Subjected to $x_j^{(l)} \le x_j \le x_j^{(u)},\ j=1,2,....,n$ (6)

Where Φ is a general penalty function define as:

$$\Phi=\left(Z\right)=\left\langle Z\right\rangle^2 \quad (7)$$

Where $\left\langle Z\right\rangle=\begin{cases} Z & if \quad Z>0 \\ 0 & if \quad Z\le 0 \end{cases}$ (8)

R is the constant penalty parameter.

Maximizing the fitness objective function, F(X), the second alteration function is minimized as:

$$F(X)=F_{\max}-\left(f(\mathrm{X})+R\sum_{i=1}^{n}\Phi\left(g_i(\mathrm{X})\right)\right)=F_{\max}-f'(X) \quad (9)$$

Where, $F_{\max} > f'(X)$ (10)

F(X) denotes the general fitness function.

It usually works with structures of typically binary numbers (0-1) repressing the problem variables. A binary structure can consider as a biological chromosome.

Analysis of The Result for Multi-Objective Global Optimization

The following conditions are contemplated during the computation when the population is double vector type, with a population size of 50, a constraint dependent creation function, null initial population and initial scores. In case of selection, it is having tournament selection function, 2 number of tournament size. The reproduction crossover fraction is 0.8 and mutation function is constant dependent. The crossover function is intermediate having ratio 1. The migration has forward direction, fraction of 0.2 and interval of 20. The distance measure function has a crowding with a pareto front population fraction of 0.35 and no hybrid function. In case of stopping criteria, the generations have a 100x number of variables, infinite time limit, infinite fitness limit, 100 stall generations, infinite stall time limit, 1x10-4 function tolerance and $1\text{x}10^{-3}$ constrain tolerance. In display to command window, the level of display is off, and the evaluation function fitness is in serial. Figure 4 shows the plot for GA where opposing objectives are optimized simultaneously.

Figure 4. Plot functions for GA

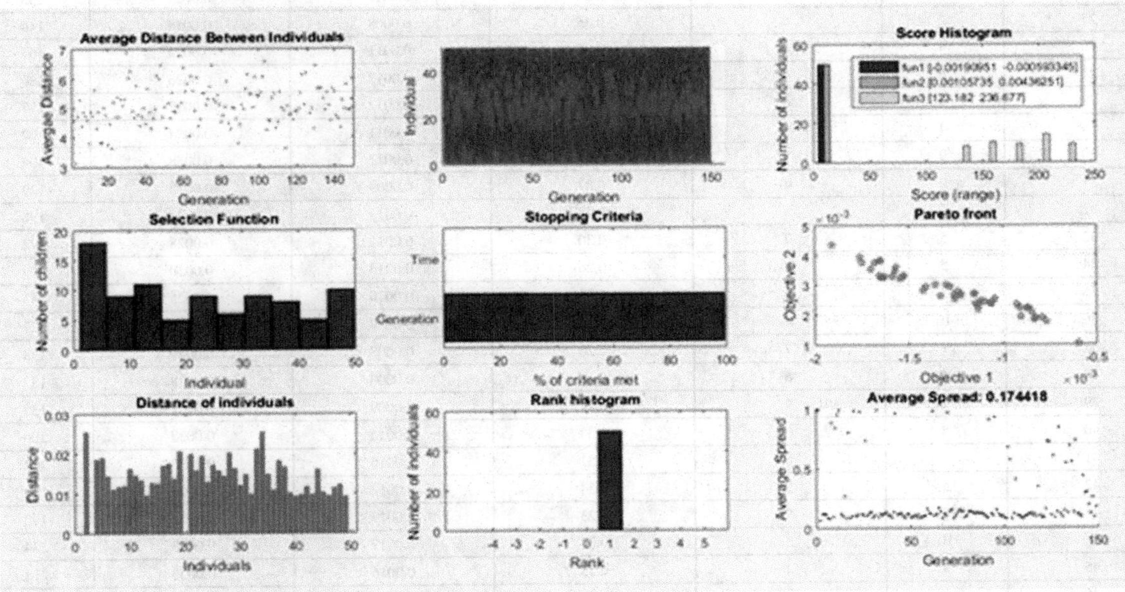

Here the total number of iterations required for optimization is 102 and it gives 50 combinations for the control parameters which also gives the corresponding responses. The output combination is illustrated in table 3. Optimization terminated as the average change in the spread of Pareto solutions has been attained to its tolerance value. As the general setting of the genetic algorithm is to minimize

Table 3. Parametric combination with responses

Sl. No	Control Parameters			Response		
	I (A)	POT (μsec)	Pr (kg/cm²)	MRR (gm/min)	TWR (gm/min)	OC (mm)
1	10	1	0.44	0.0016	0.0032	237
2	1	10	0.39	0.0009	0.0022	126
3	1	1	0.15	0.0006	0.0011	150
4	5	3	0.27	0.0011	0.0023	184
5	4	8	0.19	0.0012	0.0027	156
6	5	8	0.39	0.0013	0.0029	172
7	10	10	0.35	0.0019	0.0044	211
8	1	9	0.16	0.0008	0.0021	129
9	10	6	0.16	0.0018	0.0038	219
10	8	7	0.34	0.0016	0.0035	198
11	8	2	0.36	0.0014	0.0028	217
12	7	4	0.19	0.0014	0.0029	201
13	9	8	0.19	0.0018	0.0040	206
14	5	4	0.33	0.0011	0.0024	181
15	4	6	0.24	0.0011	0.0024	164
16	4	6	0.18	0.0011	0.0025	165
17	6	1	0.21	0.0011	0.0022	194
18	6	7	0.16	0.0014	0.0030	182
19	7	9	0.31	0.0016	0.0036	187
20	1	10	0.14	0.0009	0.0022	123
21	3	4	0.30	0.0009	0.0019	158
22	8	4	0.36	0.0015	0.0032	215
23	2	5	0.23	0.0008	0.0018	146
24	10	2	0.39	0.0016	0.0033	235
25	2	6	0.36	0.0008	0.0019	140
26	4	6	0.25	0.0011	0.0024	161
27	6	4	0.33	0.0013	0.0026	189
28	5	6	0.32	0.0012	0.0027	177
29	4	6	0.33	0.0011	0.0024	162
30	9	8	0.34	0.0017	0.0038	204
31	2	10	0.27	0.0009	0.0023	129
32	6	3	0.28	0.0013	0.0025	196
33	5	7	0.30	0.0012	0.0028	172
34	5	8	0.26	0.0013	0.0030	169
35	3	9	0.35	0.0010	0.0025	143
36	10	4	0.35	0.0017	0.0035	227
37	1	7	0.26	0.0008	0.0019	133
38	1	6	0.15	0.0008	0.0018	137
39	2	9	0.24	0.0009	0.0022	135
40	8	6	0.33	0.0015	0.0033	200
41	8	5	0.31	0.0015	0.0033	204
42	5	5	0.34	0.0012	0.0026	179
43	8	10	0.23	0.0017	0.0038	192
44	10	2	0.37	0.0017	0.0033	234
45	9	4	0.33	0.0016	0.0033	218
46	8	10	0.31	0.0017	0.0038	190
47	10	2	0.37	0.0016	0.0033	231
48	7	2	0.22	0.0013	0.0026	208
49	4	9	0.16	0.0012	0.0027	154
50	10	10	0.35	0.0019	0.0044	211

the objective function, the negative sign is eliminated for maximizing MRR. From Figure 6 it is evident that the responses are varied within a range. For MRR the range is 0.0019 gm/min to 0.0006 gm/min, for TWR it varies between 0.0044 m to 0.0011 µm, for OC it is 237 µmm to 123 µmm. Therefore, in order to accomplish at an optimal or near optimal parametric combination which will all together satisfy opposing nature of the responses, Fuzzy Gray Relational Analysis is conducted.

MULTI OBJECTIVE MODEL USING GREY RELATION ANALYSIS

Grey Relation Analysis (GRA) can utilize to optimize reliable responses simultaneously which opposes one another in nature. The grey system theory was developed by Deng in 1989's and at the present time it is frequently used for analysing experimental design in which the model is undetermined or the information is not complete indicating a combination of known and unknown information's.

GRA buildsthe relationship in between desired (best/ ideal) with real experimental data. Grey grade is computed by averaging the grey coefficient of respective response. In this study multiple response optimizations are found out by converting into a single grey relational grade. The calculated grey relational grade range varies in between 0 to 1, where closer to 1 value indicate its closeness towards the global possible idle solution. Finally, among all the combinations of process control variables, one that attains the maximum grey relational grade is taken to be the best parametric combination.

If higher value is for the better performance such as MRR then it is normalized as per equation,

$$X_{ij} = \frac{Y_{ij} - Min[Y_{ij,} i = 1,2,....n]}{Max[Y_{ij,} i = 1,2,....n] - Min[Y_{ij,} i = 1,2,....n]} \tag{11}$$

If lower value for the better performance such as TWR and OC then it is expressed as,

$$X_{ij} = \frac{Max[Y_{ij,} i = 1,2,....n] - Y_{ij}}{Max[Y_{ij,} i = 1,2,....n] - Min[Y_{ij,} i = 1,2,....n]} \tag{12}$$

The grey relational co-efficient is employed to articulate the relationship between actual normalized experimental data with reference. This relation co-efficient can be evaluated as;

$$Y(X_{oj}, X_{ij}) = \frac{\nabla_{min} + \varsigma \nabla_{max}}{\nabla_{ij} + \varsigma \nabla_{max}} [i = 1,2,....n \,\&\, j = 1,2,...m] \tag{13}$$

Where, $\nabla_{ij} = \left| X_{oj} - X_{ij} \right|, \nabla_{min} = Min[\nabla_{ij}, i = 1,2,....n \,\&\, j = 1,2,...m]$ and
$\nabla_{max} = Max[\nabla_{ij}, i = 1,2,....n \,\&\, j = 1,2,...m]$

ζ = Distinguished co-efficient (range 0-1)

Generally, the notable co-efficient can be regulated to fit the partial requirements. MRR and Ra both are given equal weights that assume a value of 0.5. The expression is as follows:

$$\Gamma\left(X_0, X_i\right) = \frac{1}{m}\sum_{i=1}^{m} Y\left(X_{0j}, X_{ij}\right) \tag{14}$$

Where, m = Number of response parameter.

To optimize both the response at a time by single combination of process variables, GRA is performed. The combination with the rank 1 full fill multiple response parameters optimization.

Fuzzy Set Theory

Fuzzy set theory is the finest controlling tool to solve the uncertainty in decision making problem. Rarely unclear judgments of decision maker(s) make it difficult to evaluate accurate mathematical assessment. Use of linguistic assessments values of weights of the conditions in the problem is a more valuable approach as compared to numerical values (Keufmann& Gupta, 1991). Decision matrix can be changed into a fuzzy decision matrix and associated with weighted normalized fuzzy decision matrix while considering the decision makers' fuzzy ratings. In a cosmos of discussion X, a fuzzy set $\tilde{A}$ is characterized by an associated function $\mu_{\tilde{A}}(x)$ i.e., degree of association of x in $\tilde{A}$ which maps each element x in X to a real number in the interval [0-1]. Triangular fuzzy number (TFN), $\tilde{A}$ can be defined as a triplet (d_1, d_2, d_3) and the membership function is defined (Dubois &Prade, 1979) as shown by equation 15.

$$\mu_{\tilde{d}}(x) = \begin{cases} 0, & x \le d_1 \\ \dfrac{x - d_1}{d_2 - d_1}, & d_1 \le x \le d_2 \\ \dfrac{d_3 - x}{d_3 - d_2}, & d_2 \le x \le d_3 \\ 0, & x > d_3 \end{cases} \tag{15}$$

The transformation technique of fuzzy number into non-fuzzy number, that is, crisp value is recognized as defuzzyfication. In this study 'centroid of area' technique for determining Best Non-Fuzzy Performance (BNP) value is applied.

$$BNP = \frac{[(d_3 - d_1) - (d_2 - d_1)]}{3} + d_1 \tag{16}$$

Choosing the linguistic ratings for criteria:

These linguistic variables can be shown in positive triangular fuzzy numbers as table 4.

Table 4. Linguistic terms for criteria

Linguistic terms	Fuzzy number
Very High (VH)	(0.9,1.0,1.0)
High (H)	(0.7,0.9,1.0)
Moderate High (MH)	(0.5,0.7,0.9)
Moderate (M)	(0.3,0.5,0.7)
Moderate Low (ML)	(0.1,0.3,0.5)
Low (L)	(0.0,0.1,0.3)
Very Low (VL)	(0.0,0.0, 0.1)

Multi Criteria Decision Making (MCDM) Analysis

In the present research study, the four contradictory responses i.e. MRR, TWR and OC have got different level of importance. Here importance is given on OC rather than on other parameters because micro EDM is mainly used for very accuracy purpose.

From fuzzy set theory, the criteria weights are calculated for respective criteria as tabulated in table 5.

Table 5. Weight criteria for deference responses

Criteria	Linguistic terms	Fuzzy number	BNP
MRR	M	0.3,0.5,0.7	0.1833
TWR	H	0.7,0.9,1	0.3667
OC	VH	0.9,1,1	0.4500

Here 50 experimental data set as obtained through GA are further evaluated. In this MCDM analysis of the MRR is aimed to be maximum i.e. larger is better and other responses are aimed to be minimum, i.e. smaller is better.

Optimization of the Parameters

The calculated weights for MRR, TWR and OC are 18.33%, 36.67%, and 45% respectively. Table 6 illustrate the grey relation co-efficient along with grades corresponding to parametric settings and responses for table 3 material.

The results show that experiment number 3 has the maximum grey relational grade value. As defined above, this testing setup fulfils multiple response parameter optimizations. Hence, the experimental run of 3 which having parametric combination as I 1 (unit), POT 1 (unit) and Pr. 0.15 (unit) the best among other experimental setup for having high MRR as 0.0006 (unit), low TWRas 0.0011 (unit)and also low OC as 150 (unit).

The confirmation experiment performed with the above optimal combination results in grey relational grade MRR, TWR and OC obtained 0.0009 (unit), 0.001 (unit)and 151 (unit)respectively. It is found

Table 6. Grey relation co-efficient along with grades and ranks

Exp No.	Response			Grey Co-efficient			Grey Grade	Rank
	MRR	TWR	OC	MRR	TWR	OC		
1	0.0016	0.0032	237	0.48	0.36	0.31	0.38	41
2	0.0009	0.0022	126	0.19	0.52	1.01	0.57	3
3	**0.0006**	**0.0011**	**150**	**0.15**	**1.04**	**0.68**	**0.62**	**1**
4	0.0011	0.0023	184	0.24	0.50	0.46	0.40	31
5	0.0012	0.0027	156	0.24	0.43	0.63	0.43	18
6	0.0013	0.0029	172	0.28	0.40	0.53	0.40	29
7	0.0019	0.0044	211	1.04	0.27	0.37	0.56	5
8	0.0008	0.0021	129	0.18	0.55	0.96	0.56	4
9	0.0018	0.0038	219	0.61	0.31	0.35	0.43	20
10	0.0016	0.0035	198	0.42	0.34	0.41	0.39	36
11	0.0014	0.0028	217	0.33	0.41	0.36	0.37	50
12	0.0014	0.0029	201	0.33	0.40	0.40	0.37	48
13	0.0018	0.0040	206	0.63	0.30	0.38	0.44	16
14	0.0011	0.0024	181	0.24	0.49	0.48	0.40	30
15	0.0011	0.0024	164	0.23	0.48	0.57	0.43	21
16	0.0011	0.0025	165	0.23	0.47	0.56	0.42	22
17	0.0011	0.0022	194	0.24	0.53	0.43	0.40	34
18	0.0014	0.0030	182	0.31	0.39	0.47	0.39	37
19	0.0016	0.0036	187	0.42	0.33	0.45	0.40	32
20	0.0009	0.0022	123	0.19	0.52	1.08	0.60	2
21	0.0009	0.0019	158	0.19	0.59	0.61	0.47	14
22	0.0015	0.0032	215	0.40	0.36	0.36	0.38	47
23	0.0008	0.0018	146	0.18	0.62	0.72	0.51	12
24	0.0016	0.0033	235	0.48	0.36	0.31	0.39	39
25	0.0008	0.0019	140	0.18	0.60	0.79	0.52	11
26	0.0011	0.0024	161	0.22	0.49	0.60	0.44	17
27	0.0013	0.0026	189	0.27	0.44	0.44	0.38	40
28	0.0012	0.0027	177	0.26	0.43	0.50	0.40	33
29	0.0011	0.0024	162	0.22	0.49	0.59	0.43	19
30	0.0017	0.0038	204	0.52	0.31	0.39	0.41	25
31	0.0009	0.0023	129	0.20	0.50	0.95	0.55	9
32	0.0013	0.0025	196	0.27	0.46	0.42	0.38	43
33	0.0012	0.0028	172	0.27	0.42	0.52	0.40	28
34	0.0013	0.0030	169	0.28	0.39	0.54	0.40	26
35	0.0010	0.0025	143	0.22	0.46	0.76	0.48	13
36	0.0017	0.0035	227	0.55	0.33	0.33	0.40	27
37	0.0008	0.0019	133	0.18	0.61	0.89	0.56	7
38	0.0008	0.0018	137	0.17	0.65	0.84	0.55	8
39	0.0009	0.0022	135	0.19	0.52	0.87	0.53	10
40	0.0015	0.0033	200	0.39	0.35	0.40	0.38	44
41	0.0015	0.0033	204	0.39	0.36	0.39	0.38	46
42	0.0012	0.0026	179	0.26	0.44	0.49	0.40	35
43	0.0017	0.0038	192	0.50	0.31	0.43	0.41	23
44	0.0017	0.0033	234	0.49	0.35	0.32	0.39	38
45	0.0016	0.0033	218	0.43	0.36	0.35	0.38	45
46	0.0017	0.0038	190	0.49	0.31	0.44	0.41	24
47	0.0016	0.0033	231	0.47	0.36	0.32	0.38	42
48	0.0013	0.0026	208	0.30	0.44	0.38	0.37	49
49	0.0012	0.0027	154	0.24	0.43	0.65	0.44	15
50	0.0019	0.0044	211	1.04	0.27	0.37	0.56	6

that MRR, TWR and OC improved considerably as appeared from computational results by using ideal machining variables combinations. Table 7 displays the validation results while machining at elevate condition.

Table 7. Results of machining performance using optimal machining parameters

Settings Levels	Predicted result	Experimental result
MRR	0.0006	0.0009
TWR	0.0011	0.0010
OC	150	151
Grey Grade	0.62	0.65
Improvement of the grey relation grade: **0.03**		

CONCLUSION

An initial and basic study has been done on SS 304 with the help of Response Surface Methodology and Multi Criteria Decision Making. Linear regression equation has been generated for MRR, TWR and Overcut. Application of MCDM technique has been found to be satisfactory for the generated results. It was found that MRR depends significantly on Pulse on Time and Gap Current and minutely on Flushing pressure. It is the major performance characteristics for industrial applications. On the other hand, Overcut decreases with decrease in Gap current and increase in Pulse On time up to some extent. After a certain value of Pulse on Time approximately greater than 2, Overcut increases. Approximately after a range 0.5-1 kg/cm^2 of flushing pressure TWR decreases.

However, future scope reveals to look further on modeling of other machining aspects like type of dielectrics, powder additives, harder conductive materials.

REFERENCES

Bhattacharyya, B., Gangopadhyay, S., & Sarkar, B. R. (2007). Modelling and analysis of EDMED job surface Integrity. *Journal of Materials Processing Technology*, *189*(1-3), 169–177. doi:10.1016/j.jmatprotec.2007.01.018

Bobbili, R., Madhu, V., & Gogia, A. K. (2013). Effect of Wire-EDM Machining Parameters on Surface Roughness and Material Removal Rate of High Strength Armor Steel. *Materials and Manufacturing Processes*, *28*(4), 364–368. doi:10.1080/10426914.2012.736661

Chen, S. T., & Yang, H. Y. (2011). Study of micro electro discharge machining (micro-EDM) with onmachine measurement-assisted techniques. *Journal of Micromechanics and Microengineering*, 22.

Dastagiri, M., & Kumar, A. H. (2014). Experimental Investigation of EDM parameters on stainless steelEn41b. *12th Global Congress on Manufacturing and Management*, *97*, 1551-1564.

Deng, J. (1989). Introduction to Grey System. *Journal of Grey System*, *1*(1), 1–24.

Dubois, D., & Prade, H. (1979). Operations in a Fuzzy-Valued Logic. *Information and Control*, *43*(2), 224–240. doi:10.1016/S0019-9958(79)90730-7

Ekmekci, B., Sayar, A., Opoz, T.T., &Erden, A. (2009). Geometry and surface damage in micro-electrical discharge machining of micro-holes. *Journal of Micromechanics and Microengineering, 19*, 105030-45.

Garg, R., & Mittal, S. (2014). Optimization by Genetic Algorithm. *International Journal of Advanced Research in Computer Science and Software Engineering*, *4*(4), 587–589.

Jahan, M. P., Wong, Y. S., & Rahman, M. (2009). A study on the fine finish die sinking micro-EDM oftungsten-carbide using different electrode materials. *Journal of Materials Processing Technology*, *209*(8), 3956–3967. doi:10.1016/j.jmatprotec.2008.09.015

Keufmann, A., & Gupta, M. M. (1985). *Introduction to Fuzzy Arithmetic: Theory and Applications*. Van Nostrand Reinhold.

Kiran, M. P. S. K., & Joshi, S. S. (2007). Modelling of Surface Roughness andthe Role of Debris inMicro-EDM. *Journal of Manufacturing Science and Engineering*, *129*(2), 265–273. doi:10.1115/1.2540683

Kuriachen, B., Somashekhar, K. P., & Mathew, J. (2015). Multi response optimization of micro- wire electrical discharge machining process. *International Journal of Advanced Manufacturing Technology*, *76*(1-4), 91–104. doi:10.100700170-014-6005-2

Kurikose, S., & Shanmugham, M. S. (2005). Multi objective optimization of wire EDM process bynon-dominated sorting genetic algorithms. *Journal of Materials Processing Technology*, *170*, 133–141. doi:10.1016/j.jmatprotec.2005.04.105

Liao, Y. S., Chuang, T. J., & Yu, Y. P. (2014). Study of machining parameters optimization for different materials in WEDM. *International Journal of Advanced Manufacturing Technology*, *70*(9-12), 2051–2058. doi:10.100700170-013-5458-z

Maradia, U., Scuderi, M., Knaak, R., Boccadoro, M., Beltrami, I., Stirnimann, J., & Wegener, K. (2013). Super finished surfaces using meso-micro EDM. *The Seventeenth CIRP Conference on Electro Physical and Chemical Machining (ISEM)*, 6, 157-162.

Rajmohan, T., Prabhu, R., Subbarao, G., & Palanikumar, K. (2012). Optimization of Machining parametersinElectricaldischarge Machining (EDM) of 304 Stainless Steel. *Journal of Procedia Engineering*, *38*, 1030–1036. doi:10.1016/j.proeng.2012.06.129

Rao, B. T., & Krishna, A. G. (2014). Selection of optimal process parameters in WEDM while machining Al7075/SiCp metal matrix composites. *International Journal of Advanced Manufacturing Technology*, *73*(1-4), 299–314. doi:10.100700170-014-5780-0

Somashekhar, K. P., Ramachandran, N., & Mathew, J. (2010). Optimization of Material Removal Rate in Micro-EDM Using Artificial Neural Network and Genetic Algorithms. *Materials and Manufacturing Processes*, *25*(6), 467–475. doi:10.1080/10426910903365760

Tong, H., Li, Y., Zhang, L., & Li, B. (2013). Mechanism design and process control of micro EDM for drilling spray holes of diesel injector nozzles. *Precision Engineering*, *37*(1), 213–221. doi:10.1016/j.precisioneng.2012.09.004

Chapter 3

Multi-Objective Optimization of EDM Process on AISI P-20 Tool Steel Using Multi-Criteria Decision-Making Technique

Souvick Chakraborty
Bengal Institute of Technology and Management, India

ABSTRACT

The optimization technique is introduced to overcome the problem. Here the author introduces multi-criteria decision-making technique to get the optimization value. Electrical discharge machining (EDM) in nontraditional machining process is applied for machining complicated or intricate geometries on raw materials. The present work attempts to optimize several responses of machining operation using multi-criteria decision making (MCDM) by employing different machining parameters like current, voltage, pulse. The Taguchi L9 orthogonal experimental design is followed during electrical discharge machining of AISI P20 tool steel. Four responses, namely metal removal rate, tool life, surface roughness, and over cut, are considered for optimization. The present work is aimed at multi-response optimization (i.e., higher MRR, higher tool life, lower surface roughness, and minimum overcut), which is conducted using MCDM technique.

INTRODUCTION

From the very beginning of civilization, man has been continuously engaged in converting the natural resources into useful products. Basically, entire discipline of engineering is mainly concerned with this. Among all of engineering, manufacturing is perhaps most important because it involves the conversion of a raw material into a final product. The metal cutting process is the part of manufacturing process. The metal cutting refers to only those processes where material removal is affected by relative motion between tool made of harder material and work piece. Now is the time for flexible manufacturing.

DOI: 10.4018/978-1-7998-3624-7.ch003

So, there was a new process introduces in metal cutting process, called Non-Traditional machining process. Some of the notable Non-Traditional machines are the Electrochemical machining, Electrical discharge machining, Electrochemical grinding, Ultrasonic machining, Electron beam machining, Laser beam machining, Plasma arc machining etc. Our present work based on Electrical discharge machining process.

A brief literature review on EDM process is presented here. G. K. Bose et. al. (Bose & Mahapatra, 2014) studied the experimental performance were conducted within the L27 orthogonal array based on the Taguchi method and significant process parameters were identified using analysis of variance (ANOVA) using electric discharge machining (EDM) of AISI H 13, W.-Nr. 1.2344 Grade for finding out the effect of machining parameters such as discharge gap current (GI), pulse on time (POT), pulse off time (POF) and spark gap (SG) on performance responses such as material removal rate (MRR), surface roughness (*Ra*) and overcut (OC)using a square-shaped Cu tool with lateral flushing. It was found that MRR is affected by gap current and *Ra* is affected by pulse on time. Selvakumar et al. (Selvakumar et al., 2013) studied the experimental performance based on L-18 orthogonal array with pulse on time, pulse off time, peak current, wire tension, servo feed setting and corner angle as control factors. ANOVA was performed to find the significance of the factors considered. Kapoor et al. (Kapoor et al., 2012) investigated the effect of cryogenic treated brass wire electrode on surface roughness and material removal rate for WEDM. They described the influence of various machining parameters (including pulse width, time between two pulses, wire tension and wire feed) on surface roughness and material removal rate by using one variable at a time approach. Goutam Kumar Bose et. al (Bose & Pritam, 2018) studied the experimental performance based on Taguchi Methodology, Regression analysis and Response Surface Methodology (RSM). A die sinking EDM is applied to machine mild steel in order to measure the different multi-objective results like Material Removal Rate (MRR) and Over Cut (OC) and this contradictory objective is accomplished by using the control parameters like a pulse on time, duty factor, gap current and spark gap employing copper tool with lateral flushing. Goutam Kumar Bose et al. (Bose & Pritam, 2016) studied the experimental performance based on L9 orthogonal array with four different control parameters such as pulse on time, pulse off time, gap current, and Spark gap are considered to study the effect on the performance of responses like material removal rate, surface roughness and overcut using a square shape copper tool with lateral flushing. Based on Taguchi methodology the significant process parameters affecting the responses are identified applying ANOVA for each material. A well-known Grey relational analysis is carried out where the weights are calculated using entropy method to full fill the multi criteria decision making process.

MCDM Method

Multiple criteria decision making (MCDM) is the approach dealing with the ranking and selection of one or more vendors from a pool of providers (Shyur & Shih, 2006). The MCDM provides an effective framework for comparison based on the evaluation of multiple conflict criteria. MCDM has been one of the fastest growing areas of operational research, as it is often realized that many concrete problems can be represented by several (conflicting) criteria. It was described as the most well-known branch of decision making (Triantaphyllou, 2000). Multiple criteria decision making (MCDM) is widely used in ranking one or more alternatives from a set of available alternatives with respect to multiple criteria. The criteria for MCDM problem can be classified into two groups: beneficial (B) for which higher values are desirable and non-beneficial (NB) or cost for which lower values are desirable. In the basis of criteria

MCDM technique can be classified in to three categories: (i) objective, (ii) subjective, and (iii) critical, irrespective of beneficial or non-beneficial in nature.

There are many types of MCDM techniques are present like VIKOR, COPRAS, ELECTRE, PROMETHEE, TOPSIS and MOORA. Out of these following MCDM techniques we used in our research only MOORA and TOPSIS.

Multi Objective Optimization by Ratio Analysis (MOORA)

MOORA method based on two components (a) The ratio system and (b) the reference point approach that relies on the concept that the chosen alternative should have the highest composite score which represent the difference between benefit and non-benefit scores. In MOORA, the set of ratio has the square root of the sum of square responses as denominators.

The stepwise procedures of MOORA technique is presented below.

Step 1: *Formation of decision matrix with performance scores. Performance score or performance rating is the value of alternative on each criterion provided by the decision maker.*

$$\begin{array}{cc} & \begin{array}{ccccc} C_1 & \ldots & C_j & \ldots & C_n \end{array} \\ D = \begin{array}{c} A_1 \\ \ldots \\ A_i \\ \ldots \\ A_m \end{array} & \begin{bmatrix} x_{11} & \ldots & x_{1j} & \ldots & x_{1n} \\ \ldots & \ldots & \ldots & \ldots & \ldots \\ x_{i1} & \ldots & x_{ij} & \ldots & x_{in} \\ \ldots & \ldots & \ldots & \ldots & \ldots \\ x_{m1} & \ldots & x_{mj} & \ldots & x_{mn} \end{bmatrix} \end{array} \quad (1)$$

x_{ij} is the performance rating of alternative A_i with respect to criterion C_j. m is the number of alternatives and n is the number of criteria. Here the performance rating x_{ij} is crisp

Step 2: *Formation of weight matrix.*

$$W = \left[\tilde{w}_1 \ \ldots \ \tilde{w}_j \ \ldots \ \tilde{w}_n \right] \quad (2)$$

Step 3: *Normalization of performance ratings*

$$r_{ij} = \frac{x_{ij}}{\sqrt{\sum_{i=1}^{m} \left(x_{ij}^2 \right)}} \quad (3)$$

Step 4: *Computations of sum of benefit criteria measures (SoB) and sum of non-benefit criteria measures (SoNB) by following equations*

$$SoB = \sum_{j \in B} w_j r_{ij} \tag{4}$$

$$SoNB = \sum_{j \in NB} w_j r_{ij} \tag{5}$$

where, w_j is the weight of jth criterion.

Step 5: *Computation of composite score*In most of the real life problems different weights are given to the attributes of the alternatives as per their relative importance. When the weights of attributes are taken into consideration then the Eq. 3 can be expressed as

$$y_i^* = \sum_{j \in B} w_j r_{ij} - \sum_{j \in NB} w_j r_{ij} \tag{6}$$

where y_i^* is composite score of alternative *i*. The value of y_i^* may be positive, negative or zero. The best alternative is one which is associated with the highest y_i^* value and the worst alternative is one which is associated with the lowest y_i^* value.

Step 6: *Ranking the products in descending order of composite score* y_i^*.

Technique for Order Preference by Similarity to the Ideal Solution (TOPSIS)

The TOPSIS is proposed by Hwang and Yoon (Hwang & Yoon (1981)). The primary concept of TOPSIS approach is that the most preferred alternative should not only have the shortest distance from the positive ideal solution (PIS), but also have the farthest distance from the negative ideal solution (NIS). General speaking, the advantages for TOPSIS include (i) simple, rationally comprehensible concept, (ii) good computational efficiency, (iii) ability to measure the relative performance for each alternative in a simple mathematical form.

The stepwise procedures of TOPSIS are as follows.

Step 1: *Normalize performance ratings*

Normalization of performance ratings in TOPSIS method is carried out by using the same formula used in MOORA.

Step 2: *Construct weighted normalized decision matrix*

$$\tilde{D}_{wn} = \left[v_{ij}\right]_{m \times n} = \left[r_{ij} \times \bar{w}_j\right]_{m \times n} \tag{7}$$

Step 3: *Determine Positive Ideal Solution (PIS) and Negative Ideal Solution (NIS)*

$$\text{PIS} = \left[v_1^+, \ldots, v_j^+, \ldots, v_n^+\right],\ v_j^+ = \max_i \left(v_{ij}\right), \text{if } j \in B;\ v_j^+ = \min_i \left(v_{ij}\right), \text{if } j \in NB \tag{8}$$

NIS= $\left[v_1^-,...,v_j^-,...,v_n^-\right]$, $v_j^- = \min\limits_i\left(v_{ij}\right)$, if $j \in B$; $v_j^- = \max\limits_i\left(v_{ij}\right)$, if $j \in NB$ (9)

Step 4: *Calculate separation measures*

Separation measures are calculated by the Euclidean distances of each alternative from PIS (S_i^+) and NIS (S_i^-) respectively using following equations

$$S_i^+ = \sqrt{\sum_{j=1}^{n}\left(v_j^+ - v_j\right)^2} \qquad (10)$$

$$S_i^- = \sqrt{\sum_{j=1}^{n}\left(v_j - v_j^-\right)^2} \qquad (11)$$

Step 5: *Determine closeness coefficient and rank the alternatives*

Closeness coefficient (CC_i) is measured by the following relation

$$CC_i = \frac{S_i^-}{S_i^- + S_i^+} \qquad (12)$$

CC_i maximizes the benefit criteria and minimizes the cost criteria.

WEIGHT CALCULATION METHOD

The Entropy Method for Determination of Weight

The Entropy method is used for determine the weigh in the present work. The entropy weight method was originally a concept of thermodynamics, which firstly added into the information theory by C.E.S hannon and it is now applied widely in the field of engineering technology, social economy, etc. Based on the basic principle of information theory, the information is a measure of system orderly degree, but the entropy is a measure of the system's disorder. Their absolute value is equal, but the symbol instead.

The stepwise procedures of Entropy method is presented below.

Step 1: *Construct the decision matrix as shown in equation* 1.

Step 2: *Normalize the decision matrix using the following equation.*

$$\tau_{ij} = \frac{\left|x_{ij}\right|}{\sum_{i=1}^{m}\left|x_{ij}\right|}, \text{ where, } 0 \le \tau_{ij} \le 1, i=1, 2...m. \qquad (13)$$

Step 3: *Calculate the entropy using the following relationship*

$$e_j = \frac{1}{\ln m} \sum_{i=1}^{m} \left| \tau_{ij} \ln \tau_{ij} \right| \quad (14)$$

Here, e_j represents the entropy of the corresponding criteria.

Step 4: Determine the weight (w_j) of jth criterion using the following equation

$$w_j = \frac{1 - e_j}{\sum_{j=1}^{t} (1 - e_j)} \quad (15)$$

Experimentation

In this experimental work is carried out during Electrical Discharge Machining of AISI P20 tool steel. Machining was performed on EDM machine in Mechanical Engineering Department. The chemical composition of the work piece material is provided in Table 1.

Table 1. Chemical composition

C %	Si%	Mn%	Cr%	Mo%	Fe%
0.28-0.40	0.20-0.80	0.60-1.00	1.40-2.00	0.30-0.55	Balance

Electrical Discharge Machining was conducted on AISI P20 tool steel using EDM machine in order to find out the maximum allowable range of machining parameters (current, voltage, pulse) that can be used. Cutting parameters are classified in to three levels which shown in Table 2. Taguchi L9 orthogonal array design is selected to employ different parametric combinations for test run, as shown in Table 3.

MRR is calculated using mathematical formula. The surface roughness Ra (micron) is measured using stylus type profilometer Talysurf (Taylor Hobson Surtronic 3+). The different experimental runs along with the responses are presented in Table 4.

Table 2. Machining parameters and their levels

Factors	Cutting Parameters	Units	Low (-1)	Medium (0)	High (+1)
A	Current(IP)	Amp	15	20	25
B	Voltage(V)	V	45	50	55
C	Pulse(TON)	μs	1000	2000	3000

Table 3. Experimental layout using an L_9 Orthogonal array

Experimental Run	Cutting factor		
	A Current	B Voltage	C Pulse
E_1	1	1	1
E_2	1	2	2
E_3	1	3	3
E_4	2	1	3
E_5	2	2	1
E_6	2	3	2
E_7	3	1	2
E_8	3	2	3
E_9	3	3	1

RESULTS AND DISCUSSION

The various performances considered here are *Metal removal rate* (C_1), *Tool life* (C_2), *Surface roughness* (C_3) and *Over cut* (C_4). The initial decision matrix is shown in Table 5. The normalized decision matrix and the final weight matrix (as evaluated by entropy method) are shown in Table 6 and Table 7 respectively.

The initial decision matrix combined with weight matrix is presented in Table 8. Normalization technique of MOORA and TOPSIS being same, a common normalized decision matrix along with the weight matrix is presented in Table 9.

The weighted normalized decision matrix, SoB, SoNB, y_i^* and ranking of experiments following MOORA are shown in Table 10. The weighted normalized decision matrix, PIS, NIS,, , and ranking of experiments by TOPSIS are shown in Table 11.

Table 4. Experimental run for MRR, Tool life, Surface roughness and Over cut

Experimental Run	MRR	Tool life	Surface roughness	Over cut
E_1	0.3515	3.56	12.241	0.244
E_2	0.3926	2.89	11.8482	0.332
E_3	0.3364	22.81	12.8656	0.304
E_4	0.2443	33.55	9.126	0.096
E_5	0.4811	3.09	14.0822	0.232
E_6	0.5075	2.19	12.4748	0.352
E_7	0.4829	13.89	13.2504	0.36
E_8	0.5982	25.8	17.6182	0.216
E_9	0.6341	3.29	14.1882	0.272

Table 5. Initial decision matrix

Experimental Run	Criteria →	C_1 (+)	C_2 (+)	C_3 (-)	C_4 (-)
E_1		0.3515	3.56	12.241	0.244
E_2		0.3926	2.89	11.8482	0.332
E_3		0.3364	22.81	12.8656	0.304
E_4		0.2443	33.55	9.126	0.096
E_5		0.4811	3.09	14.0822	0.232
E_6		0.5075	2.19	12.4748	0.352
E_7		0.4829	13.89	13.2504	0.36
E_8		0.5982	25.8	17.6182	0.216
E_9		0.6341	3.29	14.1882	0.272

The output of MOORA method exhibits that E_4>E_8>E_3>E_7>E_9>E_5>E_6>E_1>$E_2$and that of TOPSIS yields E_4>E_8>E_3>E_7>E_9>E_6>E_5>E_2>E_1.The ranking of the experimental runs obtained by two methods are compared and presented in Figure 1.

For investigate the existence of any correlation between two different sets of ranks obtained by MOORA and TOPSIS, the Spearman's rank correlation coefficient () is computed.

(16)

Table 6. Normalized decision matrix for Entropy weight calculation

Experimental Run	Criteria →	C_1 (+)	C_2 (+)	C_3 (-)	C_4 (-)
E_1		0.087	0.032	0.104	0.101
E_2		0.097	0.026	0.100	0.137
E_3		0.083	0.205	0.109	0.126
E_4		0.060	0.302	0.077	0.039
E_5		0.119	0.027	0.119	0.096
E_6		0.125	0.019	0.105	0.146
E_7		0.119	0.125	0.112	0.149
E_8		0.148	0.232	0.149	0.089
E_9		0.157	0.029	0.120	0.112

Table 7. The final weight matrix

Criteria →	C_1 (+)	C_2 (+)	C_3 (-)	C_4 (-)
e_j →	0.016	0.193	0.006	0.022
w_j →	0.307	0.416	0.181	0.094

Table 8. Initial decision matrix combined with weight matrix

Experimental Run	Criteria →	C_1 (+)	C_2 (+)	C_3 (-)	C_4 (-)
	Weight →	**0.307**	**0.416**	**0.181**	**0.094**
E_1		0.3515	3.56	12.241	0.244
E_2		0.3926	2.89	11.8482	0.332
E_3		0.3364	22.81	12.8656	0.304
E_4		0.2443	33.55	9.126	0.096
E_5		0.4811	3.09	14.0822	0.232
E_6		0.5075	2.19	12.4748	0.352
E_7		0.4829	13.89	13.2504	0.36
E_8		0.5982	25.8	17.6182	0.216
E_9		0.6341	3.29	14.1882	0.272

NB: Benefit criteria are marked (+) and non-benefit criteria are marked (-).

Where is the difference between the rank of each experimental run obtained by two methods, and is the number of experiments. The method is fairly simple, yet reliable for testing both the strength and direction (positive or negative) of any correlation between two variables. The result is presented in Table 12.

The Spearman's coefficient is determined and found to assume a healthy value of 0.967. That means there are strong relationship exists between the two different rank sets (MOORA and TOPSIS).

CONCLUSION

Presently all industries are focused on enhancement the productivity with respect to less of time and believed on flexible manufacturing system in metal cutting area. This will be possible if we introduce the optimization techniques with metal cutting process. We get best optimal values of cutting parameter

Table 9. Normalized decision matrix along with weight matrix for MOORA & TOPSIS

Experimental Run	Criteria →	C_1 (+)	C_2 (+)	C_3 (-)	C_4 (-)
	Weight →	**0.307**	**0.416**	**0.181**	**0.094**
E_1		0.2528	0.0705	0.3079	0.2918
E_2		0.2824	0.0572	0.2981	0.3970
E_3		0.2420	0.4516	0.3236	0.3635
E_4		0.1757	0.6643	0.2296	0.1148
E_5		0.3461	0.0612	0.3542	0.2774
E_6		0.3651	0.0434	0.3138	0.4209
E_7		0.3474	0.2750	0.3333	0.4305
E_8		0.4303	0.5108	0.4432	0.2583
E_9		0.4561	0.0651	0.3569	0.3253

Table 10. Weighted normalized decision matrix, SOB, SONB, y_i^* and ranking for MOORA

Experimental Run	C_1 (+)	C_2 (+)	C_3 (-)	C_4 (-)	SOB	SONB	y_i^*	Rank
E_1	0.0776	0.0294	0.0559	0.027	0.1070	0.0835	0.0235	8
E_2	0.0867	0.0238	0.0541	0.037	0.1106	0.0917	0.0189	9
E_3	0.0743	0.1882	0.0587	0.034	0.2625	0.0932	0.1693	3
E_4	0.0540	0.2768	0.0417	0.010	0.3308	0.0525	0.2783	1
E_5	0.1063	0.0255	0.0643	0.026	0.1318	0.0906	0.0412	6
E_6	0.1121	0.0181	0.0569	0.039	0.1302	0.0968	0.0333	7
E_7	0.1067	0.1146	0.0605	0.040	0.2213	0.1013	0.1200	4
E_8	0.1321	0.2129	0.0804	0.024	0.3450	0.1049	0.2401	2
E_9	0.1401	0.0271	0.0648	0.030	0.1672	0.0956	0.0716	5

in metal cutting process with help of optimization techniques. The recent work is done by Multi criteria decision making technique to optimization the Electrical discharge machining process of AISI P20 tool steel. The Taguchi L9 orthogonal array utilized for experimental design. There are three cutting parameters, IP, V, TON selected for optimization. Among many MCDM techniques MOORA and TOPSIS are selected for analysis. The weight is calculated using the Entropy method. And finally, we get the best parametric combination like, medium current- low voltage-high pulse with respect to ideal rank 1 (E_4) and also said that MCDM techniques have more advantages, likely easily implementation, less time effort, simple techniques, base only ranking system.

Table 11. Weighted normalized decision matrix, PIS, NIS, S_i^+, S_i^-, CC_i and ranking (TOPSIS)

Experimental Run	C_1 (+)	C_2 (+)	C_3 (-)	C_4 (-)	S_i^+	S_i^-	CC_i	Rank
E_1	0.077	0.029	0.055	0.027	0.256	0.038	0.129	9
E_2	0.086	0.023	0.054	0.037	0.260	0.042	0.140	8
E_3	0.074	0.188	0.058	0.034	0.114	0.172	0.602	3
E_4	0.053	0.276	0.041	0.010	0.086	0.263	0.753	1
E_5	0.106	0.025	0.064	0.026	0.255	0.057	0.182	7
E_6	0.112	0.018	0.056	0.039	0.262	0.062	0.192	6
E_7	0.106	0.114	0.060	0.040	0.169	0.111	0.397	4
E_8	0.132	0.212	0.080	0.024	0.076	0.210	0.733	2
E_9	0.140	0.027	0.064	0.030	0.251	0.088	0.260	5
PIS	0.140	0.276	0.041	0.010				
NIS	0.053	0.018	0.080	0.040				

Figure 1. Comparison of ranking of experimental run by MOORA and TOPSIS

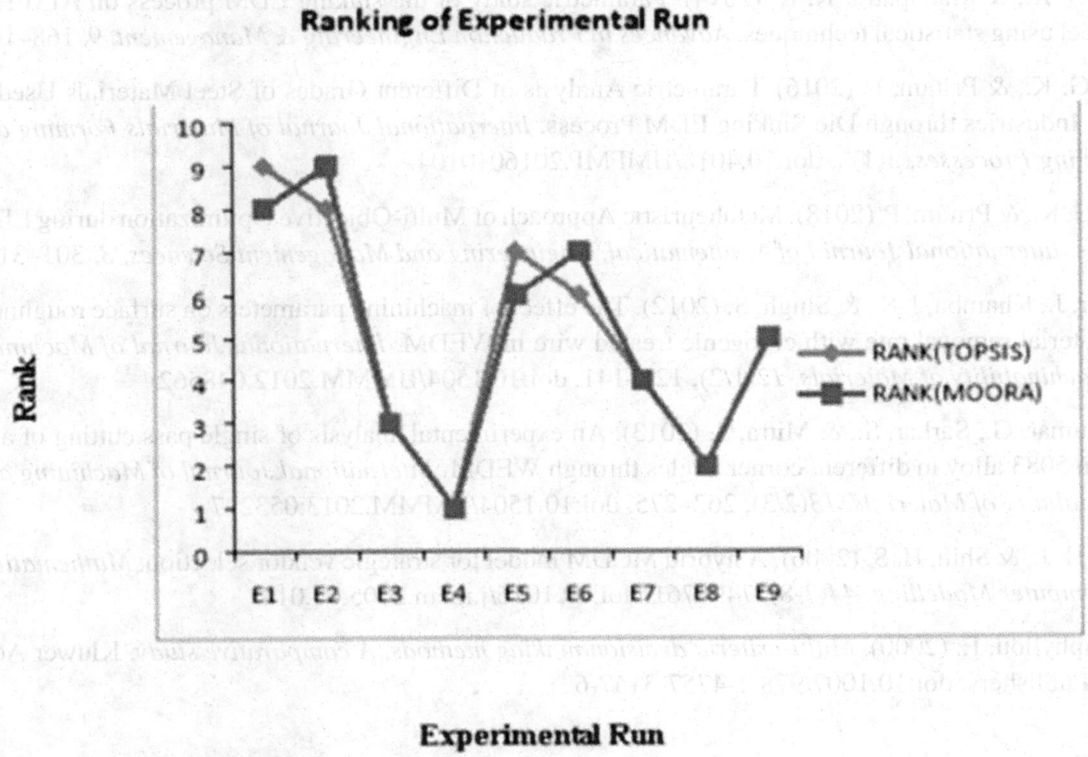

Table 12. Spearman's Coefficient between ranks sets by MOORA and TOPSIS

Experimental Run	Priority by MOORA	Priority by TOPSIS	d_i	$\sum d_i^2$
E_1	9	8	1	1
E_2	8	9	-1	1
E_3	3	3	0	0
E_4	1	1	0	0
E_5	7	6	1	1
E_6	6	7	-1	1
E_7	4	4	0	0
E_8	2	2	0	0
E_9	5	5	0	0

REFERENCES

Bose, G. K., & Mahapatra, K. K. (2014). Parametric study of die sinking EDM process on AISI H13 tool steel using statistical techniques. *Advances in Production Engineering & Management, 9,* 168–180.

Bose, G. K., & Pritam, P. (2016). Parametric Analysis of Different Grades of Steel Materials Used in Plastic Industries through Die Sinking EDM Process. *International Journal of Materials Forming and Machining Processes, 3*(1). . doi:10.4018/IJMFMP.2016010104

Bose, G. K., & Pritam, P. (2018). Metaheuristic Approach of Multi-Objective Optimization during EDM Process. *International Journal of Mathematical, Engineering and Management Sciences, 3,* 301–314.

Kapoor, J., Khamba, J. S., & Singh, S. (2012). The effect of machining parameters on surface roughness and material removal rate with cryogenic treated wire in WEDM. *International Journal of Machining and Machinability of Materials, 12*(1/2), 126–141. doi:10.1504/IJMMM.2012.048562

Selvakumar, G., Sarkar, S., & Mitra, S. (2013). An experimental analysis of single pass cutting of aluminium 5083 alloy in different corner angles through WEDM. *International Journal of Machining and Machinability of Materials, 13*(2/3), 262–275. doi:10.1504/IJMMM.2013.053227

Shyur, H. J., & Shih, H. S. (2006). A hybrid MCDM model for strategic vendor selection. *Mathematical and Computer Modelling, 44*(7-8), 749–761. doi:10.1016/j.mcm.2005.04.018

Triantaphyllou, E. (2000). *Multi-criteria decision making methods. A comparative study*. Kluwer Academic Publishers. doi:10.1007/978-1-4757-3157-6

Chapter 4
Analysis of Performance Characteristics by Firefly Algorithm–Based Electro Discharge Machining of SS 316

Premangshu Mukhopadhyay
https://orcid.org/0000-0001-8892-5443
Haldia Institute of Technology, India

ABSTRACT

The process of combining two or more non-conventional machining processes to obtain the required machining performance is known as hybridisation. Hybrid electro discharge machining came into the picture of macro machining due to the requirement of more rapid machining process with improved efficiency of non-conventional machining process. The technique of vibration assisted EDM process did not prove to be successful due to some disadvantages like increase in tool wear for low melting and comparatively softer tool material. Therefore, a need for more advanced hybridised process has been realized to improve the overall machining efficiency specially circularity and radial overcut. A permanent magnetic field force assisted EDM process was carried out on SS 316 plate with tungsten carbide tool of 5 mm diameter. MRR, TWR, and diametral overcut have been optimized by firefly algorithm technique which showed satisfactory results. It has been found that tool wear and diametral overcut has been found to be reduced with magnetic field-assisted EDM than conventional EDM processes.

INTRODUCTION

Electro Discharge Machining is a process of spark erosion in which removal of materials is caused by melting and vaporisation of metals with the help of positive and negative polarity electrodes from the workpiece surface in the form of chips or debris particles to get the required product. A very high temperature of about 10000ºC is generated in the plasma region created by dissociation of ions. Pulse On-Time, Peak Current, Duty Factor, Voltage, Frequency are generally considered as process param-

DOI: 10.4018/978-1-7998-3624-7.ch004

eters. Metal Removal Rate (MRR), Tool Wear Rate (TWR), Overcut, Surface Roughness are mostly considered as machining / performance criteria / responses. The process of combining two or more non-conventional machining processes in order to obtain the required machining performance is known as hybridisation. Hybrid electro discharge machining came into the picture of macro machining due to the requirement of more rapid machining process with improved efficiency of non conventional machining process. The technique of vibration assisted EDM process did not proved to be successful due to some disadvantages like increase in tool wear for low melting and comparatively softer tool material. EDM is an indispensable machining process for the drilling of metals and its alloys with required dimensional accuracy and precision. But there are some obstacles like tool wear, overcut, etc. which directly affect the dimensional accuracy of machined surface during EDMing of SS 316. Therefore a need for more advanced hybridised process is essential to bring a revolution in the field of micro-manufacturing which will be helpful to achieve required aspect ratio and dimensional accuracy of machined features / products. This type of improvement is possible by induction of external force assisted processes called Hybridised Electro Discharge Machining Technology (HEDMT). Govindan et al (2013) improved the Metal removal rate (MRR) to nearly 130% by the induction of magnetic field (MF) assisted dry-EDM. Rise into MRR improved the depth and decreased crater diameter by 80% thereby improving uniformity into material erosion in liquid EDM. Walkar et al (2014) increased the machining performance was improved by rapid elimination of debris from the inter-electrode gap. Magnetic field (MF) induced EDM helps in improvement of the process stability. Bains et al (2018) observed about 22% reduction into the micro-hardness values of surface and formation of thinnest recast layer at magnetic field united high discharge energy was recorded for EDMing of Al-SiC composites. The sparks obtained from magnetic field induced EDM generated better surface finishing features than the conventional electro-discharge machining of tool steel material (AISI 420 mod.) by the application of graphite electrode. Efendee et al. (2019) observed that craters due to discharges developed on the surface after machining were very thin and small with the application of magnetic field. Based on the experimental results, Ming et al (2019) performed a comparative study on the magnetic field (MF) induced electro-discharge machining and conventional electro-discharge machining to analyze the flow of discharge energy due to spark discharges and workpiece temperature distribution, tool and debris particles. Leppert et al. (2018) conducted a study on the characteristics of EDM which may cause a risk to the atmosphere and physical fitness of EDM machine representatives was performed. Prakash et al. (20180 conducted the experiments based on L_{27} orthogonal array and an empirical model has been established to interpret the co-relation amongst input and output parameters. Mukhopadhyay et al (2019) discussed and analyzed the effects on MRR, TWR and Diametral Overcut with permanent magnetic field assisted EDMing of SS 316. A number of optimal solutions (~100) were obtained by MO-PSO technique, where all responses were optimized. The XRD pattern investigations of modified surface confirmed the formation of various biocompatible phases, which enhanced the mechanical properties, corrosion and osseintegration characteristics.

This study presents a brief investigation of the effects of process parameters like pulse on-time, gap voltage and flushing pressure on performance characteristics i.e. Metal removal rate (MRR), Tool wear rate (TWR) and Diametral overcut (DOC) for conventional and magnetic field assisted EDMing of SS 316 using tungsten carbide as tool electrode. It has been also proved that there is a need to optimize those response parameters to meet the industrial prototype. Also, optimized values of measured responses would be helpful for future engineers and researchers to meet the industrial demands.

TAGUCHI METHODOLOGY

The technique of laying out the conditions of experiments involving multiple factors was first proposed by the Englishman, Sir R.A.Fisher. The method is very commonly known as the factorial design of experiments. A full factorial design will identify all possible combinations for a given set of factors. Since most industrial experiments usually involve a significant number of factors, a full factorial design results in a large number of experiments. To reduce the number of experiments to a practical level, only a small set from all the possibilities is selected. The method of selecting a limited number of experiments which produces the most information is known as a partial fraction experiment. Although this method is well known, there are no general guidelines for its application or the analysis of the results obtained by performing the experiments. This problem is solved by development of new technique called Taguchi methodology.

The Taguchi method was developed by Genichi Taguchi. He developed a method for designing experiments to investigate how different parameters affect the mean and variance of a process performance characteristic that defines how well the process is functioning. Taguchi constructed a special set of general design guidelines for factorial experiments that cover many applications. The Taguchi method involves reducing the variation in a process through robust design of experiments. The overall objective of the method is to produce high quality product at low cost to the manufacturer. The experimental design proposed by Taguchi involves using orthogonal arrays to organize the parameters affecting the process and the levels at which they should be varied. Instead of having to test all possible combinations like the factorial design, the Taguchi method tests pairs of combinations. This allows for the collection of the necessary data to determine which factors most affect the product quality with a minimum amount of experimentation, thus saving time and resources. Taguchi has envisaged a new method of conducting the design of experiments which are based on well defined guidelines. This method uses a special set of arrays called orthogonal arrays. These standard arrays stipulate the way of conducting the minimal number of experiments which could give the full information of all the factors that affect the performance parameter. The crux of the orthogonal arrays method lies in choosing the level combinations of the input design variables for each experiment. While there are many standard orthogonal arrays available, each of the arrays is meant for a specific number of independent design variables and levels . For example, if one wants to conduct an experiment to understand the influence of 4 different independent variables with each variable having 3 set values (level values), then an L9 orthogonal array might be the right choice. The L9 orthogonal array is meant for understanding the effect of 4 independent factors each having 3 factor level values. This array assumes that there is no interaction between any two factor. While in many cases, no interaction model assumption is valid, there are some cases where there is a clear evidence of interaction. A typical case of interaction would be the interaction between the material properties and temperature. Once the orthogonal array is selected, the experiments are conducted as per the level combinations. It is necessary that all the experiments be conducted. The interaction columns and dummy variable columns shall not be considered for conducting the experiment, but are needed while analyzing the data to understand the interaction effect. The performance parameter under study is noted down for each experiment to conduct the sensitivity analysis. In Taguchi's design method the design parameters (factors that can be controlled by designers) and noise factors (factors that cannot be controlled by designers, such as environmental factors) are considered influential on the product quality. The Signal to Noise (S/N) ratio is used in this analysis which takes both the mean and the variability of the experimental result into account. The S/N ratio depends on the quality characteristics of the product/process to be optimized.

EXPERIMENTAL SCHEME AND SET-UP

At first, pilot experiments were conducted randomly to select the significant process parameters. Range of process parameters have been determined by conducting experiments using chosen process parameters called Pulse on-time (T_{ON}), Gap voltage (V_g) and Flushing pressure (P). Experiments have been performed using SS 316 as workpiece and tungsten carbide tool of 5 mm diameter. Peak current of 10 A and duty factor of 50% were used as fixed process parameters. Total numbers of experimental runs have been designed based on taguchi L_9 orthogonal array method has been used for the design of experiments. Taguchi methodology based experimental design technique for the conventional EDMing of SS 316 has been given in Table 1.

Table 1. Taguchi L_9 technique based Orthogonal Array design for EDMing of SS 316

Expt. No.	Pulse On-Time (μsec)	Gap Voltage (V)	Flushing Pressure (kg/cm²)	Pulse On-Time (μsec)	Gap Voltage (V)	Flushing Pressure (kg/cm²)
	Coded Values			Actual Values		
1	1	1	1	10	30	0.1
2	1	2	2	10	40	0.2
3	1	3	3	10	50	0.3
4	2	1	2	20	30	0.2
5	2	2	3	20	40	0.3
6	2	3	1	20	50	0.1
7	3	1	3	30	30	0.3
8	3	2	1	30	40	0.1
9	3	3	2	30	50	0.2

A total of 9 number of experiments have been conducted with non magnetic field assisted EDMing of SS 316 and 3 number of experiments with permanent magnetic field assisted EDMing of SS 316. Weights of SS 316 plates and tungsten carbide tool as shown in Fig.1 were measured previous to and following machining by the suitable weighing device and dimensions of both tool and SS 316 plates were measured by a Mitituyo Vernier Caliper. Effects of constant magnetic field on MRR, TWR and Overcut generated by two permanent bar magnets as shown in Figure 1 were placed in opposite directions, parallel to the edge of SS 316 plate in the machining chamber have been analyzed for different values of pulse on-time (10μsec, 20 μsec, 30 μsec) and flushing pressure (0.1kg/cm², 0.2 kg/cm², 0.3 kg/cm²) at fixed gap voltage (30V).

EXPERIMENTAL RESULTS AND DISCUSSIONS

Both conventional and magnetic field assisted EDMing of SS 316 have been conducted to determine the values of Metal removal rate (MRR), Tool wear rate (TWR) and Diametral overcut (DOC). The experimental results for conventional and magnetic field assisted EDMing of SS 316 have been shown in Table 2 and Table 3 respectively.

Table 2. Experimental Results for Conventional EDMing of SS 316

Expt.No.	MRR (g/min)	TWR (g/min)	Diametral overcut (mm)
1	0.015	0.0028	0.040
2	0.012	0.0021	0.010
3	0.009	0.0015	0.030
4	0.010	0.0012	0.030
5	0.011	0.0004	0.080
6	0.009	0.0004	0.080
7	0.011	0.0004	0.130
8	0.012	0.0009	0.030
9	0.012	0.0010	0.030

The formulae for calculations of MRR, TWR and DOC are given as below in Eq.1, Eq.2 and Eq.3.

$$MRR = \frac{W_{bw} - W_{aw}}{T_{m/c}} \text{.........Eq.1}$$

$$TWR = \frac{W_{bt} - W_{at}}{T_{m/c}} \text{.........Eq.2}$$

$$DOC = D_{t-}D_{w} \text{.........Eq.3}$$

Where W_{bw} = Weight of workpiece previous to machining

Table 3. Experimental Results for Magnetic Field assisted EDMing of SS 316

Expt.No.	Pulse On-Time (μsec)	Gap Voltage (V)	Flushing Pressure (kg/cm²)	MRR (g/min)	TWR (g/min)	Diametral overcut (mm)
1	10	30	0.1	0.013	0.0012	0.010
2	20	30	0.2	0.008	0.0007	0.025
3	30	30	0.3	0.009	0.0002	0.120

W_{aw} = Weight of workpiece following machining
W_{bt} = Weight of tool previous to machining
W_{at} = Weight of tool following machining
$T_{m/c}$ = Time of machining
D_t = Tool diameter
D_w = Diameter of workpiece

Figure 1 represents the magnetic field assisted EDMed drilled holes on SS 316 plates with 5 mm diameter tungsten carbide tool. Figure 2 represents the S/N Ratio Plot for MRR.

Figure 1. EDMed drilled holes on SS 316 plates with Tungsten Carbide tool and Permanent magnets

After the determination of values of performance characteristics i.e. Metal Removal Rate (MRR), TWR (Tool Wear Rate) and Diametral Overcut (DOC), the results have been analyzed using signal to noise ratio plots obtained by a suitable software. Figure 2, Figure 3, Figure 4 represent the signal to noise ratio plots obtained for MRR, TWR and DOC. From Figure 2 it is observed that maximum value of signal to noise ratio represent the optimum parametric combination based on 'bigger the better' principle. So, the maximum MRR is depicted for pulse on-time of 10 μsec, gap voltage of 30V and flushing pressure of 0.1 kg/cm^2 i.e. at least chosen values of process parameters. Figure 2 represents the signal to noise ratio plot for MRR.

This may be due to the reason that at the least chosen values of process parameters, discharge energy is least which results into less deposition of the debris particles into the gap between the electrodes.

Figure 2. S/N Ratio Plot for MRR

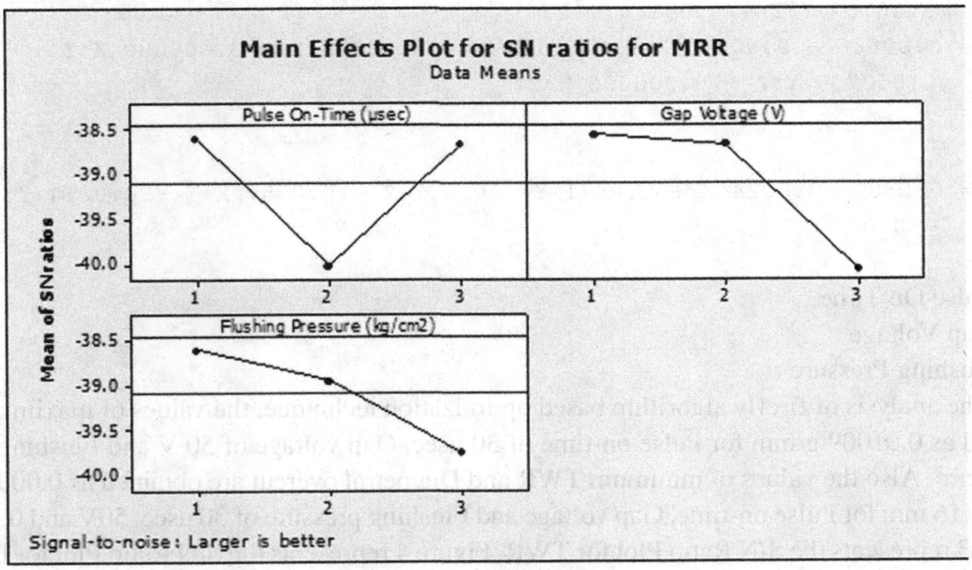

This helps in more amount of erosion from parent metal causing high metal removal rate (MRR). But at this setting of parametric values, MRR is found to be decreased with magnetic field assisted EDMing of SS 316. Due to magnetic vulnerability of SS 316, debris particles get dispersed in the machining region causing unstable machining conditions which results in the reduction of MRR. From Figure 3 it has been observed that minimum TWR is found for pulse on-time of 20 µsec, gap voltage of 30 V and flushing pressure of 0.3 kg/cm^2 based on 'smaller is better' principle i.e. at chosen lowest value of gap voltage and highest value of flushing pressure. This may be because at lowest value of gap voltage, removal of debris particles are very less and highest value of flushing pressure helps in elimination of these particles from the gap between the electrodes. It further leads to stable machining conditions so that minimum tool wear is recorded. Now with application of magnetic field at same value of 20 µsec pulse on-time, TWR is found to be further reduced because of segregation of debris particles already present in the machining region. From Figure 4 it is observed that minimum diametral overcut (DOC) has been found for pulse on-time of 10 µsec, gap voltage of 40 V and flushing pressure of 0.2 kg/cm^2 based on 'smaller is better' principle i.e. at chosen least pulse on-time value and moderate values of gap voltage and flushing pressure. This is due to the reason that with less accumulation of debris particles in the machining region and removal of these particles with moderate value of flushing pressure helps in uniformity of sparking at the periphery of machined surface. Ultimately, a reduced diametral overcut is recorded. With the application of permanent magnetic field it is observed that diametral overcut (DOC) is reduced at highest chosen values of process parameters. This is due to the reason that with the combination of both magnetic field and increased flushing pressure in the machining region, debris particles get removed from the margin of machined surface. As such, sparking is uniform at the border of EDMed surface lead to the condensed DOC. Finally, performance characteristics like MRR, TWR and Overcut is optimized by firefly algorithm and following results are obtained.

A regression analysis is carried out using the suitable software to find the regression equations for MRR, TWR and Diametral Overcut as given below.

MRR, $Y_u = 0.0255 - 0.00310 X - 0.00500 Y - 0.00590 Z + 0.00071 X*Y + 0.00157 Y*Z + 0.00114 X*Z$

TWR, $Y_u = 0.00666 - 0.00093 X - 0.00150 Y - 0.00230 Z + 0.000000 X*Y + 0.000700 Y*Z + 0.000300 X*Z$

DOC, $Y_u = 0.030 - 0.0024 X + 0.0871 Y - 0.091 Z - 0.0357 X*Y - 0.0014 Y*Z + 0.0457 X*Z$

X = Pulse On-Time
Y = Gap Voltage
Z = Flushing Pressure

From the analysis of firefly algorithm based optimization technique, the values of maximized MRR is obtained as 0.01009 g/min for Pulse on-time of 30 μsec, Gap voltage of 50 V and Flushing pressure of 0.3 kg/cm². Also the values of minimum TWR and Diametral overcut are obtained as 0.00092 g/min and 0.049116 mm for Pulse on-time, Gap voltage and Flushing pressure of 30 μsec, 50V and 0.1 kg/cm².

Figure 3 represents the S/N Ratio Plot for TWR. Figure 4 represents the S/N Ratio Plot for Diametral Overcut (DOC).

Figure 3. S/N Ratio Plot for TWR

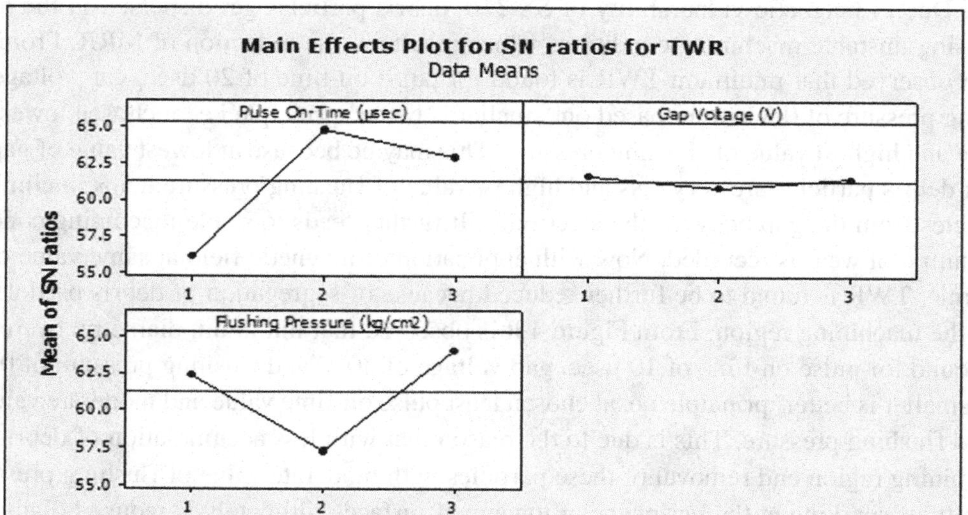

CONCLUSION

The following conclusions can be depicted from the experimental results of experimentation and analysis for conventional EDMing and magnetic field assisted EDMing of SS 316.

Figure 4. S/N Ratio Plot for DOC

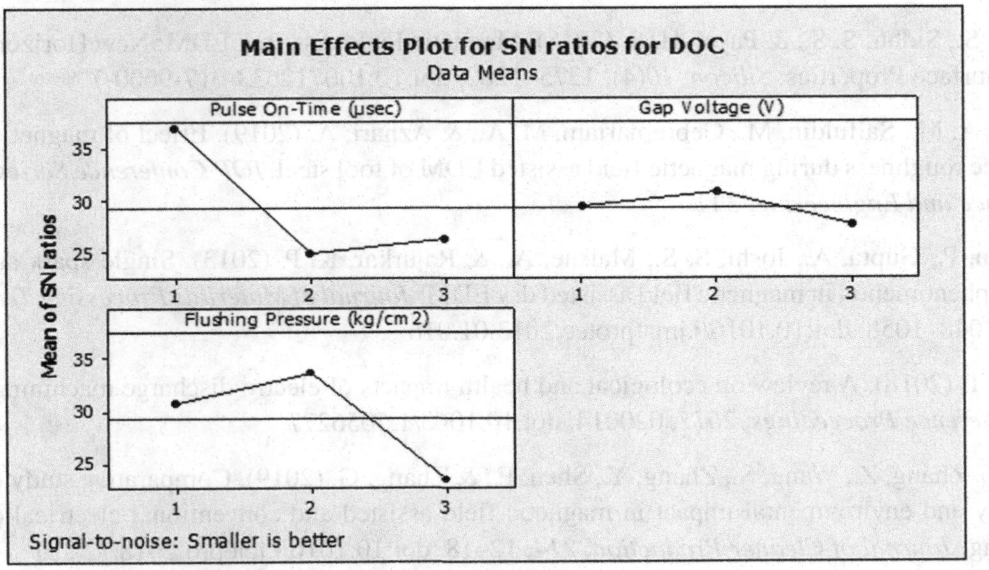

- From the analysis of S / N ratio plot for MRR, maximum MRR is cited for pulse on-time of 10µsec, gap voltage of 30V and flushing pressure of 0.1 kg/cm^2.
- From the analysis of S / N ratio plots for TWR & DOC, minimum TWR and DOC are recorded for pulse on-time of 20 µsec, gap voltage of 30 V and flushing pressure of 0.3 kg/cm^2 and pulse on-time of 10 µsec, gap voltage of 40 V and flushing pressure of 0.2 kg/cm^2 respectively.
- Introduction of magnetic field by permanent magnets, MRR is decreased to 13%, TWR reduced to 57% and DOC reduced to 75% as compared to conventional EDMing of SS 316.
- From the analysis of firefly optimization method, maximum MRR was obtained as 0.01009 g/min, whereas minimum TWR and Diametral overcut were determined as 0.00092 g/min and 0.049116 mm respectively for firefly algorithm based optimization of performance features.
- Firefly algorithm has been proved to be ideal optimization technique for magnetic field assisted EDM process.

Hence, the outcomes determined as such will help the future researchers, engineers and scientists for successful application of firefly optimization based electro-discharge machining of SS 316 with external force assisted technique such as induced magnetic field.

REFERENCES

Bains, P. S., Sidhu, S. S., & Payal, H. S. (2018). Magnetic Field Assisted EDM: New Horizons for Improved Surface Properties. *Silicon, 10*(4), 1275–1282. doi:10.100712633-017-9600-7

Efendee, A. M., Saifuldin, M., Gebremariam, M. A., & Azhari, A. (2019). Effect of magnetic polarity on surface roughness during magnetic field assisted EDM of tool steel. *IOP Conference Series: Materials Science and Engineering*, 342.

Govindan, P., Gupta, A., Joshi, S. S., Malshe, A., & Rajurkar, K. P. (2013). Single spark analysis of removal phenomenon in magnetic field assisted dry EDM. *Journal of Materials Processing Technology, 213*(7), 1048–1058. doi:10.1016/j.jmatprotec.2013.01.016

Leppert, T. (2018). A review on ecological and health impacts of electro discharge machining (EDM). *AIP Conference Proceedings, 2017*, 020014. doi:10.1063/1.5056277

Ming, W., Zhang, Z., Wang, S., Zhang, Y., Shen, F., & Zhang, G. (2019). Comparative study of energy efficiency and environmental impact in magnetic field assisted and conventional electrical discharge machining. *Journal of Cleaner Production, 214*, 12–18. doi:10.1016/j.jclepro.2018.12.231

Mukhopadhyay, P., Adhikary, S., Samanta, A. K., Maiti, S., Khan, S., & Mudi, S. (2019). External Force Assisted Electro Discharge Machining of SS 316. *Materials Today: Proceedings, 19*, 626–629. doi:10.1016/j.matpr.2019.07.743

Mukhopadhyay, P. B. R., & Sarkar, B. R. (2019). Advancement in Utrasonic Vibration and Magnetic Field Assisted Micro-EDM Proces: An Overview. *International Journal of Advanced Research in Engineering & Technology, 10*(2), 362–373. doi:10.34218/IJARET.10.2.2019.035

Prakash, C., Singh, S., Singh, M., Verma, K., Chaudhary, B., & Singh, S. (2018). Multi-objective particle swarm optimization of EDM parameters to deposit HA-coating on biodegradable Mg-alloy. *Vacuum, 158*, 180–190. doi:10.1016/j.vacuum.2018.09.050

Walkar, H., Jatti, V. S., & Singh, T. P. (2014). Magnetic field Assisted Electrical Discharge Machining of AISI 4140. *Applied Mechanics and Materials, 592-594*, 479–483. doi:10.4028/www.scientific.net/AMM.592-594.479

Chapter 5
Programming for Machining in Electrical Discharge Machine:
A Non-Conventional Machining Technique

Chikesh Ranjan
https://orcid.org/0000-0003-1197-601X
RTC Institute of Technology, India

Hridayjit Kalita
Birla Institute of Technology, Mesra, India

T. Vishnu Vardhan
CMR Institute of Technology, India

Kaushik Kumar
Birla Institute of Technology, Mesra, India

ABSTRACT

The correct selection of manufacturing conditions is one of the most important aspects to take into consideration in most manufacturing processes and, particularly, in processes related to electrical discharge machining (EDM). It is a capable of machining geometrically complex or hard material components that are precise and difficult-to-machine such as heat-treated tool steels, composites, super alloys, ceramics, carbides, heat resistant steels, etc. being widely used in die and mold making industries, aerospace, aeronautics, and nuclear industries. This chapter highlights the programming for machining in electrical discharge machine.

DOI: 10.4018/978-1-7998-3624-7.ch005

INTRODUCTION

Electric discharge machining (EDM) is the most commonly used and versatile non-traditional technique (technique having no physical interaction between the tool and the workpiece) of cutting conducting metals and alloys using the heat of the electric spark from an electrode tool in presence of a flow of di-electric fluid (Bleys, P et al, 2002). It is basically an electro thermal process where the metal is melted and vaporized employing electric spark discharges at regular intervals (recurring) on the surfaces of both the electrode and the workpiece, producing a metal erosion effect (Abbas et al., 2007). The electric spark is generated due to voltage difference across the tool surface and the workpiece applied externally from the supply. EDM is extensively employed in industries such as automobile, aerospace, communication, biotechnology, and manufacturing in cutting high precision products of conducting materials such as graphite, ceramics, metals and alloys (Adrian Iosub et al,2010). An important aspect of EDM is its ability to melt and machine even hard and brittle material with ease considering the metal is electrically conductive (Vikas, Roy, A. K. et al, (2013). The components in an EDM process is shown schematically in Figure 1.

Figure 1. Schematic diagram of Electrical discharge machining

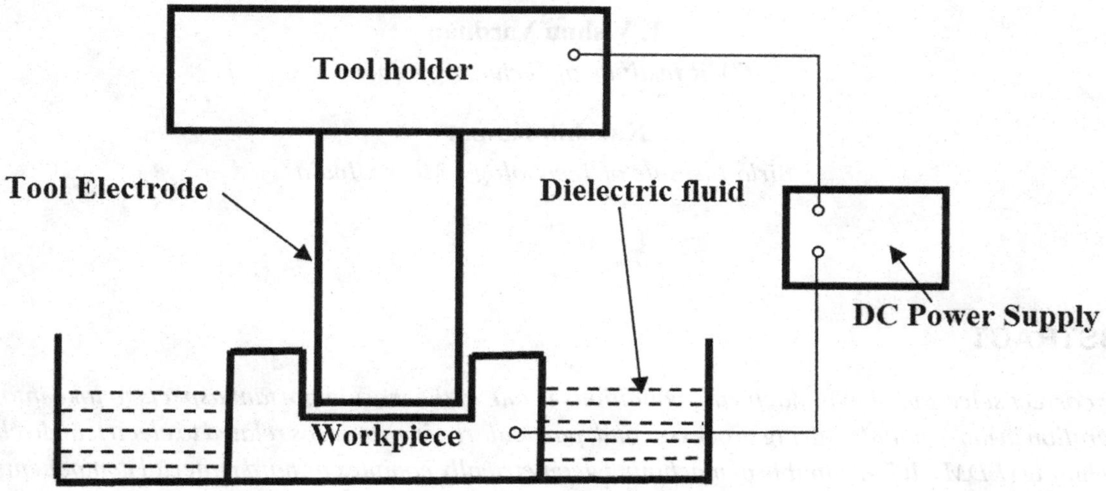

Though EDM machining technique was first discovered in 1770 by an English scientist, it was not fully developed and precise until 1943 when Russian scientists independently learned the effect of an electric spark on the erosion of a work material which can be controlled and utilized for machining purposes. Wire EDM was developed for commercial use in around mid-1970's which tremendously benefitted the metal cutting industries and is continuing to evolve till the present time. The implementation of EDM as machine tools in industries has made it a widely used, reliable and appealing over other traditional methods in machining.

Non-traditional techniques of machining employ non – conventional energy sources like electrical, ions and electrons, chemical, water pressure, sound, light and even indirect mechanical interactions which eliminate the risk of frictional tool wear due to direct metal contact and interactions and higher power consumptions. With the rapid rise in industrial technological growth and development and with introduction of new exotic materials (Zhou, M. And Han, F., 2009) such as engineered metallic materials, composite, high tech ceramics possessing high hardness, strength to weight ratio and heat resistance qualities (Debroy, A. & Chakraborty, S., 2013), it has become necessary to machine these materials with higher precision, accuracy and surface finish in industries like aerospace and nuclear energy (Liao, Y. S. et al, 2005). Complex shapes and sizes of products and structures can be machined suitably using the non-traditional techniques of machining with sufficient material removal rate which is improving as new advancement been made in past few years, thus yielding enhanced effectiveness, efficiency and active use of non- traditional techniques.

Tools and dies that are heat treated, super alloys, carbides, heat resistant steels, ceramics, and composites are now commonly used materials that are machined using EDM process and replacing the traditional approaches of drilling, milling, machining and grinding. The presence and importance of EDM technique has also been appreciated and felt in different other fields such as medical and surgical,

Figure 2. Electrical discharge machine

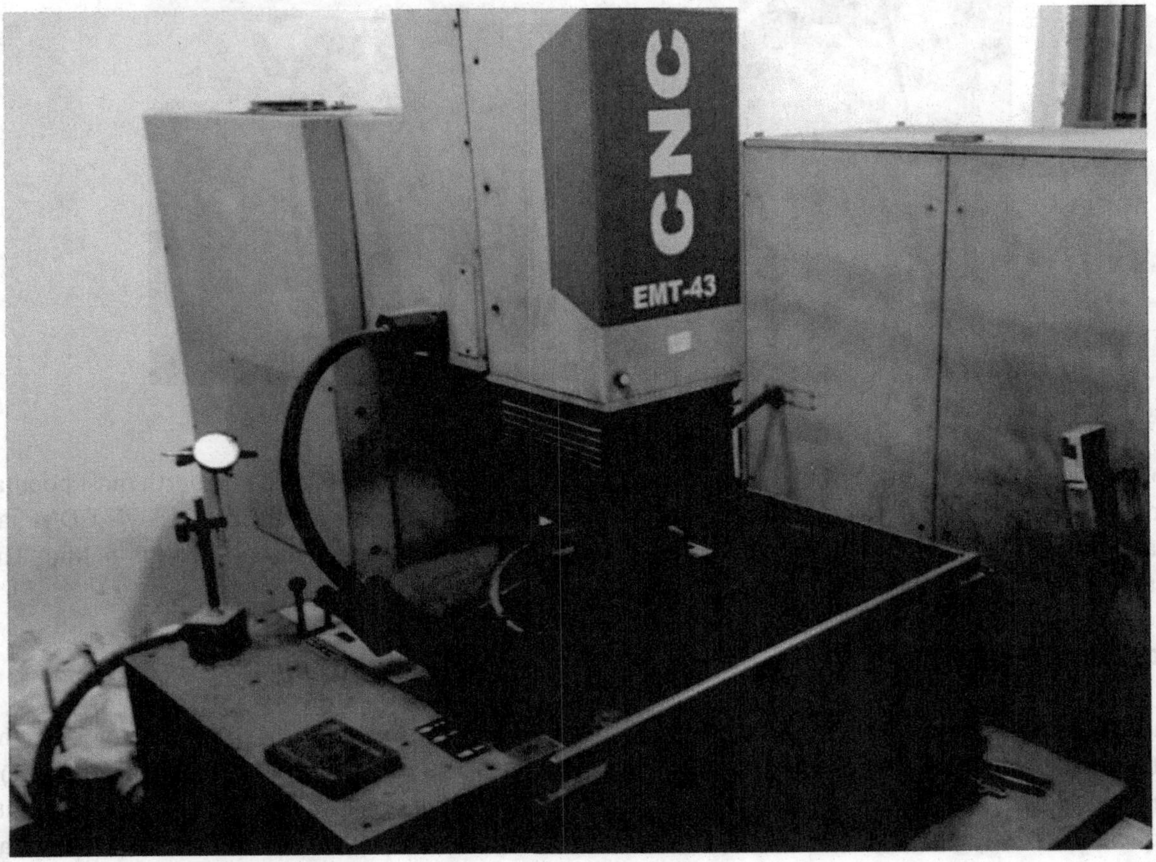

Figure 3. Electrical discharge machine Programme unit

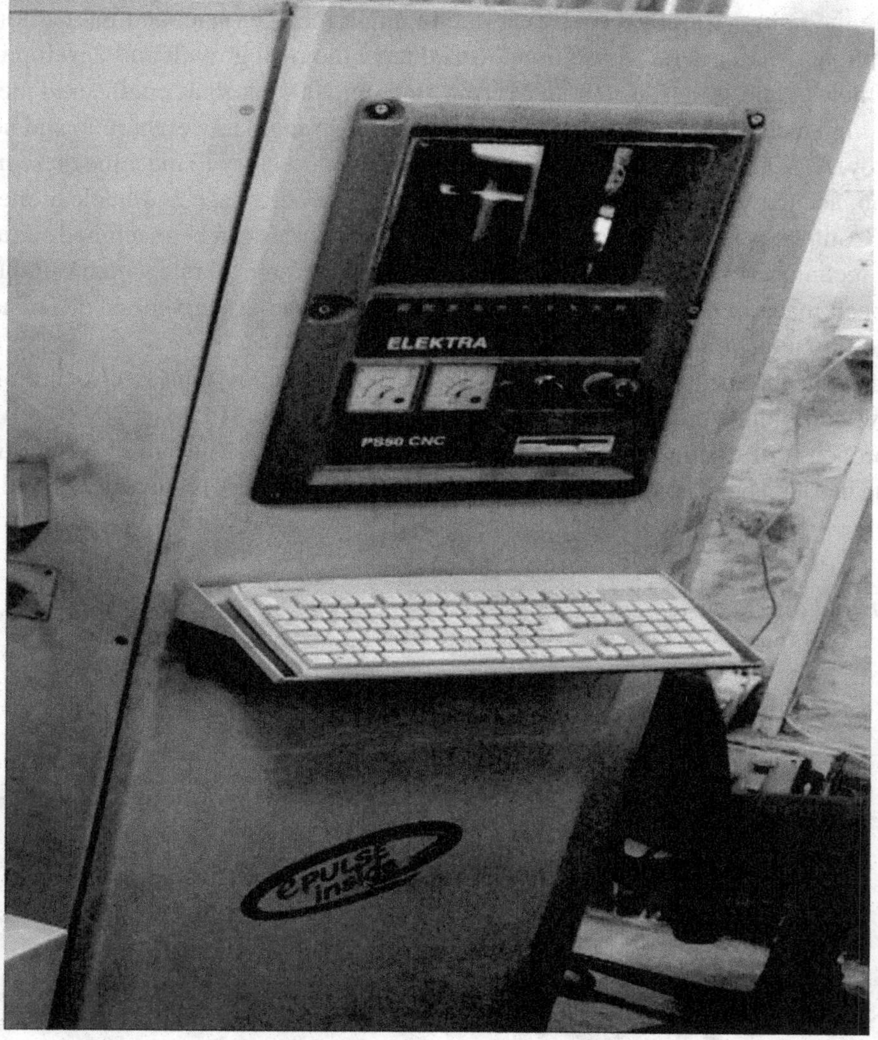

optical, automotive R and D, sports, instrumentation, etc and is now considered the fourth most popular technique in machining next to milling, turning and grinding. The cutting speeds of today's EDM had dramatically increased which served as a major advantage in gaining attention from the public. The actual EDM machine has been shown in Figures 2 and 3.

Part Programming

Part programming is the most important, critical and fundamental stage in EDM machining process, the efficiency, correctness and accuracy of which influences the performance and operation of the machining for a better and trouble free one. The part program is basically defined as the set of instructions and its sequence for describing the work that has to be done on the part. These instructions are transferred in the form understandable to the computer controlled by CNC computer program (Zivanovic, S.Puzovic, R., 2015). Part programming basically includes the operations of collecting necessary data for machining the part, calculation of the tool path and rotation of components in a format acceptable to the machine control unit (MCU) or in the form of standardized punched tape. It is basically the transfer of an idea from drawing sheets to well-defined and systematic computer programs sheets. The methods of part programming can be of 4 types (Krzic, P., Stoic, A., Kopac, J., 2009) such as Manual Part programming, computer assisted part programming, part programming using CAD/CAM and Manual data input, out of which Manual part programming and Computer assisted part programming will be discussed in the section.

Manual Part Programming

In manual part programming, the data required for machining is written in a standard format known as program manuscripts. Each horizontal line in a manuscript represents a 'block' of information. It may include the route sheet or the list of instructions. In order to prepare a part program, the part programmer must know all the codes for all the operations and functions. The manuscript is typed with the help of a flexo writer, by the operator form the hand written list of coded instructions.

Part programs that are based on point to point type of tool movement are performed basically for simple parts while contouring is performed for complex parts. Manual part programming facilitates the application of both point to point operations such as drilling and contouring operations on jobs though contouring is done for simple milling and turning operations involving two axis system. For complex shaped 3D parts, computer assisted part programming is generally recommended due to their advantages.

Computer-Assisted Part Programming

Manual part programming can be time consuming, tedious, and subject to errors for parts possessing operations. In these cases, and even for simpler jobs, it is advantageous to use computer-assisted part programming. Various CNC part programming language software been developed which allows the user to write programs in high level languages such as statements in English. These high level languages are then compiled into a low level language or machine language to be directly interpreted by the machine tool. Computer assisted part programming enhances the accuracy, efficiency, and effectiveness of the part programming operation which saves time and manpower. The computer assisted part programming includes tasks that are to be followed in the sequence as under:

1. Input translation;
2. Arithmetic and cutter offset computations;
3. Editing and
4. Post processing.

NC Words

NC words are basically a collection of characters that are itself a combination of binary digits (bits) arranged in rows. These NC words provide instruction for the movement of the machine tool in its X-Y-Z

Figure 4. Tasks in computer-assisted part programming

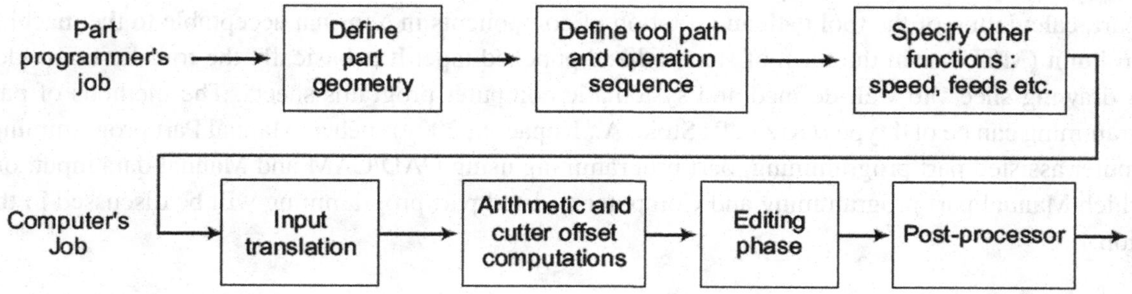

positions, feed rates, etc. NC words combine to form a block which is a complete program. In many CNC machines, there might be no requirements of NC words as mentioned in (Zhang, Y. et al, (2012).

Sequence number: sequence is the first word in any block that basically helps in identifying the block. It holds a sequence of numbers proceeded by a letter N and is executed from lower sequence number to higher one such as N01, N02, etc. The numbers can be started from 01 to 10 in steps of 5 or 10 to insert the access omitted block.

Preparatory Function (G-words): The preparatory function popularly known as G codes are generally represented by two digits that are preceded by the letter G as per ISO specifications such as G01, G02, etc with current day controllers even accepting up to 3 to 4 digits. It interprets the instructions to be followed by the controller for the job to be done on the part with various tool axis movements. This function is generally succeeded by the words for the co-ordinate axis (x, y, z).

Coordinates (x, y and z- words): This word is generally used to assign the final positions of the machine tool for its X, Y,Z motions. Two co-ordinate words are generally used in a 2- axis CNC system for position specification while in 3-axis systems additional words such as a-word and b-word are employed to specify angular positions. For circular interpolation, the arc center position is generally specified by the words I, J, K in addition to the co-ordinate words. Different formats for specifying the coordinates of the part are employed by various CNC machines with few systems where the decimal point does not need to be coded by the programmer and automatically gets into the program by the control system at a pre-set position.

Feed Function (F-word): Feed function or F word is generally used to specify the feed rate of the machining operation which is basically expressed in millimeters per minute (mm/min) or millimeters per revolution (MM/rev) based on the appropriate G codes (G94 or G85) specified in the machine. For a feed of 200 mm/min, the F-word will be specified as F 200.

Spindle speed Function (S-Word): The spindle speed function is used to specify the speed of the spindle in revolutions per minute (rpm) or in meters per minute with the necessary calculation by the control unit in converting it to rpm using appropriate formulae. For a machine to run at a spindle speed of 800 rpm, the speed will be specified as S800.

Tool Selection Function (T-word): The T-word is generally used for CNC machines having the provision for automatic tool changer or the tool turret to denote the tool required for specified operation. Each pocket in the tool turret is assigned a distinct tool number which is identified by the machine and which is represented by words from T00 to T99.

Miscellaneous Function (M-word): Various auxiliary functions having no relevance to the actual dimensional movements of the machine tool like Coolant ON/OFF, spindle START/STOP, etc are generally represented by M-words. M code is generally supposed to be stored in a single block with some controllers even accepting more than two provided the codes are mutually inclusive as can be observed from the commands M07 and M09 for coolant ON and OFF respectively which cannot be included in a single block. Less number of M codes is standardized by ISO specifications in comparison to the G codes which generally depends on the controls exercised by the machine tools.

End of Block (EOB): The EOB symbol identifies the end of the instruction block.

A typical NC word format is shown in figure 5.

Programming Formats

Format is the method for writing the words in a block of instruction. The three program formats that are used for part programming are the fixed block format, tab sequential format, and word address format. NC systems are generally adapted to understand and work with a single type of program format while for a CNC system, all types of program formats can be identified by the control unit.

Fixed Block Format: Instructions are arranged sequentially in a fixed block format where every block stores all instructions including the instructions stored in the preceding block without any change.

Tab sequential format: Instructions are as well arranged in the same sequence as in the case of fixed block format and words (in order) need to be separated from one another by the TAB character. The words from the preceding block if remaining unchanged need not be repeated again but TAB character maintained to arrange the order of the words in the same sequence. The address letters as well are not required in this format.

Word Address Format: In the word address format, each data is preceded by an address letter and identified in sequence like the letter X that precedes and identifies the x-coordinate, F identifies the feed rate, etc. The word that has been included in the preceding block need not be repeated in the current block. A typical block in word address format is written as shown below:

N01 G00 X01 Y05 F200 S000 T010.01 M30 EOB

Part Programs in EDM

The major challenge in the part programming phase of the EDM process is to deal with various complex shapes and structure to be machined which requires a complicated set of part programs that needs to be highly efficient, less time consuming and error free. Few complicated programming associated with the EDM process are the Vector circular orbit, vector cycle, spherical cycle, polygon cycle and sub program, the samples of which are discussed below.

Vector circular orbit: Vector circular orbit (G81) (Figure 6) is generally used for lateral finishing of round. A general cavity is also possible with Z-lock mode and circular pattern. A program to develop vector circular orbit is shown below which performs a polygon cycle with the given parameters as absolute co-ordinates. The syntax used is

G81 X Y Z P Q L U V W T

A typical sample program for the same is shown in figure 7.

Given: X = 0, Y = 0, Z = 50, P = 0.05, Q = 0.3, L = 10, U= 0, V = 0, W = 5

Figure 5. NC Word Formats

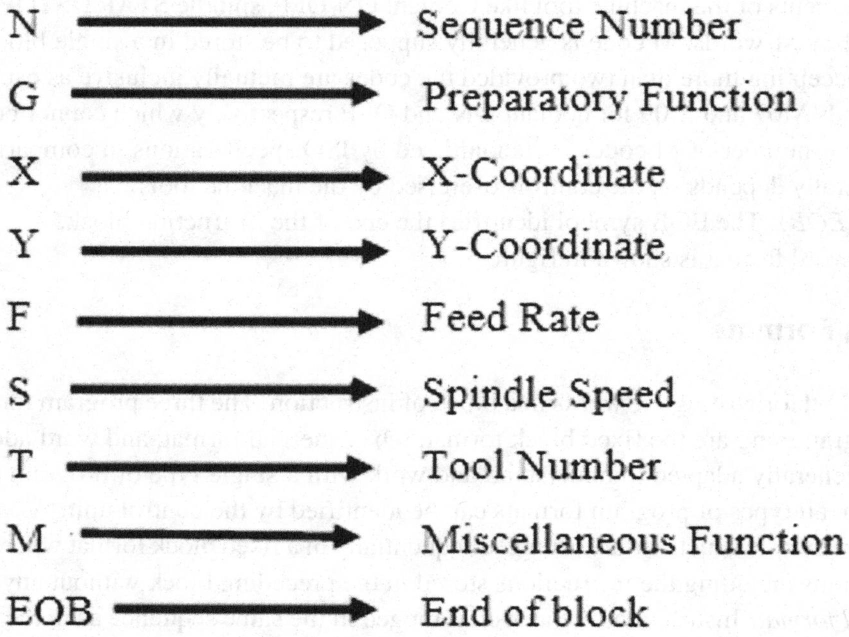

Vector cycle: This program is mainly used when accurate compensation in machining is required. A program is shown below which performs a vector cycle (G87) (Figure 8) with the given parameters as absolute coordinates. The syntax used is

G87 X Y Z P Q L U V W T

X = 0, Y = 0, Z = -5, P = 0.05, Q = 0.3, L = 10, U = 45, V = 45, R =4, W= -5

A typical sample program of the same is illustrated in figure 9

Spherical cycle: This cycle (Figure 10) is basically used for the surface finishing of curved surfaces. A program is shown below to develop a spherical cycle (G80) with given parameters as absolute coordinates. The syntax used is

G80 X Y Z P W

X = 0, Y = 0, Z = -50, P = 5, W= -5

A typical sample program of the same is depicted in figure 11

Polygon cycle: Polygon cycle shown in Figure 12 is used for EDM machining. A program has been shown to develop this cycle (G84) with the given parameters as absolute coordinates. The syntax used is

G84 X Y Z P Q L U R W

X = 0, Y = 0, Z = -5, P = 0.05, Q = 0.3, L = 10, U = 60, R = 6, W= -5

A typical sample program of the same is provided in figure 13

Sub programs: This cycle is basically used for mirroring of the objects (Figure 14). A program consisting of the main program (Figure 15) and 2 sub programs (Figures 16 and 17) are shown below to develop triangles in the first, second, third and fourth quadrant by mirroring in Y axis.

Figure 6. Schematic diagram of Circular cycle

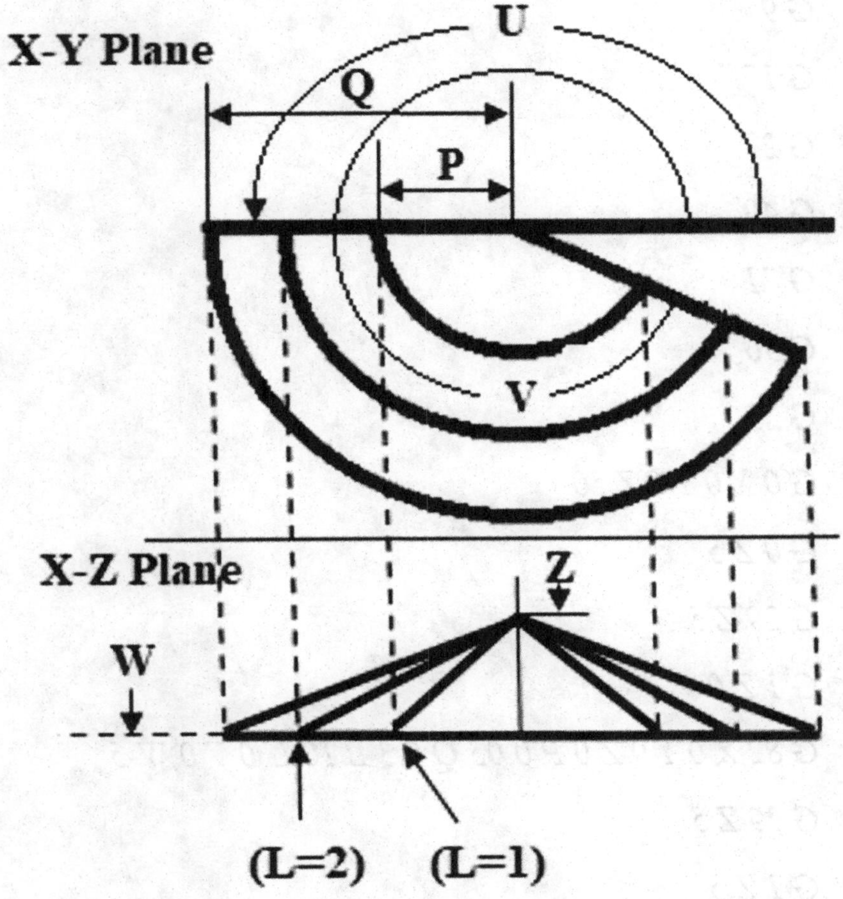

Main Program

Sub Program (003)

Sub Program (002)

CONCLUSION

With the recent advancements in the material technologies and introduction of exotic materials that are hard to machine, having high strength and high heat resistivity there is a requirement of the EDM

Figure 7. Typical sample program for the circular cycle

```
G9
G17
G27
G40
G71
G90
G29
G0X0Y0Z50
G0Z5
G29Z5
G1Z0
G82X0Y0Z0P0.05Q0.3L10U0V0W-5
G29Z5
G1Z5
G0Z50
```

machines fulfilling the requirement of several cutting industries. Due to the adoption of the EDM processes in complex 2D and 3D shape and size cutting of these materials, EDM part programming plays a significant role in elevating accuracy, precision and surface finish of the finished product. Efficient and effective part programs which consume less time with defined optimized operations and sufficient accuracy is the need of the current metal working industries. In the above discussion, various fundamental concepts in the part programming, guidelines and the components involved are described in detail along with few sample programs for the development of complicated part programs in EDM operations such as Vector circular orbit, vector cycle, spherical cycle, polygon cycle, and sub program. The major advantage of the EDM process is its independency on the hardness of the material and the ability to machine intricate shapes.

Figure 8. Schematic diagram of the vector cycle

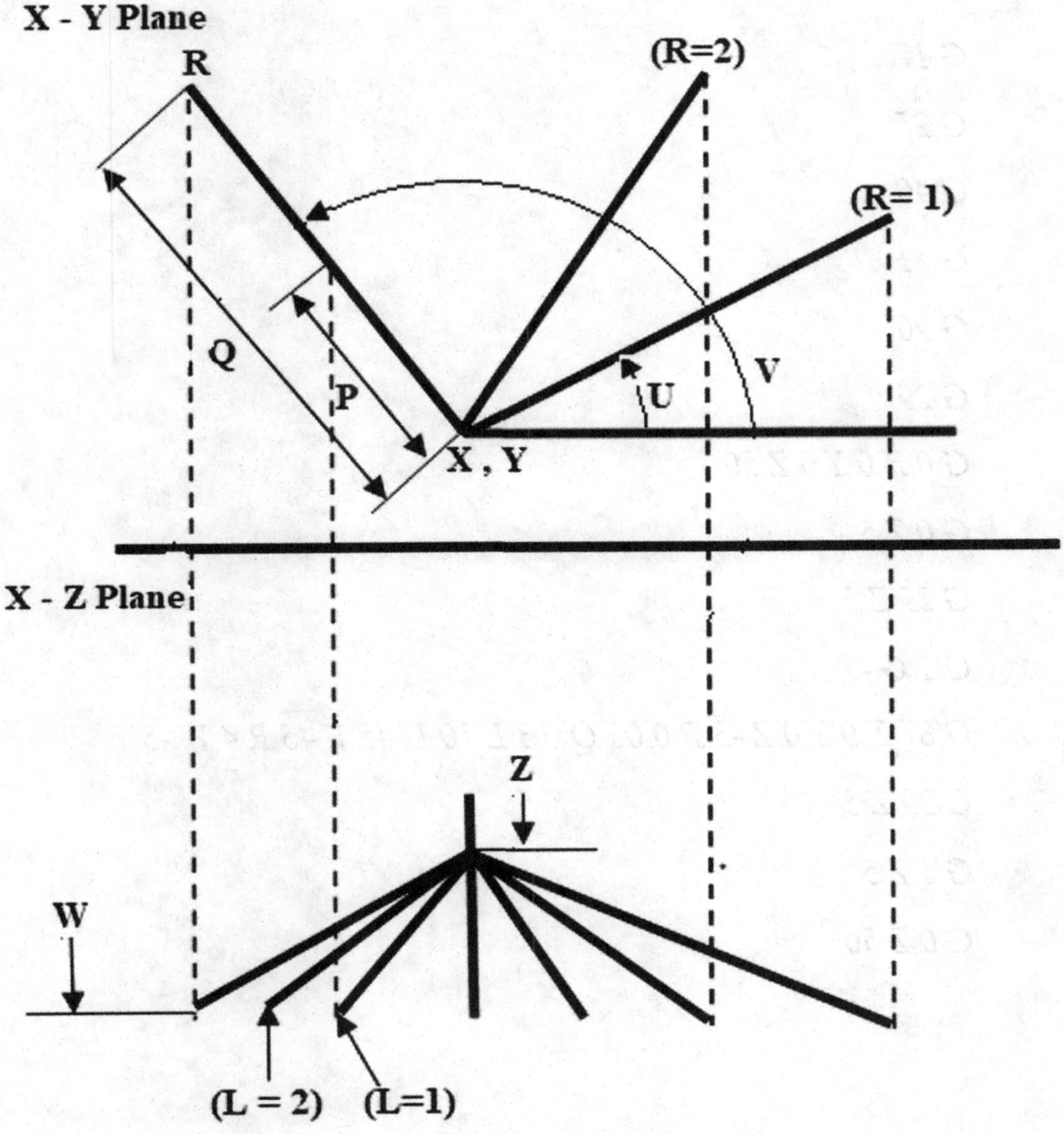

Figure 9. Typical sample program for the vector cycle

```
G 9
G 17
G 27
G 40
G 71
G 90
G 29
G 0 X 0 Y 0 Z 50
G 0 Z 5
G 29 Z 5
G 1 G -5
G 87 X 0 Y 0 Z -5 P 0.05 Q 0.3 L 10 U 45 V 45 R 4 W -5
G 29 Z 5
G 1 Z 5
G 0 Z 50
```

Figure 10. Schematic diagram of the sphere cycle

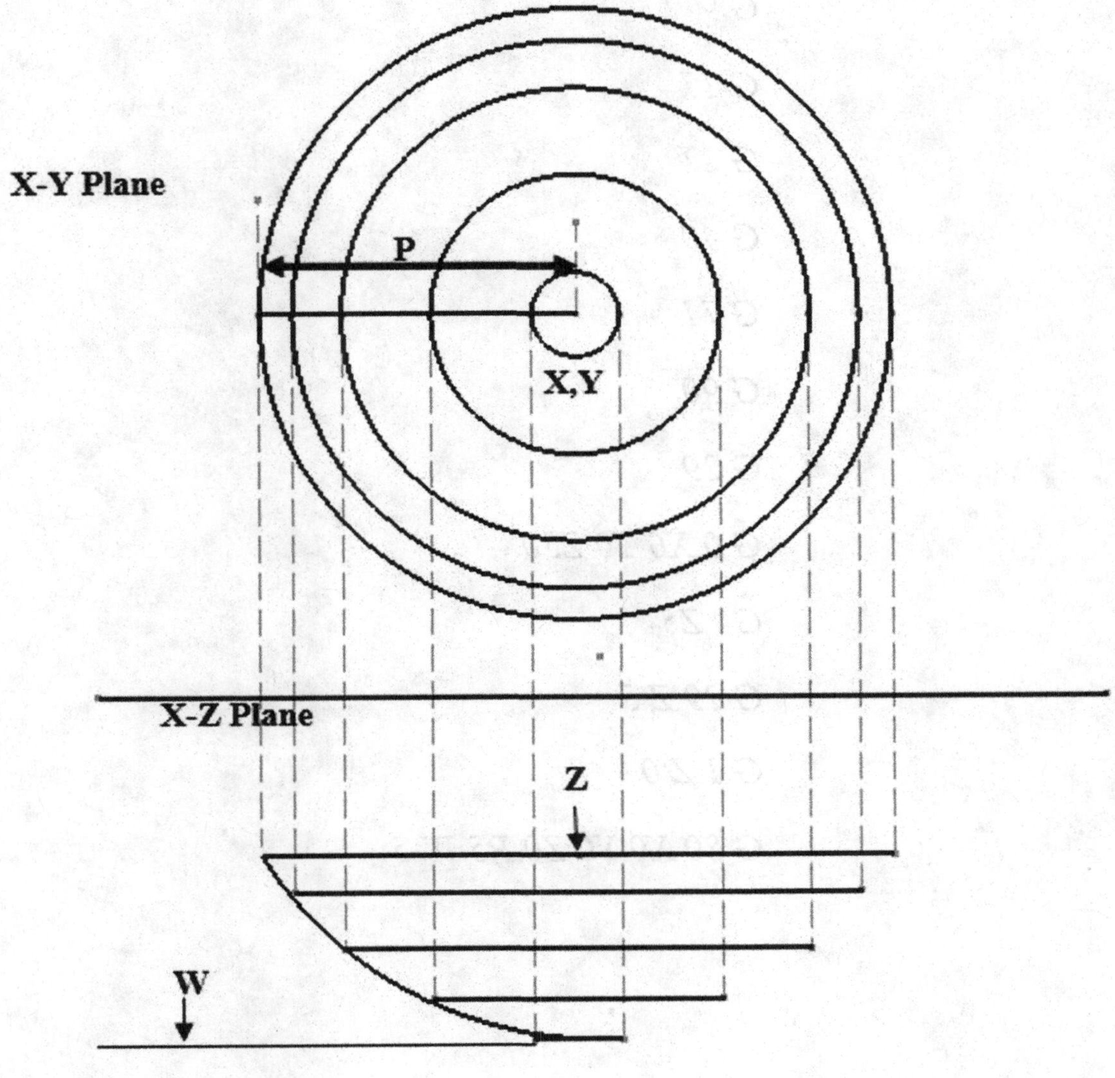

Figure 11. Typical sample program for Spherical cycle

```
G 9
G 17
G 27
G 40
G 71
G 90
G 29
G 0 X0 Y0 Z50
G0 Z5
G 29 Z 5
G 1 Z 0
G 80 X0 Y0 Z0 P5 W-5
```

Figure 12. Schematic diagram of the polygon cycle

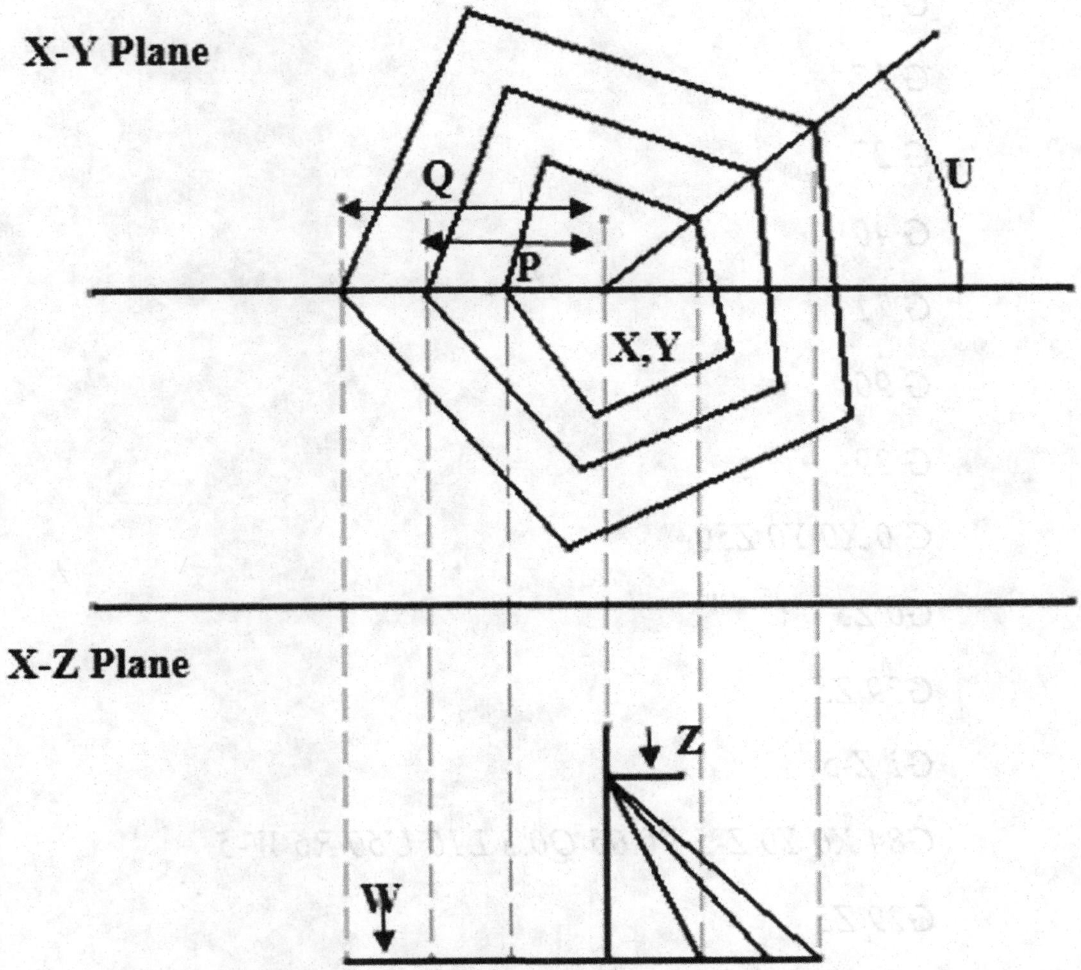

Figure 13. Typical sample program for Polygon Cycle

```
G 9
G 17
G 27
G 40
G 71
G 90
G 29
G 0 X0 Y0 Z50
G0 Z5
G29 Z5
G1 Z-5
G84 X0 Y0 Z-5 P0.05 Q0.3 L10 U60 R6 W-5
G29 Z5
G1 Z5
```

Figure 14. Schematic diagram of Mirroring in Y axis

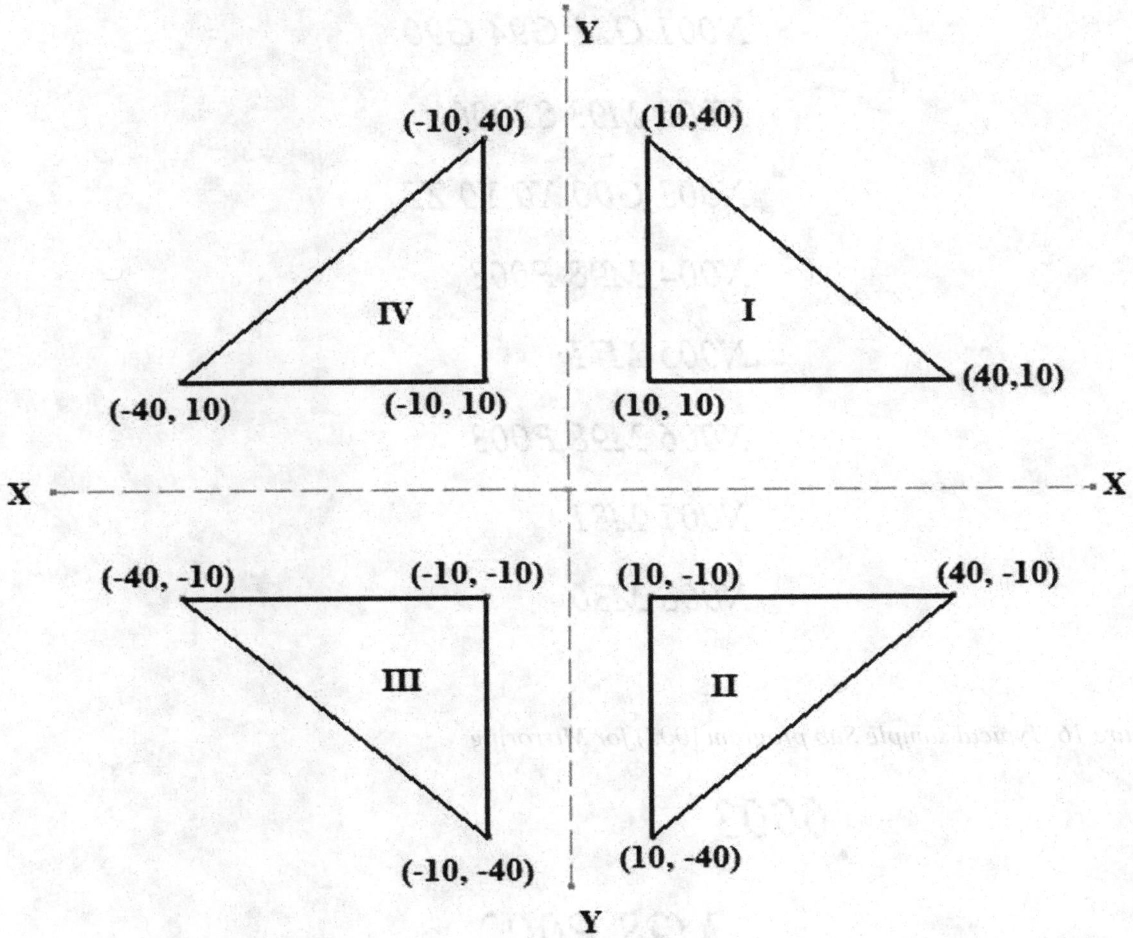

Figure 15. Typical sample Main program for Mirroring

```
N001 G21 G94 G90
N002 M03 S2000
N003 G00 X0 Y0 Z2
N004 M98 P003
N005 M71
N006 M98 P003
N007 M81
N008 M30
```

Figure 16. Typical sample Sub program (003) for Mirroring

```
0003
    M98 P002
    M70
    M98 P002
    M80
    M99
```

Figure 17. Typical sample Sub program (002) for Mirroring

```
0002

G00 X10 Y10

G001   Z0 F25

G91

G01   Z-2 F25
G90

G01 X10 Y40 F40

G01 X40 Y10

G01   X10

G00 X0 Y0

M99
```

REFERENCES

Abbas, M. N., Solomon, D. G., & Fuad Bahari, M. (2007). A review on current research trends in electrical discharge machining (EDM). *International Journal of Machine Tools & Manufacture*, *47*(7), 1214–1228. doi:10.1016/j.ijmachtools.2006.08.026

Bleys, P., Kruth, J., Lauwers, B., Zryd, A., Delpretti, R., & Tricarico, C. (2002). Realtime tool wear compensation in milling EDM. *CIRP Annals - Manufacturing Technology, 51*(1), 157-160.

Debroy, A., & Chakraborty, S. (2013). Non-conventional optimization techniques in optimizing non-traditional machining processes: A review. *Management Science Letters*, *3*(1), 23–38. doi:10.5267/j.msl.2012.10.038

Ding, S., & Jiang, R. (2004). Tool path generation for 4-axis contour EDM rough machining. *International Journal of Machine Tools & Manufacture*, *44*(14), 1493–1502. doi:10.1016/j.ijmachtools.2004.05.010

Ho, K. H., Newman, S. T., Rahimifard, S., & Allen, R. D. (2004). State of art in wire electrical discharge machining (WEDM). *International Journal of Machine Tools & Manufacture*, *44*(12-13), 1247–1259. doi:10.1016/j.ijmachtools.2004.04.017

Hoang, K. T., & Yang, S. H. (2013). A study on the effect of different vibration-assisted methods in micro-WEDM. *Journal of Materials Processing Technology*, *213*(9), 1616–1622. doi:10.1016/j.jmatprotec.2013.03.025

Hoang, K. T., & Yang, S. H. (2015). A new approach for micro-WEDM control based on real-time estimation of material removal rate. *International Journal of Precision Engineering and Manufacturing*, *16*(2), 241–246. doi:10.100712541-015-0032-2

Iosub, A., Axinte, E., & Negoescu, F. (2010). A study about micro-drilling by electrical discharge method of an Al/SiC hybrid composite. *International Journal of Academic Research*, *2*(3), 6–12.

Krzic, P., Stoic, A., & Kopac, J. (2009). STEP-NC A New Programming Code for the CNC Machines. *Strojniskivestnik - Journal of Mechanical Engineering.*, *55*(6), 406–417.

Kumar Senthil, K. L., Sivasubramanian, R., & Kalaiselvan, K. (2009). Selection of Optimum Parameters in Non-Conventional Machining of Metal Matrix Composite. *Portugaliae Electrochimica Acta*, *27*(4), 477–486. doi:10.4152/pea.200904477

Liao, Y. S., Chen, S. T., & Lin, C. S. (2005). Development of a high precision tabletop versatile CNC wire-EDM for making intricate micro parts. *Journal of Micromechanics and Microengineering*, *15*(2), 245–253. doi:10.1088/0960-1317/15/2/001

Raghuraman, S., Thiruppathi, K., Panneerselvam, T., & Santosh, S. (2013). Optimization of EDM parameters using taguchi method and grey relational analysis for mild steel IS 2026. *International Journal of Innovative Research in Science, Engineering and Technology*, *2*(7), 3095–3104.

Saha, S. K., & Choudhury, S. K. (2009). Experimental investigation and empirical modeling of the dry electric discharge machining process. *International Journal of Machine Tools & Manufacture*, *49*(3-4), 297–308. doi:10.1016/j.ijmachtools.2008.10.012

Sohani, M. S., Gaitonde, V. N., Siddeswarappa, B., & And Deshpande, A. S. (2009). Investigations into the effect of tool shapes with size factor consideration in sink electrical discharge machining (EDM) process. *International Journal of Advanced Manufacturing Technology*, *45*(11-12), 1–15. doi:10.100700170-009-2044-5

Vikas, R. A. K., & Kumar, K. (2013). Effect and Optimization of Machine Process Parameters on Material Removal Rate in EDM for EN41 Material Using Taguchi. *International Journal of Mechanical Engineering and Computer Applications*, *1*(5), 35–39.

Yan, B. H. (2005). Examination of wire electrical discharge machining of Al2O3p/6061Al composites. *International Journal of Machine Tools & Manufacture*, *45*(3), 251–259. doi:10.1016/j.ijmachtools.2004.08.015

Yan, M. T. (2010). An adaptive control system with self-organizing fuzzy sliding mode control strategy for micro wire-EDM machines. *International Journal of Advanced Manufacturing Technology*, *50*(1-4), 315–328. doi:10.100700170-009-2481-1

Yoo, H. K., Kwon, W. T., & Kang, S. (2014). Development of a new electrode for micro-electrical discharge machining (EDM) using Ti (C, N)-based cermet. *International Journal of Precision Engineering and Manufacturing*, *15*(4), 609–616. doi:10.100712541-014-0378-x

Younis, M. A., Abbas, M. S., Gouda, M. A., Mahmoud, F. H., & Allah, S. A. A. (2015). Effect of electrode material on electrical discharge machining of tool steel surface. *Ain Shams Engineering Journal*, *6*(3), 977–986. doi:10.1016/j.asej.2015.02.001

Zhang, Y., Bai, X.-L., Xu, X., & Liu, Y.-X. (2012). STEP-NC Based High-level Machining Simulations Integrated with CAD/CAPP/CAM. *International Journal of Automation and Computing*, *9*(5), 506–517. doi:10.100711633-012-0674-9

Zhou, M., & And Han, F. (2009). Adaptive control for EDM process with a self-tuning regulator. *International Journal of Machine Tools & Manufacture*, *49*(6), 462–469. doi:10.1016/j.ijmachtools.2009.01.004

Zivanovic, S., & Puzovic, R. (2015). Off-line Programming and Simulation for 2-axis Wire EDM. FME Transactions, 43, 138-143. doi:10.5937/fmet1502138z

Chapter 6
Multi-Objective Optimization in WEDM of Al 7075 Alloy Using TOPSIS and GRA Method

K. Mandal
https://orcid.org/0000-0001-6684-129X
Jadavpur University, India

S. Sarkar
Jadavpur University, India

S. Mitra
Jadavpur University, India

Dipankar Bose
National Institute of Technical Teachers' Training and Research, Kolkata, India

ABSTRACT

In this research study, Taguchi grey relational analysis (GRA) has been coupled with the technique for order of preference by similarity to ideal solution (TOPSIS) to optimize the multi-performance characteristics in WEDM of Al 7075 alloy. The influence of process factors such as pulse duration (Ton), pulse interval (Toff), flushing pressure (Fp), and servo voltage (Sv) on output responses machining speed (Vc) and corner inaccuracy (Ce) have been considered. The analysis of variance (ANOVA) for the grey relational grade (GRG) and order of preference value generated by TOPSIS have been carried out to justify the optimal results. The recommended input factor settings are found to be Ton = 1.1 μs, Toff = 20 μs, Fp = 9 kg/cm2, and Sv = 20 volt from TOPSIS, and from GRA is Ton = 1.1 μs, Toff = 10 μs, Fp = 12 kg/cm2, and Sv = 40 volt. Finally, surface roughness and surface topography evaluation have been carried out in-depth understanding of influencing factors.

DOI: 10.4018/978-1-7998-3624-7.ch006

INTRODUCTION

Now a day, high strength to weight ratio material like Al 7075 alloy become extremely useful in high temperature and wear resistant application. These extremely useful materials are difficult to machine by conventional process (Ezugwu, 2005 & Selvakumar et. al. 2013; 2014; 2016). Non-conventional machining technique like WEDM is the potential solution to successfully machine of this alloy. (Abbas et. al. 2007) WEDM is a non-traditional machining process, where machining takes place due to the potential difference between tool electrode and work piece. The principle criterion of this machining process is that the work piece must be electrically conductive (Ho et. al. 2003 & Sundaram et. al 2008). Melting and evaporation of material in WEDM takes place due to thermal heating within the machining zone. Heat is generated by the spark in each pulse. Any kind of complex 3D shape and contour can be manufactured with the aid of WEDM (Mandal et. al. 2019). The main aim of WEDM process is to improving the efficiency of the machining as well as quality of the product after manufacturing. Thereby, contribution of WEDM in manufacturing field plays a pivotal role (Sarkar et. al. 2005; 2006; 2008; 2011). The performance characteristics of the WEDM process are strongly influenced by input process parameters. However, the main problem is to selection of appropriate process parameters, which completely depends on machining material. An appropriate selection of process parameters in WEDM process relies deeply on the machining operator and their experiences (Sundaram et. al. 2008). In general, process parameters table supplied by machine tool manufacturer cannot meet the requirement of the manufacturing operator. Since, for a particular requirement of job; builder cannot provide the optimal parameter settings (Garg et. al. 2010 & Jawahir et. al. 2011). Hence, the selection of optimal process parameters is important to attain the desire quality characteristics and productive efficiency in WEDM.

Multi attribute optimization (MAO) is the most prominent approach to choose the optimum variable process parameters in WEDM. The sophisticated MAO methods such as analytical hierarchy process (AHP), technique for order of preference by similarity to ideal solution (TOPSIS), multi objective optimization on the basis of ratio analysis (MOORA), quality function deployment (QFD) and grey relational analysis (GRA) are generally used to solve the engineering problems (Yuan et. al. 2008; Saaty, 1980; Roy, 1990; Kumar et al. 2014 & Tripathy et. al. 2016). Tosun et al. 2004 assessed the significance of process variables and proposed mathematical model on kerf width and surface roughness. Buckingham pi theorem also has been employed in this study to find out the correlation between process variables and responses. Chiang et. al. 2006 employed the grey relational analysis to optimize the process parameters in WEDM with multiple outputs measure such as material removal rate and surface roughness and confirmatory experiments also carried out to validate the optimum results. Somasekhar et. al. 2010 established the artificial neural network model and optimizes the process parameters in micro-WEDM using genetic algorithm. On the other hand, so many research works have been carried out over the past few years on parametric optimization in WEDM using different kind of MAO technique (Pradhan et. al. 2013). A combined approach of RSM based GRA is implemented for reckoning the influence of input factors on surface integrity of WEDM for tool steel. The collective approach of GRA has been decoratively clarified for multi-attribute optimizations in WEDM of Inconel 825 alloy (Rajyalakshmi et. al 2013). A combine approach of Taguchi and Fuzzy-TOPSIS has been developed to solve the multi response optimization problem in different manufacturing field (Sivapirakasam et. al. 2011). An extensive research work is required in WEDM of Al 7075 alloy for the analysis of machining speed and corner inaccuracy. Therefore, it is demanding to optimize the process parameters using combine approach in WEDM for this alloy.

Researchers have detailed studied the effect of input factors on machining speed and corner inaccuracy of Al 7075 alloy. Optimal parameter selection for Al 7075 alloy in WEDM using cohesive methodology has been employed in this work. Weighting factors related to the output parameters have been resolute via entropy method and the most influenced parametric combinations are identified using TOPSIS and grey relational analysis (GRA). In both the optimization technique, multiple characteristics transmute into the single factor for better understanding. The importance of respective characteristics is recognized by comparing the GR grade and relative closeness value. Finally, confirmatory experiments have been conducted based on the statistical analysis of the experimental results to verify the optimal outcome.

EXPERIMENTAL SET-UP AND PROCEDURE

Experiments have been performed on EX 40 WEDM to explore the machining speed (V_c) and corner inaccuracy (e_r). Pulse duration (T_{on}), pulse interval (T_{off}), flushing pressure (F_p) and servo voltage (S_v) have been considered as input factors in this research. L_{16} orthogonal array with four process variables are selected for the experiment. Fig. 1 shows that the machining table unit where the experimentation has been carried out and slot produced by the tool electrode is shown in Fig. 2. Input process parameters and their levels are given in Table 1. Higher the better (HB) for machining speed and lower the better (LB) for corner inaccuracy have been considered to acquire the optimum machining criteria in Taguchi methodology. The input factors and results for the respective output are exhibited in Table 2. Al 7075 workpiece of thickness 20 mm has been used for the experiments. Square block of dimension 8 mm × 8mm × 20mm were sliced from the main workpiece using coated brass electrode with diameter of 250 μm. Deionized water is used as dielectric fluid to remove the material and also used as cooling agent while machining.

Machining speed (V_c) is observed from the monitor of the machine tool. Corner inaccuracy (e_r) measurement has been carried out using high precision contour measuring instrument. Roughness profile is traced by SJ 410 surface roughness testing instrument. Average value of three different measurements has been taken into consideration to minimize the measurement error. Finally, SEM image analysis has been carried out to observe the microstructural changes on the machine surface.

TECHNIQUE FOR ORDER OF PREFERENCE BY SIMILARITY TO IDEAL SOLUTION (TOPSIS)

TOPSIS can assist from the finite set to define the most suitable substitute. The principle selection process of this technique is to find out the nearest from +ve best solution and farthest from –ve best solution w.r.t. the selection criteria. Technique for order of preference by similarity to ideal solution (TOPSIS) is followed eight major steps, which are explained bellow:

Step 1: Decision matrix formation

The decision matrix is consisting of '*j*' attributes and '*i*' alternatives. It can be expressed as-

Figure 1. WEDM table unit

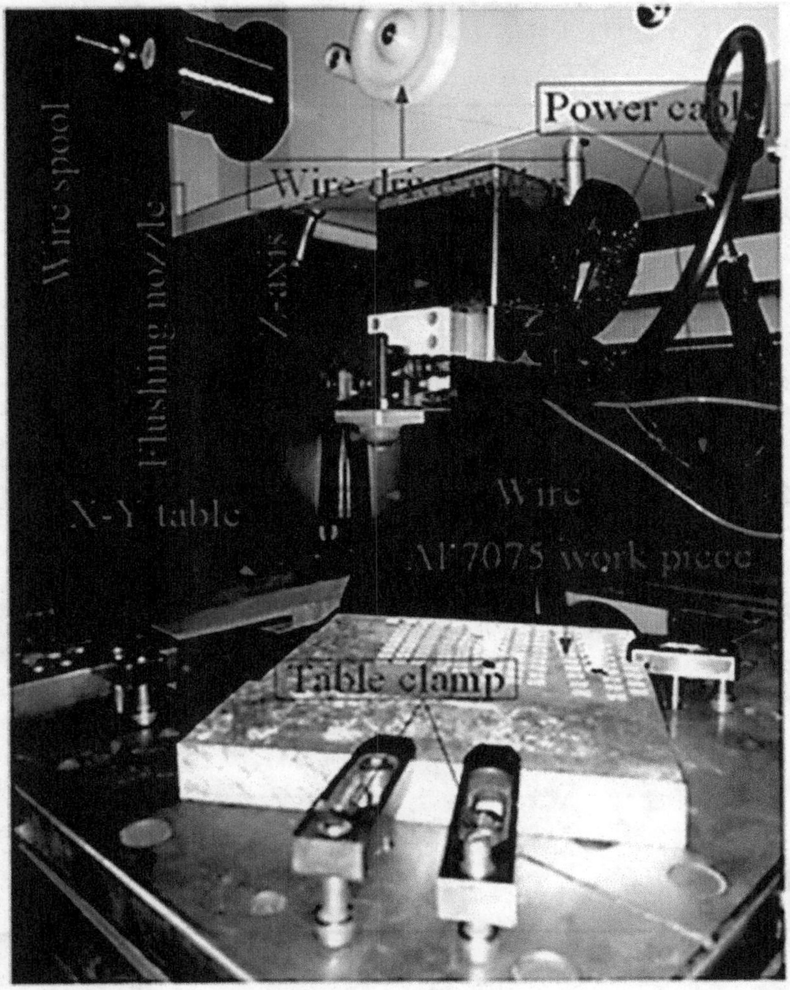

$$x_{ij} = \begin{bmatrix} x_{11}x_{12} \cdots\cdots\cdots\cdots x_{1n} \\ x_{21}x_{22} \cdots\cdots\cdots\cdots x_{2n} \\ x_{31}x_{32} \cdots\cdots\cdots\cdots x_{3n} \\ \cdots\cdots\cdots\cdots\cdots\cdots \\ \cdots\cdots\cdots\cdots\cdots\cdots \\ x_{m1}x_{m2} \cdots\cdots\cdots\cdots x_{mn} \end{bmatrix} \quad (1)$$

Where x_{ij} is the function of ith alternative relative to the jth attribute.

Step 2: Normalization of decision matrix

Normalized values are calculated by following expression

Figure 2. Slot produced by WEDM

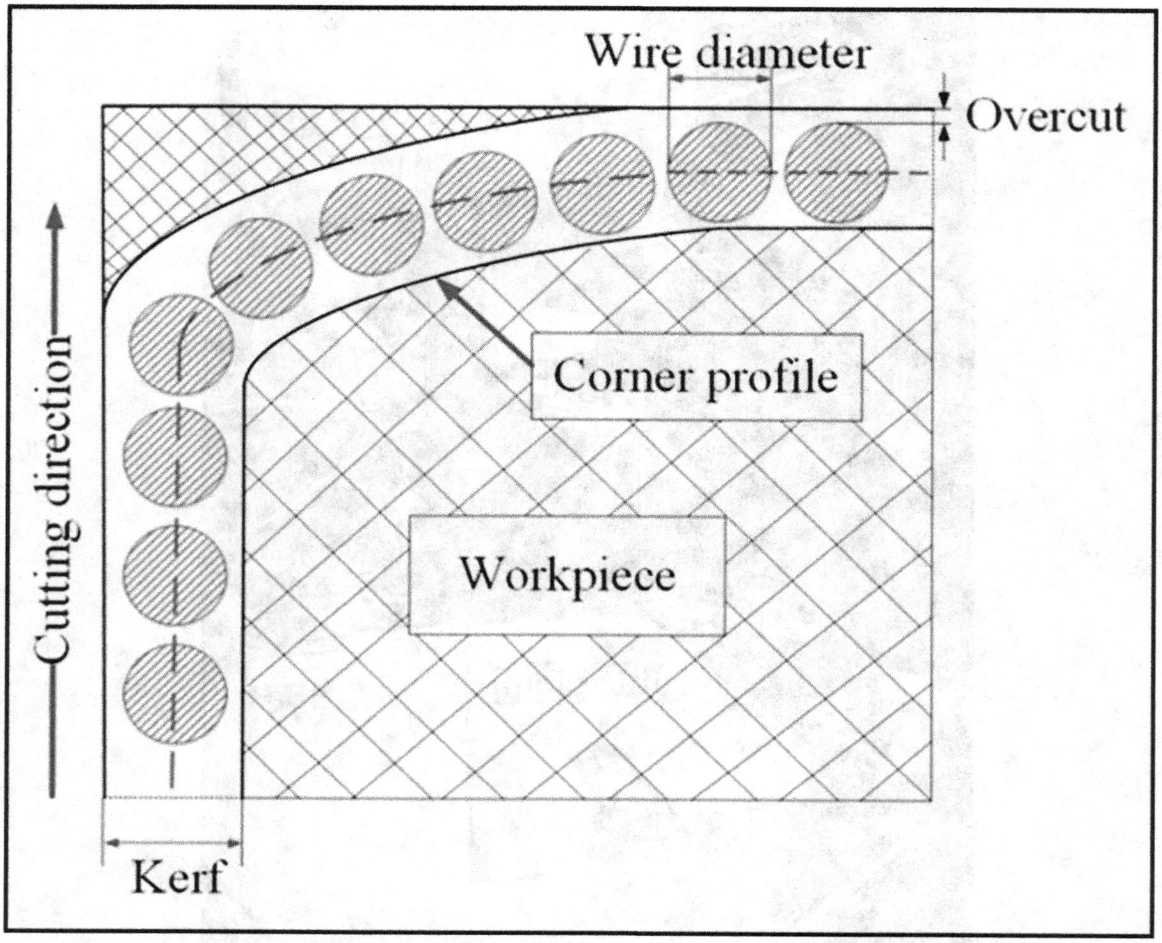

$$x_{ij}^{*} = \frac{a_{ij}}{\sqrt{\sum_{i=1}^{m} a_{ij}^{2}}} \quad (2)$$

Where, x_{ij}^{*} is the order after data normalization.

Step 3: Entropy based weight calculation

Table 1. Process parameters and their levels

Parameters	Units	Levels			
		1	2	3	4
Pulse duration (T_{on})	μs	0.2	0.5	0.8	1.1
Pulse interval (T_{off})	μs	10	20	30	40
Flushing Pressure (F_p)	kg/cm²	3	6	9	12
Servo voltage (S_v)	volt	20	40	60	80

Table 2. L_{16} design table with response variables

Sl. No.	T_{on} (μs)	T_{off} (μs)	F_p (kg/cm²)	S_v (volt)	V_c (mm/min)	e_r (mm)
1	0.2	10	03	20	2.29	0.113
2	0.2	20	06	40	1.91	0.096
3	0.2	30	09	60	1.37	0.076
4	0.2	40	12	80	1.12	0.069
5	0.5	10	06	60	2.89	0.122
6	0.5	20	03	80	2.41	0.121
7	0.5	30	12	20	2.13	0.102
8	0.5	40	09	40	1.72	0.082
9	0.8	10	09	80	3.84	0.133
10	0.8	20	12	60	3.56	0.124
11	0.8	30	03	40	2.91	0.126
12	0.8	40	06	20	1.89	0.097
13	1.1	10	12	40	6.24	0.146
14	1.1	20	09	20	5.33	0.138
15	1.1	30	06	80	4.11	0.132
16	1.1	40	03	60	3.31	0.121

The weight can be calculated by Entropy method and it is expressed by following equation-

$$y_j = -k\sum_{i=1}^{m} x_{ij}^* \ln\left(x_{ij}^*\right), j = 1, 2, 3, \ldots\ldots n \tag{3}$$

Where b_j is the entropy value of jth criterion, k is a constant $\{=1/ln\ (m)\}$.

The degree of divergence (d_j) can be find out by the following Equation-

$$d_j = \left|1 - y_j\right| \tag{4}$$

The Entropy of jth criterion can be given as-

$$w_j = \frac{1}{\sum_{i=1}^{n} d_j} \tag{5}$$

$w_j \leq 1$ (i.e. 100%)

The weighted normalized decision matrix $U = [u_{ij}]$ can be given by

$$U = w_j u_{ij} \tag{6}$$

Step 4: Searching ideal solution

The +ve ideal and –ve ideal solutions are obtained by following equations-

$$U^{+} = \left\{ \left(\sum_{i}^{max} u_{ij} \left| j \in J \right| \right), \left(\sum_{i}^{min} \left| j \in J \right| i = 1,2,3,\ldots\ldots m \right) \right\} \tag{7}$$

$$= \left\{ u_1^{+} u_2^{+} u_3^{+} \ldots\ldots\ldots u_n^{+} \right\}$$

$$U^{-} = \left\{ \left(\sum_{i}^{min} u_{ij} \left| j \in J \right| \right), \left(\sum_{i}^{max} \left| j \in J \right| i = 1,2,3,\ldots\ldots m \right) \right\} \tag{8}$$

$$= \left\{ u_1^{-} u_2^{-} u_3^{-} \ldots\ldots\ldots u_n^{-} \right\}$$

Step 5: Separation measurements

The separation between alternatives and +ve ideal solution is-

$$U_i^{+} = \sqrt{\sum_{j=1}^{n} (u_{ij} - u_j^{+})^2}, \; i = 1,2,3 \ldots\ldots,m \tag{9}$$

The separation between alternatives and –ve ideal solution is-

$$U_i^{-} = \sqrt{\sum_{j=1}^{n} (u_{ij} - u_j^{-})^2}, \; i = 1,2,3 \ldots\ldots,m \tag{10}$$

Step 6: Relative closeness calculation

The relative closeness value is calculated by following equation-

$$z_i = \frac{U_i^{-}}{U_i^{+} + U_i^{-}} \; i = 1,2,3 \ldots\ldots,m \tag{11}$$

Step 7: Ranking

The z_i value has been ranked to identify the most and least preferred solutions of the alternatives. This ranking system is following the descending order.

Step 8: ANOVA for relative closeness value

ANOVA has been done on relative closeness value to identify the main influencing factors and to evaluate the predicted optimal solution criteria.

GREY RELATIONAL ANALYSIS (GRA)

Generally, in grey relation analysis provides an effective solution of multiple input and distinct data problem. The co-relation between input process parameters and output have been determined using GRA. Following steps are required in GRA to determine the co-relation between process factor and responses i.e. machining speed and corner inaccuracy.

Step 1: Normalization of raw data

Normalization of experimental data has been carried out to analysis where the original sequence is transformed to a comparable sequence. Measured output responses are first normalized within the limit 0 to 1.

According to the process criteria, three types of normalization process [i.e. lower-is-Better (LB), higher-is-Better (HB), and nominal-is-best (NB)] have been carried out.

For machining speed (Higher-the-better kind of problem)

$$x_{ij}^{*} = \frac{(x_{ij}) - \min(x_{ij})}{\max(x_{ij}) - \min(x_{ij})} \tag{12}$$

For corner inaccuracy (Lower-the-better kind of problem)

$$x_{ij}^{*} = \frac{max(x_{ij}) - (x_{ij})}{\max(x_{ij}) - \min(x_{ij})} \tag{13}$$

Where, x_{ij}^{*} is the order after data normalization, x_{ij} is the ith sequence of raw data, (i = 1, 2, 3 ….. 16), $max(x_{ij})$ is the highest value of x_{ij} and $\min(x_{ij})$ is the lowest value of x_{ij}.

Step 2: Grey relational coefficient calculation

To establish the relations between reference (best) data and the actual (normalized) data, grey relational coefficient has to be calculated. The GRC calculation can be expressed as follows:

$$\epsilon_{ij} = \frac{\partial_{min} + £\partial_{max}}{\partial_i + £\partial_{max}} \tag{14}$$

$$0 < \epsilon_{ij} \leq 1$$

Where, ϵ_{ij} is the grey relational coefficient (GRC) and £ ($0 < £ \leq 1$) is the distinguishing coefficient, is considered as 0.5 in this study. ∂_i is the comparability sequence, ∂_{max} and ∂_{min} are the maximum and minimum comparability sequence of the allocating sequence.

Step 3: Grey relational grade generation

The grey relational grade can be obtained as follows:

$$A_j = w_j \times \frac{1}{n}\sum_{i=1}^{n} \in_{ij} \tag{15}$$

Where, A_j is the grey relational grade and n is the performance characteristics. Higher the value of grey relational grade indicates the better quality. By allocating entropy based weight for machining speed $\{w_j = 0.5314\}$ and corner inaccuracy $\{w_j = 0.4686\}$, grey relational grade is generated.

Step 4: Ranking

The GRG value has been ranked to recognize the most and least desired solutions of the performance characteristics. The GRG ranking system is following the descending in order.

Step 5: Perform analysis of variance (ANOVA)

ANOVA has been carried out to identify the significant factors and estimate the predicted optimal solution criteria.

RESULTS AND DISCUSSIONS

The efficiency of the WEDM process can be characterised by the machining speed (V_c). The main aim behind machining should be higher corner accuracy. The Al 7075 alloy for machining is selected based upon the industrial application that this material can resist corrosion and high temperature in any environmental condition. From the experimental study it has been observed that, when pulse duration (T_{on}) increase V_c and e_r are consistently increases (Shown in Fig. 3 and 4). This is happening due to increases of electrical power, additional thermal energy that is generated in each spark while machining. Similarly, reverse trend is observed in case of pulse interval (T_{off}) as shown in Fig. 5 and Fig. 6. Higher pulse interval gives low aggressive pulse parameter setting i.e. energy consumption and power generation by each pulse become small. It is the better strategy to increase machining speed with the increase of pulse duration. However, as such corner accuracy also decreases due to the aggressive pulse parameter setting, that is not satisfactory. Similarly, corner accuracy can be improved by increasing pulse interval but machining speed will be significantly decreased due to low pulse parameter setting. As per these two pulse parameters are conflicting in nature, it is recommended to adjust the pulse parameter without negotiating machining efficiency and accuracy.

Multi Attribute Optimization-Using TOPSIS

The preference value for every experimental run can be obtained using Equ. (1–10). The preference value for the alternative is calculate considering the respective comparative closeness to the ideal best solution. From +ve and –ve ideal solution, the separation has been measured using Equ. 11. The corresponding weightage 0.5314 and 0.4686 have been assigned to the machining speed (V_c) and corner inaccuracy (e_r), which is calculated by Entropy method. The multi response is converted into a single response using a combine approach Taguchi's design and TOPSIS. The rank order from the relative closeness value obtained by TOPSIS is given in Table 3.

It has been found that the experimental run fourteen (#14) is the preeminent multiple performance characteristics with highest preference value, hence it is the best optimal setting followed by run number thirteen (#13) and fifteen (#15). The optimal parametric combination can be determined by considering

Figure 3. Pulse duration vs. machining speed

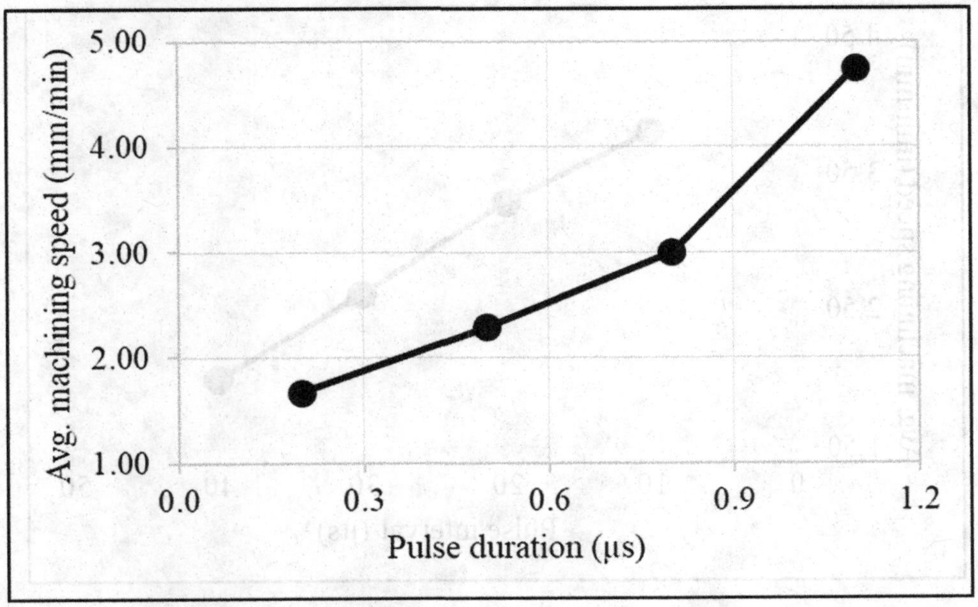

Figure 4. Pulse duration vs. corner inaccuracy

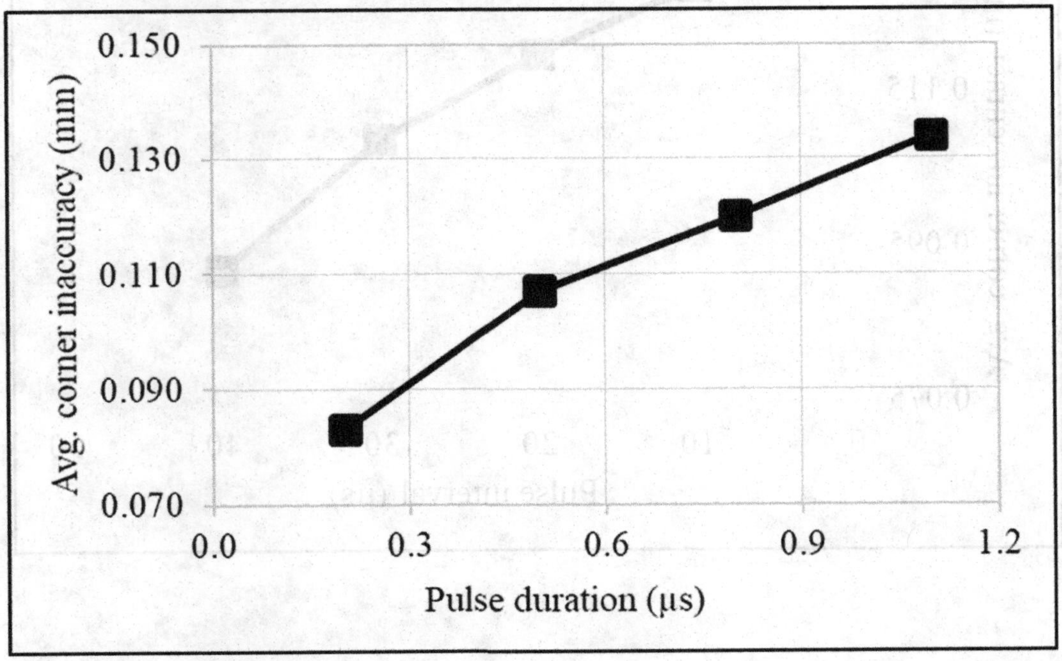

Figure 5. Pulse interval vs. machining speed

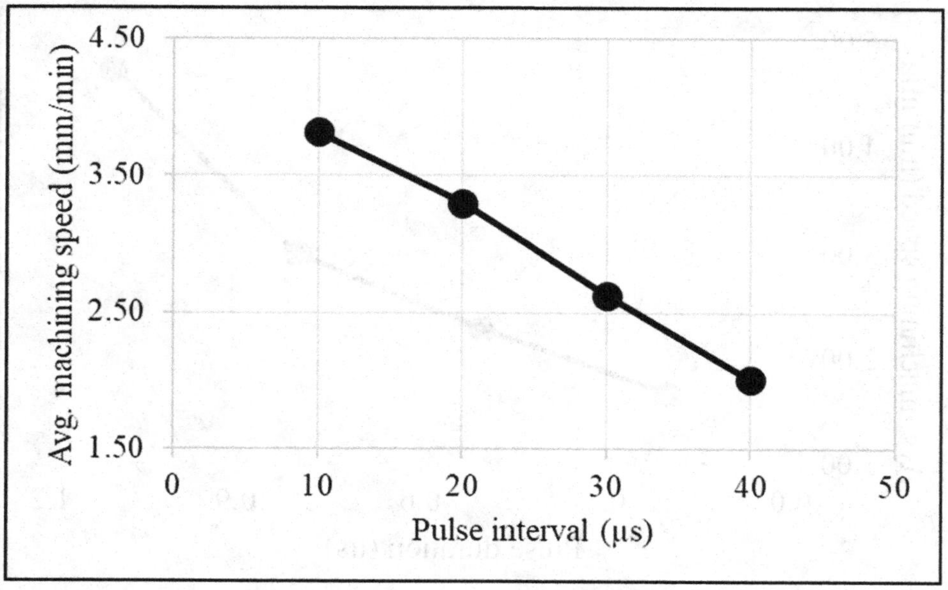

Figure 6. Pulse interval vs. corner inaccuracy

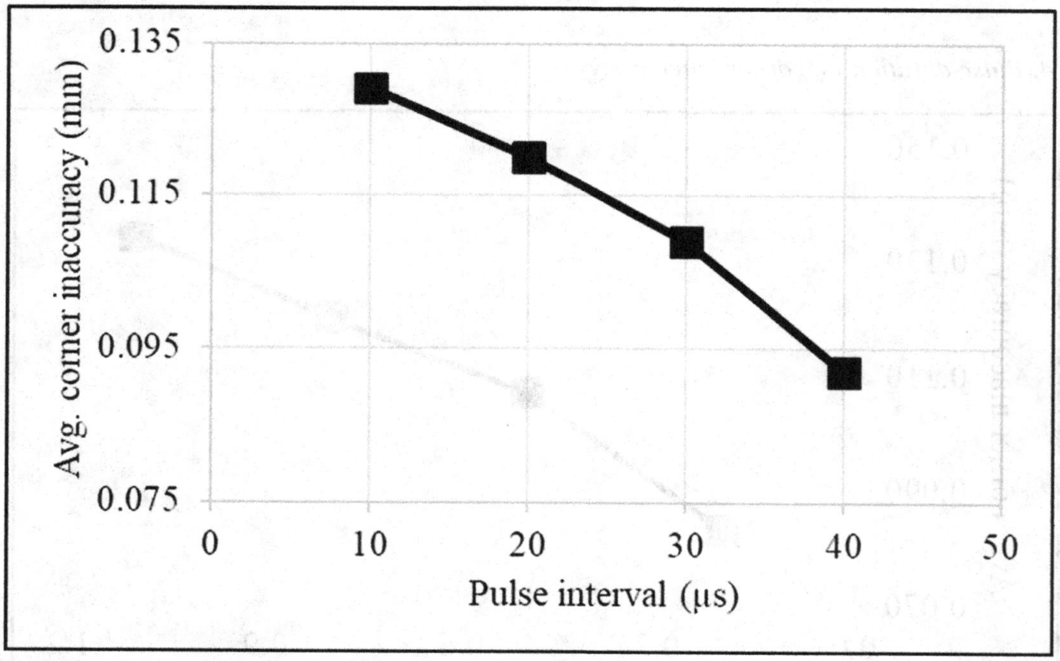

Table 3. Estimation of relative closeness and rank order for TOPSIS

Sl. No.	Responses		Normalized responses		Weighted normalized		Separation measurement		Relative closeness	Rank order
	Vc	e_r	V_c	e_r	V_c	e_r	S^+	S^-	z_i	R
1	2.29	0.113	0.0487	0.0629	0.0259	0.0295	0.0454	0.0177	0.3119	10
2	1.91	0.096	0.0406	0.0535	0.0216	0.0250	0.0506	0.0115	0.2372	13
3	1.37	0.076	0.0291	0.0423	0.0155	0.0198	0.0580	0.0035	0.5132	6
4	1.12	0.068	0.0238	0.0379	0.0127	0.0177	0.0613	0.0001	0.1875	14
5	2.89	0.122	0.0615	0.0679	0.0327	0.0318	0.0384	0.0245	0.3656	9
6	2.41	0.121	0.0512	0.0674	0.0272	0.0316	0.0438	0.0201	0.2547	12
7	2.13	0.102	0.0453	0.0568	0.0241	0.0266	0.0478	0.0144	0.2837	11
8	1.72	0.082	0.0366	0.0457	0.0194	0.0214	0.0537	0.0077	0.1570	16
9	3.84	0.133	0.0817	0.0741	0.0434	0.0347	0.0273	0.0351	0.6140	4
10	3.56	0.124	0.0757	0.0690	0.0402	0.0324	0.0308	0.0312	0.5349	5
11	2.91	0.126	0.0619	0.0702	0.0329	0.0329	0.0380	0.0252	0.3756	8
12	1.89	0.097	0.0402	0.0540	0.0214	0.0253	0.0508	0.0115	0.1751	15
13	6.24	0.146	0.1327	0.0813	0.0705	0.0381	0.0000	0.0613	0.7503	2
14	5.33	0.137	0.1133	0.0763	0.0602	0.0357	0.0105	0.0508	0.8045	1
15	4.11	0.132	0.0874	0.0735	0.0464	0.0344	0.0243	0.0377	0.6394	3
16	3.31	0.121	0.0704	0.0674	0.0374	0.0316	0.0337	0.0283	0.5082	7

Figure 7. Relative closeness vs. run order

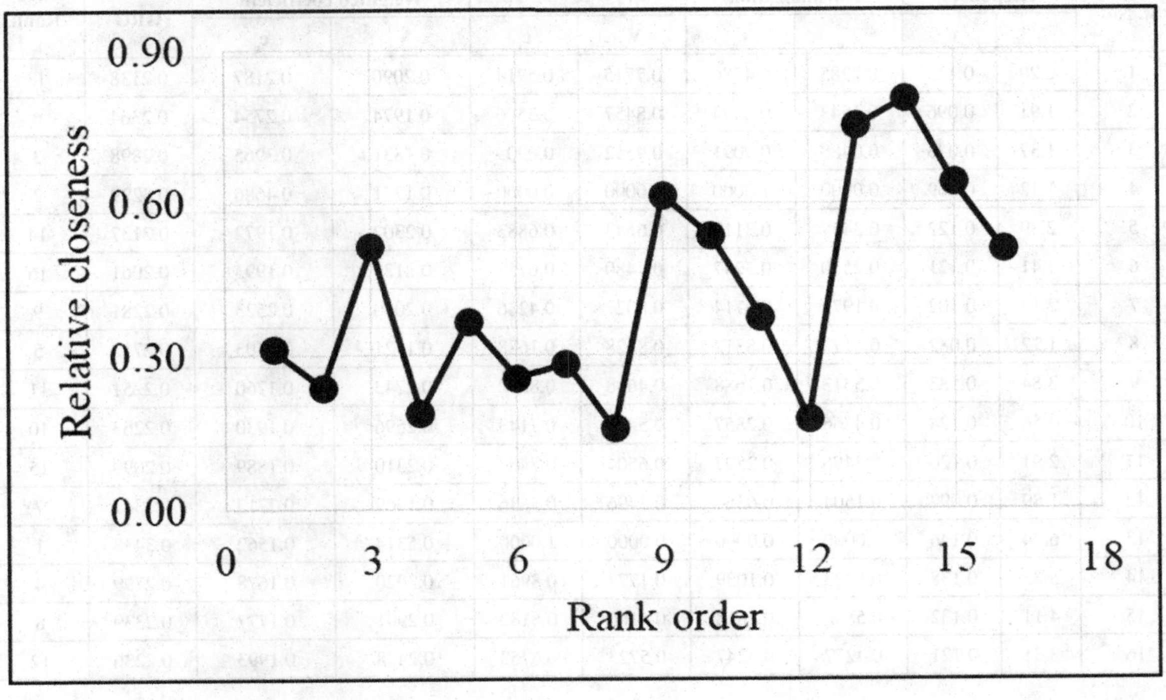

Table 4. Confirmatory experiments for TOPSIS

Optimal parameters setting	Predicted results		Actual results		z_i	
	V_c	C_e	V_c	C_e	Predicted	Actual
$T_{on4}T_{off2}F_{p3}S_{v1}$	5.33	0.137	5.35	0.136	0.8045	0.8009

Table 5. ANOVA table for relative closeness

Source	DF	Adj SS	Adj MS	F-value	P-value	Percentage contribution
Pulse duration (T_{on})	3	0.403476	0.134492	282.64	0.000	62%
Pulse interval (T_{off})	3	0.149135	0.049712	104.47	0.002	23%
Flushing pressure (F_p)	3	0.073647	0.024549	51.59	0.004	11%
Servo voltage (S_v)	3	0.023824	0.007941	16.69	0.022	4%
Error	3	0.001428	0.000476			
Total	15	0.651510				
Model summary						
S 0.0218136	R-sq 99.78%	R-sq (adj) 98.90%	R-sq (pred) 93.77%			

Table 6. Estimation of grey relational grade and rank order

Sl. No.	Responses		Normalization		δ		Weighted coefficient		GRG	Rank
	V_c	e_r	V_c	e_r	V_c	e_r	V_c	e_r		
1	2.29	0.113	0.2285	0.4286	0.7715	0.5714	0.2090	0.2187	0.2138	13
2	1.91	0.096	0.1543	0.6494	0.8457	0.3506	0.1974	0.2754	0.2364	6
3	1.37	0.076	0.0488	0.9091	0.9512	0.0909	0.1831	0.3965	0.2898	3
4	1.12	0.069	0.0000	1.0000	1.0000	0.0000	0.1771	0.4686	0.3229	2
5	2.89	0.122	0.3457	0.3117	0.6543	0.6883	0.2302	0.1972	0.2137	14
6	2.41	0.121	0.2520	0.3247	0.7480	0.6753	0.2129	0.1993	0.2061	16
7	2.13	0.102	0.1973	0.5714	0.8027	0.4286	0.2040	0.2523	0.2281	9
8	1.72	0.082	0.1172	0.8312	0.8828	0.1688	0.1921	0.3503	0.2712	5
9	3.84	0.133	0.5313	0.1688	0.4688	0.8312	0.2743	0.1760	0.2251	11
10	3.56	0.124	0.4766	0.2857	0.5234	0.7143	0.2596	0.1930	0.2263	10
11	2.91	0.126	0.3496	0.2597	0.6504	0.7403	0.2310	0.1889	0.2099	15
12	1.89	0.097	0.1504	0.6364	0.8496	0.3636	0.1969	0.2713	0.2341	7
13	6.24	0.146	1.0000	0.0000	0.0000	1.0000	0.5314	0.1562	0.3438	1
14	5.33	0.138	0.8223	0.1039	0.1777	0.8961	0.3920	0.1678	0.2799	4
15	4.11	0.132	0.5840	0.1818	0.4160	0.8182	0.2901	0.1777	0.2339	8
16	3.31	0.121	0.4277	0.3247	0.5723	0.6753	0.2478	0.1993	0.2236	12

the higher values of preference order. The optimal parameter setting is obtained as $T_{on4}T_{off2}F_{p3}S_{v1}$. Relative closeness and run order has been plotted in Fig. 7.

Confirmatory Experiment for TOPSIS

Predicted and experimental result has been carried out to verify the optimal parameter setting. Most effective set of input factors and quality characteristics improvement also have been carried out on optimal result. From Table 4, it is observed that the optimal parameters setting obtained from the TOPSIS gives an increased cutting speed with optimum corner inaccuracy, thus improving the quality characteristic and productivity. The improvement in relative closeness value for ideal solution is (0.8045-0.8009) i.e. 0.0036.

ANOVA for TOPSIS

The effects of process parameters on the performance characteristics have been resolute using ANOVA. ANOVA result of relative closeness is enlisted in Table 5. Results of the output are considered as 'higher-the-better' for V_c and 'lower the better' for e_r. Table 5 implies that T_{on}, T_{off}, F_p and S_v are parameters which have significant contribution towards the improvement of relative closeness. From the percentage of contribution, it has been observed that the most dominating parameters are pulse duration (62%) and pulse interval (23%). Flushing pressure (11%) and servo voltage (4%) are also significant factors on machining speed and corner inaccuracy.

GRA of the Experimental Results

The multi-responses are transformed into a single response in term of grey relational grade (GRG). The GR grade for individual experimental run has been developed using Equ. (12–15). Optimal parametric combination has been recognized by allowing the higher value of GRG. Normalized data and GRG values for respective experimental run are given in Table 6. It has been found that the number thirteen (#13) experimental run is the best fit of performance characteristics with highest GR grade (0.3438). Hence, the optimal setting from most suitable set followed by number four (#4) and three (#3). Fig. 8 shows that the GR grade value in different experimental run.

Confirmatory Experiment for GRA

After the assessment of optimal process parameter setting, predicted and confirmatory experiment for the improvement of quality characteristics using the optimal parameter setting have been carried out. From the optimum level of process parameters, estimated GRG (φ) is calculated as:

$$\varphi = \varphi_m + \sum_{i=1}^{q} \blacklozenge - \varphi_m \tag{16}$$

Where, φ is the total mean GR grade φ_m is the GR grade at the utmost favourable setting and q is the number of process variables effecting the performance characteristics. The predicted and confirmatory experimented results are exhibited in Table 7.

ANOVA for GRA

The effect of input factors on the output can be specified by analysis of variance at 95% confidence level. The outcome of response factors are calculate by using 'higher-the-better' for machining speed and 'lower-the-better' for corner inaccuracy. ANOVA results for GRG with percentage contribution are shown in Table 8. It is specified that the pulse duration (52%), pulse interval (27%) are the most dominating factors having highly significant in respect of other process parameters. However, flushing pressure (10%) and servo voltage (11%) are less influencing factors with respect to T_{on} and T_{off} towards improvement in GRG.

SURFACE ROUGHNESS AND SURFACE TOPOGRAPHY ANALYSIS

Many craters and globules that have resulted from individual electrical discharges of entire surfaces machined by WEDM. These carried about microscopic elements of the material, which are partially flushed away by the jet of deionized water (dielectric liquid). The morphology of the specified area surface display traces that are emblematic of material which is molten and consequently rapidly cooled. Using surface roughness tester, the surface of each sample subject to the experiment has been investigated. On the surfaces of two different machined samples (i.e. for low and high pulse duration), the evolution profile shown in Fig. 9 (a-b) has been found.

After metallographic preparations of machined sample, sub-surface area of samples has been inspected using scanning electron microscope at 500X magnified resolution. The incomplete melting and successive rapid cooling of the machined material ensued in the development of a resolidification stratum, which are shown in Fig. 10 (a-b). The rate of crater occurrence on the machined surfaces varies widely. Some areas are enclosed with a constellation of deep craters, micro voids (Shown in Fig. 10a-b).

When the pulse duration is longer (i.e. smaller the T_{off}), the number of discharge takes place within a small period of time becomes larger, prominent too rapid cooling and heating within the machining zone. This induced larger craters, micro voids and huge amount of recast metal within the machining zone. From the Fig.10 (a-b), it is clear that the number of micro pores and deep crates are simultaneously varies as the parameters are varied.

CONCLUSIONS

In present experimental investigation, single pass rough cutting operation in WEDM of Al 7075 alloy have been carried out. Pulse duration (T_{on}), pulse interval (T_{off}), flushing pressure (F_p) and servo voltage have been considered as variable input factors and Taguchi design technique is used to conduct the experiments. TOPSIS and GRA based multi objective optimization technique have been employed to determine the most significant set of input factors on machining speed (V_c) and corner inaccuracy (e_r). The following conclusions are drawn from the present study:

1. The optimal parameter settings from TOPSIS is T_{on} = 1.1 µs, T_{off} = 20 µs, F_p = 9 kg/cm², S_v = 20 volt and GRA is T_{on} = 1.1 µs, T_{off} = 10 µs, F_p = 12 kg/cm², S_v = 40 volt.

Figure 8. Grey relational grade vs. run order

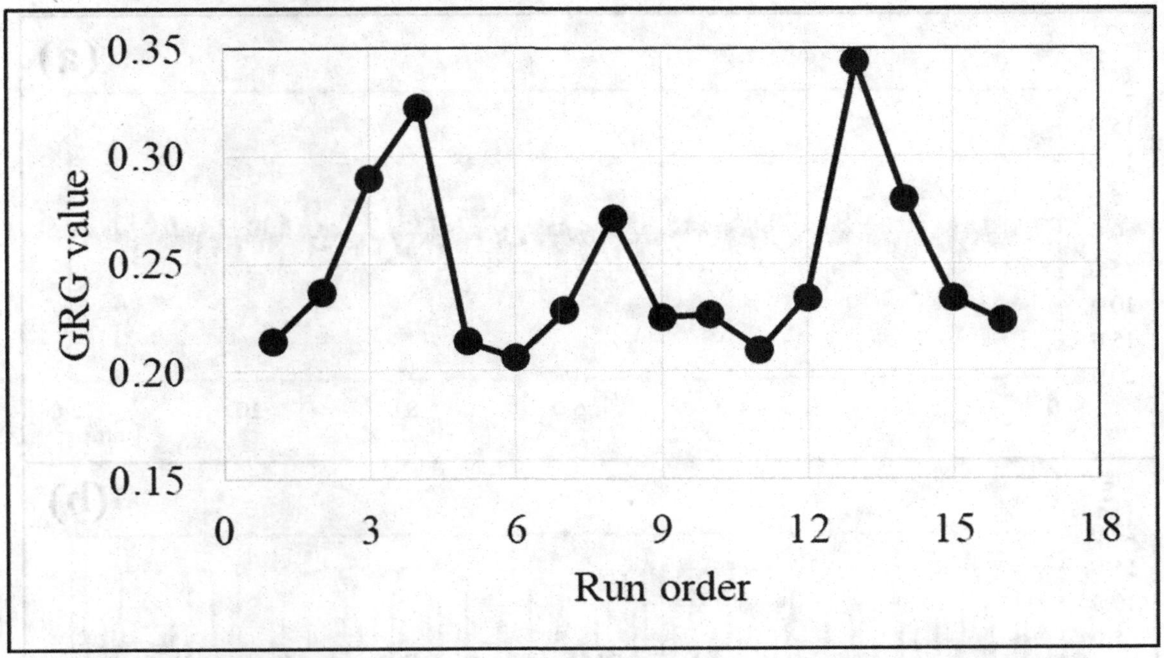

Table 7. Confirmatory experimentation for GRA

Optimal parameters setting	Predicted results		Actual results		GRG	
	V_c	e_r	V_c	e_r	Predicted	Actual
$T_{on4}T_{off1}F_{p4}S_{v2}$	6.24	0.146	6.14	0.151	0.3505	0.3438

Table 8. ANOVA for GRG

Source	DF	Adj SS	Adj MS	F-Value	P-Value	Percentage contribution
Pulse duration (T_{on})	3	0.044937	0.014979	139.62	0.001	52%
Pulse interval (T_{off})	3	0.023295	0.007765	72.38	0.003	27%
Flushing pressure (F_p)	3	0.008160	0.002720	25.35	0.012	10%
Servo voltage (S_v)	3	0.009455	0.003152	29.38	0.010	11%
Residual error	3	0.000322	0.000107			
Total	15	0.086169				
Model Summary						
S	R^2	R^2(adj)	R^2(pred)			
0.010358	99.63%	98.13%	92.38%			

Figure 9. Surface roughness profile traced by SJ 400 (a) Ton = 0.2 μs (b) Ton = 1.1 μs

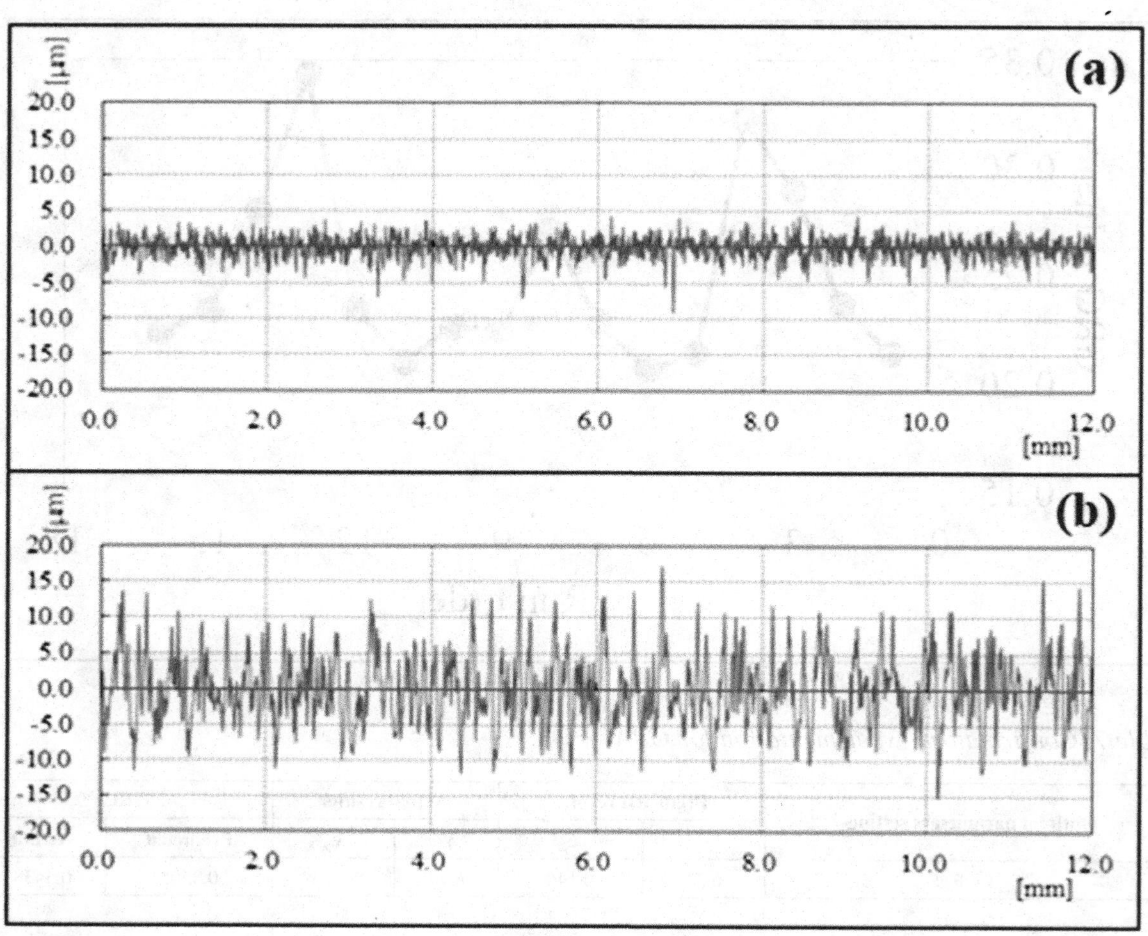

2. Confirmatory experiment shows that the improving of relative closeness value from TOPSIS is 0.0036 and GR grade value from GRA is 0.0067, which are satisfactory.
3. From the ANOVA, pulse duration (T_{on}) has been found the most dominating factor (more than 50% contribution on V_c and e_r) in TOPSIS and GRA. Other process parameters are also significant but not as much as pulse duration.
4. Percentage contribution in TOPSIS is found to be T_{on} (62%), T_{off} (23%), F_p (11%), S_v (4%) and for GRA is T_{on} (52%), T_{off} (27%), F_p (10%), S_v (11%).
5. Therefore, both optimization methods are suitable to establish the preeminent possible solution for the set of input factors depending upon the desired performance characteristics.
6. From the roughness evolution, it has been found that pulse parameter setting directly decides the surface roughness (i.e. surface roughness is increased as the pulse duration increases). SEM micrographs represent the defects, pores and recast metal in the machined surface, which is directly decided by process parameter settings.

Figure 10. SEM image of machined surface in two different optimal parameter setting (a) #13 (b) #14

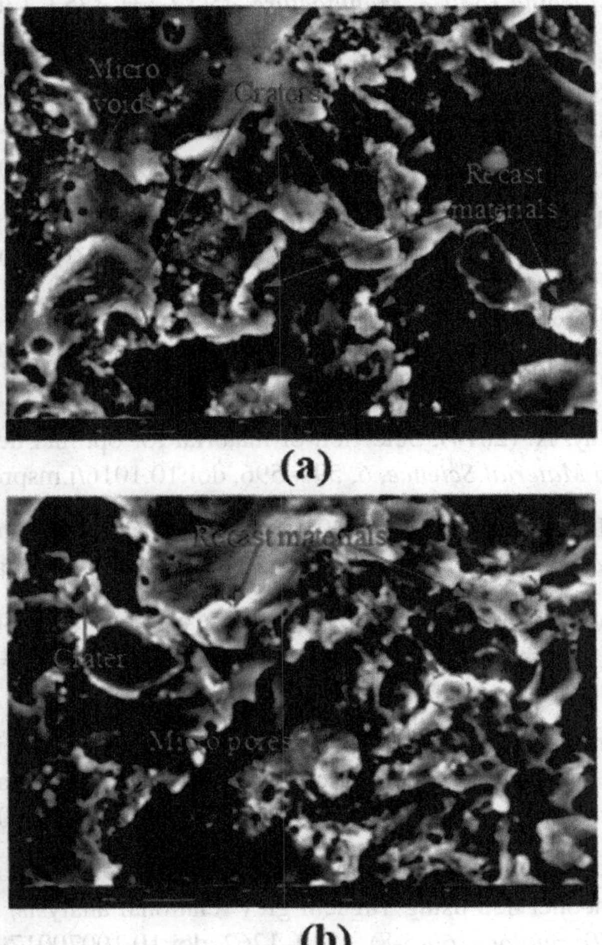

The experimental outcome of present research study will be a substantial support to the modern manufacturing industries for quality improvement in processing using WEDM.

REFERENCES

Abbas, N. M., Solomon, D. G., & Bahari, M. F. (2007). A review on current research trends in electrical discharge machining (EDM). *International Journal of Machine Tools & Manufacture*, *47*(7-8), 1214–1228. doi:10.1016/j.ijmachtools.2006.08.026

Chiang, K., & Chang, F. (2006). Optimization of the WEDM process of particle reinforced material with multiple performance characterises using Grey relational grade. *Journal of Materials Processing Technology*, *180*(1-3), 96–101. doi:10.1016/j.jmatprotec.2006.05.008

Ezugwu, E. O. (2005). Key improvements in the machining of difficult-to-cut aerospace superalloys. *International Journal of Machine Tools & Manufacture*, *45*(12-13), 1353–1367. doi:10.1016/j.ijmachtools.2005.02.003

Garg, R. K., Singh, K. K., Sachdeva, A., Sharma, V. S., Ojha, K., & Singh, S. (2010). Review of research work in sinking EDM and WEDM on metal matrix composite materials. *International Journal of Advanced Manufacturing Technology*, *50*(5-8), 611–624. doi:10.100700170-010-2534-5

Ho, K. H., & Newman, S. T. (2003). State of the art electrical discharge machining (EDM). *International Journal of Machine Tools & Manufacture*, *43*(13), 287–1300. doi:10.1016/S0890-6955(03)00162-7

Jawahir, I. S., Brinksmeier, E., Saoubi, R. M., Aspinwall, D. K., Outeiro, J. C., Meyer, D., Umbrell, D., & Jayala, A. D. (2011). Surface integrity in material removal processes: Recent advances. *CIRP Annals*, *60*(2), 603–626. doi:10.1016/j.cirp.2011.05.002

Kumar, R., Jagadish, & Ray, A. (2014). Selection of material for optimal design using multi-criteria decision making. *Procedia Material Science*, *6*, 590–596. doi:10.1016/j.mspro.2014.07.073

Mandal, K., Sarkar, S., Mitra, S., & Bose, D. (2019). Multi-Attribute Optimization in WEDM Light Metal Alloy. *Materials Today: Proceedings*, *18*, 3492–3500. doi:10.1016/j.matpr.2019.07.277

Mandal, K., Sarkar, S., Mitra, S., & Bose, D. (2019). Surface roughness and surface topography evaluation of Al 6065-T6 alloy using wire electrodischarge machining (wire EDM). *Advances in Materials and Processing Technologies*.

Pradhan, M. K. (2013). Estimating the effect of process parameters on surface integrity of EDMed AISI D2 tool steel by response surface methodology coupled with grey relational analysis. *International Journal of Advanced Manufacturing Technology*, *67*(9-12), 2051–2062. doi:10.100700170-012-4630-1

Rajyalakshmi, G., & Ramaiah, P. V. (2013). Multiple process parameter optimization of wire electrical discharge machining on Inconel 825 using Taguchi grey relational analysis. *International Journal of Advanced Manufacturing Technology*, *69*(5-8), 1249–1262. doi:10.100700170-013-5081-z

Roy, B. (1990). Decision-aid and decision-making. *European Journal of Operational Research*, *45*(2-3), 324–331. doi:10.1016/0377-2217(90)90196-I

Saaty, T. L. (1980). *The Analytic Hierarchy Process*. McGraw-Hill.

Sarkar, S., Mitra, S., & Bhattacharyya, B. (2005). Parametric analysis and optimization of wire electrical discharge machining of γ-titanium aluminide alloy. *Journal of Materials Processing Technology*, *159*(3), 286–294. doi:10.1016/j.jmatprotec.2004.10.009

Sarkar, S., Mitra, S., & Bhattacharyya, B. (2006). Parametric optimisation of wire electrical discharge machining of γ titanium aluminide alloy through an artificial neural network model. *International Journal of Advanced Manufacturing Technology*, *27*(5–6), 501–508. doi:10.100700170-004-2203-7

Sarkar, S., Mitra, S., & Bhattacharyya, B. (2011). A novel method of determination of wire lag for enhanced profile accuracy in WEDM. *Precision Engineering*, *35*(2), 339–347. doi:10.1016/j.precisioneng.2011.01.001

Sarkar, S., Sekh, M., Mitra, S., & Bhattacharyya, B. (2008). Modelling and optimization of wire electrical discharge machining of γ-TiAl in trim cutting operation. *Journal of Materials Processing Technology*, *205*(1-3), 376–387. doi:10.1016/j.jmatprotec.2007.11.194

Selvakumar, G., Jiju, K. B., Sarkar, S., & Mitra, S. (2016). Enhancing die corner accuracy through trim cut in WEDM. *International Journal of Advanced Manufacturing Technology*, *83*(5–8), 791–803. doi:10.100700170-015-7606-0

Selvakumar, G., Sarkar, S., & Mitra, S. (2013). An experimental analysis of single pass cutting of aluminium 5083 alloy in different corner angles through WEDM. *International Journal of Machining and Machinability of Materials*, *13*(2/3), 262. doi:10.1504/IJMMM.2013.053227

Selvakumar, G., Sornalatha, G., Sarkar, S., & Mitra, S. (2014). Experimental investigation and multi-objective optimization of wire electrical discharge machining (WEDM) of 5083 aluminum alloy. *Transactions of Nonferrous Metals Society of China*, *24*(2), 373–379. doi:10.1016/S1003-6326(14)63071-5

Sivapirakasam, S. P., Mathew, J., & Surianarayanan, M. (2011). Multi-attribute decision making for green electrical discharge machining. *Expert Systems with Applications*, *38*(7), 8370–8374. doi:10.1016/j.eswa.2011.01.026

Somashekhar, K. P., Ramachandram, N., & Mathew, J. (2010). Optimization of material removal rate in micro-WEDM using artificial neural network and genetic algorithms. *Materials and Manufacturing Processes*, *25*(6), 467–475. doi:10.1080/10426910903365760

Sundaram, M. M., Pavalarajan, G. B., & Rajurkar, K. P. (2008). A Study on Process Parameters of Ultrasonic Assisted Micro EDM Based on Taguchi Method. *Journal of Materials Engineering and Performance*, *17*(2), 210–215. doi:10.100711665-007-9128-x

Tosun, N., Cogun, C., & Tosun, G. (2004). A study on kerf and material removal rate in wire electrical discharge machining based on Taguchi method. *Journal of Materials Processing Technology*, *152*(3), 316–322. doi:10.1016/j.jmatprotec.2004.04.373

Tripathy, S., & Tripathy, D. K. (2016). Multi-attribute optimization of machining process parameters in powder mixed electro-discharge machining using TOPSIS and grey relational analysis. *Engineering Science and Technology, an International Journal*, *19*, 62-70.

Yuan, J., Wang, K., Yua, T., & Fanga, M. (2008). Reliable multi-objective optimization of high-speed WEDM process based on Gaussian process regression. *International Journal of Machine Tools & Manufacture*, *48*(1), 47–60. doi:10.1016/j.ijmachtools.2007.07.011

Chapter 7
Experimental Evaluation on Corner Accuracy in WEDM for Aluminium 6061 Alloy

Debal Pramanik
https://orcid.org/0000-0003-1899-3197
Jadavpur University, India

Dipankar Bose
National Institute of Technical Teachers' Training and Research, Kolkata, India

ABSTRACT

An important electro-thermal process known as wire electrical discharge machining (WEDM) is applied for machining of conductive materials to generate most precisely. All cutting inaccuracies of WEDM arise out of the major cause of wire bending. At the time of cutting a sharp corner or cut profile, bending of the wire leads to a geometrical error on the workpiece. Though this type of error may be of a few hundred microns, it is not suitable for micro applications. In this research study, an experimental investigation based on response surface methodology (RSM) has been done on wire EDM of Aluminium 6061 t6 alloy. This chapter studies the outcome of input process variables (i.e., wire feed rate, pulse on time, pulse off time, and gap voltage) on machining output responses (i.e., corner inaccuracy) extensively. Experimental validation of the proposed model shows that corner inaccuracy value may be reduced by modification of input parameters.

INTRODUCTION

Due to a lot of problems faced by the machining process wire electrical discharge machining was evolved. The success of this process of machining comes out of its extensive capabilities to achieve production in the fields of automobile, telecommunication and electronics industries, aerospace, medical sector and has qualitative superiority in all the fields of conductive material machining (Puri et al. 2003). Such features have been considered to be the best and this process has no other alternatives to produce

DOI: 10.4018/978-1-7998-3624-7.ch007

intricate shapes and profiles. Being a special mode of electrical discharge machining (EDM) process wire electrical discharge machining (WEDM) has a continuous moving wire serving the purpose of the electrode. For the purpose of to drive away the eroded particles from the workpiece and wire electrode are separated. Numerical controller of the wire movement is done to achieve required complex shape, smooth surface finish and corner accuracy in the workpiece. Precision and accuracy are the demands of various industries for further improvement in the area. The manufacturers and users have main target to achieve higher machining rate with optimum surface finish. Even a highly skilled operator who is working with a state of art of WEDM may probably to unable to reach the optimal performance level when wire breakage and surface damage are highly advanced in nature. Only the performance of the procedure and its controllable process parameters may figure out the problem efficiently with the use of appropriate mathematical techniques.

WIRE ELECTRO DISCHARGE MACHINING (WEDM) PROCESS

Application of potential difference between the tool and work piece is made in WEDM. Commonly, conductivity of both the tool and work material to electricity is a pre-condition for the process. Kerosene or deionized water are the best dielectric medium in which the tool and the work material are emerged. Maintenance of a gap between the tool and the work piece is necessary for the effectively of the process and electric field that depends upon the application of potential variance and gap between the tool and work piece should be created. Commonly the tool is attached to the negative pole of the generator and the work piece is connected to positive pole. As a result of the establishment of an electric field between the tool and the job, the free electrons on the tool become subject to electro static forces. In a situation of the work function or the bonding energy of the electrons become less the electrons would come out from the tool if it is connected to the negative terminal. This sort of emission of electrons is well-defined as cold emission. Acceleration of the "Cold emitted" electrons towards the job is made possible through dielectric medium. Collisions between the electrons and dielectric particles happen when the electrons and the dielectric molecules happen when the electrons gain velocity and energy and start moving near the job. The work function or ionization energy of the electrons is the guiding factors for such collision which may ultimately lead to ionization of the dielectric molecules. In this way when the accelerations of the electrons are done collisions would produce generation of more positive ions and electrons. Increase of concentration of electrons and ions in the dielectric medium between the tool and the job at the spark gap is caused by this cyclic process. If the concentration becomes higher than the matter existing in that channel could be feature as 'Plasma'. Such plasma channel would contain very less electrical resistance. Suddenly a large number of electrons from the tool to the job and ions for the job to the tool will start moving. This condition is termed as avalanche motion of electrons. In reality it can be run as a spark when electrons and ions move in such way. The electrical energy is transformed into the thermal energy of the spark. Then impingement of the high-speed electrons on the job and ions on the tool is done. The impact of the kinetic energy of the electrons and ions on the surface of the job and the tool respectively would become thermal energy or heat flux. As an effect of the intense localized heat flux extremely confined rise in temperature up to 10,000°c would appear instantaneously. This localized extreme rise in temperature causes material removal. Melting and instant vaporization of material are responsible for such material removal, through the molten metal is removed only partially. As the potential difference is drawn back, the plasma channel is no longer continued. As the plasma downfall, it produces pressure or shock waves, which evacuates the molten material forming a crater of removed material around the position of the spark (Ghosh et al. 1985, Benedict, 1987; Mishra, 1997, Jain, 2004). Thus, to summarize the material removal in WEDM typically occurs due to making of shock waves as the plasma channel downfall owing to discontinuation of applied potential difference. A schematic diagram of wire electro discharge machining is shown in Figure 1.

Figure 1. Illustration of the WEDM process

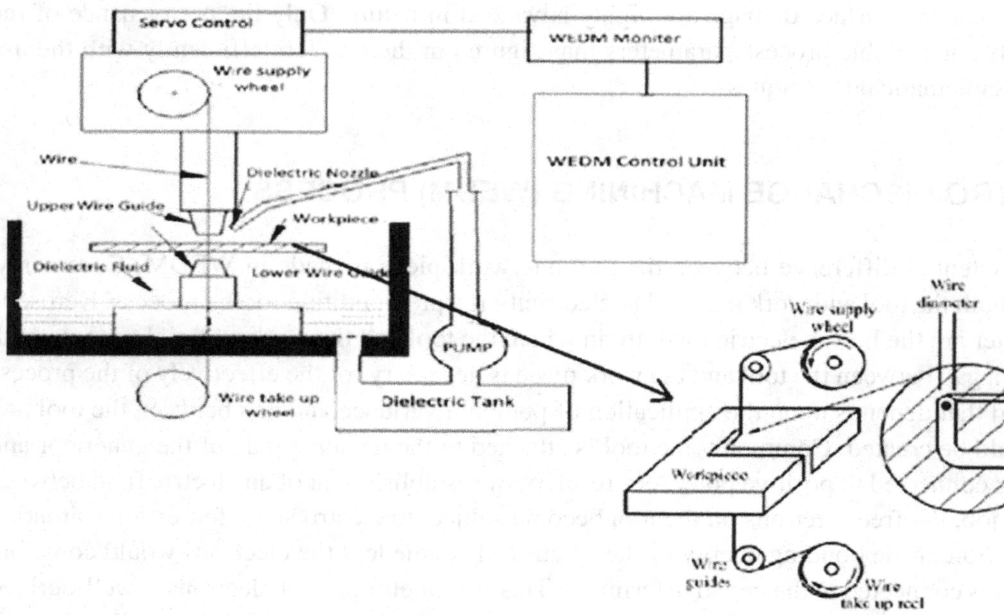

ESSENTIAL OF WIRE ELECTRICAL DISCHARGE MACHINING (WEDM)

For ultra-precision fabrication utilization of non-conventional machining process such as electrical discharge machining (EDM), ultra-sonic machining (USM), electro chemical micro machining (ECM), and laser beam machining (LBM) has been used into operation. As EDM and LBM are basically thermal processes they create formation of the heat affected zone and micro cracks on work piece. But thermal or mechanical stresses on the work piece material are not produce by the WEDM machining techniques. When versatile machining can be done on any kind of material by them, additional advantages of absence of heat affected layer and production of some tool wear are also associated with them. The anodic behaviour of the work piece material in a given electrolyte controls WEDM is very promising as a future micro machining technique as it includes higher machining rate, better precision and control material removal and wider range of material which can be machined (Tosun et al. 2004). Removal and patterning of metal films and foils requiring highly localized precision material can be done effectively by it. Classification of wide range of thesis works relating to the WEDM process may be done into their main areas such as optimization of the process variables, WEDM developments and modelling and control of the process.

LITERATURE REVIEW

The manufacturers and users have main target to achieve higher machining rate with optimum accuracy. In spite of most of the available WEDM machines having same kind of process control features selection and maintenance of optimal setting is an extremely difficult job. Han et al. 2007 have gone through the relationship between the wire electrode drive and the NC drive with the application of new simulation method for WEDM in corner machining of rough cutting. The wire vibration analysis and geometry model between the wire electrode path and the NC path of the newly established Wire EDM are the basic factors in carrying out a corner error simulation. Results of simulation and experiment are compared it proves that the simulation method is possible. The outcome of the reported work is that a new method for simulating corner machining is introduced by it. Sanchez et al. 2007 have observed the corner geometry produced by successive cuts (i.e. finishing cuts after rough cut) in view of different aspects such as work piece thickness, corner radius and number of trim cuts. Their work exposes that the first cut leaves the amount of material which primarily regulates the final corner accuracy. Limiting of the cutting speed through process parameter modification considerably removes the corner error. The factors such as work piece thickness, corner radius, and number of finishing cuts are the guiding parameters in the value of limitation in cutting speed. The reduction of corner error is largely possible when the numbers of finishing cuts are increased. Dodun et al. 2009 have developed a permanent bending at the crest of sharp corners, which leads to a significant deviation from the prescribed geometrical shape. They have focused on establishing a means for characterizing this shape error. They have also developed the influence applied by certain factors, such as the corner angle and the thickness of the work piece. Experimentally they have proved that the use of WEDM to obtain outside corners with small corner angle and small thickness is accompanied by a machining error having the shape of a post yield bending. They have used the material of carbon steel. Sarkar et al. 2011 have developed gap force intensity and wire lag phenomenon on the impact of wire deflection on profile accuracy during cutting cylindrical job. They have developed an analytical model also. An effective method has been suggested to eliminate this inaccuracy using wire lag compensation method. Experimentally they have proved that the required wire lag compensation technique is inversely proportional to programmed radius and interesting outcome from the experimental result is that the gap force intensity is inversely proportional to job height for a given mechanical condition with servo feed control model. Super cut 734 is used for conducting the experiments with a typical die steel. Plaza et al. 2009 have developed the prediction of angular error in Wire EDM tapper cutting. Material of test part is AISI D2 tool steel and the wire used is 0.25 mm in diameter which is uncoated Cu Zn. They have also developed a method to reduce the experimental load and to contribute a more general approach to this angular cutting problem. Two original models i.e. DOE based model for the prediction of an angular error and a numerical model of wire deformation for the prediction of angular error in WEDM tapper cutting are presented. Experimentally they have proved that part thickness and taper angle are the most influencing variables in the problem. Experimental validation of the proposed model shows that angular error can be reduced below 3'45" in 75% cases. Firouzabodi et al. 2015 have made their studies for improving accuracy of carved corners in wire EDM successive cutting. Error in cutting small radius corner poses to be one of the major problems. The factors responsible for wire deflection to influence the accuracy of the corner cutting are processing forces acting on the wire and low rigidity of the wire. Small radius convex and concave corners are pointed out in this research study. Alternative solution is proposed for having successive cuts (one roughing and two finishing). Primarily considering frequency of discharges and feed speed as input variables experiment are made for roughing operation. Revaluation of the results is that these optimum input parameters have a better influence on controlling the residual material thickness on straight paths than on small radius convex curved corners. Abyar et al. 2019 have made their experimental studies regarding machining errors of the arced paths through consecutive machining steps. The machining faults of a three-stage WEDM on both straight and arced paths are primary experimentally analysed. Mathematical formulas are deduced to relate a very new theoretical ideas, including spark density and spark angle, for each final stage on both straight and arced paths. Then, the results of these ideas on machining faults of the final stages are determined. The experimental machining faults of the first and second finishing steps on the different arced paths are compared and assessed with associated theoretical ones. Outcomes reveal that the statistical methodology predicts and compensates the machining faults of the first finishing step with the accuracy of 78% and of the second finishing step with the accuracy of 83%. There is a well improvement which can be employed in WEDM applications and to increase the wire electrical discharge machine capability.

MACHINING ACCURACY IN WEDM

Evaluation of past research shows that method of improving accuracy may broadly be divided into two categories. Modification of the cutting parameters (pulse on time, pulse off time, peak current etc.) for reduction of the wire deflection is the first one. The resultant effects of this method lower down the cutting speed at the corner. The second procedure consists of modification of the wire path for correction of the geometrical inaccuracy in an online manner. For smaller angle the second procedure is comparatively poorer than the first procedure and though there is no reduction in the cutting speed the accuracy level becomes poorer. The information of wire deflection in relation to a machining parameter is most essential for implementation of anyone of the above procedure. Optical sensor or electrical contact between wire and work piece helps researchers to evaluate the wire displacement. But measurement of wire position by the sensor with accuracy is not a very an easy task. (Huang et al. 2013; Chen et al. 2017; Selvakumar et al. 2013) To keep up sufficient flushing in the machining region the sensor is required to be very small and simultaneously it needs to be strong enough to tolerate very high dielectric fluid pressure. More difficulties arise out of the presence of debris in the dielectric medium and electromagnetic disturbances by EDM process. Besides this technique of wire deflection measurement is a very costly affair and it is the reason for which the said method remains far away from success in the field of industrial application. Actual value of wire deflection in view of different machining condition cannot be measured in a straight forward way. Presently improvement of inaccuracy in WEDM remains to be a major difficulty due to this (Sinha, 2010; Pramanik et al. 2019; Chen et al. 2014).

COMPONENTS OF WIRE ELECTRO DISCHARGE MACHINING SYSTEM

The machine tool constitutes of a main worktable (called X-Y table) and wire drive mechanism based on computerised numerical control (CNC). A photographic view of wire electro discharge machining is shown on Figure 2. The U and V axis are parallel to X and Y axis respectively and are also impelled by stepper motors. The travelling wire is flowed from wire feed drum. The wire goes through the work piece and is affirmed under tension between a pair of wire rollers, which are settled at the opposite sides of the work piece. The lower wire roller is stationary whereas the upper wire roller, which is affirmed by the U-V table, can be terminated transversely, along U and V axis, with respect to the lower wire roller. A WEDM system is comprised of four main components.

1. Computerised Numerical Control (CNC)
2. Power Supply- Provides energy to the spark.
3. Mechanical Section- Machine tool, taper unit, worktable, and wire drive mechanism.
4. Dielectric System- Water reservoir provides for filtration and controls the condition and temperature of the water.

DISCUSSION ON INPUT PARAMETERS

Figure 2. Photographic view of experimental set up (EZEECUT PLUS wire cut EDM)

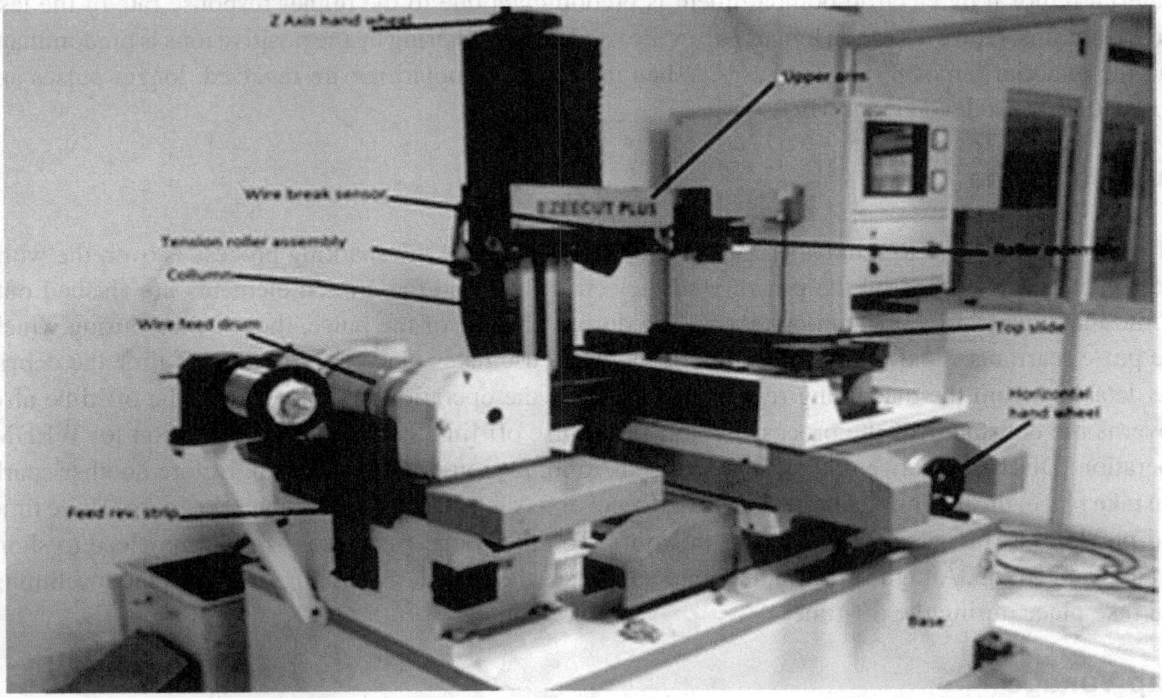

Based on the discharge phenomena discussed above, the various input parameters are discussed below

Wire Feed Rate

This wire feed rate setting controls the speed of wire feed motor. The travelling wire is fed from wire feed drum. The wire travels through the work piece and is supported and maintained under tension between a pair of wire rollers, which are positioned at the opposite sides of the work piece. The lower wire roller is fixed whereas the upper wire roller, which is maintained by the U-V table, can be displaced transversely, along U and V axis, with respect to the lower wire roller. The upper wire roller can also be positioned vertically along Z axis by moving the quill. A series of electrical pulses generated by the pulse generator unit is applied between the work piece and the travelling wire electrode, to cause the electro-erosion of the work piece material.

Pulse on Time

Throughout on time-controlled spark erodes material because dielectric fluid acts as a resistor until enough voltage is applied. Then the fluid ionizes and sparks happen between the wire electrode and the work piece. Spark precisely melt and vaporize the material. The spark gap is bridged, current is generated and the work is accomplished. The longer the spark is sustained more is the material removal. This is ON time pulse width in μ sec. When the tool electrode is at negative potential, material removal from the anode (work piece) takes place by bombing of high energy electrons ejected from the wire surface. At the same time positive ions transfer towards the cathode. When pulses with small on times are used, material removal by electron bombardment is predominant due to the higher response rate of the less huge electrons. However, when longer pulses are used, energy sharing by the positive ions is predominant and the material removal rate decreases. When the electrode polarities are reversed, longer pulses are originating to produce higher MRR.

Pulse off Time

Off time permits fluid to remove eroded particles because once the sparking process is over, the work piece material is cooled by the pressurized dielectric fluid and the eroded elements are flushed out. While maximum of the machining takes place during on time of the pulse, the off time during which the pulse rearranges and the re-ionization of the dielectric takes place. During the off time the debris are detached from the machining region and speed up the operation in a large way. The off time also governs the constancy of the process. A non-zero pulse off time is an essential condition for WEDM operation. Discharge between the electrode leads to ionization of the spark gap. Before another spark can take place, the medium must de-ionize and recover its dielectric strength. This takes some finite time and power must be switched off during this time. Too low values of pulse off time may lead to short circuits and arcing. A high value on the other hand rises the overall machining time since no machining can take place during the off-time

Gap Voltage

A gap voltage indicator in a wire-cut electrical discharge machine is rendered, which is capable of removing an adverse outcome due to a variation in an electric discharge location, thereby sensing a gap voltage between a wire electrode and a work piece in a precise method. A functioning amplifier of the gap voltage indicator is provided at one input terminal with the sum of a voltage between an upper bound conductor and the work piece detected by a voltage divider and a voltage between a lower bound conductor and the work piece sensed by another voltage divider and is supplied at another input terminal through adjustable resistors, with an output from a detection coil corresponding to a differentiation of the electric discharge current, as a signal for correcting the voltage drop components sum attributable to the wire resistance and inductance between the conductors, to thereby generate the corrected sum by using the voltage drop components as a gap voltage.

DIELECTRIC MEDIUM IN WEDM

In the current research water to oil ratio (20:1) is used as dielectric/coolant material. To wash out the metal particles and to assist in the machining or erosion process the dielectric fluid must be circulated under constant pressure. If the water supplied insufficient red sparks come out during the cutting operation. Increasing the flow of water may solve this problem till the appearance of blue spark. The removal of the metal particles (i.e. not chips) from the working gap remains to be one of the most vital factors for the success in WEDM operation. Flushing of these elements out of the gap between the works pieces hinder them to form bridges causing short circuits. The machining zone is cooled by the dielectric medium as it drives away excess heat from the wire electrode and the work piece.

WIRE MATERIAL

Though the die sinker EDM and the WEDM expose itself in a quite different way in the current situation the wire performs a function of the electrode. As it moves constantly it does not necessitate to process the EDM wear or erosion resistance. As a result of the constant feeding of new wire during the machining process, there are three main important criteria for the ideal wire electrode material for the process, high conductivity, high mechanical strength and ideal spark and flush characteristic. No wire can meet all this optimal criterion like most other variables in machining. But all three factors are inter related and inter dependent. Materials with low meeting point and high vapor pressure rating are known to be the ideals.

In the present investigation the cutting tool or the wire are selected to be of CuZn37 Master Brass wire with 0.25 mm diameter and 900N/mm^2 tensile strength.

PROBLEM IDENTIFICATION

Extreme level of difficulty lies in the nature of the mechanical aspect of wire when it is placed into machining zone. The purpose of this is that the magnitudes and directions of various forces act along or upon the wire are constantly variable in nature as the sparks seem in a stochastic mode (Selvakumar et al. 2016). Distribution of dielectric, fluctuation in voltage and current interaction of two successive discharges, random ionic migration and presence of debris particles in machining zone are the combination of influences responsible for the attribution of the stochastic nature of the WEDM processes. Figure 3 shows the uncut area between the real profile and the optimum profile of the workpiece to explain the corner inaccuracy. The main reason of corner inaccuracy occurs due to discharge concertation, wire deflection and vibrational imbalance of external load.

1. Wire deflection

Being tiny and flexible the wire electrode has actually some rigidity under discharge spark force. When the machining process actually runs the wire centre is always pulled back of the CNC path

2. Discharge concentration

The accumulation of the electric discharges and change of the discharge angle can increase the electric field intensity. More outstanding performance would have been done by the discharge concentration phenomenon and washing away of the removed material cannot be performed easily as the line cutting.

3. The imbalance of the external load on wire electrode

Wire tension, discharge spark force, electro static force, hydraulic force etc are the resultant sufferings of the wire electrode in the WEDM process.

Figure 3. WEDM corner error

ASSUMPTIONS DURING EXPERIMENT

Wire tension is enforced on the wire due to thinness and flexibility deformities come to it for gap force and as an effect deflection of wire reverse to the cutting direction results and the real wire location continuously remains behind the wire guide. The force applied on the wire does not remain constant as the nature of the plasma channel is mainly unstable and the nature of the sparking remains to be unfamiliar or uncertain. The following assumptions are neglected when a mathematical model is set out of the static deflection of a stretched wire which is

1. Constancy of the axial tensile force (F) between the wire guides.
2. Absolutely flexibility of the wire, which means that it has no resistance to bending.
3. Consistently stretching of the wire along its length. The vibration of the wire can be overlooked because the damping co- efficient is considerable.

4. The resistance of the viscous force to the bend of the wire in the dielectric medium is very slight in comparison to other gap forces and axial tensile force.
5. The interposing forces inducing per unit length of the wire vertical to the axial force remain constant or static all through the span of the wire between the guides.

PROCEDURE AND PLANNING OF WIRE ELECTRO DISCHARGE MACHINING

Experiments have been conducted according to response surface methodology, on an EZEECUT PLUS wire-cut electrical discharge machine, with aluminium 6061 alloy plate of 5 mm thickness as the work-piece (anode) and a brass wire of 250 μm diameter as the tool electrode (cathode) and decided corner angle is 60 ° . Table 1 shows the machine specification of wire electro discharge machining setup.

Table 1. Machine specification

1	Control mode	CNC close loop.
2	Simultaneously controlled axis	X, Y, U, V.
3	X, Y axis travel	320 x 400 mm.
4	Maximum workpiece size	360 x 600 mm.
5	Max Z height	360 / 480 mm.
6	Wire diameter	0.2 to 0.25 mm. (Brass) :0.12 to 0.25 mm. (Molybdenum).
7	Overload protection	With siemens contactor & 3 Ph thermal OL relay.
8	Power requirement	415 v / 50Hz / 3 ph / 1.5 Kva max

PROCESSES PARAMETER IDENTIFICATION

WEDM is a very complicated machining process and is controlled by a large number of process parameters. Selection of proper level setting of these parameters is truly difficult for high precision applications. Besides, it is exceedingly tricky to find out the different parametric combinations needed for optimal machining of different materials. The identification of controllable parameters and to define the level of each factor has been found to be equally crucial to the successes of any optimization problem. Experiments have been performed on Response Surface Methodology (RSM), the central composite rotatable second order design based. Total 31 experiments have been performed and replicate with two times. After successful completion of the experiments, microscopic images of corner inaccuracy have been captured by the LEICA VZ80RC digital video microscope (zoom 150x) which is later measured by image analysis software. The controllable input process parameters in the present investigation have been chosen as Wire feed rate (WFR), pulse-on-time (T_{on}), pulse-off-time (T_{off}), and gap voltage (GV). The range of process parameters are selected from the previous research work carried out and trail experiments. The ranges of each controllable process parameters are listed in Table 2.

Table 2. Controllable parameters and their limits

Notations (Coded names)	Controllable parameters	Units	Levels/Limits				
			-2	-1	0	1	2
A	Wire feed rate	m/min	35	50	65	80	95
B	Pulse-on-time	µ sec	12	27	42	57	72
C	Pulse-off-time	µ sec	3	5	7	9	11
D	Gap voltage	Volts	10	20	30	40	50

EXPERIMENTAL RESULTS AND DISCUSSION

A second order rotatable polynomial model has been developed to carry out further analysis. Minitab 17 software is used for analysis the response. In this graphical Figure 4, the experiment number indicates the experimental settings corresponding to the settings of central composite design (CCD) technique. Determination of the mathematical model with best fits is specified below as equation no. 1

$$\begin{aligned} Corner\ Inaccuracy &= 0.054600 - 0.001567A - 0.001908B \\ &-0.004342C - 0.001108D + 0.004200A \times A + 0.007263B \times B \\ &-0.000712C \times C + 0.003050D \times D + 0.001750A \times B + 0.001750A \times C \\ &-0.001613A \times D - 0.000575B \times C + 0.006212B \times D + 0.002387C \times D \end{aligned} \quad (1)$$

DATA ANALYSIS

The adequacy of the new developed mathematical models for corner inaccuracy, analysis of variance (ANOVA) and subsequently F and P value tests have been done. ANOVA of the quadratic model with other adequacy measures R^2, adjusted R^2 and predicted R^2 are shown in Table 3.

From Table 3 it is detected that the associated p-value of less than 0.05 for the model (i.e. α=0.05, or 95% confidence level) shows that the model terms are statistically significant (Cocharam et al. 1977; Montgomery, 1997; Deb, 2001). The developed new second order regression equation for this response is significant and linear interaction of parameters are also significant. F value (2.86) and P value (0.105) of the lack of fit suggests that it is not important relative to the pure error as this is wanted.

Figure 5 shows the combined effect of pulse on time and pulse off time on corner accuracy when wire feed rate and gap voltage are taken at constant value 65 m/min and 30 volt respectively. It is observed that corner inaccuracy is reduced with increase of pulse off time and gradually reduces with the implementation of pulse on time following a non-linear path. This is because of the fact that the rise in pulse off time means less sparking period and lower cutting speed, marks better corner accuracy. The pulse off time is fit at higher value, the sparking period of machine decreases with cutting speed. The external forces produced lateral sparks and due to this wire in pulses in the perpendicular direction.

Figure 4. Experimental measured value of corner inaccuracy

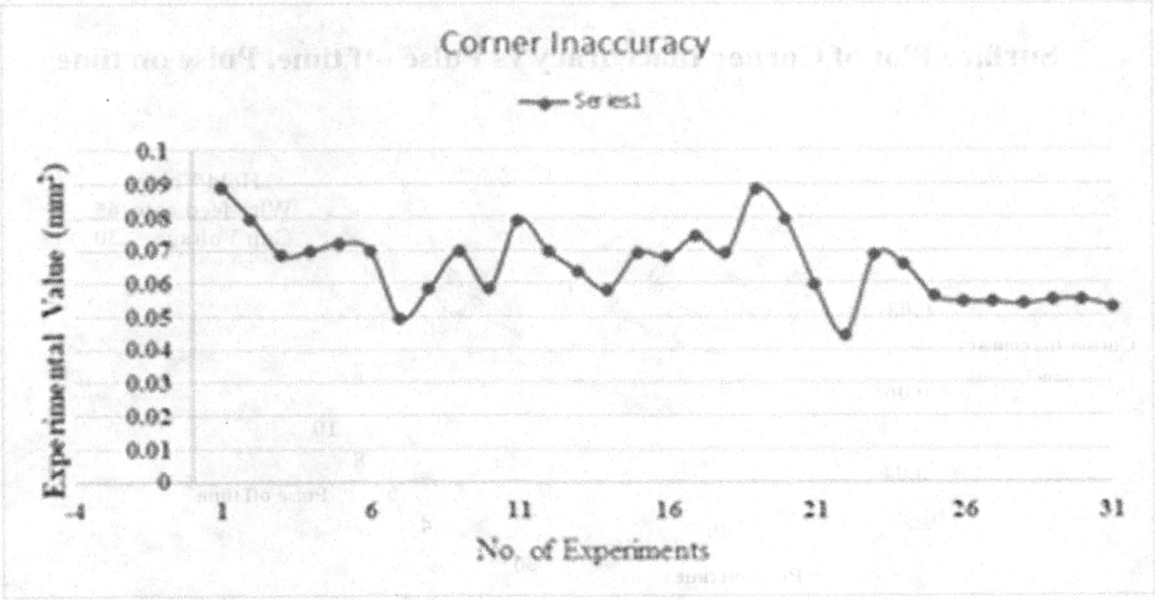

From the Figure 6 shows the combined effect of wire feed rate and pulse on time on corner inaccuracy. Pulse off time and gap voltage are kept constant at 7 μsec and 30 volt. Surface plot reveals that corner inaccuracy decreases with moderate value of pulse on time and wire feed rate. The reason behind that pulse on time increases, sparking time will be more. A higher pulse on time generates higher thermal

Table 3. ANOVA table for corner inaccuracy

Source	DF	Adj. SS	Adj. MS	F-Value	P-Value
Model	14	0.003557	0.000254	121.40	0.000
Linear	4	0.000628	0.000157	75.05	0.000
A	1	0.000059	0.000059	28.15	0.000
B	1	0.000087	0.000087	41.77	0.000
C	1	0.000452	0.000452	216.20	0.000
D	1	0.000029	0.000029	14.09	0.002
Square	4	0.002075	0.000519	247.87	0.000
2-way interaction	6	0.000854	0.000142	67.99	0.000
Error	16	0.000033	0.000002	-	-
Lack of fit	10	0.000028	0.000003	2.86	0.105
Pure Error	6	0.000006	0.000001	-	-
Total	30	0.003590	-	-	-
S = 0.0014466, R-sq =99.07%, R-sq (adj) = 98.25%, R-sq (pred) =95.34%					

Figure 5. Surface plot of corner inaccuracy with pulse on time and pulse off time

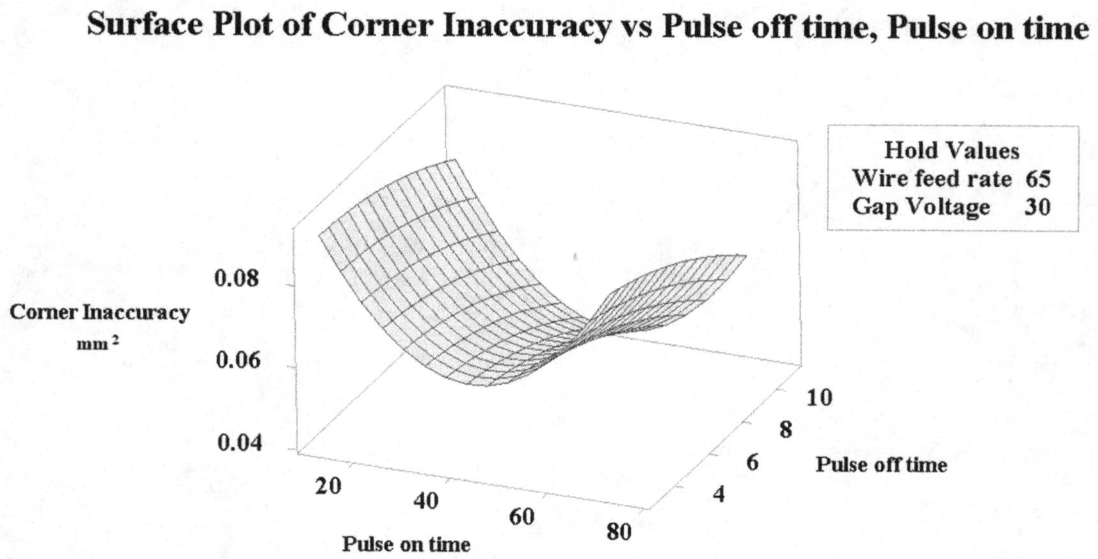

Figure 6. Surface plot of corner inaccuracy with wire feed rate and pulse on time

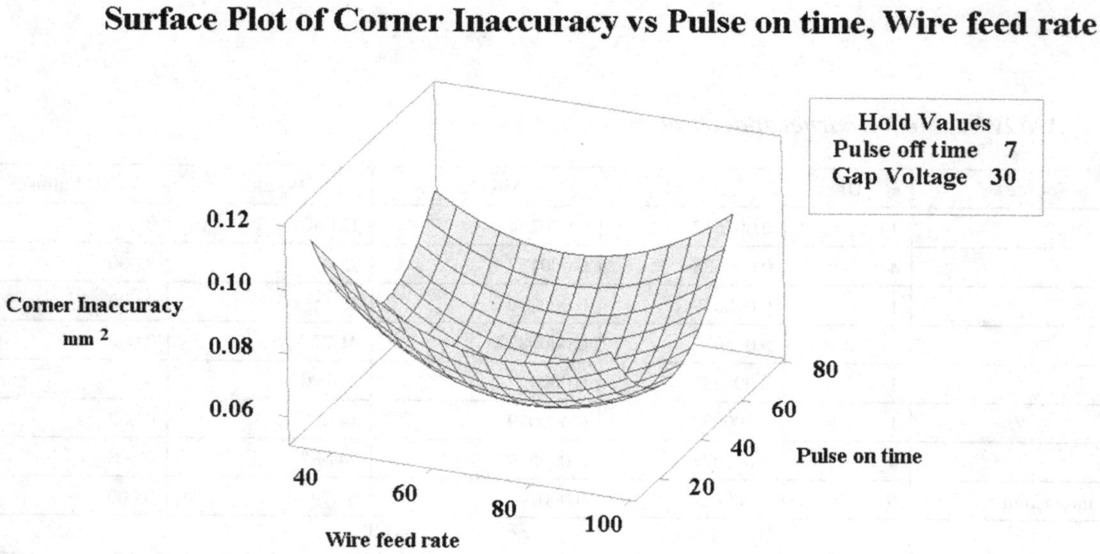

Figure 7. Surface plot of corner inaccuracy with pulse off time and wire feed rate

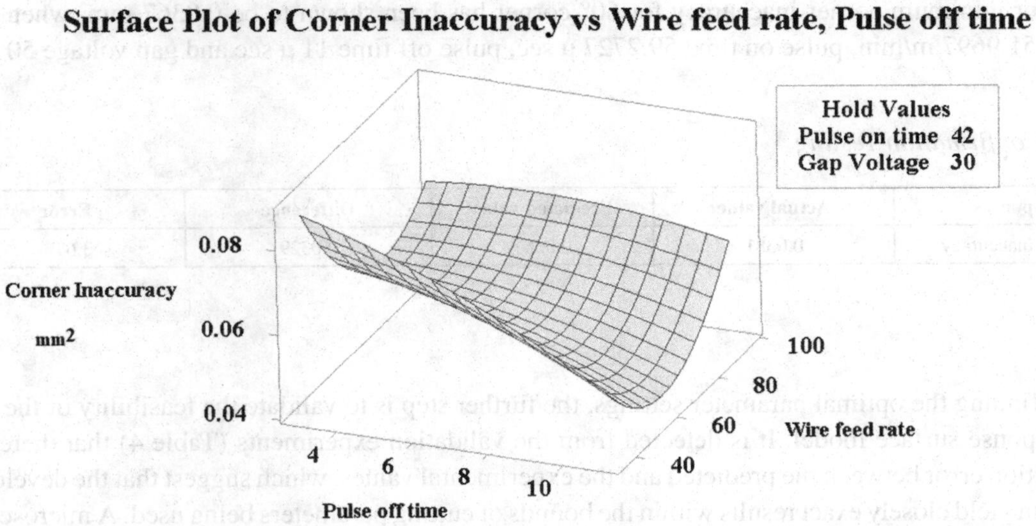

energy and low pulse on time generates bow effect on the wire. So, mid-range of wire feed rate and pulse on time generates lower accuracy in the corner portion.

From the surface plot in Figure 7 show the combined effect of pulse off time and wire feed rate on corner inaccuracy. The pulse on time and gap voltage are kept constant at 42 μ sec and 30 volt respectively. Surface plot reveals that a non-linear path following that corner accuracy merely decrease with decrease of pulse off time whereas a certain limit of decrease with increase in wire feed rate. Increase in pulse off time means less flashing period. Besides decrease of wire vibration is insured by wire feed rate.

Figure 8. Optimization result of corner inaccuracy

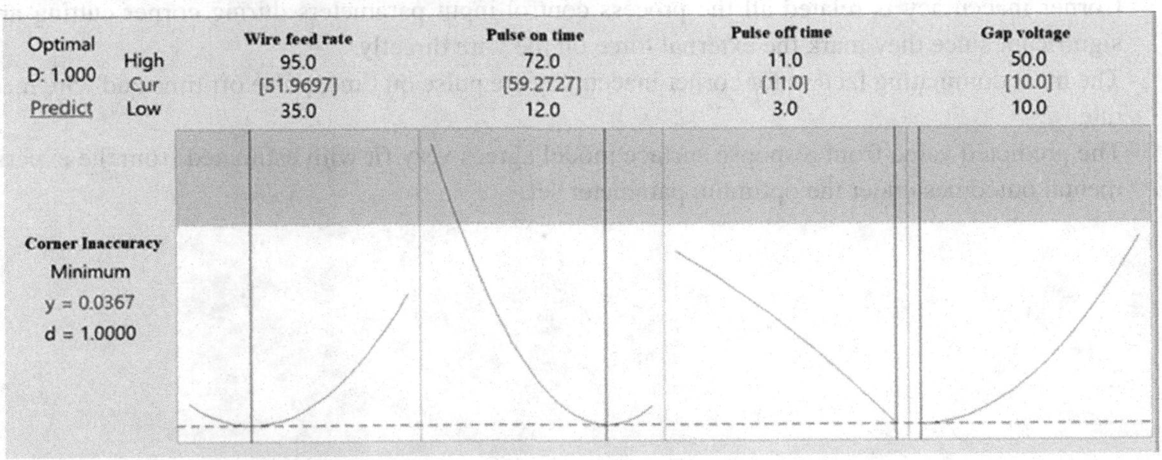

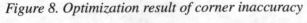

Figure 8 confirmations the optimization result for minimum corner inaccuracy created on the established mathematical model i.e. equation 1. The linear desirability function (d) value is set as 1. The parameters settings for minimum corner inaccuracy for 60° corner has been shown to be 0.0367 mm^2 when wire feed rate 51.9697 m/min, pulse on time 59.2727 μ sec, pulse off time 11 μ sec and gap voltage 50 volt.

Table 4. Confirmation Testing

Responses	Actual value	Predicted value	Difference	Error
Corner Inaccuracy	0.0381	0.0367	0.0329	3.67%

After finding the optimal parameter settings, the further step is to validate the feasibility of the proposed response surface model. It is detected from the validation experiments (Table 4) that there is a small fraction error between the predicted and the experimental values, which suggest that the developed models can yield closely exact results within the bounds of cutting parameters being used. A microscopic image of corner inaccuracy for 60° is shown in Figure 9.

CONCLUSION

Productions of highly precisive intricate jobs which resemble die/punch face a challenge in WEDM. This present work deals with the measurement of corner accuracy of the uncut area which has been left between the actual profile and optimum profile (programmed) of the job. Experiments relating to extensive studies regarding minimization of corner inaccuracy relating to controllable machining conditions has been made. Response surface methodology is employed to determine the main parameters that affect the machining criteria such as corner inaccuracy caused due to wire bending in the present set of research study. Observations coming out of the experiment and resultant modelling and optimization of WEDM draw the following general conclusion:

1. Corner inaccuracy is related all the process control input parameters during corner cutting are significant since they mark the external force on the wire directly.
2. The most dominating factors for corner inaccuracy are pulse on time, pulse off time and wire feed rate.
3. The predicted value from response surface model agrees very fit with estimated from the experimental outcomes under the optimum parameter set.

Figure 9. A microscopic image of comer inaccuracy (ϴ=60°)

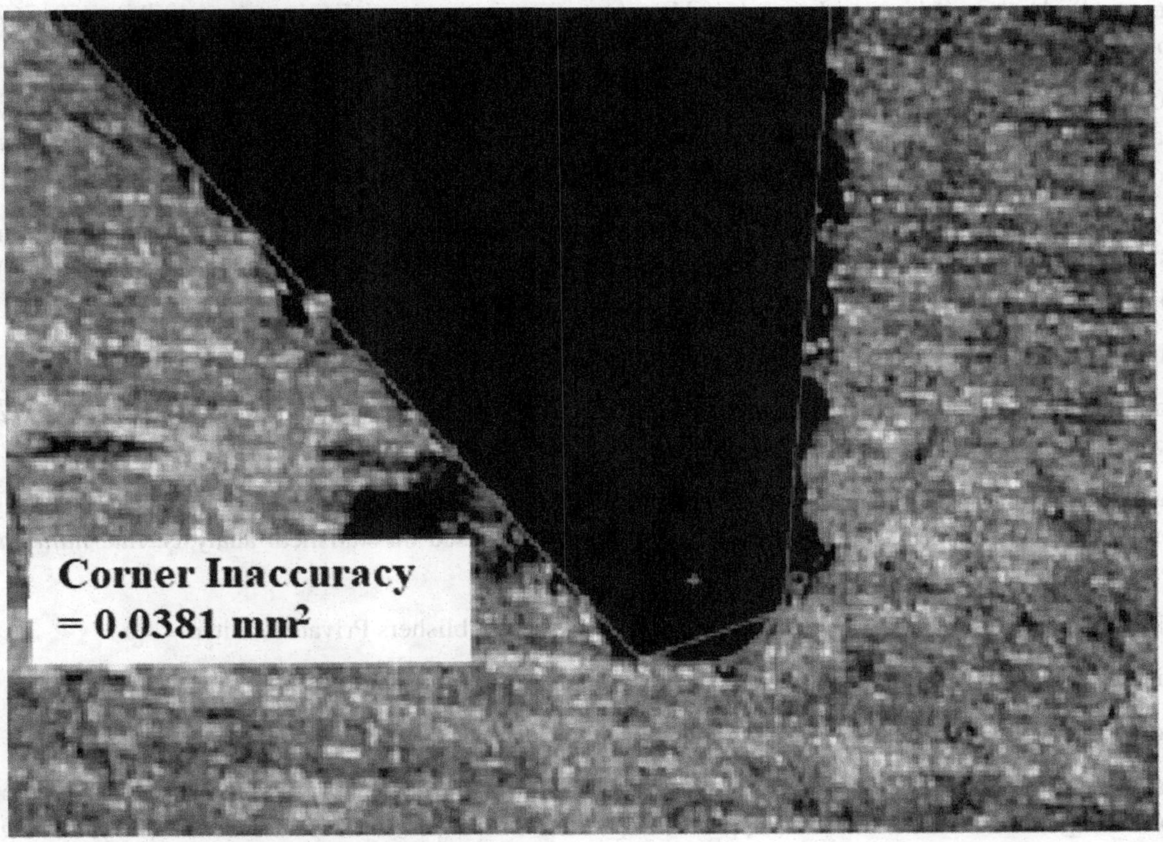

REFERENCES

Abyar, H., Abdullah, A., & Shafaroud, A. A. (2019). Theoretical and experimental analysis of machining errors during WEDM finishing stages. *Machining Science and Technology*, *23*(5), 734–757. doi:10.1080/10910344.2019.1575410

Benedict, G. F. (1987). Non-Traditional manufacturing processes. Taylor & Francis.

Chen, Z., Huang, Y., Zhang, Z., Li, H., Ming, W., & Zhang, G. (2014). An analysis and optimization of the geometrical inaccuracy in WEDM rough corner cutting. *International Journal of Advanced Manufacturing Technology*, *74*(5-8), 917–929. doi:10.100700170-014-6002-5

Chen, Z., Zhang, Y., Zhang, G., Huang, Y., & Liu, C. (2017). Theoretical and experimental study of magnetic assisted finish cutting ferromagnetic material in WEDM. *International Journal of Machine Tools & Manufacture*, *123*, 36–47. doi:10.1016/j.ijmachtools.2017.07.009

Cochran, W. G., & Cox, G. M. (1977). *Experimental designs* (2nd ed.). Asia Publishing House.

Deb, K. (2001). *Multiobjective optimization using evolutionary algorithms* (3rd ed.). Wiley.

Dhanik, S., & Joshi, S. S. (2005). Modeling of a single resistance capacitance pulse discharge in micro-electro discharge machining. *Journal of Manufacturing Science and Engineering*, *127*(4), 759–767. doi:10.1115/1.2034512

Dodun, O., Goncalvascoclho, A. M., Slatineanu, L., & Nagit, G. (2009). Using wire electrical discharge machining for improved corner cutting accuracy of thin parts. *International Journal of Advanced Manufacturing Technology*, *41*(9-10), 858–864. doi:10.100700170-008-1531-4

Firouzabadi, H. A., Parvizian, J., & Abdullah, A. (2015). Improving accuracy of curved corners in wire EDM successive cutting. *International Journal of Advanced Manufacturing Technology*, *76*(1-4), 447–459. doi:10.100700170-014-6270-0

Ghosh, A., & Mallick, A. K. (1985). *Manufacturing science*. East-West Press Private Limited.

Han, F., Zhang, J., & Soichiro, I. (2007). Corner error simulation of rough cutting in wireEDM. *Precision Engineering*, *31*(4), 331–336. doi:10.1016/j.precisioneng.2007.01.005

Huang, Y., Ming, W., Guo, J., Zhang, Z., Liu, G., Li, M., & Zhang, G. (2013). Optimization of cutting conditions of yg15 on rough and finish cutting in wedm based on statistical analysis. *International Journal Advanced Technology*, *69*(6), 993–1008.

Jain, V. K. (2004). *Advanced Machining Processes*. Allied Publishers Private Limited.

Mishra, P. K. (1997). Non -Conventional machining. Narosa Publishers.

Montgomery, D. C. (1997). *Design and analysis of experiments* (4th ed.). Wiley.

Plaza, S., Ortega, N., Sanchez, J. A., Pombo, I., & Mendikute, A. (2009). Original models for the prediction of angular error in wire EDM tapper cutting. *International Journal of Advanced Manufacturing*, *44*(5-6), 529–538. doi:10.100700170-008-1842-5

Pramanik, D., Kuar, A. S., & Bose, D. (2019). *Effects of Wire EDM machining variables on material removal rate and surface roughness of Al 6061 alloy. In Renewable Energy and Its Innovative Technologies*. Springer.

Puri, A. B., & Bhattacharyya, B. (2003). An analysis and optimization of the geometrical inaccuracy due to wire lag phenomenon in WEDM. *International Journal of Machine Tools & Manufacture*, *43*(2), 151–159. doi:10.1016/S0890-6955(02)00158-X

Sanchez, J. A., Rodil, J. L., Herrero, A., Lacalle, L. N., & Lamikiz, A. (2007). On the Influence of Cutting Speed Limitation on the Accuracy of Wire EDM Corner Cutting. *Journal of Materials Processing Technology*, *182*(1-3), 574–579. doi:10.1016/j.jmatprotec.2006.09.030

Sarkar, S., Sekh, M., Mitra, S., & Bhattacharyya, B. (2011). A novel method of determination of wire lag for enhanced profile accuracy in WEDM. *Precision Engineering*, *35*(2), 339–347. doi:10.1016/j.precisioneng.2011.01.001

Selvakumar, G., Jiju, K. B., Sarkar, S., & Mitra, S. (2016). Enhancing die corner accuracy through trim cut in WEDM. *International Journal of Advanced Manufacturing Technology*, *83*(5-8), 791–803. doi:10.100700170-015-7606-0

Selvakumar, G., Sarkar, S., & Mitra, S. (2013). An experimental analysis of single pass cutting of aluminium 5083 alloy in different corner angles through WEDM. *International Journal of Machining and Machinability of Materials*, *13*(2/3), 262–275. doi:10.1504/IJMMM.2013.053227

Sinha, S. K. (2010). Effects of wire lag in wire electrical discharge machining (WEDM). *International Journal of Engineering Science and Technology*, *2*, 6622–6625.

Tosun, N., Cogun, C., & Tosun, G. (2004). A study on kerf and material removal rate in wire electrical discharge machining based on Taguchi method. *Journal of Materials Processing Technology*, *152*(3), 316–322. doi:10.1016/j.jmatprotec.2004.04.373

Werner, A. (2016). Method for enhanced accuracy in machining curvilinear profiles on wire-cut electrical discharge machines. *Precision Engineering*, *44*, 75–80. doi:10.1016/j.precisioneng.2015.10.004

Chapter 8
Evaluation of Surface Roughness in Wire Electrical Discharge Turning Process

Sibabrata Mondal
Society for Applied Microwave Electronics Engineering and Research (SAMEER), Kolkata, India

Dipankar Bose
National Institute of Technical Teachers' Training and Research (NITTTR), Kolkata, India

ABSTRACT

This investigation presents an experimental investigation in developing small cylindrical pins in electrolytic tough pitch copper (ETP Cu) material using wire electrical discharge turning (WEDT) to evaluate surface roughness of the cylindrical turning faces. The material ETP Cu is soft in nature and has growing range of application in the field of aerospace and electronics industries for advanced applications. In this process, a customized rotary spindle has been developed and added to five-axis CNC wire electrical discharge machine (WEDM) and straight turning of the cylindrical pin has been done up to a length of 15mm with 0.5mm diameter. Under this investigation, 31 experiments along with two confirmation tests have been carried out to study the influence of four design factors—pulse on time, pulse off time, spindle speed, and servo voltage—on the machining performance of surface roughness by means the technique of design of experiment (DOE).

INTRODUCTION

In 1974, D.H. Dulebohn utilized the optical-line follower system which controls the shape of the component automatically by WEDM process (Qu et al., 2002). In 1975, the process and its capabilities were better understood by the industry. As a result, they have started to utilize this process rapidly. Actually, the end of 1970s, when computer numeric control (CNC) system was introduced into WEDM process, from that time onward a major evolution happened in the manufacturing process (Scott et al. 2004). The

DOI: 10.4018/978-1-7998-3624-7.ch008

common applications of WEDM include the fabrication of dies, stamping and extrusion tools, fixtures and gauges and medical parts, prototypes etc.

Basic Principle of WEDM Process

The CNC WEDM has five axes control like XYZUV. The XY axes relate to the movement of the work table on which job is clamped for machining. The UV axes relate to the angular movement of the upper nozzle head in the U and V directions with respect to Z-axis. The Z-axis moves the upper nozzle head up or down before start the cutting operation. Schematic diagram of WEDM process is shown in Figure 1. Actually, in WEDM process, a thin single-strand wire of diameter 0.25mm and generally made of brass material is fed through a work piece which is submerged in a tank of dielectric fluid. The wire which is act as the electrode, is constantly fed from a spool through different stage of wire guides to maintain the wire tension to a desire level and finally the wire, is fed from upper guide to lower guide through the work piece to generate components with intricate shapes and profiles with very small inner corner radii of size half of the diameter of the wire used.

Figure 1. Schematic diagram of WEDM

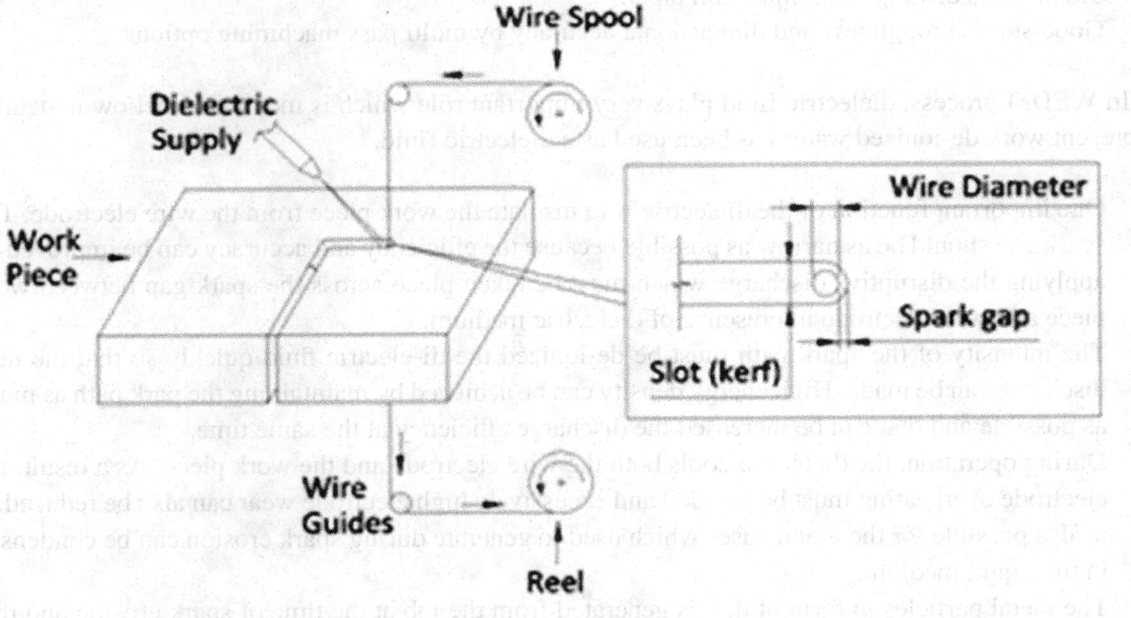

Wire EDM is widely used in the medical, aerospace, and injection-mold industries to produce parts in complex shapes that cannot be achieved with traditional cutting tools (Hadad, M., 2004) (Gieldum, et al., 2014). In WEDM process, the electrical energy produces a channel of plasma between the cathode which is connected with wire electrode and anode which is connected with job and which is converted into thermal energy at the temperature range of 8000°C - 12,000°Cwhich actually melting of job material as well as wire electrode on the surface of each pole. When the pulsating direct current power supply occurring between 20,000 and 30,000 Hz, then plasma channel generated and during pulse off time, the plasma channel break down. As a result, sudden reduction in temperature will be happened and allowing the dielectric fluid rushed towards the plasma channel and flush the molten particles from the job in the form of debris. Because the wire EDM uses a thin wire to erode material surface through a predefined path which is nothing but some lines of systematic NC codes which can be generated by different offline software for different wire Cut machine (Scoot, et al., 2004) (Haddad and Tehrani, 2008). In present experimentation Pc Fact Cut software is used. In that software initially the desired path profile is required to be generated in any 2D generation software followed by some standard steps, the NC codes for the desired path can be generated. Ultimately the generated NC code is required to be fed to the machine to cut the desire path in the job. The wire EDM process is ideal for (Mohammad and Alireza, 2008):

- Cutting hardened metals and even some conductive ceramics.
- Cutting soft material like Copper which is difficult to machine in small shape & size in conventional machining process.
- Cutting small & intricate contours or cavities.
- Cutting internal corners with extremely small radii in microns using 0.1mm diameter wire electrode.
- Cutting complex tapers up to a certain height of the job with the help of U and V axes.
- Small holes drilling with minimum taper.
- Good surface roughness and dimensional accuracy by multi pass machining options.

In WEDM process, dielectric fluid plays very important role which is mentioned bellow in details. In present work de-ionized water has been used as a dielectric fluid.

- One important function of the dielectric is to insulate the work piece from the wire electrode. The spark gap should be as narrow as possible because the efficiency and accuracy can be improved by applying the disruptive discharge which must be taken place across the spark gap between work piece and wire electrode in presence of dielectric medium.
- The intensity of the spark path must be de-ionized the di-electric fluid quickly so that the next discharge can be made. High energy density can be achieved by maintaining the park path as much as possible and that can be increased the discharge efficiency at the same time.
- During operation, the dielectric cools both the wire electrode and the work piece. As a result, the electrode overheating must be avoided and excessively high electrode wear can also be reduced. It is also possible for the metal gases which used to generate during spark erosion can be condensed in the liquid medium.
- The metal particles in form of debris generated from the job at the time of spark erosion and that can be removed from the area of spark erosion by the dielectric fluid to avoid disruptions in the sparking process.
- There will be a chance of less smoke if the spark erosion between the work piece and wire electrode can be submerged in the dielectric medium.

Basic Principle of WEDT Process

Wire electrical discharge turning (WEDT) process, rotary table is mounted on the work table of the wire CUT machine rigidly and the rotary table can allow the programming of continuous variable high-speed rotation and indexing during WEDT operation. Instead of clamping the job to the work table, it is held in a chuck mounted on a rotary table. The rotary table then allows the rotation to the job to form desired intricate shape.This process is capable for machining different types of cylindrical forms like straight, tapered and stepped on hard and difficult to machine material, as well as the miniature cylindrical parts with comparatively long length in soft material but those are very difficult to machining in the conventional machining process because of frequent formation of build-up edge at cutting tool tip and the tendency of the part getting bend due to the presence of tool pressure.

The WEDT process is similar to straight turning in Lathe. Both the cases work specimen to be hold on the rotary chuck which is required to rotate in counter clockwise direction. But only difference is cutting tool which is fixed to the tool holder in Lathe whereas in WEDT process, the wire electrode continuously travel to the downward direction during cutting operation shown in Figure 2 and the process of introducing depth of cut and feed of wire electrode and cutting tool are similar in both the WEDT and Lathe operations respectively.

Several researchers have developed the concept of wire electrical discharge machining process. Hadad(2014) noticed that the surface roughness(R_a) can be increased with the increase of both voltage and power and decrease of pulse off time and spindle rotational speed. Qu etal.(2002) reported that the precision spindle was the key factor in the system for micro machining applications. Masuzawa and Tonshoff (1997) developed the small size of pins of diameter 5μm using WEDM turning process. Mohammadiet

Figure 2. Schematic diagram of WEDT

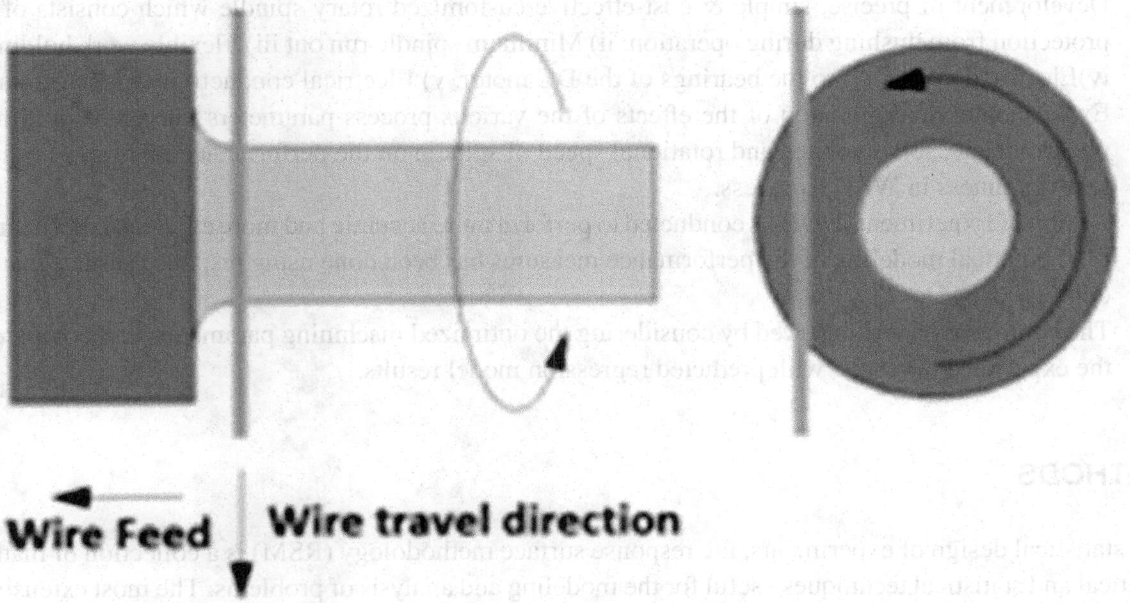

al.(2008) reported that for getting good surface finish in CWEDM work piece, power and voltage should be fixed as high as possible and pulse off time and spindle rotational speed should be fixed as low as possible. Pasamet al. (2010) obtained surface roughness of 1.85μm with selected optimal parameters in the WEDM process of Ti6A14V alloy. Goswami and Kumar(2014) observed that re-cast layer on the machined surface was thicker when the sample machined at high discharge energy level compared to the sample machined at low discharge energy level. Haddad and Tehrani(2008) developed the CWEDT process by introducing precise, flexible and corrosion resistance submerged rotary spindle for generating precise cylindrical forms on hard and difficult to machine materials. In case of micro-machining the rotary EDM has biggest benefits. Small dynamically balanced parts that require a high surface quality can be cut accurately with high-speed erosive turning because the absence of tool pressure allows for minimal diameters. Notches or other flat features can also be cut in the same setup (Mohammadi, et al., 2008). Conventional milling or turning methods, the small, intricate parts cannot be machined efficiently with high quality. But the EDM process is the perfect solution for cutting intricate parts because there are no cutting forces involved in the process. It is more effective for machining difficult-to-cut materials, such as titanium (Ti-6Al-4V) or Inconel or Hastelloy (Qu, et al., 2002) (Padhee, et al., 2012).Actually, these materials are very tough and "springy". The chattering is a huge problem when conventional mechanical processes are used to cut them, causing high tool wear, poor surface finish and broken work pieces. The rotary wire EDM can produce parts with an excellent surface roughness and roundness. This process involved comparatively low tooling costs and less chance of broken parts causing minimum wastage of material (Janardhan and Samuel 2010). For many manufacturers, there is great potential for adding rotary-axis EDM technology to their current capabilities. In many cases, it is a better alternative of machining processes in place of use of traditional tooling because by introducing the rotary wire EDM, it is possible to generate cost effective quality product.

Objective of the Present Study

- Development of precise, simple & cost-effective customized rotary spindle which consists of i) protection from flushing during operation. ii) Minimum spindle run out iii) Flexible work holding. iv)Electrical insulation to the bearings of the DC motor. v) Electrical conductivity to the ground. Experimental determination of the effects of the various process parameters like pulse on time, pulse off time, servo voltage and rotational speed of spindle on the performance measures i.e surface roughness in WEDT process.
- Design of Experiment (DOE) is conducted to perform more accurate and more efficient experiment.
- Mathematical modeling of the performance measures has been done using response surface methodology (RSM).
- The confirmation test followed by considering the optimized machining parameters and compared the experimental results with predicted regression model results.

METHODS

The statistical design of experiments, the response surface methodology (RSM) is a collection of mathematical and statistical techniques useful for the modeling and analysis of problems. The most extensive application of RSM is in the particular situations where several input variables influence some performance measure or quality characteristic is called the response (Rao and Kalyankar, 2013) (Datta and Mahapatra 2010). The approximating model is based on observed data from the process or system and is an empirical model. Multiple regressions are the collection of statistical techniques useful for building the types of empirical models required in RSM.

The first-order multiple linear regression models with two independent variables is mentioned in Eq. 1 and the independent variables are often called predictor variables or repressors. The term "linear" is used because Eq.1is a linear function of the unknown parameters β_0 β_1 and β_2. In general, the response variable y may be related to k regressor variables.

$$y = \beta_0 + \beta_1 x_1 + \beta_2 x_2 + \varepsilon \tag{1}$$

The said model is called a multiple linear regression model with k regressor variables. The parameters, β_j $j = 0, 1 \ldots k$, are called the regression coefficients

$$y = \beta_0 + \beta_1 x_1 + \beta_2 x_2 + \ldots\ldots + \beta_k x_k + \varepsilon \tag{2}$$

WEDM Machine Tool Specification

- Make: FANUC Corporation
- Design: Fixed column, moving table
- Machining Method: Submerge/Flushing
- Maximum work piece dimension: 700 x 600 x 250mm
- Maximum work piece mass: 500 Kg
- X-axis travel: 370mm
- Y- axis travel: 270mm
- Z-axis travel: 255mm
- U axis travel: ± 60mm
- V axis travel: ± 60mm
- Maximum taper angle: ± 30°/80mm
- Wire diameter: ø0.05- ø0.3mm
- Maximum wire mass: 16Kg
- Machine Mass: Approx. 1800Kg
- Part program storage size: 4MB
- Input power supply: 200V AC, 3 phase
- Compressed Air: 6.5 bar
- Controlled axes: X Y, U, V simultaneous / independent
- Interpolation: Linear & Circular
- Least input increment: 0.0001mm
- Least command input (X, Y, U & V): 0.0005mm

Development of Customized Rotary Axis Setup

The purpose of development of precise, simple and cost-effective customized rotary axis setup is to give rotary motion to the work piece during discharge (Mohammadi, et al. 2008). The required run out of the spindle should be as minimum as possible for wire electrical discharge turning process. Following are the basic requirements for the setup (Vishal et al. 2010):

- Protection from flushing due to small clearance in the range of few microns between any metallic bodies.
- High current electrical conductivity to the ground.
- Minimum run out of the spindle during rotation.
- Holding flexibility of the job in the chuck.
- Electrical insulation to the bearings used in the DC motor. The bearing balls and races may get eroded during the discharge due to the small clearance between them which will affect the rotational accuracy of the bearings.

Figure 3. Customized Rotary Axis Setup Mounted on WEDM Machine Bed

Proper construction of customized rotary setup is very much important and it follows some sequential steps to maintain minimum run out of the spindle which will also be reflected to the work piece to be machined in WEDT process. Following steps have to be maintained carefully to construct the customized rotary axis setup. First following parts are to be fabricated as per dimension to establish the customized rotary axis setup shown in Figure 3.

- One no. of insulator of rexolite material.

- One no of inner ring of aluminum material.
- One no. of outer ring with M2 tapped hole of aluminum material.
- L-clamp with through holes of diameter 2mm at both end of the clamp of aluminum material.
- Two nos of circular insulators of Teflon material.
- Two nos of curved shaped clamps (upper & lower) of aluminum material

Digital Tachometer Setup

In the present investigation, the digital tachometer is required to find out the RPM of the spindle rather drill chuck which is mounted on the spindle and that RPM is transmitted to the job made of ETP Cu because it is mounted on the self-centered drill chuck. In WEDT experimental setup, the customized rotary axis does not have CNC controller to get specific rpm. Actually, the DC motor is connected with DC power supply and the RPM of the motor spindle can directly control by changing the voltage at a specific current of the DC power supply. Initially by using the digital tachometer shown in Figure 4, different approximate RPM is tabulated with their corresponding voltage value from DC power source. The tabulated input voltage Vs PRM is shown in Table 1.

Best on said input voltage vs corresponding RPM chart mentioned above, it can be easily be found out the corresponding voltage value for a particular RPM value without digital tachometer. Accordingly,

Table 1. Input voltage Vs. Corresponding RPM chart

Sl. No.	Input Voltage (V)	Corresponding Speed (RPM)
01	10	621
02	15	932
03	20	1235
04	25	1550
05	30	1920

Figure 4. Digital Tachometer Setup and DC Power Supply Setup

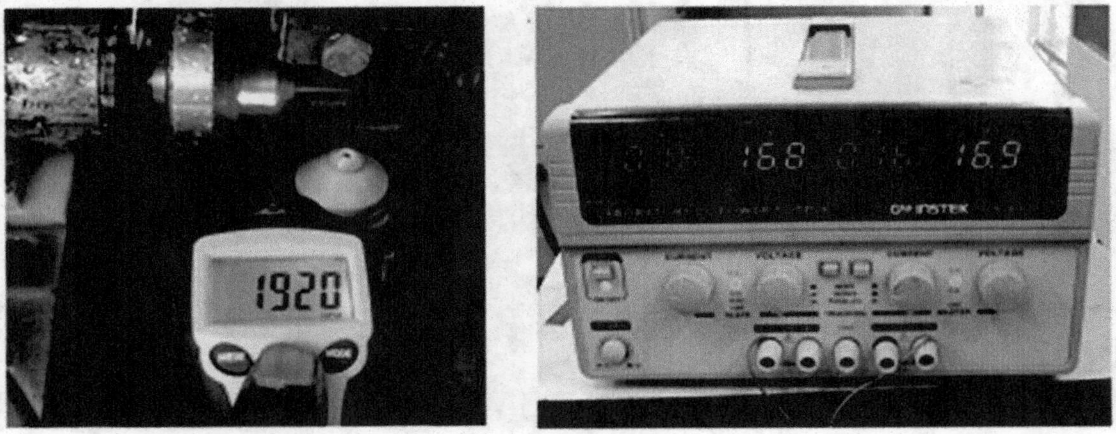

five different RPM have been selected best on pilot experiments and find out their corresponding voltage value which can be set easily in DC power source to carry out the successful WEDT experiment and the same is shown in Table 2.

Table 2. Input voltage Vs. Corresponding RPM chart

Sl. No.	Corresponding Speed (RPM)	Required Voltage (V)
01	930	14.9
02	1005	16.2
03	1080	17.4
04	1155	18.6
05	1230	19.6

Figure 5. Fabricated Specimens by WEDT Process

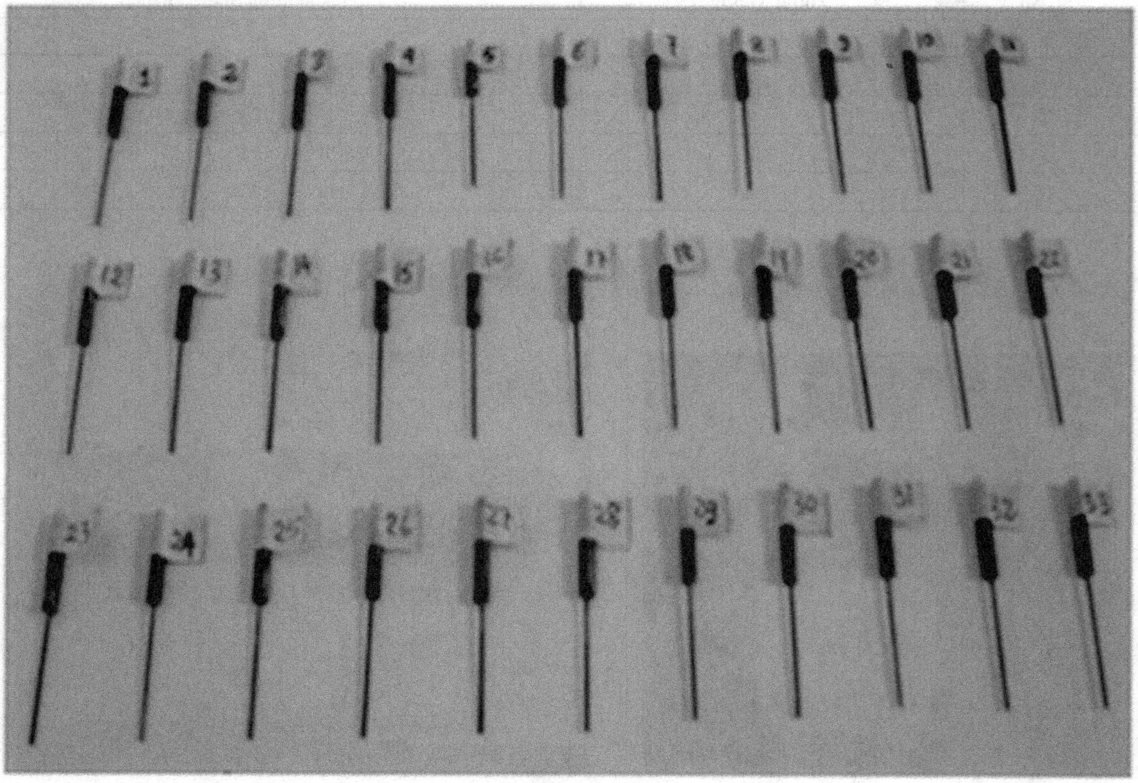

Table 3. Chemical Composition of ETP Cu

Chemical composition of ETP Cu	
Copper	Oxygen
99.90%	0.04%

Work Piece Material

The fabricated pins shown in Figure 5 can be used as a bias pin for biasing the microwave Oscillator cavity and as an electrode for generating small diameter holes by EDM process. The chemical composition & physical properties of ETP Cu is mentioned in Table 3 and Table 4respectively.

Table 4. Physical and Mechanical Properties of ETP Cu

Malting Point	1065°C
Density	8.91gm/cm³
Electrical Resistivity	1.71microhm-cm
Electrical Conductivity	0.591 Mega Siemens/cm
Thermal Conductivity	391.1W/m-°K
Coefficient of Thermal Expansion	17.6 x 10^{-6} per °C
Specific Heat	393.5 J/Kg-°K
Modulus of Elasticity	117000MPa
Hardness	87 Rockwell F Scales
Tensile Strength	48 KSI
Yield Strength	44 KSI
Elongation	10% in 2 inch

Selection of Process Parameters and Ranges

In the present investigation, pulse on time (Ton), pulse off time (Toff), servo voltage (SV) and spindle speed (SS) are considered as the input parameters which are independent variables and that can be varied during the experiment to get desired output in WEDT process. The non-variable parameters are generally called as fixed factor. These factors are set apart from the experiment and they are neither having effect on the process, nor can vary because of the equipment setup (Matoorian, et al. 2008).

- Wire tension (machine unit): 1700
- Flow rate (machine unit): 1
- Maximum depth of cut (mm): 0.1
- Specimen material: ETP Copper (C11000)
- Size of the specimen (mm): Diameter: 2.0, length: 25

- Machining length (mm): 15

Ishikawa cause and effect diagram has been constructed for better understanding about the categories of the main parameters like electrical parameters, Electrode parameters, non-electrical parameters and the information about the work piece and variety of different type process parameters under those main parameters and their effects on performance parameters at a glance which is shown in Figure 6. Initially some experiments have been carried out to identify the important process parameters which may affect more on the machining characteristics of the parts. Considering those parameters further final experimentations have been done.

Figure 6. Ishikawa Cause and Effect Diagram for process parameter selection of WEDT

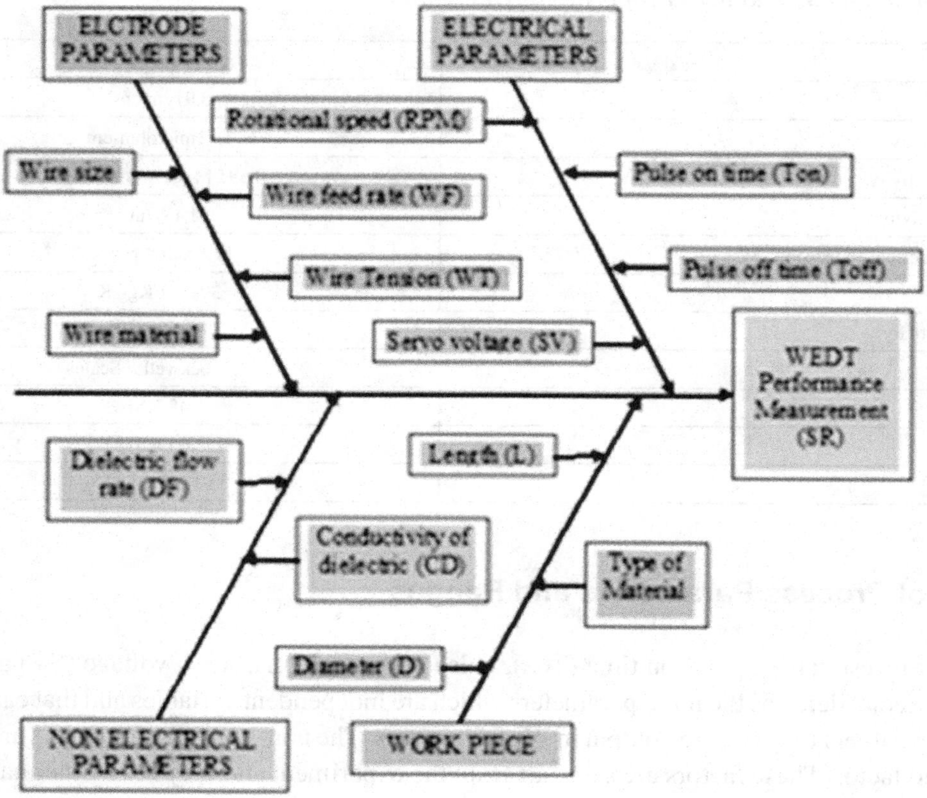

The pilot experiments have been carried out by varying the process parameters to understand the effective maximum and minimum ranges of the parameters by which desired output can be established. The process parameters like pulse on time, pulse off time, servo voltage and spindle speed have been selected to study their actual effect on performance parameters like surface roughness. The ranges of these process parameters are given in Table 5. From these ranges of the individual process parameter, the actual range has been selected through the pilot experiment. A proper design of experiments (DOE) has been constructed to perform more accurate and more efficient experiment. The analysis of variance (ANOVA) has been conducted to determine significant factors and regression analysis has been used to establish a relationship between factors & responses by using response surface methodology (RSM) (Islam, et al. 2010) (Lertphokanont, et al. 2012). The combined use of these techniques has been allowed us to create models which make it possible to explain the variability associated with each of the technological variables studied in this work.

Table 5. Process Parameters, Symbols and their Ranges

Process Parameters	Symbol	Units	Range (machine units)	Range (actual units)
Pulse on Time	Ton	µs	1-16	6-10 µs
Pulse off Time	Toff	µs	6-300	30 -38 µs
Servo Voltage	SV	V	2-255	70-78 volt
Spindle Speed	SS	rpm	50-1500	930-1230 rpm

The pulse off time is referred as Toff and it represents the duration of time in micro seconds (µs), between the two simultaneous sparks shown in Figure 7. The voltage is absent during this part of the cycle. The Toff setting time range available on the machine tool is 6 – 300. The lower value of Toff means more number of discharges in a given time and its increase the sparking efficiency. As a result, the cutting rate also increased.

Figure 7. Waveform used in WEDT Process

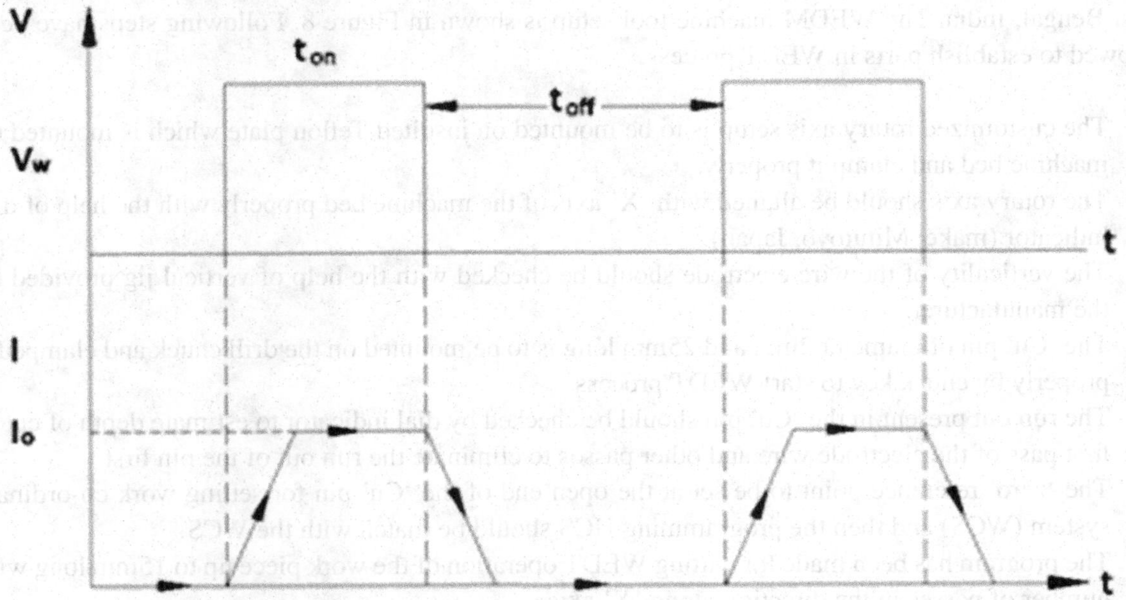

The pulse on time is referred as 'Ton' and the duration of time in micro seconds (μs) for which the current is flowing in each cycle shown in Figure 7. During this time the voltage is applied across the electrodes (Srivastava, et al. 2014). The 'Ton' setting time range available on the machine tool is 1-16. Where,

- The open circuit voltage: V_0
- The working voltage: V_w
- The maximum current: I_0
- The pulse on time (the duration for which the voltage pulse is applied): t_{on}
- The pulse off time: t_{off}
- The gap between the work piece and the tool is spark gap: δ
- The polarity, straight polarity, wire electrode: -ve
- The dielectric medium
- External flushing through the spark gap.

Servo voltage (SV) is used for controlling advances and retracts of the wire electrode. Mean machining voltage varies depending on the state of the machining between the work piece and the wire electrode. When the mean machining voltage is higher than the set voltage level then the wire advances and if it is lower, the wire retracts. Higher the value for SV, the wider the gap between the work piece and the electrode becomes and vice versa (Kalajahi et al. 2013).

Actually the work piece is mounted on the drill chuck which is mounted on the DC motor spindle. So at the time of WEDT operation, the rotational speed of the work piece is nothing but the spindle speed of the motor. Surface roughness of the specimen is depend on the rotational speed of the specimen, If rotational speed will increase then surface roughness will be better (Ghiculescu, et al. 2013). Wire feed also dependent on rotational speed, it decreases with the increase of rotational speed and vice versa.

The experiments have been carried out on a wire-cut EDM machine (FANUC ROBOCUT, Alpha-OiD) manufactured by M/s FANUC Ltd. which installed at SAMEER Kolkata Centre, Kolkata-106, West Bengal, India. The WEDM machine tool setup is shown in Figure 8. Following steps have been followed to establish parts in WEDT process.

- The customized rotary axis setup is to be mounted on insulted Teflon plate which is mounted on machine bed and clamp it properly.
- The rotary axis should be aligned with 'X' axis of the machine bed properly with the help of dial indicator (make: Mitutoyo, Japan)
- The verticality of the wire electrode should be checked with the help of vertical jig provided by the manufacturer.
- The 'Cu' pin of diameter 2mm and 25mm long is to be mounted on the drill chuck and clamped it properly by chuck key to start WEDT process.
- The run out present in the 'Cu' pin should be checked by dial indicator to estimate depth of cut in first pass of the electrode wire and other passes to eliminate the run out of the pin first.
- The 'zero' reference point to be set at the open end of the 'Cu' pin for setting work co-ordinate system (WCS) and then the programming UCS should be match with the WCS.
- The program has been made for cutting WEDT operation of the work piece up to 15mm long with number of passes in the direction along 'X' axis.

Figure 8. Setup of WEDM Machine Tool

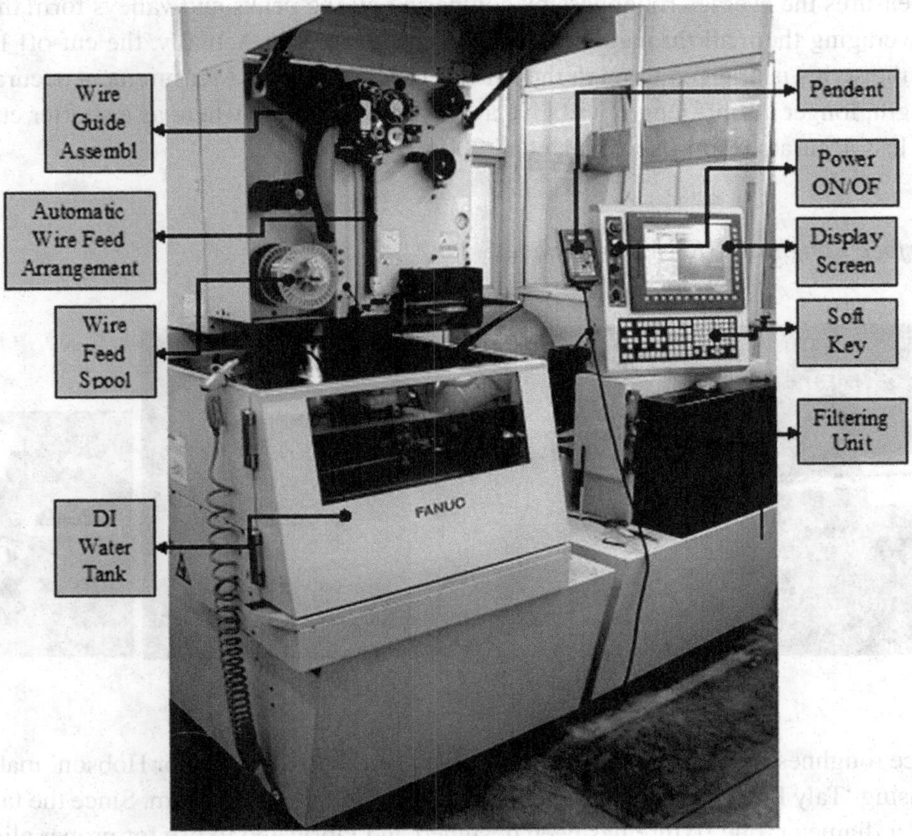

- The cable connection between the DC power sources with customized rotary axis setup to be checked before starting the operation.
- The cutting parameters which need not to be changed should be put along with the value of variable parameters like pulse on time, pulse off time, rpm, servo voltage and wire feed as optimized for different test run.
- The DC power source to be switched on with specific voltage value to get desired rpm of the motor spindle as well as the work piece also.
- Finally, the wire electrical discharge turning (WEDT) operation should be start by putting the depth of cut as estimated and the operation is continued until the desired diameter of the pin with specified length is achieved.
- Before dismantle the final work piece (stepped pin) from the drill chuck, preliminary inspection has been made using wire electrode.

After fabrication of specimens shown in Figure 5 by WEDT process, it is very important to measure the surface roughness (SR) to understand whether these results are meeting the desire accuracy level or not. Roughness is nothing but the vertical deviations of a real surface from its ideal form. Surface is rough if the deviation is large and the surface is smooth if small deviation is there. Basically, surface roughness measures the average roughness by comparing all the peaks and valleys form the mean line and finally averaging them all throughout the entire cut-off length. Actually, the cut-off length is the length when the stylus is dragged through the surface to be measured. Measurement accuracy depends on cutoff length, longer cut-off length will give a more average value where as a shorter cut-off length might give a less accurate result (Newman, et al. 2004).

Figure 9. Surface Roughness (R_a) Measurement Setup

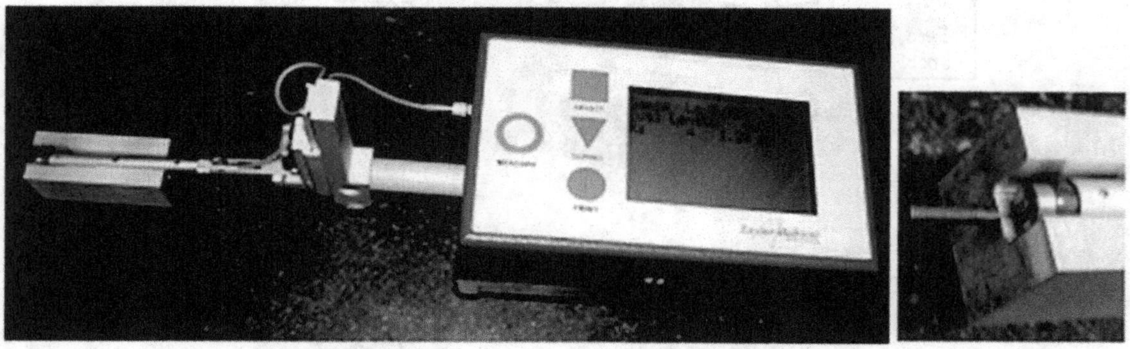

The surface roughness of the machined components is measured by 'Taylor Hobson' make 'Talysurf instrument' using 'Taly Profile Lite' software, with a cut-off length of 0.25 mm. Since the fabricated Cu pin has smaller diameter, one fixture has been designed and fabricated to use for proper alignment and holding the pin at the time of measurement of Ra and after measurement also the pin can be taken out from the fixture easily without any damage of pin. The setup used for measuring the surface roughness of the specimen is shown in Figure 9.

In Figure 10 shows the surface roughness plot of the specimens in two different machining conditions. One figure shows that the measured surface roughness (Ra) is 1.77μm when the pulse off time 34μs, pulse on time 6μs, rotational speed 1080rpm and servo voltage 74volt and another figure shows the achieved roughness value of 2.04 μm with different set of parametric value like pulse off time 34μs, pulse on time 8μs, rotational speed 930rpm and servo voltage 74volt. Considering both the plots, it is evident that surface roughness changes with the change of pulse on time and spindle speed because in both the cases pulse off time and servo voltage remains same. It is also noticed that better surface roughness can be achieved by decreasing pulse on time with the increase of comparatively moderate spindle speed.

Figure 10. Surface Roughness (Ra) Plots of the Pins with Two Different Machining Conditions

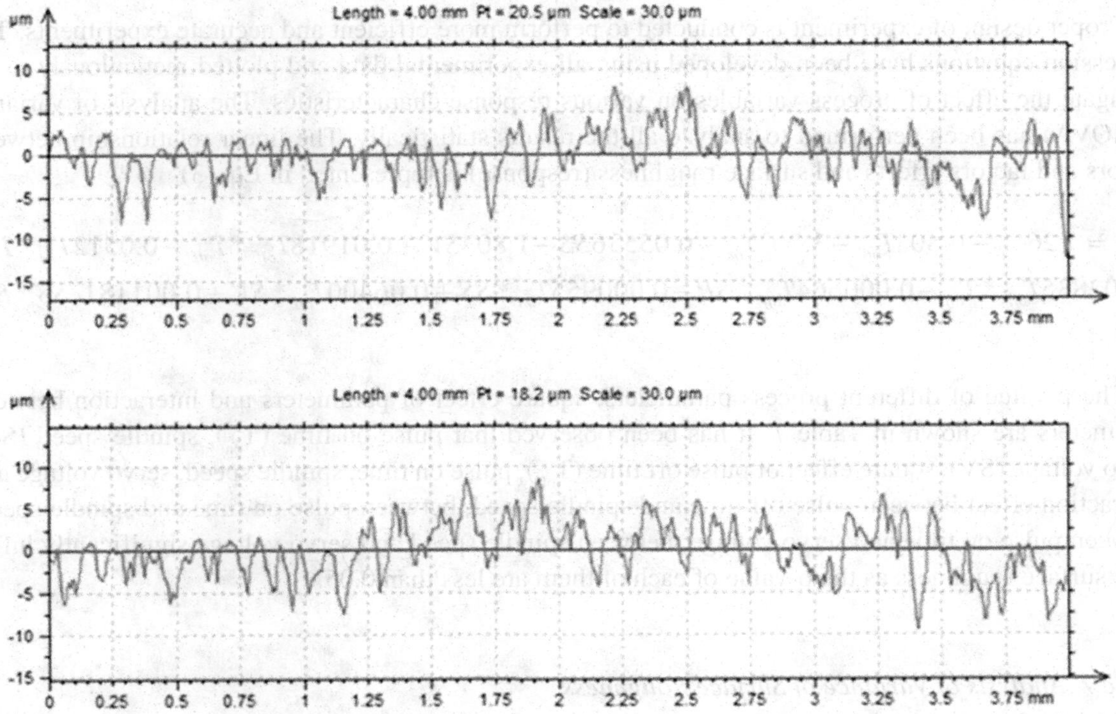

RESULT AND DISCUSSION

The scheme under 'response surface methodology' has been developed for carrying out the experiments to investigate the effect of process parameters on output parameters. The maximum and minimum range of process parameters have been selected based on the pilot experiments.

The experiments have been executed on the central composite rotatable second order design of response surface methodology. Total 31 experiments have been conducted because the mode of variation of surface roughness is considered and modeled using a statistical approach in Minitab 16 software. Also, it has been observed that the central composite full (unblocked) design requires much fewer test

Table 6. Process Parameters and their Levels

Parameters	Level				
	(-2)	(-1)	0	(+1)	(+2)
Pulse off time (µs)	30	32	34	36	38
Pulse on time (µs)	6	7	8	9	10
Spindle speed (rpm)	930	1005	1080	1155	1230
Servo voltage (volt)	70	72	74	76	78

runs and found to be sufficient to describe the responses. The process parameters and their levels are shown in Table 6.

Proper design of experiment is conducted to perform more efficient and accurate experiments. The regression equations have been developed using all experimental data and plotted meticulously to investigate the effect of process variables on various response characteristics. The analysis of variance (ANOVA) has been performed to analyze all the results statistically. The linear relationship between factors and factors effects and surface roughness (response) is represented in Eq. (3).

$$Ra = 126.2 - 0.803T_{off} - 3.703T_{on} - 0.05536SS - 1.803SV + 0.01918T_{off} * T_{off} - 0.0512T_{on} * T_{on} + 0.02835T_{off} * T_{on} - 0.000664T_{off} * SP - 0.000955T_{on} * SS + 0.06400T_{on} * SV + 0.001181\ SS * SV \tag{3}$$

The p-value of different process parameters, square effect of parameters and interaction between parameters are shown in Table 7. It has been observed that pulse on time (T_{on}), spindle speed (SS), servo voltage (SV), square effect of pulse off time (T_{off}), pulse on time, spindle speed, servo voltage and interaction effect between pulse off time and spindle speed, between pulse on time and spindle speed, between pulse on time and servo voltage, between spindle speed and servo voltage significantly influence surface roughness as the p-value of each of them are less than 0.05.

Table 7. Analysis of Variance of Surface Roughness

Source	DF	Adj. SS	Adj. MS	F-Value	P-Value
Model	11	0.2304	0.2940	51.99	0.000
Linear	4	0.9771	0.2442	60.63	0.000
T_{off}	1	0.01036	0.01036	2.57	0.125
T_{on}	1	0.51512	0.51512	127.85	0.000
SS	1	0.4258	0.04258	105.69	0.000
SV	1	0.02583	0.02582	6.41	00.02
Square	2	0.2705	0.1352	33.58	0.000
2-way interaction	5	1.0563	0.21126	52.44	0.000
Error	19	0.0765	0.00402	-	-
Lack of fit	13	0.05706	0.0043	1.35	0.373
Pure Error	6	0.01949	0.0032	-	-
Total	30	2.3805			
S = 0.0634, R-sq =96.78%, R-sq(adj) = 94.92%, R-sq(pred) =89.54%					

The values of S, R-Sq and R-Sq (adj) of regression analysis for the surface roughness is shown in Table 7. It has been observed that the S-value of the responses is smaller and R-Sq and R-Sq (adj) values of the responses are comparatively high. Reference to this it can be concluded that the data for each response are well fitted in the developed models. Also it is observed that for circularity error, pulse on

Figure 11. Response Surface of SR vs. SS and T_{on}

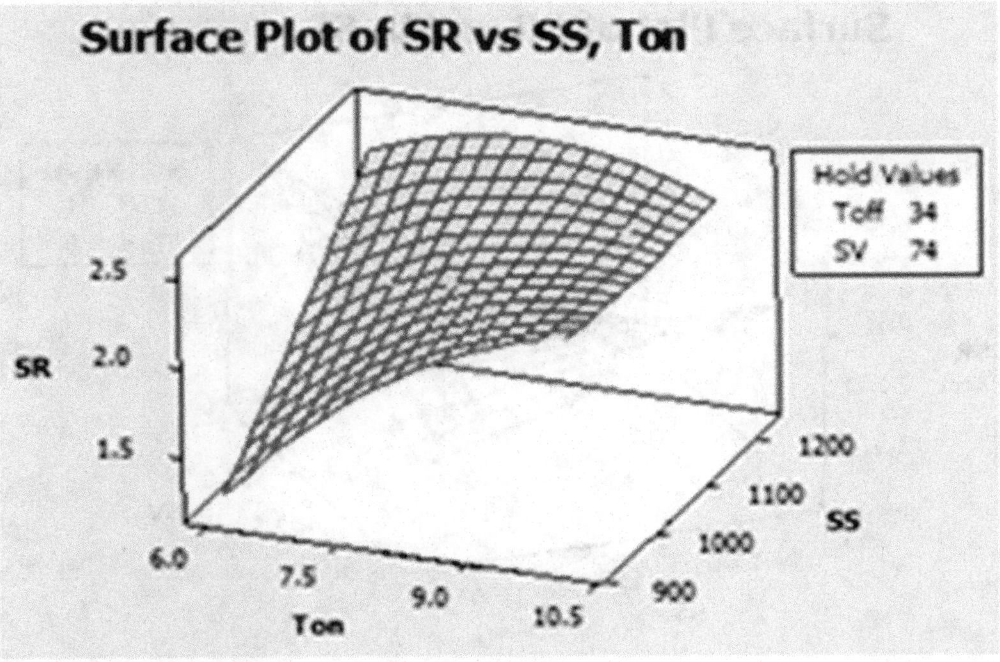

time (52.71%) is the most dominating factor followed by spindle speed (43.57%), servo voltage (2.64%) and pulse off time (1.05%).

Figure 11 shows the estimated response of surface roughness (SR), varying the factors of spindle speed and pulse on time, whilst the pulse off time and servo voltage remains constant in their central values. It is observed that SR decreases linearly with the decrease of spindle speed. It can be seen that decreasing pulse on time with decreasing spindle speed surface roughness decreases strongly. It can also be noted that the higher values of pulse on time, by decreasing spindle speed values, the surface roughness increases. This is because that the decreasing pulse on time means less sparking time and slower material removal rate which results good surface finish.

Figure 12 shows the estimated response of surface roughness (SR), varying the factors of spindle speed and servo voltage, whilst the pulse off time and pulse on time remains constant in their central values. It is observed that SR decreases linearly with the decrease of servo voltage. It can be seen that increasing servo voltage with higher spindle speed SR increases strongly. It can also be clearly seen that SR decreases linearly by increasing spindle speed values. Actually, higher the value for servo voltage (SV), the wider the gap between the work piece and the electrode which results less effective spark between them. As a result, poor surface finish will come. On the other hand, better surface finish can be achieved if the spindle speed increases gradually because the spindle run out present in the rotary axis can be minimized with comparatively moderate spindle speed.

Figure 13 shows the estimated response of surface roughness (SR), varying the factors of pulse off time and pulse on time, whilst the spindle speed and servo voltage remains constant in their central values. It is observed that decreasing pulse on time with higher value of pulse off time, surface roughness decreases strongly. It is because of the fact that the increase in pulse off time means less sparking time

Figure 12. Response Surface of SR vs. SV and SS

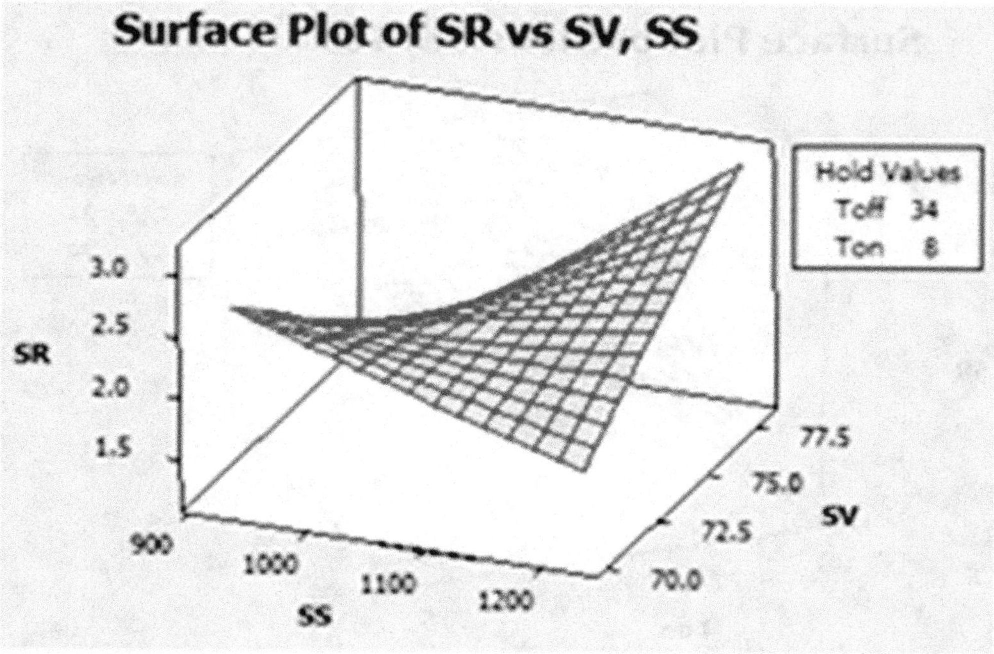

and comparatively lower cutting speed which results better surface finish. If the pulse off time is set at higher value then the sparking time of machine decreases with cutting speed, results comparatively good surface finish.

To minimize the response, equal importance has been given on the higher, target and on the lower bound of the linear desirability function. For linear desirability function (D), the value of the weight is considered as 1. In Figure14 shows the optimization result for the minimum surface roughness (SR) is 1.2471μm when the pulse off time, pulse on time, spindle speed and servo voltage are set at their optimal parametric setting of 35μs, 6μs, 1100rpm and 78 volt respectively.

Final Verification of the Experiment

After getting the optimal parameter settings for desired surface finish characteristics, the next step is to verify the feasibility of the proposed response surface equations. It is observed from the validation experiments that there is a small percentage error between the estimated and the experimental values, which suggest that the developed models can yield nearly exact results within the limits of cutting parameters being used during experimentation. The experimental results and the predicted optimal results along with the predication errors have been shown in Table 8.

These small prediction errors have been occurred may be due to inherent inaccuracy in setting of the customized rotary table setup during operation and the measurements of surface roughness measuring instrument setup. Actually, the predicted value of surface roughness is 1.24μm and experimental value

Figure 13. Response Surface of SR vs. T_{on} and T_{off}

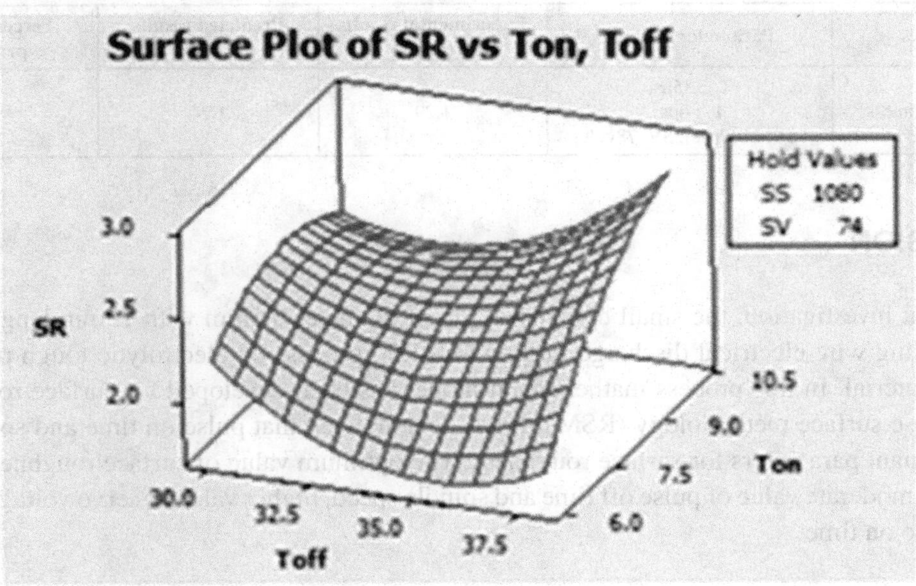

of surface roughness is 1.29µm and the involved error is 3.78%. So, the developed model can be useful in predicting output surface roughness within the limits of range taken in the analysis.

Figure 14. Optimization Result of Minimum SR

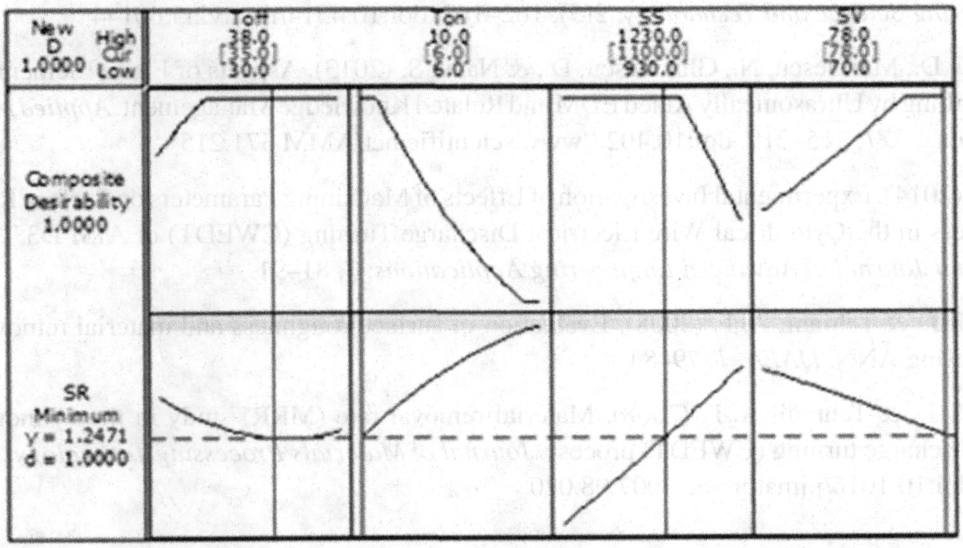

Table 8. Confirmation Test of Surface Roughness

Responses	Parameter settings	Experimental results (μm)	Predicted results (μm)	Percent error in prediction
Surface Roughness	T_{off}: 35μs, T_{on}: 6μs, SS: 1100rpm, SV: 78volt	1.29	1.24	3.87

CONCLUSION

In the present investigation, the small cylindrical pin of diameter 0.5mm with 15mm length has been fabricated using wire electrical discharge turning (WEDT) process on electrolytic tough pitch copper (ETP Cu) material. In this process mathematical model has been developed for surface roughness by using response surface methodology (RSM). It has been noticed that pulse on time and spindle speed are the dominant parameters for surface roughness. The optimum value of surface roughness has been calculated at moderate value of pulse off time and spindle speed, higher value of servo voltage and lower value of pulse on time.

ACKNOWLEDGMENT

Authors would like to thank to SAMEER Kolkata Centre (R & D laboratory, Govt. of India) for providing work materials as well as machine facilities to carry out all the experiments for this study.

REFERENCES

Datta, S., & Mahapatra, S. S. (2010). Modeling, simulation and parametric optimization of wire EDM process using response surface methodology coupled with grey-Taguchi technique. *International Journal of Engineering Science and Technology*, *2*(5), 162–183. doi:10.4314/ijest.v2i5.60144

Ghiculescu, D., Marinescu, N., Ghiculescu, D., & Nanu, S. (2013). Aspects of Finite Element Analysis of Microdrilling by Ultrasonically Aided EDM and Related Knowledge Management. *Applied Mechanics and Materials*, *371*, 215–219. doi:10.4028/www.scientific.net/AMM.371.215

Hadad, M. (2014). Experimental Investigation of Effects of Machining Parameters on Surface Roughness & Roundness in the Cylindrical Wire Electrical Discharge Turning (CWEDT) of AISI D3 Tool Steel. *International Journal of Advanced Engineering Applications*, *7*, 81–91.

Haddad, M. J., & Tehrani, A. F. (2008). Evaluation of surface roughness and material removal rate in CWEDM using ANN. *IJAEA*, *1*, 79–84.

Haddad, M. J., & Tehrani, A. F. (2008). Material removal rate (MRR) study in the cylindrical wire electrical discharge turning (CWEDT) process. *Journal of Materials Processing Technology*, *199*(1-3), 369–378. doi:10.1016/j.jmatprotec.2007.08.020

Islam, M. N., Rafai, N. H., & Subramanian, S. S. (2010) An Investigation into Dimensional Accuracy achievable in Wire-cut Electrical Discharge Machining. *Proceedings of the World Congress on Engineering*, 3.

Janardhan, V., & Samuel, G. L. (2010). Pulse train data analysis to investigate the effect of machining parameters on the performance of wire electro discharge turning (WEDT) process. *International Journal of Machine Tools & Manufacture*, *50*(9), 775–788. doi:10.1016/j.ijmachtools.2010.05.008

Kalajahi, M. H., Ahmadi, S. R., & Oliaei, S. N. B. (2013). Experimental and finite element analysis of EDM process and investigation of material removal rate by response surface methodology. *International Journal of Advanced Manufacturing Technology*, *69*(1-4), 687–704. doi:10.100700170-013-5059-x

Lertphokanont, V., Sato, T., Ota, M., Yamaguchi, K., & Egashira, K. (2012). Micro-structuring on Cylindrical Inner Surface using Whirling Electrical Discharge Texturing. *Advanced Materials Research*, *565*, 430–435. doi:10.4028/www.scientific.net/AMR.565.430

Masuzawa, T., & Tonshoff, H. K. (1997). Three-Dimensional Micromachining by Machine Tools. *Annals of the CIRP*, *46*(2), 621–628. doi:10.1016/S0007-8506(07)60882-8

Matoorian, P., Sulaiman, S., & Ahmad, M. M. H. M. (2008). An experimental study for optimization of electrical discharge turning (EDT) process. *Journal of Materials Processing Technology*, *204*(1-3), 350–356. doi:10.1016/j.jmatprotec.2007.11.058

Mohammad, J. H., & Alireza, F. T. (2008). Investigation of cylindrical wire electrical discharge turning (CWEDT) of AISI D3 tool steel based on statistical analysis. *Journal of Materials Processing Technology*, *198*(1-3), 77–85. doi:10.1016/j.jmatprotec.2007.06.059

Mohammadi, A., Tehrani, A. F., Ehsan, E. E., & Karimi, D. (2008). A new approach to surface roughness and Circularity Error improvement in wire electrical discharge turning based on statistical analyses. *International Journal of Advanced Manufacturing Technology*, *39*(1-2), 64–73. doi:10.100700170-007-1179-5

Newman, K. H. (2004). State of the art in wire electrical discharge machining (WEDM). *International Journal of Machine Tools & Manufacture*, *44*(12-13), 1247–1259. doi:10.1016/j.ijmachtools.2004.04.017

Padhee, S., Nayak, N., Panda, S. K., Dhal, P. R., & Mahapatra, S. S. (2012). Multi-objective parametric optimization of powder mixed electro-discharge machining using response surface methodology and non-dominated sorting genetic algorithm. *Indian Academy of Sciences*, *37*(2), 1–18. doi:10.100712046-012-0078-0

Pasam, V. K., Battula, S. B., Madar, P. V., & Swapna, M. (2010). Optimizing Surface Finish in WEDM Using the Taguchi Parameter Design Method. *Journal of the Brazilian Society of Mechanical Sciences and Engineering*, *32*(2), 107–113. doi:10.1590/S1678-58782010000200002

Qu, J., Shih, A. J., & Scattergood, R. O. (2002). Development of the cylindrical wire electrical discharge machining process, part 1: Concept, design, and material removal rate. *Journal of Manufacturing Science and Engineering*, *124*(3), 702–707. doi:10.1115/1.1475321

Rao, R. V., & Kalyankar, V. D. (2013). Parameter optimization of modern machining processes using teaching–learning-based optimization algorithm. *Engineering Applications of Artificial Intelligence*, *26*(1), 524–531. doi:10.1016/j.engappai.2012.06.007

Scott, F. M. (2005). Investigation of wire electrical discharge machining of thin cross-sections and compliant mechanisms. *International Journal of Machine Tools & Manufacture*, *45*(15), 1717–1725. doi:10.1016/j.ijmachtools.2005.03.003

Scott, F. M., Albert, J. S., & Qu, J. (2004). Investigation of the spark cycle on material removal rate in wire electrical discharge machining of advanced materials. *International Journal of Machine Tools & Manufacture*, *44*(4), 391–400. doi:10.1016/j.ijmachtools.2003.10.005

Srivastava, A., Dixit, A. R., & Tiwari, S. (2014). Experimental Investigation of Wire EDM Process Parameters on Aluminium Metal Matrix Composite Al2024/SiC. *International Journal of Advance Research and Innovation*, *2*, 511–515.

Vishal, P., Rehman, A., Bhagoria, J. L., & Puri, Y. M. (2010). Kerfs width analysis for wire cut electro discharge machining of SS 304L using design of experiments. *Indian Journal of Science and Technology*, *3*(4), 369–373. doi:10.17485/ijst/2010/v3i4.4

Chapter 9
Laser Trepan Drilling of Monel k-500 Superalloy in Low Power Laser Beam Machining

D. Pramanik
https://orcid.org/0000-0003-1899-3197
Jadavpur University, India

N. Roy
Jadavpur University, India

A. S. Kuar
Jadavpur University, India

S. Sarkar
Jadavpur University, India

S. Mitra
Jadavpur University, India

Dipankar Bose
National Institute of Technical Teachers' Training and Research (NITTTR), Kolkata, India

ABSTRACT

In the field of micro processing of materials, laser has great importance as a source of heat and for its ability to deliver a coherent beam. The use of 50-watt average power for through-hole is impossible to achieve good quality drilling of the metal sheet upto 2 mm thickness. But the use of unique parameter sawing angle and constant focal point distance plays a significant role on hole diameter and circularity in laser trepan drilling. In the present research study, laser trepan drilling is investigated through multi diode pulsed fiber laser beam machining. Experimental analysis based on central composite design (CCD) of response surface methodology (RSM) has been fulfilled to find out the mathematical model.

DOI: 10.4018/978-1-7998-3624-7.ch009

A study of the effect of sawing angle with other process parameters such as cutting speed, power, duty cycle, and pulse frequency on overcut bottom diameter and circularity at bottom for a monel k-500 has been conducted. Experimental validation of the proposed model shows that desired hole quality can be obtained by optimization of controllable of suitable process parameters.

INTRODUCTION

The earliest machining process for making different types of hole is drilling. Non-traditional drilling techniques like electro discharge machining (EDM), electro chemical machining (ECM), ultrasonic machining (USM), plasma arc machining (PAM), laser beam machining (LBM) and abrasive jet machining (AJM) etc. have come into the arena of drilling methods as a result of the development of materials and requirement of high precise holes with higher drilling rate (Dahotre et al. 2007; Jain 2005; Liu et al. 2012; Biffi et al. 2011). The laser beam drilling is more acceptable than other non-conventional drilling techniques due to the fact laser beam drilling has better techniques for higher production rate over the wide range of materials of conductive and non-conductive by nature (Meijer 2004). Their advantages are precession of operation, high speed processing and low cost. Laser drilling has involvement of high temperature processing of materials with solid phase heating, melting and evaporation. For reduction in the oxidation reactions in the cutting section use of assist gas is made in metallic material processing. An extensive heating in the cutting section via high temperature exothermic reaction is caused by oxidation reactions cutting section is devoid of cutting asperities like sidewall burning, overcut, dross attachment, taperness and thermal erosion. The defects portions along the cut section are minimized when cutting parameters are selected approximately in laser cutting or drilling process with proper control. The quality assessment of the final product requires important aspects like laser cutting process and assessment of the cutting parameters on kerf size and geometry. Improvement of process control and achieving of quality of the final product can be optimized through optimization of studies on laser drilling (Gautam et al. 2018; Mishra et al. 2013; Majumdar et al. 2013).

LASER ABLATION WITH NANO SECOND LASER

Material ejection and generation of nano particles are caused by photo thermal process in ns laser ablation. Rate of energy deposition being slow it combines with electronic and vibrational mode of the work-piece to hit the target material. Thermal penetration depth gives the estimated depth of effective laser energy absorption at low laser value (Roy et al. 2015). Thermal evaporation dominates the ablation process in the regime of thermal penetration. Direct heating of laser radiation causes ionization of vapor plume when the laser value comes near the threshold value. As the laser intensity goes to be higher than the gas ionization threshold optical break down process helps the ionization phenomenon to occur. The laser irradiant being greater than 10^9 w/cm^2 and surface temperature being equal to thermo dynamic critical point phase explosion phenomenon happens to change the matter from an overheated liquid droplet. Creation of plasma with high temperature and pressure occurs at the end of the laser pulse, leading to ejection of molten droplets at supersonic velocity. Re-solidification of the expelled liquid into thin films helps to alter topography at the rim and surroundings area of the ablated region (Pramanik et al. 2018; 2019; Sharma et al. 2018; Chien et al. 2007; Ghoreishi et al. 2002). Figure 1 shows the schematic representation of laser material interaction.

Figure 1. Schematic picture of laser material interaction

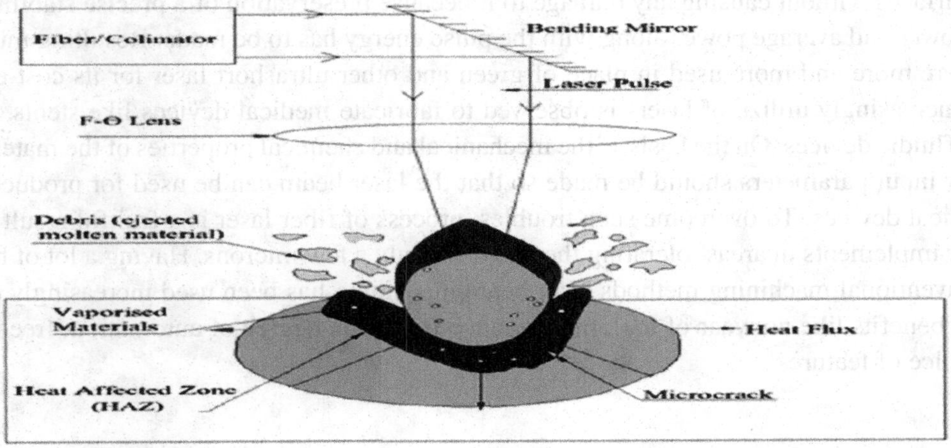

ADVANTAGES OF FIBER LASER OVER OTHER SOLID-STATE LASERS

The significance of fiber laser system for the micro machining domain is inevitable. Evolving of fiber lasers in the most versatile and rapid developing laser system for the recent years is a significant achievement in various fields of manufacturing, medical, metrological and military applications which were perform by conventional solid-state laser including gas lasers. Fiber laser has the qualities like high efficiency, high beam quality, less maintenance and ability to process highly reflective material, for which it is acquiring the fields of CO_2 and Nd: YAG laser in different manufacturing fields (Lopez et al. 2017; Ezugwu et al. 1999). Due to following reasons fiber laser become more acceptable from other type of laser.

1. High output power efficiency: Active regions of optic fiber can be several meters long, for which it can give very high optical gain. Fibers' high surface part proportionate to volume ratio, allowing cooling competently is the cause of supporting of kilowatt levels of continuous powers by lasers.
2. High optical quality: Wave guiding properties of fiber decrease or remove thermal deformation of the optical path, which creates a high-quality optical beam with limited diffraction. The better beam quality provides cleaner cut edges and faster cutting speed.
3. Compact machine size: In comparison with rod or gas lasers, diode pumped fiber lasers remain to be compact and to take small space. No chilling unit is vital for such kind of fiber laser machine.
4. Reliability: Vibrational strength at high level with extension of lifetime and maintenance-free procedure is in fiber laser.

APPLICATIONS OF FIBER LASER IN THE AREA OF MICRO-MACHINING

Fiber laser micro drilling, micro-cutting, micro-marking, are more broadly used than the lamp current Nd: YAG lasers in the field of manufacturing industrial application and medical sciences. As the surgical medical equipments are small in dimension, expensive in material and able to be fixed into small areas production of them is a very intricate task. Laser beam drilled high aspect ratio holes are used in various applications, including aerospace turbine engine cooling holes, oil gallery of engine blocks, laser fusion components and printed circuit board. It is extremely hard task to make laser beam machining on such surfaces without causing any damage to it because preservation of a precise stability between the peak power and average power along with the pulse energy has to be made. Resulting multi diode fiber lasers are more and more used in place of green and other ultrashort laser for its cost-effective class. Also, increasingly utilize of lasers is observed to fabricate medical devices like stents, catheters, and micro-fluidic devices. On the basis of the mechanical and chemical properties of the materials, selection of laser input parameters should be made so that the laser beam can be used for production of variety of medical devices. To overcome such troubles, process of fiber laser is a fruitful result for costly and smaller implements in areas tolerating the power of only a few microns. Having a lot of beneficial over the conventional machining methods laser beam machining has been used increasingly due to the following benefits like no wear of tool, maintenance free, high degree of automation, free programming, and choice of features.

TYPES OF LASER BEAM DRILLING

Different techniques have been practiced for different materials in their laser beam drilling. On the basis of the relative movement of the laser beam and CNC work table techniques of the fiber laser drilling have been divided into two types like static drilling and dynamic drilling. Static drilling requires a stationary condition of both the work-piece and laser beam and removal of the material is done through action of a number of pulses. When a single pulse helps to complete the drilling action it is termed as single pulse drilling. With the increase in the thickness of the sheet it needs an increase in the number of pulses. Percussion drilling remains to be one of the popular state laser drilling technique, which striking of successive pulses on the work-piece is done for removal of material. Laser dynamic drilling technique makes use of the laser beam in piercing at the centre of the hole and later movement to the circumference of the hole. This type of laser drilling includes the laser trepan drilling and it is commonly used in industrial fields. In this process vaporization and/or by the ejection of melting material are done for removal of material. When compared with dynamic drilling processes static techniques fail to maintain the quality of the drilled hole as done through dynamic drilling processes. For inclination of laser beam upto 0-5° placement of optical wages are done in helical drilling when compared with the other drilling techniques rate of percussion of helical drilling remains to be higher (Yilbas,1997; 2004; 2013).

As the annular volume for heating, melting and vaporizing and ejecting remains to be smaller than the cylindrical volume in dynamic laser drilling it requires less energy for the same diameter hole in-comparison to the static laser drilling. The heat affected zone remains to be small due to reduction in laser energy input to the work-piece and it is very much advantageous. Frequent use of the Nd: YAG laser beam drilling is seen in the fields of drilling in oil gallery of engine blocks, inject printer nozzle, nozzle guided vane holes, turbine cooling holes etc. (Bandyopadhyay et al. 2005).

ADVANTAGES OF LASER TREPAN DRILLING OVER PERCUSSION DRILLING OPERATION

Due to straight impingement of laser pulses in laser percussion drilling (LPD) the processing time in laser percussion drilling (LPD) is lesser, but hole feature is poor compared with laser trepan drilling (LTD) due to the formation of recast layer, spatter, and heat- affected zone (HAZ). Higher dimensional precision and stringent hole-quality necessities in aerospace components result in holes with better-quality attributes. LTD may provide this purpose more proficiently than LPD if the processing input parameters are optimized appropriately in order to overcome the geometrical inaccuracies (Yilbas et al. 2011).

IMPORTANCE OF MONEL K-500 MICRO DRILLING IN RESEARCH AND INDUSTRIAL PERCEPTION

Excellent strength to ratio, strong corrosion resistant and ability to retain high strength at high temperature are the superior properties of nickel copper-based Monel k-500 superalloy for which in an extensive use of marine and chemical environments. Pump, shafts, sea water valves, strainer baskets and trolling wire etc. High-quality resistance against corrosion by acids and oxygen makes Monel a superior material for chemical engineering. But in conventional drilling methods face many problems in machining of Monel alloys for their peculiar properties. But alloys have poor thermal conductivity and high reactivity at elevated temperature for which laser beam faces difficulties in cutting such alloys. For this increasing demand it has become necessary to increase machining speed and resultantly the material removal rate and productivity.

LITERATURE REVIEW ON LASER DRILLING

In the laser trepan drilling (LTD) method focusing of high intensity beam on work piece material with micro beam spot is done which results in very high-power density. The targeted object or material of any kind is melted or vaporized due to sufficient heat flux of the laser trepan drilling technique. Assist gas jet helps to expel the molten material appropriately from the machining region. Removal of the material along the region of the cut hole is done by the laser beam. Innate qualities of laser drilling may cause defects like spatter formation, heat affected zone (HAZ), hole taper, surface defects (roughness & micro cracks), hole non-circularity and thermal residual stresses in a drilled hole. Efforts are made by the researchers for minimization of these defects so that required quality laser drilled holes in different materials may be obtained. Yilbas et al. 2017 have made investigation regarding the temperature and residual stress distribution adjacent to the laser drill hole at the time of trepanning of 4 mm diameter hole in 3 mm thick titanium alloy (Ti6Al4V) sheet. In their opinion use of optimum process parameter may result in reduction of stresses near the drilled hole area. Moreover, validation of the numerical simulation results with experimental results by the use of thermocouple and x-ray diffraction technique. Kuar et al. 2006 have made experimental investigation to find out the influence of laser machining parameters on the heat affected zone thickness and phenomenon regarding taper in course of CNC pulsed Nd: YAG laser micro drilling of ($ZrO_{2)}$ zirconium. Low et al. 2000 have found out the characteristic of the spatter deposited on the drilled holes in a nimonic alloy. They have also made investigation regarding various laser processing parameters with the use of a fiber optic delivered Nd: YAG laser. Biswas et al. 2010 have found out a strategy to predict machining parameter setting to generate maximum circularity at entry and exit and minimum hole taper in Nd: YAG laser micro drilling of titanium nitride alumina composite (TiN-Al_2O_3). Use of an artificial neural network (ANN) has been made relating to process modeling of laser micro drilling. And a feed forward back propagation network has been utilized for modeling the machining process. Okasha et al. 2010 have made experimental investigation to find out the feasibility and fundamental characteristics of a new approach for micro drilling Inconel 718 alloy sheets at an acute angle, using sequential laser and mechanical drilling. The outcome reveals that sequential laser mechanical micro drilling alleviates the defects related with laser drilled holes, reduces burr size and machining time and increases the tool life compared with mechanical drilling. Dhaker et al. 2019 have experimentally investigated the behavior of hole geometry features hole circularity and hole taper in laser trepan drilling of Inconel 718 sheet. Computational intelligence technique particle swarm optimization has helped much to find out optimum value of laser input parameters for the improvement of hole circularity and reduction of hole taper. Goyel et al. 2016 have made investigation regarding laser trepan drilling process performance in terms of geometrical quality characteristics, such as hole taper and circularity for drilling small diameter hole in difficult to cut titanium alloy sheet. Due to concern of variant input process parameters such as pulse width, laser power, pulse frequency, workpiece thickness, cutting speed, stand of distance and assist gas pressure, the laser cutting is a extremely nonlinear and complex method. To grip this nonlinearity and complexity, genetic algorithm has been used for the optimization. The result of major process parameters on hole characteristics are discussed on the basis of data obtained through a well-designed orthogonal array experimental matrix. Reliable observed models have been developed for different quality characteristics. Marimuthu el al. 2017 have investigated the basic aspects of millisecond pulsed fiber laser drilling of aerospace nickel based Nimonic superalloy. The main study concentrates on perceptive the fiber laser parameters on laser trepanning drilled hole quality and speed. The most important findings are based on controlling the oxide layer, recast layer, hole surface quality and fatigue performance of the laser drilled samples. The outcome showed that the high average power of the fiber laser can be efficiently used to attain increased trepanning drilling speed without deflation the drilling quality, which is not viable with a free space Nd: YAG laser.

COMPONENTS OF FIBER LASER MACHINING SYSTEM

Optical fiber, rare earth dopant ions, pump sources and fiber coupler remain to be the essentials of fiber laser. A number of parameters including laser source, (mainly wave length and emission regime) and characteristic of the material itself are the depending factors for laser interface with the optical fiber material. As a very low failure material silica glass make cylindrical wave guide which possesses to be optical fiber as a major part. Doping with as rare earth materials like ytterbium yb^{3+} and neodium Nd^{3+} help out to get better the optical properties. Incomparision among other rare earth materials Yb^{3+} have several advantages for its longer higher state life span, a very small quantum defect (resulting in lower thermal load per unit length of pump power) and lack of the excited state absorption. Different types of mirrors are used in fiber lasers to form cavity. Several diode lasers are used for increasing the pump power reaching to the fiber. To avoid the emitted light to return to-words the source fiber couplers are used either one side of input fibers or one side of output fibers. Figure 2 shows the photographic view of fiber laser machining system.

Figure 2. Photographic view of fiber laser machining system

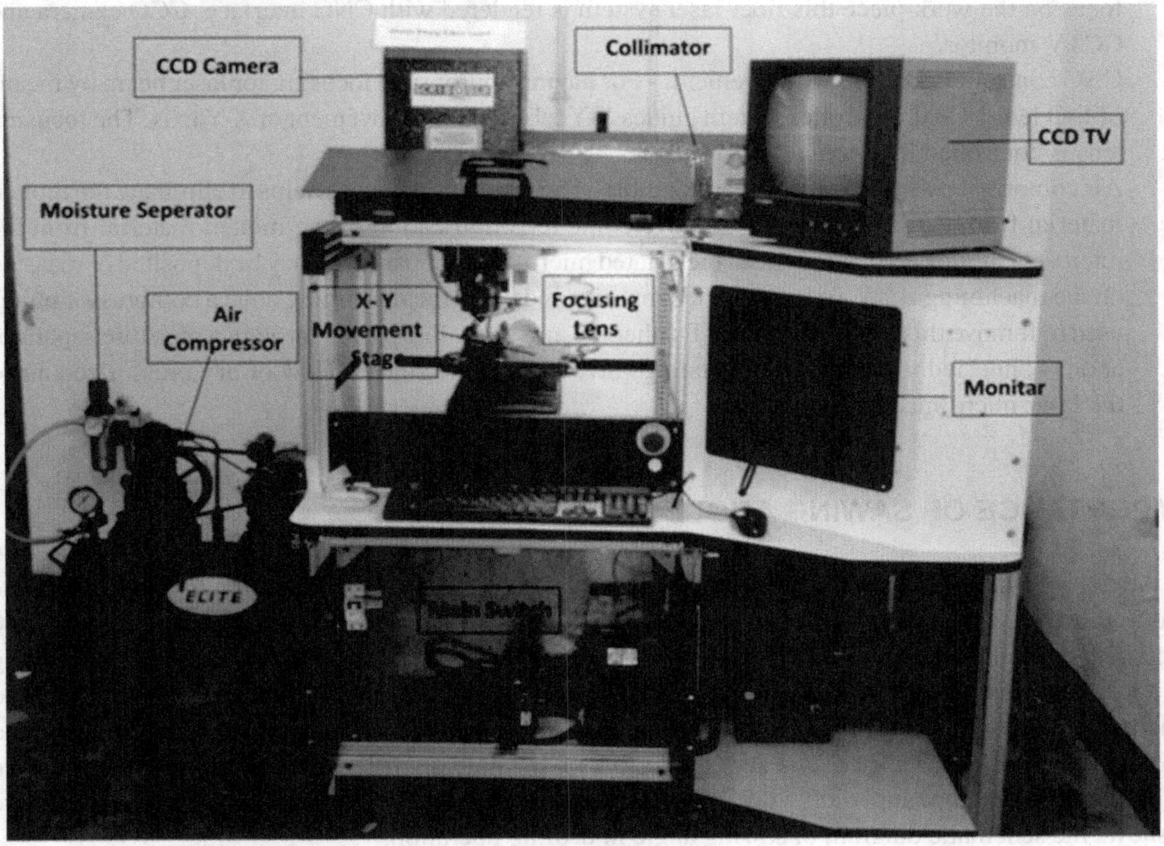

The main essentials of fiber laser marching system are laser source unit, beam delivery unit, laser beam focusing control system, CNC controller unit for axis movement and air compressor with moisture separator unit.

1. Laser source unit: - Pumping of fiber laser is made with special high-power multimode diodes throughout cladding of surrounding as single mode core. In contrast to conventional diode pump solid-state laser (DPSSL) life of this individual multimode is quite higher, when a single diode bar pumps DPSSL multiple equal diodes, all feeding the similar gain medium, pump fiber laser.
2. Beam delivery unit: - Generally constructive advantage of fiber laser is the gain medium remains to be fiber and the delivery is also throughout the optic fiber. As a result, probability of breakdown at coupling point between gain medium and delivery, extending to the FΘ lens remain to be very less. A collimator is used and act as a beam expander i.e. the laser can propagate to the required distance.
3. Laser beam focusing control unit: - To adjust the power density and the depth of focus made by the laser of a specified beam diameter the focal length of the focusing lens may be adjusted. A lower focal length lens achieves superior power density. The significance of the alignment of the focusing lens really regulates the coincidence of the beam core with centre of the lens and the beam after the

lens if it not straight it will radically let down the efficiency of the cutting. For getting appropriate focus on the work-piece this fiber laser system is rendered with CNC interface, CCD camera and CCTV monitor.

4. CNC controller unit for axis movement: - For having appropriate focusing for laser beam by means of F-Θ lens a CNC controller system guides X-Y table and the movement of X-Y axis. The focusing lens is controlled by Z axis.
5. Air compressor with moisture separator unit: - The jet of assisting gas helps to eliminate the molten material from the cutting region and overcome re-solidification of the molten material from the micro-machining area. Sometimes the ablated micro-chips or particles may be deposited or recasted on the machining zone. To remove this impurity and clean the machining zone a compressor unit is used to remove this adhere particles. Further the air supply line passes through a moisture separator and is connected to a pressure regulating valve. It results in the jet flow of dry pressurized air to the laser micro-machining zone.

IMPORTANCE OF SAWING ANGLE

In the field of fine and precise micro cutting requiring the combination of both continuous mode and pulse mode with the help of fusion cutting to sublimation cutting fiber lasers of an average laser power of 10-50 watt bear a good market value. But this average value of fiber laser used only for channeling, scribing and marking operation etc. Use of 50-watt average power for through hole is impossible to achieve good quality drilling of the metal sheet upto 2 mm thickness. But use of unique parameter sawing angle and constant focal point distance play a significant role on the hole diameter and circularity in laser trepan drilling of Monel k500 super alloy 0.7 mm thickness in low power fiber laser beam machining. Figure 3 shows the schematic diagram of sawing angle in drilling operation.

INPUT PARAMETERS IN LASER BEAM MACHINING

A quality machining of any material is a complicated method in which a number of different parameters are to be followed at the same point. Laser beam machining (LBM) process requires the mainly important parameters like power setting, duty cycle, cutting speed and pulse repetition frequency, which are elaborated below:

1. Sawing Angle

Sawing Angle is used for smooth and easy laser machining. In high power laser machining, laser impact on the metal and immediate evaporation of metal takes place. But in case of low power laser molten metal solidifies immediately after the melting. To overcome the recasting, an offset is provided on the metal but the depth of the offset is taper in nature for easy removal of molten and evaporated metal.

Figure 3. Schematic diagram of sawing angle

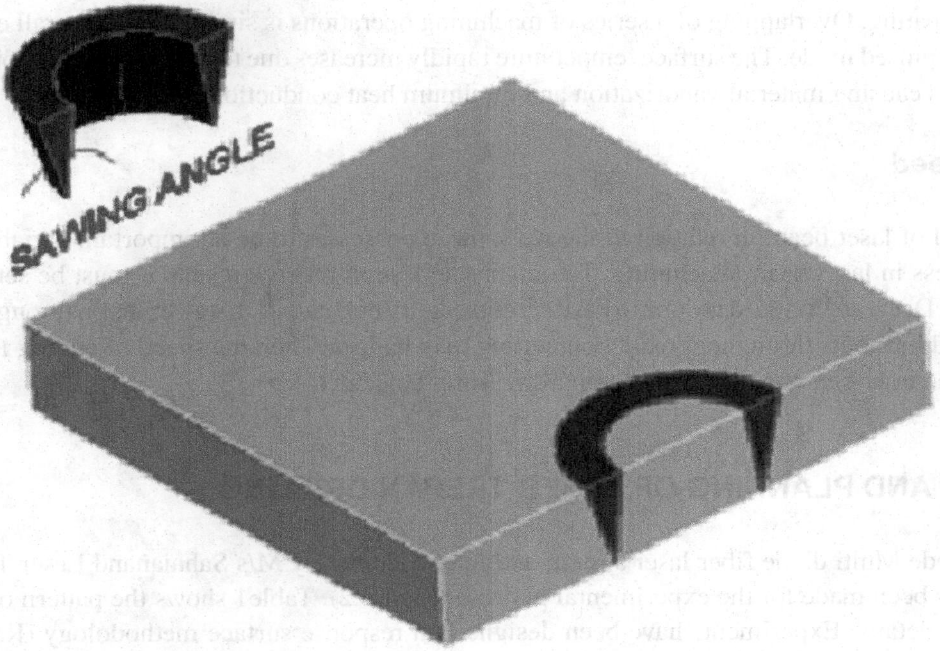

2. Power Setting

As the metal is heated up by a laser beam, the absorbed energy is extended into surrounding colder metal. Threshold power is the least amount of power impact required for initiating evaporation as it is showing to laser radiation. The main mechanism of material removal from the target remains to be vaporization even higher absorption rate.

3. Duty Cycle

The definition of the time required for vaporization of the material is known to be pulse width or duty cycle. The penetration time of the beam should be shorter than the pulse width. The pulse energy and the penetration time have an inverse relation, i.e., when one increases the after decreases. Duty cycle or pulse width refers to the fraction of time its on and active in its application. It can be expressed as a fraction real number or as a percentage of the fraction multiplied by 100. A laser that's on continuously can be said to have 100% duty cycle.

4. Pulse Frequency

The system of pulsed laser cutting differs from continuous wavelength laser beam cutting due to the cyclic nature of heating. Overlapping of a series of machining operations is similar to the overall effect of laser cutting in pulsed mode. The surface temperature rapidly increases due to high peak power pulses at low frequencies causing material vaporization and minimum heat conduction into the part.

5. Cutting Speed

The cutting speed of laser beam in relation to the work-piece possesses to be an important variable in the thermal process in laser beam machining. To obtain the desired process results it must be set to a definite schedule. Decrease in speed is done to have certain quality demands. Dross formation throughout fusion cutting and burnouts throughout oxidation cutting may happen when the speed of cutting is too low. Pulsing of the laser beam may assist to keep away from the defect.

PROCEDURE AND PLANNING OF LASER TREPAN DRILLING

Use of pulsed mode Multi diode fiber laser system and manufactured by M/s Sahajanand Laser Technology, India, has been made for the experimental purpose (Figure 2). Table1 shows the pattern of the machine setup in details. Experiments have been designed on response surface methodology (RSM), central composite rotatable design (CCD) based. Total 52 runs have been conducted and replicate with four times. Monel k-500 Ni based alloy metal sheet specimens, having a thickness of 0.7 mm are used as sample material. The range of different process parameters are determined based on pilot experiments for entire through drilled holes of targeted diameter 0.5 mm. A digital vernier calliper with the efficacy of least count of 0.01 mm is used to evaluate the thickness of the job sample. On experimental end, microscopic images of bottom diameter have been taken at 10x magnification by using an optical measuring microscope (Olympus STM 6), which is later measured by image analysis software. The controllable process parameter in the present research has been chosen as sawing angle, power setting, duty cycle, pulse frequency and scanning speed at 3 bar constant air pressure. The range of process parameters are selected by basic pilot experiments. The range of every controllable process parameters as per CCD techniques is listed in Table 2.

BOTTOM DIAMETER

A laser drilled hole has deviation as a inherent feature. When laser strikes and go through into the material, melting and evaporation takes place from the inner and bottom section of the material also. A small overcut is also there at the bottom surface like the top surface. An investigation on the overcut of bottom diameter has been done in that experiment. In general, the overcut is mostly depending upon the power setting, sawing angle, duty cycle, pulse frequency and scanning speed. In the present experiment the relation between that process parameters and bottom diameter has been developed.

Table 1. Machine specification

Specification	Description
Laser type	Multi diode fiber laser
Wave length	1064 nm
Average power	50 Watt
Mode of operation	Pulsed mode
Mode of laser Beam	Fundamental/ Gaussian mode (TEM_{00})
Beam diameter $1/e^2$	9mm (after collimator)
Laser beam spot diameter	21 µm
Pulse repetition rate	50-120 kHz

CIRCULARITY

The circularity is used to explain how close an object should be to a accurate circle. Sometimes it is called roundness; circularity is a 2-Dimensional tolerance that controls the overall form of a circle assuring it is not too oblong, square, or out of round. The hole circularity has a functional relationship with the extent of variation of hole diameter in course of cutting along the circular path or trepanning path. The cutting front and nearby area of the material along the kerf path is heated by the irradiating laser beam. As a result, distribution of a heat along the laser trepanning path does not result in a uniform way. An investigation on the circularity has been done in that experiment. In general, the circularity is mostly depending upon the power setting, sawing angle, duty cycle, pulse frequency and scanning speed. In the present experiment the relation between that process parameters and bottom surface circularity has been developed.

Table 2. Controllable process parameter and their range

Controllable Parameters	Units	Levels				
		-2	-1	0	1	2
Sawing Angle (A)	Θ	0.1	0.4	0.7	1	1.3
Power Setting (B)	watt	32.50	35	37.50	40	42.50
Duty Cycle (C)	%	80	83	86	89	92
Pulse Frequency (D)	kHz	50	55	60	65	70
Scanning Speed (E)	mm/sec	0.2	0.4	0.6	0.8	1

EXPERIMENTAL RESULT

The experimental values of different quality characteristics are revealed in Figure 4 and Figure 5. In these graphical figures, the experiment number indicates the experimental settings corresponding to the settings of central composite design (CCD) technique. For example, experiment 1 shows the first experimental settings of CCD technique.

Figure 4. Experimental measured value of bottom diameter

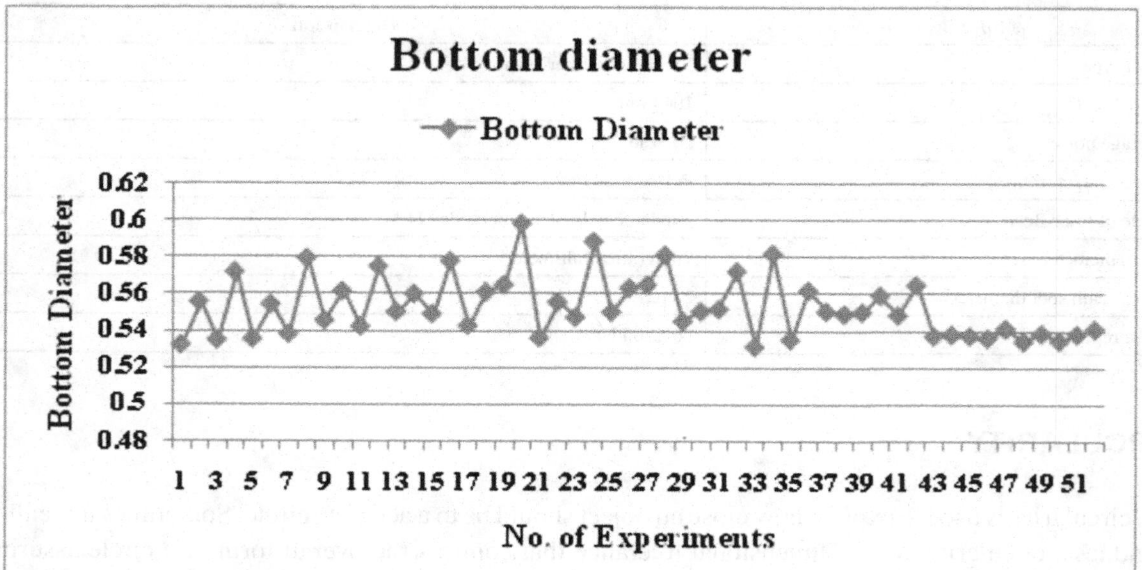

DEVELOPING THE MATHEMATICAL MODELS

The current study develops response surface model for establishing the mathematical relationship between the two responses (i.e. bottom diameter and circularity at bottom surface) and laser cutting parameters.

Figure 5. Experimental measured value of circularity at bottom

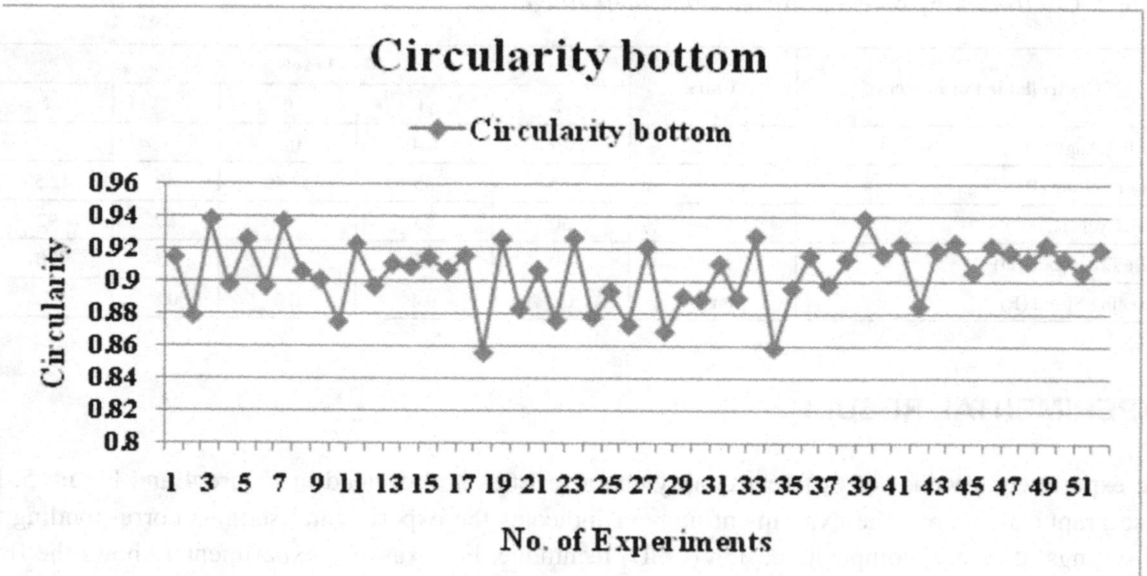

A second order polynomial equation has been evolved to perform the analysis. Minitab 17 software is used for analyzing the response i.e. bottom diameter and circularity at bottom surface and determination of mathematical model with best fits is given below as Equation 1 and Equation 2 respectively.

Bottom Diameter = .0527601 + .0011957 A + .0007302 B - .0001437 C + 0.001587 D + .0003578 E + 0.004001 A ... . (1)

Circularity at Bottom = 0.01701 - 0.015275 A + 0.006275 B + 0.002625 C - 0.003325 D - 0.007575 E - 0.00652 A×A - 0.00329 B×B ... . (2)

ANOVA TABLE

The present study covers the adequacy of the developed mathematical model for bottom diameter and circularity at bottom, analysis of variance (ANOVA) and subsequent F and P value test. For validation of the developed models and for evaluating their fitness calculation of the S-values, R-sq and adjusted R-sq value has been made for individual of each model (Cochram et al. 1977; Montgomery et al. 1997; Deb 2001). ANOVA of the bottom diameter and circularity at bottom quadratic model with other adequacy measures R^2, adjusted R^2 and predicted R^2 are shown in Table 3 and Table 4. First order, second order and interaction between different machining controlling factors have been considered to realize the effect of controlling factors on the responses. It appears quite low level of P-values and all remain to be below 0.01. Significance and adequacy of developed regression models related to all the responses appear to be necessary to predict the response values.

Figure 6 shows the combined effect of sawing angle and power setting when duty cycle, pulse frequency and scanning speed are taken at constant value 86%, 60 KHz and 0.6 mm/sec respectively. When power setting will be higher with low sawing angle bottom diameter will be lower. If sawing angle is high the kerf width will also be high. Due to high kerf width diameter deviation will be high. In low power laser when power setting value is low at bottom surface changes of re-solidification after melting will be higher. So, keeping of power at moderate value and sawing angle within moderate value to lower value will lead to less bottom diameter deviation.

The combined effect of sawing angle and scanning speed is shown in Figure 7 when power setting, duty cycle and pulse frequency are taken as constant value 37.5 watt, 86% and 60Khz respectively. If scanning speed at moderate value is on lower site along with low sawing angle bottom diameter deviation will be less. If sawing angle is low due to low offset value from top to bottom, diameter deviation will be less. In case of low scanning speed interaction time between the material and laser beam will be higher. As a result, at the time of material removal re-deposition or re-solidification will be less. So, keeping of scanning speed at moderate value and sawing angle within moderate value to lower value will lead to less bottom diameter deviation.

The combined effect of power setting and scanning speed on bottom diameter is shown in Figure 8 when sawing angle, duty cycle and pulse frequency are taken as constant value0.7°, 86% and 60 Khz respectively. As power setting will be higher from moderate value and scanning speed will be lower

Table 3. ANOVA table for bottom diameter

Source	DF	Adj. SS	Adj.MS	F-Value	P-Value
Model	20	0.013392	0.000670	84.08	0.000
Linear	5	0.008547	0.001709	214.63	0.000
A	1	0.005719	0.005719	718.15	0.000
B	1	0.002133	0.002133	267.84	0.000
C	1	0.000082	0.000082	10.23	0.003
D	1	0.000101	0.000101	12.66	0.001
E	1	0.000512	0.000512	64.28	0.000
Square	5	0.003125	0.000625	78.48	0.000
2-Way interaction	10	0.001720	0.000172	21.60	0.000
Error	31	0.000247	0.000008	-	-
Lack of fit	22	0.000195	0.000009	1.55	0.253
Pure Error	9	0.000052	0.000006	-	-
Total	51	0.013639	-	-	-
S =0.0028220, R-sq = 98.19%, R-sq (adj) = 97.02%					

from moderate value diameter deviation in the bottom will be lesser. If power setting is high at bottom surface material re-deposition will be less and if scanning speed remains to be low, interaction effect to the material will be much. Poor penetration uneven melting, uneven recast formation may influence low hole circularity. Scanning speed and power setting are the two important factors regarding the influence

Table 4. ANOVA table for hole circularity at bottom

Source	DF	Adj. SS	Adj.MS	F-Value	P-Value
Model	20	0.019336	0.000967	25.25	0.000
Linear	5	0.014294	0.002859	74.66	0.000
A	1	0.009456	0.009456	246.95	0.000
B	1	0.001575	0.001575	41.13	0.000
C	1	0.000526	0.000526	13.73	0.001
D	1	0.000442	0.000442	11.55	0.002
E	1	0.002295	0.002295	59.94	0.000
Square	5	0.003004	0.000601	15.69	0.000
2-Way interaction	10	0.002038	0.000204	5.32	0.000
Error	31	0.001187	0.000038	-	-
Lack of fit	22	0.000798	0.000036	0.84	0.651
Pure Error	9	0.000389	0.000043	-	-
Total	51	0.020523	-	-	-
S = 0.0061879, R-sq = 94.22%, R-sq (adj) = 90.48%					

Figure 6. Surface plot of bottom diameter vs. power setting and sawing angle

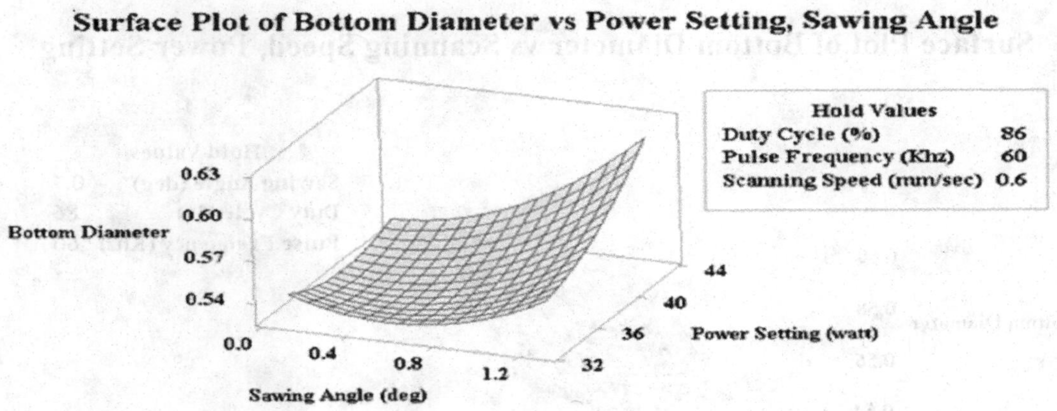

of simultaneous variation on hole circularity. So, with the increase in average power along with low value of scanning speed, bottom diameter deviation decreases.

Figure 9 shows the combined effect of sawing angle and power setting on hole circularity at bottom when duty cycle, pulse frequency and scanning speed are taken at constant value 86 %, 60 Khz and 0.6 mm/sec respectively. Alongwith the low sawing angle if power setting is high, circularity will be better. Generation of high thermal energy is made by a high-power setting, resulting in the melting and immediate vaporization of the material and it causes more disorder in the process of the material removal

Figure 7. Surface plot of bottom diameter vs. sawing angle and scanning speed

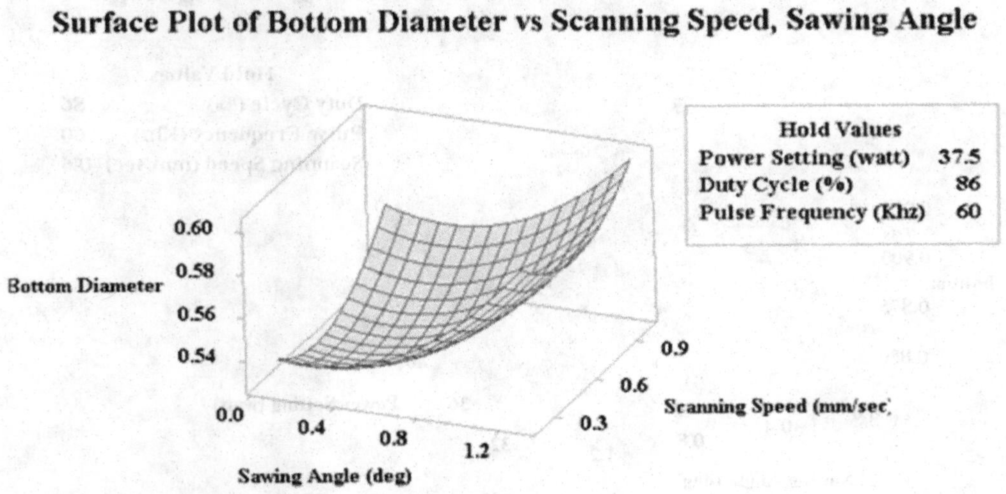

Figure 8. Surface plot of bottom diameter vs. power setting and scanning speed

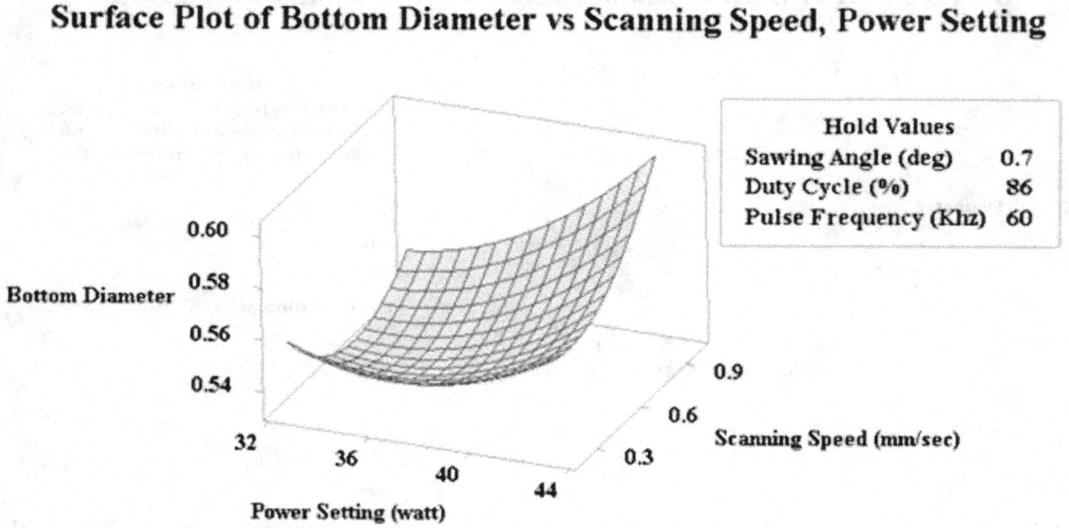

and lower circularity comes up of this. So, keeping of power setting at higher value and sawing angle at lower value will lead to high circularity at bottom surface.

Figure 9. Surface plot of hole circularity bottom vs. sawing angle, power setting

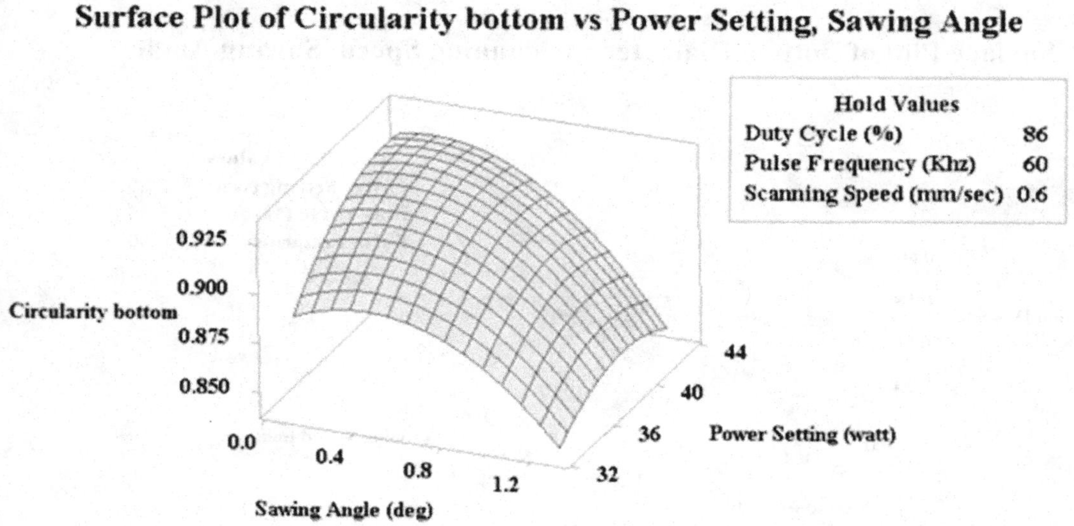

Figure 10. Surface plot of hole circularity bottom vs sawing angle, scanning speed

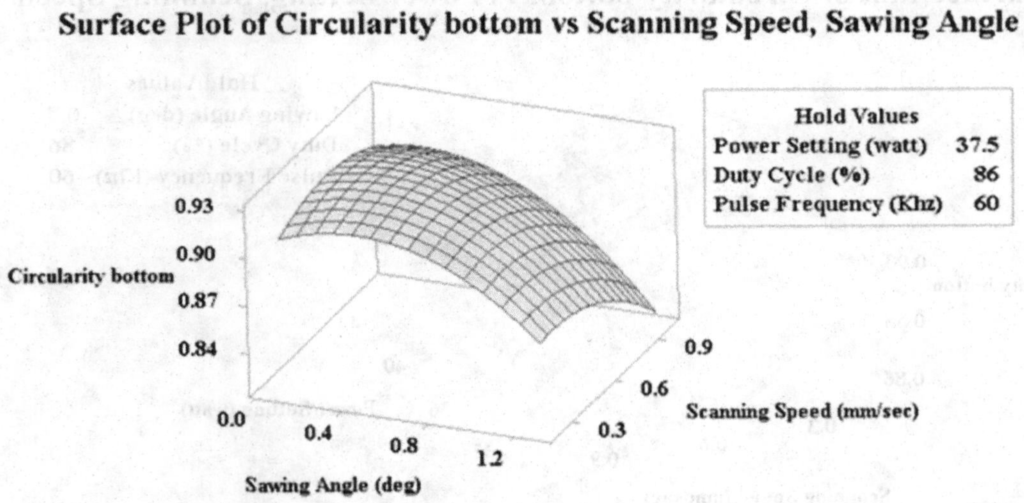

The combined effect of sawing angle and scanning speed on hole circularity at bottom is shown in Figure 10 when power setting, duty cycle and pulse frequency are taken as constant value 37.5 watt, 86% and 60Khz respectively. When sawing angle remains to be low from moderate value and scanning speed is also low, circularity will be much higher. Sawing angle increases the kerf width will also be increases and it is very hard to maintain uniform kerf width. On the additional low interaction due to high scanning speed will reason low circularity at the bottom surface.

Figure 11 shows the combined effect of scanning speed and power setting on hole circularity at bottom when sawing angle, duty cycle and pulse frequency are taken at constant value 0.7°, 86% and 60 Khz respectively. If power setting is on the higher side and scanning speed remains to be low, circularity will be higher. Poor circularity is the outcome of random heating and melting at low energy level of power. When power increases instant melting will occur and low scanning speed will lead to better circularity at bottom surface.

CONCLUSION OF OPTIMAL PROCESS PARAMETER OF BOTTOM DIAMETER

The optimization results for minimum bottom diameter and maximum circularity at bottom based on the developed mathematical model i.e. Equation 1 and Equation 2 is shown in Figure 12 and Figure 13 respectively. The value count for linear desirability function (d) remains to be 1 i.e. all input parameters are within their working limit. The parameter setting for minimum bottom diameter value has been shown to be 0.5256 mm when sawing angle 0.2212°, power setting 37.2475 watt, duty cycle 85.3333%, pulse frequency 55.2525 Khz and scanning speed 0.4343 mm/sec and maximum hole circularity at bottom

Figure 11. Surface plot of hole circularity bottom vs scanning speed, power setting

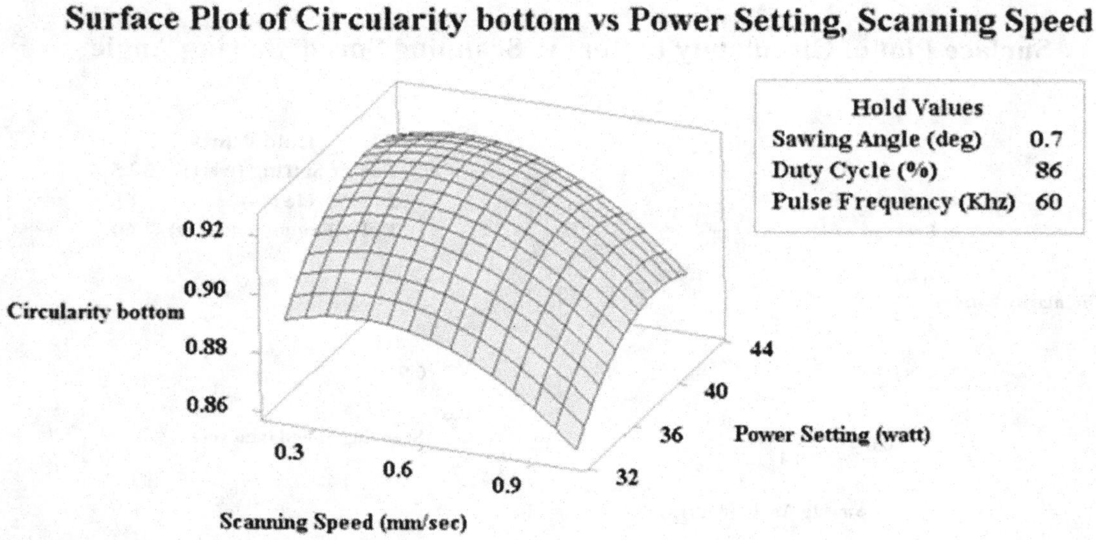

value has been shown to be 0.9654 when sawing angle 0.1375 °, power setting 42.0284 watt, duty cycle 84.1771%, pulse frequency 51.3773 Khz and scanning speed 0.3847 mm/sec.

MULTI OBJECTIVE OPTIMIZATION

Optimization method with Multi-objective deals with troubles of optimization requiring more than one objective function optimization simultaneously. Problems relating to multi objective optimization emerge in different areas like engineering, logistic, economics as optimal decisions are required to be accepted in the presence of tradeoffs between two or more opposite objectives [31]. Micro drilling operation of

Figure 12. Single objective optimization of bottom diameter

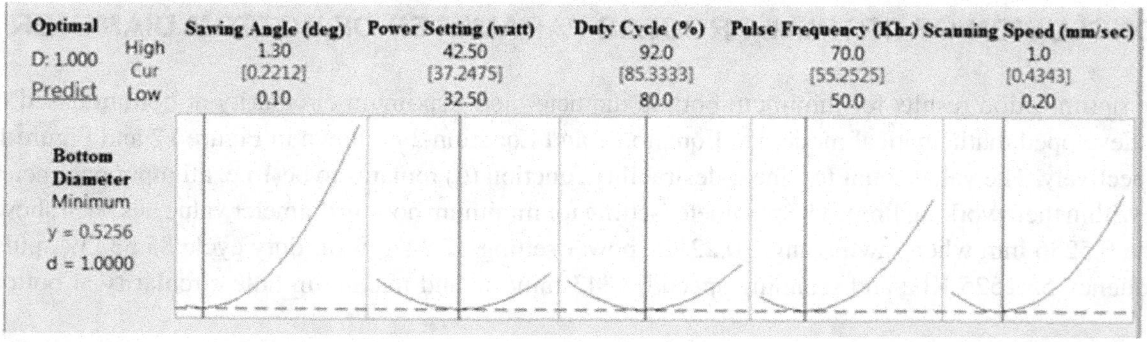

Figure 13. Single objective optimization of hole circularity at bottom

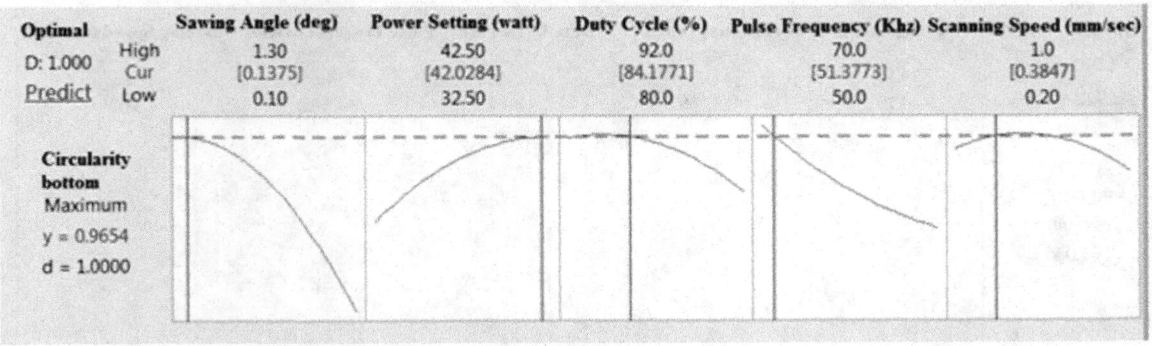

Monel k-500 alloy sheet has been performed to analyze multi response optimization and Figure 14 shows the results of optimization hole circularity bottom and bottom diameter. Optimization of two outputs has been performed together in one setting. To further confirm the intended mathematical model, a new set of experiments have been prepared according to the parameter settings i.e. sawing angle 0.10°, power setting 41.7393 watt, duty cycle 83.1515%, pulse frequency 54.8618 Khz and scanning speed 0.2566 mm/sec, obtained from the multi objective optimization result, shown in Figure 14.

CONFIRMATION TESTING

It is found from the validation experiments from Table 6 that there is a slight % of error between the predicted values and the experimental values. So, it is cleared that using the developed model form, it is relatively possible to attain the desired bottom diameter and circularity at bottom with good accuracy. Figure 15 shows the microscopic images of bottom diameter of Monel k-500 super alloy sheet.

CONCLUSION

Fiber laser trepan drilling has a great potential for generating hole on Monel K-500 alloy sheet. The present chapter mainly deals with the influence of five process parameters such as sawing angle, power setting, scanning speed, pulse frequency and duty cycle during laser micro-drilling on Monel K-500 superalloy using low power 50-watt diode pumped fiber laser. In low average power fiber laser drilling the sawing strategy remains to be very significant and attractive well-organized, helping a through drill hole by altering focal point distance or steady movement of Z axis remaining within the appropriate focusibility. The effect of the sawing angle on bottom diameter and circularity at bottom is that when the sawing angle becomes greater the kerf width will be larger accordingly and due to this deviation of diameter and circularity may appear also. Apply of an assisting gas flow for shield of the drilling section from elevated temperature oxidation reaction and purging of the molten metal from the cut section in laser drilling process.

Figure 14. Multi-objective optimization

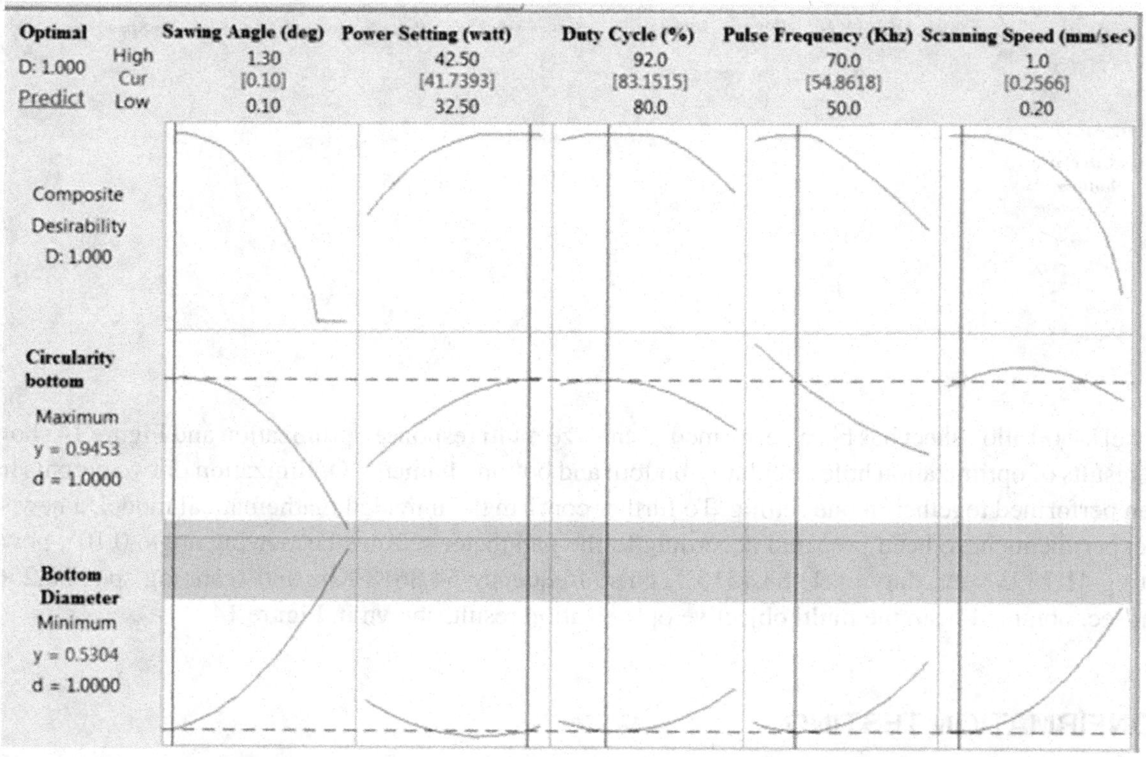

Table 6. Final confirmation experiments

Responses	Experimental results	Predicted results	% error in prediction
Minimum bottom diameter	0.5311mm	0.5256 mm	1.03%
Maximum circularity at bottom	0.9511	0.9654	1.50%
Minimum bottom diameter and maximum Circularity at bottom	0.5381 mm &0.9556	0.5304 mm & 0.9453	1.43% & 1.05%

Figure 15. Microscopic image of bottom diameter and nature of circularity

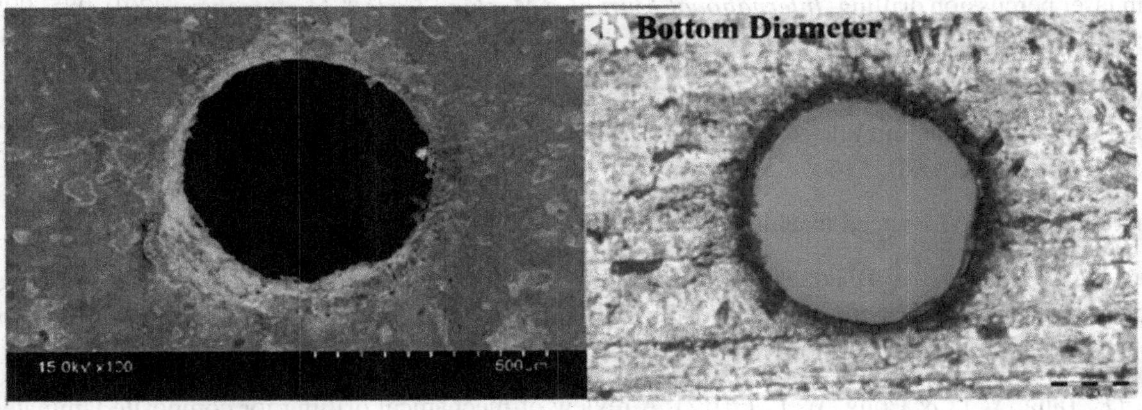

REFERENCES

Bandyopadhyay, S., Gokhale, H., Sarin Sundar, J. K., Sundararajan, G., & Joshi, S. V. (2005). A statistical approach to determine process parameter impact in Nd: YAG laser drilling of IN718 and Ti-6Al-4V sheets. *Optics and Lasers in Engineering*, *43*(2), 163–182. doi:10.1016/j.optlaseng.2004.06.013

Biffi, C. A., Lecis, N., Previtali, B., Vedani, M., & Vimercati, G. M. (2011). Fiber laser micro drilling of titanium and its effect on material microstructure. *International Journal of Advanced Manufacturing Technology*, *54*(1-4), 149–160. doi:10.100700170-010-2918-6

Biswas, R., Kuar, A. S., Biswas, S. K. S., & Mitra, S. (2010). Effects of process parameters on hole circularity and taper in pulsed Nd: YAG laser micro-drilling of TiN-Al_2O_3 composites. *Materials and Manufacturing Processes*, *25*(6), 503–514. doi:10.1080/10426910903365737

Chien, W., & Hou, S. (2007). Investigating the recast layer formed during the laser trepan drilling of inconel 718 using the taguchi method. *International Journal of Advanced Manufacturing Technology*, *33*(3-4), 308–316. doi:10.100700170-006-0454-1

Cochran, W. G., & Cox, G. M. (1977). *Experimental designs* (2nd ed.). Asia Publishing House.

Dahotre, N. B., & Harimkar, S. P. (2007). *Laser fabrication and machining of materials*. Springer.

Deb, K. (2001). *Multi-objective optimization using evolutionary algorithms* (3rd ed.). Wiley.

Dhaker, K. L., & Pandey, A. K. (2019). Particle swarm optimization of hole quality characteristics in laser trepan drilling of Inconel 718. *Defence Science Journal*, *69*(1), 37–45. doi:10.14429/dsj.69.12879

Ezugwu, E. O., Wang, Z. M., & Machado, A. R. (1999). The machinability of nickel-based alloys-A review. *Journal of Materials Processing Technology*, *86*(1-3), 1–16. doi:10.1016/S0924-0136(98)00314-8

Gautam, G. D., & Pandey, A. K. (2018). Pulsed Nd: YAG laser beam drilling: A review. *Optics & Laser Technology*, *100*, 183–215. doi:10.1016/j.optlastec.2017.09.054

Ghoreishi, M., Low, D. K. Y., & Li, L. (2002). Comparative statistical analysis of hole taper and circularity in laser percussion drilling. *International Journal of Machine Tools & Manufacture*, *42*(9), 985–995. doi:10.1016/S0890-6955(02)00038-X

Goyal, R., & Dubey, A. K. (2016). Modelling and optimization of geometrical characteristics in laser trepan drilling of titanium alloy. *Journal of Mechanical Science and Technology*, *30*(3), 1281–1293. doi:10.100712206-016-0233-3

Jain, V. K. (2005). Advanced machining processes (4th ed.). Allied Publishers Private Limited.

Kuar, A. S., Doloi, B., & Bhattacharyya, B. (2006). Modelling and analysis of pulsed Nd: YAG laser machining characteristics during micro drilling of zirconia (ZrO_2). *International Journal of Machine Tools & Manufacture*, *46*(12-13), 1301–1310. doi:10.1016/j.ijmachtools.2005.10.016

Liu, D., Tang, Y. J., & Cong, W. L. (2012). A review of mechanical drilling for composite laminates. *Composite Structures*, *94*(4), 1265–1279. doi:10.1016/j.compstruct.2011.11.024

Lopez, A. B., Assuncao, E., Quintino, L., Blackburn, J., & Khan, A. (2017). High power fiber laser cutting parameter optimization for nuclear decommissioning. *Nuclear Engineering and Technology*, *49*(4), 865–872. doi:10.1016/j.net.2017.02.004

Low, D. K. Y., Li, L., & Byrd, P. J. (2000). The effects of process parameters on spatter deposition in laser percussion drilling. *Optics & Laser Technology*, *32*(5), 347–354. doi:10.1016/S0030-3992(00)00079-7

Majumdar, J. D., & Manna, I., (2013). Introduction to laser-assisted fabrication of materials. *Laser Assisted Fabrication of Materials*, 1–67.

Marimuthu, S., Antar, M., Dunleavey, J., Chantzis, D., Darlington, E., & Hayward, P. (2017). An experimental study on quasi-CW fibre laser drilling of nickel superalloy. *Optics & Laser Technology*, *94*(1), 119–127. doi:10.1016/j.optlastec.2017.03.021

Meijer, J. (2004). Laser beam machining (LBM), State of the art and new opportunities. *Journal of Materials Processing Technology*, *149*(1-3), 2–17. doi:10.1016/j.jmatprotec.2004.02.003

Mishra, S., & Yadava, V. (2013). Modeling and optimization of laser beam percussion drilling of thin aluminum sheet. *Optics & Laser Technology*, *48*, 461–474. doi:10.1016/j.optlastec.2012.10.035

Montgomery, D. C. (1997). *Design and analysis of experiments* (4th ed.). Wiley.

Okasha, M.M., Mativenga, P.T., Driver, N., & Li, L. (2010). Sequential laser and mechanical micro drilling of Ni superalloy for aerospace application. *CIRP Annals - Manufacturing Technology*, *59*(1), 199-202.

Pramanik, D., Das, S., Sarkar, S., Debnath, S.K., Kuar, A.S., & Mitra, S. (2018). Experimental investigation of fiber laser micro marking on aluminium 6061 alloy. *Advances in Materials Mechanical and Industrial Engineering,* 273–294.

Pramanik, D., Goswami, S., Kuar, A. S., Sarkar, S., & Mitra, S. (2019). A parametric study of kerf deviation in fiber laser micro cutting on Ti6Al4V superalloy. *Materials Today: Proceedings*, *18*, 3348–3356. doi:10.1016/j.matpr.2019.07.257

Roy, N., Kuar, A. S., Mitra, S., & Acherjee, B. (2015). Nd: YAG laser micro drilling of Sic-30 BN Nanocomposite: experimental study and process optimization, *Laser Based Manufacturing*. In *Topics in Mining, Metallurgy and Materials Engineering* (pp. 317–341). Springer.

Sharma, S., Mandal, V., Ramakrishna, S. A., & Ramkumar, J. (2018). Numerical simulation of melt hydrodynamics induced hole blockage in Quasi- CW fiber laser micro-drilling of TiAl6V4. *Journal of Materials Processing Technology*, *262*, 131–148. doi:10.1016/j.jmatprotec.2018.06.038

Yilbas, B. S. (1997). Parametric study to improve laser hole drilling process. *Journal of Materials Processing Technology*, *70*(1-3), 264–273. doi:10.1016/S0924-0136(97)00076-9

Yilbas, B. S. (2013). *Laser drilling-practical applications, manufacturing and surface engineering*. Springer.

Yilbas, B. S., Akhtar, S. S., & Karatas, C. (2011). Laser trepanning of a small diameter hole in titanium alloy: Temperature and stress fields. *Journal of Materials Processing Technology*, *211*(7), 1296–1304. doi:10.1016/j.jmatprotec.2011.02.012

Yilbas, B. S., & Aleem, A. (2004). Laser hole drilling quality and efficiency assessment. *Proceedings of the Institution of Mechanical Engineers. Part B, Journal of Engineering Manufacture*, *18*(2), 225–233. doi:10.1243/095440504322886541

Yilbas, B. S., Shaukat, M. M., & Ashraf, F. (2017). Laser cutting of various materials: Kerf width size analysis and life cycle assessment of cutting process. *Optics & Laser Technology*, *93*(1), 67–73. doi:10.1016/j.optlastec.2017.02.014

Chapter 10
Experimental Investigation on Laser Transmission Welding of Polycarbonate and Acrylic

Dhiraj Kumar
Jadavpur University, India

Sudipta Paitandi
Jadavpur University, India

Arunanshu Shekhar Kuar
Jadavpur University, India

Dipankar Bose
National Institute of Technical Teachers' Training and Research (NITTTR), Kolkata, India

ABSTRACT

This chapter presents the effect of various process parameters, namely laser power, pulse frequency, and welding speed, on the weld shear strength and weld width using a diode laser system. Here, laser transmission welding of transparent polycarbonate and black carbon filled acrylic each of 2.8 mm thickness have been performed to create lap joint by using low power laser. Response surface methodology is applied to develop the mathematical model between the laser welding process parameters and the responses of weld joint. The developed mathematical model is tested for its adequacy using analysis of variance and other adequacy measures. It has been observed that laser power and welding speed are the dominant factor followed by frequency. A confirmation test has also been conducted to validate the experimental results at optimum parameter setting. Results show that weld strength of 34.3173 N/mm and weld width of 2.61547 mm have been achieved at optimum parameter setting using desirability function-based optimization technique.

DOI: 10.4018/978-1-7998-3624-7.ch010

INTRODUCTION

The use of lasers for industrial, scientific and medical applications has gained tremendous attention because of the beneficial ability to control precise heat transfer parameters. Laser-material processing has been introduced for various applications in flexible electronics, processors, displays, and other peripheral electronic components, in order to overcome temperature problems with plastic substrates (J. J. Daniel et al., 2017). Numerous efforts have been made to implement lasers in advanced electronic processing. Laser stands for Light Amplification by Stimulated Emission of Radiation. It is a device that emits amplified light from an emitting source by stimulating photon emission. Lasers have played an important role in the joining of materials since the advent of high-power gas and solid-state lasers. Innovative developments over the past decade have been the subject of diode lasers and diode pumped solid state lasers. For materials processing applications, the latest diode pumped fiber lasers have been developed with attractive features (L. Quintino et al., 2007).

Plastics have been the fast-growing basic material. The applications of plastics are essentially limitless. Now a days, plastics are replacing metals and non-metals in certain applications due to its light-weight, flexibility, weather-resistance, strong and relatively inexpensive. Major applications have been found for plastics in the aerospace, adhesives, coating, construction, electrical, electronic, medical, packaging, textile, household products and automotive industries. The everincreasing demand for plastic products and the widespread use in both technologically advanced fields and everyday life require new methods that are more versatile, quicker and environmental friendly. As a new alternative to meeting these requirements, laser processing of plastic materials is emerging. Laser transmission welding provides an attractive alternative to defeat the limits of traditional plastic joining technologies. With the more common use of plastic components, joining techniques play an important role in their production. Since it is not always feasible or cost-effective to produce the complex plastic components in one piece, various joining techniques have been developed over the years. It is possible to split the joining of plastic materials and their composites into mechanical fastening and bonding. Therefore, bonding can be categorized as adhesive bonding, solvent bonding, and welding. Mechanical fastening and adhesive bonding can be used for joining all materials. On the other hand, welding allowing the materials to melt at the joint interface is only applicable to thermoplastics as it is not possible to melt thermosets. This process's versatility is second to none and the weld quality is better than most other plastic joining techniques. The flexibility of Laser allowed plastic welding techniques to be replaced based on ultrasonic energy, friction, vibration, electrical resistance and hot tool. The gradual replacement of conventional tools by Laser in welding in plastics industries can be justified by process reproducibility, process simplicity, decreased rejection rate, and productivity increase. The fundamental principle of the method of transmission laser welding is to pass or transmit laser radiation through one piece of plastic to create a weld. Unlike standard welding, where the energy is applied to the surface of the materials, the purpose of transmission welding is to apply the energy at their interface between two plastic parts.

Laser beams can be used for welding plastics by transmitting a laser beam through a laser transmitting material and welding at the laser absorbing material interface. In laser transmission welding, a laser beam is aimed at two overlapping thermoplastic pieces with different optical properties. The first part is designed to be transparent to the laser wavelength and the second part is designed to absorb the radiation. Based on the thickness and absorption coefficient of the absorbing component, the transmitted energy is absorbed over a certain depth of a surface and converted to heat. In this way, the heat generated is transported to the transparent portion. Consequently, at the joining interface, both pieces are melted and result in a solid joint as a weld seam. The laser source of 0.8-1.1 μm wavelength is used for the transmission laser welding, as plastics have high transmittance at this wavelength range. Fig. 1 shows the operation of through transmission laser welding.

Figure 1. operation of laser transmission welding

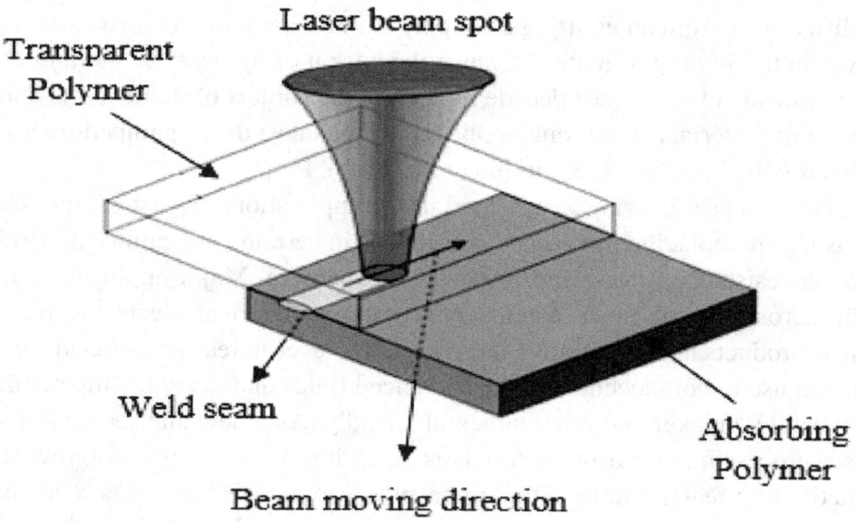

Laser transmission welding of polymer for large industrial applications is at an emerging stage. However, several applications have already been adapted into industrial production. At present, many industries are investigating this process to replace conventional plastic joining processes. Laser transmission welding is now being used in a wide range of applications such as Automotive Sensor housings, Lighting systems, Fluid control. There is also a continuous growth in the use of a laser transmission welding technique in the manufacture of micro parts such as joining of micro fluid devices. In most of their applications, the electronics and medical devices industry requires micro-assembly of dissimilar materials. The joining process should not use any third material that is not bio-compatible when joining biomedical products. The laser transmission welding process meets this condition. The laser transmission welding is a non-contact process and does not result in damage in the usable areas of the biomedical products. Laser transmission welding process is now used to join biomedical implants and for encapsulation of biomedical devices due to its high precision and biocompatibility property. Joining process need to keep pace with the development of new materials. Lasers play a vital role in joining of materials. Diode lasers and diode pumped solid state laser are being used since last decade. Recently, diode pump fiber lasers with innovative characteristic for materials processing is being used. A core of fiber doped with rare-earth is used as an active medium of a fiber laser.

The simultaneous optimization of through transmission laser welding of transparent acrylic and 0.2% black carbon filled acrylic has been performed. Grey relational analysis with the taguchi method have been applied to solve the problem of multi-criteria optimization in TTLW. Grey relational analysis changes the multiple quality characteristics into grey relational grade (B. Acherjee et al., 2011). The taguchi method gives the optimal welding condition by using the grey relational grade. The welding process parameters are optimized with respect to response. It has been observed that this optimization technique simplifies the process of optimization. The microstructure of the laser transmission welding of polypropylene has been studied. The thermal effect on weld width of welded polypropylene (semi-crystalline polymer) has also been observed (S. Abed et al., 2001). Optical penetration depth decreases with an increase in additive contents in absorbing material which also affects the shape of the weld seam. A thin skin layer and bulk pp material can be seen in the microstructure. Melt zone shows a transition between initial material and heat affected zone which bound by shell structure. The absorption coefficient (apparent) and Bouguer Lambert law are used to define the laser energy reduction in scattering polymers with or without black carbon through transmission laser welding of thermoplastics. Experimentally, a linear relationship has been found between the absorption coefficient and black carbon for PA6GF, PC and PA6 (M. chen et al., 2011). This model has been validated using measured transmittance which is a function of part thickness. It has been seen that laser energy is diminished more quickly in PA6GF than in PA6 for the same black carbon content. This happens because of the higher density and light scattering by glass fibers. The absorption coefficient of PC is higher than that of PA6 for the same black carbon due to higher density. The influence of carbon black (CB) on weld profile and temperature distribution during transmission laser welding of polymers has been investigated (B. Acherjee et al., 2012). The Gaussian heat source is assumed as only heat input to this model. The finite element is used to calculate the numerical results, then the numerical results of weld pool dimensions are compared to that of theoretical results. It has been found out that weld width and molten ratio increases with the CB of absorbing polymers. Weld geometry is asymmetric with a lesser amount of carbon black content. The influence of glass fiber and crystallinity during transmission laser welding of thermoplastics have been observed (X.F. Xu et al., 2015). It can be concluded from the results that a linear relationship between absorption coefficients (apparent) and the volume fraction of glass fiber of reinforced polymers have been established. Crystallinity increases the backscattering that leads to an increment of apparent reflection. It has been found out that the absorption coefficient is a material-dependent parameter. It has been investigated that the absorption coefficient initially declines and then rises for all glass-fiber reinforced materials.

Through transmission laser welding of dissimilar thermoplastic materials such as ABS and PMMA have been performed to see the effect of process parameters on responses (B. Acherjee et al., 2012). RSM has been used for the design of experiments and multi-objective optimization based on desirability function have been used to optimize the responses. RSM has different features such as orthogonality, rotatabilty and uniformity (uniform precision) for which it is being widely used. Orthogonality allows the model equation with minimal variance estimates. Several surface response problems deal with analyzing various responses. The laser heat input is responsible for fractional decomposition and overheating of the material which also controls the weld strength and quality of the weld. Lesser the heat input results in a lack of fusion. Standoff distance is the dominant parameter followed by laser power and speed. There is always a challenging to join two dissimilar thermoplastic materials which are not soluble to each other. The concept of the intermediate material comes into the role to increase the solubility of two dissimilar thermoplastic materials. Through transmission laser welding has been performed between PMMA and PBT using polycarbonate (PC) as intermediate material for increment of weld strength (X. Wang et al., 2016). It has been found out that weld strength increases four times with an only insertion of intermediate material as a comparison to without the use of intermediate material. The reason behind the increment of weld strength is observed from the micro morphology of the weld region that bubble formation can be used to form micro mechanical riveting. The equilibrium interfacial width also plays an important role for the development of weld strength. Laser transmission spot welding of PMMA materials has been investigated by Nd: YAG pulse laser (X. Wang et. al., 2017). The effect of different process parameters such as defocusing distance, peak voltages and the welding type on responses have been observed. The bubble forms during the welding produce a micro anchor between upper and lower layer which improves the welding strength. It can be seen that weld pool diameter to depth ratio greatly influences the joint quality. The geometry and microstructure of the welded zone of polypropylene have been investigated through transmission laser welding (E. Ghorbel et al., 2009). It can be observed from the microscopic observation that increment of laser power and reduction of scanning speed results in a greater volume of weld zone with a depth penetration. The Elliptic type of structure is generated in the weld area. Thermal degradation of polypropylene occurs due to unsystematic chain scission. The outcomes show that both optical properties of absorbing polymer and process parameter have a larger impact on weld seam width. When the correct laser intensity, the right amount of energy and correct laser parameters are applied then good joint quality can be produced (J. Brodhun et al., 2018). By adjusting the proper amount of laser energy and intensity, the resin layer is removed from the joining zone without suddenly evaporating the resin. However, it has been observed that low laser intensity leads to weakening the joint. The problem of joining optical transparent thermoplastic materials might occurs due to unmeant coloration (M. Devrient et al., 2011). This is because of the thermoplastic material are doped with different absorbers. Therefore, an approach has been made to investigate the joint strength without using absorber. It has been observed that transparent materials can be joined using short focusing length, feed speed, and focal dislocations to the joining plane.

Desirability function based optimization technique has been applied to optimize the weld strength and weld width through transmission laser welding of thermoplastic materials (B. Acherjee et al., 2009) Increment of laser power and drop in scanning speed give the optimize responses. It has been observed that line energy increases the weld width until its maximum limit. The optimization of the hardness, depth of hardness and ferrite percentage of laser hardening process has been performed to achieve the best optimal parameter by desirability approach (M. Moradi et al., 2020). Different metaheuristic optimization technique along with desirability approach has been developed. Grey wolf optimization is a recent popular technique which works on leadership hierarchy and hunting process. A cricket algorithm has been recently introduced in which good features of few swarm intelligence based optimization technique have been incorporated (S. Datta et al., 2020). Desirability function approach works on the basis of reduced gradient algorithm. Beginning with multiple solutions, eventually it achieves the maximum desirability to choose the optimal solution. RSM designs statistical prediction models for MRR and SR. It is used to model the performance measures of material removal rate and surface roughness (M.S. Rao et al., 2015). It has been investigated that Artificial bee colony algorithm is most recent swarm-based algorithms. The experiment result shows that the response of ABC is better than other algorithms such as PSO algorithm, genetic algorithm differential evolution algorithm and evolution strategies with the advantage of employing fewer control parameters (D. Karaboga et al., 2009). The desirability approach has been used to find the optimum process parameter settings. Artificial neural network and response surface methodology have been compared and correlated (N. Sivagurumanikandan et al., 2018). The desirability approach has been found the suitable optimization technique to obtain the weld bead profile.

It is revealed from the literature survey that research has been done to a large extent in the area of transmission laser welding of thermoplastics. There is a few literatures covering the through transmission laser welding of two dissimilar thermoplastics. To the best knowledge of the author, very few investigations has been done in the area of laser transmission welding of transparent polycarbonate and black carbon filled acrylic by low power laser. It is always challenging to join two dissimilar thermoplastic materials. The problem happens such as that the materials to be joined must have similar melting temperatures, joining member must be soluble with each other in order to permit diffusion of melts. In the present experimental work, an attempt has been made to join polycarbonate and acrylic.

METHODOLOGY

Response Surface Methodology (RSM) is a statistical technique which is used for empirical model building and analysis of problems in which a response of interest is concerned and determined by a number of input variables. By the use of design of the experiment, the key objective is to enhance the output parameter which is influenced by many independent variables. Design of experiment and multi-regression techniques are joined through this technique. RSM establishes the relationship between several input variables and output variables. The main clue of RSM is to choose a design of experiment to achieve a response parameter. In the present work, RSM has been used for the design of experiments and to model the responses in terms of process parameters. A central composite full factorial unblocked design with three continuous factors P (power), frequency (F) and scanning speed (S) have been used for modeling of DOE. As a linear model is not found to be suitable for this process therefore a quadratic polynomial regression equation has been used as shown in equation (1).

$$y = a_0 + \sum_{i-1}^{n} a_i x_i + \sum_{i-1}^{n} a_{ii} x_i^2 + \sum_{i<j}^{n} a_{ij} x_i x_j + \in \quad (1)$$

Where,

y = f (P, F, S)

Here y is the desired response and f is the output function.

x_i and x_j are the design variables

n is the number of an independent process variable

a_0 is the constant in the regression model

a_i is the linear effect of x_i

a_{ii} is the quadratic effect of x_i

a_{ij} is the line to line interaction between x_i and x_j

$\in$ is the response error

ANOVA has been applied after the experiments as per the design of experiment. It has provided information regarding the significance of the parameters and their contribution to the obtained responses. A regression equation has also been generated.

DESIRABILITY FUNCTION BASED OPTIMIZATION

Derringer and Suich intoduced desirability function based optimization method in 1980 (G. Derringer et al., 1980). A desirability function approach is broadly used in multi objective optimization because of its simplicity. All the qualitative and quantitative responses need to be optimized simultaneously in order to enhance quality of the product. The response parameters are typically influenced by the setting combination of input variables. In order to optimize all response parameters, it is therefore important to choose the best selection of input process variables. This approach deals with the solving multi objective optimization problems by combining multiple response in to dimensionless performance measurement, called Overall Desirability function. It is a process in which each response is translated into the corresponding values of desirability. The variability of the response variables is considered to be constant. Desirability value depends on appropriately tolerance range and target response. When responses reach their target value, then unity value is assigned which is the best desired situation. Desirability value is assumed to be zero beyond a certain range. The response variable's desirability function value (D) is increased by moving the response to the targeted output condition. The desirability function condenses the problem of multivariate optimization into one univariate. The ability to plot D as a function of one or more independent variables is an added advantage of the process In the present analysis, individual desirability function contains one of the following two characteristics:-

For maximization of Goal, the desirability (d_i) can be defined as,

$0 \quad ;if\ response(y_i) \leq lowvalue(L_i)$

978-1-7998-3624-7. ch010.m14

$D_i =$

978-1-7998-3624-7. ch010.m15

For minimization of Goal, the desirability (d_i) can be defined as,

978-1-7998-3624-7.ch010.m16

978-1-7998-3624-7.ch010.m17

$D_i =$

978-1-7998-3624-7.ch010.m18

For maximization of Goal, the desirability (d_i) can be defined as, w stands for weight and it can be allotted to a goal to emphasize the particular desirability function. The importance of weight can vary from 0.1 to 10. When weight is greater than 1 it gives the goal more pressure when weight less than 1 places less focus on the goal.

The objective desirability function, D, is the geometric mean (GM) of each individual responses:

978-1-7998-3624-7.ch010.m19

This single value of D provides an overall evaluation of the desirability of the combined level of response. The range of D clearly varies from 0 to 1 and it rises as the balance of properties becomes more favorable. If any one of the response variable is unaccepted ($d_i = 0$), then overall product is unacceptable i.e. D = 0. This is why the geometric mean is used in this method unlike other method. Here n gives the number of responses in the measure. Each response can be consigned importance relative to other responses. Importance (r_i) values vary from 1, the least important to 5, the most important. Some responses may be critical (5); while some may be of medium importance (3) and some are of the lowest importance (1). Higher value of D indicates more desirable and greatest function of the system (M. Ragavendran et al., 2017). Optimum parameters are determined from the individual desirability function (d) which maximizes the overall desirability objective function.

EXPERIMENTATION ON LASER TRANSMISSION WELDING OF DISSIMILAR THERMOPLASTIC: A CASE STUDY

An electrox EMS 100 raptor laser system has been used in the present research work. The Nd:YVO_4 (Neodymium doped yttrium orthovanadate) laser with 1064 nm wavelength, the average power of 9.28W and continuous wave have been used for transmission laser welding of thermoplastics in Fig. 2. It works by its own control unit and computer interface. The computer interface contains a software name marker comsol, by which the laser unit is operated. When the main power supply of the laser unit and the control unit are switched ON, the control unit establishes a communication to computer interface via the marker comsol software.

Figure 2. Photographic view of Experimental setup

LASER SYSTEM

The Laser produces a monochromatic light of high intensity beam at the wavelength of 1064 nm. Light is properly focused through a lens and it has adequate power to vaporize materials or change the thermal and mechanical characteristics of the material. The light beam is steered by two motorized moving mirrors which is controlled by a computer. Raptor laser system contains laser enclosure and scanning system, controller and control unit. The units are interconnected by fiber optics and cable which give light, power and data communications. Laser enclosure and the control unit are in Fig. 3.

LASER SPECIFICATIONS

Laser type Q-switched, solid state.

- Wavelength 1064±4nm
- Peak laser power > 10kW
- Pulse energy > 0.2mJ
- Beam diameter 0.8 – 1.2mm
- Beam divergence <2 mrad
- Q-switch pulse frequency 0.1 – 250kHz and CW.

Figure 3. Pictorial view of (A) raptor laser enclosure and, (B) laser control unit

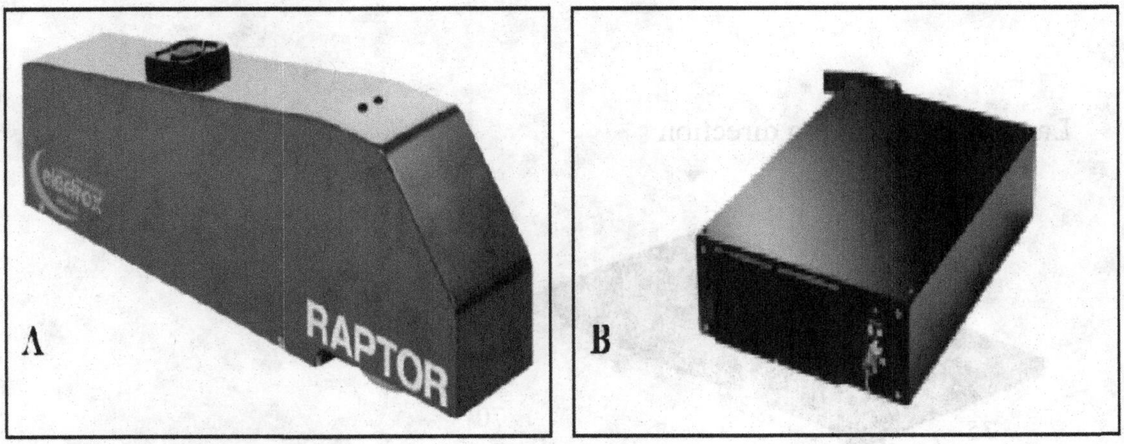

Pulse width 24-100ns

LASER CONTROL SYSTEM

Raptor laser consists of a central processing unit (CPU) that controls the laser function. It is inside the control unit with other electronics. The control units comprise the following electric modules:

Diode laser power supply, Q-switch power supply, Auxiliary power supplies, DSP (Laser beam scanner) PCB, CPU PCB, Laser Interface PCB, I/O PCB (interface PCB), Fiber-coupled laser diode.

EXPERIMENTAL PROCEDURE

A transparent polycarbonate and black carbon filled acrylic plates each of size 70 mm x 35mm x 2.8mm are used in this experimental work. A transparent polycarbonate is used as the upper part while black carbon filled acrylic is placed on the bottom part to perform the transmission laser welding. Black carbon filled acrylic absorbs the laser and after that melting and vaporization happen. A lap joint is created with an overlap area of 20 mm. The laser beam has scanned the middle of the overlap length in Fig. 4.

Acrylic is useful plastic that looks like glass, but it has severe properties which makes it different to glass in many ways. It is used in bath enclosures, door, windows skylights and to make various products. Polycarbonate is a clear, colorless polymer, having high strength, toughness, heat resistance and excellent dimensional stability, which is used extensively for engineering and optical applications.

LEXAN is its most popular trade name. PC is one of the high-performance polymeric heterochain materials comprising the thermoplastics engineering family. Not only because of its qualities but also because its manufacturing is environmentally friendly and it can be recycled, PC is a great material option in the industry. The workpiece material which needs to be joined in Fig. 5.

Figure 4. Weld lap joint configuration

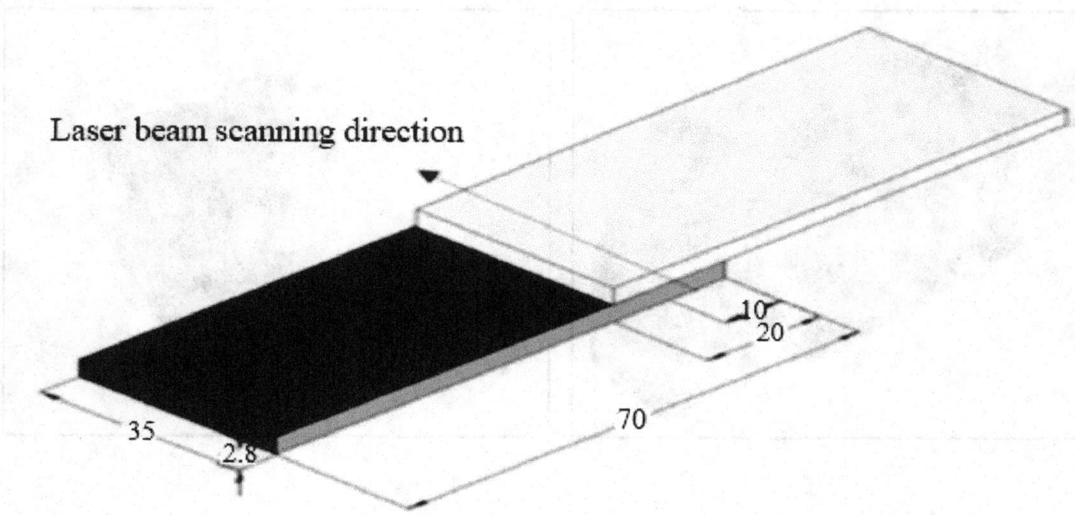

After trial and error experiment, literature survey and machine constraint, the working range is decided by inspecting the weld seam width for smooth appearance in Table 1.

TEST PROCEDURES

An Instron universal tensile testing machine is used for lap shear test of laser welded sample. It is performed to determine the joint strength. The specimen is labelled approximately 25 mm from the weld centerline before pulling the test and the end of the grips is matched with these markings. There is some adjustment to the sample. To avoid bending moments in Fig. 6, two plastic sheets measuring 35mm×35mm×2.8mm are pasted with each specimen, thus, the weld is close to the pulling path centerline. After that, each specimen is roughened to avoid slip during the lap-shear test on both sides of two ends. Mitutoyo Tool maker's microscope is used to measure the weld width of all welded-samples with an accuracy of 0.005mm. The average weld strength and weld width of at least three tests are taken and considered for analysis.

RESULTS AND DISCUSSION

Development of Mathematical Models

Design expert v17 software has been used for the analysis of output and estimating the mathematical models. The suitability of the model is tested using the ANOVA technique. Fig. 7 represents the graphical illustration of experimental results.

Figure 5. Photographic view of work material (A) Acrylic (B) Polycarbonate

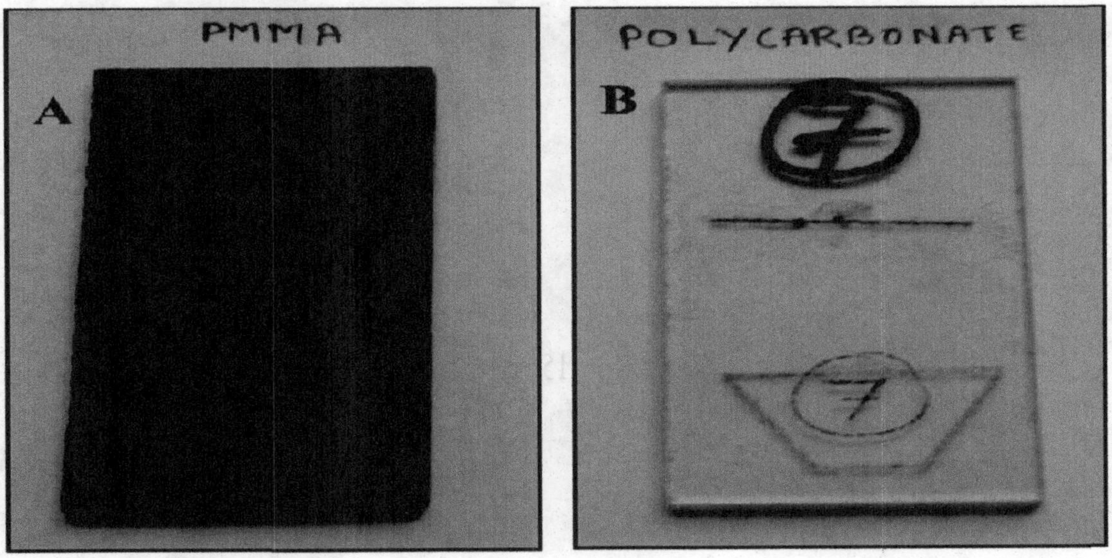

Analysis of Weld Shear Strength

The fit for weld strength proposes the quadratic model and the model is not aliased. ANOVA has been analyzed to see the influence of each parameter on weld shear strength. The model having a p-value of less than 0.05 (i.e. 95% confidence level) is considered significant parameter. Since the p-value of interaction of power on frequency is 0.705, thus, it is considered insignificant parameter and it does not impact much on weld strength. Therefore, in order to improve model accuracy, it is eliminated by the backward elimination process. P-value of lack of fit shows its insignificance model, which is desirable. ANOVA for shear strength is in Table 2. The final regression equation generated from the mathematical model is given in equation 2.

Table 1. Process parameter and their ranges

Parameter	Symbol	Units	Levels				
			-1.68179	-1	0	+1	+1.68179
Laser Power	P	W (%)	51.5910	55	60	65	68.409
Welding Speed	S	mm/min.	0.15910	0.5	1	1.5	1.84089
Frequency	F	kHz	18.2955	20	22.5	25	26.7044

Figure 6. Diagram of welded sample used for lap shear test

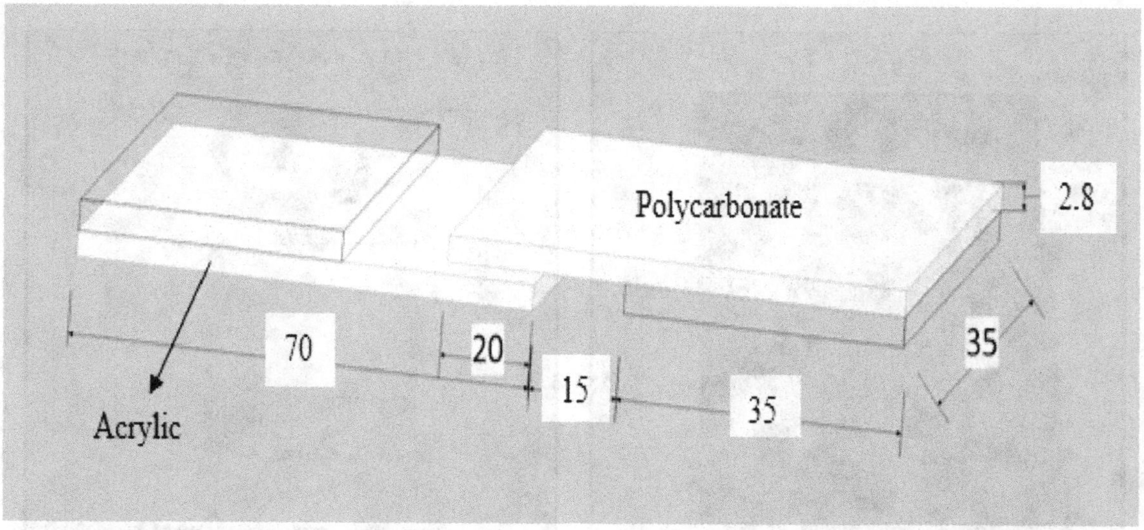

Analysis of Weld Seam Width

The fit for weld width proposes the quadratic model and the model is not aliased. ANOVA has been analyzed to see the influence of each parameter on weld seam width. The model having a p-value of less than 0.05 (i.e. 95% confidence level) is considered significant parameter. Since p-value of interaction of frequency on scanning speed is 0.219, thus, it is considered an insignificant parameter and it does not impact much on weld width. Therefore, in order to improve model accuracy, it is eliminated by the backward elimination process. P-value of lack of fit shows its insignificance model, which is desirable. ANOVA for weld width is in Table 3. The final regression equation generated from the mathematical model is given in equation 3.

Effect of Process Parameter on Weld Shear Strength

Fig. 8 shows weld shear strength interaction with laser power and scanning speed. It is evident from the figure that welding or scanning speed has a negative effect on weld shear strength. This happens because heat diffusion and deposition of energy into the material depends on the time of irradiation and the density of power. Higher scanning speed decreases the irradiation time, causes less heat input to the weld zone, resulting in less material being melted, resulting in decreased weld strength. Laser power has also been found to have a positive impact on weld strength. The reason for the positive effect is that higher laser power increases the input of laser heat to the material, increases the melting area and increases the weld shear strength. It can be clearly observed from the figure that weld strength tends to maximum when laser power is maximum and scanning speed is minimum. This is due to the increased laser power and lower scanning speed that increases the line energy and thus increases the bond strength. Line energy, described as laser heat energy per unit length, is basically defined as the ratio of laser power to the scanning speed.

Figure 7. Graphical illustration of experimental results

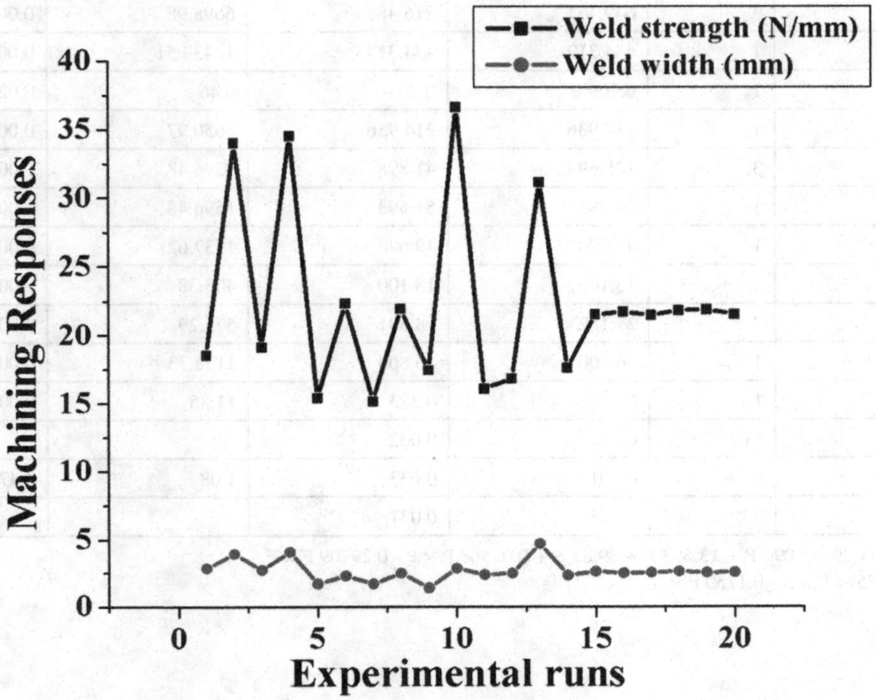

Fig. 9 shows weld shear strength interaction with scanning speed and frequency. It is evident from the figure that weld shear strength is maximum at low scanning speed and at F = 22 kHz. This happens due to the fact that losses in heat conduction have a higher impact at low speed. At a high value of welding speed, the heat loss is minimal because there is less heat dissipation time available. Higher scanning speed decreases the irradiation time, causes less heat input to the weld zone, and thus weld shear strength decreases. Too low frequency tends to narrow the laser beam, causing less amount of laser energy deposition whereas too high frequency spread the laser beam. Here welding speed is most dominant parameter.

Effect of Process Parameter on Weld Seam Width

Fig. 10 shows weld seam width interaction with laser power and scanning speed. The weld width is maximum at high value of laser power and low value of welding speed. It is evident from the result that welding speed has a negative effect on weld seam width. This is because increased welding speed decreases irradiation time and allows less heat to be supplied with reduced molten volume resulting in narrow and weak weld formation. It can also be observed that weld width increases with laser power, as higher laser power melts the large amount of base material, thus increasing the weld zone width.

Table 2. ANOVA Table for weld strength

Source	DF	Adj. SS	Adj. MS	F-value	P-value
Model	8	811.921	101.490	3140.51	0.000
Linear	3	649.461	216.487	6698.98	0.000
P	1	434.317	434.317	13439.51	0.000
F	1	0.209	0.209	6.46	0.027
S	1	214.936	214.936	6650.97	0.000
Square	3	125.693	41.898	1296.48	0.000
P × P	1	51.593	51.593	1596.48	0.000
F × F	1	49.690	49.690	1537.62	0.000
S × S	1	13.100	13.100	405.38	0.000
2-way interaction	2	37.182	18.591	575.29	0.000
P × S	1	36.800	36.800	1138.73	0.000
F × S	1	0.383	0.383	11.85	0.006
Error	11	0.355	0.032		
Lack-of-fit	6	0.201	0.033	1.08	0.476
Pure error	5	0.155	0.031		

Weld Strength = 31.29 – 7.096 P + 13.593 F + 39.85 S + 0.07568 P × P - 0.29709 F × F + 3.817 S × S- 0.8579 P × S - 0.1750 F × S

Table 3. ANOVA Table for weld width

Source	DF	Adj. SS	Adj. MS	F-value	P-value
Model	8	12.1525	1.51906	580.99	0.000
Linear	3	9.6669	3.22230	1232.42	0.000
P	1	2.9463	2.94631	1126.87	0.000
F	1	0.0141	0.01410	5.39	0.040
S	1	6.7065	6.70649	2565.01	0.000
Square	3	2.3176	0.77253	295.47	0.000
P × P	1	0.3109	0.31094	118.93	0.000
F × F	1	0.0240	0.02403	9.19	0.011
S × S	1	1.7851	1.78513	682.75	0.000
2-way interaction	2	0.1750	0.08751	33.47	0.000
P × F	1	0.0272	0.02721	10.41	0.008
P × S	1	0.1478	0.14781	56.53	0.000
Error	11	0.0288	0.00261		
Lack-of-fit	6	0.0160	0.00267	1.05	0.490
Pure error	5	0.0127	0.00255		

Weld Width = -21.95 + 0.7473 P + 0.027 F – 0.956 S – 0.005875 P × P - 0.00653 F × F + 1.4089 S × S + 0.00467 P × F - 0.05437 P × S

Figure 8. Surface interaction plot of P and S on the weld strength

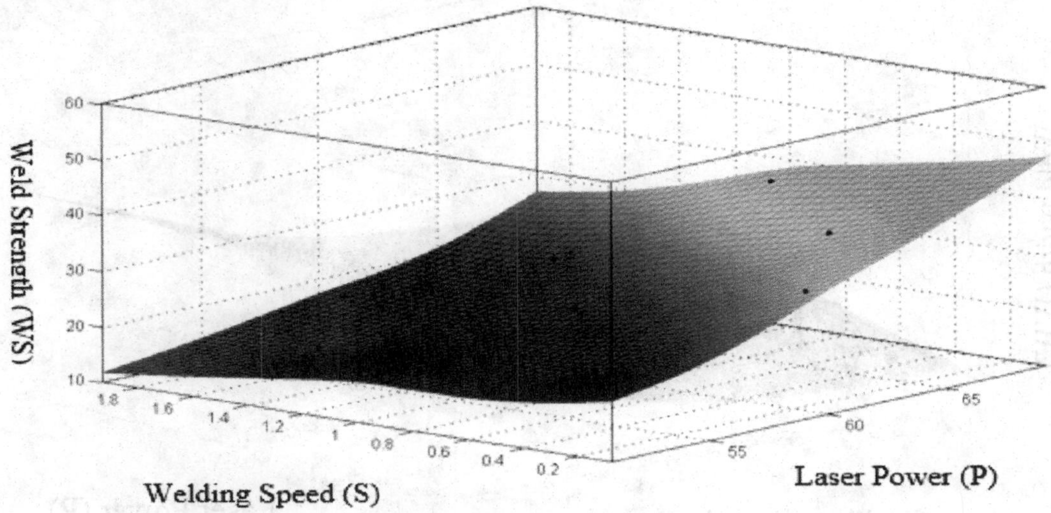

Fig. 11 shows weld seam width interaction with scanning speed and frequency. It is revealed from the figure that weld width tends to the maximum at a low value of welding speed and F = 22 kHz. This

Figure 9. Surface interaction plot of F and S on the weld strength

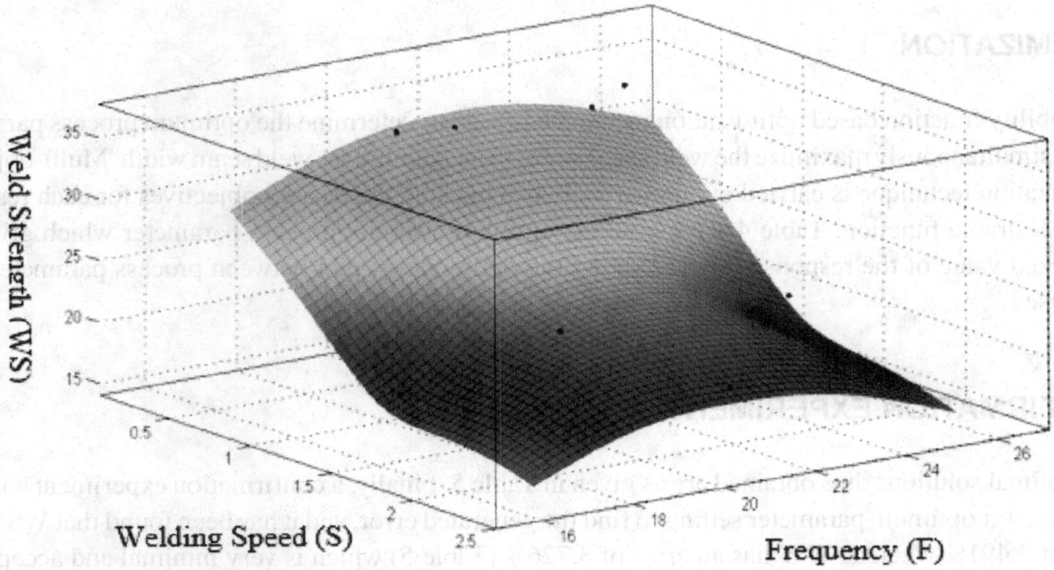

Figure 10. Surface interaction plot of P and S on the weld width

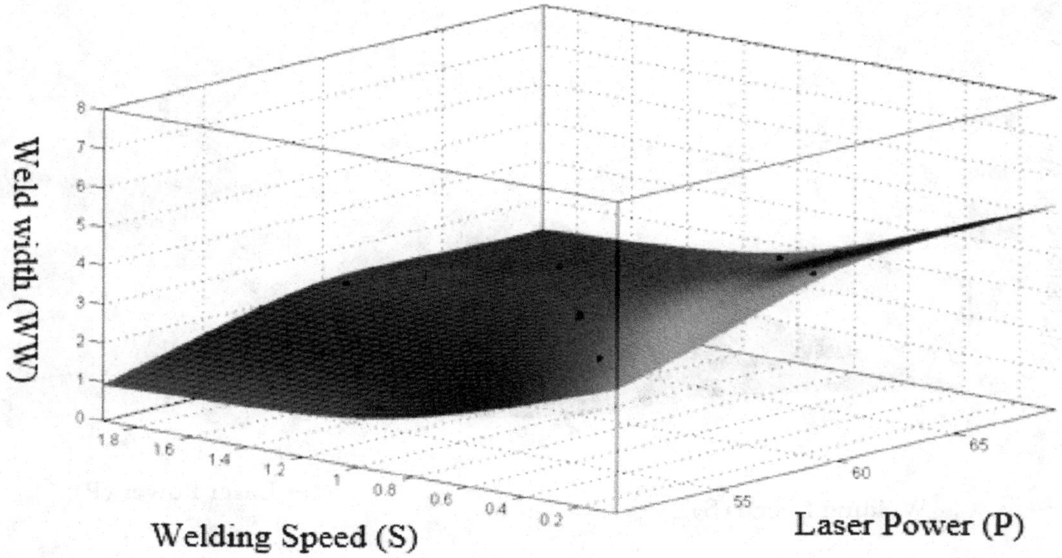

is because increment of welding speed reduces the irradiation time, causes less heat is delivered with a reduction in molten volume resulting in the formation of narrow and weak weld. Too low frequency tends to narrow the laser beam, causing less amount of laser energy deposition whereas too high frequency spread the laser beam. The Optimum value of welding speed and frequency are required to get the optimum weld seam width.

OPTIMIZATION

Desirability function based optimization technique is used to determine the optimum process parameter which simultaneously maximize the weld shear strength and minimizes weld seam width. Multi-objective optimization technique is carried out numerically by choosing the desired objectives for each response using desirable function. Table 4 represents the optimum welding process parameter which gives the optimized value of the response. Fig. 12 shows the optimization plot between process parameters and response.

CONFIRMATION EXPERIMENT

The optimal solutions thus obtained are as given in Table 5. Finally, a confirmation experiment has been conducted at optimum parameter setting to find the generated error, and it has been found that WS has an error of 3.491% whereas WW has an error of 3.726% (Table 5) which is very minimal and acceptable.

Figure 11. Surface interaction plot of F and S on the weld width

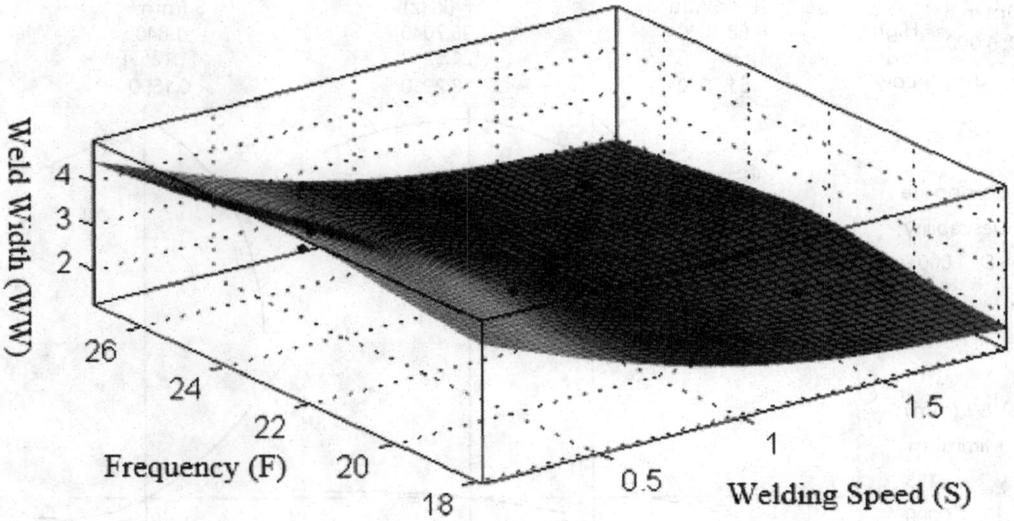

CONCLUSION OF CASE STUDY

From the experimental study and research within the specified set of parameters considered in the present study, the following inference can be said.

1. The thermoplastic materials can be joined by low power laser.
2. Increasing laser power increases the weld shear strength and weld width; while, welding speed has a negative impact on both responses.
3. From the ANOVA table, it has been found that laser power and welding speed have a strong effect on both responses followed by frequency.
4. The developed surface response models estimate the responses within the limit of process parameters for laser welding.
5. Laser power, frequency and speed have a better interaction effect on weld shear strength and weld width. Such parameters regulate the laser heat input to the weld area.
6. The weld strength is limited by very high laser heat input, which causes the material to overheat and decompose. On the other hand, very low laser heat input results in a lack of fusion.

Table 4. Optimal welding process parameter

P (%Watt)	F (kHz)	S (mm/sec.)	Weld shear strength (N/mm)	Weld seam width (mm)
68.409	21.523	1.12689	34.3173	2.61547

Figure 12. Optimization plot of machining responses

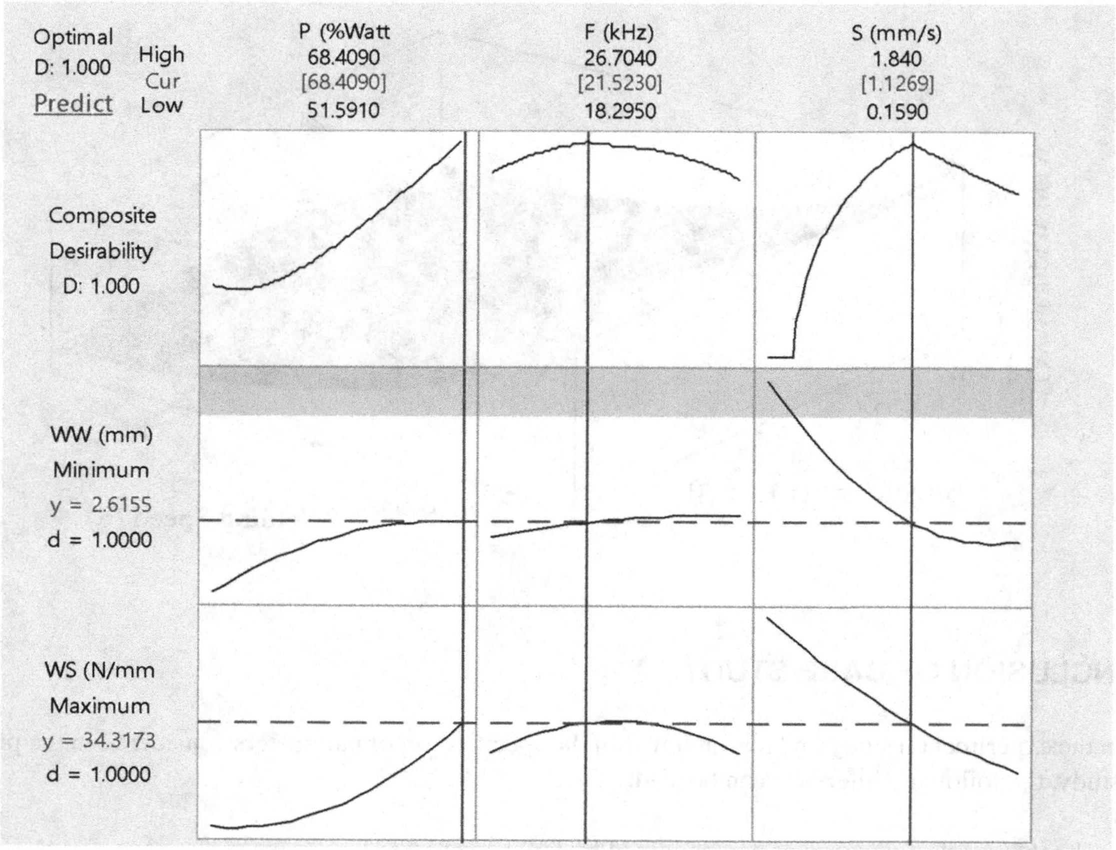

SUMMARY

In this chapter, a brief study on laser transmission welding using a diode laser system of dissimilar polymers has been documented. Previous research works on laser welding as well as laser transmission welding is provided in this chapter. Disadvantages of laser welding which lead to the necessity of laser

Table 5. WS and WW values from Optimization and after confirmation test

Optimized value from Desirability analysis			Confirmation test	%Error
Process Parameters	P	68.409	68.409	
	F	21.523	21.523	
	S	1.12689	1.12689	
Performance Parameters	WS	34.3173	33.119	3.491
	WW	2.61547	2.518	3.726

transmission welding briefly described in the chapter. This chapter also provides a case study on laser transmission welding of transparent polycarbonate and black carbon filled acrylic. Effectiveness of low power laser to weld dissimilar polymer via laser transmission welding is the main outcome of the case study. The Methodology used for the experimental study is also elaborately explained in this chapter. In the case study the effect of various process parameters, namely, laser power, pulse frequency and welding speed on the weld shear strength and weld width have been investigated. Experimental data indicates a deviation on values of weld strength and weld width. It also observed that deviation in weld strength is comparatively more than weld width in the same design space. Experimental results show that weld strength of 34.3173 N/mm and weld width of 2.61547 mm have been achieved at optimum parameter setting using the Desirability function based optimization technique.

REFERENCES

Abed, S., Laurens, P., Carretero, C., Deschamps, J. R., & Duval, C. (2001). Diode laser welding of polymers Microstructures of the welded zones for polypropylene. *International Congress on Applications of Lasers & Electro-Optics*, 1499-1507. 10.2351/1.5059820

Acherjee, B., Kuar, A. S., Mitra, S., & Misra, D. (2011). Application of grey-based Taguchi method for simultaneous optimization of multiple quality characteristics in laser transmission welding process of thermoplastics. *International Journal of Advanced Manufacturing Technology*, *56*(9-12), 995–1006. doi:10.100700170-011-3224-7

Acherjee, B., Kuar, A. S., Mitra, S., & Misra, D. (2012). Effect of carbon black on temperature field and weld profile during laser transmission welding of polymers: A FEM study. *Optics & Laser Technology*, *44*(3), 514–521. doi:10.1016/j.optlastec.2011.08.008

Acherjee, B., Kuar, A. S., Mitra, S., Misra, D., & Acharyya, S. (2012). Experimental investigation on laser transmission welding of PMMA to ABS via RSM modeling. *Optics & Laser Technology*, *44*(5), 1372–1383. doi:10.1016/j.optlastec.2011.12.029

Acherjee, B., Misra, D., Bose, D., & Venkadshwaran, K. (2009). Prediction of weld strength and seam width for laser transmission welding of thermoplastic using response surface methodology. *Optics & Laser Technology*, *41*(8), 956–967. doi:10.1016/j.optlastec.2009.04.007

Brodhun, J., Blass, D., & Dilger, K. (2018). Laser transmission joining of thermoplastic fasteners Application for thermoset CFRP. *Proceedings of the Institution of Mechanical Engineers, Part L: Journal of Materials: Design and Applications, 233*(3), 475-484. 10.1177/1464420718804571

Chen, M., Zak, G., & Bates, P. J. (2011). Effect of carbon black on light transmission in laser welding of thermoplastics. *Journal of Materials Processing Technology*, *211*(1), 43–47. doi:10.1016/j.jmatprotec.2010.08.017

Daniel, J. J., Seungjun, K., Jung, H. P., Dae, Y. P., Han, E. L., Tae, H. I., Insung, C., Rodney, S. R., & Keon, J. L. (2017). Laser–Material Interactions for Flexible Applications. *Advanced Materials*, *29*(26), 1606586. doi:10.1002/adma.201606586 PMID:28370626

Datta, S., Raza, M. S., Das, A. K., Saha, P., & Pratihar, D. K. (2020). Experimental investigations and parametric optimization of laser beam welding of NiTinol sheets by metaheuristic techniques and desirability function analysis. *Optics & Laser Technology*, *214*, 105982. doi:10.1016/j.optlastec.2019.105982

Derringer, G., & Suich, R. (1980). Simultaneous Optimization of Several Response Variables. *Journal of Quality Technology*, *12*(4), 214–219. doi:10.1080/00224065.1980.11980968

Devrient, M., Frick, T., & Schmidt, M. (2011). Laser transmission welding of optical transparent thermoplastics. *Physics Procedia*, *12*, 157–165. doi:10.1016/j.phpro.2011.03.020

Ghorbel, E., Casalino, G., & Abed, S. (2009). Laser diode transmission welding of polypropylene Geometrical and microstructure characterization of weld. *Materials & Design*, *30*(7), 2745–2751. doi:10.1016/j.matdes.2008.10.027

Karaboga, D., & Akay, B. (2009). A comparative study of Artificial Bee colony algorithm. *Applied Mathematics and Computation*, *214*(1), 108–132. doi:10.1016/j.amc.2009.03.090

Moradi, M., Arabi, H., & Shamsborhan, M. (2020). Multi-Objective Optimization of High Power Diode Laser Surface Hardening Process of AISI 410 by means of RSM and Desirability Approach. *Optik (Stuttgart)*, *202*, 163619. doi:10.1016/j.ijleo.2019.163619

Quintino, L., Costa, A., Miranda, R., Yapp, D., Kumar, V., & Kong, C. J. (2007). Welding with high power fiber lasers – A preliminary study. *Materials & Design*, *28*(4), 1231–1237. doi:10.1016/j.matdes.2006.01.009

Ragavendran, M., Chandrasekhar, N., Ravikumar, R., Saxena, R., Vasudevan, M., & Bhaduri, A. K. (2017). Optimization of hybrid laser – TIG welding of 316LN steel using response surface methodology (RSM). *Optics and Lasers in Engineering*, *94*, 27–36. doi:10.1016/j.optlaseng.2017.02.015

Rao, M. S., & Venkaiah, N. (2015). Parametric optimization in machining of Nimonic-263 alloy using RSM and particle swarm optimization. *Procedia Materials Science*, *10*, 70–79. doi:10.1016/j.mspro.2015.06.027

Sivagurumanikandan, N., Saravanan, S., Kumar, G. S., Raju, S., & Raghukandan, K. (2018). Prediction and optimization of process parameters to enhance the tensile strength of Nd: YAG laser welded super duplex stainless steel. *Optik (Stuttgart)*, *157*, 833–840. doi:10.1016/j.ijleo.2017.11.146

Wang, X., Liu, B., Liu, W., Zhong, X., Jiang, Y., & Liu, H. (2017). Investigation on the Mechanism and Failure Mode of Laser transmission Spot Welding using PMMA material for the automotive industry. *Materials (Basel)*, *10*(1), 22. doi:10.3390/ma10010022 PMID:28772383

Wang, X., Zhong, X., Liu, W., Liu, B., & Liu, H. (2016). Investigation on enhancement of weld strength between PMMA and PBT in laser transmission welding—Using intermediate material. *Journal of Applied Polymer Science*, *133*(44), 44167. doi:10.1002/app.44167

Xu, X. F., Bates, P. J., & Zak, G. (2015). Effect of glass fiber and crystallinity on light transmission during laser transmission welding of thermoplastics. *Optics & Laser Technology*, *69*, 133–139. doi:10.1016/j.optlastec.2014.12.025

Chapter 11
Application of Evolutionary Optimization Techniques Towards Non-Traditional Machining for Performance Enhancement

Chikesh Ranjan
https://orcid.org/0000-0003-1197-601X
RTC Institute of Technology, India

Hridayjit Kalita
Birla Institute of Technology, Mesra, India

B. Sridhar Babu
https://orcid.org/0000-0002-3721-813X
CMR Institute of Technology, India

Kaushik Kumar
Birla Institute of Technology, Mesra, India

ABSTRACT

Electro-chemical machining is a non-conventional machining method that is used for machining of very complicated shape. In this chapter an attempt has been made to carry out multi-objective optimization of the surface roughness (SR) and material removal rate (MRR) for the ECM process of EN 19 on a CNC ECM machine using copper electrode through evolutionary optimization techniques like teaching-learning-based optimization (TLBO) technique and biogeography-based optimization (BBO) technique. The input parameters considered are electrolyte concentration, voltage, feed rate, inter-electrode gap. TLBO and BBO techniques were used to obtain maximum MRR and minimum SR. In addition, obtained optimized values were validated for testing the significance of the TLBO and BBO techniques, and a very small error value of MRR and SR was found. BBO outperformed TLBO in every aspect like less percentage error and better-optimized values; however, TLBO took less computation time than the BBO.

DOI: 10.4018/978-1-7998-3624-7.ch011

INTRODUCTION

Conventional machining processes employ tools that are tougher than the workpieces to take the work material to its plastic state (beyond the yield stress) until it gets removed from the parent work material. Alloys consisting of alloying elements such as wolfram, chromium, metallic elements, vanadium etc possess high hardness value, high strength to weight ratio and high heat resistance which makes it impossible for conventional machining processes to work efficiently, effectively and with ease of cutting due to the physical interaction between the tool and the work material(Aggarwal et al., (2015)). These drawbacks can be overcome by implementing non-conventional machining processes which employs other sources of energy for metal cutting rather than by physical interaction between the work and the tool. These sources of energy can be light, heat, electricity, water pressure and kinetic energy of the abrasive particles, based on which non conventional machining processes can be divided into various types. Electro chemical machining (ECM) is one such type which employs electrolytes between the electrode work and the tool to remove the material from the surface.

ECM process works on the principle that when electric voltage is applied across the anode and cathode electrodes under the presence of an electrolytic medium, material starts to get remove material from the anode surface due to electron exchange resulting in removal of material. During ECM process, work piece is treated an anode, while the tool as a cathode and a voltage of 5-30 V is applied with a current density of 10-200 A/cm. The electrolytic aqueous solution commonly used is of NaCl or NaNO3 and is selected to prevent from any alteration in the shape of the tool. A pump speed (3 to 60m/s) of the electrolyte is maintained to expel the removed material from the gap between the cathode tool and the anode work surface. A constant feed (about 0.02mm/s) of the tool towards the work surface is maintained and a steady state gap is reached which generates a negative profile of the cathode tool on the work surface and gradually deepening for complete cut. The components of a general ECM machine are shown in figure 1.

In the current chapter ECM machining of EN19 was performed for finding the optimal values of the input parameters using two different optimization technique which are the Biogeography based optimization (BBO) and Teaching learning based optimization techniques (TLPO). Results from these techniques are validated by conducting experiments considering the optimal input parameters and finding the error percentages of the output parameter values with the theoretical one as obtained from the two techniques. A thorough literature review, experimental setups, input and output parameters, the BBO and TLBO techniques, the results and discussions are all described in the subsequent sections.

One of the most significant parts of industries associated with manufacturing is the machining process. The intricate shapes are machined using the non-traditional machining process. Engineers are required to give their best and produce products with higher performance and better effectiveness. As such ample effort have been made to identify optimal solution for the machining processes using different optimization techniques as such Particle Swarm Optimization (PSO), Artificial Neural Network (ANN), Simulated Annealing (SA), Genetic Algorithm etc. (Anitha et al. (2016). Owing to the importance of optimization techniques, researchers have developed several optimization techniques that depict the nature in their operation which resulted in reduced cycle time and better machining.

Biogeography based optimization (BBO) comes under the category of heuristic optimization technique which was first introduced by Dan Simon (professor at Cleveland State University in the Department of Electrical and Computer Engineering) in the year 2008 and is based on an iterative technique to optimize stochastic functions by improving the fitness function. This technique is motivated by the nature of the biological species in their locomotion, distribution, evolution, emergence and extinction patterns. The

Figure 1. Schematic diagram of ECM process

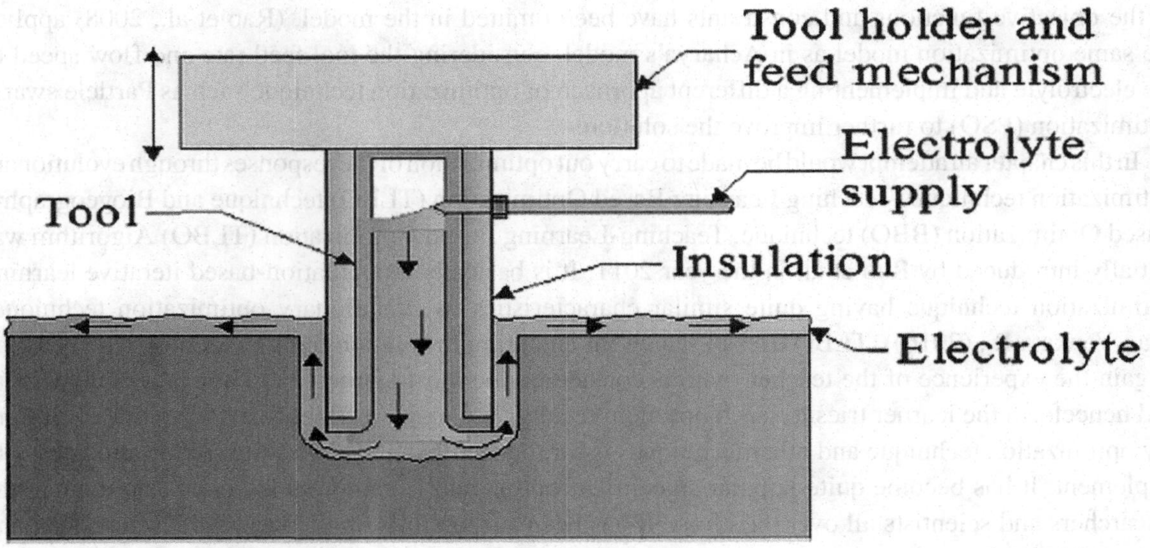

suitability of the habitat is computed and is given a habitat suitability index (HSI), the definition of which complies with the nature of the objective function of the optimization technique and is basically a fitness value as in the case of TLBO.

LITERATURE REVIEW

In a 2-dimensional ECM inter electrode gap model proposed by Bhattacharyya et al. (1999), metal removal rate (MRR) is analyzed as an objective response to the flow speed of the electrolyte and the feed rate of the tool in a numerical model assuming a constant electrical conductivity (or constant void fraction) and a uniform pressure throughout the flow path of the electrolyte.

(El-Dardery M.A. 1982) proposed a cost model of the ECM considering various machining costs but did not yield practical results due to lack of constraints in the model. (Hewidy et al., 1984) did a similar study on the various costs involved in the ECM machining process considering machining costs, electrolyte cost, cost of power consumption and labor costs in their study. (Hewidy et al., 2007) in some other work also gave an analytical modeling approach for performing an ECM operation, one which is assisted with low frequency vibrations.

(Acharya et al., 1986) considered a multi objective optimization model with the objective of minimizing the dimensional accuracy, maximizing the MRR and the tool life of the ECM process but without taking into account the variables for the 'tool feed rate' and the 'inter electrode gap' as in (Bhattacharyya et al., 1999). The shortcomings of Achaya's model were tackled later in (Choobineh and Jain, 1993) where a vertex method was employed to determine the weights given to each objective function and was solved in the same way as in (Acharya et al., 1986).

(Jain et al., 2007) modified the Acharya's multi objective optimization model by including the variables for tool feed rate and the flow speed of the electrolyte and expanding their range though linearization of the objective functions and constraints have been omitted in the model. (Rao et al., 2008) applied the same optimization model as in Acharya's model, considering the tool feed rate and flow speed of the electrolyte and implementing a different approach of optimization technique such as Particle swarm optimization (PSO) to further improve the solution.

In this chapter an attempt would be made to carry out optimization of the responses through evolutionary optimization techniques Teaching Learning Based Optimization (TLBO) technique and Biogeography-Based Optimization (BBO) technique. Teaching-Learning Based Optimization (TLBO) Algorithm was initially introduced by Rao et al. in the year 2011. It is basically a population-based iterative learning optimization technique having quite similar characteristics to evolutionary optimization techniques (Rao, Venkata R . (2016)). TLBO tries to search for an optimum solution through learner, who is trying to gain the experience of the teacher (who is considered the most learned and knowledgeable person) and henceforth the learner tries to reach optimum results. The major difference between this evolutionary optimization technique and other techniques is for the fact that TLBO is quite simple and is easy to implement. It has become quite popular since its inception and is gaining wide popularity among the researchers and scientists all over the globe. It has been successfully applied to many engineering and real-world problems.

EXPERIMENTAL SETUP

An experimental setup is initiated where experiments were conducted on METATECH electrochemical machining involving 3 major functional units which are: the control panel, machining chamber and an electrolyte circulation system. The machining chamber and the control panel are shown in Figure 2 and 3 respectively. The setup consists of tool which is attached to the main screw operated by a servo feed system and a machining chamber with fixtures for holding workpieces (Dhobe et al. (2014)). A feedback loop system involving a high current sensor circuit is utilized to interface the movement of the tool or the feed to the stepper motor controller. As the current in the circuit surges due to alteration in approach of the tool towards the work surfaces, a signal is sent to the controller for reversing the downward approach of the tool or completely shutting the machine down. Potassium chloride (KCl) which is taken as an Electrolyte is circulated from the KCl tank to the machining chamber and back using a pneumatically pumping system (Chen et al. (2016)).

In this chapter, apart from finding the optimal solution, surface morphology would also be studied using Scanning Electron Microscope (SEM). The obtained optimized values would then be validated foresting the significance of the TLBO and BBO technique. Moreover, the performance of these would be compared against the performance indices like percentage error, optimized values, computation time etc.

Input Parameters and Output Parameters

In the experimentation, the input parameters that are considered are the electrolyte concentration (%), feed rate (mm/min), voltage (V) and inter-electrode gap (mm). the parameters are taken from the literature considering a larger influence on the material removal rate (MRR) and surface roughness (SR).

Figure 2. Electrochemical Machine Chamber

MRR and SR are taken as the output parameters. MRR (in cubic centimeter/min) for ECM process is determined as given by equation 1:

$$MRR = \frac{w_i - w_f}{t} \quad (1)$$

where

Figure 3. Control Panel

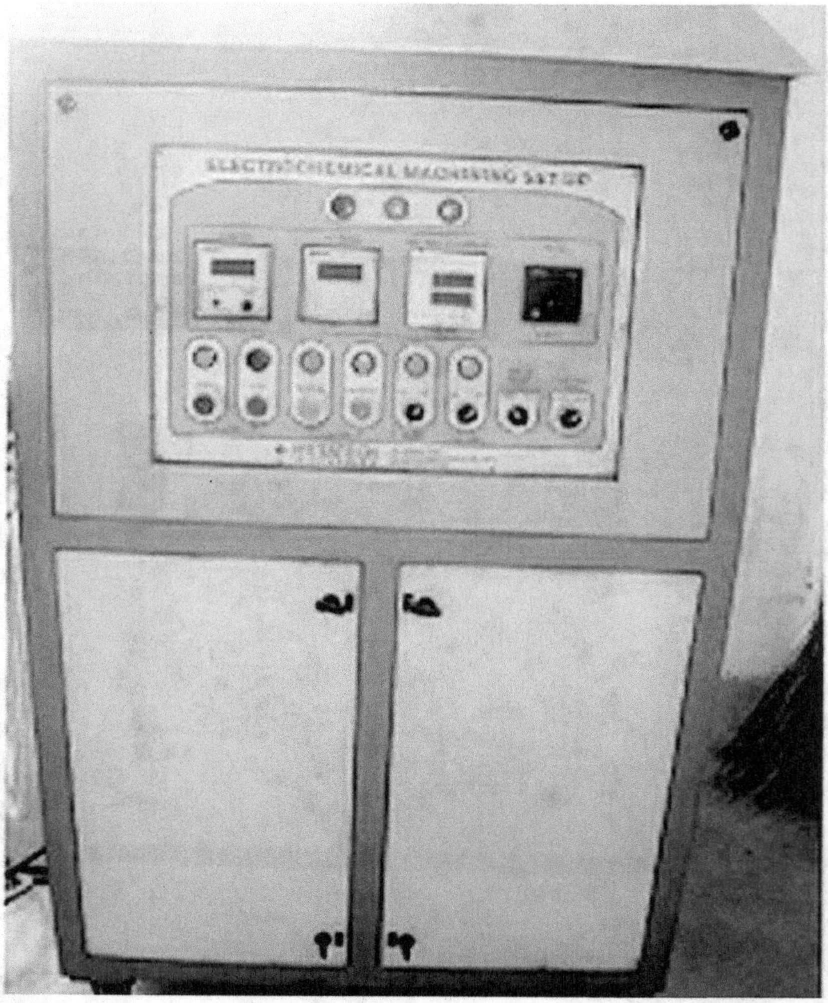

Wi =initial weight of the work piece before machining
Wf= final weight of the work piece after machining
t = time period of the trials.

MRR is directly proportional to the current passed through the electrode gap, pulse ON and pulse OFF time. MRR also have the effect of voltage applied across the electrodes.

SR can be defined by ISO 4287:1997 international standards. SR generally determines the surface texture of the work material which is basically a deviation of the surfaces from its theoretical average value or the centre line of the roughness. The surface roughness is considered high when this deviation is more while surface is smooth in case of smaller deviations. This is also termed as arithmetic mean surface roughness.

Table 1. Input Parameters with Levels

Process Parameter(unit)	Symbol	Level 1	Level 2	Level 3
Electrolyte conc. (%)	A	10	15	20
Voltage (V)	B	8	10	12
Feed rate (mm/min)	C	0.1	0.21	0.32
Inter-electrode gap, mm	D	0.2	0.25	0.3

EXPERIMENTATION

The experimentation is carried out considering the variations in the input parameters as described in the previous section and their responses in the form of the output parameters i.e. MRR and SR. The experimentation values of the input and output parameters are shown in Table 2.

Regression Model: In order to determine the relationship between the input and the output parameters, a statistical tool of regression analysis was utilized using Minitab 16. The regression relationships of MRR and SR with the input parameters are given by equations 2 and 3.

$$MRR = 0.000253A + 0.011500B + 0.008014C - 0.250000D + 0.058007 \quad (2)$$

$$SR = 0.0254\,A + 1.3904B + 0.3726C + 0.5101D + 2.0411 \quad (3)$$

Here, 'A', 'B', 'C' and 'D' represents Electrolyte conc, Voltage, Feed rate and Inter-electrode gap respectively.

TEACHING LEARNING BASED OPTIMIZATION TECHNIQUE

Teaching-Learning based optimization (TLBO) algorithm was initially introduced by Rao et al. (2011). It is basically a population-based iterative learning optimization technique having quite similar characteristics to evolutionary optimization techniques. TLBO tries to search for an optimum solution through learners, who are trying to gain the experience of the teacher (who is considered the most learned and knowledgeable person). Thus the learners tries to approach towards an optimal solution after each iterations to become a teacher. The major difference between this evolutionary optimization technique and other techniques is for the fact that TLBO is quite simple and is easy to implement (Rao, (2016)). It has become quite popular since its inception and is gaining wide popularity among the researchers and scientists all over the globe. It has been successfully applied to many engineering and real-world problems.

The major importance of when solving an optimization problem using evolutionary optimization is given to convergence rate over the quality of solutions. TLBO is divided into two parts. One part consists of the "Teacher Phase" where learning from a teacher is involved whereas the second part is "Learner Phase" where learning through interaction between learners is involved. TLBO is implemented as described below.

In the TLBO technique let 'N' be the number of learners or the class size, 'D' be the number of courses for the learners and 'MAXIT' representing the maximum number of iterations permitted.

A population represented by 'X' is randomly selected from a search space bounded by a matrix of N rows and D columns, the i-jth element of which are assigned using equation 4 below.

$$x_0(ij) = xj_{\min} + rand[x(xj_{\max} - xj_{\min}) \quad (4)$$

where,

rand = random variable uniformly distributed and having a range between (0,1)
xjmin= minimum value for the j_{th} parameter,
xjmax= maximum value for j_{th} parameter,
The ith learner in the generatin 'g' is given by the equation 5 below:

$$x_g(i) = [x_g(i,1), x_g(i,2), x_g(i,3)..............x_g(i,\mathrm{j}),............x_g(i,\mathrm{D})] \quad (5)$$

Teacher Phase: Mean parameter Mg of every subject taken by the learner at generation g is given as (Eq. 6)

$$M_g = [\mathrm{m}_{g1,}\mathrm{m}_{g2,}\mathrm{m}_{g3,}\ ....\mathrm{m}_{gj},.........,\mathrm{m}_{gD}] \quad (6)$$

Learner having minimum objective function value is regarded as teacher *XgTeacher* for every iteration. Optimization algorithm proceeds further when teacher phases shift the mean of learner towards its teacher. Now, for obtaining improved learner, randomly weighted differential vector is formed from current mean & desired mean parameters and is subsequently added to the existing population of learners with the formula (Eq. 7)

$$Xnew_g(i) = x_g(i) + rand[x(\mathrm{X}_g\, Teacher - TFM_g) \quad (7)$$

where,

TF= teaching factor ranging from 1 or 2. It can be calculated from Eq. 8 given below:

$$TF = round[1 + round(0,1)\{2-1\}] \quad (8)$$

where *TF* is not a parameter of the TLBO algorithm. When *Xnewg(i)* is found to be superior to *Xg(i)* in a generation, then Xg(i) in the matrix phase is replaced with the superior one.

Learner Phase: In this phase the interaction among the learners is initiated which enhances the knowledge of the learners and the learner Xg(i) is randomly selected as (i≠r).

The interaction between the learner takes place with each other in this phase. The interaction between the learner tends to increase the knowledge of the learner. For any learner, *Xg(i)* another learner *Xg(i)*is randomly selected as *(i≠r)*. For matrix *Xnew* in learner phase the ith parameter is given as follows (Eq. 9):

Table 2. Experimental observation for MRR and SR

Exp. No.	A	B	C	D	MRR	SR (Ra) (μm)
1	1	1	1	1	21.6561	2.666
2	1	1	2	2	17.6	2.4
3	1	1	3	3	19.7235	1.635
4	1	2	1	2	12.1189	3.089
5	1	2	2	3	11.837	20.7
6	1	2	3	1	15.135	1.285
7	1	3	1	3	19.7745	1.65
8	1	3	2	1	24.2038	1.403
9	1	3	3	2	23.0828	2.062
10	2	1	1	2	12.2484	1.616
11	2	1	2	3	16.7	2.653
12	2	1	3	1	16.35	1.919
13	2	2	1	3	15.1783	2.35
14	2	2	2	1	25.4777	1.255
15	2	2	3	2	26.95	1.33
16	2	3	1	1	24.1401	2.957
17	2	3	2	2	25.3715	3.022
18	3	3	3	3	22.8238	2.225
19	3	1	1	3	23.0998	5.514
20	3	1	2	1	21.8259	3.176
21	3	1	3	2	23.5669	2.2
22	3	2	1	1	22.1806	3.422
23	3	2	2	2	25.2529	2.062
24	3	2	3	3	33.3931	1.882
25	3	3	1	2	22.293	3.125
26	3	3	2	2	24.7134	2.553
27	3	3	3	1	37.207	1.32
28	1	2	2	1	22.6561	2.666
29	1	3	3	1	16.2399	2
30	1	1	2	2	18.7452	1.693
31	1	2	3	2	13.1189	3.089
32	1	3	1	2	10.837	20.7
33	1	1	3	3	14.135	1.285
34	1	2	1	3	19.7985	1.777
35	1	3	2	3	24.2038	1.403
36	2	1	2	1	23.0828	2.062
37	2	2	3	1	11.2484	1.616
38	2	3	1	1	15.8153	1.5
39	2	1	3	2	16.4968	1.919
40	2	2	1	2	14.1783	2.35
41	2	3	2	2	25.4777	1.255
42	2	1	1	3	26.86	1.33
43	2	2	2	3	24.1401	2.957
44	3	3	3	3	25.3715	3.022
45	3	1	3	1	22.8238	2.225
46	3	2	1	1	23.0998	5.514
47	3	3	2	1	21.8259	3.176
48	3	1	1	2	23.5669	2.2
49	3	2	2	2	22.1806	3.422
50	3	3	3	2	25.2529	2.062
51	3	1	2	3	32.3931	1.882
52	3	2	2	3	22.293	3.125
53	3	3	1	3	24.7134	2.553
54	2	1	1	2	31.207	1.32
55	3	1	1	3	21.6561	2.666
56	1	1	2	2	17.2399	2
57	2	1	2	3	19.7452	1.693
58	3	1	2	1	11.1189	3.089
59	1	1	3	3	12.837	20.7
60	2	1	3	1	17.135	1.285

continued on following page

Table 2. Continued

Exp. No.	A	B	C	D	MRR	SR (Ra) (μm)
61	3	1	3	2	19.6895	1.865
62	1	2	1	2	24.2038	1.403
63	2	2	1	3	23.0828	2.062
64	3	2	1	1	13.2484	1.616
65	1	2	2	3	16.6	1.2
66	2	2	2	1	17.4968	1.919
67	3	2	2	2	11.1783	2.35
68	1	2	3	1	25.4777	1.255
69	2	2	3	2	26.9	1.33
70	3	3	3	3	24.1401	2.957
71	1	3	1	3	25.3715	3.022
72	2	3	1	1	23.8238	2.225
73	3	3	1	2	21.0998	5.514
74	1	3	2	1	21.8259	3.176
75	2	3	2	2	22.5669	2.2
76	3	3	2	3	21.1806	3.422
77	1	3	3	2	24.2529	2.062
78	2	3	3	2	31.3931	1.882
79	3	3	3	1	20.293	3.125
80	2	2	2	2	25.7134	2.553
81	3	3	3	3	35.207	1.32

$$Xnew_g = x_g(i) + rand[x(X_g(i) - X_g(r)]\text{if}(X_g(i) > X_g(r) \tag{9}$$

BIOGEOGRAPHY BASED OPTIMIZATION (BBO) TECHNIQUE

Biogeography based optimization (BBO) comes under the category of heuristic optimization technique which was first introduced by Dan Simon (professor at Cleveland State University in the Department of Electrical and Computer Engineering) in the year 2008 and is based on an iterative technique to optimize stochastic functions by improving the fitness function. This technique is motivated by the nature of the biological species in their locomotion, distribution, evolution, emergence and extinction patterns. The suitability of the habitat is computed and is given a habitat suitability index (HSI), the definition of which complies with the nature of the objective function of the optimization technique and is basically a fitness value as in the case of TLBO.

Rate of mutation of the species in BBO technique can be calculated as given in Eq. 10 below:

$$m_k = m_{\max} \frac{1 - p_k}{p_{\max}} \tag{10}$$

where, m_k represents mutation rate, m_{max} representing maximum mutation rate, P_k represents probability of the number of species and P_{max} is the maximum probability.

Habitat is altered with the older habitat getting replaced by the new ones having the best solutions. The best possible solution with the highest probability (P_k) in the previous habitat is passed on to the new one without any alteration.

Let there be 'S' number of species in the recipient island having probability (t) and λs and μs be the immigration and emigration rates with 'S' species on that island. The variation from Ps (t) to Ps(t + Δt) can be given by equation 11.

$$p_s(t+\Delta t) = p_s(t)(1-\lambda_s \Delta t - \mu_s \Delta t) + p_{s-1}(t)\lambda_{s-1}\Delta t + p_{s+1}(t)\mu_{s+1}\Delta t \quad (11)$$

Thus, using the known values of Ps(t)and Ṗs(t), the value of Ps (t + Δt) given in Eq. 11 can be approximated as:

$$p_s(t+\Delta t) = p_s(t) + p_s(t+\Delta t) \quad (12)$$

The above equation (Eq. 12) will be used in the programming of BBO for calculating (t +Δt). The algorithm for the BBO is shown below in Figure 4:

Figure 4. Algorithm for Biogeography-based optimization

```
Initialize a population of N candidate solutions {x_k}
While not(termination criterion)
   For each x_k, set emigration probability μ_k ∝ fitness of x_k,
      with μ_k ∈ [0,1]
   For each x_k, set immigration probability λ_k = 1 − μ_k
   {z_k} ← {x_k}
   For each individual z_k(k = 1,···,N)
      For each independent variable index s ∈ [1,n]
         Use λ_k to probabilistically decide whether to immigrate to z_k
         If immigrating then
            Use {μ_i} to probabilistically select the emigrating individual x_j
            z_k(s) ← x_j(s)
         End if
      Next independent variable index: s ← s + 1
      Probabilistically mutate z_k
   Next individual: k ← k + 1
   {x_k} ← {z_k}
Next generation
```

RESULTS AND DISCUSSION

TLBO technique is run to obtain the most optimized values of the input parameters for the minimum S.R. value and maximum MRR value. The optimized values of the input parameters obtained are: A=12, B=8, C=0.31, D=0.297 while the MRR and SR values obtained are 25 mm/min and 1.24 μm respectively from the optimal input values.

While running the BBO algorithm, after completion of the maximum number of iterations the optimized values of all input parameters are obtained for the best output values of MRR and SR. The input parameters obtained are: A=12, B=8, C=0.31 and D=0.297 while the MRR and SR values are 25.04 mm/min and 1.241 µm respectively.

The validation test results for ECM through TLBO and BBO are shown in Table 3 and 4 respectively and the error percentages of MRR and SR experimental values (considering the optimal values of the input parameters) with the theoretical value are evaluated.

It has been observed that BBO technique predicts a more accurate result for both MRR and SR than the TLBO technique. On the other hand, TLBO algorithm is easy and simple to use and requires lesser computational time (being a sorted algorithm-based technique) when compared to BBO and hence TLBO is very effective under time constraint situation.

Table 3. Validation test results for ECM through TLBO

Concentration %	Voltage (V)	Feed rate (mm/min)	Gap (mm)	MRR (mm3/min)			Surface roughness (µm)		
				Experimental	Optimized	Error %	Experimental	Optimized	Error %
12	8	0.31	0.297	25.149	25	**0.59**	1.25	1.24	**0.8**

CONCLUSION

In the current chapter, BBO and TLBO techniques of multi objective optimization for the ECM machining parameters are performed to evaluate for the effectiveness comparison between the two techniques. Experiments were performed considering the optimal values of the input parameters and the error percentages of the MRR and SR values with the theoretical values from BBO and TLBO techniques were compared. BBO technique was found to yield a higher accuracy, less relative percentage error and cost effective though it consumes higher computational time as compared to the TLBO technique. Both TLBO and BBO techniques have proven to be a cost effective one for fulfilling specific requirements of the ECM process in the production system.

Table 4. Validation test results for ECM through BBO

Concentration %	Voltage (V)	Feed rate (mm/min)	Gap (mm)	MRR (mm3/min)			Surface roughness (µm)		
				Experimental	Optimized	Error %	Experimental	Optimized	Error %
12	8	0.31	0.297	25.149	25.04	**0.433**	1.25	1.241	**0.72**

REFERENCES

Abuzeid, H. H., Awad, A. M., & Senbel, A. H. (2012). Prediction of electrochemical machining process parameters using artificial neural networks. *International Journal on Computer Science and Engineering*, *4*, 125–132.

Acharya, B. G., Jain, V. K., & Batra, J. L. (1986). Multiobjective optimization of ECM process. *Precision Engineering*, *8*(2), 88–96. doi:10.1016/0141-6359(86)90091-7

Aggarwal, V., Khangura, S. S., & Garg, R. K. (2015). Parametric modeling and optimization for wire electrical discharge machining of Inconel 718 using response surface methodology. *International Journal of Advanced Manufacturing Technology*, *79*(1-4), 31–47. doi:10.100700170-015-6797-8

Anitha, J., Das, R., & Pradhan, M. K. (2016). Multi-objective optimization of electrical discharge machining processes using artificial neural network. *Jordan Journal of Mechanical and Industrial Engineering*, *10*(1), 11–18.

Bahre, D., Weber, O., & Rebschlager, A. (2013). Investigation on pulse electrochemical machining characteristics of lamellar cast iron using a response surface methodology-based approach. *Procedia CIRP*, *6*, 363–368. doi:10.1016/j.procir.2013.03.028

Bhattacharyya, B., & Sorkhel, S. K. (1999). Investigation for controlled electrochemical machining through response surface methodology-based approach. *Journal of Materials Processing Technology*, *86*(1-3), 200–207. doi:10.1016/S0924-0136(98)00311-2

Chen, D., Lu, R., Zou, F., & Li, S. (2016). Teaching-learning-based optimization with variable-population scheme and its application for ANN and global optimization. *Neurocomputing*, *173*, 1096–1111. doi:10.1016/j.neucom.2015.08.068

Choobineh, F., & Jain, V. K. (1993). A fuzzy sets approach for selecting optimum parameters of an ECM process. *Advanced Materials & Processes*, *3*, 225–232.

Crichton, M., & McGough, J. A. (1985). Studies of the discharge mechanisms in electrochemical arc machining. *Journal of Applied Electrochemistry*, *115*(1), 113–119. doi:10.1007/BF00617748

Derakhshan, G., Shayanfar, H. A., & Kazemi, A. (2016). The optimization of demand response programs in smart grids. *Energy Policy*, *94*, 295–306. doi:10.1016/j.enpol.2016.04.009

Dhobe, S. H., Doloi, B., & Bhattacharya, B. (2014). Optimisation of ECM process during machining of titanium using quality loss function. *International Journal of Manufacturing Technology and Management*, *28*(1-3), 19–38. doi:10.1504/IJMTM.2014.064631

El-Dardery, M. A. (1982). Economic study of electrochemical. *International Journal of Machine Tool Design and Research*, *22*(3), 147–158. doi:10.1016/0020-7357(82)90023-3

Hewidy, M. S., Ebeid, S. J., El-Taweel, T. A., & Youssef, A. H. (2007). Modelling the performance of ECM assisted by low frequency vibrations. *Journal of Materials Processing Technology*, *189*(1-3), 455–472. doi:10.1016/j.jmatprotec.2007.02.032

Hewidy, M. S., Fattouh, M., & Elkhabeery, M. (1984), Some economical aspects of ECM processes. *Proceedings of the 1st AME Conference*, 87-94.

Jain, N. K., & Jain, V. K. (2007). Optimization of electrochemical machining process parameters using genetic algorithm. *Machining Science and Technology*, *11*(2), 235–258. doi:10.1080/10910340701350108

Kulkarni, A., Sharan, R., & Lal, G. K. (2002). An experimental study of discharge mechanism in electrochemical discharge machining. *International Journal of Machine Tools & Manufacture*, *42*(10), 1121–1127. doi:10.1016/S0890-6955(02)00058-5

Mediliyegedara, T. K. K. R., De Silva, A. K. M., Harrison, D. K., & McGeough, J. A. (2004). An intelligent pulse classification system for electro-chemical discharge machining (ECDM)— A preliminary study. *Journal of Materials Processing Technology*, *149*(1-3), 499–503. doi:10.1016/j.jmatprotec.2004.04.002

Montes, M. E., & Coello, C. A. C. (2005). A simple multimembered evolution strategy to solve constrained optimization problems. *IEEE Transactions on Evolutionary Computation*, *9*(1), 1–17. doi:10.1109/TEVC.2004.836819

Rao, R. (2016). Review of applications of TLBO algorithm and a tutorial for beginners to solve the unconstrained and constrained optimization problems. *Decision Science Letters*, *5*(1), 1–30.

Rao, R. V., Pawar, P. J., & Shankar, R. (2008). Multi-objective optimization of electrochemical machining process parameters using a particle swarm optimization algorithm. *Proceedings of the Institution of Mechanical Engineers. Part B, Journal of Engineering Manufacture*, *222*(8), 949–958. doi:10.1243/09544054JEM1158

Rao, R. V., Savsani, V. J., & Vakharia, D. P. (2011). Teaching–Learning-Based Optimization: A Novel Method for Constrained Mechanical Design Optimization Problems. *Computer Design (Winchester)*, *43*(3), 303–315. doi:10.1016/j.cad.2010.12.015

Rao, V. R. (2016). Teaching-Learning-Based Optimization Algorithm. In Teaching Learning Based Optimization Algorithm. Springer International Publishing.

Samanta, S., & Chakraborty, S. (2011). Parametric optimization of some non-traditional machining processes using artificial bee colony algorithm. *Engineering Applications of Artificial Intelligence*, *24*(6), 946–957. doi:10.1016/j.engappai.2011.03.009

Chapter 12
Analysis of Non-Traditional Machining Processes Using Machine Learning

Somnath Das
Swami Vivekananda Institute of Science and Technology, India

ABSTRACT

The nature of manufacturing systems faces increasingly complex dynamics to meet the demand for high quality products efficiently. One area, which experienced rapid development in terms not only of promising results but also of usability, is machine learning. New developments in certain domains such as mathematics, computer science, and the availability of easy-to-use tools, often freely available, offer great potential to transform the non-traditional machining domain and its understanding of the increase in manufacturing data. However, the field is very broad and even confusing, which presents a challenge and a barrier that hinders wide application. Here, this chapter helps to present an overview of the available machine learning techniques for improving the non-traditional machining process area. It provides a basis for the subsequent argument that the machine learning is a suitable tool for manufacturers to face these challenges head-on in non-traditional machining processes.

INTRODUCTION

Machine learning (ML) is the scientific study of algorithms and statistical models that computer systems use to perform a specific task effectively without using explicit instructions, relying on patterns and inference instead (Harding et al., 2006). It is seen as a subset of artificial intelligence. Machine learning algorithms build a mathematical model based on sample data, known as "training data," to make predictions or decisions without being explicitly programmed to perform the task (Esmaeilian et al., 2016).

Machine learning is not a device you can plug into a production line and make the production line operate better than it did before. Machine learning is a process that needs inputs from many devices to feed data to it so that data can be collected, evaluated, and used to develop knowledge about how a production line produces the products and parts it does (Kang et al., 2016). That knowledge can then be

DOI: 10.4018/978-1-7998-3624-7.ch012

used to determine how production line can have a higher throughput of parts, operate at a lower cost, and run more reliably (Shin et al., 2014).

Machine learning uses data, or more explicitly, training data, to teach its computer algorithm on what to expect from the production machines it's monitoring to obtain that training data, relying on pattern recognition and inference to develop the capability for the algorithm to make decisions and predictions without having to write code to be explicitly programmed to perform that task. The training data is collected, processed, and evaluated in a structured sequence of steps to prepare that data for use in the machine learning algorithm. That structured sequence of steps is a process, and the creation of that process introduces a new technology that includes (Vogl et al., 2016):

- IoT devices to create the data
- Networks to store and process the data
- Computers process to clean the data for accuracy and relevancy

Today the manufacturing industry has never seen increase in available data. These data comes from variety of different formats e.g. sensor data from the production line, environmental data, machine tool parameters, etc. Different names are used for this phenomenon, e.g. Industrie 4.0 (Germany), Smart Manufacturing (USA), and Smart Factory (South Korea). This increase and availability of large amounts of data is often referred to as Big Data. The availability of quality-related data offers potential to improve process and product quality sustainably. However, it has been recognized that much information can also propose a challenge and may have a negative impact as it can, e.g. distract from the main issues/causalities or lead to delayed or wrong conclusions about appropriate actions. Overall, it can be safely concluded, the manufacturing industry has to accept that in order to benefit from the increased data availability, e.g. for quality improvement initiatives, manufacturing cost estimation and/or process optimization, better understanding of the customer's requirements, etc., support is needed to handle the high dimensionality, complexity. New developments in certain domains like mathematics and computer science e.g. statistical learning and availability of easy-to-use, often freely available software tools offer great potential to transform the manufacturing domain and their grasp on the increased manufacturing data repositories sustainably. One of the most exciting developments in the area of machine learning is data mining (DM), artificial intelligence (AI), knowledge discovery (KD) etc. For many manufacturing practitioners, this represents a barrier regarding the adoption of these powerful tools and thus may hinder the utilization of the vast amounts of data increasingly being available (Xie, 2008).

The aims of the chapter to argue from a manufacturing perspective why machine learning is an appropriate and promising tool for today's and future challenges and to introduce the terminology used in the respective fields. In this chapter an overview of the different areas of machine learning and propose an overall structuring is also presented.

MACHINE LEARNING APPLICATION IN NON TRADITIONAL MACHINING PROCESSES

The dynamic business environment of today's manufacturing companies is affected by uncertainty. Especially looking at domains most likely to being optimized, e.g. monitoring and control, scheduling and diagnostics, it becomes apparent that the increasing availability of data is adding another challenge:

besides the large amounts of available date e.g. sensor data, the high dimensionality and variety e.g. due to different sensors or connected processes of data of manufacturing optimization problems (Esmaeilian et al., 2016).

Machine learning (ML) has been successfully utilized in various process optimization, monitoring and control applications in manufacturing, and predictive maintenance in different industries. ML techniques were found to provide promising potential for improved quality control optimization in different non traditional machining processes, especially in complex manufacturing environments where detection of the causes of problems is difficult. However, often ML applications are found to be limited focusing on specific processes instead of the whole manufacturing system (Scholz-Reiter et al., 2012).

There are many different ML methods, tools, and techniques available, each with distinct advantages and disadvantages. The domain of ML has grown to an independent research domain. Therefore, within this section, the goal is to find a suitable ML technique for application in non traditional machining processes.

To overcome some of today's major challenges of complex manufacturing systems the machine learning techniques are the only option. These data-driven approaches are able to find highly complex and non-linear patterns in data of different types and sources and trans- form raw data to features spaces, so-called models, which are then applied for prediction, detection, classification, regression, or forecasting (Wuest et al., 2016).

REVOLUTIONIZE NON TRADITIONAL MACHINING PROCESS BY MACHINE LEARNING

Manufacturers care most about finding new ways to grow, excel at product quality while still being able to take on short lead-time production runs from customers. New business models often bring the paradox of new product lines that strain existing ERP, CRM and PLM systems by the need always to improve time-to-customer performance. New products are proliferating in manufacturing today, and delivery windows are tightening. Manufacturers are turning to machine learning to improve the end-to-end performance of their operations and find a performance-based solution to this paradox ().

The machine learning is revolutionizing the manufacturing industry include the following:

1. Improving semiconductor manufacturing yields up to 30%, reducing scrap rates, and optimizing operations are is achievable with machine learning. Attaining up to a 30% reduction in yield detraction in semiconductor manufacturing, reducing scrap rates based on machine learning-based root-cause analysis and reducing testing costs using AI optimization are the top three areas where machine learning will improve semiconductor manufacturing.
2. McKinsey also found that AI-enhanced predictive maintenance of industrial equipment will generate a 10% reduction in annual maintenance costs, up to a 20% downtime reduction and 25% reduction in inspection costs.
3. Manufacturer's adoption of machine learning and analytics to improve predictive maintenance is predicted to increase 38% in the next five years according to PwC. Analytics and MI-driven process and quality optimization are predicted to grow 35% and process visualization and automation, 34%. PwC sees the integration of analytics, APIs and big data contributing to a 31% growth rate for connected factories in the next five years.

4. McKinsey predicts machine learning will reduce supply chain forecasting errors by 50% and reduce lost sales by 65% with better product availability. Supply chains are the lifeblood of any manufacturing business. Machine learning is predicted to reduce costs related to transport and warehousing and supply chain administration by 5 to 10% and 25 to 40%, respectively. Due to machine learning, overall inventory reductions of 20 to 50% are possible.
5. Improving yield rates, preventative maintenance accuracy and workloads by the asset is now possible by combining machine learning and Overall Equipment Effectiveness (OEE). OEE is a pervasively used metric in manufacturing as it combines availability, performance, and quality, defining production effectiveness. Combined with other metrics, it's possible to find the factors that impact manufacturing performance the most and least. Integrating OEE and other datasets in machine learning models that learn quickly through iteration are one of the fastest growing areas of manufacturing intelligence and analytics today.

PREDICTIVE QUALITY ANALYTICS WITH MACHINE LEARNING

The quality of output is crucial and product quality deterioration can also be predicted using Machine Learning. Knowing beforehand that the quality of products being manufactured is destined to drop prevents the wastage of raw materials and valuable production time.

Machine Learning can be split into two main techniques – Supervised and Unsupervised machine learning (Wuest, Liu, Lu et al, 2014).

4.1 Supervised Machine Learning

In manufacturing use cases, supervised machine learning is the most commonly used technique since it leads to a predefined target: we have the input data; we have the output data; and we're looking to map the function that connects the two variables.

Supervised machine learning demands a high level of involvement – data input, data training, defining and choosing algorithms, data visualizations, and so on. The goal is to construct a mapping function with a level of accuracy that allows us to predict outputs when new input data is entered into the system (Wuest et al., 2016).

Initially, the algorithm is fed from a training dataset, and by working through iterations, continues to improve its performance as it aims to reach the defined output. The learning process is completed when the algorithm reaches an acceptable level of accuracy.

In manufacturing, one of the most powerful use cases for Machine Learning is Predictive Maintenance, which can be performed using two Supervised Learning approaches: Classification and Regression. Fig. 1 shows the difference between Classification and Regression.

These two approaches share the same goal: to map a relationship between the input data (from the manufacturing process) and the output data (known possible results such as part failure, overheating etc.) (Opitz & Maclin, 1999).

Classification

When data exists in well-defined categories, Classification can be used. An example of Classification that we're all familiar with is the email filter algorithm that decides whether an email should be sent to our spam folder, or not. Classification is limited to a boolean value response, but can be very useful since only a small amount of data is needed to achieve a high level of accuracy.

In machine learning, common Classification algorithms include naive Bayes, logistic regression, support vector machines and Artificial Neural Networks.

Predictive Maintenance makes use of multi-class classification since there are multiple possible causes for the failure of a machine or component. These are possible outcomes that are classified as potential equipment issues, calculated using a number of variables including machine health, risk levels and possible reasons for malfunction (Monostori, 2003).

Regression

Regression is used when data exists within a range (e.g. temperature, weight), which is often the case when dealing with data collected from sensors.

In manufacturing, regression can be used to calculate an estimate for the Remaining Useful Life (RUL) of an asset. This is a prediction of how many days or cycles we have before the next component/machine/system failure (Lu, 1990).

For regression, the most commonly used machine learning algorithm is Linear Regression, being fairly quick and simple to implement, with output that is easy to interpret. An example of linear regression would be a system that predicts temperature, since temperature is a continuous value with an estimate that would be simple to train (Wuest, Liu, Lu et al, 2014).

Unsupervised Machine Learning

With Supervised machine learning we start off by working from an expected outcome and train the algorithm accordingly. Unsupervised learning is suitable for cases where the outcome is not yet known.

Clustering

In some cases, not only will the outcome be unknown to us, but information describing the data will also be lacking (data labels). By creating clusters of input data points that share certain attributes, a Machine Learning algorithm can discover underlying patterns.

Clustering can also be used to reduce noise (irrelevant parameters within the data) when dealing with extremely large numbers of variables (Monostori, 2003).

Artificial Neural Networks

In the manufacturing sector, Artificial Neural Networks are proving to be an extremely effective unsupervised learning tool for a variety of applications including production process simulation and Predictive Quality Analytics.

The basic structure of the Artificial Neural Network is loosely based upon how the human brain processes information using its network of around 100 billion neurons, allowing for extremely complex and versatile problem solving. Fig. 2 exhibits that the basic schematic of a feed-forward Artificial Neural Network (Sun et al., 2004).

Every node in one layer is connected to every node in the next. Hidden layers can be added as required, depending on the complexity of the problem.

This ability to process a large number of parameters through multiple layers makes Artificial Neural Networks very suitable for the variable-rich and constantly changing processes common to manufacturing. Moreover, once properly trained, an Artificial Neural Network can demonstrate a high level of accuracy when creating predictions regarding the mechanical properties of processed products, enabling cuts in the cost of raw materials (Thomas et al., 2012).

Data Preparation

Machine learning is all about data, so understanding some key elements about the quality and type of data needed is extremely important in ensuring accurate results. With Predictive Maintenance, for example, we're focused on failure events (Wuest et al., 2016). Therefore, it makes sense to start by collecting historical data about the machines' performance and maintenance records in order to form predictions about future failures. Since the operational life span of production machines is usually a number of years, historical data should reach back far enough to properly reflect the machines' deterioration processes. Additionally, other static information about the machine/system is also useful such as data about a machine's features, its mechanical properties, typical usage behaviour and environmental operating conditions (Lu, 1990).

THE GROUNDBREAKING BENEFITS OF MACHINE LEARNING IN OVERALL MANUFACTURING

The introduction of Machine Learning to industry represents a sea change with many benefits that can result in advantages well beyond efficiency improvements, opening doors to new business opportunities (Monostori, 2003).

Some of the direct benefits of Machine Learning in manufacturing include (Sun et al., 2004).

1. **Cost reduction through Predictive Maintenance**. PdM leads to less maintenance activity, which means lower labor costs and reduced inventory and materials wastage.
2. **Predicting Remaining Useful Life (RUL)**. Knowing more about the behavior of machines and equipment leads to creating conditions that improve performance while maintaining machine health. Predicting RUL does away with "unpleasant surprises" that cause unplanned downtime.
3. **Improved supply chain management** through efficient inventory management and a well monitored and synchronized production flow.
4. **Improved Quality Control** with actionable insights to constantly raise product quality.
5. **Improved Human-Robot** collaboration improving employee safety conditions and boosting overall efficiency.

6. **Consumer-focused manufacturing** – being able to respond quickly to changes in the market demand.

CONCLUSION

In this chapter, at first the challenges of advance manufacturing systems, e.g. escalating complexity, dynamic and chaotic structures are highlighted. Following, machine learning (ML) limitations and advantages from a manufacturing perspective are discussed. Revolutionize non traditional machining process by machine learning is also been discussed here and from this discussion it is concluded that machine learning is reducing all types of additional cost involved in any production system. At last it is concluded that within intelligent manufacturing systems and smart manufacturing the machine learning (ML) is already a powerful tool for many applications and its importance will amplify further in the future. Its interdisciplinary nature presents a big opening but also a momentous risk at the same time as collaboration between different disciplines, like Computer Science, Electrical Engineering, Mathematics and Industrial Engineering is essential to drive advancement.

REFERENCES

Esmaeilian, B., Behdad, S., & Wang, B. (2016). The evolution and future of manufacturing: A review. *Journal of Manufacturing Systems*, *39*, 79–100. doi:10.1016/j.jmsy.2016.03.001

Harding, J. A., Shahbaz, M., & Srinivas Kusiak, A. (2006). Data mining in manufacturing: A review. *Journal of Manufacturing Science and Engineering*, *128*(4), 969–976. doi:10.1115/1.2194554

Kang, H. S., Ju, Y. L., Choi, S. S., Kim, H., & Park, J. H. (2016). Smart manufacturing: Past research, present findings, and future directions. *Int J Precision Eng Manuf Green Technol*, *3*(1), 111–128. doi:10.100740684-016-0015-5

Lu, S. C.-Y. (1990). Machine learning approaches to knowledge synthesis and integration tasks for advanced engineering automation. *Computers in Industry*, *15*, 105–120.

Monostori, L. (2003). AI and machine learning techniques for managing complexity, changes and uncertainties in manufacturing. *Engineering Applications of Artificial Intelligence*, *16*(4), 277–291. doi:10.1016/S0952-1976(03)00078-2

Neogi, N., Mohanta, D. K., & Dutta, P. K. (2014). Review of vision-based steel surface inspection systems. *EURASIP Journal on Image and Video Processing*, *1*(1), 1–19. doi:10.1186/1687-5281-2014-50

Opitz, D., & Maclin, R. (1999). Popular ensemble methods: An empirical study. *Journal of Artificial Intelligence Research*, *11*, 169–198. doi:10.1613/jair.614

Pernkopf, F., & O'Leary, P. (2002). Visual inspection of machined metallic high-precision surfaces. *EURASIP Journal on Advances in Signal Processing*, *7*(7), 667–668. doi:10.1155/S1110865702203145

Scholz-Reiter, B., Weimer, D., & Thamer, H. (2012). Automated surface inspection of cold-formed micro-parts. *CIRP Ann Manuf Technol*, *61*(1), 531–534. doi:10.1016/j.cirp.2012.03.131

Shin, S. J., Woo, J., & Rachuri, S. (2014). Predictive analytics model for power consumption in manufacturing. *Procedia CIRP*, *15*, 153–158. doi:10.1016/j.procir.2014.06.036

Sun, J., Rahman, M., Wong, Y., & Hong, G. (2004). Multiclassification of tool wear with support vector machine by manufacturing loss consideration. *International Journal of Machine Tools & Manufacture*, *44*(11), 1179–1187. doi:10.1016/j.ijmachtools.2004.04.003

Thomas, A. J., Byard, P., & Evans, R. (2012). Identifying the UK's manufacturing challenges as a benchmark for future growth. *Journal of Manufacturing Technology Management*, *23*(2), 142–156. doi:10.1108/17410381211202160

Vogl, G. W., Weiss, B. A., & Helu, M. (2016). A review of diagnostic and prognostic capabilities and best practice for manufacturing. *Journal of Intelligent Manufacturing*, •••, 1–17. PMID:30820072

Wuest, T., Irgens, C., & Thoben, K.-D. (2014). An approach to monitoring quality in manufacturing using supervised machine learning on product state data. *Journal of Intelligent Manufacturing*, *25*(5), 1167–1180. doi:10.100710845-013-0761-y

Wuest, T., Liu, A., Lu, S. C.-Y., & Thoben, K.-D. (2014). Application of the stage gate model in production supporting quality management. *Procedia CIRP*, *17*, 32–37. doi:10.1016/j.procir.2014.01.071

Wuest, T., Weimer, D., Irgens, C., & Thoben, K. D. (2016). Machine learning in manufacturing: Advantages, challenges, and applications. *Production & Manufacturing Research*, *4*(1), 23–45. doi:10.10 80/21693277.2016.1192517

Xie, X. (2008). A review of recent advances in surface defect detection using texture analysis techniques. *Elcvia Electron Lett ComputVision Image Anal*, *7*(3), 1–22. doi:10.5565/rev/elcvia.268

Chapter 13
Role of Non-Traditional Machining Equipment in Industry 4.0

Tarun Kanti Jana
Haldia Institute of Technology, India

ABSTRACT

The manufacturing industry is undergoing drastic changes owing to a steep rise in business competition and growing complexities in other business perspectives. The highly turbulent market is characterized by ever-increasing mass customization, wide volume-mix, shorter lead time, and low cost, which along with varieties of internal disturbances have complicated the business stability. The multi-agent-based systems comprising of fundamental entities called agents and characterized by autonomy, cooperation, and self-organizing abilities have already made remarkable breakthrough to deal with the challenges through increased robustness, scalability, and enhanced adaptability through their dynamic capabilities. The decision-making ability of the agents can be augmented if equipped with cognitive abilities like that of human beings. The chapter discusses cyber-physical production system (CPPS) to realize cognitive manufacturing in non-conventional machining environments.

INTRODUCTION

The highly turbulent global market is characterized by ever-increasing mass customization, wide volume-mix, shorter lead time, and low cost, which along with varieties of internal disturbances has complicated the business stability by many-fold. This has compelled the factories to adopt new approaches in manufacturing to combat these unprecedented challenges and survive in the highly competitive business world. The proliferation of Information and Communication Technologies (ICT) in the recent years has fueled the challenges on one hand and simultaneously provides solution on the other. Against the backdrop of the rising complexities and disturbances, the Industry is now passing through the fourth Industrial Revolution, identified as Industry 4.0. Industry 4.0 emphasizes on digital technology to add a new dimension with the help of interconnectivity through the Internet of Things (IoT), access to real-time data and its

DOI: 10.4018/978-1-7998-3624-7.ch013

analysis, and the use of cyber-physical systems. Industry 4.0 offers a more comprehensive, interlinked, and holistic approach to manufacturing. It connects physical world with the digital world, and allows for better collaboration and access across departments, partners, product, and people. Industry 4.0 harnesses the factories with the weapon to better control the processes and operations, and allows them to utilize instant data to enhance productivity, improve processes, and boost growth.

THE BACKGROUND

The chronological development in manufacturing philosophy that had taken place since the ancient times till the beginning of the 21st Century is shown in Table 1.

Table 1. Chronological evolution of revolution in manufacturing paradigm

Stone age	Pyramid age	Mediaeval age	Victorian age	Early 20th Century	Late 20th Century	Early 21st Century
Craft	Craft	Craft	Craft	Craft	Craft	Craft
	Project	Project	Project	Project	Project	Project
		Process	Process	Process	Process	Process
			Batch	Batch	Batch	Batch
				Line	Line	Line
					Lean	Lean
						Agile

The aforesaid development can also be categorized under different industrial revolution.

1st Industrial Revolution

The first industrial revolution started around 1760 and continued till 1840 with a focus on replacement of muscle power by non-living system for execution of work through mechanization and generation of mechanical power. Steel production, Hydel power generation, Chemical manufacturing, machine tools etc. are some of the prominent developments of this era of revolution.

2nd Industrial Revolution

The second industrial revolution, spanned between 1870 and 1920, is characterized by electrification that boosted industrialization and mass production. During this period rapid industrial development took place. Interchangeable part production, assembly line, standardization of parts, and hard automation are key features of the development.

3rd Industrial Revolution

The advent of digital electronics and proliferation of digital computer triggered the third industrial revolution in 21st Century. Use of PLCs and microprocessors added a new dimension to the control systems in terms of reliability, flexibility, improved functionality, and compactness. Emergence of NC/CNC machine tools, industrial robots, batch production, Flexible automation, and Computer Integrated Manufacturing (CIM) feature this revolution. With the advent of hard and temperature-resistant materials, the need for non-traditional ways of machining was felt and subsequently different types of nonconventional machining processes were developed during 1960's.

4th Industrial Revolution

Currently, the industry is undergoing the fourth industrial revolution, popularly identified as Industry 4.0, which is triggered by the development of Information and Communications Technologies (ICT) and internet enabled systems and services. It harnesses with smart automation leading to cyber-physical systems with decentralized control and advanced connectivity (IoT functionalities).

PRESENT DAY'S MARKET REQUIREMENTS

The manufacturing industries across the globe have experienced the radical changes in the recent times in view of rising complexities in business perspective. The highly tumultuous global market is characterized by more complex customer-specific product design, stringent quality requirements, wide varieties, different volume-mix and shorter lead time. The various attributes that govern the manufacturing business is shown in Figure 1.

Proliferation of ICT along with several external and internal disturbances has further aggravated the situation. The survival of manufacturing industries therefore hinges on how successfully these volatile and unexpected situations are dealt with. Considering the customer's requirements of better quality product, low-cost customization and innovative product, present day's manufacturing is currently undergoing a revolutionary transition with focus shifting from mass production to mass customization. Thus the business philosophy which was earlier characterized by 'Make-to-stock (MTS)' has now been modified to what is called 'Engineer-to-order (ETO)'. Accordingly, the earlier concept of manufacturer's market has changed to customer's market. A high degree of customization coupled with increased shop floor disturbances inhibits quick responsiveness of the enterprises.

To address these challenges, the international business fraternity ought to adopt and adapt new manufacturing strategies and control requirements so as to migrate from the traditional hierarchical control to a more flexible and agile heterarchical control.

INDUSTRY 4.0

Industry 4.0 is a strategic initiative of the German government and the idea was put forward in public in Hannover Fair in 2011. The main theme of Industry 4.0 is *computerization of manufacturing* with an objective of realization of mass customization with the efficiency of mass production in a flexible

Figure 1. The attributes of present day's manufacturing business

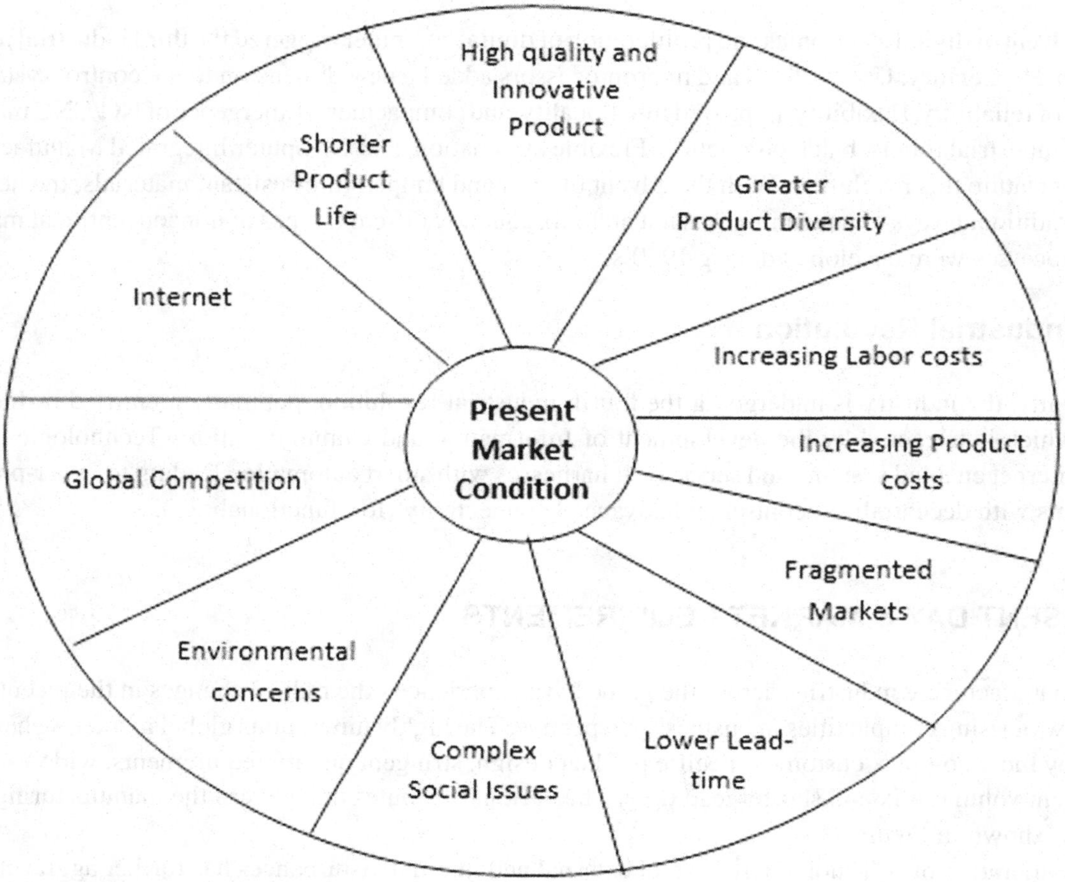

manner through self-optimization, self-organization, self-diagnosis, cognition and intelligent support of workers in their increasingly complex work. Germany has already proved its market leadership in the areas of manufacturing, particularly heavy machinery and automotive industries. To retain the same position and maintain a sustainable growth in this sector, even in the present day's highly traumatic business environment, German government emphasis on the need for advanced automation as reflected in Industry 4.0. Since its introduction, Industry 4.0 has gained substantial attention in research, industries and in academia.

Industry 4.0 hinges on advanced automation and computing such as Internet of Things (IoT), Cloud computing, Data Analytics, Machine Learning, Artificial Intelligence (AI) and seamless interconnectivity among the facilities through a communication network. It is characterized by the integration along three dimensions: horizontal integration through value networks, vertical integration together with networked manufacturing systems, and end-to-end digital integration of engineering across the value chain of a product's life-cycle. The horizontal integration implies that the machines or production units communicate and share their performance status and respond autonomously to dynamic production variations. The ultimate goal is that such production units will be able to produce goods economically and reduce downtime through predictive maintenance. However, if an enterprise has multiple production facilities, horizontal integration establishes a coordinated Manufacturing Execution Systems (MES) so as to share production facility data across the entire enterprise and, wherever possible, production tasks are shifted automatically among facilities in order to respond quickly and efficiently to production variables. Vertical integration in Industry 4.0 aims to connect all logical layers within the organization from the shop-floor up through R&D, quality assurance, product management, IT, sales and marketing, and so on. Data flows up and down through these layers by establishing two-way communication so that both strategic and tactical decisions can be data-driven. The vertically integrated enterprise based on Industry 4.0 have a significant competitive edge by being able to respond appropriately and with agility to changing market demands and new opportunities. Using the Internet of Services (IoS), both internal and external services are offered and used by stakeholders of the entire value chain. The successful implementation of Industry 4.0 leads to realization of Smart Factory which implies smart production in all areas of manufacturing and smart products. Some of the potential benefits that can be accrued from Industry 4.0 are (i) Quick responsiveness to customer requirements, (ii) Better adaptation to the mass customization, (iii) Optimization of processes and rationalization of resources and facilities, and (iv) overall reduction of cost.

Concept of Smart Factory

A factory equipped with the facilities having a vision in compliance with the Industry 4.0 is popularly known as Smart factory. A smart factory is therefore envisaged as a network of self-organized production units which allows production processes to be globally optimized and adaptive to cope with the unexpected changes and disturbances. A smart factory is therefore having smart design, smart manufacturing, smart scheduling etc. so as to cover entire range of activities under its purview and at the same time each activity is characterized by data collection, data analysis, which would be eventually used for smart decision-making.

Products in such factories are also 'smart', with embedded sensors that are used via wireless network to enable real-time data collection and its analysis to assess the product performance, predict the future, and environment conditions. Smart products having their built-in processing capabilities, can decide their processing path, negotiate and bargain with the resources for their processing considering various issues, and can also optimize these requirements. Additionally, smart products are capable of progress monitoring during production and self-health checking for their entire life cycle.

Cyber Physical Systems (CPS)

Rapid development in ICT has usher a new arena of technologies such as cloud computing, Internet of Things (IoT), big data analytics, artificial intelligence (AI) etc. (S. Wang et. al., 2016, Monostori et. al., 2016, Vaidya et. al., 2016) which brings physical world together with virtual world, giving rise to the Cyber Physical systems (CPS). The advent of these new technologies enables the creation of a smart, networked world, in which "things" are endowed with a certain degree of intelligence, and moreover, being increasingly connected to each other.

Cyber-physical systems find its application in transportation, energy, health and well-being, manufacturing, and smart infrastructures and cities. A Cyber Physical Production Systems (CPPS) is the integration of physical manufacturing equipment and sensors with the virtual world through internet coupled with big data analytics, AI, and cloud computing so as to convert the existing manufacturing system to a more powerful and smart through enhanced decision-making, computing, and communication. The domain of CPS can be best understood by set theoretic approach as: ''CPPS is about the intersection, not the union, of the physical and the cyber world (Monostori et. al., 2016). The scheme of such a system is shown in Figure 2.

A CPPS manifest three key characteristics:

1. **Intelligence:** The entities are capable of sensing and acquiring information from their surroundings and can act autonomously with higher level decision-making based on the collected data.
2. **Connectivity:** Establishing connection with the other elements of the system for necessary co-operation and collaboration including human being. Moreover, entities will be able to access the internet for available knowledge and services.
3. **Responsiveness:** Ability to respond to changes by providing solution at the earliest.

A CPS therefore provides a new paradigm of manufacturing by establishing communication and cooperation among equipment and devices (physical world) and information systems (digital world) in a decentralized manner and in real time to derive enhanced benefits in the wake of rising business challenges.

AGENT BASED SYSTEM TO REALIZE CPPS

Another underlying concept of smart automation is migration from orthodox hierarchical automation systems to self-organizing cyber physical production system so as to leverage the benefit of traditional mass production in mass customized production. It is therefore imperative to adopt agent based approach for better control of Manufacturing Execution Systems (MES), which rely on heterarchical control architecture in sharp contrast to the traditional and orthodox hierarchical control. Agent based control offers higher flexibility and agility to deal with the changing circumstances. Since, negotiation and cooperation based work is at the core of an agent based system, manufacturing systems following such an approach would be able to implement CPPS successfully.

In recent past, agent technology has become a popular approach under distributed problem solving paradigm for decentralized control of the shop floor. Instead of having one large computing system, cooperative intelligent agents are being used as fundamental entities of the systems to realize flexibility and adaptability in the wake of dynamic variations in the system. An agent is a small distinguishable, self-reliant and autonomous entity having decision making ability to plan its own work and its execution. The concept of an agent can be extended further in terms of its ability in the environment where it is supposed to work. Wooldridge and Jennings (1995) defined agent as an autonomous and flexible computational system situated in some environment that is capable of flexible and autonomous action in order to meet its design objectives. From the objected-oriented programming view point, agents are a special type of software objects which, have their own internal algorithms, use a common language for communication and in contrast with objects, have the possibility to reason, interpret incoming messages, and take decisions according to its specific beliefs and objectives. Monostori et al. (2006) defined agent as a computational system that is situated in a dynamic environment and is capable of exhibiting

Figure 2. The Scheme of Cyber Physical System

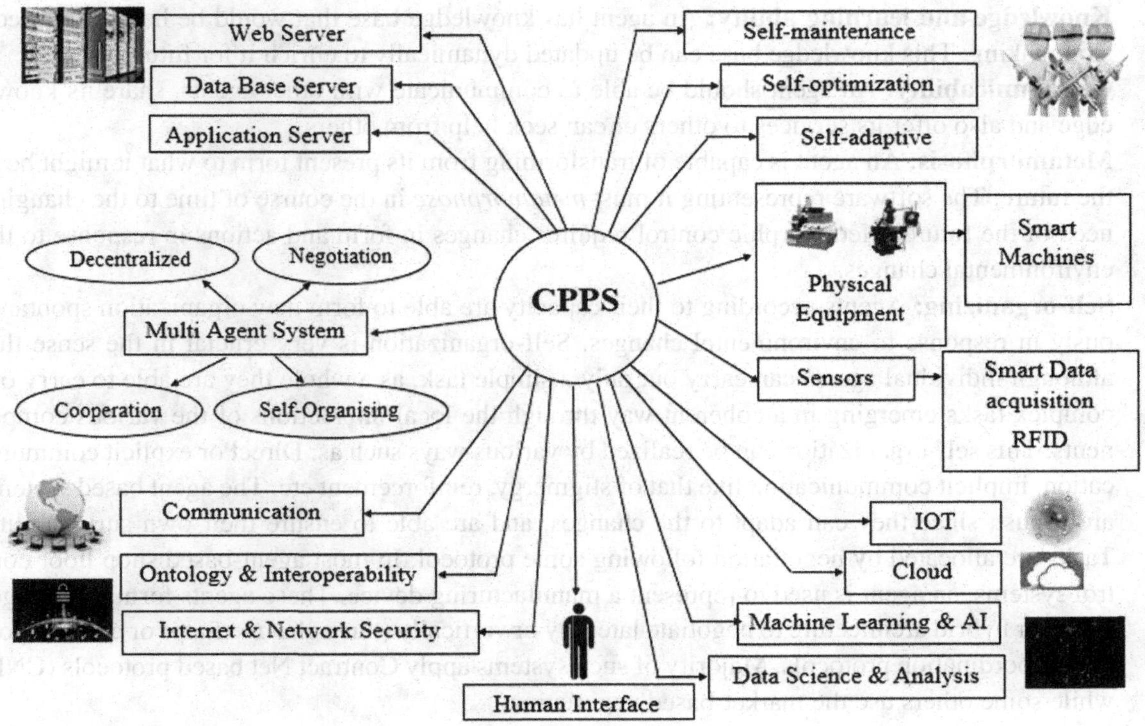

autonomous and intelligent behavior. The gross behavior of an agent is characterized by the attributes like autonomy, intelligence, adaptation and co-operation.

A multi-agent system (MAS) is collection a set of agents having heterarchical control structure capable of interacting with each other, in order to achieve their individual goals when they do not have adequate knowledge and/or skills to accomplish the same in standalone mode. According to Li and Yang (2008), a MAS is a collection of autonomous agents working together to solve problems that are beyond the overall capability of individual agents. Meyer et al. (2009) defined MAS as a federation of software agents interacting in a shared environment that cooperate and coordinate their actions given their own goals and plans. Lou et al. (2010) viewed MAS as a distributed computing system composed of a number of interacting agents.

MAS is fundamentally a software technology, where an agent possess behavioral attributes like *autonomy* (ability to take one's own decision by virtue of proactiveness), *social ability* (interacts with other agents by mutual message-based communication), *reactivity* (agents can sense and respond to changes in the environment), and *proactiveness* (ability to take initiatives). The behavior of an agent is predominantly governed by autonomy and cooperation which help exhibits high performance against disturbances and remain fault-tolerant. Reconfiguration is rather easier according to the changing need of the system. The aforesaid properties can be explored further to few distinct and multi-faceted attributes that would be useful for implementation. These are listed as follows:

- **Cognition:** An agent would be able to sense the environment in which it is working by virtue of awareness, perception, reasoning and judgment.
- **Knowledge and learning ability:** An agent has knowledge base that would be helpful for decision making. This knowledge base can be updated dynamically to enrich it for future use.
- **Communicability:** An agent should be able to communicate with other agents, share its knowledge and also offer its services to others or can seek help from others.
- **Metamorphosis:** An agent is capable of transforming from its present form to what it might be in the future. The software representing it must *metamorphose* in the course of time to the changing need of the future. Metamorphic control requires changes in form and actions in response to the environmental changes.
- **Self-organizing:** Agents according to their capacity are able to form new organization spontaneously in response to environmental changes. Self-organization is very crucial in the sense that although individual agents can carry out only a simple task, as a whole they are able to carry out complex tasks emerging in a coherent way through the local interactions of the various components. This self-organization can be realized by various ways such as: Direct or explicit communication, implicit communication like that of stigmergy, reinforcement etc. The agent based systems are robust, since they can adapt to the changes, and are able to ensure their own survivability. Tasks are allocated by negotiation following some protocol. In most agent-based shop floor control systems, an agent is used to represent a manufacturing device. These agents form a heterogeneous or hybrid architecture to negotiate laterally or vertically (through a mediator or coordinator) using coordination protocols. Majority of such systems apply Contract Net based protocols (CNP) while some others use the market-based negotiation.

Agents manifest two contradictory properties: Under normal situation they are highly competitive and vie with each other for lucrative jobs to augment their prosperity and credentials. On the contrary, they are altruistic and benevolent when disturbances prevail. This implies that under disturbances they collaborate and cooperate to solve problems. The communication is the means for negotiation and cooperation. Thus an agent communication language having specific ontology with necessary interoperability is the backbone of establishing communication.

However, agents are only being aware of a small problem, global optimization is difficult. Nevertheless, being intelligent, an agent always tries to improve local performance that eventually leads to global optimization. Thus global optimization is implicit. Successful implementation of agent based systems helps rationalize the load distribution, better address the need of the customer, and would be less affected from the negative consequences of a machine failure and other disturbances and therefore adaptive to changes and stay unperturbed. It therefore emerges that MAS platform is the potential platform for implementation of CPPS.

Concept of Cognitive Factory

Further advancement of MAS is possible, if agents are augmented with cognitive properties. Cognitive manufacturing is inspired by cognitive science wherein machines and equipment are capable of human-like decision making. It is the cognitive properties that enable human being to deal with the uncertainties by higher level decision-making. Cognitive manufacturing attempts to infuse cognitive properties such as perception, reasoning, learning and planning in machines so as to enable human like decision-making by machines. It is a promising approach to deal with uncertainties and to offer flexibility and agility in production systems. The Cognitive Factory learns from its tasks history and gain experience and is, therefore, easily adaptable to new products. This ensures small lot size and customized production at a competitive cost level. Furthermore, self-maintenance of the system components accomplishes preventive maintenance, which eventually reduces down time and improves productivity. Since factories and equipment get smarter and augmented with sensors, embedded systems, IoT, AI, Machine learning etc. cognitive factory can fulfill realization of Industry 4.0. Thus, a cognitive agent based system is the potential and promising platform to realize Industry 4.0 in its true sense.

Machine Tool 4.0

Machine Tools play a crucial role in metal working industries and envisaged as an integral part of it since its emergence in late 17th century. Since then, it has undergone several developments namely from Machine Tool 1.0 to Machine Tool 3.0 in synchronization with the three stages of industrial revolutions. To fit in the new era of industrialization marked by Industry 4.0, the further reform of machine tools can in no way be overlooked.

Cyber Physical Machine Tool (CPMT) is the integration of the machine tool, machining processes, computation and networking, where embedded computations monitor and control the machining processes, with feedback loops in which machining processes can affect computations and vice versa. Machine Tool 4.0 (MT 4.0) defines a new generation of machine tools that are smart, connected in a network, more adaptive and more autonomous than before. MT 4.0 makes use of sensory and embedded systems, IOT, and cloud computing technologies in CNC machine tools so as justify its presence in CPS.

In comparison to Machine Tool 3.0 which is essentially a CNC machine tool, MT 4.0 exhibits advanced features like network connectivity, adaptability, predictability, intelligence, with real-time feedback loops and human-machine interface. In addition to the position and velocity transducers inherent with any CNC systems, MT 4.0 incorporates various advanced sensors to capture real-time data pertaining to process and machine tool components. These real-time data from the physical systems are captured by sensors and data acquisition systems and transferred into the cyber space through various networks to build a Machine Tool Cyber Twin (MTCT). As communication tool, one can make use of either of embedded controllers, radio frequency identification devices (RFIDs), and Quick Response (QR)/bar codes. The MTCT acting as a digital world of the machine tool, has built-in computation and decision-making systems, which monitor and control the physical components and processes and provide the data to the cloud for further analysis. Process parameters monitoring and automatic adjustments helps the machine for better adaptability to the changes and can also optimize the performance by adaptive control. Self- health checking of components and analysis allows self-awareness, predictability and self-healing of the critical components. MT 4.0 utilizes the information models and knowledge base to work intelligently through higher level decision-making. With the passage of time, the knowledge base expands with added data. The history stored in the data warehouse can be utilized for assessment of performance and prediction of credibility.

NTM Equipment as MT 4.0

Traditionally, Machine Tool 3.0 are CNC machine tools intended for complex shape generations where metal removal takes place following the principles of conventional metal cutting, in which the tool path is generated by coded instructions and machine tool functions are controlled by a dedicated computer. However, it is misnomer to consider that applications of CNCs are limited to conventional metal cutting only. There are applications like profile cutting (Gas cutting), Rapid prototyping, Coordinate measuring etc. where CNC technology has got its prominence in industry.

Nontraditional machining (NTM) is yet another prospective approach to intricate and accurate shape generations by metal removal using varieties of fundamental principles of physics and chemistry instead of conventional approach. With the rapid development of advanced high strength materials which are not amenable for machining by conventional means, NTM processes offer potential solutions. Furthermore, very stringent dimensional accuracy together with extremely good surface finish requirements in difficult to machine materials also justify NTM as a promising technique. Some prominent NTM processes are EDM, ECM, CM, USM, LBM, AJM, WAJM, IBM etc. which can be catered to different materials and for various types of shapes generation with the associated attributes.

With the advancement of CNC technology, the NTM processes are increasingly controlled by it. We argue hereby that the equipment used for nontraditional machining can be successfully upgraded so as to consider them under the banner MT 4.0. The integration of physical NTM equipment and the sensors with the digital world would help accrue potential benefits of CPPS similar to that of metal cutting machine tools. Some salient generic parameters pertaining to NTM processes are Material removal rate (MRR), Surface finish, close dimensional tolerance, tool wear etc. which are functions of different process parameters.

In mechanical production the role of automation is crucial and undeniable. Increased automation in process control can considerably reduce the throughput time, production cost and inventory. Automatic monitoring of process parameters, real-time computation of output responses, and subsequent adjustments of the process variables can lead to self-adaptive optimization. This approach can be implemented in some cases with some non-conventional machining methods. EDM wire cutting is an appropriate example. Also NC controlled LASER or electron beam cutting are applied partially because of the improved automation in data transmission. For example, Knowledge of existing ECM processes can be used to develop knowledge rules for the selection of machining conditions. The optimization and tool-electrode design is carried out using ECM process models. Thus, the system combines the modern techniques of knowledge engineering and process simulation to automate the traditional ECM parameters selection. Another prominent approach to NTM process control is use of fuzzy rules. The quality of machining can be determined using fuzzy rules developed using experimental knowledge for recognizing instability in machining. Information provided by a signal processor is then used to decide on the appropriate electro-machining conditions. Artificial neural network is yet another approach for optimization. Neural nets are already used in EDM for monitoring and off-line process planning. In a simple application, pulse duration and current are used as inputs, and normal and abnormal (undesired) pulses are classified in the output stage. In the neural net, cutting depth, roughness, accuracy can be correlated with cutting conditions at the output stage.

NTM equipment can be made smart, if upgraded with sensors and embedded systems and integrated with digital world for higher level decision-making, thereby befitting its role in Industry 4.0. The equipment can be connected to the web server through the common interface. Varieties of application software are used to implement Machine learning, data analytics, ANN, GA etc. for analysis and optimization of process and machine performance through cloud. Monitoring the status and performance of critical components features self-prediction of machine health, thereby avoiding catastrophic failure. This automatically reduces machine down time and improves utilization. Database server records the past data, which could be used for analysis and prediction. NTM equipment suitably upgraded and integrated with digital world makes much promise to satisfy the present day's business requirements and therefore contribute significantly in CPPS environment in realization of Industry 4.0.

REFERENCES

Cengarle, M. V., Bensalem, S., McDermid, J., Passerone, R., Sangiovanni-Vincentelli, A., & Törngren, M. (2013). Characteristics, Capabilities, Potential applications of Cyber-Physical Systems: A Preliminary Analysis. *Cyber-Physical European Roadmap & Strategy*. http://www.cyphers.eu

De Silva, A. K. M., & McGeough, J. A. (2000). Computer applications in Unconventional machining. *Journal of Materials Processing Technology*, *107*(1-3), 276–282. doi:10.1016/S0924-0136(00)00722-6

Kanti, S. (2019). How cognitive technologies are redefining the future of manufacturing. *Analytics Insight.* Retrieved from https://www.analyticsinsight.net/how-cognitive-technologies-are-redefining-the-future-of-manufacturing/

Li, L., & Yang, Y. (2008). Agent-based ontology mapping and integration towards interoperability. *Expert Systems: International Journal of Knowledge Engineering and Neural Networks*, *25*(3), 197–220. doi:10.1111/j.1468-0394.2008.00460.x

Liu, C., & Xu, X. (2017). Cyber-Physical Machine Tool – the Era of Machine Tool 4.0. *Procedia CIRP*, *63*, 70–75. doi:10.1016/j.procir.2017.03.078

Liu, Y., & Xu, X. (2017). Industry 4.0 and cloud manufacturing: A Comparative Analysis. *Journal of Manufacturing Science and Engineering*, *139*(3), 034701–034708. doi:10.1115/1.4034667

Lou, P., Ong, S. K., & Nee, A. Y. C. (2010). Agent-based distributed scheduling for virtual job shops. *International Journal of Production Research*, *48*(13), 3889–3910. doi:10.1080/00207540902927918

Meyer, G. G., Framling, K., & Holmstrom, J. (2009). Intelligent Products: A survey. *Computers in Industry*, *60*(3), 137–148. doi:10.1016/j.compind.2008.12.005

Mills, K. (2019). *What is cognitive manufacturing? by Metrology news.* Retrieved from https://metrology.news/what-is-cognitive-manufacturing

Mohammadi, M., Al-Fuqaha, A., Sorour, S., & Guizani, M. (2018). Deep Learning for IoT Big Data and Streaming Analytics: A Survey. *IEEE Communications Surveys and Tutorials*, *20*(4), 2923–2960. doi:10.1109/COMST.2018.2844341

Monostori, L. (2014). Cyber-physical production systems: Roots, expectations and R&D challenges. *Procedia CIRP*, *17*, 9–13. doi:10.1016/j.procir.2014.03.115

Monostori, L., Kádár, B., Bauernhansl, T., Kondoh, S., Kumara, S., Reinhart, G., Sauer, O., Schuh, G., Sihn, W., & Ueda, K. (2016). Cyber-physical systems in manufacturing. *CIRP Annals - Manufacturing Technology, 65*(2), 621-641.

Monostori, L., Váncza, J., & Kumara, S. R. T. (2006). Agent-Based Systems for Manufacturing. *Annals of the CIRP*, *55*(2), 1–24. doi:10.1016/j.cirp.2006.10.004

Shen, W., Hao, Q., Yoon, H. J., & Norrie, D. H. (2006). Applications of agent-based systems in intelligent manufacturing: An updated review. *Advanced Engineering Informatics*, *20*(4), 415–431. doi:10.1016/j.aei.2006.05.004

Shen, W., Norrie, D. H., & Barthes, J.-P. (2001). *A Multi-Agent Systems for Concurrent Intelligent Design and Manufacturing*. Taylor & Francis Inc. doi:10.4324/9780203305607

Snoeys, R., Staelens, F., & Dekeyser, W. (1986). Current Trends in Non-Conventional Material Removal Processes. *Annals CIRP*, *35*(2), 467–480. doi:10.1016/S0007-8506(07)60195-4

Törngren, M., & Grogan, P. T. (2018). How to Deal with the Complexity of Future Cyber-Physical Systems. *Designs*, *2*(40), 2–16. doi:10.3390/designs2040040

Vaidya, S., Ambad, P., & Bhosle, S. (2018). Industry 4.0 – A Glimpse. *Procedia Manufacturing*, *20*, 233–238. doi:10.1016/j.promfg.2018.02.034

Wang, S., Wan, J., Li, D., & Zhang, C. (2016). Implementing Smart Factory of Industries 4.0: An Outlook. *International Journal of Distributed Sensor Networks*, 1–10.

Wooldridge, M., & Jennings, N. R. (1995). Intelligent agents: Theory and practice. *The Knowledge Engineering Review*, *10*(2), 115–152. doi:10.1017/S0269888900008122

Wu, D., Greer, M. J., Rosen, D. W., & Schaefer, D. (2013). Cloud Manufacturing: Strategic Vision and State-of-the-Art. *Journal of Manufacturing Systems*, *32*(4), 564–579. doi:10.1016/j.jmsy.2013.04.008

Xu, X. (2017). Machine Tool 4.0 for the new era of manufacturing. *International Journal of Advanced Manufacturing Technology*, *92*(5-8), 1893–1900. doi:10.100700170-017-0300-7

Zaeh, M. F., Reinhart, G., Ostgathe, M., Geiger, F., & Lau, C. (2010). A holistic approach for the cognitive control of production systems. *Advanced Engineering Informatics*, *24*(3), 300–307. doi:10.1016/j.aei.2010.05.014

Zheng, P., Wang, H., Sang, Z., Zhong, R. Y., Liu, Y., Liu, C., Mubarok, K., Yu, S., & Xu, X. (2018). Smart manufacturing systems for Industry 4.0: Conceptual framework, scenarios, and future perspectives. *Frontiers of Mechanical Engineering*, *13*(2), 137–150. doi:10.100711465-018-0499-5

Chapter 14
Finite Element–Based Optimization of Additive Manufacturing Process Using Statistical Modelling and League of Champion Algorithm

Anoop Kumar Sood
https://orcid.org/0000-0001-5702-4108
National Institute of Foundry and Forge Technology, India

ABSTRACT

The study develops a 2D (two-dimensional) finite element model with a Gaussian heat source to simulate powder bed-based laser additive manufacturing process of Ti6Al4V alloy. The modelling approach provides insight into the process by correlating laser power and scan speed with melt pool temperature distribution and size. To tackle the FEA result in optimization environment, statistical approach of data normalization and regression modelling is adopted. Statistical treatment is not only able to deduce the interdependence of various objectives consider but also make the representation of objectives and constraint computationally simple. Adoption of a new stochastic algorithm namely league of a champion algorithm (LCA) together with penalty function approach for non-linear constraint handling reduces the effort required and computational complexity involved in determining the optimum parameter setting.

INTRODUCTION

Additive manufacturing (AM) is a term which encompasses a group of technologies which can build a part by consolidating the feedstock in a layer by layer manner as per the part digital information (Gibson, 2015). These technologies can be grouped into seven categories namely (a) powder bed fusion (PBF); (b) direct energy deposition (DED); (c) Sheet lamination; (d) Binder jetting; (e) material jetting; (f) Extrusion based process; (g) Vet photopolymerization process (Sames, 2016). Ability to manufacture complex

DOI: 10.4018/978-1-7998-3624-7.ch014

functional parts with minimum part count and low buy to fly ratio makes them viable manufacturing alternative in aerospace, automobile and dental industries to name a few (Uriondo, 2015). The majority of AM systems worldwide utilize a laser powder bed fusion process (Gu, 2012). In the framework of this process, a laser heat source scans the selected locations of the powder bed at the controlled rate and melts the powder and fuse it with previously solidified layer or substrate which then solidifies and form a solid layer of the part to be produced. The inherent nature of process induces non-uniform temperature gradient affecting part quality in terms of distortion, non-uniform microstructure growth, residual stress development, poor surface quality and uncertainty in part performance (Abdulhameed, 2019).

The previous effort to improve part quality is related to in-situ process monitoring and control (Malekipour, 2018) or restoring to experimental methods to optimize the process parameters (Wang, 2019). Experimental methods are costly in terms of AM and outcome depends upon the choice of parameters and their range and will not give the insight of the process mechanism, associated uncertainty or cause of uncertainty and effect of processing parameters on them. In situ monitoring and control may aid AM part quality improvement but such type of feedback control mechanism works well when parameters are set to near optimum values, especially for the case when response time is very small.

To overcome the challenges in improving part quality, modelling and simulation (M&S) is the current direction of research to understand the physics of process (Foteinopoulos, 2019). Most of the past studies in this direction are concentrated on the development of a model based on transient nature of the process, Gaussian heat distribution, temperature dependent material properties, complex heat and mass transfer phenomena and phase changes involved (Luo, 2018). Few of the researchers extended modelling approach to predict residual stress develops in the part (Mukherjee, 2017), distortion and shrinkage calculation for reducing part geometric dimensioning and tolerancing errors (Paul, 2014), controlling the microstructure growth within the part (Song, 2018), simulate the solid-liquid phase transition (Li, 2018) predict melt pool size (Cheng, 2016) and heat and mass transfer phenomena within the melt pool (Gan, 2017). Despite vast growth in the AM related research especially in the area of M&S, there are certain issues which are unaddressed or need new insight; like integrating M&S with optimization techniques especially under the constraint environment. In this direction present work adopted M&S approach to identify key factors and related assumptions to explain variation during the part build with minimum simulation time. For this 2D (two dimensional) metamodel is proposed to simulate laser-based powder bed fusion (LPBF) of Ti6Al4V alloy. Influence of important process parameters namely laser power and laser scan speed on a maximum temperature of the melt pool and melt pool size is studied using finite element analysis (FEA). To tackle the FEA result in optimization environment statistical approach of data normalization and regression modelling is adopted. Statistical treatment not only able to deduce the interdependence of various objectives consider but also make the representation of objectives and constraint computationally simple. A novel meta-heuristic algorithm namely league of a champion algorithm (LCA) (Husseinzadeh, 2014) which was originally design for the unconstrained optimization problem is model for constrained optimization involve in this study and use to determine the optimum value of laser power and scan speed.

In the next section detail of the LCA algorithm with a constraint handling approach is provided. This section is followed by a section on finite element (FE) modelling of LPBF process. Methodology to analyse the results is proposed in Section 4. Detail discussion on results together with the statistical relationship between input parameters and output response is presented in section 5, followed by confirmation experiment results. Finally, in the last section, major conclusions drawn from the study is presented.

LEAGUE OF CHAMPIONS ALGORITHM (LCA)

LCA is a stochastic algorithm to search global optimum in a continuous search space. Different to nature-inspired algorithms like particle swarm optimization (PSO) (Wang, 2018), bacteria forging algorithm (BFOA) (Huang, 2018), genetic algorithm (Wang, 2016). LCA mimic a sporting coemption between various teams in a regulated framework. The algorithm is successfully implemented in a number of real-life engineering problems like the design of pin-jointed structures (Jalili, 2017), performing job scheduling (Subbaraj, 2019) and many more (Abdulhamid, 2015).

In the assumed scenario of LCA, teams will play matches as per the pre-declare schedule such that after completion of a single season all teams have played an equal number of matches. The team which has a maximum number of wins or points after completion of all the seasons will be declared the winner. The outcome of the match between two teams depend upon their playing strength but the probability of a win is assumed to be equal for both the teams. If each team is considered as a population in a decision variable search space and individuals in teams are nothing but the decision variable themselves then to be considered as a winner, the variable must have the values which will optimize the objective function or maximize the playing strength under given set of constraints. To achieve this, the value of the variable is updated after each iteration in accordance with team formation strategies. Team formation, in turn, depends upon its own strength and weakness and strength and weakness of its opponent scheduled to be played in the current week. Strength and weakness of teams are measured with respect to their respective match outcomes in the previous week. For a team point of view, the strength of the opponent is considered as a threat and weakness of the opponent is considered as an opportunity. Based on using its own strengths for diffusing the threats or exploiting the opportunities and minimizing its weakness to avoid threats or taking advantages of opportunities team formation for each match is decided. The important stages or elements of the algorithm are described below.

League Schedule

League schedule defines a schedule of matches between various teams in a single season. In general, single round robin schedule is assumed where each team will play other team only once. To understand the way schedule is generated consider 6 teams in a league. Each team is assigned a number from 1 to 6. For the first week teams are paired randomly as shown in Fig. 1. That is 1 with 6, 2 with 5 and 3 with 4. To generate remaining weeks schedule fix one team, say team 1 and change the position of each team in clockwise direction. It is necessary that total teams in the league must be even. For generation of schedule if odd number of teams are present one dummy team can be added. Outcome of match of any team with dummy team will be decided in favour of team.

Figure 1. League schedule for single season

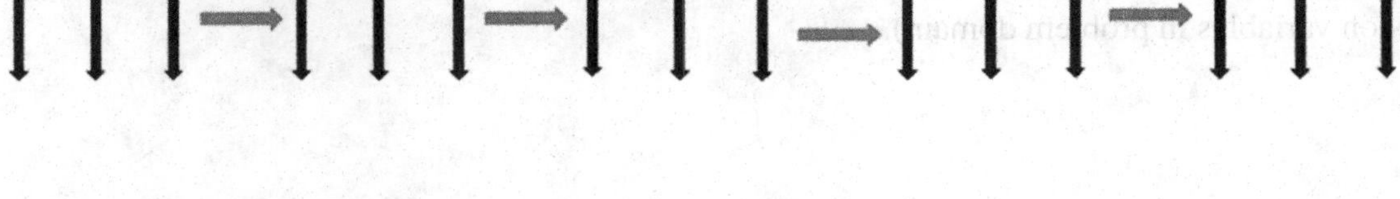

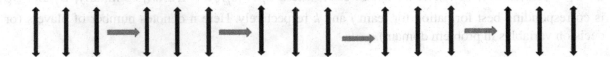

Winner-Loser Recognition

Chance of winning a match by any team depends upon its playing strength which is proportional to its degree of fit. Degree of fit is measured in terms of team playing strength from the fix reference point. Suppose team *i* and *j* are competing each other in a particular week *t*. X_i^t and X_j^t are their respective team formation with $f\left(X_i^t\right)$ and $f\left(X_j^t\right)$ their corresponding playing strength. Let p_i^t denotes the probability of team *i* beating team *j* and p_j^t is probability of team *j* beating team *i*. Accordingly we can write

$$\frac{f\left(X_i^t\right)-\hat{f}}{f\left(X_j^t\right)-\hat{f}}=\frac{p_j^t}{p_i^t} \tag{1}$$

where

$$p_i^t + p_j^t = 1 \tag{2}$$

In this equation $\hat{f}$ is an ideal value or an optimum value of objective function *f*. In most of the cases as in this work it is not known in advance hence is taken as best function value found so far. In Eq. 1 if say $f\left(X_i^t\right) = \hat{f}$ this means that $p_j^t = 0$ and $p_i^t = 1$.

From Eq. 1 and Eq. 2

$$p_i^t = \frac{f\left(X_j^t\right)-\hat{f}}{f\left(X_j^t\right)-2\hat{f}} \tag{3}$$

Since match outcome is stochastic, therefore random number $r \in [0,1]$ is generated and if $r < p_i^t$ team *i* will be adjust winner else team *j* will win the match.

New Team Formation

New team formation depends upon its current strength and weakness and threat and opportunity it faces. To understand this mathematically let,

l = index of team that will play with team *i* at week *t*+1,

j = index of the team that has played with team *i* at week *t* and

k = index of the team that has played with team *l* at week *t*.

B_i^t = best team formation for team *i* at week *t*, where $B_i^t = \{b_{id}^t \mid d = 1,2,..n\}$. Similarly, B_j^t and B_k^t is corresponding best formation for team *j* and *k* respectively. Here n denotes number of players (or decision variables in problem domain).

New team formation $X_i^{t+1} = \{x_{id}^{t+1} \mid d = 1,2,\ldots n\}$ for team *i* at week *t*+1 is decided based on conditions define below.

if *i* and *l* were winner at week *t*,

$$x_{id}^{t+1} = b_{id}^t + y_{id}^t \times \left\{\psi_1 \times r_1 \times \left(b_{id}^t - b_{kd}^t\right) + \psi_1 \times r_2 \times \left(b_{id}^t - b_{jd}^t\right)\right\} \ \forall d = 1,2,\ldots n \quad (4)$$

if *i* was a winner and *l* was a loser at week *t*,

$$x_{id}^{t+1} = b_{id}^t + y_{id}^t \times \left\{\psi_2 \times r_1 \times \left(b_{kd}^t - b_{id}^t\right) + \psi_1 \times r_2 \times \left(b_{id}^t - b_{jd}^t\right)\right\} \ \forall d = 1,2,\ldots n \quad (5)$$

if *i* had lost and *l* had won at week *t*,

$$x_{id}^{t+1} = b_{id}^t + y_{id}^t \times \left\{\psi_1 \times r_2 \times \left(b_{id}^t - b_{kd}^t\right) + \psi_2 \times r_1 \times \left(b_{jd}^t - b_{id}^t\right)\right\} \ \forall d = 1,2,\ldots n \quad (6)$$

if *i* and *l* had lost their matches at week *t*,

$$x_{id}^{t+1} = b_{id}^t + y_{id}^t \times \left\{\psi_2 \times r_2 \times \left(b_{kd}^t - b_{id}^t\right) + \psi_2 \times r_1 \times \left(b_{jd}^t - b_{id}^t\right)\right\} \ \forall d = 1,2,\ldots n \quad (7)$$

In these equations, $0 < \psi_1 < 1.5$ and $0 < \psi_2 < 1.5$ and $\psi_2 > \psi_1$ are constant coefficients. r_1 and r_2 are uniform random number between [0,1]. y_{id}^t is a binary variable. d^{th} element in current best formation will be changed only when $y_{id}^t = 1$. Let, $Y_{id}^t = (y_{i1}^t, y_{i2}^t, \ldots y_{in}^t)$ is a binary change array in which number of ones is equal to q_i^t given by Eq. 8.

$$q_i^t = \left\lceil \frac{\ln\left(1-\left(1-p_c\right)^{n-q_o+1}\right) \times r}{\ln\left(1-p_c\right)} \right\rceil + q_o - 1 \quad (8)$$

$r \in [0,1]$ is a random number. The greater positive (negative) of p_c, the smaller (greater) number of changes more than q_o is recommended. q_o is the least number of changes realized.

Constraint Handling

During team updating it may be possible that certain variable may assume out of bound value. In such cases, variable value is updated as per following conditions.

Let, $x_i^{lb} \le x_i \le x_i^{ub}$, here x_i^{lb} and x_i^{ub} are lower and upper bond of variable x_i.

if $x_i < x_i^{lb} : x_i = x_i + r \times \left(x_i^{ub} - x_i^{lb}\right)$ (9.a) if $x_i > x_i^{ub} : x_i = x_i - r \times \left(x_i^{ub} - x_i^{lb} \right)$ (9.b)

r∈[0,1] is a random number.

Numerous methods like special representations and operators, repair methods, methods based on the separation of objectives and constraints, penalty function approach etc. have been proposed for handling constraints (Deb, 2010). Among all these methods the most common approach for handling constraints is the method of a penalty function and is adopted in this study. This approach transforms the constrained problem into an unconstrained problem by adding high penalty value in objective function based on the amount of constraint violation present in the solution. This enhances the searchability in a feasible region as the infeasible solutions responsible for enhancing the objective function value are automatically neglected based on algorithm search criteria.

To exploit the LCA in function optimization problem the steps of algorithm are given as follows.

1. Initialize problem parameters, League size (L), total seasons (S), playing schedule, teams and iteration counter t=1.
2. Calculate the fitness function value.
3. If t=1, fitness function value of each team is considered as best personal fitness value else best personal fit value is the best fitness obtain till step t. Out of all personal best fitness values store the best fitness as global best fitness value.
4. Based on particular week schedule conduct the matches between team and choose winner and looser as explained n sub-section 2.2.
5. Update teams based on methodology explained in sub-section 2.3.
6. t=t+1;
7. If t>(L-1) ×S stop, else go to step b.

Finite Element Modelling

The thermal problem to be solved involves a laser beam traversing the surface of the powder bed at a constant speed, define as scan speed. The 2D heat transfer equation for an isotropic material, assuming there is no internal heat generation or sink inside the material, is written as (Cengel, 2002):

$$K\frac{\partial^2 T}{\partial x^2} + K\frac{\partial^2 T}{\partial z^2} = \rho C_p \frac{\partial T}{\partial t} \quad (10)$$

The assumptions that have been made in this study are the following:

1. The part created is situated in a 2D space and its shape is rectangular and continuous.
2. The heat transfer through radiation is neglected in comparison to that due to conduction.
3. The thermal conductivity (K), specific heat capacity (C_p) and density (ρ), are temperature dependent. Any other material properties used are constant and not temperature dependent.
4. The metal's vaporization is not taken into account, as it is negligible in the processes at hand.

5. The machine building platform is considered having an infinite heat capacity as a result, its temperature remains constant.
6. Changes in dimensions due to temperature induced differences in density or the powder/solid state change of the material have been neglected.

The fundamental mode of the Gaussian beam (TEM_{00}) is selected for the heat source model (Roberts, 2009). According to it irradiance of the laser can be written as:

$$q(r) = \alpha \frac{2P}{\pi r_o^2} \exp\left(-\frac{2r^2}{r_o^2}\right) \tag{11}$$

Here, $r = \sqrt{(x - x_o)^2 + z_o^2}$. P is laser power, d is laser spot diameter, (x_o, z_o) is centre of laser spot in Cartesian coordinate system. r_o is the radial distance from laser centre where irradiance is $\frac{1}{e^2}$ of maximum irradiance. α is absorptivity of powder.

Figure 2. Model with boundary conditions

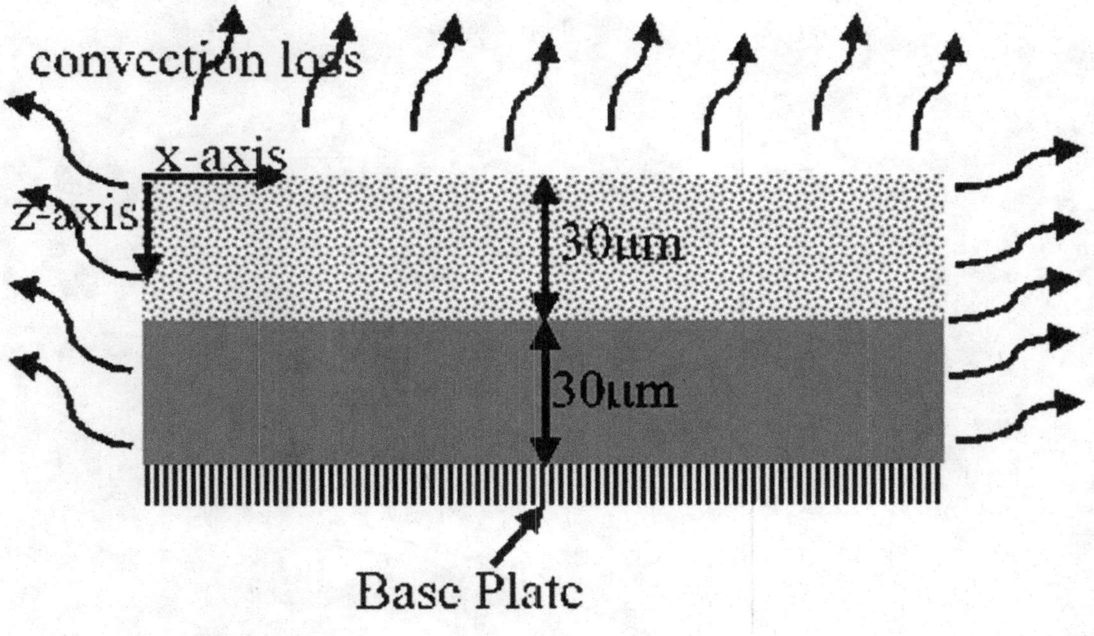

A two-layer model is used to simulate the laser deposition process, each layer thickness is taken as 30μm and length is taken as 0.6mm. The reference system is fixed at the top left corner of the model as shown in Fig. 2. It is assumed that the bottom layer is completely solidified whereas the top layer is a layer of just deposited powder particles. The part build chamber temperature is considered as constant and equals to 300K and the newly deposited layer of powder is assumed to be pre-heated to this temperature before depositing it over already solidified layer. Convection heat loss from the top, and side surfaces are assumed with constant convection coefficient h=10 W/(m²K). Base plate over which part is built is considered as a heat sink at a constant temperature of 300K. Four node square plane element of side length 3.7974μm, with a single degree of freedom corresponding to the temperature, is selected to generate finite element mesh. Heat flux given by Eq. 11 is applied at the centre of a top surface of powder layer for time $t = \frac{d}{v}$. Here d is the laser spot diameter and v is a laser scan speed.

Figure 3. Variation of Ti6Al4V thermal properties with temperature

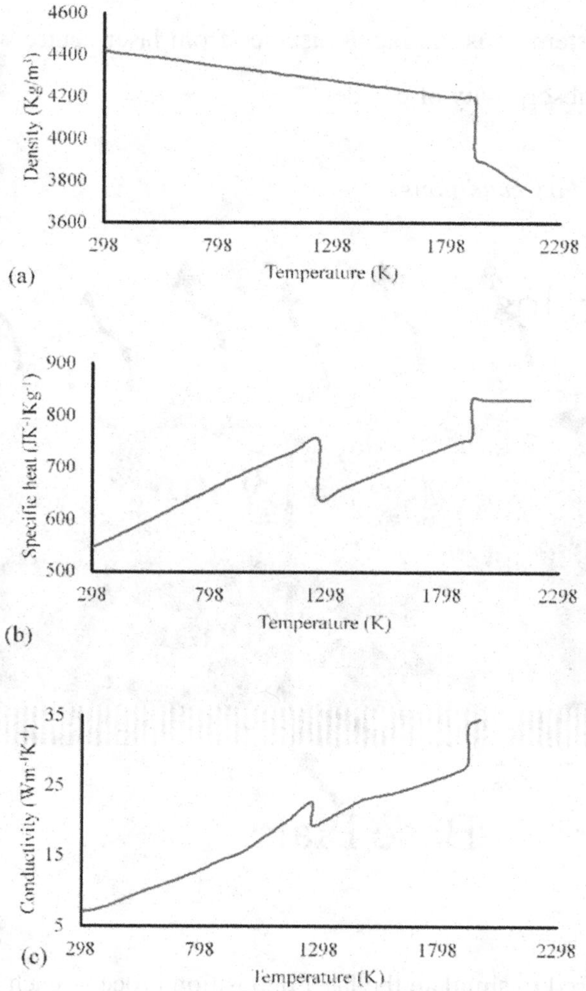

Temperature dependent material properties of Ti6Al4V alloy are taken from (Mills, 2002) and are presented in Fig 3. For the case of powder these properties depend upon the porosity (Chua, 2018). The porosity of powder bed is temperature dependent as the powder particles changes to liquid and then solid. The process is so fast it can be considered that the reduction in porosity due to solid-state sintering is minimal under the present laser densification condition. As such, the porosity of material has been simplified at two levels, that is, the initial porosity (65% in this study) before the powder converts to liquid, and zero porosity (fully dense) after the powder has converted to liquid and subsequently to a fully dense solid once the liquid is cooled below 1893 K (melting temperature of Ti6Al4V). In terms of powder bed porosity (φ), temperature depended properties of powder is given from Eq. 12 to Eq. 14.

$$K = \frac{(1-\varphi)}{(1+11\varphi)} K_s \tag{12}$$

$$C_p = (1-\varphi) C_{ps} \tag{13}$$

$$\rho = (1-\varphi) \rho_s \tag{14}$$

Here, K_s, C_{ps} and ρ_s are thermal conductivity, specific heat and porosity of solid.

METHODOLOGY

To understand the effect of the variation of scan speed (v) and laser power (P) on the maximum temperature produced and the melt pool geometry, simulation is performed for various combinations of v and P as per the experimental plan presented in Table 1. The model used for simulation with required boundary and initial condition is already explained in section 3. For conducting these simulations five equally spaced values of v and P from 1m/s-3m/s and 100W-300W respectively are considered. After each simulation run maximum melt pool temperature (T), melt pool width (w) and melt pool depth (d) is calculated from the coordinate positions of all the points whose temperature is more than the melting temperature of Ti6Al4V.

Fig. 4 shows the variation of T, w, d with respect to P at various values of v. From these results it is clear that increase in laser power increases the T, w and d of melt pool and this increase is prominent with decrease in scanning velocity. The observe effects are in accordance to heat input per unit time which increases with laser power and decrease with scanning velocity and as cited in (Foteinopoulos, 2018). The obtained values of T, w and d are validated by comparing with the work of Huang et al. (Huang, 2019). They studied temperature distribution, cooling rate and molten pool dimensions of the single-track multi-layer thin wall structure under laser power varying between 20-80W. The temperature obtained by (Huang, 2019) varies from 4059°C to 1286°C and width lies in the range of 0.04-0.16mm and depth of melt pool lies in between 0.01-0.06mm. After interpolation of results of present study for the laser power in the range of 150W to 300W are found to be in agreement with that of (Huang, 2019).

Figure 4. (a) Maximum Temperature (b) width (c) depth of melt pool with respect to laser power and scan speed (v)

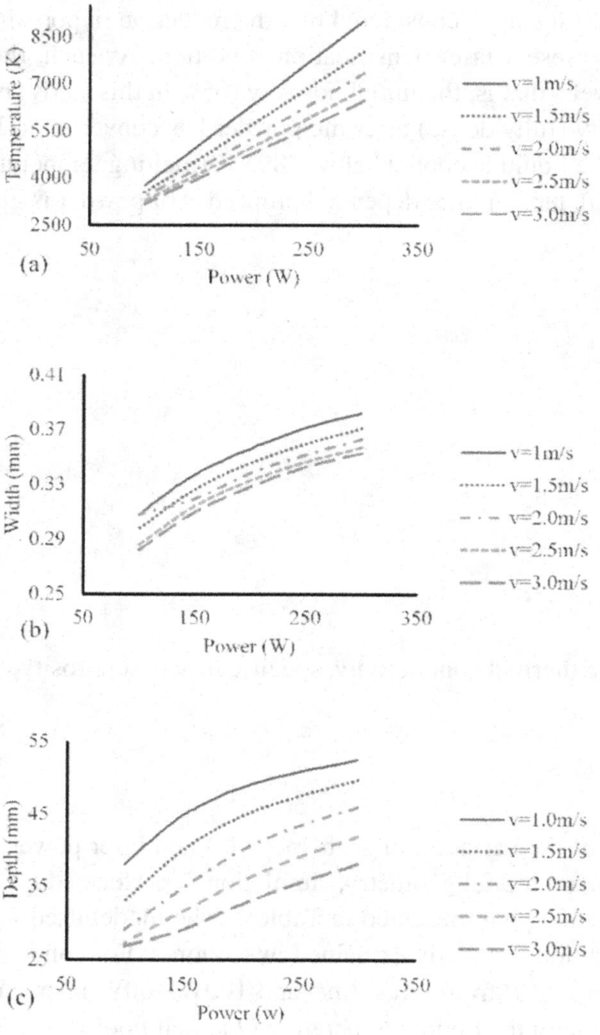

The requirement of laser base metal additive manufacturing system is that input heat flux must be enough to melt the top layer of powder particles and generate adequate heat so that top surface of bottom layers melts and form the strong joint by the diffusion and solidification of melt pool. Excessive heat may result in heat penetration to bottom solid layers and result in the formation of keyholes or development of residual stress (King, 2014, Li, 2018). Whereas insufficient heat input may not able to produce the sound bounding. As shown in Fig.3 for high heat input, high laser power at low scan speed is a suitable choice. But the requirement is that there should not be a large temperature difference between the maximum temperature of melt pool and melting temperature (T_m) of alloy, and width and depth of melt pool should be small so that heat affected region is as small as possible. With this, it is necessary that the depth of melt pool must be more than the single layer thickness (l_t) but less than the twice of layer thickness ($2l_t$). Mathematically this can be stated as:

minimize T and w

subject to

$$l_t < d < 2l_t$$

and

$$T > T_m, v > 0, P > 0 \tag{15}$$

Presence of two objectives makes this problem a multi objective constrain problem. For problem to be multi objective it is necessary that all the consider objectives must be independent to each other and conflicting in nature so that single solution will not satisfy all the objectives (Deb, 2010). In present case it can be observed from the simulation results depicted in Fig. 4 that both temperature and width will be minimum at low value of laser power and at high scan speed. To further strengthen this observation Pearson correlation coefficient is calculated using Eq. 16.

$$r_{12} = \frac{\sum_{j=1}^{n}\left(y_{1j} - \bar{y}_1\right)\times\left(y_{2j} - \bar{y}_2\right)}{\sqrt{\sum_{j=1}^{n}\left(y_{1j} - \bar{y}_1\right)^2}\times\sqrt{\sum_{j=1}^{n}\left(y_{2j} - \bar{y}_2\right)^2}} \tag{16}$$

Here, r_{12} is a correlation coefficient between variable y_1 and y_2. In this equation $\bar{y}_i = \frac{\sum_{j=1}^{n} y_{ij}}{n}$ for i=1,2 and n=total number of experimental runs. Correlation coefficient varies from -1 to +1. Where +1 is total positive linear correlation, 0 is no linear correlation, and −1 is total negative linear correlation. For determining correlation coefficient data corresponding to *T* and *w* are normalized. Normalization will make all the data unitless and in the same range of 0 to 1 so that they can be compared and results should not be affected by the scaling factor. Since the temperature should be minimum and must be greater than the melting temperature (T_m), nominal the better criteria define by Eq. 17 is used for normalizing *T*.

$$\hat{T} = 1 - \frac{\left|T_j - T_m\right|}{\max imum\{T^{\max} - T_m),\left(T_m - T^{\min}\right)\}}; j = 1,2,\ldots n \tag{17}$$

In this equation $\tilde{T}$ is the normalize value, T^{max} is the maximum value and T^{min} is minimum value of T in Table 1.

Width of melt pool need to be minimized, hence lower the better criteria define by Eq. 18 is used.

$$\tilde{w} = \frac{w^{max} - w_j}{w^{max} - w^{min}}; j = 1, 2, \ldots n \tag{18}$$

In Eq. 18 $\tilde{w}$ is the normalized value of w, w^{max} is the maximum value and w^{min} is the minimum value of w in Table 1. In both, the equations j indicates an experiment run (Exp. No.) in Table 1 and varies from 1 to 25. It is important to mention here d is appearing as a constraint in Eq. 15 which need to vary between lower and upper bound. To maintain the consistency in results d is also normalized with the criteria lower the better as depicted by Eq. 18. In this equation, w is replaced by d and $d^{min} = l_t$ and $d^{max} = 2l_t$ are considered. Since d vary within the limit defined by the problem constraint hence its normalize values also varies between its lower and upper bound values and not between 0 to 1 as in the case of T and w.

The normalization procedure adopted indicates that for keeping the maximum temperature near to melting temperature or for minimization of the width of melt pool, desire value must be 1 or near to 1 and the worst value near to zero. This will make all the objectives to maximize type and reduce the number of constraints. The normalization procedure will also make a regression analysis to find the relationship between output variables and input variables computationally simple.

The full quadratic linear model in two variables is used to predict the relationship between the input variables and the dependent output variable (Wu, 2010). The t-test was performed to determine the individual significant terms at 95% of confidence level. The significance of regression is established by the analysis of variance (ANOVA). For significance check probability of F-value greater than calculated F-value due to noise is indicated by p-value. p-value gives the probability under the null hypothesis that the F statics value for an experiment conducted in comparable condition will exceed the observed F value. The smaller the p-value, the stronger is the evidence that the null hypothesis does not hold. In the present case, the null hypothesis is that the terms are not significant. Since 95% of confidence level means that 5% of error is acceptable. Hence any p-value less than 0.05 establishes the significance of the term. The proportion of total variation in response data explained by the fitted model is measured by the coefficient of determination R^2. A higher R^2 value indicates a better fit of the regression model.

RESULTS

Finite element simulation based on the procedure described above is performed and the temperature distribution and the melt pool size are determined.

Fig. 5 shows the temperature distribution in the part for the case when power is 200W and scan speed is 1 m/s. It can be seen that the region of maximum temperature distribution is small and near to the laser centre. The melting point of Ti6Al4V alloy is 1080°C. The temperature contours up to this temperature are taken as a melt pool. Despite the lower thermal conductivity of powder in comparison to the solid, spread of heat affected zone is more at the powder layer in comparison to the sold layer. This is due to

Figure 5. Temperature distribution in powder bed (a) Temperature distribution for P=200 W, v=1m/s (b) Temperature distribution for P=150 W, v=2.86 m/s

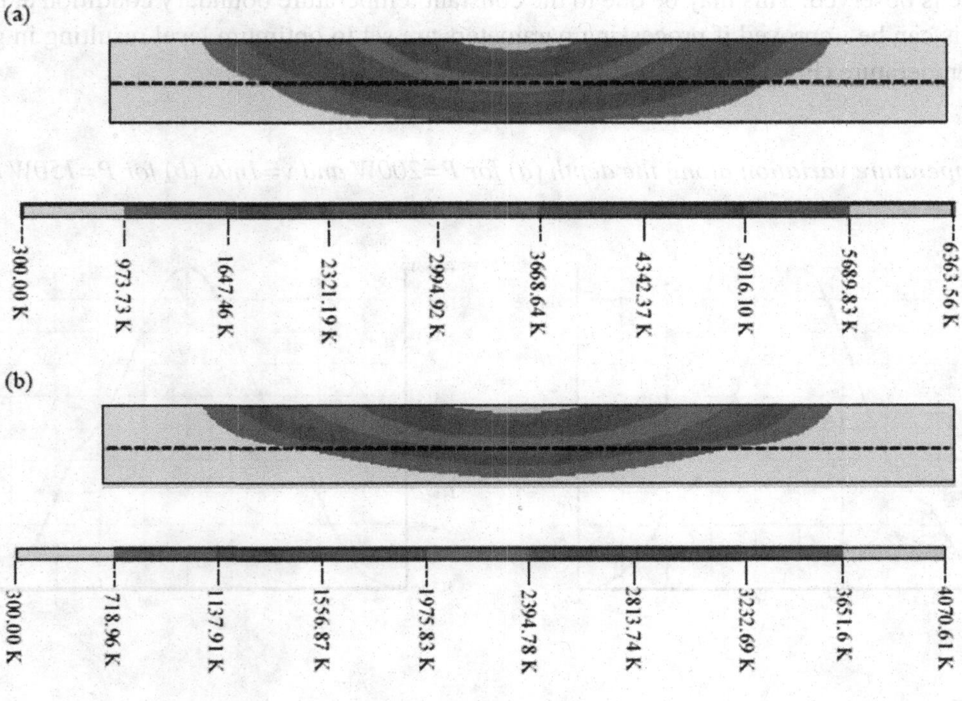

the fact that thermal conductivity is a function of temperature and increase with it as can be seen from material property data. The powder layer due to exposure to laser is at a higher temperature in comparison to the solid bottom layer and hence due to the difference in temperature its conductivity is more.

Figure 6. Temperature variation along the depth (a) for P=200W and v=1m/s (b) for P=150W and v= 2.86m/s

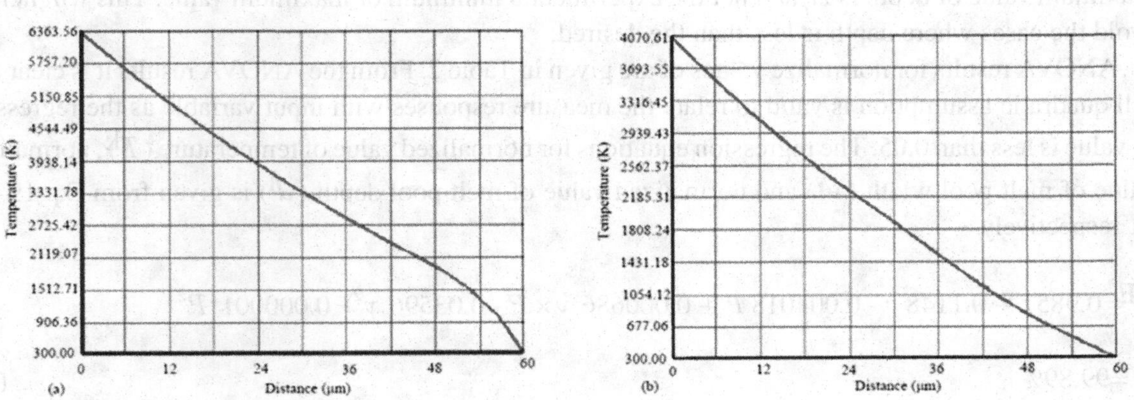

Variation of temperature along the depth is shown in Fig. 6. There is a gradual decrease resulting in the development of a large temperature gradient. For the case in Fig. 6(a) near the end sharp decrease in temperature is observed. This may be due to the constant temperature boundary condition at the bottom layer. This can be improved if processing parameters are set to optimum level resulting in gradual decrease in temperature (Fig. 6(b)).

Figure 7. Temperature variation along the depth (a) for P=200W and v=1m/s (b) for P=150W and v= 2.86m/s

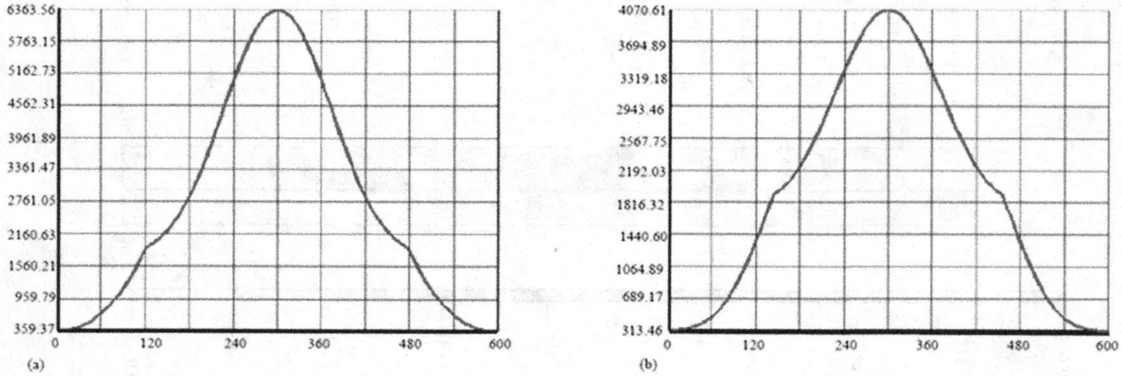

The distribution of temperature along the width shown in Fig. 7 and this is as per the Gaussian intensity distribution of the laser source.

The results given in Table 1 are normalized using Eq.17 for temperature. In this equation melting point of the alloy is considered as a target temperature. For the case of melt pool width and depth, Eq. 18 is used for normalization. The normalized results are presented in Table 1. Comparing the observed values given in Table 1 and their corresponding normalized values, it can be said better values are those which are equal to one or approaching one. In the case of depth, it can be seen that normalized values are more than one. This is because minimum value of depth is taken as single layer thickness (l_t) and maximum value of depth is $2l_t$ and not the experimental minimum or maximum value. This will help to avoid the cases where depth is less than the desired.

ANOVA results for normalize values of are given in Table 2. From the ANOVA results it is clear that full quadratic assumption is valid to relate the measure responses with input variable as the regression p- value is less than 0.05. The regression equations for normalized value of temperature ($\hat{T}$), normalized value of melt pool width ($\hat{w}$) and normalized value of melt pool depth ($\hat{d}$) is given from Eq. 19-Eq. 21 respectively.

$$\hat{T} = 0.9851 + 0.1148\, v - 0.004018\, P + 0.000686\, v \times P - 0.03596\, v^2 - 0.000001\, P^2$$

$$R^2 = 99.89\% \qquad (19)$$

Table 2. ANOVA of Simulation results

		$\hat{T}$				$\hat{w}$				$\hat{d}$			
Source	**DF**	**SS**	**V**	**F**	**P**	**SS**	**V**	**F**	**P**	**SS**	**V**	**F**	**P**
Regression	5	1.21864	0.243727	3537.97	0.00	1.73083	0.34617	283.96	0.00	1.54906	0.3098	283.2	0.00
v	1	0.00301	0.003012	43.720	0.00	0.01071	0.01071	8.79	0.01	0.02580	0.0258	23.58	0.00
P	1	0.03687	0.036875	535.28	0.00	0.12243	0.12243	100.43	0.00	0.07093	0.0709	64.84	0.00
$v \times P$	1	0.02942	0.029425	427.13	0.00	0.00057	0.00057	0.47	0.50	0.00283	0.0028	2.580	0.13
v^2	1	0.00566	0.005657	82.120	0.00	0.00266	0.00266	2.18	0.16	0.00471	0.0047	4.300	0.05
P^2	1	0.00015	0.000151	2.1900	0.16	0.03779	0.03779	31.0	0.00	0.01972	0.0197	18.03	0.00
Error	19	0.00131	0.000069			0.02316	0.00122			0.02079	0.0011		
Total	24	1.21994				1.75399				1.56985			
DF=degree of freedom; SS=sum of square; V=variance; F=F-value; p=p-value													

$$\hat{w} = 1.155 + 0.2165\, v - 0.007320\, P + 0.000095\, v \times P - 0.0247\, v^2 + 0.000009\, P^2$$

R^2=98.68% (20)

$$\hat{d} = 0.8938 + 0.3360\, v - 0.005572\, P + 0.000213\, v \times P - 0.0328\, v^2 + 0.000007\, P^2$$

R^2=98.68% (21)

A Pearson correlation coefficient calculated using Eq. 16 is 0.972 between $\hat{T}-\hat{w}$ and 0.88 between $\hat{T}-\hat{d}$. It shows that there is high degree of correlation between T and w as compare to d. It means the studies which are devoted to control the melt pool size by considering temperature develop may not give the correct result. This fact is also highlighted in studies which incorporate surface temperature monitoring to control the melt pool size (Criales, 2017). High degree of correlation between $\hat{T}-\hat{w}$ is advantageous in our case also as it will reduce the computational complexity for LCA algorithm as we need to consider only $\hat{T}$ or $\hat{w}$ as an objective function, instead of considering both.

The single objective nonlinear constraint optimization problem formulated as:

$\max imize\ \hat{T}$

subject to

$0 < \hat{d} < 1$

$1 \leq v \leq 3$

$$100 \leq P \leq 300 \tag{22}$$

LCA parameter consider in present study are league size=20, total seasons=10, ψ_1=0.5, ψ_2=1.0 and p_c=0.7.

Figure 8. LCA convergence curve

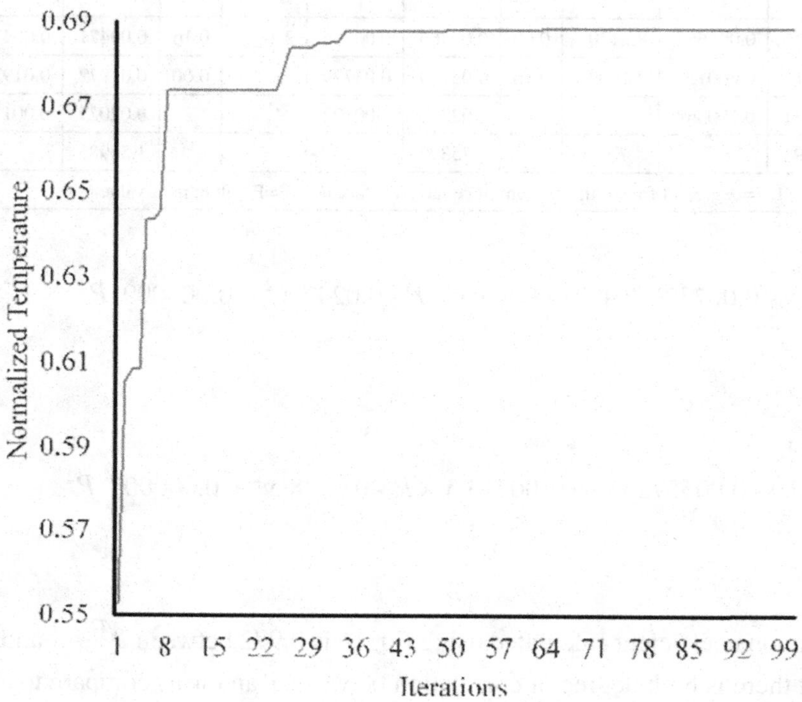

The convergence curve of LCA algorithm is given in Fig. 8. It can be seen that optimum T^A value is 0.68, when v=2.86m/s and P=150W. The results can be verified from Table 1, itself. We can see from Table 1 that it is not possible to have normalized value of temperature greater than calculated without violating the constraint related with depth of melt pool. Simulation is run at the optimum v and P values and the maximum temperature obtained is 4070.6K, depth is 30.0788μm and width is 0.3124mm. These values are close to the values obtained by LCA algorithm. The temperature distribution at these optimum values in melt pool, along the depth and width is shown in Fig 4.b, Fig 5.b and Fig. 6.b respectively. It can be seen that temperature change is gradual and smooth even at the boundary when optimum parameters are selected.

CONCLUSION

In this study, a 2D finite element model with fixed gaussian heat source was used to simulate layered additive manufacturing process of Ti6Al4V. The aim of this study was to find temperature distribution in the model, maximum depth of melt pool and maximum width of melt pool. This was done for different combinations of laser power and scan speed. Then using the given constraints of power, scan speed and depth of melt pool, optimum values of scan speed and laser power were determined so as to minimize difference between maximum temperature and melting temperature, minimize width of melt pool and contain depth of melt pool between bottom surface of first layer and second layer. The study presented following important results which may be useful to understand or predict the behaviour or laser-based AM process.

1. Maximum temperature increases with increase in laser power and decrease in scan speed and vice versa.
2. Maximum depth of melt pool and width of melt pool temperature increases with increase in laser power and decrease in scan speed and vice versa.
3. Temperature is maximum at the centre of the model and decreases away from the centre.
4. Keeping lower value of laser power or higher value of scan speed is not a recommended criterion as it will not grantee the proper melting of powder layer.
5. Considering only temperature distribution at the top surface will not give a proper estimate of melt pool size.
6. To reduce the chance of sharp decrease in temperature it is necessary to properly control the process by working in optimum parameter setting.
7. LCA is efficient and simple algorithm for constraint-based optimization of non-linear objective function.

REFERENCES

Abdulhameed, O., Al-Ahmari, A., Ameen, W., & Mian, S. H. (2019). Additive manufacturing: Challenges, trends, and applications. *Advances in Mechanical Engineering*, *11*(2), 1–27. doi:10.1177/1687814018822880

Abdulhamid, S. M., Latiff, M. S. A., Madni, S. H., & Oluwafemi, O. (2015). A Survey of League Championship Algorithm: Prospects and Challenges. *Indian Journal of Science and Technology*, *8*(3), 101–110. doi:10.17485/ijst/2015/v8iS3/60476

Cengel, Y. A. (2002). *Heat transfer: A practical approach*. Tata McGraw-Hill Publishing Company Limited.

Cheng, B., & Chou, K. (2016). *A numerical investigation of thermal property effects on melt pool characteristics in powder-bed electron beam additive manufacturing*. Academic Press.

Chua, B. L., Lee, H. J., & Ahn, D. G. (2018). Estimation of effective thermal conductivity of Ti-6AL-4V powders for a powder bed fusion process using finite element analysis. *International Journal of Precision Engineering and Manufacturing*, *19*(2), 257–264. doi:10.100712541-018-0030-2

Criales, L. E., & Ozel, T. (2017). Temperature profile and melt depth in laser powder bed fusion of Ti-6Al-4V titanium alloy. *Progress in Additive Manufacturing*, *2*(3), 169–177. doi:10.100740964-017-0029-8

Deb, K. (2010). *Multi-objective optimization using evolutionary algorithms*. Wiley India.

Foteinopoulos, P., Papacharalampopoulos, A., & Stavropoulos, P. (2018). On thermal modeling of additive manufacturing processes. *CIRP Journal of Manufacturing Science and Technology*, *20*, 66–83. doi:10.1016/j.cirpj.2017.09.007

Gan, Z., Liu, H., Li, S., He, X., & Yu, G. (2017). Modeling of thermal behaviour and mass transport in multi-layer laser additive manufacturing of Ni-based alloy on cast iron. *International Journal of Heat and Mass Transfer*, *111*, 709–722. doi:10.1016/j.ijheatmasstransfer.2017.04.055

Gibson, I., Rosen, D., & Stucker, B. (2015). *Additive Manufacturing Technologies: 3D Printing, Rapid Prototyping, and Direct Digital Manufacturing*. Springer-Verlag. doi:10.1007/978-1-4939-2113-3

Gu, D. D., Meiners, W., Wissenbach, K., & Poprawe, R. (2012). Laser additive manufacturing of metallic components: Materials, processes and mechanisms. *International Materials Reviews*, *57*(3), 33–164. do i:10.1179/1743280411Y.0000000014

Huang, M. L., & Lin, C. J. (2018). Nonlinear system control using a fuzzy cerebellar model articulation controller involving reinforcement-strategy-based bacterial foraging optimization. *Advances in Mechanical Engineering*, *10*(9), 1–12. doi:10.1177/1687814018797426

Huang, W., & Zhang, Y. (2019). Finite element simulation of thermal behaviour in single track multiple layers thin wall without support during selective laser melting. *Journal of Manufacturing Processes*, *42*, 139–148. doi:10.1016/j.jmapro.2019.04.019

Husseinzadeh, K. A. (2014). Championship Algorithm (LCA): An algorithm for global optimization inspired by sport championships. *Applied Soft Computing*, *16*, 171–200. doi:10.1016/j.asoc.2013.12.005

Jalili, S., Kashan, A. H., & Hosseinzadeh, Y. (2017). League Championship Algorithms for Optimum Design of Pin-Jointed Structures. *Journal of Computing in Civil Engineering*, *31*(2), 04016048. doi:10.1061/(ASCE)CP.1943-5487.0000617

King, W. E., Barth, H. D., Castillo, V. M., Gallegos, G. F., Gibbs, J. W., Hahn, D. E., Kamath, C., & Rubenchik, A. M. (2014). Observation of keyhole-mode laser melting in laser powder-bed fusion additive manufacturing. *Journal of Materials Processing Technology*, *214*(12), 2915–2925. doi:10.1016/j.jmatprotec.2014.06.005

Li, C., Liu, Y., Fang, X. Y., & Guo, Y. B. (2018). Residual Stress in Metal Additive Manufacturing. *Procedia CIRP*, *71*, 348–353. doi:10.1016/j.procir.2018.05.039

Li, J., Fan, T., Taniguchi, T., & Zhang, B. (2018). Phase-field modeling on laser melting of a metallic powder. *International Journal of Heat and Mass Transfer*, *117*, 412–424. doi:10.1016/j.ijheatmasstransfer.2017.10.001

Luo, Z., & Zhao, Y. (2018). A survey of finite element analysis of temperature and thermal stress fields in powder bed fusion additive manufacturing. *Additive Manufacturing*, *21*, 318–332. doi:10.1016/j.addma.2018.03.022

Malekipor, E., & El-Mounayri, H. (2018). Common defects and contributing parameters in powder bed fusion AM process and their classification for online monitoring and control: A review. *International Journal of Advanced Manufacturing Technology*, *95*(1-4), 527–550. doi:10.100700170-017-1172-6

Mills, K. C. (2002). *Recommended Values of Thermophysical Properties for Selected Commercial Alloys*. Woodhead Publishing Limited. doi:10.1533/9781845690144

Mukherjee, T., Zhang, W., & Debroy, T. (2017). An improved prediction of residual stresses and distortion in additive manufacturing. *Computational Materials Science*, *126*, 360–372. doi:10.1016/j.commatsci.2016.10.003

Paul, R., Anand, S., & Garner, F. (2014). Effect of thermal deformation on part errors in metal powder based additive manufacturing processes. *Journal of Manufacturing Science and Engineering*, *136*(3), 031009–0310021. doi:10.1115/1.4026524

Proceedings of the Institute of Mechanical Engineering Part B. (n.d.). Article. *Proceedings of the Institution of Mechanical Engineers. Part B, Journal of Engineering Manufacture*, *232*(9), 1615–1662. doi:10.1177/0954405416673105

Roberts, I. A., Wang, C. J., Esterlein, R., Stanford, M., & Mynors, D. J. (2009). A three-dimensional finite element analysis of the temperature field during laser melting of metal powders in additive layer manufacturing. *International Journal of Machine Tools & Manufacture*, *149*(12-13), 916–923. doi:10.1016/j.ijmachtools.2009.07.004

Sames, W. J., List, F. A., Pannala, S., Dehoff, R. R., & Babu, S. S. (2016). The metallurgy and processing science of metal additive manufacturing. *International Materials Reviews*, *61*(5), 315–360. doi:10.1080/09506608.2015.1116649

Song, J., Chew, Y., Bi, G., Yao, X., Zhang, B., Bai, J., & Seung, K. M. (2018). Numerical and experimental study of laser aided additive manufacturing for melt-pool profile and grain orientation analysis. *Materials & Design*, *137*, 286–297. doi:10.1016/j.matdes.2017.10.033

Subbaraj, S., Thiagarajan, R., & Rengaraj, M. (2019). Multi-objective league championship algorithm for real-time task scheduling. *Neural Computing & Applications*, 1–12.

Uriondo, A., Esperon-Miguez, M., & Perinpanayagam, S. (2015). The present and future of additive manufacturing in the aerospace sector: A review of important aspects. *Proceedings of the Institution of Mechanical Engineers. Part G, Journal of Aerospace Engineering*, *229*(11), 2132–2147. doi:10.1177/0954410014568797

Wang, L., Cai, J. C., & Li, M. (2016). An adaptive multi-population genetic algorithm for job-shop scheduling problem. *Advances in Manufacturing*, *4*(2), 142–149. doi:10.100740436-016-0140-y

Wang, S., Jia, Z., Lu, X., Zhang, H., Zhang, C., & Liang, S. Y. (2018). Simultaneous optimization of fixture and cutting parameters of thin-walled workpieces based on particle swarm optimization algorithm. *Simulation*, *94*(1), 67–76. doi:10.1177/0037549717713850

Wang, Z., Xiao, Z., Tse, Y., Huang, C., & Zhang, W. (2019). Optimization of processing parameters and establishment of a relationship between microstructure and mechanical properties of SLM titanium alloy. *Optics & Laser Technology*, *112*, 159–167. doi:10.1016/j.optlastec.2018.11.014

Wu, C. F. J., & Hamada, M. (2010). *Experiments Planning, analysis, and Parameter Design Optimization*. Wiley-India.

Chapter 15
A Novel Approach Towards Selection of Role Model Cluster Head for Power Management in WSN

Ramkrishna Ghosh
KIIT University (Deemed), India

Suneeta Mohanty
KIIT University (Deemed), India

Prasant Kumar Pattnaik
KIIT University (Deemed), India

Sabyasachi Pramanik
https://orcid.org/0000-0002-9431-8751
Haldia Institute of Technology, India

ABSTRACT

In this chapter, the authors present an innovative, smart controller to sustain mobility in wireless sensor networks (WSNs). Principally, the focal point is dependent on the arrangement of fuzzy input variables (i.e., remaining battery power [RBP], mobility, and centrality solution) to crucial usages, similar to personnel safety in an industrialized atmosphere. A mobility controller dependent upon type-1 fuzzy logic (T1FL) is planned to support sensor mobile nodes (MN). Here, a role model cluster head (RMCH) is picked out among the cluster heads (CHs) that may simply convey the message to the mobile base station (BS) by determining the appropriate type-1 fuzzy (T1F) descriptors such as RBP, mobility of the sink, and the centrality of the clusters. Type-1 fuzzy inference system (Mamdani's rule) is utilized to opt for the possibility to be RMCH. The validity of the introduced model is carried out by means of multiple linear regressions.

DOI: 10.4018/978-1-7998-3624-7.ch015

INTRODUCTION

WSN is a swiftly rising specialized stage with noteworthy usages in numerous fields similarly militant, cultivation, architectural observation, healthcare vigilance, homeland networks etc. (Akyildiz, Su, Sankarasubramaniam & Cayirci, 2002).

A WSN comprises of a quantity of tiny inferior potential sensor nodes (SNs) competent of perceiving physical occurrence, which are comprised of power system, processing power, and bandwidth. Since WSNs typically are structured in unsecured and vulnerable regions, these are susceptible to different kinds of attacks (Wang, Yan, Wang &Liu, 2011). WSNs comprised of wirelessly organized SNs those can assemble, allocate and progress information in a range of functional areas. Typical WSNs are intended for linking real electronic or mechanical sensors across wireless communication. At the present time, WSNs are allotted with other technologies, for instance big data and cloud computing for the management of data. In WSN, if all the sensors are in direct communication with high end network (like internet), then an ample of energy will be utilized. Power expenditure in WSNs is a chief difficulty. WSN is a technology with a massive potential that can be used in a high quantity of wide-ranging applications of attention to society such as traffic control, environmental monitoring, structural monitoring of buildings, tracking of people and objects, aided living and many more.

WSN is vastly thought as one of the most noteworthy technologies of the twenty-first century (Raghavendra et al., 2004; Cayirci et al., 2003; Kaur et al., 2013; Nayak & Devulapalli, 2015). In the past decades, it attained massive awareness from equally academic circles and industry all over the globe. WSNs are attaining an ample of research attention in the recent scenario because of its gigantic and versatile usages. WSN offers several advantages like movability, adaptability, better efficiency, deplorability, transportability and lesser setting up prices. WSNs are disseminated network of totally tiny and slight SNs that can perceive substantial specifications for instance heat, pressure, comparative humidity etc. Those SNs commune across the little space along a wireless means and perform cooperatively to accomplish a general job. In a range of WSN usages, the arrangement of SNs is accomplished in an ad hoc mode. The SNs perform at four means which include i. Transmit state ii. Receive state iii. Idle state and iv. Sleep state. The expenditure of power throughout receive and idle state is somewhat equal. Every SN is made up of three different subsystems. The power utilization throughout communicating is significantly higher compared to the power utilization throughout sensing and processing.

LEACH is the first well-known hierarchical routing protocol that is proven to be generally competent over conventional routing protocol. In LEACH, the CH is designated in a probabilistic method and attempt to balance the load at every SN based on rotation. Even though many studies show the competence of LEACH protocol, it has certain drawbacks that require to be examined. As LEACH depends upon probabilistic value, this might happen that in every round more than one CHs are elected or no CH is selected.

RELATED WORK

Khan et al. (2012) have presented a fault detection scheme for WSNs. The scheme was based on forming a SN by Takagi-Sugeno-Kang (TSK) T1FIS, where a sensor measurement function of the neighboring SNs approximates sensor quantity of SN.

Lin et al. (2017) have developed a T1FIS and an algorithm for study of big data which introduced to consider the threat of fire and computed the measurable possible risk of fire. The elements transformed into a triangular type-1 fuzzy quantity are evaluated by defuzzification techniques and wanted output level for fire rating. The incessant day-and -night information for climate that could mirror the tremendous exact standing of woodland surroundings, was gathered by the energized WSN.

Zinonos et al. (2014) developed an intelligent controller to carry mobility in WSNs. The spotlight built upon exploitation of similar mobility way out to essential usages, similar to personnel safety in a manufacturing atmosphere. A mobility controller based upon T1FL is introduced to serve sensor MN to make a decision even if they have to activate handover process and achieve handover to a fresh link location or not.

Shokouhifar and Jalali (2017) have proposed an adaptive type-1 fuzzy clustering protocol, named as low energy adaptive clustering hierarchy (LEACH-SF) for the purpose of overcoming stated demerits. An algorithm fuzzy c-means in LEACH-SF is applied to collect all SNs into balanced clusters, and afterwards proper CHs are chosen via Sugeno T1FIS.

Chanana and Arora (2013) have built up a fresh model together with programmable communicating thermostat (PCT) in air conditioning load has been planned. Outcomes demonstrate that the preface of PCT in an air conditioner is functional in diminishing spending for electricity of consumers besides dropping the peak requirement.

The major aim of smart grid incentives is to progress vision for the purpose of reducing network voltages as well as to facilitate customer's involvement in the function of power system, fundamentally by means of Smart meters (U.S. Department of Energy, 2009), Smart homes (Vojdani, 2008) PCTs and price responsive thermostats (Woolley et al., 2014.) and occupancy responsive thermostats (Lu, 2010) are utilized broadly to routinely handle HVAC systems for residential purposes as users load their daily plans and selections i.e. set point temperatures.

Authors in (Oldewurtel, 2012) mentioned that current devices dedicated to the management of energy for smart home cannot save power for all time because of their reliance on customer attachment. Users commonly readjust the predefined offsets for the purpose of upholding their thermal comforts. A synergy of predictive control model and climate information was built up to progress competence of power in commercial buildings whilst supplying thermal comforts. Nevertheless, this technology would be high-priced for putting into operation in residential buildings because the processing is completed by tiny embedded micro controller integrated into thermostats. Additionally the abilities of WSNs to perceive, scrutinize and quantify various variables have been assessed to progress the boundaries of current management schemes for power similar to thermostats (Lu, 2010; Cao et al., 2010; Redfern, 2012).

Hamzah et al. (2019) in their research work have proposed a model for CH selection based on fuzzy logic. The planned model uses 5 descriptors to decide the chance for every node to turn into a CH. Those descriptors are: i. residual energy ii. Location suitability, iii. Density, iv. Compacting, and v. distance from the BS. They apply this model in suggesting the Fuzzy Logic-dependent power-proficient clustering for WSN based on smallest amount separation Distance enforcement between CHs. Additionally, they implement the Gini index to determine the clustering algorithms' energy efficiency with regard to their capability to equilibrium the allocation of power during WSN SNs. They compare the proposed method FL-EEC/D with a fuzzy logic-dependent CH selection method, a *k*-means dependent method for clustering, and LEACH. Simulation outcomes explain improvements in power competence in respect of WSN lifespan and power utilization balancing between SNs for various network sizes and topologies. Outcomes demonstrate an average development in respect of death of the first node and last node.

According to Rizwana et al. (2019) in their work, they have proposed an Artificial Bee Colony algorithm. It is a power competent algorithm and utilizes power with balancing to amplify the network lifespan with best possible path and diminish a loss. Of a packet Algorithm rapidly recognizes the shortest path on every SN. This is optimizing the paths for routing and offers a successful multipath data communication.

Xue et al. (2007) have initiated an approach for active power management depends upon forecast. A particle filter was set up to forecast an objective status, which was accepted to wake up wireless SNs for their long-term sleep time. With the scattered computing competence of SNs, a scheme for optimization of distributed genetic algorithm and annealing for simulation was planned to diminish the power expenditure of capacity. Taking into account usage of goal tracking, they developed prediction for goal position, SN sleep scheduling and election of the optimal sensing node. Furthermore, a scheme for routing of forwarding SNs was demonstrated to attain further power preservation. Investigation outcomes of goal tracking confirmed that competence of power is improved by active power management dependent upon forecast.

According to Azfar et al. (2019) in their paper, they present a fuzzy logic dependent system for a two hop energy harvesting (EH) WSN. Integrating data and power causality constraints, discrete communication rates, finite energy and data buffers, a fuzzy model have been built up that utilizes WSN throughput, battery level and channel gain as inputs. This technique is subsequently evaluated with most favourable, modified most favourable, and Markov decision process (MDP) techniques in respect of computational complexity, throughput, battery level and data buffer capacity. The throughput outcomes demonstrate that the fuzzy online system achieves closely to the evaluated methods and evades battery depletion when the quantity of discrete communication rates is enhanced.

Zadeh(1965) first proposed T1FL for decision making, and is capable to offer precise outcomes based on uncertain and unclear information. The most well-liked T1FIS models are Mamdani (Mamdani, 1975) and Sugeno (Sugeno, 1985). Usually, each model can be signified as "If antecedence then consequence". The antecedence is identical for every T1F models, but the consequence has various kinds for every model.

MAIN FOCUS OF THE CHAPTER

1. T1FL control technique for forecast of various kinds of chance in building of WSN.
2. Interval T1FLC aids to outline inputs and output in a well-ordered approach for constructing inference train so as to different kinds of chance evaluation may be forecasted.
3. Qualitative aspects accountable for enhancing chance assessment might be simply incorporated in the model of T1F forecasts for enhancing exactness.
4. Validity of planned model is carried out by means of Statistical Analysis and Multiple Linear Regression.

The current chapter demonstrates a complete T1F WSN model which gives a crucial indicator of parameters of chance estimation in WSN. There are various chances to choose operations and operators besides inference, implication, aggregation and defuzzification techniques, so the investigation of the ideal mathematical representation can be incorporated among largely crucial topics in improvement of models built upon fuzzy rules.

Because of this, we have prepared a chief analysis on the specifications directing the chance evaluation and opt for the uttermost fitting variables for input and output. Mamdani interval type 1 fuzzy inference systems (MFT1IS) are subsequently improved applying those inputs and output. Building upon the membership functions (MFs), a WSN model has been set up and by sensitivity analyses we choose the top suitable model amongst these.

Ultimately, with a few graphical demonstrations we authenticate the selected model with substantial hypothetical representations.

MODEL DEVELOPMENT

T1FL is applied for indicating human understanding and decision making performance. Furthermore, it can hold doubts of usages in real time further exactly than the probabilistic demonstration. T1FL is accepted into this scheme for the purpose of handling the uncertainties for selecting RMCH. The most essential benefit by means of T1FL controller is to control the overheads of gathering and computing power and position information of every SN. Many T1FL dependent clustering algorithms regard as the BS as static sensor node. But sink movement can lessen the network traffic, delay and as a consequence develops energy efficiency.

Figure 1. Proposed model for WSN

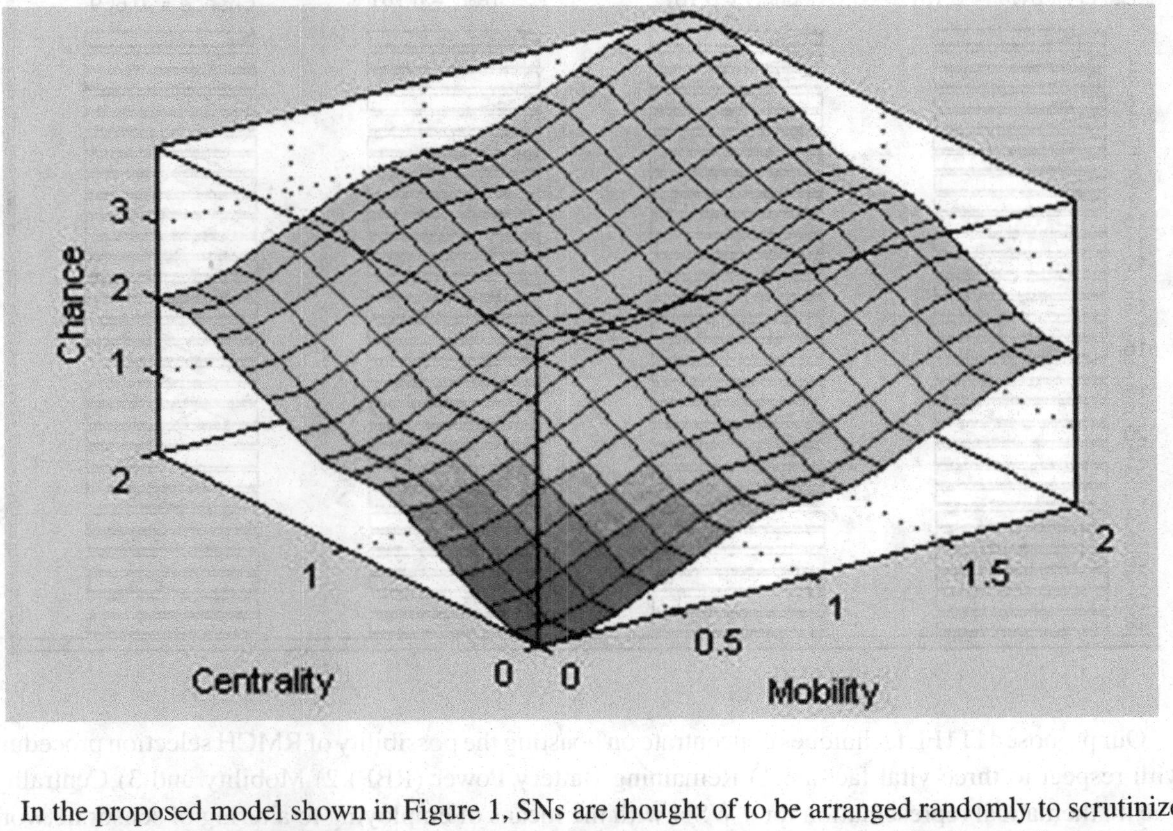

In the proposed model shown in Figure 1, SNs are thought of to be arranged randomly to scrutinize the atmosphere endlessly. Here all the SNs are static apart from the base static that is mobile in nature. Here all the SNs have initial equal energy. On the basis of receiving signal power the distance between the SN and the BS can be computed. The projected clustering approach goes after the chief rule of LEACH. The cluster is made in every round, each SN creates a number between 0 and 1at random .If the generated number at random is less than the threshold value T, the SN will be a CH. The most favorable value of K in LEACH can be decided systematically by means of power model. For example, there are N SNs arranged at random across an M ×*M* region and clusters of quantity k are determined. So there is N/k SN every cluster out of which 1 CH and (N/k) -1 normal SNs. Every CH scatters power by getting a signal, combines and transmits the average signal to sink. To save energy we have planned one RMCH among the CHs that can convey the information to BS. This technique can decrease energy consumption and boost up energy efficiency.

In this investigation, Mamdani's technique IT1FIS is utilized to opt for the RMCH because this is mainly regularly utilized inference method. The inference systems and T1F scheme applied for our introduced model are displayed in Figure 2.

Figure 2. Fuzzy Interference Engine

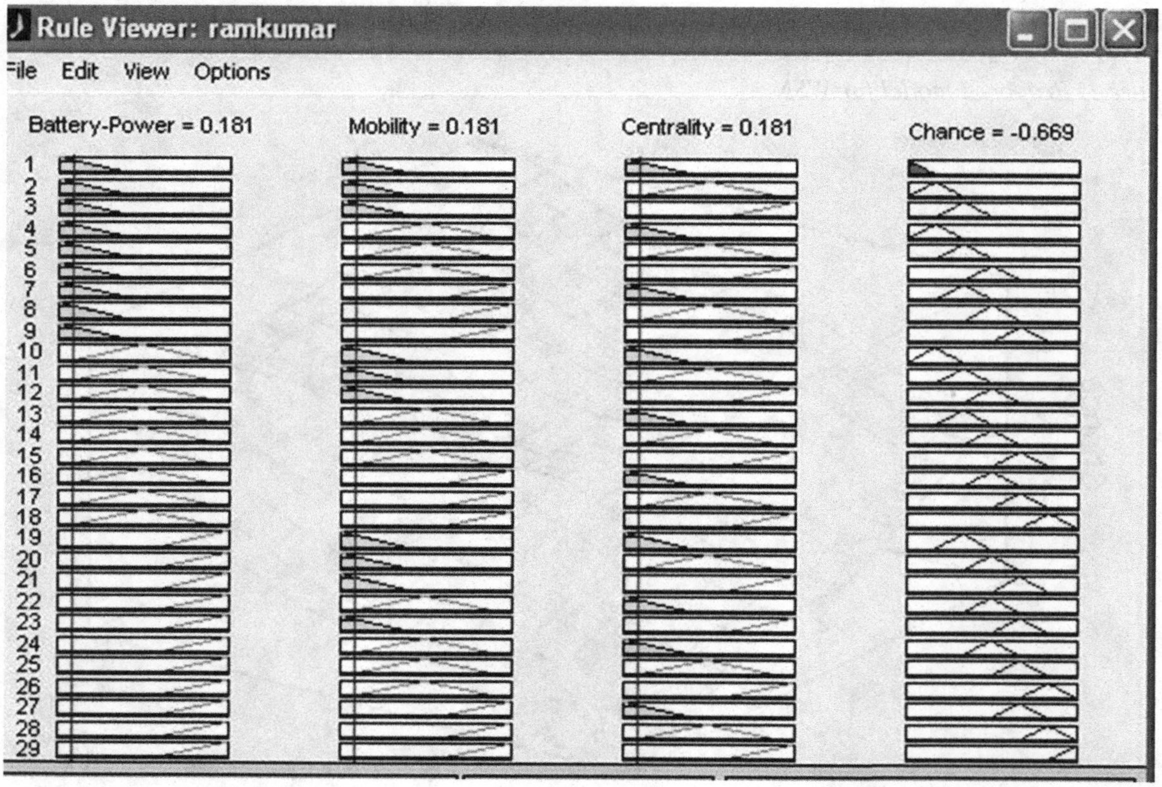

Our proposed IT1FL techniques concentrate on boasting the possibility of RMCH selection procedure with respect to three vital factors: 1) Remaining Battery Power (RBP) 2) Mobility and 3) Centrality. The mathematical representation for a WSN with the means of employing to altering of sensor network ambience is not only hard to build but also impractical and unreasonable way out. These mathematical representations are not flexible and appropriate for accurate configurations of static networks. IT1F rule dependent method has become a usual preference as they offer us with a finest means for controlling vagueness of measurements achieved in WSNs. IT1FL method is efficient while there is a quantity of vagueness in analysis procedure. Fuzzy MFs specify the scale of certainty of variables for input and output and signify these quantitative measures in a distinct set of variables. The IT1F set of values for variables of input and output have become well thought-out relying on WSNs performance and optimal power saving necessities of WSN. The interval T1F set values for variables of input and output are described below.

Remaining Battery Power{Less(LE), Medium(M), High(H)}, Mobility {Low(L), Moderate(MO), frequent(FR)}, Centrality{Close(C), Adequate(A), Far(F)}, Chance{Very Weak(VW), Weak(W), Lower Medium(LM), Medium(M), Higher Medium(HM), Strong(S), Very Strong(VS)}.

The T1F set that signifies the first input variable, i.e. RBP. The linguistic variables for T1F set is less, medium and high. MF of type Gaussian has been regarded as for less and high. For medium, MF of type triangular has been thought.

Remaining Battery Power

Sensor nodes are controlled by non renewable batteries. Battery power (BP) is the warning factor in the lifespan of WSN. Power Consumption in WSN is a major problem. Power management is significant to be dealt with to sensors to work for a long time. After every round power level of CH decreases. It is quite impossible to restore battery and to preserve WSN lifespan. More RBP power will maximize the network lifetime. Progress of network dynamics like topology, routing, security, based on WSN is controlled by power constraints of the nodes. Suitable CH Selection can improve the battery power. Interval type 2 fuzzy variables have taken for Battery Power.

Mobility

In important usages, such as personnel safety in industrialized surroundings, a system for surveillance in real time can always be obtained. For the purpose of resourcefully tracking or controlling a person travelling in a WSN region, mobile entity is intelligent to carry out the handover between various assisting/anchoring SNs or WSNs while achieving its shift. Consequently, the subsistence of an appropriate mobility protocol to organize the handover method is essential in WSN. Mobility based communication can extend the lifetime of WSNs and enhance the connectivity of sensor nodes and clusters For this reason using mobility control to reduce energy consumption in WSNs has lately captured attention. Mobility means that when sink travels in specific track the distance between the sink and RMCH raises or diminishes with respect to speed and route of travelling sink. The linguistic variable for the input parameter mobility is considered as IT1FV since planned WSN protocol reflects on the BS as mobile.

Centrality

Centrality measure defines the importance and position of a node within a network. It helps in computing its importance and connection with its neighbouring nodes. Furthermore, centrality measures help in determining a variety of intrinsic problems and developing efficient and robust algorithms for WSNs. It concentrates on the position of RMCH what extent this is located centrally to converse with all new CHs. The linguistic variables mobility is considered as third input variable.

Chance

The appropriate prediction the quality of chance to be the RMCH based on three input variables, namely Battery Power, Mobility and Centrality that can send information to the BS after collecting data from all other CHs. Chance can be measured in the following formula .The linguistic term of MFs of Chance is.

Chance = (Battery Power -1) +Mobility + Centrality

In this analysis, we have considered a T1F dependent way out which does not alter current typical algorithms, but employs the actions of these so to offer a control scheme which would handle to manage the handover process and present enhanced presentations. The choice of T1FL system was built upon its easiness and reality that it undertakes specialists-determined Mamdani's rules directing objective control scheme, it may be altered and pinched smoothly to develop or significantly modify the performance of control system. Investigation of uncertain situation of the ability in this region makes known that there is a complete push of assignments and proposals covering an extensive range of connected study demanding, scientific difficulties and teamwork performances in WSNs. Nonetheless, the interest of this operation is the actuality that there is no procedure planned and assessed to sustain the mobility method in uncertain T1F surroundings; consequently, this effort offers successful resolution to chance. This matter is assumed of extreme significance for nowadays industrialized and managerial usages.

This surface describes in a compressed means all the information in the IT1FLC. An examination of that nonlinear control surface and the rules for linguistic variables are displayed in Figure 3 to Figure 6. It gives an indication of the procedure of T1FLC. The decision likelihood activities under the area of equilibrium are smoothly evaluated from the past data set. In any other way, the fuzzy rules are destructive by raising assessment likelihood roughly in the area over and above the equilibrium point, where the excellence begins to get affected and activating of handover is essential. The active technique of computing the result likelihood by an inference method for fuzzy receives from the reality that as stated in the immediate values of WSN and a distinctive set of T1F rules.

For the purpose of building a T1F control scheme a precise process must be pursued. The method engages recognizing and identifying T1F inputs (Battery Power, Mobility and Centrality) and outputs (Chance), generating T1FMFs for each, building the rule base, and making a decision how the activity will be completed. The input/output variables in a Fuzzy Control (FC) system are in general mapped into fuzzy sets. The practice of transferring a crisp (deterministic) input value to a T1F value is called "fuzzification", where "defuzzification" is a mapping from a space of T1FL control activities defined over an output universe of discourse into a space of non T1FL control action. A T1F set is defined by a MF that can be any real quantity in the interval [0; 1], stating the status of membership for which an element belongs to that T1F set.

SOLUTION PROCEDURE

In fuzzy sets, every element is mapped to [0, 1] by MF. [0, 1]→A: X μ Where [0, 1] means real quantities between 0 and 1 (including 0 and 1).

The value of membership degree might contain uncertainty. If the value of MF is provided by a fuzzy set, it is a T1F set. This facilitates one to perform in doubtful and confusing circumstances and resolve indistinct (vague) difficulties or difficulties with partial information. There are 2 infrastructures for Fuzzy Systems 1) Improvement reliant on crisp mathematical representation and fuzzifying a few parts:

Model 1: Mathematical representation for Fuzzy Example: Fuzzy – K means clustering 2) Improvement built upon Fuzzy Inference rules: Model 2: Fuzzy Logical representation Example: Decision Support System for Fuzzy.

In our research work, we are applying MFIS to forecast the excellence of chance. For computing the output of this FIS given the inputs, 6 steps have to be pursued:

(i) Decide a group of rules built upon fuzzy.
(ii) Fuzzify inputs applying the input MFS (transforms crisp input to a linguistic variable applying the MFs saved in fuzzy knowledge base).
(iii) Incorporate fuzzified inputs just as rules for fuzzy to set up rule power (fuzzy actions).
(iv) Discover the outcome of the rule by integrating the rule power and the MF for output (implication).
(v) Integrate the outcomes to obtain an output assigning (aggregation).
(vi) Defuzzify the output dissemination (which transforms output for fuzzy of the inference engine to crisp applying MFs similar to particulars utilized by fuzzifier).

The following rule base comprises of 27 rules. All fuzzy rules are displayed in Table 1. These have been designed just as the principle depicted above. In Table 1, input variables for fuzzy have been symbolized by A, B, C. These stand for the input variables for fuzzy viz., Battery Power, Mobility and Centrality. The output variable for fuzzy i.e., Chance is symbolized by O. The rule viewer for fuzzy is shown in Figure 6.

The values of fuzzification are handled by means of inference engine that comprises of a rule base and a variety of techniques for inferring the rules. This is basically a sequence of IF-THEN rules that describe fuzzy variables for input to fuzzy variables for output by means of linguistic variables, each of that is outlined by a fuzzy set, and operators for fuzzy implications such as AND, OR etc. The mixed truth of predicate is decided by rules of implication such as MIN-MAX and limited arithmetic sums. All rules in rule-base are prepared in a concurrent approach by means of inference engine for fuzzy. Any rule that fires presents to the ultimate fuzzy solution space. Based on variations of Battery-Power, Mobility and Centrality chance will be varied from Type 1 Fuzzy Controller. Based on the values of input variables (Battery-Power, Mobility and Centrality) and output variable (Chance) the linear regression graph is shown in Figure 7.

It is concluded from the result that T1FL transmits additional data signal to the BS. The traffic load is disseminated uniformly among all the SNs that can boost the life span of the sensor network. The performance of T1FL is superior. The throughput of the data packet is measured.

CONCLUSION AND FUTURE RESEARCH DIRECTIONS

WSN transports a fresh example of embedded systems in real time with restricted calculation, transmission, storage, and resources for power that are being utilized for enormous series of usages where conventional infrastructure WSN is chiefly not suitable. In this investigation, a power resourceful clustering algorithm has been projected for WSN using T1FLC System. By picking appropriate type-1 fuzzy descriptors one RMCH is chosen among the CHs that are the indicatives for conveying information to a moving BS. The concept of BS movement along with the T1FL enhances WSN lifespan considerably. The planned thought can be relevant in numerous useful usages such as medical management, farming

Table 1. Fuzzy Rules and Chance values

Sl. No	A	B	C	O
1	LE(0)	L(0)	C(0)	VW(-1)
2	LE(0)	L(0)	A(1)	W(0)
3	LE(0)	L(0)	F(1)	LM(1)
4	LE(0)	MO(1)	C(0)	W(0)
5	LE(0)	MO(1)	A(1)	LM(1)
6	LE(0)	MO(1)	F(2)	M(2)
7	LE(0)	FR(2)	C(0)	LM(1)
8	LE(0)	FR(2)	A(2)	M(2)
9	LE(0)	FR(2)	F(2)	HM(3)
10	M(0)	L(0)	C(0)	W(0)
11	M(0)	L(0)	A(1)	LM(1)
12	M(0)	L(0)	F(2)	M(2)
13	M(0)	MO(1)	C(0)	LM(1)
14	M(0)	MO(1)	A(1)	M(2)
15	M(0)	MO(1)	F(2)	HM(3)
16	M(0)	FR(2)	C(0)	M(2)
17	M(0)	FR(2)	A(1)	HM(3)
18	M(0)	FR(2)	F(2)	S(4)
19	H(2)	L(0)	C(0)	LM(1)
20	H(2)	L(0)	A(1)	M(2)
21	H(2)	L(0)	F(2)	HM(3)
22	H(2)	M0(1)	C(0)	M(2)
23	H(2)	MO(1)	A(1)	HM(3)
24	H(2)	MO(1)	F(2)	S(4)
25	H(2)	FR(2)	C(0)	HM(3)
26	H(2)	FR(2)	A(1)	S(4)
27	H(2)	FR(2)	F(2)	VS(5)

field, disaster heat regions, militant usages etc. Statistical outcome demonstrates that planned protocol presents superior to LEACH protocol with respect to death of 1st node, alive status of half SNs, death of last node, improved stability and enhanced WSN lifespan. For additional research work, we will exploit and incorporate various bright techniques, similar to analytical organizational modelling technique, simulink, artificial neural network (ANN) for fuzzy, etc., to assess the extent of competence of our recent activity.

Figure 3. Battery-Power, Centrality Vs Chance

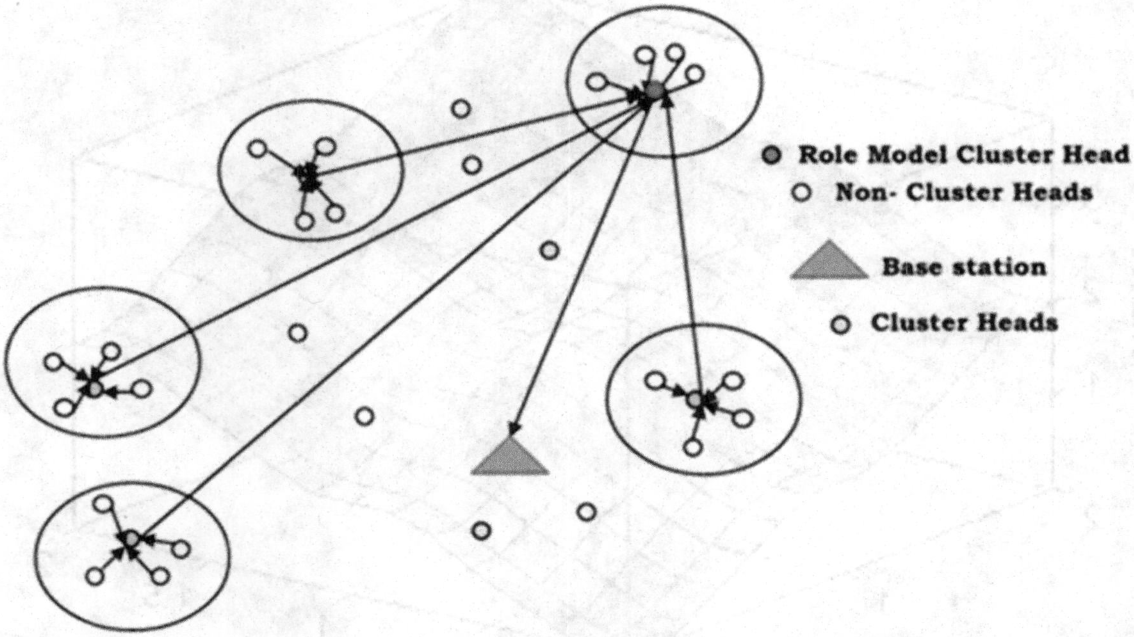

Figure 4. Battery-Power, Mobility Vs Chance

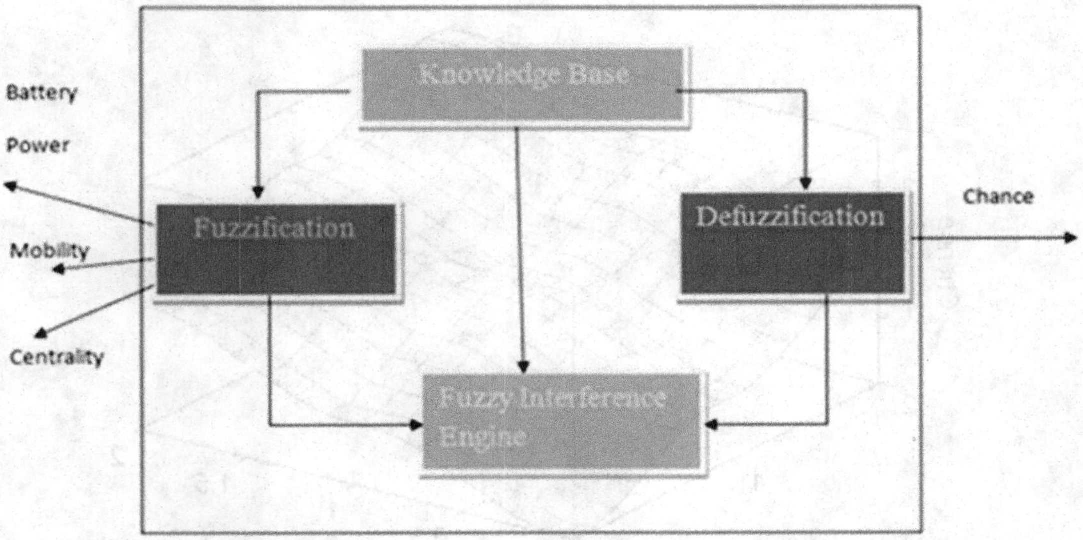

Figure 5. Mobility, Centrality Vs Chance

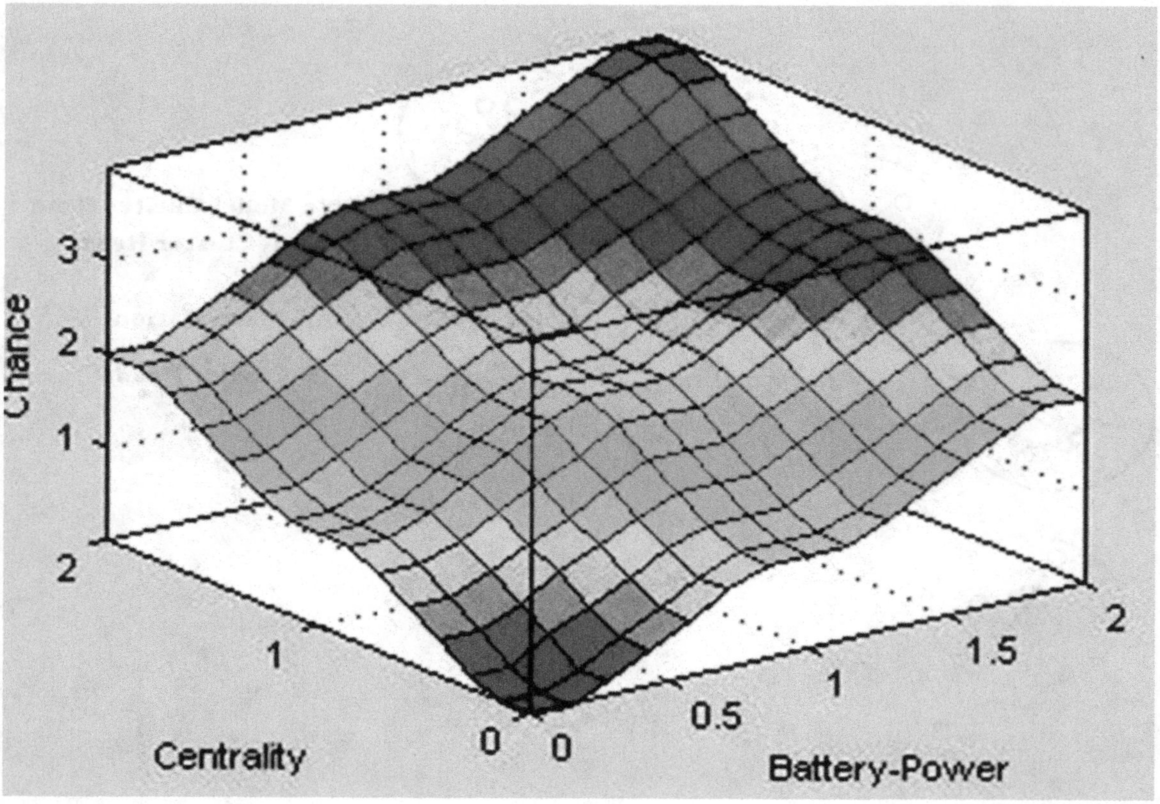

Figure 6. Fuzzy Rule Viewer

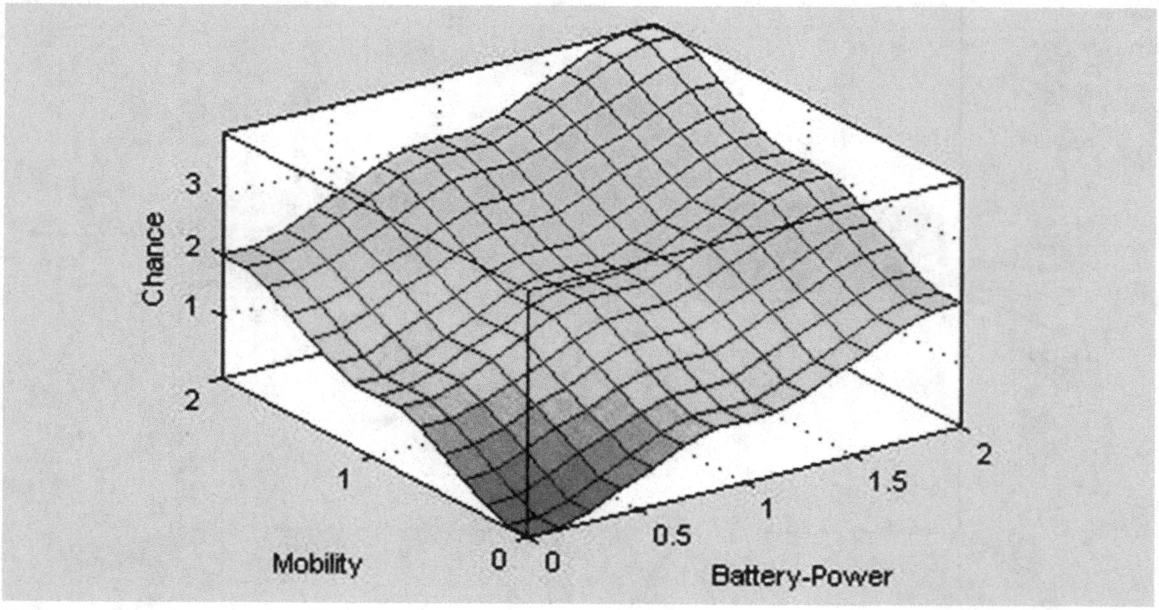

Figure 7. Linear Regression graph on Input and output values

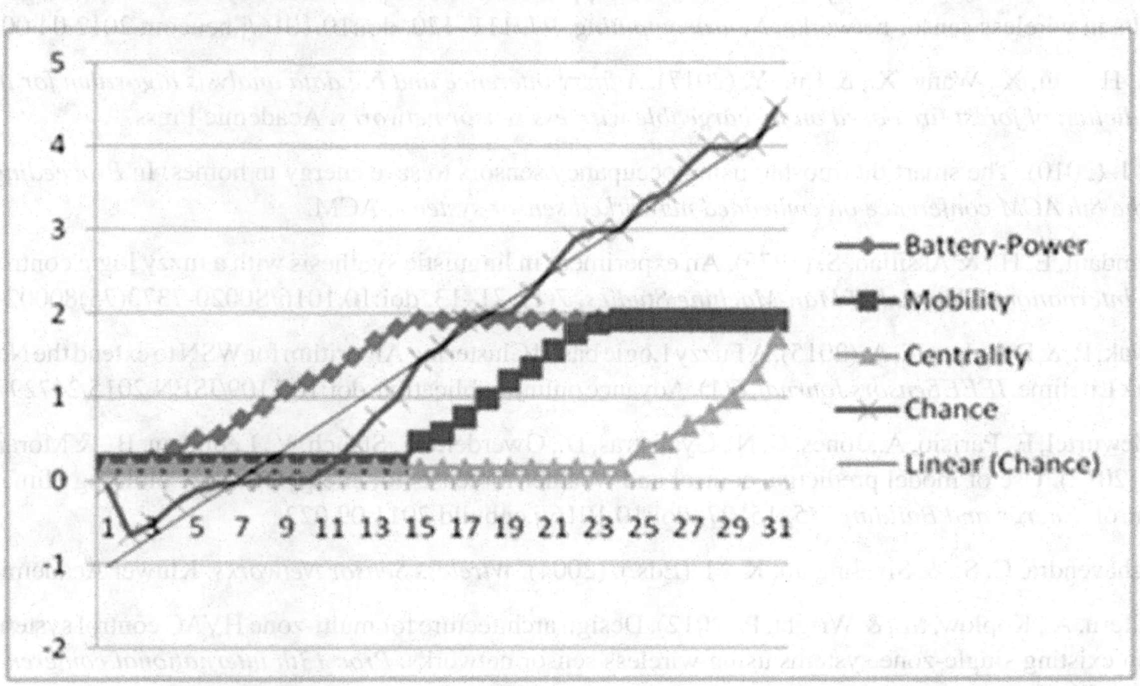

REFERENCES

Akyildiz, I. F., Su, W., Sankarasubramaniam, Y., & Cayirci, E. (2002). Wireless sensor networks: A survey. *Computer Networks*, *38*(4), 393–422. doi:10.1016/S1389-1286(01)00302-4

Azfar, T., Ahmed, W., Haseeb, A., Ahmad, R., Gul, S. T., & Zheng, F.-C. (2019, April). Zheng, Fu-C. (2019). A low complexity online controller using fuzzy logic in energy harvesting WSNs. *Science China. Information Sciences*, *62*(4), 42305. Advance online publication. doi:10.100711432-018-9751-5

Cao, X. (2010). Building-environment control with wireless sensor and actuator networks: Centralized versus distributed. *IEEE Transactions on Industrial Electronics*, *57*(11), 3596–3605. doi:10.1109/TIE.2009.2029585

Cayirci, E., Govindam, R., Znati, T., & Srivastava, M. (2003). Wireless sensor networks. *Int. J. Conmput. Telecommun.Netw*, *43*(4).

Chanana, S., & Arora, M. (2013). Demand response from residential air conditioning load using a programmable communication thermostat. *Int J Electr Comput Energetic Eng*, *7*(12).

Hamzah, A., Shurman, M., Al-Jarrah, O., & Taqieddin, E. (2019). Energy-Efficient Fuzzy-Logic-Based Clustering Technique for Hierarchical Routing Protocols in Wireless Sensor Networks. *Sensors (Basel)*, *19*(3), 561. doi:10.339019030561 PMID:30700022

Kaur, R., Sharma, D., & Kaur, N. (2013). Comparative analysis of LEACH and its descendant protocols in wireless sensor network. *Int. J. P2P Netw. Trends Technolol.*, *3*(1).

Khan, A., Daachi, S. S., & Djouani, K. (2012). Application of fuzzy inference systems to detection of faults in wireless sensor networks. *Neurocomputing*, *94*, 111–120. doi:10.1016/j.neucom.2012.04.002

Lin, H., Liu, X., Wang, X., & Liu, Y. (2017). *A fuzzy inference and big data analysis algorithm for the prediction of forest fire based on rechargeable wireless sensor networks*. Academic Press.

Lu, J. (2010). The smart thermostat: using occupancy sensors to save energy in homes. In *Proceedings of the 8th ACM conference on embedded networked sensor systems*. ACM.

Mamdani, E. H., & Assilian, S. (1975). An experiment in linguistic synthesis with a fuzzy logic controller. *International Journal of Man-Machine Studies*, *7*(1), 71–13. doi:10.1016/S0020-7373(75)80002-2

Nayak, P., & Devulapalli, A. (2015). A Fuzzy Logic based Clustering Algorithm for WSN to extend the Network Lifetime. *IEEE Sensors Journal*, *6*(1). Advance online publication. doi:10.1109/JSEN.2015.2472970

Oldewurtel, F., Parisio, A., Jones, C. N., Gyalistras, D., Gwerder, M., Stauch, V., Lehmann, B., & Morari, M. (2012). Use of model predictive control and weather forecasts for energy efficient building climate control. *Energy and Building*, *45*, 15–27. doi:10.1016/j.enbuild.2011.09.022

Raghavendra, C. S., & Sivalingam, K. M. (Eds.). (2004). *Wireless Sensor Networks*. Kluwer Academic.

Redfern, A., Koplow, M., & Wright, P. (2012). Design architecture for multi-zone HVAC control systems from existing single-zone systems using wireless sensor networks. *Proc 13th international conference on intelligence systems application to power systems, 6414*.

Rizwana, S., Gayathri, K. M., & Thangadurai, N. (2019). Fuzzy Logic Based Routing Algorithm for Wireless Sensor Networks to Enhance the Network Lifetime. *International Journal of Innovative Technology and Exploring Engineering*, *8*(8), 2272–2279.

Shokouhifar, M., & Jalali, A. (2017). Optimized sugeno fuzzy clustering algorithm for wireless sensor networks. *Engineering Applications of Artificial Intelligence*, *60*, 16–25. doi:10.1016/j.engappai.2017.01.007

Sugeno, M. (1985). *Industrial applications of fuzzy control*. North-Holland. Sole distributors for the U.S.A. and Canada, Elsevier Science Publishing company.

U.S. Department of Energy. (2009). *Smart grid system report; July 2009*. Author.

Vojdani, A. (2008). Smart integration. *IEEE Power & Energy Magazine*, *6*(6), 71–79. doi:10.1109/MPE.2008.929744

Wang, S. S., Yan, K. Q., Wang, S. C., & Liu, C. W. (2011). An integrated intrusion detection system for cluster based wireless sensor networks. *Expert Systems with Applications*, *38*(12), 15234–15243. doi:10.1016/j.eswa.2011.05.076

Woolley, J., Pritoni, M., & Modera, M. (2014).Why occupancy-responsive adaptive thermostats do not always save and the limits for when they should. *ACEEE summer study on energy efficiency in buildings*, 337-350.

Xue, W., Jun-Jie, M., Sheng, W., & Dao-Wei, B. (2007). Prediction-based Dynamic Energy Management in Wireless Sensor Networks. *Sensors (Basel)*, *7*(3), 251–266. doi:10.33907030251

Zadeh, L. A. (1965). Fuzzy sets. *Information and Control*, *8*(3), 338–353. doi:10.1016/S0019-9958(65)90241-X

Zinonos, Z., Chrysostomou, C., & Vassiliou, V. (2014). Wireless sensor networks mobility management using fuzzy Logic. *Ad Hoc Networks*, *16*, 70–87. doi:10.1016/j.adhoc.2013.12.003

Chapter 16
Synthesis and Characterization of Nanocomposites for the Application in Hybrid Solar Cell

Sakshi Tyagi
Haldia Institute of Technology, India

Pawan Kumar Singh
Indian Institute of Technology (Indian School of Mines), Dhanbad, India

Arun Kumar Tiwari
Institute of Engineering and Technology, Lucknow, India

ABSTRACT

In today's era, a lot of interest is gained by solar cell formed by combination of organic and inorganic nano-particle semiconductors mainly because of its major features such as scalable solar power conversion and cost effectiveness, which makes the cell a desirable photovoltaic device. This piece of work is an attempt to make a solar cells by the combination of zinc oxide (ZnO) and graphite. ZnO is a good n-type material for the application in photovoltaic (PV) devices due to its better optical, electrical, structural, and environmentally friendly properties, and on the other hand, graphite, an organic semiconductor, enhances the rate of charge transfer in the device. These materials are so designed to help bring in more understanding in a wider range of the solar spectrum. This work focuses on developing solid-state polymer and hybrid solar cells.

INTRODUCTION

There has always been need of alternative source of energy, be it renewable or non-renewable. The crisis of the same has resulted into environmental disbalance. In order to survive, research and development has picked up a great pace so as to ensure energy sustainability in future. One of the rapidly growing alternative energies in the world is solar energy. Solar energy is luminous light and heat from the sun

DOI: 10.4018/978-1-7998-3624-7.ch016

that is exploited using a range of continuously upgrading technologies such as photovoltaics, heating, artificial photosynthesis, solar architecture, solar thermal energy and molten salt power plants (Blouin et al., 2008). In today's era, technology and population is growing rapidly. With the developing pace many countries are facing shortage of fossil fuel resources. By the year passes, increasing needs of society are resulting into shortage of raw material of non-renewable energy. In order to meet human demand, it is vital to develop energy sources that are inexpensive and clean.

Solar energy is the cleanest and easily available form of energy. Also, there are many applications for the free radiation energy obtained from the sun. Photovoltaics is one of the prominent fields in which effective application of solar energy can be observed The prominent field in which the application of solar energy can be seen rapidly is the electronic devices such as photovoltaics, which is on its increasing pace year after year. (Coakley et al., 2003).

MATERIAL USED

Zinc Oxide (ZnO) is an inorganic compound. As ZnO is insoluble in water, it is preferably used as an additive in numerous materials and products like rubbers, plastics, ceramics, glass, cement, lubricants. ZnO is a wide-band gap semiconductor. The native doping of the semiconductor is due to oxygen vacancies or zinc interstitials is n- type (Chiang et al., 1977). Hence the semiconductor has many desirable properties like high electron mobility, good transparency, strong room-temperature luminescence and wide band gap. Those propertiesare valuable in emerging applications for: transparent electrodes in liquid crystal displays, energy-saving windows, and electronics as thin-film transistors and light-emitting diodes. ZnO has a relatively large direct band gap of approximately 3.3 eV at room temperature (Dayal et al., 2009). The band gap of ZnO can further be tuned to approximately 3-4 eV by its alloying with grapheneoxide.

Even in the absence of intentional doping, most ZnO has n-type character. An alternative explanation has been proposed, based on theoretical calculations, that unintentional substitutional hydrogen impurities are responsible for the same (Dutta et al., 2012). Substitution of Zn with group- III elements such as Al, Ga, in is done to achieve controlled n-type doping. In past few decades, considerable attention has been paid to the research in the production of conductive polymers and organic molecules (Dutta et al., 2012). It has been on top interests of scientists to produce a new solar cell, they decided to construct the device using organic materials as shown in figure 1. This structure is known as bilayer solar cell. Layer by layer fabrication is done to fabricate a bilayer solar cell. As a basic solar cell, the device consists of four layers such as anode layer, two contact layers of ZnO and Graphite, the cathode (Halls et al., 1995). At the interface, excitons are dissociated into electrons and holes and successively there occurs diffusion of electrons at the cathode following which the electrons enter the external to generate electrical flow and complete the cell. To generate electric current, conversion of photon to electron is necessary. Light is absorbed by electron donor material to bind the excitons and the energy used in binding excitons is called Frenkel exciton (Hou et al., 2009).

Methodology

Usually, construction of polymer solar cells is accomplished by sandwiching an active layer between two coplanar electrodes, along with a layer of Zinc Oxide and Graphite. The bottom electrode (anode) and the upper electrode (cathode) is made of a transparent substrate (glass) coated with a conducting film

Figure 1. Device architecture of Hybrid Cell

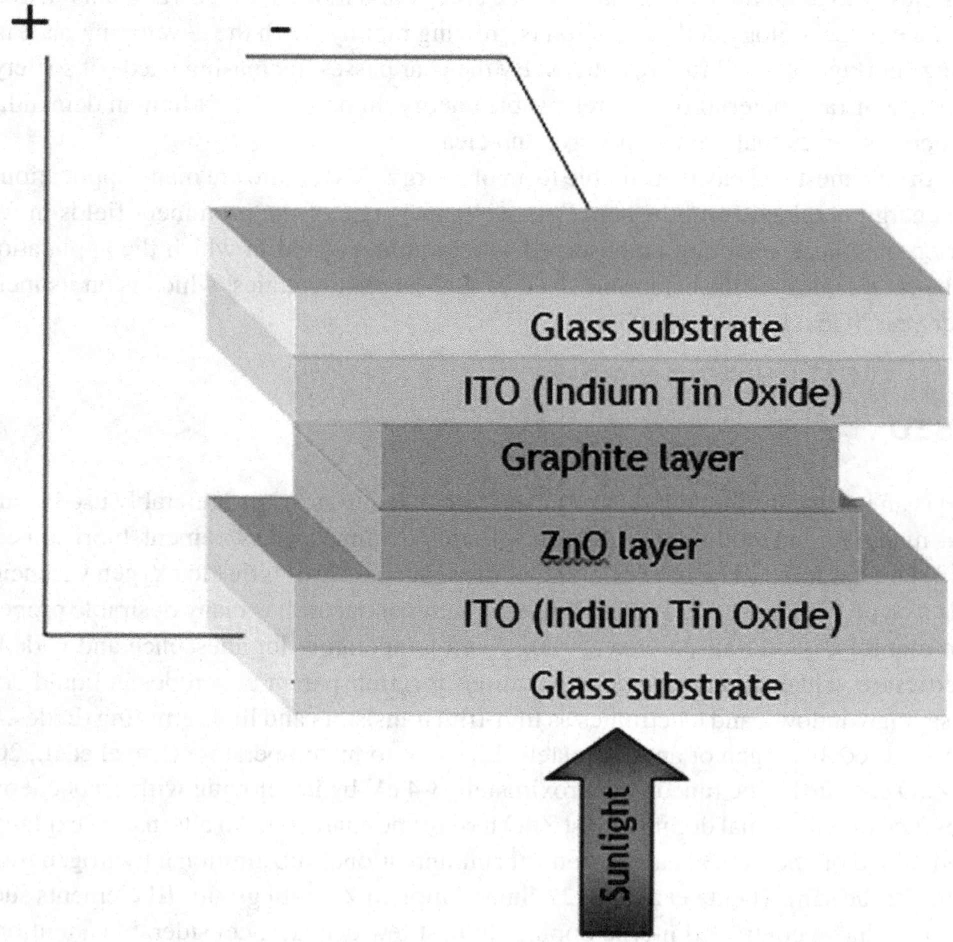

such as indium tin oxide (ITO). Advantage of incorporating conductive polymer as electrode is its simple film-forming techniques. The conductive polymer in solution can be moulded into different geometric drawings, and after baking it becomes conductive film (Kannan et al., 2003). Polymer electrode successfully replaces metal film making flexible plastic large-scale photovoltaic cells a future possibility.

Experimental Procedure

The device architecture is shown in figure 1. To start with, it is visible that the first layer that is the anode is made up of conductive glass substrate coated with ITO (Indium Tin Oxide). A thin layer of ZnO is spread over the ITO coated glass. As a bilayer solar cell involves layer by layer fabrication, therefore the device is constituted by four layers such as anode layer, contact layer made of Zinc Oxide, the graphite layer, and the cathode. These layers comply with the architecture of the cell (Lenes et al., 2006). Sol gel of ZnO which is to be spread over the ITO coated glass is prepared by Wet Chemical Technique. (WCT is a method for producing solid material from small molecules).

Figure 2. (A) Compounds required in preparation of ZnO sol gel(B) Other chemicals used from Chemistry lab, Agra college#*

** Powdered zinc oxide has been doggled in blue.*

 # Source of research, Department of Chemical Technology and Department of Zoology, Agra college.

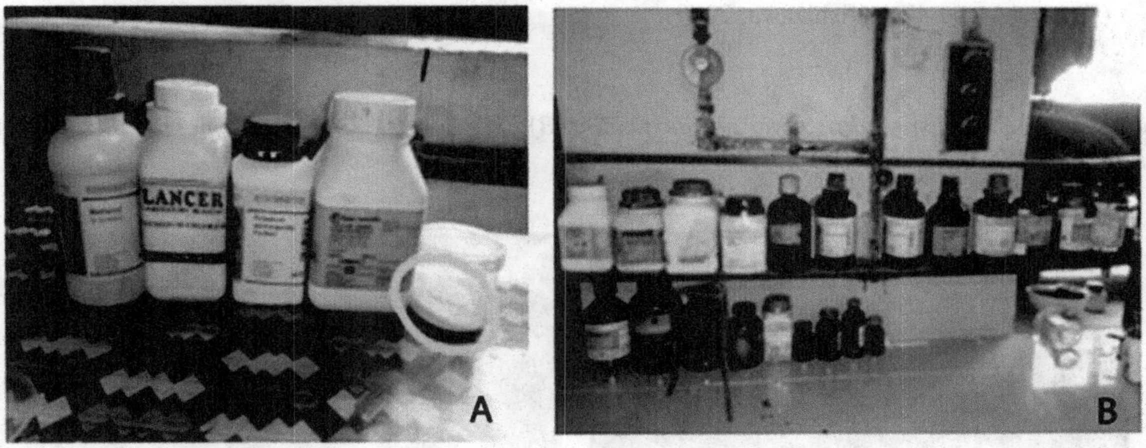

All these compounds are mixed in following proportions:

1. Zinc Acetate dihydrate (ZnADH- 3.636g)
2. Ethylene di-amine tetra acetic acid (0.72ml)
3. Potassium Chloride (0.52g)
4. Methanol (21ml)
5. Potassium Permanganate purified (1ml)
6. HCl (3.2ml)

The above prepared solution is stirred for 3, 4, 5 hours. The variation in stirring time is done to observe different morphology of ZnO molecules.

For film deposition these steps are to be followed:

1. A pair of Indium Tin Oxide (ITO) coated glass substrate purchased from Shilpa enterprises, Nagpur. Specification of the substrates is as follows (25 mm x 75 mm x 1mm). Substrates are first cleaned by distilled water and then byAcetone, 2-Isopropanol and de-ionized water (Liu et al., 2012) one after the other.
2. Pure ZnO solution samples are prepared by Wet chemical Technique. In this work synthesis of ZnO nanostructures is done by wet chemical route having Zinc Acetate Dihydrate (ZnADH), Ethylene di-amine tetra acetic acid, Potassium Chloride, Methanol in the proportion mentioned earlier. ZnO has to be spread on the substrate after performing mechanical stirring of the sol gel at 500 rpm for 3,4,5 hours. Stirring has to be done to separate the molecules from forming colloidal solution (Muhlbacher, 2006). Now place the glass substrate on a clean surface with the help of transparent tape, placing the tape on the three sides, so that glass gets coated properly, as shown in figure

3A. Layer of ZnO is spread evenly with the help of another glass piece. Remove the side tapes to observe the fine finish,figure 3B.

3. Substrate coated with ZnO layer which is stirred up to 3 hours is heated on the hot plate for up to 10 minutes, increasing the energy by 10 units after each 2 minutes with the help of energy regulator (figure 4A and 4B) (Nishizawa, 2009).

Figure 3. (A) Evenly spreading layer of Zinc Oxide. (B) Fine layer of ZnO after removing the transparent tape from the three sides

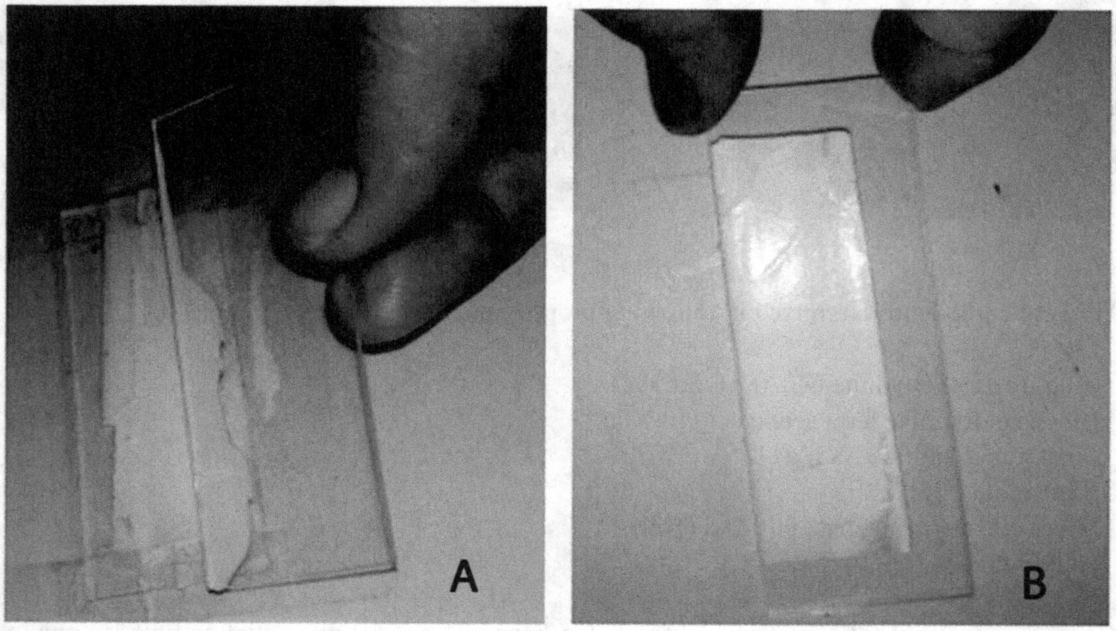

4. Now after deposition of ZnO, the films are left to dry at room temperature for 30 minutes (figure 5) (Peet et al., 2007).

5. Sketch a mesh of Graphite with the help of pencil to provide a layer of organic semiconductor which is in contact with ZnO (Inorganic semiconductor layer) and ITO glass (figure 6). Graphene oxide (GO) is a better option as compared to graphite because it is prepared in a regulated environment with all possible parameters taken care of (Peumans et al., 2003).
6. Final step is to assemble the glass substrate with the help of alligator clip (figure7) so that it can hold both anode and cathode close to each other. Now put one to two drops of the solution between the two pieces of glass, formed by mixing three parts of Potassium Iodide with one part of Ethanol, i.e. in a ratio of 3:1 (Ren at al., 2011).

Figure 4. (A) Glass substrate being dried on hot plate for 10 minutes, increasing energy by 10 units after 2 minutes each (B) Dried ZnO layer after 10 minutes

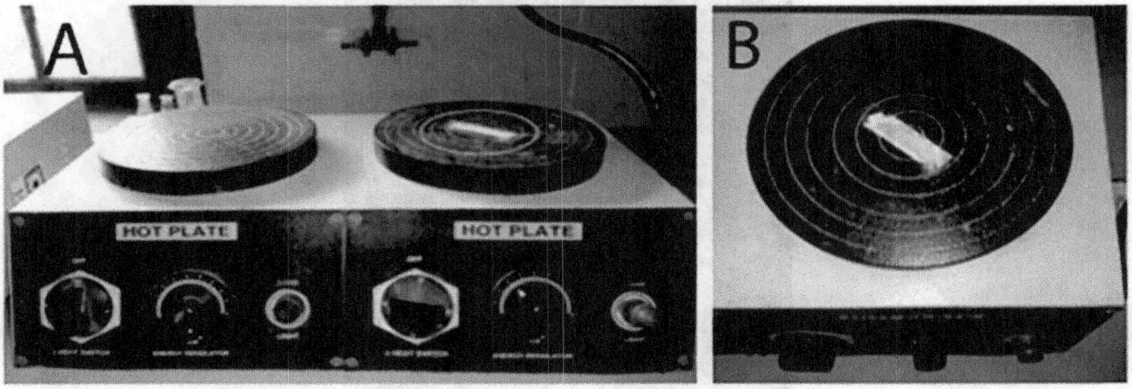

Note: An iodine solution is an ideal electrolyte.

7. Three such sample solar cells are prepared whose J-V characteristics vary with respect to the time donated in oxide sol gel being stirred, i.e. for 1stcell, oxide sol gel is stirred for 3 hours, 2ndfor 4 hours, 3rdfor 5 hours (Shinar et al., 2004).
8. The current density–voltage (*J–V*) measurements of the fabricated sample cell were performed by using a conventional circuit which measures the current corresponding to a certain potential difference across the junction. High impedance electrometers (Keithley 610 and Keithley 617 as the voltage source and current meter) are used to measure the voltage across the junction and current passing through it. The dark current–voltage characteristics were obtained in a complete dark chamber at room temperature or inside a dark furnace in case of measurements at higher temperatures. For measuring the temperature of the specimen NiCr–NiAl thermocouple is connected to a digital thermometer. (Tanveer et al., 2012)
9. Halogen lamp (white light) is used for the illumination of the specimen with intensity of 80 mW cm^{-2}. For measuring the intensity of incident light, a digital Lux-meter (BCHA, model 93408) is used. The distance of 15 cm is maintained in between the device and the halo- gen lamp.(Wang et al., 2010)

RESULTS AND OBSERVATION

It is known that ZnO layer is used as electron selective film to enhance the performance of photovoltaic cell (Xu et al., 2011). And the ZnO layer which is contact with ITO shows the same function of electron selection, which is desirable from a PV device (Yu et al. 1995). Figure 9 illustrates the current density–voltage (*J–V*) characteristics of the fabricated cell at some fixed temperatures. By the formation of p–n heterojunction, forward and reverse carrier's builds a barrier at the interface and limits the flow across the junction.

The modified ideal diode equation is used to represent the dark forward current–density, *J*

Figure 5. Drying the layer at room temperature for 30 minutes

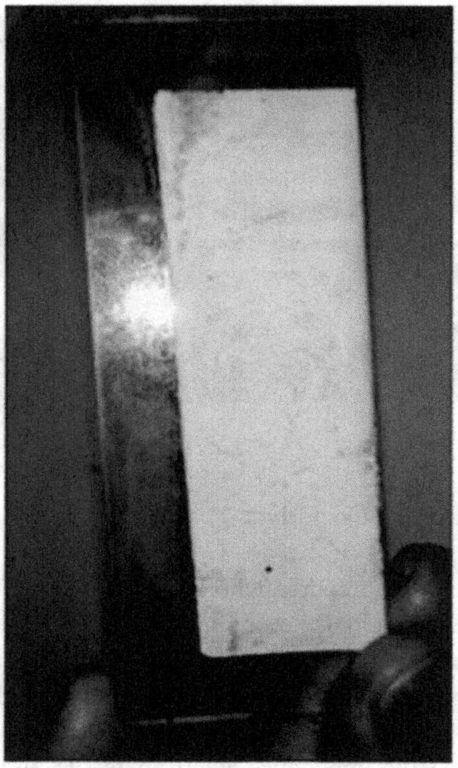

$$j = j_0\left[\frac{e^{q(V-JR_s)}}{nk_bT}-1\right]+v-\frac{JR_s}{R_{sh}} \tag{1}$$

where J_o is the reverse saturation current density, q is the electronic charge, n is the diode quality factor, k_B is Boltzmann constant, T is the absolute junction temperature, R_s is the series resistance, R_{sh} is the shunt resistance and V is the applied voltage. The R_s and R_{sh} were calculated from the typical experimental results of junction resistance ($R_j = \partial V/\partial J$) and listed in Table 1. Also, the rectification ratio (RR) was evaluated at ±1Vand is enlistedinTable1. However, RR is the ratio of the forward current to the reverse current at a certain valueoftheappliedvoltage(RR=J_F/J_R). The forward J–V characteristics (Figure9) can be divided into two regions according to the applied voltages. In the first region there is lower voltage, where the temperature is dependent on the forward currents. Analysis of the same is done by Schottky emission mechanism.

Modeling the J–V Characteristics Using ANNs

Neurons are the basic processing element of a neural network. is made up of one or more neurons, which is. A neuron comprises of one or more individually weighted inputs. A neuron has one or more output

Figure 6. Graphitemesh

that is weighted when connecting to other neurons. A function is included in neuron that integrates its inputs by summing them and then classifying the outputs by a transfer function. (see figure 10). (Luo et al., 2012)

Amulti-layerfeed-forwardnetworkis prepared which comprises of *l*inputneurons,thefirsthiddenlayer contains $m_1$neuronsin it,inthesecondhiddenlayers *there are* m_2 neurons,andtheoutputlayer comprising of$n_o$outputneurons which is represented as (l–m_1– m_2–n_o) or(l–m–n_o).The proposed ANN model of the *J–V* characteristics can be viewed as a two-input one-output model where the inputs are: the junction temperature, *T* ranging from 298 to 373 K and the applied voltage, *V* (from 2 to 2 V) while the output is: the current density, *J*, as shown in figure 6. As the nature of the outputs (*J*) is completely different from each other, the authors chose to internally model the problem with neural networks trained using experimental data. The ANN model is simply shown as a block diagram in figure11. (Zhu et al., 2007). With the help of input–output arrangement, tests on different (four) network configurations were performedtoattaingoodmean-squareerror(MSE)andgoodperformanceforthenetworkasinTable2.MSE on predicting performance(Δw) presents the learning and generalization error of the normalizedvaluesofthe currentdensity,*J*(seeTable2and12(a)–(d)).ItiscomputedusingtheLevenberg– Marquardt equationswhere:

$$\Delta w = (J^T J_{ac} + ml)^{-1} J^T e \tag{2}$$

Figure 7. Assembling the two glass substrates with the help of alligator clips

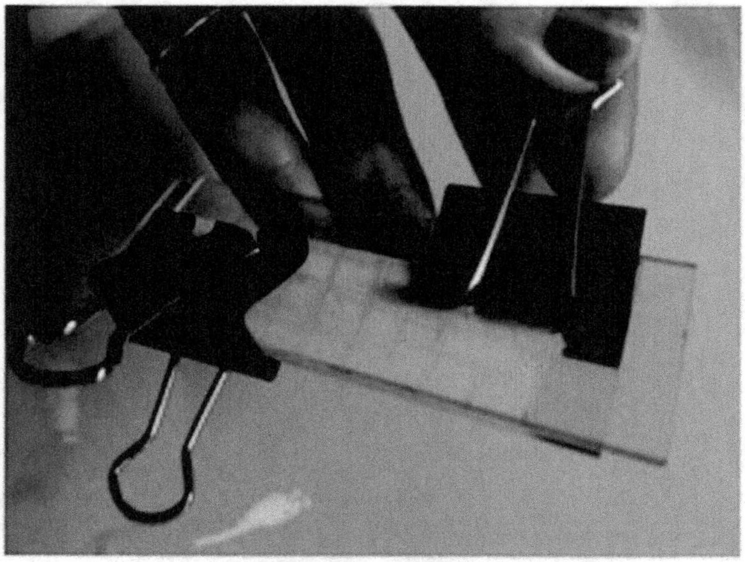

where J_{ac} is the Jacobian matrix of derivatives of each error with respect to each weight; J^T is the transposed matrix of 'J; I' is the identity matrix that has the same dimensions as those of J^TJ; m is a scalar changed adaptively by the algorithm and e is an error vector. When $\Delta w \rightarrow$ zero, this means that the network has beenlearnt (Liu et al., 2012)

Structure of ANN Model and Simulation Results

For the purpose of improving the predictor's training current density, J. A couple of simulation tests were performed to identify the structure that gave the best prediction results, (as in Table 2). Using the experimental data, four individual neural networks at different temperatures (T = 298, 303, 323 or 363 K) are trained separately as shown in figure 11. The network transfer function is a log sigmoid function expressedas

$$f(x) = \frac{1}{1+e^{-x}} \tag{3}$$

The following are the appropriate parameters for the ANNs predictor, including the number of hidden layers (5, 5, 5, 5), number of neurons (see Table 2), number of epochs (218, 700, 800, 2000) and the performance (see Table 2). 12(a)–(d) presents the training procedure. It reveals that the mean squared error of the network starting at a large value and decreasing to a smaller value. It shows the network is learning. After the network memorizes the training set, training is stopped and the obtained equation (which represents the current density, J) for all four networks is given in Appendix A.

Figure 8. Current produced (in milli-amperes) after keeping in sunlight for 3-4 hours

The results of ANNs calculation from the obtained function are represented in 13(a)–(d) together with the corresponding experimental data. A very good agreement between the simulated results (Appendix A) and the validating data was achieved. This indicates that the trained ANNs take on optimal generalization performance. Simulation capability of the ANNs models for current density, J, is calculated also, at lower and higher of the applied voltage (2 ± 2). Then, the results of the current density based ANNs showed almost exact fit to the obtained experimental data. This is not usually the case with other conventional theoretical techniques.

CONCLUSION

In India, the most promising role of renewable energies remains with the poorest and remote population of major centres. In the near time, renewable energies are still a ray of hope for coping with the climate changes. From the investigation regarding nanocomplex cells we came across the fact that as compared to common conductive metal, ZnO/Graphite nanocomplex can be an interesting alternative electrode used in hybrid solar cell. The IV characteristic of the cell goes on improving by increasing the sol gel stirring time. The efficiency of photovoltaic devices with polymer anode is comparatively better to that of conventional devices using Al as electrodes (Zhou et al., 2011).

Figure 9. Dark J–V characteristics for ZnO/GO junction at some fixed temperatures in both forward and reverse bias

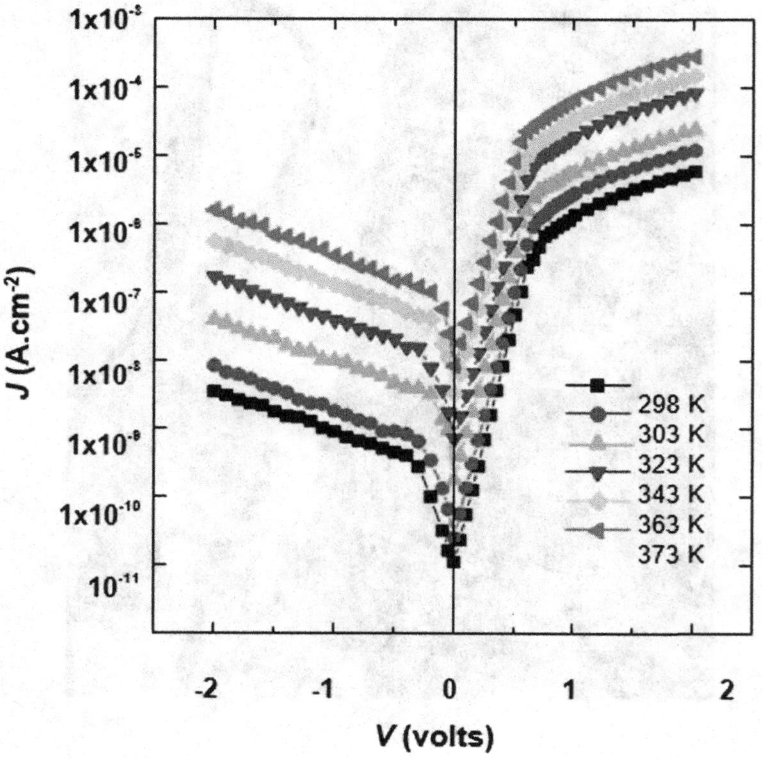

A heterojunction cell was fabricated by the deposition of InSe thin film onto p-Si. Electrical and photoelectrical measurements involving the current density–voltage (J–V) have been performed in order to characterize the electrical properties of the junction. The junction exhibited rectifying characteristics showing diode-like behavior. When voltage is kept low, Schottky emission mechanism is used to control the dark forward current density; whereas a space charge-limited- conduction mechanism is dominated at a relatively high voltage. The cell exhibited a photovoltaic characteristic with a power conversion efficiency of 3.42%. The current article presents an efficient approach for computing the J–V through the obtained functions using the ANN model. (Zhou et al., 2012). The simulation results show a clear and excellent match to the experimental data. Finally, the present work has proved that the ANN approach

Table 1. Junction parameters for n-InSe/p-Si junction cell at some fixed temperatures

S. No	T(K)	RR	R_s(kX)	R_{sh}(MX)	N	J_o(A cm^{-2})
1	298	1495	347.2	837.4	2.32 ± 0.05	1.16×10^{-11}
2	303	1551	168.1	405.2	2.31±0.05	2.66×10^{-11}
3	323	568	85.2	76.2	2.30±0.05	1.81×10^{-10}
4	363	260	16.1	6.3	2.33±0.05	3.35×10^{-9}

Figure 10. Simple neuron with biological equivalents

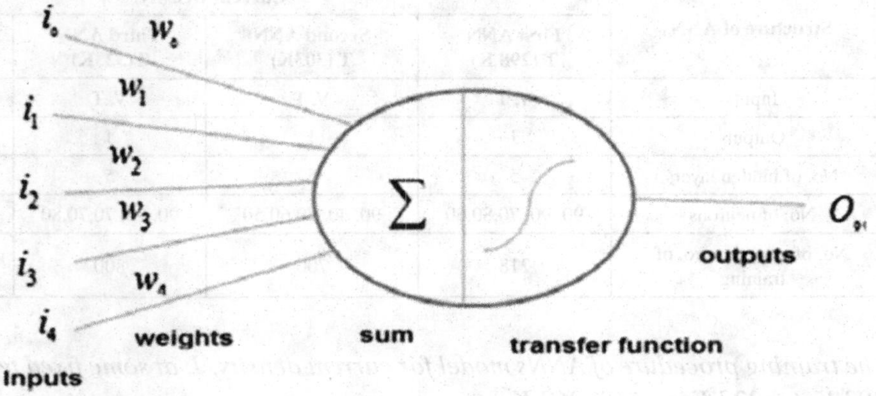

Figure 11. Block diagram of the current density, J, ANNs based modeling

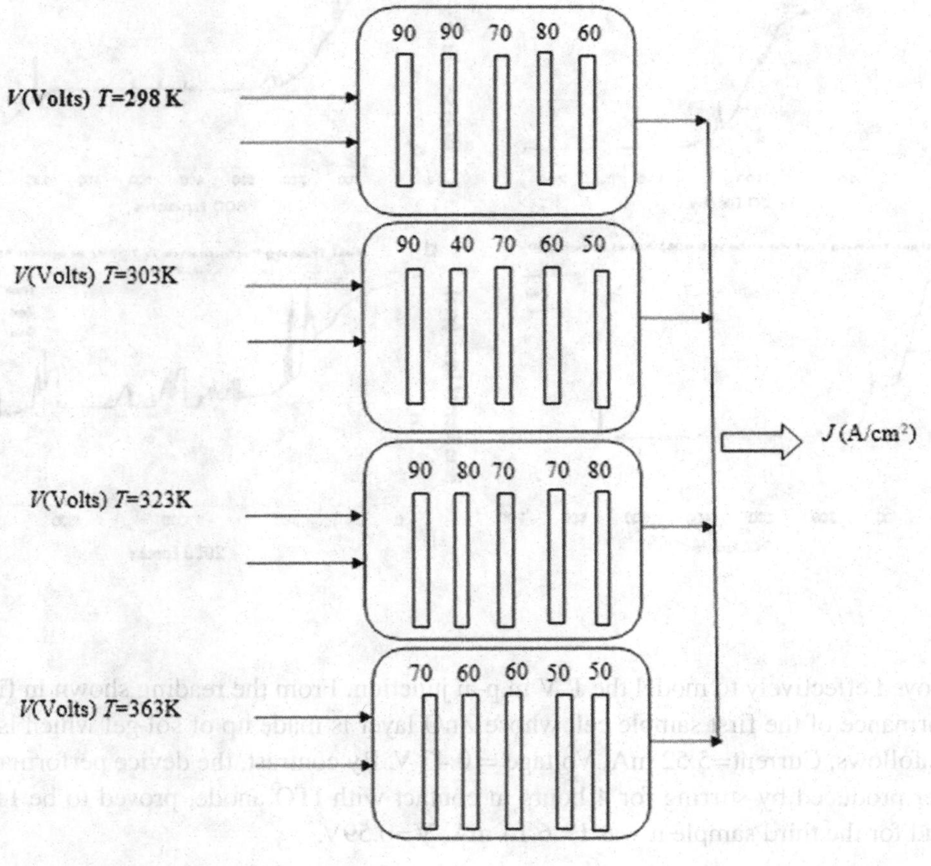

Table 2. Overview of all parameters in the ANNs for the current density, J of n-InSe/p-Si junction

S.No	Structure of ANN	Current Density			
		First ANN T (298 K)	Second ANN T (303K)	Third ANN T(323K)	Fourth ANN T(363K)
1	Inputs	V, T	V, T	V, T	V, T
2	Outputs	J	J	J	J
3	No. of hidden layers	5	5	5	5
4	No. of neurons	90, 90, 70,80,60	90, 40, 70,60,50	90, 80, 70,70,80	70, 60, 60, 50,50
5	No. of epochs = no. of training	218	700	800	2000

Figure 12. The training procedure of ANNs model for current density, J, at some fixed temperatures: (a) 298 K, (b) 303 K, (c) 323 K, and (d) 363 K

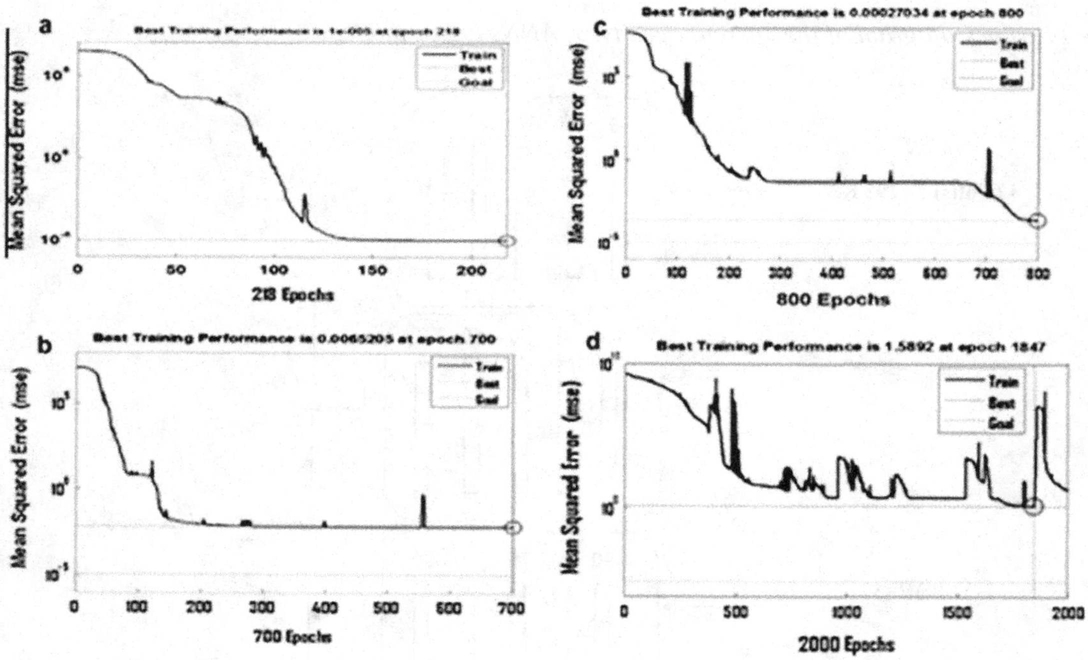

can be employed effectively to model the J–V in p–n junction. From the reading shown in figure 8, the device performance of the first sample cell whose ZnO layer is made up of sol gel which is stirred for 3 hours is as follows, Current=5.52 mA, Voltage = 0.43 V. By contrast, the device performance, which is using layer produced by stirring for 4 hours in contact with ITO anode, proved to be I = 5.7 mA, V=0.51V and for the third sample it was I= 6.14 mA, V=0.59V.

Figure 13. Simulation results for the current density, J, at some fixed temperatures: (a) 298 K, (b) 303 K, (c) 323 K, and (d) 363 K

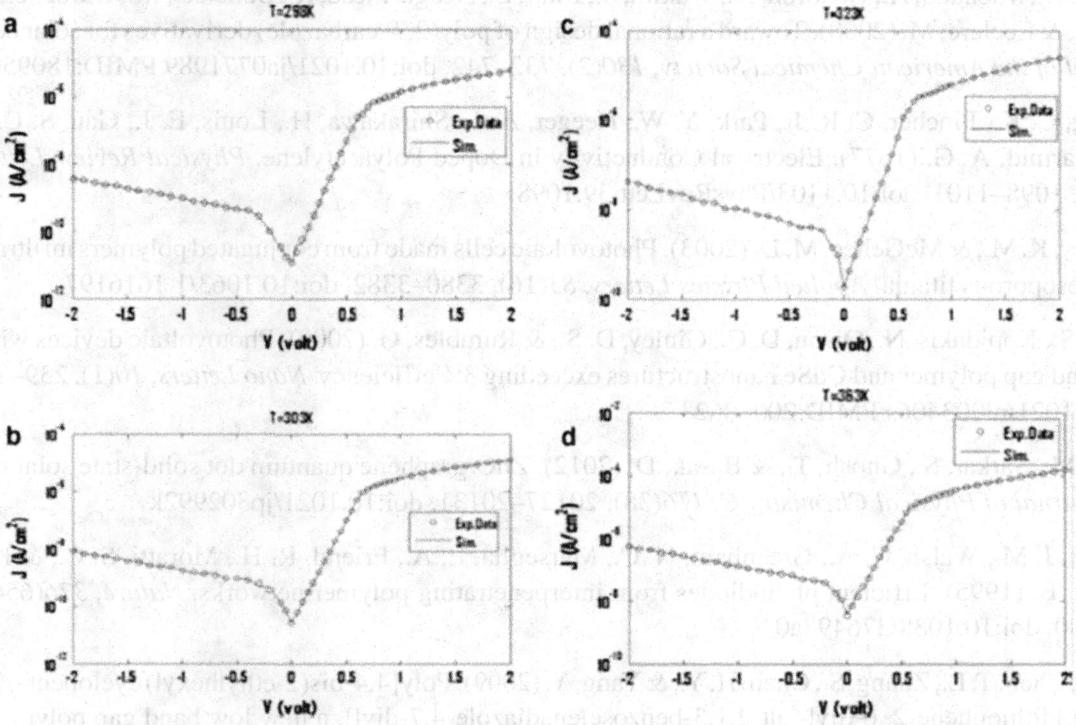

Table 3. Effect of mechanical stirring on IV characteristics of hybrid solar cell

S.No.	ZnO sol gel stirring time (hours)	Current (mA)	Voltage (V)
1.	3	5.52	0.43
2.	4	5.7	0.51
3.	5	6.14	0.59

REFERENCES

Blouin, N., Michaud, A., Gendron, D., Wakim, S., Blair, E., Neagu-Plesu, R., Belletête, M., Durocher, G., Tao, Y., & Leclerc, M. (2008). Toward a rational design of poly(2,7- carbazole) derivatives for solar cells. *Journal of the American Chemical Society*, *130*(2), 732–742. doi:10.1021/ja0771989 PMID:18095689

Chiang, C. K., Fincher, C. R. Jr, Park, Y. W., Heeger, A. J., Shirakawa, H., Louis, E. J., Gau, S. C., & MacDiarmid, A. G. (1977). Electrical Conductivity in Doped Polyacetylene. *Physical Review Letters*, *39*(17), 1098–1101. doi:10.1103/PhysRevLett.39.1098

Coakley, K. M., & McGehee, M. D. (2003). Photovoltaic cells made from conjugated polymers infiltrated into mesoporous titania. *Applied Physics Letters*, *83*(16), 3380–3382. doi:10.1063/1.1616197

Dayal, S., Kopidakis, N., Olson, D. C., Ginley, D. S., & Rumbles, G. (2009). Photovoltaic devices with a low band gap polymer and CdSe nanostructures exceeding 3% efficiency. *Nano Letters*, *10*(1), 239–242. doi:10.1021/nl903406s PMID:20000623

Dutta, M., Sarkar, S., Ghosh, T., & Basak, D. (2012). ZnO/graphene quantum dot solid-state solar cell. *The Journal of Physical Chemistry C*, *116*(38), 20127–20131. doi:10.1021/jp302992k

Halls, J. J. M., Walsh, C. A., Greenham, N. C., Marseglia, E. A., Friend, R. H., Moratti, S. C., & Holmes, A. B. (1995). Efficient photodiodes from interpenetrating polymer networks. *Nature*, *376*(6540), 498–500. doi:10.1038/376498a0

Hou, J., Chen, T. L., Zhang, S., Chen, H. Y., & Yang, Y. (2009). Poly[4,4-bis(2-ethylhexyl) cyclopenta[2,1-b;3,4-b]dithiophene-2, 6-diyl- alt-2,1,3-benzoselenadiazole-4,7-diyl], a new low band gap polymer in polymer solar cells. *The Journal of Physical Chemistry C*, *113*(4), 1601–1605. doi:10.1021/jp808255b

Hou, J., & Guo, X. (2013). Chapter. In W. C. H. Choy (Ed.), Active layer materials for organic solar cells (pp. 17–42). Springer. doi:10.1007/978-1-4471-4823-4_2

Kannan, B., Castelino, K., & Majumdar, A. (2003). Design of Nanostructured Heterojunction Polymer Photovoltaic Devices. *APC Nano Letter*, *3*(12), 1729–1733. doi:10.1021/nl034810v

Kim, M. (2009). *Understanding Organic Photovoltaic Cells Electrode. In Nanostructure, Reliability and Performance*. University of Michigan.

Lenes, M., Koster, L. J. A., Mihailetchi, V. D., & Blom, P. W. M. (2006). Thickness dependence of the efficiency of polymer: Fullerene bulk heterojunction solar cells. *Applied Physics Letters*, *88*(24), 243502–243503. doi:10.1063/1.2211189

Liu, X., Pan, L., Zhao, Q., Lv, T., Zhu, G., Chen, T., Lu, T., Sun, Z., & Sun, C. (2012). UV-assisted photocatalytic synthesis of ZnO reduced grapheme oxide composites with enhanced photocatalytic activity in reduction of Cr(VI). *Chemical Engineering Journal*, *183*, 238–243. doi:10.1016/j.cej.2011.12.068

Luo, Q. P., Yu, X.-Y., Lei, B.-X., Chen, H.-Y., Kuang, D.-B., & Su, C.-Y. (2012). Reduced graphene oxide-hierarchical ZnO hollow sphere composites with enhanced photocurrent and photocatalytic activity. *The Journal of Physical Chemistry C*, *116*(14), 8111–8117. doi:10.1021/jp2113329

Muhlbacher, D., Scharber, M., & Moranaetal, M. (2006). Highphotovoltaicperformanceof a low-bandgappolymer. *Advanced Materials, 18*(21), 2884–2889.

Nicolaidis, N. C., Routley, B. S., Holdsworth, J. L., Belcher, W. J., Zhou, X., & Dastoor, P. C. (2011). Fullerene contribution to photocurrent generation in organic photovoltaic cells. *The Journal of Physical Chemistry C, 115*(15), 7801–7805. doi:10.1021/jp2007683

Nishizawa, T., Lim, H. K., Tajima, K., & Hashimoto, K. (2009). Efficient dyad-based organic solar cells with a highly crystalline donor group. *Chemical Communications (Cambridge), 18*(18), 2469–2471. doi:10.1039/b902060h PMID:19532859

Peet, J., Kim, J. Y., Coates, N. E., Ma, W. L., Moses, D., Heeger, A. J., & Bazan, G. C. (2007). Efficiency enhancement in low-bandgap polymer solar cells by processing with alkane dithiols. *Nature Materials, 6*(7), 497–500. doi:10.1038/nmat1928 PMID:17529968

Peumans, P., Yakimov, A., & Forrest, S. R. (2003). Small molecular weight organic thin-film photodetectors and solar cells. *Journal of Applied Physics, 93*(7), 3693–3723. doi:10.1063/1.1534621

Ren, S., Chang, L.-Y., Lim, S.-K., Zhao, J., Smith, M., Zhao, N., Bulović, V., Bawendi, M., & Gradečak, S. (2011). Inorganic and organic hybrid solar cell: Bridging quantum dots to conjugated polymer nanowires. *Nano Letters, 11*(9), 3998–4002. doi:10.1021/nl202435t PMID:21859097

Shinar, J., & Savvateev, V. (2004). Introduction to Organic Light-Emitting Devices. In J. Shinar (Ed.), *Organic Light-Emitting Devices*. Springer. doi:10.1007/978-0-387-21720-8_1

Soci, C., Hwang, I. W., Moses, D., Zhu, Z., Waller, D., Gaudiana, R., Brabec, C. J., & Heeger, A. J. (2007). Photoconductivity of a low-bandgap conjugated polymer. *Advanced Functional Materials, 17*(4), 632–636. doi:10.1002/adfm.200600199

Tanveer, M., Habib, A., & Khan, M. B. (2012). Improved efficiency of organic/inorganic photovoltaic devices by electrospunZnO nanofibers. *Materials Science and Engineering B, 177*(13), 1144–1148. doi:10.1016/j.mseb.2012.05.025

Wang, X., Liu, D., & Li, J. (2010). Organic photovoltaic materials and thin-film solar cells. *FrontiersofChemistryinChina, 5*(1), 45–60. doi:10.100711458-009-0208-3

Xu, T., Zhang, L., Cheng, H., & Zhu, Y. (2011). Significantly enhanced photocatalytic performance of ZnOvia graphene hybridization and the mechanism stud. *Applied Catalysis B: Environmental, 101*(3), 382–387. doi:10.1016/j.apcatb.2010.10.007

Yu, G., Gao, J., Hummelen, J. C., Wudl, F., & Heeger, A. J. (1995). Polymer Photovoltaic Cells: Enhanced Efficiencies via a Network of Internal Donor-Acceptor Heterojunctions. *American Association for the Advancement of Science, 270*(5243), 1789–1790. doi:10.1126cience.270.5243.1789

Zheng, Q., Fang, G., Cheng, F., Lei, H., Wang, W., Qin, P., & Zhou, H. (2012). Hybrid graphene ZnO nanocomposites as electron acceptor in polymer based bulk-heterojunction organic photovoltaics. *Journal of Physics. D, Applied Physics, 45*(45), 455103. doi:10.1088/0022-3727/45/45/455103

Zhou, M., Eck, Y., & Krueger, M. (2011). *Solar Cells—New Aspects and Solutions*. Freiburg Materials Research Centre University of Freiburg.

Zhou, R., Zheng, Y., Qian, L., Yang, Y., Holloway, P. H., & Xue, J. (2012). Solution- processed, nanostructured hybrid solar cells with broad spectral sensitivity and stability. *Nanoscale*, *4*(11), 3507–3514. doi:10.1039/c2nr30210a PMID:22543410

Zhou, R. J., & Xue, J. G. (2012). Hybrid Polymer-Nanocrystal Materials for Photovoltaic Applications. *ChemPhysChem*, *13*(10), 2471–2480. doi:10.1002/cphc.201101016 PMID:22461231

Zhu, Z., Waller, D., Gaudiana, R., Morana, M., Mühlbacher, D., Scharber, M., & Brabec, C. (2007). Panchromatic conjugated polymers containing alternating donor/acceptor units for photovoltaic applications. *Macromolecules*, *40*(6), 1981–1986. doi:10.1021/ma062376o

Chapter 17
Intelligent Investment Approaches for Mutual Funds: An Evolutionary Model

Dipankar Majumdar
RCC Institute of Information Technology, India

Arup Kumar Bhattacharjee
RCC Institute of Information Technology, India

Soumen Mukherjee
https://orcid.org/0000-0002-8211-0507
RCC Institute of Information Technology, India

ABSTRACT

Investment in the right fund at the right time happens to be the key to success in the stock trading business. Therefore, for strategic investment, the selection of the right opportunity has to be executed crucially so as to reap the maximum returns from the market. Predicting the stock market has always been known to be very critical and needs years of experience as it involves lots of interleaving parameters and constraints. Intelligent investment in mutual funds (MF) can be done when various machine learning tools are used to predict future fund value using the past fund value. In this chapter, an elaborate discussion is presented on the different types of mutual funds and how these data can be used in prediction by machine learning in different literature. In this work, the NAV of a total of 17 different mutual funds have been extracted from the website of AMFI, and thereafter, ANFIS is used to forecast the time series of the NAV of the MF. They have been trained using ANFIS and thereafter tested for prediction with satisfactory results.

DOI: 10.4018/978-1-7998-3624-7.ch017

INTRODUCTION

Recent times have witnessed a general concept that massive volumes of capital are being sold by the Stock Markets throughout the world. Every country's economy happens to be associated and influenced severely by the behavior of the Stock Markets. Additionally, in the last few years or precisely more than a decade or two, the stock markets has become an easily available investment option for professional investors and also for common investor as well. As a result they did not remain related only to macroeconomic factors, but they have begun influencing day to day life directly. Therefore they have assumed significance and direct social impacts. Stock prices had always been a significant parameter for development of the companies, the constituting sector as well as the economic stability and growth of the country as a whole. One common characteristic of all Stock Markets is that they are uncertain, and they are correlated with short and long term future status. This characteristic, although an unwanted one from the investor's point of view, but at the same time is also unavoidable one whenever he or she takes the Stock Market into consideration as the asset building option. The best option that one can try is to attempt to reduce this uncertainty. Stock Market prediction is one of the tool under this condition. Mutual Fund (MF) is a platform which collects money from various investors and the fund manager invests the money in various stocks and bonds. These bonds and stocks on which the investment is made constitute the portfolio of the fund. A mutual fund is managed by a company called fund house which hires a team of experts who executes the crucial investment of the investors' money into selected stocks so as to provide maximum returns to the investors. The earning from the mutual fund is dispersed to the investors after paying the operating costs of the fund house. Every mutual fund comes with a certain objective and the investments made are also as per the offer documents. Investors also known as unit holder invest their money in a mutual fund which in turn is invested across a range of sectors thus minimizing the risk. Usually a fund house comes with a number of mutual funds each with certain objectives. Stock prices determine the development of banking operations viz. deposit and loan interest rates which in turn determines the mobility of money in the market and a whole lot of other economic factors of day to day life. Consequently, all through last few decades, the task of stock price speculation has assumed paramount importance in the capital market. Mutual Funds and other financial houses, who work on equity linked investments always, have the tremendously heavy task of speculating the stock prices so as to provide proper returns to the investors. If the same is not done accurately, either the investment will cease or the company will incur loss giving returns. Therefore, an accurate prediction is always essential so as to sustain in the market. Thanks to the field of Business Intelligence which offers varied metaheuristic approaches for accomplishing the above using the statistical knowledge base and input from external factors. The models involve extracting the data from statistics of past years, modeling them appropriately, adjusting them with external factors and finally speculating the trajectory of the prices for the time to come. The proposed chapter endeavors to model the past history of certain sectors of stocks so as to give a realistic prediction of the same in the time to come. The neuro fuzzy inference system is quite an established tool for forecast of data based on available data. Consequently, the authors have resorted to the same so as to predict the prices of stocks. There may be two different views of investment (return) maximization: viz. Long term investments and Short Term Investments. Analogously we also have two types of mutual funds viz. close ended and open ended that fetches returns likewise. The current chapter we confine our strategy to open ended mutual funds. We execute the same using historic patterns of the statistical data over the last 4 years, starting from the year 2014. In the next portion a history of the Mutual Fund, Net Asset Value and different types of mutual fund schemes are given. In the related work section the literature survey on the use of machine learning in portfolio management is given. Finally the data set preparation for the work and the proposed work is discussed with result and discussion.

History of Mutual Funds

The concept of mutual was introduced way back in early 18th century in Europe while it becomes popular in United States almost a century later around 1920s. In India, Unit Trust of India (UTI) was the initial mutual fund established in 1963. In India, a mutual fund needs to be registered with Securities and Exchange Board of India (SEBI). SEBI comes with an objective to promote the development of the securities market and shield investors from any unwanted situation. SEBI supervises all mutual fund schemes in India, regulates and formulates various policies for standardization of mutual funds. Even SEBI holds control over funds promoted by foreign entities. The Association of Mutual Funds in India (AMFI) is a non-profit organization established in 1995 to maintain standards in all areas of Mutual Fund Industries in India. AMFI is the representation of the mutual fund industry to the Government of India regarding all issues of mutual fund as well as to secure the investment of the investors in this industry.

Net Asset Value (NAV)

Net Asset Value (NAV) determines the performance of a mutual fund scheme. NAV is the measure of market value of the securities held under a MF scheme. NAV value of a scheme varies every day as market holding of a security changes on daily basis. As per SEBI rule NAV per unit of all schemes must be uploaded on the website of AMFI every day.

Categories of Mutual Fund Schemes

Mutual fund schemes can be divided into various categories based on different views –

- Based on maturity period: The classification of mutual funds based on maturity period may be enlisted as follows:
    - Open Ended Fund: This type of fund have no fixed maturity period. Investor can buy or sell units with no lock in period. The biggest advantage of these schemes is their liquidity.
    - Close Ended Fund: These schemes have stipulated maturity period of 3-5 years. Subscription to these funds is open only during specified period of time.
- Based on Investment Objective: The classification of mutual funds may also be done based on the objective with which the investment is made. Such categories have been enlisted below.
    - Growth / Equity Oriented Fund: Under this category, majority of the fund is invested in equities. These happen to involve comparatively more risks and they are suitable for long duration as the growth of the fund is of prime importance.
    - Income/ Debt Oriented Fund: Funds of this category is invested in government securities, bonds, debentures and money market instruments. They are known to be less risky than equity oriented funds. However they are not suitable for long term investments.
- Balanced/Hybrid Fund: These funds invest in equity and debt domain in 40-60 ratios. They are known to be less risky than equity funds which is suitable for moderate growth.

- Liquid Fund: These funds are invested in government securities, treasury bills, commercial papers etc. They are further less risky than balanced fund and suitable for short duration.
- Index Fund: These funds follow the index of NSE 50 index, BSE Sensitive Index etc. Their rise or fall depends on the index values. Index of these funds is generally influenced by tracking errors.
- Gilt Fund: This type of fund exclusively invests in government securities and consequently known to involve very low risk. The NAVs vary with change in interest rates.
- Sector Specific Fund: These funds invest in securities of specific sector or industry. More risky than diversified funds since their portfolio is very specific and hard coded. The exit from these funds depends on the performance of those sectors.
- Tax Saving Funds: These funds offer tax rebates. The nature of risks involved is same as that of equity oriented funds. The schemes are growth oriented.
- Exchange Traded Funds: Investor need to have demat and trading accounts for purchasing these funds. Purchasing and selling of units for these funds are executed through stock exchange.
- Capital Protection Oriented Fund: These funds invests mostly in fixed income securities that do not offer any guaranteed return. They are generally closed ended funds.

Based on the requirement and expectation of the investor, the funds can be selected for investment with correct timing for entry as well as duration of holding. Consequently a critically organized, dynamic portfolio is required to be maintained for funds of different categories for fulfillment of the interests of investors.

Related Work

Data Mining is extensively used for various analyses in financial domain (Shen et al., 2012). Neural network, classification, regression etc. are used for making different types of analysis on stocks, portfolio and other financial operations (Charkha, 2008). Even time series prediction has a great role on predicting mutual funds and stock price determination (Naeini et al. 2010). Artificial Intelligence has huge influence in every aspect of human life. Since mutual fund is an area of huge interest for business community so there is large scope of research in analysis in mutual fund domain using artificial intelligence. Genetic algorithm, support vector machines, K nearest neighbors, etc. are some prominent techniques used in mutual fund analysis with great analysis (Pathak, 2014). Pathak has suggested various studies on Adaptive Neuro Fuzzy Inference System (ANFIS). ANFIS provides a hybridization of neural network and fuzzy inference system (Jang, 1993; Alizadeh, et al. 2009). Many work being done using ANFIS for predicting sales forecast stock market prediction etc. (Kablan, 2009; Wang, et al., 2011, Wei, et al. 2011, Boyacioglu, et al. 2010). Also it is found that ANFIS has given good result over other techniques. ANFIS and neural network is used by B. S. Trinkle, to forecast the annual profits of 3 companies using autoregressive moving average (ARMA) model (Trinkle, 2006).

On studying the literature we find several methods which have been applied with an aim for prediction of Stock Market return on investment. These methods have been categorized in four major categories in (Kalyvas, 2001). Technical analysts, specialists in chart preparation, attempt to speculate the market trends by tracing the patterns that yield through the study of charts that describes the pattern of the trend of the market. Fundamental analysts again on the other hand study the inherent value of a stock and target them for investment if the current value as estimated is lower than the pre-calculated inherent value. Traditional Time Series forecasting is an attempt to fit the past data into a linear prediction model. These linear prediction models have further been categorized into two subcategories: namely uni-variate and multi-variate regression models, depending on use of one of more variables to model the Stock Market time series.

Finally several of approaches have been proposed and developed using Machine Learning methods which use datasets and try to find linear or non-linear patterns, to generate the underlying function that generated by the data.

For Banking, Insurance and other similar sectors, an impartial balance between risks and returns has to be controlled by any investor to deduce a conclusion at the best standpoint as mentioned in (Brown, 2004; McNeil, et al. 2005). In the area of portfolio selection, several models have been proposed and have come up throughout the years, which comprise the early mean variance models in condition to Markowitz's work (Markowitz, 1952). Once again, moderation of stochastic optimization methods based on the market scenario has counterfeited the significance in (Bhattacharya, et al. 2010; Ray, & Bhattacharyya, 2015).

The management methodologies of mutual fund asset allocation in recent times are heavily relying on the management of crucial asset allocations in disparate sectors of the volatile market. Financial sectors, information technology sector, core industrial sectors, and the acceptance and the investment strategies in the volatile market. Analysis of a financial portfolio of various sectors associates a comprehensive behavior of the inter relation between time, money, risk, and return. This can often be characterized in terms of the relation between the compatible assets existing within a specific market condition. Thus preferring an appropriate portfolio is therefore contingent in respect to the risk–reward trade-off (the trade-off experienced by an investor between risk and return considering investment decisions in turn) in the distribution of investments to a divergent group of assets. The aim of such a selection procedure through proper supervision of the underlying assets is for maximizing the investment returns or for minimizing the risks in stipulated time duration. Numerous efforts been devoted to accomplishing one of the aforesaid goals in the unpredictable market condition as mentioned in (Markowitz, 1952; Boyle, et al., 1997; Zenios, 1996; Crouhy, et al., 2001).

Common Errors in Computation

A deviation from perfection in a calculation may be termed as an error. This may be due to the difference between the feedback value and a reference evaluated using a comparator or the deviation of an experimental result with its ideal value. The most common errors that we encounter in our regular empirical research works are:

Mean Square Error (MSE)

In analysis of empirical results, the mean squared error (MSE) of a predictor calculates the mean of the squares of the error i.e., the average of squared difference in between the calculated value and the estimated value. The value of MSE is always non-zero positive number. The MSE is a value by which the quality of a predictor can be measured.

Root Mean Square Error (RMSE)

The root mean square error (RMSE) is a commonly used method to calculate the dissimilarity between sample values estimated by a model and the experimental value. The RMSE used to sum up all the magnitudes of the errors in estimations into a single value of prediction. RMSE is a measure of correctness, at the time of comparison between forecasting errors of different models. The value of RMSE is every time non negative. If a value of zero is found, it specifies a completely fit to the data. Lower RMSE value is better than a higher value.

Mean Absolute Error (MAE)

In empirical analysis, mean absolute error (MAE) is a measure of difference between two variables found from the experimented result, denoted by A and predicted result denoted by B. If a scattered 2D plot of n number of points is taken, let the point i has a coordinate (A_i, B_i). The MAE is the mean perpendicular distance between each point in the plot and the B=A straight line, It is known as 1-to-1 line. The Mean Absolute Error can be represented by:

$$\text{MAE}=\frac{\sum_{i=1}^{n} B_i - A_i \vee}{n}$$

Error in Standard Deviation

In predictive empirical analysis, the mean of the deviation of the individual error values from the Mean Absolute Error (MAE) may be termed as Error in Standard Deviation. It may be used to portray how the error in speculation varies over a given period of distribution of actual values. It may be calculated as:

$$\sigma_{\text{Error}} = \frac{\sum_{i=1}^{n} B_i - \text{MAE} \vee}{n}$$

Regression

In the domain of statistical modeling, the concept of regression analysis happens to me a set of statistical procedures for calculating (approximately) the associations amid the variables. Regression consists of several procedures for modeling and analysis of the said variables viz. independent variable(s) and dependent variables(s). To say it precisely, regression analysis aids us to recognize how the characteristic value of the dependent variable(s) change when the value of any particular independent variable is altered, keeping the values of all other independent variables(s) static. Regression models of the type B $\approx$ func(A, μ) comprise of the following parameters and variables:

- Other parameters 'μ' that are influencing the function 'func' (scalar / vector).

- Independent variables, A
- Dependent variables, B

Adaptive Neuro Fuzzy Inference System (ANFIS)

ANFIS or the adaptive network based fuzzy inference system happens to be a type of artificial neural network based on Takagi Sugeno fuzzy inference system. This methodology was designed during early 90's (Jang, 1991). The design happens to be a technique which is a hybrid of neural networks as well as fuzzy logic principles; and hence it is expected to have the benefits of both the techniques in a single framework.

The inference system it nests corresponds to a set of fuzzy IF/THEN rules which have a learning competence to approximate nonlinear functions (Abraham, 2005). Therefore, ANFIS is recognized as a universal estimator (Mizutani, 1997). In order to harness the true potential of ANFIS optimally, genetic algorithm can be used (Tahmasebi, 2012) for estimating the parameters of ANFIS accurately.

In this paper we attempt to trace the variations in the Net Asset Value (NAV) with time with our model.

Proposed Work Description

In this section details about the proposed work is given including data preparation and work done.

Data Preparation

In this work, authors have taken data from the web site of Association of mutual funds in India (AMFI) www.amfiindia.com. All experiments being done on Open End Mutual Fund data between January 2014 and April 2018. Information from 17 different fund houses are collected and processed. Following information are collected for each fund under different fund house:

1. Scheme Code
2. Scheme Name
3. Net Asset Value
4. Repurchase Price
5. Sale Price
6. Date

To maintain confidentiality instead of giving the original name of the mutual fund house, they are given name like MF1, MF2... MF17. For each fund house data of different funds are taken. 5000 different NAV value are taken for each fund house.

Proposed Work

In this proposed work Adaptive Network/Neuro Based Fuzzy Inference System (ANFIS) is used for nonlinear regression of the Mutual Fund dataset. It is an ANN based Takagi Sugeno inference system. It is used for time series prediction problem of Mutual Fund NAV. The program for ANFIS is written using MATLAB 16A ver. The details of the system implementation are given in the result and discussion section. ANFIS represented by fuzzy if/then rule. The ANFIS model is useful to forecast with good predictive capability with moving average model. In time series analysis the old values the data series can be used only to construct the model.

$$a_{t+1} = func(a_t, a_{t-1}, \ldots, a_{t-N+1})$$

Here the value a_{t+1} ($t+1^{th}$ time value) can be estimated from present and previous values of a. The arguments of the function func are taken from dataset with varying time.

Result and Discussion

For each fund house, time series data are predicted using FCM. The different parameters that have been considered are enlisted as follows:

- No. of clusters considered: 10
- Partition Matrix Exponent value: 2
- Maximum iteration: 100
- Minimum improvement per iteration: 0.00001
- Maximum no. of epochs: 100
- Preliminary step length: 0.01
- Step length reduce rate: 0.9
- Step length raise rate: 1.1

Various measurements are calculated for all data as well as for partitioned training and testing data. Various features measured for each mutual fund are shown enlisted as follows:

- Mean Square Error
- Root Mean Square Error
- Mean Error
- Error in Standard Deviation
- Regression

Value for each of the above mentioned feature for all the data are shown below. Table 1 corresponds to the mean square error expected for the loss, and it is found that all three category training, testing and all data set have a symmetric results for all mutual funds, but training data have less value for the mean square error as it has more data than testing data set (www.yarpiz.com).

As root mean square error measures the difference between estimated cost and experimented cost. In Table 2 for all the funds root mean square error is found to be close to zero which implies perfect fit of the data. Results of mean square error are found to be consisting for training, testing and all dataset.

Error mean refers to the mean of all errors in a set. Table 3 shows the error mean for all the three sets of data. For few funds, error mean is negative which means error in experimental value is less than the accepted value, whereas for other funds experimental value is larger than the accepted value.

Table 1. Mean Square Error for all data as well as for training and testing partitioned data

	Mean Square Error		
Data Source	**Training**	**Testing**	**All Data**
MF1	0.013374	0.042781	0.020755
MF2	47.2437	2.81E-05	35.3857
MF3	0.00019	0.005778	0.001592
MF4	5.30E-06	0.000294	7.77E-05
MF5	0.002439	0.011658	0.004753
MF6	5.04E-05	0.00514	0.001328
MF7	5.19E-06	1.79E-05	8.38E-06
MF8	1.31E-05	0.002498	0.000637
MF9	2.15E-06	0.000389	9.92E-05
MF10	4.19E-05	0.000378	0.000126
MF11	3.20E-03	0.002477	3.02E-03
MF12	2.69E-03	0.20742	0.054075
MF13	6.77E-05	1.02E-03	3.07E-04
MF14	2.68E-06	7.27E-06	3.83E-06
MF15	2.08E-03	0.007006	3.31E-03
MF16	1.16E-04	0.005366	1.42E-03
MF17	2.21E-01	375.7233	9.45E+01

Error in standard deviation measures the variation of means from the standard deviation. For most of the funds it is found to be very less and thus variation is less. In Table 4 the error in standard deviation for all data as well as for training and testing partitioned data is given.

Regression values measures the changes in dependent variable with respect to the independent variable. As shown in Table 5, regression is found to be consisting for all mutual funds which represent the relationships among data.

Software used for generating the results is MATLAB 2016A. Here authors are providing the plots for only MF1 as shown below. As per Figure 1 and Figure 3 plot of training data and all data shows target and output sample index are found to be consistent whereas from Figure 2 plot of testing data shows target and output sample index varies. Figure 4 shows the regression for different partitions which is again very consistent for training data and all dataset.

CONCLUSION

In this chapter machine learning approach is applied on different features of mutual funds. Data from 17 different fund houses are collected over 4 years for Open End Mutual Fund only. ANFIS is used here to forecast various parameters of the Mutual Funds. Variations in the Net Asset Value is shown for training, testing and entire dataset separately and their deviation for different mutual funds. This is an avenue which can be further used for applying other soft computing approach for various financial

Table 2. Root Mean Square Error for all data as well as for training and testing partitioned data

	Root Mean Square Error		
Data Source	**Training**	**Testing**	**All Data**
MF1	0.11565	0.20683	0.14407
MF2	6.8734	0.005305	5.9486
MF3	0.013776	0.76012	0.039904
MF4	0.002302	0.017139	0.008815
MF5	0.049383	0.10797	0.06894
MF6	0.007099	0.07169	0.036438
MF7	0.002279	0.004231	0.002895
MF8	0.00362	0.49977	0.025234
MF9	0.001465	0.019723	0.009962
MF10	0.006473	0.01943	0.011231
MF11	0.056544	0.049771	0.054923
MF12	0.051832	0.45544	0.23254
MF13	0.008227	0.031956	0.017522
MF14	0.001636	0.002696	0.001957
MF15	0.045567	0.083699	0.057564
MF16	0.01078	0.07325	0.037865
MF17	4.7035	19.3836	9.7196

instruments. Here neural networks and fuzzy logic principles is used for measuring time series analysis to construct the model. The work shows that if past stock market NAV data value is present then it is easy to estimate the future NAV value using machine learning tools.

Table 3. Error Mean for all data as well as for training and testing partitioned data

	Error Mean		
Data Source	**Training**	**Testing**	**All Data**
MF1	6.57E-08	0.025989	0.006523
MF2	0.006107	0.005305	0.005906
MF3	-3.00E-07	-0.02888	-0.00725
MF4	1.02E-08	-0.00195	-0.00049
MF5	-6.49E-07	0.064198	0.016113
MF6	9.30E-08	0.009129	0.002292
MF7	-1.10E-10	3.99E-04	1.00E-04
MF8	-4.38E-08	0.023003	0.005774
MF9	8.48E-09	0.008198	0.002058
MF10	-2.52E-07	0.017274	0.004336
MF11	3.88E-07	-0.00784	-0.00197
MF12	5.01E-08	-0.28097	-0.07052
MF13	6.52E-08	1.76E-02	4.41E-03
MF14	1.58E-09	1.16E-03	2.91E-04
MF15	-3.54E-03	-0.00096	-0.00289
MF16	-1.28E-07	-0.05036	-0.01264
MF17	-2.16E-05	-15.0254	-3.7713

Table 4. Error in Standard Deviation for all data as well as for training and testing partitioned data

	Error in Standard Deviation		
Data Source	**Training**	**Testing**	**All Data**
MF1	0.11596	0.20684	0.14421
MF2	6.8918	4.4512	5.9605
MF3	0.013813	0.070875	0.039319
MF4	0.002308	0.017164	0.008809
MF5	0.049515	0.087512	0.067164
MF6	0.007118	0.071678	0.036439
MF7	0.002285	0.004246	0.002899
MF8	0.00363	0.044726	0.024613
MF9	0.001469	0.018083	0.009767
MF10	0.00649	0.008967	0.010381
MF11	0.056695	0.049544	0.054997
MF12	0.05197	0.36132	0.22203
MF13	0.008249	0.02692	0.016993
MF14	0.00164	0.002454	0.001939
MF15	0.04555	0.084366	0.057606
MF16	0.010808	0.053624	0.035765
MF17	0.47161	12.3442	8.976

Table 5. Regression for all data as well as for training and testing partitioned data

	Regression		
Data Source	**Training**	**Testing**	**All Data**
MF1	0.99296	0.78711	0.98666
MF2	0.99718	1.26E-24	0.99727
MF3	0.99775	0.9202	0.99587
MF4	0.89354	0.72407	0.74721
MF5	0.99241	0.32168	0.98241
MF6	0.99903	0.66715	0.97785
MF7	8.75E-01	0.59956	7.95E-01
MF8	0.87621	0.30719	0.38353
MF9	0.75664	0.022105	0.24806
MF10	0.99967	0.9969	0.99969
MF11	0.99467	0.98098	0.99455
MF12	0.99318	0.58793	0.90824
MF13	9.63E-01	0.13507	8.75E-01
MF14	1.00E+00	0.99939	1.00E+00
MF15	0.12337	0.00084	0.050137
MF16	0.99922	0.97109	0.99834
MF17	0.9969	0.72131	0.834

Figure 1. Plot for Training Dataset

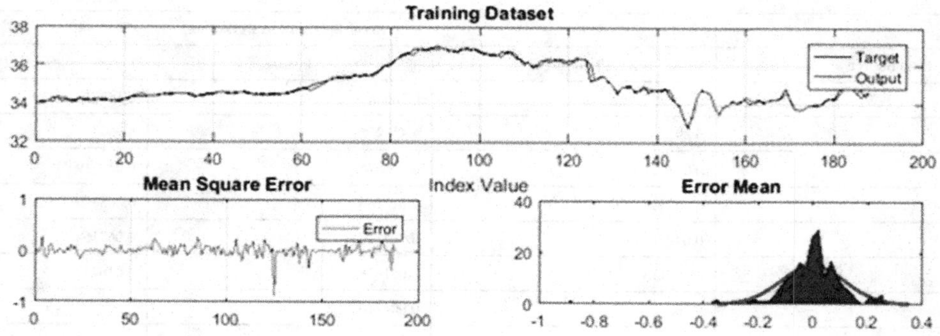

Figure 2. Plot for Testing Dataset

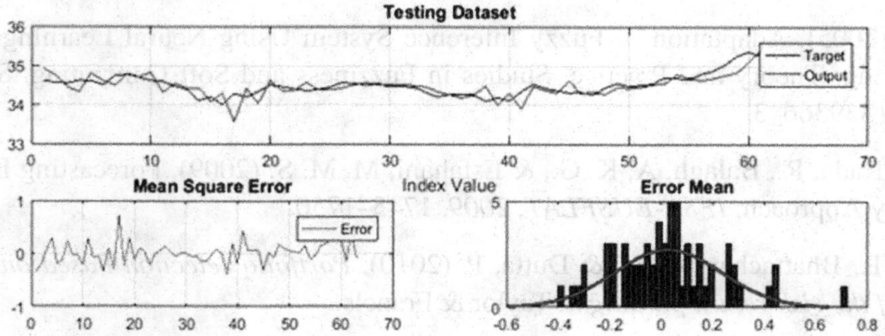

Figure 3. Plot for All Dataset

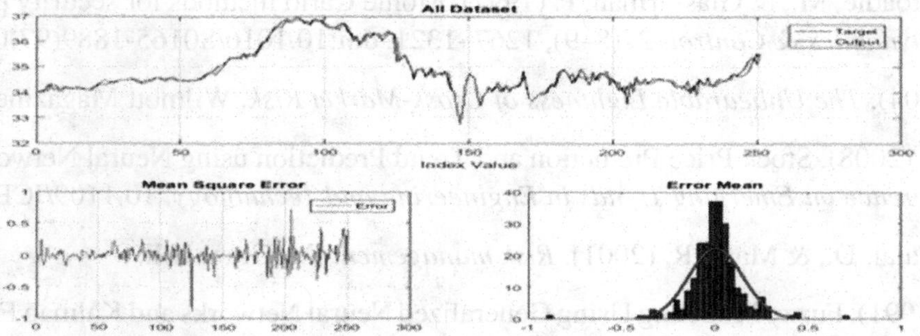

Figure 4. Regression for Train, test and All Data

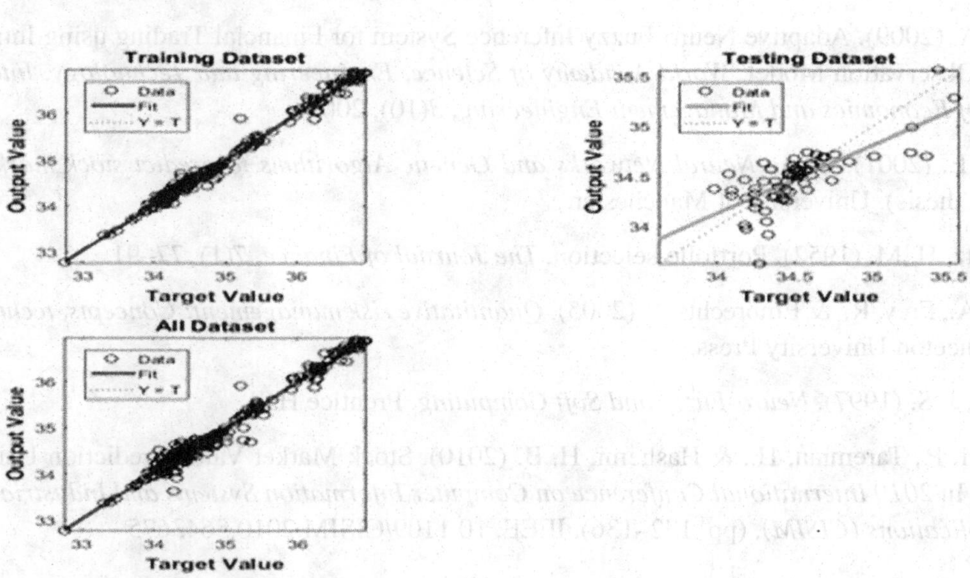

REFERENCES

Abraham, A. (2005). Adaptation of Fuzzy Inference System Using Neural Learning. In Fuzzy Systems Engineering: Theory and Practice, Studies in Fuzziness and Soft Computing. Springer Verlag. doi:10.1007/11339366_3

Alizadeh, M., Rada, R., Balagh, A. K. G., & Esfahani, M. M. S. (2009). Forecasting Exchange Rates: A Neuro-Fuzzy Approach. *IFSA-EUSFLAT*, *2009*, 1745–1750.

Bhattacharya, P., Bhattacharyya, S., & Dutta, P. (2010). *Portfolio selection based on multi-objective optimization of the risk-return paradigm*. Taylor & Francis.

Boyacioglu, M. A., & Avci, D. (2010). An Adaptive Network-Based Fuzzy Inference System (ANFIS) for the prediction of stock market return: The case of the Istanbul Stock Exchange. *Expert Systems with Applications*, *37*(12), 7908–7912. doi:10.1016/j.eswa.2010.04.045

Boyle, P. P., Broadie, M., & Glasserman, P. (1997). Monte Carlo methods for security pricing. *Journal of Economic Dynamics & Control*, *21*(8–9), 1267–1321. doi:10.1016/S0165-1889(97)00028-6

Brown, A. (2004). *The Unbearable Lightness of Cross-Market Risk*. Wilmott Magazine.

Charkha, P. R. (2008). Stock Price Prediction and Trend Prediction using Neural Networks. *First International Conference on Emerging Trends in Engineering and Technology*. 10.1109/ICETET.2008.223

Crouhy, M., Galai, D., & Mark, R. (2001). *Risk management*. McGraw-Hill.

Jang, J. S. R. (1991). Fuzzy Modeling Using Generalized Neural Networks and Kalman Filter Algorithm. *Proceedings of the 9th National Conference on Artificial Intelligence*, 762–767.

Jang, J. S. R. (1993). ANFIS: Adaptive-Network-Based Fuzzy Inference System. *IEEE Transactions on Systems, Man, and Cybernetics*, *23*(3), 665–685. doi:10.1109/21.256541

Kablan, A. (2009). Adaptive Neuro-Fuzzy Inference System for Financial Trading using Intraday Seasonality Observation Model. *World Academy of Science, Engineering and Technology*. *International Journal of Economics and Management Engineering*, *3*(10), 2009.

Kalyvas, E. (2001). *Using Neural Networks and Genetic Algorithms to predict stock market returns* (Master's thesis). University of Manchester.

Markowitz, H. M. (1952). Portfolio selection. *The Journal of Finance*, *7*(1), 77–91.

McNeil, A., Frey, R., & Embrechts, P. (2005). *Quantitative risk management: Concepts, techniques and tools*. Princeton University Press.

Mizutani, J. S. (1997). *Neuro-Fuzzy and Soft Computing*. Prentice Hall.

Naeini, M. P., Taremian, H., & Hashemi, H. B. (2010). Stock Market Value Prediction Using Neural Network. In *2010 International Conference on Computer Information Systems and Industrial Management Applications (CISIM)*, (pp. 132–136). IEEE. 10.1109/CISIM.2010.5643675

Pathak, A. (2014). Predictive time series analysis of stock prices using neural network classifier. *International Journal of Computer Science & Engineering Technology, 5*(3).

Ray, J., & Bhattacharyya, S. (2015). Value-at-risk based portfolio allocation using particle swarm optimization. *International Journal of Computer Sciences and Engineering, 3*(S1), 1–9.

Ray, J., & Bhattacharyya, S. (2017). *Conditional Value at Risk–Based Portfolio Optimization Using Metaheuristic Approaches. In Computational Intelligence Applications in BI and Big Data Analytics*. CRC Press.

Shen, S., Jiang, H., & Zhang, T. (2012). Stock Market Forecasting Using Machine Learning Algorithms. Department of Electrical Engineering, Stanford University, Tongda Zhang, Department of Electrical Engineering, Stanford University.

Tahmasebi, P., & Hezarkhani, A. (2012). A hybrid neural networks-fuzzy logic-genetic algorithm for grade estimation. *Computers & Geosciences, 42*, 18–27. doi:10.1016/j.cageo.2012.02.004 PMID:25540468

Trinkle, B. S. (2006). Forecasting annual excess stock returns via an adaptive network-based fuzzy inference system. *Intelligent Systems in Accounting, Finance & Management, 13*(3), 165–177. doi:10.1002/isaf.264

Wang, F. K., Chang, K. K., & Tzeng, C. W. (2011). Using adaptive network-based fuzzy inference system to forecast automobile sales. *Expert Systems with Applications, 38*(8), 10587–10593. doi:10.1016/j.eswa.2011.02.100

Wei, L. Y., Chen, T. L., & Ho, T. H. (2011). A hybrid model based on adaptive-network-based fuzzy inference system to forecast Taiwan stock market. *Expert Systems with Applications, 38*, 13625–13631. doi:10.1016/j.eswa.2011.04.127

Zenios, S. A. (Ed.). (1996). *Financial optimization*. Cambridge University Press.

Compilation of References

Wuest, T., Weimer, D., Irgens, C., & Thoben, K. D. (2016). Machine learning in manufacturing: Advantages, challenges, and applications. *Production & Manufacturing Research*, *4*(1), 23–45. doi:10.1080/21693277.2016.1192517

Wuest, T., Irgens, C., & Thoben, K.-D. (2014). An approach to monitoring quality in manufacturing using supervised machine learning on product state data. *Journal of Intelligent Manufacturing*, *25*(5), 1167–1180. doi:10.100710845-013-0761-y

Wuest, T., Liu, A., Lu, S. C.-Y., & Thoben, K.-D. (2014). Application of the stage gate model in production supporting quality management. *Procedia CIRP*, *17*, 32–37. doi:10.1016/j.procir.2014.01.071

Sun, J., Rahman, M., Wong, Y., & Hong, G. (2004). Multiclassification of tool wear with support vector machine by manufacturing loss consideration. *International Journal of Machine Tools & Manufacture*, *44*(11), 1179–1187. doi:10.1016/j.ijmachtools.2004.04.003

Opitz, D., & Maclin, R. (1999). Popular ensemble methods: An empirical study. *Journal of Artificial Intelligence Research*, *11*, 169–198. doi:10.1613/jair.614

Monostori, L. (2003). AI and machine learning techniques for managing complexity, changes and uncertainties in manufacturing. *Engineering Applications of Artificial Intelligence*, *16*(4), 277–291. doi:10.1016/S0952-1976(03)00078-2

Lu, S. C.-Y. (1990). Machine learning approaches to knowledge synthesis and integration tasks for advanced engineering automation. *Computers in Industry, 15*, 105–120.

Thomas, A. J., Byard, P., & Evans, R. (2012). Identifying the UK's manufacturing challenges as a benchmark for future growth. *Journal of Manufacturing Technology Management*, *23*(2), 142–156. doi:10.1108/17410381211202160

Bose, G. K., & Mahapatra, K. K. (2014). Parametric study of die sinking EDM process on AISI H13 tool steel using statistical techniques. *Advances in Production Engineering & Management, 9,* 168–180.

Harding, J. A., Shahbaz, M., & Srinivas Kusiak, A. (2006). Data mining in manufacturing: A review. *Journal of Manufacturing Science and Engineering*, *128*(4), 969–976. doi:10.1115/1.2194554

Esmaeilian, B., Behdad, S., & Wang, B. (2016). The evolution and future of manufacturing: A review. *Journal of Manufacturing Systems*, *39*, 79–100. doi:10.1016/j.jmsy.2016.03.001

Selvakumar, G., Sarkar, S., & Mitra, S. (2013). An experimental analysis of single pass cutting of aluminium 5083 alloy in different corner angles through WEDM. *International Journal of Machining and Machinability of Materials*, *13*(2/3), 262–275. doi:10.1504/IJMMM.2013.053227

Kang, H. S., Ju, Y. L., Choi, S. S., Kim, H., & Park, J. H. (2016). Smart manufacturing: Past research, present findings, and future directions. *Int J Precision Eng Manuf Green Technol*, *3*(1), 111–128. doi:10.100740684-016-0015-5

Kapoor, J., Khamba, J. S., & Singh, S. (2012). The effect of machining parameters on surface roughness and material removal rate with cryogenic treated wire in WEDM. *International Journal of Machining and Machinability of Materials*, *12*(1/2), 126–141. doi:10.1504/IJMMM.2012.048562

Bose, G. K., & Pritam, P. (2018). Metaheuristic Approach of Multi-Objective Optimization during EDM Process. *International Journal of Mathematical, Engineering and Management Sciences, 3,* 301–314.

Shin, S. J., Woo, J., & Rachuri, S. (2014). Predictive analytics model for power consumption in manufacturing. *Procedia CIRP*, *15*, 153–158. doi:10.1016/j.procir.2014.06.036

Bose, G. K., & Pritam, P. (2016). Parametric Analysis of Different Grades of Steel Materials Used in Plastic Industries through Die Sinking EDM Process. *International Journal of Materials Forming and Machining Processes, 3*(1). . doi:10.4018/IJMFMP.2016010104

Vogl, G. W., Weiss, B. A., & Helu, M. (2016). A review of diagnostic and prognostic capabilities and best practice for manufacturing. *Journal of Intelligent Manufacturing*, •••, 1–17. PMID:30820072

Shyur, H. J., & Shih, H. S. (2006). A hybrid MCDM model for strategic vendor selection. *Mathematical and Computer Modelling*, *44*(7-8), 749–761. doi:10.1016/j.mcm.2005.04.018

Xie, X. (2008). A review of recent advances in surface defect detection using texture analysis techniques. *Elcvia Electron Lett ComputVision Image Anal*, *7*(3), 1–22. doi:10.5565/rev/elcvia.268

Neogi, N., Mohanta, D. K., & Dutta, P. K. (2014). Review of vision-based steel surface inspection systems. *EURASIP Journal on Image and Video Processing*, *1*(1), 1–19. doi:10.1186/1687-5281-2014-50

Triantaphyllou, E. (2000). *Multi-criteria decision making methods. A comparative study*. Kluwer Academic Publishers. doi:10.1007/978-1-4757-3157-6

Pernkopf, F., & O'Leary, P. (2002). Visual inspection of machined metallic high-precision surfaces. *EURASIP Journal on Advances in Signal Processing*, *7*(7), 667–668. doi:10.1155/S1110865702203145

Scholz-Reiter, B., Weimer, D., & Thamer, H. (2012). Automated surface inspection of cold-formed micro-parts. *CIRP Ann Manuf Technol*, *61*(1), 531–534. doi:10.1016/j.cirp.2012.03.131

Abbas, M. N., Solomon, D. G., & Fuad Bahari, M. (2007). A review on current research trends in electrical discharge machining (EDM). *International Journal of Machine Tools & Manufacture*, *47*(7), 1214–1228. doi:10.1016/j.ijmachtools.2006.08.026

Abdulhameed, O., Al-Ahmari, A., Ameen, W., & Mian, S. H. (2019). Additive manufacturing: Challenges, trends, and applications. *Advances in Mechanical Engineering*, *11*(2), 1–27. doi:10.1177/1687814018822880

Abdulhamid, S. M., Latiff, M. S. A., Madni, S. H., & Oluwafemi, O. (2015). A Survey of League Championship Algorithm: Prospects and Challenges. *Indian Journal of Science and Technology*, *8*(3), 101–110. doi:10.17485/ijst/2015/v8iS3/60476

Abed, S., Laurens, P., Carretero, C., Deschamps, J. R., & Duval, C. (2001). Diode laser welding of polymers Microstructures of the welded zones for polypropylene. *International Congress on Applications of Lasers & Electro-Optics*, 1499-1507. 10.2351/1.5059820

Abraham, A. (2005). Adaptation of Fuzzy Inference System Using Neural Learning. In Fuzzy Systems Engineering: Theory and Practice, Studies in Fuzziness and Soft Computing. Springer Verlag. doi:10.1007/11339366_3

Abuzeid, H. H., Awad, A. M., & Senbel, A. H. (2012). Prediction of electrochemical machining process parameters using artificial neural networks. *International Journal on Computer Science and Engineering*, *4*, 125–132.

Abyar, H., Abdullah, A., & Shafaroud, A. A. (2019). Theoretical and experimental analysis of machining errors during WEDM finishing stages. *Machining Science and Technology*, *23*(5), 734–757. doi:10.1080/10910344.2019.1575410

Acharya, B. G., Jain, V. K., & Batra, J. L. (1986). Multiobjective optimization of ECM process. *Precision Engineering*, *8*(2), 88–96. doi:10.1016/0141-6359(86)90091-7

Acherjee, B., Kuar, A. S., Mitra, S., & Misra, D. (2011). Application of grey-based Taguchi method for simultaneous optimization of multiple quality characteristics in laser transmission welding process of thermoplastics. *International Journal of Advanced Manufacturing Technology*, *56*(9-12), 995–1006. doi:10.100700170-011-3224-7

Acherjee, B., Kuar, A. S., Mitra, S., & Misra, D. (2012). Effect of carbon black on temperature field and weld profile during laser transmission welding of polymers: A FEM study. *Optics & Laser Technology*, *44*(3), 514–521. doi:10.1016/j.optlastec.2011.08.008

Acherjee, B., Kuar, A. S., Mitra, S., Misra, D., & Acharyya, S. (2012). Experimental investigation on laser transmission welding of PMMA to ABS via RSM modeling. *Optics & Laser Technology*, *44*(5), 1372–1383. doi:10.1016/j.optlastec.2011.12.029

Acherjee, B., Misra, D., Bose, D., & Venkadshwaran, K. (2009). Prediction of weld strength and seam width for laser transmission welding of thermoplastic using response surface methodology. *Optics & Laser Technology*, *41*(8), 956–967. doi:10.1016/j.optlastec.2009.04.007

Aggarwal, V., Khangura, S. S., & Garg, R. K. (2015). Parametric modeling and optimization for wire electrical discharge machining of Inconel 718 using response surface methodology. *International Journal of Advanced Manufacturing Technology*, *79*(1-4), 31–47. doi:10.100700170-015-6797-8

Akyildiz, I. F., Su, W., Sankarasubramaniam, Y., & Cayirci, E. (2002). Wireless sensor networks: A survey. *Computer Networks*, *38*(4), 393–422. doi:10.1016/S1389-1286(01)00302-4

Alizadeh, M., Rada, R., Balagh, A. K. G., & Esfahani, M. M. S. (2009). Forecasting Exchange Rates: A Neuro-Fuzzy Approach. *IFSA-EUSFLAT*, *2009*, 1745–1750.

Alves, C., & Sanjurjo-Sánchez, J. (2015). Conservation of stony materials in the built environment. *Environmental Chemistry Letters*, *13*(4), 413–430. doi:10.100710311-015-0526-2

Anitha, J., Das, R., & Pradhan, M. K. (2016). Multi-objective optimization of electrical discharge machining processes using artificial neural network. *Jordan Journal of Mechanical and Industrial Engineering*, *10*(1), 11–18.

Azfar, T., Ahmed, W., Haseeb, A., Ahmad, R., Gul, S. T., & Zheng, F.-C. (2019, April). Zheng, Fu-C.(2019). A low complexity online controller using fuzzy logic in energy harvesting WSNs. *Science China. Information Sciences*, *62*(4), 42305. Advance online publication. doi:10.100711432-018-9751-5

Bahre, D., Weber, O., & Rebschlager, A. (2013). Investigation on pulse electrochemical machining characteristics of lamellar cast iron using a response surface methodology-based approach. *Procedia CIRP*, *6*, 363–368. doi:10.1016/j.procir.2013.03.028

Bains, P. S., Sidhu, S. S., & Payal, H. S. (2018). Magnetic Field Assisted EDM: New Horizons for Improved Surface Properties. *Silicon*, *10*(4), 1275–1282. doi:10.100712633-017-9600-7

Balakhnina, I. A., Brandt, N. N., Chikishev, A. Y., & Shpachenko, I. G. (2018). Single-pulse two-threshold laser ablation of historical paper. *Laser Physics Letters*, *15*(6), 065605. doi:10.1088/1612-202X/aab94e

Bandyopadhyay, S., Gokhale, H., Sarin Sundar, J. K., Sundararajan, G., & Joshi, S. V. (2005). A statistical approach to determine process parameter impact in Nd: YAG laser drilling of IN718 and Ti-6Al-4V sheets. *Optics and Lasers in Engineering*, *43*(2), 163–182. doi:10.1016/j.optlaseng.2004.06.013

Benedict, G. F. (1987). Non-Traditional manufacturing processes. Taylor & Francis.

Bhattacharya, P., Bhattacharyya, S., & Dutta, P. (2010). *Portfolio selection based on multi-objective optimization of the risk-return paradigm*. Taylor & Francis.

Bhattacharyya, B., Gangopadhyay, S., & Sarkar, B. R. (2007). Modelling and analysis of EDMED job surface Integrity. *Journal of Materials Processing Technology*, *189*(1-3), 169–177. doi:10.1016/j.jmatprotec.2007.01.018

Bhattacharyya, B., & Sorkhel, S. K. (1999). Investigation for controlled electrochemical machining through response surface methodology-based approach. *Journal of Materials Processing Technology*, *86*(1-3), 200–207. doi:10.1016/S0924-0136(98)00311-2

Biffi, C. A., Lecis, N., Previtali, B., Vedani, M., & Vimercati, G. M. (2011). Fiber laser micro drilling of titanium and its effect on material microstructure. *International Journal of Advanced Manufacturing Technology*, *54*(1-4), 149–160. doi:10.100700170-010-2918-6

Biswas, R., Kuar, A. S., Biswas, S. K. S., & Mitra, S. (2010). Effects of process parameters on hole circularity and taper in pulsed Nd: YAG laser micro-drilling of TiN-Al_2O_3 composites. *Materials and Manufacturing Processes*, *25*(6), 503–514. doi:10.1080/10426910903365737

Bleys, P., Kruth, J., Lauwers, B., Zryd, A., Delpretti, R., & Tricarico, C. (2002). Realtime tool wear compensation in milling EDM. *CIRP Annals - Manufacturing Technology, 51*(1), 157-160.

Blouin, N., Michaud, A., Gendron, D., Wakim, S., Blair, E., Neagu-Plesu, R., Belletête, M., Durocher, G., Tao, Y., & Leclerc, M. (2008). Toward a rational design of poly(2,7- carbazole) derivatives for solar cells. *Journal of the American Chemical Society*, *130*(2), 732–742. doi:10.1021/ja0771989 PMID:18095689

Bobbili, R., Madhu, V., & Gogia, A. K. (2013). Effect of Wire-EDM Machining Parameters on Surface Roughness and Material Removal Rate of High Strength Armor Steel. *Materials and Manufacturing Processes*, *28*(4), 364–368. doi:10.1080/10426914.2012.736661

Boyacioglu, M. A., & Avci, D. (2010). An Adaptive Network-Based Fuzzy Inference System (ANFIS) for the prediction of stock market return: The case of the Istanbul Stock Exchange. *Expert Systems with Applications*, *37*(12), 7908–7912. doi:10.1016/j.eswa.2010.04.045

Boyle, P. P., Broadie, M., & Glasserman, P. (1997). Monte Carlo methods for security pricing. *Journal of Economic Dynamics & Control*, *21*(8–9), 1267–1321. doi:10.1016/S0165-1889(97)00028-6

Brodhun, J., Blass, D., & Dilger, K. (2018). Laser transmission joining of thermoplastic fasteners Application for thermoset CFRP. *Proceedings of the Institution of Mechanical Engineers, Part L: Journal of Materials: Design and Applications*, *233*(3), 475-484. 10.1177/1464420718804571

Brown, A. (2004). *The Unbearable Lightness of Cross-Market Risk.* Wilmott Magazine.

Cao, X. (2010). Building-environment control with wireless sensor and actuator networks: Centralized versus distributed. *IEEE Transactions on Industrial Electronics*, *57*(11), 3596–3605. doi:10.1109/TIE.2009.2029585

Cavallaro, G., Milioto, S., Nigamatzyanova, L., Akhatova, F., Fakhrullin, R., & Lazzara, G. (2019). Pickering Emulsion Gels Based on Halloysite Nanotubes and Ionic Biopolymers: Properties and Cleaning Action on Marble Surface. *ACS Applied Nano Materials*, *2*(5), 3169–3176. doi:10.1021/acsanm.9b00487

Cayirci, E., Govindam, R., Znati, T., & Srivastava, M. (2003). Wireless sensor networks. *Int. J. Conmput. Telecommun. Netw*, *43*(4).

Cengarle, M. V., Bensalem, S., McDermid, J., Passerone, R., Sangiovanni-Vincentelli, A., & Törngren, M. (2013). Characteristics, Capabilities, Potential applications of Cyber-Physical Systems: A Preliminary Analysis. *Cyber-Physical European Roadmap & Strategy*. http://www.cyphers.eu

Cengel, Y. A. (2002). *Heat transfer: A practical approach*. Tata McGraw-Hill Publishing Company Limited.

Chanana, S., & Arora, M. (2013). Demand response from residential air conditioning load using a programmable communication thermostat. *Int J Electr Comput Energetic Eng*, *7*(12).

Charkha, P. R. (2008). Stock Price Prediction and Trend Prediction using Neural Networks. *First International Conference on Emerging Trends in Engineering and Technology*. 10.1109/ICETET.2008.223

Chen, D., Lu, R., Zou, F., & Li, S. (2016). Teaching-learning-based optimization with variable-population scheme and its application for ANN and global optimization. *Neurocomputing*, *173*, 1096–1111. doi:10.1016/j.neucom.2015.08.068

Cheng, B., & Chou, K. (2016). *A numerical investigation of thermal property effects on melt pool characteristics in powder-bed electron beam additive manufacturing*. Academic Press.

Chen, M., Zak, G., & Bates, P. J. (2011). Effect of carbon black on light transmission in laser welding of thermoplastics. *Journal of Materials Processing Technology*, *211*(1), 43–47. doi:10.1016/j.jmatprotec.2010.08.017

Chen, S. T., & Yang, H. Y. (2011). Study of micro electro discharge machining (micro-EDM) with onmachine measurement-assisted techniques. *Journal of Micromechanics and Microengineering*, 22.

Chen, Z., Huang, Y., Zhang, Z., Li, H., Ming, W., & Zhang, G. (2014). An analysis and optimization of the geometrical inaccuracy in WEDM rough corner cutting. *International Journal of Advanced Manufacturing Technology*, *74*(5-8), 917–929. doi:10.100700170-014-6002-5

Chen, Z., Zhang, Y., Zhang, G., Huang, Y., & Liu, C. (2017). Theoretical and experimental study of magnetic assisted finish cutting ferromagnetic material in WEDM. *International Journal of Machine Tools & Manufacture*, *123*, 36–47. doi:10.1016/j.ijmachtools.2017.07.009

Chiang, C. K., Fincher, C. R. Jr, Park, Y. W., Heeger, A. J., Shirakawa, H., Louis, E. J., Gau, S. C., & MacDiarmid, A. G. (1977). Electrical Conductivity in Doped Polyacetylene. *Physical Review Letters*, *39*(17), 1098–1101. doi:10.1103/PhysRevLett.39.1098

Chiang, K., & Chang, F. (2006). Optimization of the WEDM process of particle reinforced material with multiple performance characterises using Grey relational grade. *Journal of Materials Processing Technology*, *180*(1-3), 96–101. doi:10.1016/j.jmatprotec.2006.05.008

Chien, W., & Hou, S. (2007). Investigating the recast layer formed during the laser trepan drilling of inconel 718 using the taguchi method. *International Journal of Advanced Manufacturing Technology*, *33*(3-4), 308–316. doi:10.100700170-006-0454-1

Choobineh, F., & Jain, V. K. (1993). A fuzzy sets approach for selecting optimum parameters of an ECM process. *Advanced Materials & Processes*, *3*, 225–232.

Chua, B. L., Lee, H. J., & Ahn, D. G. (2018). Estimation of effective thermal conductivity of Ti-6AL-4V powders for a powder bed fusion process using finite element analysis. *International Journal of Precision Engineering and Manufacturing*, *19*(2), 257–264. doi:10.100712541-018-0030-2

Ciofini, D., Oujja, M., Cañamares, M. V., Siano, S., & Castillejo, M. (2016). Spectroscopic assessment of the UV laser removal of varnishes from painted surfaces. *Microchemical Journal, 124*, 792–803. doi:10.1016/j.microc.2015.10.031

Coakley, K. M., & McGehee, M. D. (2003). Photovoltaic cells made from conjugated polymers infiltrated into mesoporous titania. *Applied Physics Letters, 83*(16), 3380–3382. doi:10.1063/1.1616197

Cochran, W. G., & Cox, G. M. (1977). *Experimental designs* (2nd ed.). Asia Publishing House.

Criales, L. E., & Ozel, T. (2017). Temperature profile and melt depth in laser powder bed fusion of Ti-6Al-4V titanium alloy. *Progress in Additive Manufacturing*, *2*(3), 169–177. doi:10.100740964-017-0029-8

Crichton, M., & McGough, J. A. (1985). Studies of the discharge mechanisms in electrochemical arc machining. *Journal of Applied Electrochemistry*, *115*(1), 113–119. doi:10.1007/BF00617748

Crouhy, M., Galai, D., & Mark, R. (2001). *Risk management*. McGraw-Hill.

Dahotre, N. B., & Harimkar, S. P. (2007). *Laser fabrication and machining of materials*. Springer.

Daniel, J. J., Seungjun, K., Jung, H. P., Dae, Y. P., Han, E. L., Tae, H. I., Insung, C., Rodney, S. R., & Keon, J. L. (2017). Laser–Material Interactions for Flexible Applications. *Advanced Materials*, *29*(26), 1606586. doi:10.1002/adma.201606586 PMID:28370626

Dastagiri, M., & Kumar, A. H. (2014). Experimental Investigation of EDM parameters on stainless steelEn41b. *12th Global Congress on Manufacturing and Management*, *97*, 1551-1564.

Datta, S., & Mahapatra, S. S. (2010). Modeling, simulation and parametric optimization of wire EDM process using response surface methodology coupled with grey-Taguchi technique. *International Journal of Engineering Science and Technology*, *2*(5), 162–183. doi:10.4314/ijest.v2i5.60144

Datta, S., Raza, M. S., Das, A. K., Saha, P., & Pratihar, D. K. (2020). Experimental investigations and parametric optimization of laser beam welding of NiTinol sheets by metaheuristic techniques and desirability function analysis. *Optics & Laser Technology*, *214*, 105982. doi:10.1016/j.optlastec.2019.105982

Dayal, S., Kopidakis, N., Olson, D. C., Ginley, D. S., & Rumbles, G. (2009). Photovoltaic devices with a low band gap polymer and CdSe nanostructures exceeding 3% efficiency. *Nano Letters*, *10*(1), 239–242. doi:10.1021/nl903406s PMID:20000623

De Silva, A. K. M., & McGeough, J. A. (2000). Computer applications in Unconventional machining. *Journal of Materials Processing Technology*, *107*(1-3), 276–282. doi:10.1016/S0924-0136(00)00722-6

Deb, K. (2001). *Multiobjective optimization using evolutionary algorithms* (3rd ed.). Wiley.

Deb, K. (2001). *Multi-objective optimization using evolutionary algorithms* (3rd ed.). Wiley.

Debroy, A., & Chakraborty, S. (2013). Non-conventional optimization techniques in optimizing non-traditional machining processes: A review. *Management Science Letters*, *3*(1), 23–38. doi:10.5267/j.msl.2012.10.038

Deng, J. (1989). Introduction to Grey System. *Journal of Grey System*, *1*(1), 1–24.

Derakhshan, G., Shayanfar, H. A., & Kazemi, A. (2016). The optimization of demand response programs in smart grids. *Energy Policy*, *94*, 295–306. doi:10.1016/j.enpol.2016.04.009

Derringer, G., & Suich, R. (1980). Simultaneous Optimization of Several Response Variables. *Journal of Quality Technology*, *12*(4), 214–219. doi:10.1080/00224065.1980.11980968

Devrient, M., Frick, T., & Schmidt, M. (2011). Laser transmission welding of optical transparent thermoplastics. *Physics Procedia*, *12*, 157–165. doi:10.1016/j.phpro.2011.03.020

Dhaker, K. L., & Pandey, A. K. (2019). Particle swarm optimization of hole quality characteristics in laser trepan drilling of Inconel 718. *Defence Science Journal*, *69*(1), 37–45. doi:10.14429/dsj.69.12879

Dhanik, S., & Joshi, S. S. (2005). Modeling of a single resistance capacitance pulse discharge in micro-electro discharge machining. *Journal of Manufacturing Science and Engineering*, *127*(4), 759–767. doi:10.1115/1.2034512

Dhobe, S. H., Doloi, B., & Bhattacharya, B. (2014). Optimisation of ECM process during machining of titanium using quality loss function. *International Journal of Manufacturing Technology and Management*, *28*(1-3), 19–38. doi:10.1504/IJMTM.2014.064631

Ding, S., & Jiang, R. (2004). Tool path generation for 4-axis contour EDM rough machining. *International Journal of Machine Tools & Manufacture*, *44*(14), 1493–1502. doi:10.1016/j.ijmachtools.2004.05.010

Dodun, O., Goncalvascoclho, A. M., Slatineanu, L., & Nagit, G. (2009). Using wire electrical discharge machining for improved corner cutting accuracy of thin parts. *International Journal of Advanced Manufacturing Technology*, *41*(9-10), 858–864. doi:10.100700170-008-1531-4

Dubois, D., & Prade, H. (1979). Operations in a Fuzzy-Valued Logic. *Information and Control*, *43*(2), 224–240. doi:10.1016/S0019-9958(79)90730-7

Dutta, M., Sarkar, S., Ghosh, T., & Basak, D. (2012). ZnO/graphene quantum dot solid-state solar cell. *The Journal of Physical Chemistry C*, *116*(38), 20127–20131. doi:10.1021/jp302992k

Efendee, A. M., Saifuldin, M., Gebremariam, M. A., & Azhari, A. (2019). Effect of magnetic polarity on surface roughness during magnetic field assisted EDM of tool steel. *IOP Conference Series: Materials Science and Engineering*, 342.

Ekmekci, B., Sayar, A., Opoz, T.T., &Erden, A. (2009). Geometry and surface damage in micro-electrical discharge machining of micro-holes. *Journal of Micromechanics and Microengineering*, *19*, 105030-45.

El-Dardery, M. A. (1982). Economic study of electrochemical. *International Journal of Machine Tool Design and Research*, *22*(3), 147–158. doi:10.1016/0020-7357(82)90023-3

Ezugwu, E. O. (2005). Key improvements in the machining of difficult-to-cut aerospace superalloys. *International Journal of Machine Tools & Manufacture*, *45*(12-13), 1353–1367. doi:10.1016/j.ijmachtools.2005.02.003

Ezugwu, E. O., Wang, Z. M., & Machado, A. R. (1999). The machinability of nickel-based alloys-A review. *Journal of Materials Processing Technology*, *86*(1-3), 1–16. doi:10.1016/S0924-0136(98)00314-8

Firouzabadi, H. A., Parvizian, J., & Abdullah, A. (2015). Improving accuracy of curved corners in wire EDM successive cutting. *International Journal of Advanced Manufacturing Technology*, *76*(1-4), 447–459. doi:10.100700170-014-6270-0

Foteinopoulos, P., Papacharalampopoulos, A., & Stavropoulos, P. (2018). On thermal modeling of additive manufacturing processes. *CIRP Journal of Manufacturing Science and Technology*, *20*, 66–83. doi:10.1016/j.cirpj.2017.09.007

Gan, Z., Liu, H., Li, S., He, X., & Yu, G. (2017). Modeling of thermal behaviour and mass transport in multi-layer laser additive manufacturing of Ni-based alloy on cast iron. *International Journal of Heat and Mass Transfer*, *111*, 709–722. doi:10.1016/j.ijheatmasstransfer.2017.04.055

Garg, R. K., Singh, K. K., Sachdeva, A., Sharma, V. S., Ojha, K., & Singh, S. (2010). Review of research work in sinking EDM and WEDM on metal matrix composite materials. *International Journal of Advanced Manufacturing Technology*, *50*(5-8), 611–624. doi:10.100700170-010-2534-5

Garg, R., & Mittal, S. (2014). Optimization by Genetic Algorithm. *International Journal of Advanced Research in Computer Science and Software Engineering*, *4*(4), 587–589.

Gautam, G. D., & Pandey, A. K. (2018). Pulsed Nd: YAG laser beam drilling: A review. *Optics & Laser Technology*, *100*, 183–215. doi:10.1016/j.optlastec.2017.09.054

Ghiculescu, D., Marinescu, N., Ghiculescu, D., & Nanu, S. (2013). Aspects of Finite Element Analysis of Microdrilling by Ultrasonically Aided EDM and Related Knowledge Management. *Applied Mechanics and Materials*, *371*, 215–219. doi:10.4028/www.scientific.net/AMM.371.215

Ghorbel, E., Casalino, G., & Abed, S. (2009). Laser diode transmission welding of polypropylene Geometrical and microstructure characterization of weld. *Materials & Design*, *30*(7), 2745–2751. doi:10.1016/j.matdes.2008.10.027

Ghoreishi, M., Low, D. K. Y., & Li, L. (2002). Comparative statistical analysis of hole taper and circularity in laser percussion drilling. *International Journal of Machine Tools & Manufacture*, *42*(9), 985–995. doi:10.1016/S0890-6955(02)00038-X

Ghosh, A., & Mallick, A. K. (1985). *Manufacturing science*. East-West Press Private Limited.

Gibson, I., Rosen, D., & Stucker, B. (2015). *Additive Manufacturing Technologies: 3D Printing, Rapid Prototyping, and Direct Digital Manufacturing*. Springer-Verlag. doi:10.1007/978-1-4939-2113-3

Govindan, P., Gupta, A., Joshi, S. S., Malshe, A., & Rajurkar, K. P. (2013). Single spark analysis of removal phenomenon in magnetic field assisted dry EDM. *Journal of Materials Processing Technology*, *213*(7), 1048–1058. doi:10.1016/j.jmatprotec.2013.01.016

Goyal, R., & Dubey, A. K. (2016). Modelling and optimization of geometrical characteristics in laser trepan drilling of titanium alloy. *Journal of Mechanical Science and Technology*, *30*(3), 1281–1293. doi:10.100712206-016-0233-3

Gu, D. D., Meiners, W., Wissenbach, K., & Poprawe, R. (2012). Laser additive manufacturing of metallic components: Materials, processes and mechanisms. *International Materials Reviews*, *57*(3), 33–164. doi:10.1179/1743280411Y.0000000014

Hadad, M. (2014). Experimental Investigation of Effects of Machining Parameters on Surface Roughness & Roundness in the Cylindrical Wire Electrical Discharge Turning (CWEDT) of AISI D3 Tool Steel. *International Journal of Advanced Engineering Applications*, *7*, 81–91.

Haddad, M. J., & Tehrani, A. F. (2008). Evaluation of surface roughness and material removal rate in CWEDM using ANN. *IJAEA*, *1*, 79–84.

Haddad, M. J., & Tehrani, A. F. (2008). Material removal rate (MRR) study in the cylindrical wire electrical discharge turning (CWEDT) process. *Journal of Materials Processing Technology*, *199*(1-3), 369–378. doi:10.1016/j.jmatprotec.2007.08.020

Halls, J. J. M., Walsh, C. A., Greenham, N. C., Marseglia, E. A., Friend, R. H., Moratti, S. C., & Holmes, A. B. (1995). Efficient photodiodes from interpenetrating polymer networks. *Nature*, *376*(6540), 498–500. doi:10.1038/376498a0

Hamzah, A., Shurman, M., Al-Jarrah, O., & Taqieddin, E. (2019). Energy-Efficient Fuzzy-Logic-Based Clustering Technique for Hierarchical Routing Protocols in Wireless Sensor Networks. *Sensors (Basel)*, *19*(3), 561. doi:10.339019030561 PMID:30700022

Han, F., Zhang, J., & Soichiro, I. (2007). Corner error simulation of rough cutting in wireEDM. *Precision Engineering*, *31*(4), 331–336. doi:10.1016/j.precisioneng.2007.01.005

Hewidy, M. S., Ebeid, S. J., El-Taweel, T. A., & Youssef, A. H. (2007). Modelling the performance of ECM assisted by low frequency vibrations. *Journal of Materials Processing Technology*, *189*(1-3), 455–472. doi:10.1016/j.jmatprotec.2007.02.032

Hewidy, M. S., Fattouh, M., & Elkhabeery, M. (1984), Some economical aspects of ECM processes. *Proceedings of the 1st AME Conference*, 87-94.

Hoang, K. T., & Yang, S. H. (2013). A study on the effect of different vibration-assisted methods in micro-WEDM. *Journal of Materials Processing Technology*, *213*(9), 1616–1622. doi:10.1016/j.jmatprotec.2013.03.025

Hoang, K. T., & Yang, S. H. (2015). A new approach for micro-WEDM control based on real-time estimation of material removal rate. *International Journal of Precision Engineering and Manufacturing*, *16*(2), 241–246. doi:10.100712541-015-0032-2

Ho, K. H., & Newman, S. T. (2003). State of the art electrical discharge machining (EDM). *International Journal of Machine Tools & Manufacture*, *43*(13), 287–1300. doi:10.1016/S0890-6955(03)00162-7

Ho, K. H., Newman, S. T., Rahimifard, S., & Allen, R. D. (2004). State of art in wire electrical discharge machining (WEDM). *International Journal of Machine Tools & Manufacture*, *44*(12-13), 1247–1259. doi:10.1016/j.ijmachtools.2004.04.017

Hou, J., & Guo, X. (2013). Chapter. In W. C. H. Choy (Ed.), Active layer materials for organic solar cells (pp. 17–42). Springer. doi:10.1007/978-1-4471-4823-4_2

Hou, J., Chen, T. L., Zhang, S., Chen, H. Y., & Yang, Y. (2009). Poly[4,4-bis(2-ethylhexyl) cyclopenta[2,1-b;3,4-b] dithiophene-2, 6-diyl- alt-2,1,3-benzoselenadiazole-4,7-diyl], a new low band gap polymer in polymer solar cells. *The Journal of Physical Chemistry C*, *113*(4), 1601–1605. doi:10.1021/jp808255b

Huang, M. L., & Lin, C. J. (2018). Nonlinear system control using a fuzzy cerebellar model articulation controller involving reinforcement-strategy-based bacterial foraging optimization. *Advances in Mechanical Engineering*, *10*(9), 1–12. doi:10.1177/1687814018797426

Huang, W., & Zhang, Y. (2019). Finite element simulation of thermal behaviour in single track multiple layers thin wall without support during selective laser melting. *Journal of Manufacturing Processes*, *42*, 139–148. doi:10.1016/j.jmapro.2019.04.019

Huang, Y., Ming, W., Guo, J., Zhang, Z., Liu, G., Li, M., & Zhang, G. (2013). Optimization of cutting conditions of yg15 on rough and finish cutting in wedm based on statistical analysis. *International Journal Advanced Technology*, *69*(6), 993–1008.

Husseinzadeh, K. A. (2014). Championship Algorithm (LCA): An algorithm for global optimization inspired by sport championships. *Applied Soft Computing*, *16*, 171–200. doi:10.1016/j.asoc.2013.12.005

Iosub, A., Axinte, E., & Negoescu, F. (2010). A study about micro-drilling by electrical discharge method of an Al/SiC hybrid composite. *International Journal of Academic Research*, *2*(3), 6–12.

Islam, M. N., Rafai, N. H., & Subramanian, S. S. (2010) An Investigation into Dimensional Accuracy achievable in Wire-cut Electrical Discharge Machining. *Proceedings of the World Congress on Engineering*, 3.

Jahan, M. P., Wong, Y. S., & Rahman, M. (2009). A study on the fine finish die sinking micro-EDM oftungsten-carbide using different electrode materials. *Journal of Materials Processing Technology*, *209*(8), 3956–3967. doi:10.1016/j.jmatprotec.2008.09.015

Jain, V. K. (2004). *Advanced Machining Processes*. Allied Publishers Private Limited.

Jain, V. K. (2005). Advanced machining processes (4th ed.). Allied Publishers Private Limited.

Jain, N. K., & Jain, V. K. (2007). Optimization of electrochemical machining process parameters using genetic algorithm. *Machining Science and Technology*, *11*(2), 235–258. doi:10.1080/10910340701350108

Jalili, S., Kashan, A. H., & Hosseinzadeh, Y. (2017). League Championship Algorithms for Optimum Design of Pin-Jointed Structures. *Journal of Computing in Civil Engineering*, *31*(2), 04016048. doi:10.1061/(ASCE)CP.1943-5487.0000617

Janardhan, V., & Samuel, G. L. (2010). Pulse train data analysis to investigate the effect of machining parameters on the performance of wire electro discharge turning (WEDT) process. *International Journal of Machine Tools & Manufacture*, *50*(9), 775–788. doi:10.1016/j.ijmachtools.2010.05.008

Jang, J. S. R. (1991). Fuzzy Modeling Using Generalized Neural Networks and Kalman Filter Algorithm. *Proceedings of the 9th National Conference on Artificial Intelligence*, 762–767.

Jang, J. S. R. (1993). ANFIS: Adaptive-Network-Based Fuzzy Inference System. *IEEE Transactions on Systems, Man, and Cybernetics*, *23*(3), 665–685. doi:10.1109/21.256541

Jawahir, I. S., Brinksmeier, E., Saoubi, R. M., Aspinwall, D. K., Outeiro, J. C., Meyer, D., Umbrell, D., & Jayala, A. D. (2011). Surface integrity in material removal processes: Recent advances. *CIRP Annals*, *60*(2), 603–626. doi:10.1016/j.cirp.2011.05.002

Kablan, A. (2009). Adaptive Neuro-Fuzzy Inference System for Financial Trading using Intraday Seasonality Observation Model. *World Academy of Science, Engineering and Technology. International Journal of Economics and Management Engineering*, *3*(10), 2009.

Kalajahi, M. H., Ahmadi, S. R., & Oliaei, S. N. B. (2013). Experimental and finite element analysis of EDM process and investigation of material removal rate by response surface methodology. *International Journal of Advanced Manufacturing Technology*, *69*(1-4), 687–704. doi:10.100700170-013-5059-x

Kalyvas, E. (2001). *Using Neural Networks and Genetic Algorithms to predict stock market returns* (Master's thesis). University of Manchester.

Kannan, B., Castelino, K., & Majumdar, A. (2003). Design of Nanostructured Heterojunction Polymer Photovoltaic Devices. *APC Nano Letter*, *3*(12), 1729–1733. doi:10.1021/nl034810v

Kanti, S. (2019). How cognitive technologies are redefining the future of manufacturing. *Analytics Insight.* Retrieved from https://www.analyticsinsight.net/how-cognitive-technologies-are-redefining-the-future-of-manufacturing/

Karaboga, D., & Akay, B. (2009). A comparative study of Artificial Bee colony algorithm. *Applied Mathematics and Computation*, *214*(1), 108–132. doi:10.1016/j.amc.2009.03.090

Kaur, R., Sharma, D., & Kaur, N. (2013). Comparative analysis of LEACH and its descendant protocols in wireless sensor network. *Int. J. P2P Netw. Trends Technolol.*, *3*(1).

Keufmann, A., & Gupta, M. M. (1985). *Introduction to Fuzzy Arithmetic: Theory and Applications*. Van Nostrand Reinhold.

Khan, A., Daachi, S. S., & Djouani, K. (2012). Application of fuzzy inference systems to detection of faults in wireless sensor networks. *Neurocomputing*, *94*, 111–120. doi:10.1016/j.neucom.2012.04.002

Kim, M. (2009). *Understanding Organic Photovoltaic Cells Electrode. In Nanostructure, Reliability and Performance*. University of Michigan.

King, W. E., Barth, H. D., Castillo, V. M., Gallegos, G. F., Gibbs, J. W., Hahn, D. E., Kamath, C., & Rubenchik, A. M. (2014). Observation of keyhole-mode laser melting in laser powder-bed fusion additive manufacturing. *Journal of Materials Processing Technology*, *214*(12), 2915–2925. doi:10.1016/j.jmatprotec.2014.06.005

Kiran, M. P. S. K., & Joshi, S. S. (2007). Modelling of Surface Roughness andthe Role of Debris inMicro-EDM. *Journal of Manufacturing Science and Engineering*, *129*(2), 265–273. doi:10.1115/1.2540683

Krzic, P., Stoic, A., & Kopac, J. (2009). STEP-NC A New Programming Code for the CNC Machines. *Strojniskivestnik - Journal of Mechanical Engineering.*, *55*(6), 406–417.

Kuar, A. S., Doloi, B., & Bhattacharyya, B. (2006). Modelling and analysis of pulsed Nd: YAG laser machining characteristics during micro drilling of zirconia (ZrO_2). *International Journal of Machine Tools & Manufacture*, *46*(12-13), 1301–1310. doi:10.1016/j.ijmachtools.2005.10.016

Kulkarni, A., Sharan, R., & Lal, G. K. (2002). An experimental study of discharge mechanism in electrochemical discharge machining. *International Journal of Machine Tools & Manufacture*, *42*(10), 1121–1127. doi:10.1016/S0890-6955(02)00058-5

Kumar Senthil, K. L., Sivasubramanian, R., & Kalaiselvan, K. (2009). Selection of Optimum Parameters in Non-Conventional Machining of Metal Matrix Composite. *Portugaliae Electrochimica Acta*, *27*(4), 477–486. doi:10.4152/pea.200904477

Kumar, R., Jagadish, & Ray, A. (2014). Selection of material for optimal design using multi-criteria decision making. *Procedia Material Science*, *6*, 590–596. doi:10.1016/j.mspro.2014.07.073

Kuriachen, B., Somashekhar, K. P., & Mathew, J. (2015). Multi response optimization of micro- wire electrical discharge machining process. *International Journal of Advanced Manufacturing Technology*, *76*(1-4), 91–104. doi:10.100700170-014-6005-2

Kurikose, S., & Shanmugham, M. S. (2005). Multi objective optimization of wire EDM process bynon-dominated sorting genetic algorithms. *Journal of Materials Processing Technology*, *170*, 133–141. doi:10.1016/j.jmatprotec.2005.04.105

Lenes, M., Koster, L. J. A., Mihailetchi, V. D., & Blom, P. W. M. (2006). Thickness dependence of the efficiency of polymer: Fullerene bulk heterojunction solar cells. *Applied Physics Letters*, *88*(24), 243502–243503. doi:10.1063/1.2211189

Leppert, T. (2018). A review on ecological and health impacts of electro discharge machining (EDM). *AIP Conference Proceedings*, *2017*, 020014. doi:10.1063/1.5056277

Lertphokanont, V., Sato, T., Ota, M., Yamaguchi, K., & Egashira, K. (2012). Micro-structuring on Cylindrical Inner Surface using Whirling Electrical Discharge Texturing. *Advanced Materials Research*, *565*, 430–435. doi:10.4028/www.scientific.net/AMR.565.430

Liao, Y. S., Chen, S. T., & Lin, C. S. (2005). Development of a high precision tabletop versatile CNC wire-EDM for making intricate micro parts. *Journal of Micromechanics and Microengineering*, *15*(2), 245–253. doi:10.1088/0960-1317/15/2/001

Liao, Y. S., Chuang, T. J., & Yu, Y. P. (2014). Study of machining parameters optimization for different materials in WEDM. *International Journal of Advanced Manufacturing Technology*, *70*(9-12), 2051–2058. doi:10.100700170-013-5458-z

Li, C., Liu, Y., Fang, X. Y., & Guo, Y. B. (2018). Residual Stress in Metal Additive Manufacturing. *Procedia CIRP*, *71*, 348–353. doi:10.1016/j.procir.2018.05.039

Li, J., Fan, T., Taniguchi, T., & Zhang, B. (2018). Phase-field modeling on laser melting of a metallic powder. *International Journal of Heat and Mass Transfer*, *117*, 412–424. doi:10.1016/j.ijheatmasstransfer.2017.10.001

Li, L., & Yang, Y. (2008). Agent-based ontology mapping and integration towards interoperability. *Expert Systems: International Journal of Knowledge Engineering and Neural Networks*, *25*(3), 197–220. doi:10.1111/j.1468-0394.2008.00460.x

Lin, H., Liu, X., Wang, X., & Liu, Y. (2017). *A fuzzy inference and big data analysis algorithm for the prediction of forest fire based on rechargeable wireless sensor networks*. Academic Press.

Li, R., Yue, J., Shao, X., Wang, C., Yan, F., & Hu, X. (2015). A study of thick plate ultra-narrow-gap multi-pass multi-layer laser welding technology combined with laser cleaning. *International Journal of Advanced Manufacturing Technology*, *81*(1-4), 113–127. doi:10.100700170-015-7193-0

Liu, C., & Xu, X. (2017). Cyber-Physical Machine Tool – the Era of Machine Tool 4.0. *Procedia CIRP*, *63*, 70–75. doi:10.1016/j.procir.2017.03.078

Liu, D., Tang, Y. J., & Cong, W. L. (2012). A review of mechanical drilling for composite laminates. *Composite Structures*, *94*(4), 1265–1279. doi:10.1016/j.compstruct.2011.11.024

Liu, X., Pan, L., Zhao, Q., Lv, T., Zhu, G., Chen, T., Lu, T., Sun, Z., & Sun, C. (2012). UV-assisted photocatalytic synthesis of ZnO reduced grapheme oxide composites with enhanced photocatalytic activity in reduction of Cr(VI). *Chemical Engineering Journal*, *183*, 238–243. doi:10.1016/j.cej.2011.12.068

Liu, Y., & Xu, X. (2017). Industry 4.0 and cloud manufacturing: A Comparative Analysis. *Journal of Manufacturing Science and Engineering*, *139*(3), 034701–034708. doi:10.1115/1.4034667

Lopez, A. B., Assuncao, E., Quintino, L., Blackburn, J., & Khan, A. (2017). High power fiber laser cutting parameter optimization for nuclear decommissioning. *Nuclear Engineering and Technology*, *49*(4), 865–872. doi:10.1016/j.net.2017.02.004

Lou, P., Ong, S. K., & Nee, A. Y. C. (2010). Agent-based distributed scheduling for virtual job shops. *International Journal of Production Research*, *48*(13), 3889–3910. doi:10.1080/00207540902927918

Low, D. K. Y., Li, L., & Byrd, P. J. (2000). The effects of process parameters on spatter deposition in laser percussion drilling. *Optics & Laser Technology*, *32*(5), 347–354. doi:10.1016/S0030-3992(00)00079-7

Lu, J. (2010). The smart thermostat: using occupancy sensors to save energy in homes. In *Proceedings of the 8th ACM conference on embedded networked sensor systems*. ACM.

Luo, Q. P., Yu, X.-Y., Lei, B.-X., Chen, H.-Y., Kuang, D.-B., & Su, C.-Y. (2012). Reduced graphene oxide-hierarchical ZnO hollow sphere composites with enhanced photocurrent and photocatalytic activity. *The Journal of Physical Chemistry C*, *116*(14), 8111–8117. doi:10.1021/jp2113329

Luo, Z., & Zhao, Y. (2018). A survey of finite element analysis of temperature and thermal stress fields in powder bed fusion additive manufacturing. *Additive Manufacturing*, *21*, 318–332. doi:10.1016/j.addma.2018.03.022

Majumdar, J. D., & Manna, I., (2013). Introduction to laser-assisted fabrication of materials. *Laser Assisted Fabrication of Materials*, 1–67.

Malekipor, E., & El-Mounayri, H. (2018). Common defects and contributing parameters in powder bed fusion AM process and their classification for online monitoring and control: A review. *International Journal of Advanced Manufacturing Technology*, *95*(1-4), 527–550. doi:10.100700170-017-1172-6

Mamdani, E. H., & Assilian, S. (1975). An experiment in linguistic synthesis with a fuzzy logic controller. *International Journal of Man-Machine Studies*, *7*(1), 71–13. doi:10.1016/S0020-7373(75)80002-2

Mandal, K., Sarkar, S., Mitra, S., & Bose, D. (2019). Surface roughness and surface topography evaluation of Al 6065-T6 alloy using wire electrodischarge machining (wire EDM). *Advances in Materials and Processing Technologies.*

Mandal, K., Sarkar, S., Mitra, S., & Bose, D. (2019). Multi-Attribute Optimization in WEDM Light Metal Alloy. *Materials Today: Proceedings*, *18*, 3492–3500. doi:10.1016/j.matpr.2019.07.277

Maradia, U., Scuderi, M., Knaak, R., Boccadoro, M., Beltrami, I., Stirnimann, J., & Wegener, K. (2013). Super finished surfaces using meso-micro EDM. *The Seventeenth CIRP Conference on Electro Physical and Chemical Machining (ISEM)*, 6, 157-162.

Marimuthu, S., Antar, M., Dunleavey, J., Chantzis, D., Darlington, E., & Hayward, P. (2017). An experimental study on quasi-CW fibre laser drilling of nickel superalloy. *Optics & Laser Technology*, *94*(1), 119–127. doi:10.1016/j.optlastec.2017.03.021

Markowitz, H. M. (1952). Portfolio selection. *The Journal of Finance*, *7*(1), 77–91.

Masuzawa, T., & Tonshoff, H. K. (1997). Three-Dimensional Micromachining by Machine Tools. *Annals of the CIRP*, *46*(2), 621–628. doi:10.1016/S0007-8506(07)60882-8

Matoorian, P., Sulaiman, S., & Ahmad, M. M. H. M. (2008). An experimental study for optimization of electrical discharge turning (EDT) process. *Journal of Materials Processing Technology*, *204*(1-3), 350–356. doi:10.1016/j.jmatprotec.2007.11.058

McNeil, A., Frey, R., & Embrechts, P. (2005). *Quantitative risk management: Concepts, techniques and tools*. Princeton University Press.

Mediliyegedara, T. K. K. R., De Silva, A. K. M., Harrison, D. K., & McGeough, J. A. (2004). An intelligent pulse classification system for electro-chemical discharge machining (ECDM)— A preliminary study. *Journal of Materials Processing Technology*, *149*(1-3), 499–503. doi:10.1016/j.jmatprotec.2004.04.002

Meijer, J. (2004). Laser beam machining (LBM), State of the art and new opportunities. *Journal of Materials Processing Technology*, *149*(1-3), 2–17. doi:10.1016/j.jmatprotec.2004.02.003

Meyer, G. G., Framling, K., & Holmstrom, J. (2009). Intelligent Products: A survey. *Computers in Industry*, *60*(3), 137–148. doi:10.1016/j.compind.2008.12.005

Mills, K. (2019). *What is cognitive manufacturing? by Metrology news.* Retrieved from https://metrology.news/what-is-cognitive-manufacturing

Mills, K. C. (2002). *Recommended Values of Thermophysical Properties for Selected Commercial Alloys.* Woodhead Publishing Limited. doi:10.1533/9781845690144

Ming, W., Zhang, Z., Wang, S., Zhang, Y., Shen, F., & Zhang, G. (2019). Comparative study of energy efficiency and environmental impact in magnetic field assisted and conventional electrical discharge machining. *Journal of Cleaner Production*, *214*, 12–18. doi:10.1016/j.jclepro.2018.12.231

Mishra, P. K. (1997). Non -Conventional machining. Narosa Publishers.

Mishra, S., & Yadava, V. (2013). Modeling and optimization of laser beam percussion drilling of thin aluminum sheet. *Optics & Laser Technology*, *48*, 461–474. doi:10.1016/j.optlastec.2012.10.035

Mizutani, J. S. (1997). *Neuro-Fuzzy and Soft Computing*. Prentice Hall.

Mohammadi, A., Tehrani, A. F., Ehsan, E. E., & Karimi, D. (2008). A new approach to surface roughness and Circularity Error improvement in wire electrical discharge turning based on statistical analyses. *International Journal of Advanced Manufacturing Technology, 39*(1-2), 64–73. doi:10.100700170-007-1179-5

Mohammadi, M., Al-Fuqaha, A., Sorour, S., & Guizani, M. (2018). Deep Learning for IoT Big Data and Streaming Analytics: A Survey. *IEEE Communications Surveys and Tutorials, 20*(4), 2923–2960. doi:10.1109/COMST.2018.2844341

Mohammad, J. H., & Alireza, F. T. (2008). Investigation of cylindrical wire electrical discharge turning (CWEDT) of AISI D3 tool steel based on statistical analysis. *Journal of Materials Processing Technology, 198*(1-3), 77–85. doi:10.1016/j.jmatprotec.2007.06.059

Monostori, L., Kádár, B., Bauernhansl, T., Kondoh, S., Kumara, S., Reinhart, G., Sauer, O., Schuh, G., Sihn, W., & Ueda, K. (2016). Cyber-physical systems in manufacturing. *CIRP Annals - Manufacturing Technology, 65*(2), 621-641.

Monostori, L. (2014). Cyber-physical production systems: Roots, expectations and R&D challenges. *Procedia CIRP, 17*, 9–13. doi:10.1016/j.procir.2014.03.115

Monostori, L., Váncza, J., & Kumara, S. R. T. (2006). Agent-Based Systems for Manufacturing. *Annals of the CIRP, 55*(2), 1–24. doi:10.1016/j.cirp.2006.10.004

Montes, M. E., & Coello, C. A. C. (2005). A simple multimembered evolution strategy to solve constrained optimization problems. *IEEE Transactions on Evolutionary Computation, 9*(1), 1–17. doi:10.1109/TEVC.2004.836819

Montgomery, D. C. (1997). *Design and analysis of experiments* (4th ed.). Wiley.

Moradi, M., Arabi, H., & Shamsborhan, M. (2020). Multi-Objective Optimization of High Power Diode Laser Surface Hardening Process of AISI 410 by means of RSM and Desirability Approach. *Optik (Stuttgart), 202*, 163619. doi:10.1016/j.ijleo.2019.163619

Muhlbacher, D., Scharber, M., & Moranaetal, M. (2006). Highphotovoltaicperformanceof a low-bandgappolymer. *Advanced Materials, 18*(21), 2884–2889.

Mukherjee, T., Zhang, W., & Debroy, T. (2017). An improved prediction of residual stresses and distortion in additive manufacturing. *Computational Materials Science, 126*, 360–372. doi:10.1016/j.commatsci.2016.10.003

Mukhopadhyay, P. B. R., & Sarkar, B. R. (2019). Advancement in Utrasonic Vibration and Magnetic Field Assisted Micro-EDM Proces: An Overview. *International Journal of Advanced Research in Engineering & Technology, 10*(2), 362–373. doi:10.34218/IJARET.10.2.2019.035

Mukhopadhyay, P., Adhikary, S., Samanta, A. K., Maiti, S., Khan, S., & Mudi, S. (2019). External Force Assisted Electro Discharge Machining of SS 316. *Materials Today: Proceedings, 19*, 626–629. doi:10.1016/j.matpr.2019.07.743

Naeini, M. P., Taremian, H., & Hashemi, H. B. (2010). Stock Market Value Prediction Using Neural Network. In *2010 International Conference on Computer Information Systems and Industrial Management Applications (CISIM)*, (pp. 132–136). IEEE. 10.1109/CISIM.2010.5643675

Nayak, P., & Devulapalli, A. (2015). A Fuzzy Logic based Clustering Algorithm for WSN to extend the Network Lifetime. *IEEE Sensors Journal, 6*(1). Advance online publication. doi:10.1109/JSEN.2015.2472970

Nicolaidis, N. C., Routley, B. S., Holdsworth, J. L., Belcher, W. J., Zhou, X., & Dastoor, P. C. (2011). Fullerene contribution to photocurrent generation in organic photovoltaic cells. *The Journal of Physical Chemistry C, 115*(15), 7801–7805. doi:10.1021/jp2007683

Nishizawa, T., Lim, H. K., Tajima, K., & Hashimoto, K. (2009). Efficient dyad-based organic solar cells with a highly crystalline donor group. *Chemical Communications (Cambridge)*, *18*(18), 2469–2471. doi:10.1039/b902060h PMID:19532859

Okasha, M.M., Mativenga, P.T., Driver, N., & Li, L. (2010). Sequential laser and mechanical micro drilling of Ni superalloy for aerospace application. *CIRP Annals - Manufacturing Technology*, *59*(1), 199-202.

Oldewurtel, F., Parisio, A., Jones, C. N., Gyalistras, D., Gwerder, M., Stauch, V., Lehmann, B., & Morari, M. (2012). Use of model predictive control and weather forecasts for energy efficient building climate control. *Energy and Building*, *45*, 15–27. doi:10.1016/j.enbuild.2011.09.022

Padhee, S., Nayak, N., Panda, S. K., Dhal, P. R., & Mahapatra, S. S. (2012). Multi-objective parametric optimization of powder mixed electro-discharge machining using response surface methodology and non-dominated sorting genetic algorithm. *Indian Academy of Sciences*, *37*(2), 1–18. doi:10.100712046-012-0078-0

Palomar, T., Oujja, M., Llorente, I., Ramírez Barat, B., Cañamares, M. V., Cano, E., & Castillejo, M. (2016). Evaluation of laser cleaning for the restoration of tarnished silver artifacts. *Applied Surface Science*, *387*, 118–127. doi:10.1016/j.apsusc.2016.06.017

Pasam, V. K., Battula, S. B., Madar, P. V., & Swapna, M. (2010). Optimizing Surface Finish in WEDM Using the Taguchi Parameter Design Method. *Journal of the Brazilian Society of Mechanical Sciences and Engineering*, *32*(2), 107–113. doi:10.1590/S1678-58782010000200002

Pathak, A. (2014). Predictive time series analysis of stock prices using neural network classifier. *International Journal of Computer Science & Engineering Technology, 5*(3).

Paul, R., Anand, S., & Garner, F. (2014). Effect of thermal deformation on part errors in metal powder based additive manufacturing processes. *Journal of Manufacturing Science and Engineering*, *136*(3), 031009–0310021. doi:10.1115/1.4026524

Peet, J., Kim, J. Y., Coates, N. E., Ma, W. L., Moses, D., Heeger, A. J., & Bazan, G. C. (2007). Efficiency enhancement in low-bandgap polymer solar cells by processing with alkane dithiols. *Nature Materials*, *6*(7), 497–500. doi:10.1038/nmat1928 PMID:17529968

Peumans, P., Yakimov, A., & Forrest, S. R. (2003). Small molecular weight organic thin-film photodetectors and solar cells. *Journal of Applied Physics*, *93*(7), 3693–3723. doi:10.1063/1.1534621

Plaza, S., Ortega, N., Sanchez, J. A., Pombo, I., & Mendikute, A. (2009). Original models for the prediction of angular error in wire EDM tapper cutting. *International Journal of Advanced Manufacturing*, *44*(5-6), 529–538. doi:10.100700170-008-1842-5

Pradhan, M. K. (2013). Estimating the effect of process parameters on surface integrity of EDMed AISI D2 tool steel by response surface methodology coupled with grey relational analysis. *International Journal of Advanced Manufacturing Technology*, *67*(9-12), 2051–2062. doi:10.100700170-012-4630-1

Prakash, C., Singh, S., Singh, M., Verma, K., Chaudhary, B., & Singh, S. (2018). Multi-objective particle swarm optimization of EDM parameters to deposit HA-coating on biodegradable Mg-alloy. *Vacuum*, *158*, 180–190. doi:10.1016/j.vacuum.2018.09.050

Pramanik, D., Das, S., Sarkar, S., Debnath, S.K., Kuar, A.S., & Mitra, S. (2018). Experimental investigation of fiber laser micro marking on aluminium 6061 alloy. *Advances in Materials Mechanical and Industrial Engineering,* 273–294.

Pramanik, D., Goswami, S., Kuar, A. S., Sarkar, S., & Mitra, S. (2019). A parametric study of kerf deviation in fiber laser micro cutting on Ti6Al4V superalloy. *Materials Today: Proceedings*, *18*, 3348–3356. doi:10.1016/j.matpr.2019.07.257

Pramanik, D., Kuar, A. S., & Bose, D. (2019). *Effects of Wire EDM machining variables on material removal rate and surface roughness of Al 6061 alloy. In Renewable Energy and Its Innovative Technologies*. Springer.

Proceedings of the Institute of Mechanical Engineering Part B. (n.d.). Article. *Proceedings of the Institution of Mechanical Engineers. Part B, Journal of Engineering Manufacture*, *232*(9), 1615–1662. doi:10.1177/0954405416673105

Puri, A. B., & Bhattacharyya, B. (2003). An analysis and optimization of the geometrical inaccuracy due to wire lag phenomenon in WEDM. *International Journal of Machine Tools & Manufacture*, *43*(2), 151–159. doi:10.1016/S0890-6955(02)00158-X

Quintino, L., Costa, A., Miranda, R., Yapp, D., Kumar, V., & Kong, C. J. (2007). Welding with high power fiber lasers – A preliminary study. *Materials & Design*, *28*(4), 1231–1237. doi:10.1016/j.matdes.2006.01.009

Qu, J., Shih, A. J., & Scattergood, R. O. (2002). Development of the cylindrical wire electrical discharge machining process, part 1: Concept, design, and material removal rate. *Journal of Manufacturing Science and Engineering*, *124*(3), 702–707. doi:10.1115/1.1475321

Ragavendran, M., Chandrasekhar, N., Ravikumar, R., Saxena, R., Vasudevan, M., & Bhaduri, A. K. (2017). Optimization of hybrid laser – TIG welding of 316LN steel using response surface methodology (RSM). *Optics and Lasers in Engineering*, *94*, 27–36. doi:10.1016/j.optlaseng.2017.02.015

Raghavendra, C. S., & Sivalingam, K. M. (Eds.). (2004). *Wireless Sensor Networks*. Kluwer Academic.

Raghuraman, S., Thiruppathi, K., Panneerselvam, T., & Santosh, S. (2013). Optimization of EDM parameters using taguchi method and grey relational analysis for mild steel IS 2026. *International Journal of Innovative Research in Science, Engineering and Technology*, *2*(7), 3095–3104.

Rajmohan, T., Prabhu, R., Subbarao, G., & Palanikumar, K. (2012). Optimization of Machining parametersinElectrical-discharge Machining (EDM) of 304 Stainless Steel. *Journal of Procedia Engineering*, *38*, 1030–1036. doi:10.1016/j.proeng.2012.06.129

Rajyalakshmi, G., & Ramaiah, P. V. (2013). Multiple process parameter optimization of wire electrical discharge machining on Inconel 825 using Taguchi grey relational analysis. *International Journal of Advanced Manufacturing Technology*, *69*(5-8), 1249–1262. doi:10.100700170-013-5081-z

Rao, V. R. (2016). Teaching-Learning-Based Optimization Algorithm. In Teaching Learning Based Optimization Algorithm. Springer International Publishing.

Rao, B. T., & Krishna, A. G. (2014). Selection of optimal process parameters in WEDM while machining Al7075/SiCp metal matrix composites. *International Journal of Advanced Manufacturing Technology*, *73*(1-4), 299–314. doi:10.100700170-014-5780-0

Rao, M. S., & Venkaiah, N. (2015). Parametric optimization in machining of Nimonic-263 alloy using RSM and particle swarm optimization. *Procedia Materials Science*, *10*, 70–79. doi:10.1016/j.mspro.2015.06.027

Rao, R. (2016). Review of applications of TLBO algorithm and a tutorial for beginners to solve the unconstrained and constrained optimization problems. *Decision Science Letters*, *5*(1), 1–30.

Rao, R. V., & Kalyankar, V. D. (2013). Parameter optimization of modern machining processes using teaching–learning-based optimization algorithm. *Engineering Applications of Artificial Intelligence*, *26*(1), 524–531. doi:10.1016/j.engappai.2012.06.007

Rao, R. V., Pawar, P. J., & Shankar, R. (2008). Multi-objective optimization of electrochemical machining process parameters using a particle swarm optimization algorithm. *Proceedings of the Institution of Mechanical Engineers. Part B, Journal of Engineering Manufacture*, *222*(8), 949–958. doi:10.1243/09544054JEM1158

Rao, R. V., Savsani, V. J., & Vakharia, D. P. (2011). Teaching–Learning-Based Optimization: A Novel Method for Constrained Mechanical Design Optimization Problems. *Computer Design (Winchester)*, *43*(3), 303–315. doi:10.1016/j.cad.2010.12.015

Ray, J., & Bhattacharyya, S. (2015). Value-at-risk based portfolio allocation using particle swarm optimization. *International Journal of Computer Sciences and Engineering, 3*(S1), 1–9.

Ray, J., & Bhattacharyya, S. (2017). *Conditional Value at Risk–Based Portfolio Optimization Using Metaheuristic Approaches. In Computational Intelligence Applications in BI and Big Data Analytics*. CRC Press.

Redfern, A., Koplow, M., & Wright, P. (2012). Design architecture for multi-zone HVAC control systems from existing single-zone systems using wireless sensor networks. *Proc 13th international conference on intelligence systems application to power systems, 6414*.

Ren, S., Chang, L.-Y., Lim, S.-K., Zhao, J., Smith, M., Zhao, N., Bulović, V., Bawendi, M., & Gradečak, S. (2011). Inorganic and organic hybrid solar cell: Bridging quantum dots to conjugated polymer nanowires. *Nano Letters*, *11*(9), 3998–4002. doi:10.1021/nl202435t PMID:21859097

Rizwana, S., Gayathri, K. M., & Thangadurai, N. (2019). Fuzzy Logic Based Routing Algorithm for Wireless Sensor Networks to Enhance the Network Lifetime. *International Journal of Innovative Technology and Exploring Engineering*, *8*(8), 2272–2279.

Roberts, I. A., Wang, C. J., Esterlein, R., Stanford, M., & Mynors, D. J. (2009). A three-dimensional finite element analysis of the temperature field during laser melting of metal powders in additive layer manufacturing. *International Journal of Machine Tools & Manufacture*, *149*(12-13), 916–923. doi:10.1016/j.ijmachtools.2009.07.004

Roy, B. (1990). Decision-aid and decision-making. *European Journal of Operational Research*, *45*(2-3), 324–331. doi:10.1016/0377-2217(90)90196-I

Roy, N., Kuar, A. S., Mitra, S., & Acherjee, B. (2015). Nd: YAG laser micro drilling of Sic-30 BN Nanocomposite: experimental study and process optimization, *Laser Based Manufacturing*. In *Topics in Mining, Metallurgy and Materials Engineering* (pp. 317–341). Springer.

Saaty, T. L. (1980). *The Analytic Hierarchy Process*. McGraw-Hill.

Saha, S. K., & Choudhury, S. K. (2009). Experimental investigation and empirical modeling of the dry electric discharge machining process. *International Journal of Machine Tools & Manufacture*, *49*(3-4), 297–308. doi:10.1016/j.ijmachtools.2008.10.012

Samanta, S., & Chakraborty, S. (2011). Parametric optimization of some non-traditional machining processes using artificial bee colony algorithm. *Engineering Applications of Artificial Intelligence*, *24*(6), 946–957. doi:10.1016/j.engappai.2011.03.009

Sames, W. J., List, F. A., Pannala, S., Dehoff, R. R., & Babu, S. S. (2016). The metallurgy and processing science of metal additive manufacturing. *International Materials Reviews*, *61*(5), 315–360. doi:10.1080/09506608.2015.1116649

Sanchez, J. A., Rodil, J. L., Herrero, A., Lacalle, L. N., & Lamikiz, A. (2007). On the Influence of Cutting Speed Limitation on the Accuracy of Wire EDM Corner Cutting. *Journal of Materials Processing Technology*, *182*(1-3), 574–579. doi:10.1016/j.jmatprotec.2006.09.030

Sansonetti, A., Colella, M., Letardi, P., Salvadori, B., & Striova, J. (2015). Laser cleaning of a nineteenth-century bronze sculpture: In situ multi-analytical evaluation. *Studies in Conservation*, *60*(sup1), S28–S33. doi:10.1179/0039363015Z.000000000204

Sanz, M., Oujja, M., Ascaso, C., Pérez-Ortega, S., Souza-Egipsy, V., Fort, R., de los Rios, A., Wierzchos, J., Cañamares, M. V., & Castillejo, M. (2017). Influence of wavelength on the laser removal of lichens colonizing heritage stone. *Applied Surface Science*, *399*, 758–768. doi:10.1016/j.apsusc.2016.12.032

Sarkar, S., Mitra, S., & Bhattacharyya, B. (2005). Parametric analysis and optimization of wire electrical discharge machining of γ-titanium aluminide alloy. *Journal of Materials Processing Technology*, *159*(3), 286–294. doi:10.1016/j.jmatprotec.2004.10.009

Sarkar, S., Mitra, S., & Bhattacharyya, B. (2006). Parametric optimisation of wire electrical discharge machining of γ titanium aluminide alloy through an artificial neural network model. *International Journal of Advanced Manufacturing Technology*, *27*(5–6), 501–508. doi:10.100700170-004-2203-7

Sarkar, S., Mitra, S., & Bhattacharyya, B. (2011). A novel method of determination of wire lag for enhanced profile accuracy in WEDM. *Precision Engineering*, *35*(2), 339–347. doi:10.1016/j.precisioneng.2011.01.001

Sarkar, S., Sekh, M., Mitra, S., & Bhattacharyya, B. (2008). Modelling and optimization of wire electrical discharge machining of γ-TiAl in trim cutting operation. *Journal of Materials Processing Technology*, *205*(1-3), 376–387. doi:10.1016/j.jmatprotec.2007.11.194

Scott, F. M. (2005). Investigation of wire electrical discharge machining of thin cross-sections and compliant mechanisms. *International Journal of Machine Tools & Manufacture*, *45*(15), 1717–1725. doi:10.1016/j.ijmachtools.2005.03.003

Scott, F. M., Albert, J. S., & Qu, J. (2004). Investigation of the spark cycle on material removal rate in wire electrical discharge machining of advanced materials. *International Journal of Machine Tools & Manufacture*, *44*(4), 391–400. doi:10.1016/j.ijmachtools.2003.10.005

Selvakumar, G., Jiju, K. B., Sarkar, S., & Mitra, S. (2016). Enhancing die corner accuracy through trim cut in WEDM. *International Journal of Advanced Manufacturing Technology*, *83*(5–8), 791–803. doi:10.100700170-015-7606-0

Selvakumar, G., Sornalatha, G., Sarkar, S., & Mitra, S. (2014). Experimental investigation and multi-objective optimization of wire electrical discharge machining (WEDM) of 5083 aluminum alloy. *Transactions of Nonferrous Metals Society of China*, *24*(2), 373–379. doi:10.1016/S1003-6326(14)63071-5

Sharma, S., Mandal, V., Ramakrishna, S. A., & Ramkumar, J. (2018). Numerical simulation of melt hydrodynamics induced hole blockage in Quasi- CW fiber laser micro-drilling of TiAl6V4. *Journal of Materials Processing Technology*, *262*, 131–148. doi:10.1016/j.jmatprotec.2018.06.038

Shen, S., Jiang, H., & Zhang, T. (2012). Stock Market Forecasting Using Machine Learning Algorithms. Department of Electrical Engineering, Stanford University, Tongda Zhang, Department of Electrical Engineering, Stanford University.

Shen, W., Hao, Q., Yoon, H. J., & Norrie, D. H. (2006). Applications of agent-based systems in intelligent manufacturing: An updated review. *Advanced Engineering Informatics*, *20*(4), 415–431. doi:10.1016/j.aei.2006.05.004

Shen, W., Norrie, D. H., & Barthes, J.-P. (2001). *A Multi-Agent Systems for Concurrent Intelligent Design and Manufacturing*. Taylor & Francis Inc. doi:10.4324/9780203305607

Shinar, J., & Savvateev, V. (2004). Introduction to Organic Light-Emitting Devices. In J. Shinar (Ed.), *Organic Light-Emitting Devices*. Springer. doi:10.1007/978-0-387-21720-8_1

Shokouhifar, M., & Jalali, A. (2017). Optimized sugeno fuzzy clustering algorithm for wireless sensor networks. *Engineering Applications of Artificial Intelligence*, *60*, 16–25. doi:10.1016/j.engappai.2017.01.007

Sinha, S. K. (2010). Effects of wire lag in wire electrical discharge machining (WEDM). *International Journal of Engineering Science and Technology*, *2*, 6622–6625.

Sivagurumanikandan, N., Saravanan, S., Kumar, G. S., Raju, S., & Raghukandan, K. (2018). Prediction and optimization of process parameters to enhance the tensile strength of Nd: YAG laser welded super duplex stainless steel. *Optik (Stuttgart)*, *157*, 833–840. doi:10.1016/j.ijleo.2017.11.146

Sivapirakasam, S. P., Mathew, J., & Surianarayanan, M. (2011). Multi-attribute decision making for green electrical discharge machining. *Expert Systems with Applications*, *38*(7), 8370–8374. doi:10.1016/j.eswa.2011.01.026

Snoeys, R., Staelens, F., & Dekeyser, W. (1986). Current Trends in Non-Conventional Material Removal Processes. *Annals CIRP*, *35*(2), 467–480. doi:10.1016/S0007-8506(07)60195-4

Soci, C., Hwang, I. W., Moses, D., Zhu, Z., Waller, D., Gaudiana, R., Brabec, C. J., & Heeger, A. J. (2007). Photoconductivity of a low-bandgap conjugated polymer. *Advanced Functional Materials*, *17*(4), 632–636. doi:10.1002/adfm.200600199

Sohani, M. S., Gaitonde, V. N., Siddeswarappa, B., & And Deshpande, A. S. (2009). Investigations into the effect of tool shapes with size factor consideration in sink electrical discharge machining (EDM) process. *International Journal of Advanced Manufacturing Technology*, *45*(11-12), 1–15. doi:10.100700170-009-2044-5

Somashekhar, K. P., Ramachandran, N., & Mathew, J. (2010). Optimization of Material Removal Rate in Micro-EDM Using Artificial Neural Network and Genetic Algorithms. *Materials and Manufacturing Processes*, *25*(6), 467–475. doi:10.1080/10426910903365760

Song, J., Chew, Y., Bi, G., Yao, X., Zhang, B., Bai, J., & Seung, K. M. (2018). Numerical and experimental study of laser aided additive manufacturing for melt-pool profile and grain orientation analysis. *Materials & Design*, *137*, 286–297. doi:10.1016/j.matdes.2017.10.033

Srivastava, A., Dixit, A. R., & Tiwari, S. (2014). Experimental Investigation of Wire EDM Process Parameters on Aluminium Metal Matrix Composite Al2024/SiC. *International Journal of Advance Research and Innovation*, *2*, 511–515.

Striova, J., Fontana, R., Barucci, M., Felici, A., Marconi, E., Pampaloni, E., Raffaelli, M., & Riminesi, C. (2016). Optical devices provide unprecedented insights into the laser cleaning of calcium oxalate layers. *Microchemical Journal*, *124*, 331–337. doi:10.1016/j.microc.2015.09.005

Striova, J., Salvadori, B., Fontana, R., Sansonetti, A., Barucci, M., Pampaloni, E., Marconi, E., Pezzati, L., & Colombini, M. P. (2015). Optical and spectroscopic tools for evaluating Er:YAG laser removal of shellac varnish. *Studies in Conservation*, *60*(sup1), S91–S96. doi:10.1179/0039363015Z.000000000213

Subbaraj, S., Thiagarajan, R., & Rengaraj, M. (2019). Multi-objective league championship algorithm for real-time task scheduling. *Neural Computing & Applications*, 1–12.

Sugeno, M. (1985). *Industrial applications of fuzzy control*. North-Holland. Sole distributors for the U.S.A. and Canada, Elsevier Science Publishing company.

Sundaram, M. M., Pavalarajan, G. B., & Rajurkar, K. P. (2008). A Study on Process Parameters of Ultrasonic Assisted Micro EDM Based on Taguchi Method. *Journal of Materials Engineering and Performance*, *17*(2), 210–215. doi:10.100711665-007-9128-x

Tahmasebi, P., & Hezarkhani, A. (2012). A hybrid neural networks-fuzzy logic-genetic algorithm for grade estimation. *Computers & Geosciences*, *42*, 18–27. doi:10.1016/j.cageo.2012.02.004 PMID:25540468

Tanveer, M., Habib, A., & Khan, M. B. (2012). Improved efficiency of organic/inorganic photovoltaic devices by electrospunZnO nanofibers. *Materials Science and Engineering B*, *177*(13), 1144–1148. doi:10.1016/j.mseb.2012.05.025

Tong, H., Li, Y., Zhang, L., & Li, B. (2013). Mechanism design and process control of micro EDM for drilling spray holes of diesel injector nozzles. *Precision Engineering*, *37*(1), 213–221. doi:10.1016/j.precisioneng.2012.09.004

Törngren, M., & Grogan, P. T. (2018). How to Deal with the Complexity of Future Cyber-Physical Systems. *Designs*, *2*(40), 2–16. doi:10.3390/designs2040040

Tosun, N., Cogun, C., & Tosun, G. (2004). A study on kerf and material removal rate in wire electrical discharge machining based on Taguchi method. *Journal of Materials Processing Technology*, *152*(3), 316–322. doi:10.1016/j.jmatprotec.2004.04.373

Trinkle, B. S. (2006). Forecasting annual excess stock returns via an adaptive network-based fuzzy inference system. *Intelligent Systems in Accounting, Finance & Management*, *13*(3), 165–177. doi:10.1002/isaf.264

Tripathy, S., & Tripathy, D. K. (2016). Multi-attribute optimization of machining process parameters in powder mixed electro-discharge machining using TOPSIS and grey relational analysis. *Engineering Science and Technology, an International Journal*, *19*, 62-70.

U.S. Department of Energy. (2009). *Smart grid system report; July 2009*. Author.

Uriondo, A., Esperon-Miguez, M., & Perinpanayagam, S. (2015). The present and future of additive manufacturing in the aerospace sector: A review of important aspects. *Proceedings of the Institution of Mechanical Engineers. Part G, Journal of Aerospace Engineering*, *229*(11), 2132–2147. doi:10.1177/0954410014568797

Vaidya, S., Ambad, P., & Bhosle, S. (2018). Industry 4.0 – A Glimpse. *Procedia Manufacturing*, *20*, 233–238. doi:10.1016/j.promfg.2018.02.034

Vikas, R. A. K., & Kumar, K. (2013). Effect and Optimization of Machine Process Parameters on Material Removal Rate in EDM for EN41 Material Using Taguchi. *International Journal of Mechanical Engineering and Computer Applications*, *1*(5), 35–39.

Vishal, P., Rehman, A., Bhagoria, J. L., & Puri, Y. M. (2010). Kerfs width analysis for wire cut electro discharge machining of SS 304L using design of experiments. *Indian Journal of Science and Technology*, *3*(4), 369–373. doi:10.17485/ijst/2010/v3i4.4

Vojdani, A. (2008). Smart integration. *IEEE Power & Energy Magazine*, *6*(6), 71–79. doi:10.1109/MPE.2008.929744

Voltolina, S., Nodari, L., Aibéo, C., Egel, E., Pamplona, M., Simon, S., Falzacappa, E. V., Scopece, P., Gambirasi, A., Favaro, M., & Patelli, A. (2016). Assessment of plasma torches as innovative tool for cleaning of historical stone materials. *Journal of Cultural Heritage*, *22*, 940–950. doi:10.1016/j.culher.2016.05.001

Walkar, H., Jatti, V. S., & Singh, T. P. (2014). Magnetic field Assisted Electrical Discharge Machining of AISI 4140. *Applied Mechanics and Materials*, *592-594*, 479–483. doi:10.4028/www.scientific.net/AMM.592-594.479

Wang, F. K., Chang, K. K., & Tzeng, C. W. (2011). Using adaptive network-based fuzzy inference system to forecast automobile sales. *Expert Systems with Applications*, *38*(8), 10587–10593. doi:10.1016/j.eswa.2011.02.100

Wang, L., Cai, J. C., & Li, M. (2016). An adaptive multi-population genetic algorithm for job-shop scheduling problem. *Advances in Manufacturing*, *4*(2), 142–149. doi:10.100740436-016-0140-y

Wang, S. S., Yan, K. Q., Wang, S. C., & Liu, C. W. (2011). An integrated intrusion detection system for cluster based wireless sensor networks. *Expert Systems with Applications*, *38*(12), 15234–15243. doi:10.1016/j.eswa.2011.05.076

Wang, S., Jia, Z., Lu, X., Zhang, H., Zhang, C., & Liang, S. Y. (2018). Simultaneous optimization of fixture and cutting parameters of thin-walled workpieces based on particle swarm optimization algorithm. *Simulation*, *94*(1), 67–76. doi:10.1177/0037549717713850

Wang, S., Wan, J., Li, D., & Zhang, C. (2016). Implementing Smart Factory of Industries 4.0: An Outlook. *International Journal of Distributed Sensor Networks*, 1–10.

Wang, X., Liu, B., Liu, W., Zhong, X., Jiang, Y., & Liu, H. (2017). Investigation on the Mechanism and Failure Mode of Laser transmission Spot Welding using PMMA material for the automotive industry. *Materials (Basel)*, *10*(1), 22. doi:10.3390/ma10010022 PMID:28772383

Wang, X., Liu, D., & Li, J. (2010). Organic photovoltaic materials and thin-film solar cells. *FrontiersofChemistryinChina*, *5*(1), 45–60. doi:10.100711458-009-0208-3

Wang, X., Zhong, X., Liu, W., Liu, B., & Liu, H. (2016). Investigation on enhancement of weld strength between PMMA and PBT in laser transmission welding—Using intermediate material. *Journal of Applied Polymer Science*, *133*(44), 44167. doi:10.1002/app.44167

Wang, Z., Xiao, Z., Tse, Y., Huang, C., & Zhang, W. (2019). Optimization of processing parameters and establishment of a relationship between microstructure and mechanical properties of SLM titanium alloy. *Optics & Laser Technology*, *112*, 159–167. doi:10.1016/j.optlastec.2018.11.014

Wei, L. Y., Chen, T. L., & Ho, T. H. (2011). A hybrid model based on adaptive-network-based fuzzy inference system to forecast Taiwan stock market. *Expert Systems with Applications*, *38*, 13625–13631. doi:10.1016/j.eswa.2011.04.127

Werner, A. (2016). Method for enhanced accuracy in machining curvilinear profiles on wire-cut electrical discharge machines. *Precision Engineering*, *44*, 75–80. doi:10.1016/j.precisioneng.2015.10.004

Wooldridge, M., & Jennings, N. R. (1995). Intelligent agents: Theory and practice. *The Knowledge Engineering Review*, *10*(2), 115–152. doi:10.1017/S0269888900008122

Woolley, J., Pritoni, M., & Modera, M. (2014).Why occupancy-responsive adaptive thermostats do not always save and the limits for when they should. *ACEEE summer study on energy efficiency in buildings*, 337-350.

Wu, C. F. J., & Hamada, M. (2010). *Experiments Planning, analysis, and Parameter Design Optimization*. Wiley-India.

Wu, D., Greer, M. J., Rosen, D. W., & Schaefer, D. (2013). Cloud Manufacturing: Strategic Vision and State-of-the-Art. *Journal of Manufacturing Systems*, *32*(4), 564–579. doi:10.1016/j.jmsy.2013.04.008

Xue, W., Jun-Jie, M., Sheng, W., & Dao-Wei, B. (2007). Prediction-based Dynamic Energy Management in Wireless Sensor Networks. *Sensors (Basel)*, *7*(3), 251–266. doi:10.33907030251

Xu, T., Zhang, L., Cheng, H., & Zhu, Y. (2011). Significantly enhanced photocatalytic performance of ZnOvia graphene hybridization and the mechanism stud. *Applied Catalysis B: Environmental*, *101*(3), 382–387. doi:10.1016/j.apcatb.2010.10.007

Xu, X. (2017). Machine Tool 4.0 for the new era of manufacturing. *International Journal of Advanced Manufacturing Technology*, *92*(5-8), 1893–1900. doi:10.100700170-017-0300-7

Xu, X. F., Bates, P. J., & Zak, G. (2015). Effect of glass fiber and crystallinity on light transmission during laser transmission welding of thermoplastics. *Optics & Laser Technology*, *69*, 133–139. doi:10.1016/j.optlastec.2014.12.025

Yan, B. H. (2005). Examination of wire electrical discharge machining of Al2O3p/6061Al composites. *International Journal of Machine Tools & Manufacture*, *45*(3), 251–259. doi:10.1016/j.ijmachtools.2004.08.015

Yan, M. T. (2010). An adaptive control system with self-organizing fuzzy sliding mode control strategy for micro wire-EDM machines. *International Journal of Advanced Manufacturing Technology, 50*(1-4), 315–328. doi:10.100700170-009-2481-1

Yilbas, B. S. (1997). Parametric study to improve laser hole drilling process. *Journal of Materials Processing Technology, 70*(1-3), 264–273. doi:10.1016/S0924-0136(97)00076-9

Yilbas, B. S. (2013). *Laser drilling-practical applications, manufacturing and surface engineering*. Springer.

Yilbas, B. S., Akhtar, S. S., & Karatas, C. (2011). Laser trepanning of a small diameter hole in titanium alloy: Temperature and stress fields. *Journal of Materials Processing Technology, 211*(7), 1296–1304. doi:10.1016/j.jmatprotec.2011.02.012

Yilbas, B. S., & Aleem, A. (2004). Laser hole drilling quality and efficiency assessment. *Proceedings of the Institution of Mechanical Engineers. Part B, Journal of Engineering Manufacture, 18*(2), 225–233. doi:10.1243/095440504322886541

Yilbas, B. S., Shaukat, M. M., & Ashraf, F. (2017). Laser cutting of various materials: Kerf width size analysis and life cycle assessment of cutting process. *Optics & Laser Technology, 93*(1), 67–73. doi:10.1016/j.optlastec.2017.02.014

Yoo, H. K., Kwon, W. T., & Kang, S. (2014). Development of a new electrode for micro-electrical discharge machining (EDM) using Ti (C, N)-based cermet. *International Journal of Precision Engineering and Manufacturing, 15*(4), 609–616. doi:10.100712541-014-0378-x

Younis, M. A., Abbas, M. S., Gouda, M. A., Mahmoud, F. H., & Allah, S. A. A. (2015). Effect of electrode material on electrical discharge machining of tool steel surface. *Ain Shams Engineering Journal, 6*(3), 977–986. doi:10.1016/j.asej.2015.02.001

Yuan, J., Wang, K., Yua, T., & Fanga, M. (2008). Reliable multi-objective optimization of high-speed WEDM process based on Gaussian process regression. *International Journal of Machine Tools & Manufacture, 48*(1), 47–60. doi:10.1016/j.ijmachtools.2007.07.011

Yu, G., Gao, J., Hummelen, J. C., Wudl, F., & Heeger, A. J. (1995). Polymer Photovoltaic Cells: Enhanced Efficiencies via a Network of Internal Donor-Acceptor Heterojunctions. *American Association for the Advancement of Science, 270*(5243), 1789–1790. doi:10.1126cience.270.5243.1789

Zadeh, L. A. (1965). Fuzzy sets. *Information and Control, 8*(3), 338–353. doi:10.1016/S0019-9958(65)90241-X

Zaeh, M. F., Reinhart, G., Ostgathe, M., Geiger, F., & Lau, C. (2010). A holistic approach for the cognitive control of production systems. *Advanced Engineering Informatics, 24*(3), 300–307. doi:10.1016/j.aei.2010.05.014

Zanini, A., Trafeli, V., & Bartoli, L. (2018). The laser as a tool for the cleaning of Cultural Heritage. *IOP Conference Series. Materials Science and Engineering, 364*, 012078. doi:10.1088/1757-899X/364/1/012078

Zenios, S. A. (Ed.). (1996). *Financial optimization*. Cambridge University Press.

Zhang, Y., Bai, X.-L., Xu, X., & Liu, Y.-X. (2012). STEP-NC Based High-level Machining Simulations Integrated with CAD/CAPP/CAM. *International Journal of Automation and Computing, 9*(5), 506–517. doi:10.100711633-012-0674-9

Zheng, P., Wang, H., Sang, Z., Zhong, R. Y., Liu, Y., Liu, C., Mubarok, K., Yu, S., & Xu, X. (2018). Smart manufacturing systems for Industry 4.0: Conceptual framework, scenarios, and future perspectives. *Frontiers of Mechanical Engineering, 13*(2), 137–150. doi:10.100711465-018-0499-5

Zheng, Q., Fang, G., Cheng, F., Lei, H., Wang, W., Qin, P., & Zhou, H. (2012). Hybrid graphene ZnO nanocomposites as electron acceptor in polymer based bulk-heterojunction organic photovoltaics. *Journal of Physics. D, Applied Physics, 45*(45), 455103. doi:10.1088/0022-3727/45/45/455103

Zhou, M., & And Han, F. (2009). Adaptive control for EDM process with a self-tuning regulator. *International Journal of Machine Tools & Manufacture*, *49*(6), 462–469. doi:10.1016/j.ijmachtools.2009.01.004

Zhou, M., Eck, Y., & Krueger, M. (2011). *Solar Cells—New Aspects and Solutions*. Freiburg Materials Research Centre University of Freiburg.

Zhou, R. J., & Xue, J. G. (2012). Hybrid Polymer-Nanocrystal Materials for Photovoltaic Applications. *ChemPhysChem*, *13*(10), 2471–2480. doi:10.1002/cphc.201101016 PMID:22461231

Zhou, R., Zheng, Y., Qian, L., Yang, Y., Holloway, P. H., & Xue, J. (2012). Solution- processed, nanostructured hybrid solar cells with broad spectral sensitivity and stability. *Nanoscale*, *4*(11), 3507–3514. doi:10.1039/c2nr30210a PMID:22543410

Zhu, Z., Waller, D., Gaudiana, R., Morana, M., Mühlbacher, D., Scharber, M., & Brabec, C. (2007). Panchromatic conjugated polymers containing alternating donor/acceptor units for photovoltaic applications. *Macromolecules*, *40*(6), 1981–1986. doi:10.1021/ma062376o

Zinonos, Z., Chrysostomou, C., & Vassiliou, V. (2014). Wireless sensor networks mobility management using fuzzy Logic. *Ad Hoc Networks*, *16*, 70–87. doi:10.1016/j.adhoc.2013.12.003

Zivanovic, S., & Puzovic, R. (2015). Off-line Programming and Simulation for 2-axis Wire EDM. FME Transactions, 43, 138-143. doi:10.5937/fmet1502138z

About the Contributors

Goutam Kumar Bose is currently working as HOD and Professor in Mechanical Engineering Department, Haldia Institute of Technology, Haldia, India. He obtained his PhD in Production Engineering from the Jadavpur University, Kolkata, India. He has obtained a Master's in Engineering in Mechanical Engineering from the Bengal Engineering & Science University, Shibpur, India. He has worked as an Assistant Professor in the Department of Mechanical Engineering at the College of Engineering & Management, Kolaghat for ten years. He was an Engineer in R & D Centre of M/s Hindustan Motors Ltd. West Bengal, India. His active areas of interest are Metal Cutting, Non- conventional machining and Industrial and Production Management. He has published research papers in journals of International repute. He has attended several international conferences in India and abroad. [Biography pulled from the Profile]

Pritam Pain has completed his B.Tech degree from WBUT in 2014 and then completed his M.Tech degree from Haldia Institute of Technology in 2016. He is currently working as assistant professor in Haldia Institute of Technology. He had several journal papers and book chapters regarding Non-Traditional machining. He is also appointed as a reviewer in many journals. His main interest of research is in nature-inspired modern optimization algorithms.

* * *

B. Sridhar Babu has completed B.E. with Mechanical Engineering from Kakatiya University, M.Tech with Advanced manufacturing systems from JNTUH University and PhD with Mechanical Engineering from JNTUH University. He has 21 years of teaching Experience out of which 10 years of experience in CMR Institute of Technology itself. He joined in the Department of Mechanical Engineering in CMR Institute of Technology on 1st July 2009. He is Fellow of the Institution of Engineers (I), Kolkata and also Member of ISTE, IAENG and SAE India.He has published 38 papers in various International / National journals and International / National conferences. He is Author of 04 text books. He received Bharath jyothi award for his research excellence from India international friendship society New Delhi India. He is a paper setter for various universities, reviewer for various international journals and conferences and guided more than 75 B.Tech and M. Tech projects. His research interests include Manufacturing, Advanced materials and Mechanics of materials etc. He is a Guest editor for Proceedings of 1st International Conference on Manufacturing, Material Science and Engineering (ICMMSE'19), Materials Today – Proceedings (Scopus and CPCI Indexed) and AIP Proceedings (Scopus Indexed).

Arup Kumar Bhattacharjee did his Bachelors from University of Calcutta, Master of Computer Application from Kalyani University and MTech from West Bengal University of Technology. He is currently working as an Assistant Professor in RCC Institute of Information Technology, Kolkata, India. He has more than 14 years teaching experience. He has over 10 research publication in different national and international journal and conferences. He has contributed in over 20 internationally acclaimed books. He has edited 2 books. His research areas are software engineering, data mining and machine learning. He is member of various professional bodies like IETE, Indian Science Congress, Computer Society of India.

Dipankar Bose received the B.E. in mechanical engineering from Calcutta University, India in 1982 and MME & Ph.D. from Jadavpur University, India in 1984 & 2001 respectively. He has more than 31 years teaching experience in the broad field of Mechanical Engineering and he has published 50 nos. of papers, in the National /International Journals /Proceedings. Presently He is a Professor, Mechanical Engineering NITTTR, Kolkata, Block FC, Sector III, Salt Lake, Kolkata -700106. Dr. Bose is a life member of ISTE. His current research interest in the field of Fluid Mechanics, Non conventional machining, Reliability Engineering.

Souvick Chakraborty has completed his B.tech degree in 2014 in Mechanical Engineering and got his M.Tech degree in Manufacturing Science in 2016. He is now currently working as assistant professor at the Bengal Institute of Technology and Management.

Somnath Das is currently working as professor in the Department of Mechanical Engineering at Swami Vivekananda Institute of Science and Technology.

Ramkrishna Ghosh is a PhD scholar of CSE in KIIT Deemed to be University, Bhubaneswar, Odisha, India. He has total 12 years experience out of which 11 years teaching experience and 1 year industrial experience. He completed M.Tech in IT from Jadavpur University after having qualified in GATE 2007 on paper IT with score 438 and with all India rank 180. He has published many international journals and engineering books. His research interests include Wireless Sensor Network, Cryptography, Soft Computing etc. He travelled all over India through his teaching only.

T. K. Jana is currently a Professor and the dean of School of Engineering, Haldia Institute of Technology, Haldia, India. He received his BE from Bengal Engineering and Science University (BESU), Howrah, West Bengal, India in the year 1988 and he did his masters and Ph.D. in Production Engineering from the Jadavpur University. He is the co-author of two books on Mechanical Sciences – I & II, published by Tata McGraw-Hill (India). His active areas of interest are metal cutting, computer integrated manufacturing, and holonic manufacturing.

Arunanshu Shekhar Kuar graduated on 1994 in Mechanical Engineering and completed his Master's Degree in Production Engineering in the year 1996, both from Jadavpur University, India. He has been awarded PhD (Engg.) on 2005 from the same University. He has around 3 years of industrial experience. From 1999 onwards he is working as a Faculty in Production Engineering Department, Jadavpur University. He also served as Head, Production Engineering Department between 2017 and 2019. Presently, he is Professor in the said Department. His research specialisations include laser beam micro-machining, laser beam fabrication etc. He has published more than 100 national and international journals and conference papers. He has also published few reputed Book Chapter from International and national Publishers. Few of his Journal papers awarded "Most Downloaded Paper award" in a year from reputed International Journal Publishing House. Several doctoral and post graduate theses have been completed under his guidance.

Dhiraj Kumar is currently a Ph.D. Scholar under 'National Doctoral Fellowship' in the Department of Production Engineering, Jadavpur University, Kolkata, India. He obtained his M.Tech degree from National Institute of Technical Teachers' Training and Research, Kolkata in Department of Mechanical Engineering in the field of Wire-EDM process. He was awarded University Bronze Medal for securing 3rd position in M.Tech. He is working in the field of laser beam welding. He has authored/co-authored several journal papers, reputed book chapter and Conferences in the area of laser beam welding and wire electrical discharge machining processes.

Kaushik Kumar, B.Tech (Mechanical Engineering, REC (Now NIT), Warangal), MBA (Marketing, IGNOU) and Ph.D (Engineering, Jadavpur University), is presently an Associate Professor in the Department of Mechanical Engineering, Birla Institute of Technology, Mesra, Ranchi, India. He has 19 years of Teaching & Research and over 11 years of industrial experience in a manufacturing unit of Global repute. His areas of teaching and research interest are Composites, Optimization, Non-conventional machining, CAD / CAM, Rapid Prototyping and Quality Management Systems. He has 9 Patents, 35+ Book, 30+ Edited Book, 55+ Book Chapters, 150+ international Journal publications, 22 International and 1 National Conference publications to his credit. He is on the editorial board and review panel of 7 International and 1 National Journals of repute. He has been felicitated with many awards and honours. Web of Science core collection (102 publications/h-index 10+, SCOPUS/h-index 10+, Google Scholar/h-index 26+).

Dipankar Majumdar has obtained his B.E (Electrical Engg) from REC, Silchar, in the year 1999 and his M.Tech. from JU, Kolkata in the year 2006 followed by PhD(Engg) in the year 2011 and currently working as Associate Professor in the Department of Information Technology at RCC Institute of Information Technology, Kolkata, India.

Kingshuk Mandal is pursuing Ph.D. from Jadavpur University.

Souren Mitra is a professor in the Department of Production Engineering, Jadavpur University, Kolkata. His research areas include the non-traditional machining process, nano-machining, and advanced manufacturing system. He has published more than 70 research papers in international and national journals and conferences. Several Ph.D. and MProdE theses have been completed under his guidance. He is a Recipient of the Research Award of UGC, New Delhi and has completed several sponsored research project as the principal investigator. He is a Member of the Institute of Engineers (India). He has attended several international conferences abroad.

Suneeta Mohanty is an Assistant professor of School of Computer Engineering in KIIT Deemed to be University, Bhubaneswar, Odisha, India. She is a Doctorate in Computer Science and Engineering. She has published many research papers in various journals. Her research interests include Computer Security, Wireless Sensor Network, Cloud Computing, IoT, etc.

Sibabrata Mondal received the B.E. degree in mechanical engineering from Jadavpur University, Kolkata, India, in 2004, and the M.Tech. degree in manufacturing technology from the National Institute of Technical Teachers' Training and Research, Kolkata, in 2015. He has more than 12 years of experience in the field of mechanical design of critical subsystems and systems in millimeter-wave and microwave frequency bands. He is also experienced in process, planning, and execution of in-house fabrication of subsystems and systems using conventional and non-conventional machining processes. He is currently a Scientist-C and the Head of the Mechanical Division, SAMEER, Kolkata. His current research interests include nontraditional machining processes such as electro-discharge machining, wire electro-discharge machining, and wire electro-discharge turning.

Soumen Mukherjee did his B.Sc (Physics Honours) from Calcutta University, M.C.A. from Kalyani University and ME in Information Technology from West Bengal University of Technology. He is the silver medalist in ME examination for the university. He has done his Post-Graduate Diploma in Business Management from Institute of Management Technology, Center of Distance Learning, Ghaziabad. He is now working as an Assistant Professor in RCC Institute of Information Technology, Kolkata. He has 15 years teaching experience in the field of Computer Science and Application. He has over 30 research paper published in different National and International Journal and Conferences. He has contributed in over 20 internationally acclaimed books in the field of Computer Science and Engineering. He has got best paper award in the international conference, ICCAIAIT 2018. He has edited 2 books. His research fields are Image Processing and Machine Learning. He is a life member of several institutions like IETE, CSI, ISTE, FOSET, etc.

P. Mukhopadhyay is working as an Assistant Professor in Mechanical Engineering Department, Haldia Institute of Technology. He has completed his B.Tech Degree from Biju Patnaik University of Technology, Orissa. He has completed his M.Tech degree in Manufacturing Technology specialization from NITTTR Kolkata. He has published about 4 journal papers and 4 international conference papers.

Sudipta Paitandi has completed his B.Tech. in Electronics and Communication from W.B.U.T in 2008. and achieved M.Tech. in Laser Science and Technology from Jadavpur University in 2015. Since his PG research activity in laser welding, he has involved himself in research work in the same field. At Present he is working as a senior project engineer at Simplex infrastructures ltd.

Prasant Kumar Pattnaik is a Professor of School of Computer Engineering in KIIT Deemed to be University, Bhubaneswar, Odisha, India. He is a Doctorate in Computer Science and Engineering. He has published many international journals and engineering books. His research interests include Mobile Computing, Cloud Computing, and Wireless Sensor Network, etc.

Sabyasachi Pramanik is an Assistant Professor in the department of Computer Science & Engineering, Haldia Institute of Technology, Haldia, West Bengal, India. He has 12 years of teaching experience. His research interests include Data Hiding, Machine Learning and WSN.

D. Pramanik is currently a PhD student in the Department of Production Engineering, Jadavpur University, India. He obtained his M.tech degree in Mechanical Engineering department in 2015 from NITTTR, Kolkata, India. During his stay here he worked in the area of Wire EDM. He had also a position of Research Scholar of TEQIP phase III. He is working in the area of laser beam machining. He has authored/co-authored several journals, reputed book chapter and conference papers in the area of laser beam machining, wire electro-discharge machining and 3-d printing.

Chikesh Ranjan, BE (Mechanical Engineering, Marathwara Institute of Technology, Aurangabad, Maharastra, India), M.E. (Design of Mechanical Equipment, BIT Mesra), presently pursuing PhD (BIT Mesra). He has over 5 years of Teaching and Research experience. His areas of interests are Product and Process Design, CAD/CAM/CAE, Rapid prototyping and Composites. He has 10 Books, 10 international journal and 4 International Conference publications to his credit.

Nilanjan Roy submitted his PhD thesis on the field of laser based micromachining. He passed Secondary Examination under West Bengal Board of Secondary Education from Ramakrishna Vivekananda Mission High School, Barrackpore in 1999 and Higher Secondary under West Bengal Council of Higher secondary Education from Barrackpore Government High School in 2001. The author completed his graduation in Mechanical Engineering in 2006 from Birbhum Institute of Engineering and Technology under West Bengal University of Technology with first class. Author received his Post Graduation degree in Manufacturing Technology in 2009 from National Institute of Technical Teachers Training and Research under West Bengal University of Technology with first class. Then he joined in IMPS College of Engineering & Technology as Assistant Professor in March 2009. After that he Joined in Production Engineering Department, Jadavpur University as a Research Fellow under, "DST-PURSE phase II" in June 2011 and later as a National Fellow under "Rajiv Gandhi National Fellowship Programme 2014" in April 2015. He has done his research work in the area of laser beam micromachining of various materials and in different environment during entire period. Author has published 2 research papers in international referred journals and also presented 9 research papers in reputed national and international conferences related to advance manufacturing processes. Author also published 4 research articles as book chapter in various books on laser based manufacturing and non-conventional machining.

Sayantan Roy has completed his B.Tech and now currently persuing his M.Tech degree from Haldia Institute of Technology in Mechanical Engineering.

Soumya Sarkar is the Professor and Former Head of Production Engineering Department of Jadavpur University. He graduated in Mechanical Engineering in the year 1994 and completed his Master Degree in Production Engineering in the year 1996. After completion of Master Degree he served as an Assistant Manager in West Bengal Power Development Corporation for nearly 3 years and thereafter he joined Jadavpur University as Lecturer in the year 1999 and since then he is serving there. He was awarded PhD Degree in the year 2005. Prof Sarkar has research interests in the area of Advanced Manufacturing Processes. Several PhD and PG Theses have been completed under his guidance. He has published numerous research papers in international and national journals and conference. He has made significant contribution in the field of Wire EDM. Prof Sarkar has completed several sponsored research projects in field of advanced manufacturing processes.

Pawan Singh is an Assistant Professor in Department of Mechanical Engineering at IIT (ISM) Dhanbad. Specialization: Thermal and Nanofluid engineering.

Anup Kumar Sood is a professor of the Department of Manufacturing Engineering, National Institute of Foundry and Forge Technology, Ranchi. He is a member of several professional bodies like the International Society on Multiple Criteria Decision Making, International Association of Engineering, etc.

Vishnu T. has more than 15 years of teaching & research experience in the field of Mechanical Engineering. He is specialized in the areas of CAD/CAM and Robotics. He has published more than 35 technical papers in various national and international journals and published one patent. He has delivered more than 20 invited lectures in various universities and organized about 10 workshops/seminars. During his tenure as teacher he has handled administrative positions such as Dean (IIIC), Head of the Department, Chairman for Professional bodies, NAAC coordinator, NBA program coordinator for Mechanical Engineering in various colleges of repute. He is a life member of professional bodies such as IEI,ISTE. He is a faculty sponsor for five University Innovation Fellows of Stanford University's Hasso Plattner Institute of Design (d.school). a five-year National Science Foundation grant.

Arun Tiwari is Associate Professor and Head of Mechanical Engineering Department at IET Lucknow. Specialization: Heat Transfer Solar Thermal Energy Storage Nanofluids Thermal Manufacturing Computational Fluid Dynamics Electronics Cooling.

Sakshi Tyagi is presently working as Assistant Professor in Department of Mechanical Engineering at Haldia Institute of Technology, Haldia West Bengal. Specialization: Production Engineering. Pursuing PhD from IIT(ISM) Dhanbad. Topic of Research: Fabrication of Hybrid solar cell from organic and inorganic nanocomposites. Research topic reveals the vital applications of hybrid solar cell fabricated by incorporating organic as well as inorganic semiconductors. Organic semiconductor being Carbon quantum dots and inorganic semiconductor being Zinc Oxide.

Index

A

additive manufacturing 215, 224, 231-234
advance manufacturing 195, 201
agent based systems 210
Al 7075 76-78, 84, 90
Aluminium 6061 t6 alloy, 96
ANOVA 34, 76, 82, 84, 88-92, 106-107, 125, 130, 149-150, 160, 166, 170-172, 174, 177, 215, 227-228, 230
Artificial Intelligence 136, 194-196, 201, 206-207, 248, 270, 280
artificial neural network 4-5, 14, 32, 77, 94-95, 142, 164, 182, 193, 200, 212, 244, 273

B

Battery Power 235, 240-243
Biogeography-based optimization 181, 184, 191

C

CCD 106, 137, 144, 146-147
Centrality 235, 240-243, 245-246
Chance 116, 118, 217, 232, 237-238, 241-246
circular cycle 63-64
circularity 19, 45, 130, 135, 137-138, 142, 144, 147-155, 157-158
Cognitive Factory 210-211
computational time 192
corner inaccuracy 76-78, 83-86, 89-90, 96, 103, 105-110
current density 182, 255-263
Cyber Physical Production Systems 203, 207

D

Diametral Overcut 45-46, 49-53
DOE 19, 99, 114, 118, 125, 165
dry laser cleaning 1-2, 15

E

EDM 18-19, 28, 31-34, 38, 44-46, 53-58, 61-64, 73-75, 93-101, 103, 112, 115-116, 118, 123, 126, 134-136, 138, 212
electrical discharge machining 32-34, 38, 42, 54-56, 73-75, 93-98, 112-113, 117, 135-136, 193
Electro-chemical machining 181
EN 19 181
Entropy method 33-34, 37, 39, 42, 78, 81, 84
Environment friendly 250
Error in Standard Deviation 272, 274-275, 277
ETP Cu 114, 121, 123, 134

F

Feed Function 55, 60
fiber laser 4, 137, 139-140, 142-144, 146, 155, 157-159, 162
Finite Element Modelling 215, 221
firefly algorithm 4, 6-7, 12-14, 45, 51-53
Focal Length 1, 4, 7, 12-14, 143
fuzzy inference system 235, 268, 270, 273, 280-281
Fuzzy Set Theory 18, 27-28

G

GA 18-19, 22, 24-25, 28, 212, 251
GRA 25, 27, 76-78, 83, 89-92

H

hole diameter 19, 137, 144, 147
hybrid solar cell 250, 259, 263, 265
hybridisation 45-46

I

Industry 4.0 203-207, 211-214
Inorganic semiconductor 250, 254
Interval Type-1 Fuzzy Logic 235

L

Laser sawing 137
LEACH 236-237, 240, 244, 247

M

machine learning 4, 195-202, 206, 211-212, 267, 269, 271, 275-276, 281
Machine Tool 4.0 203, 211, 213-214
Machine Tool Cyber Twin 203, 211
machining speed 76-78, 83-86, 89-90, 141
magnetic field 45-46, 48-54
material removal rate 2, 15, 21, 31-32, 34, 44, 57, 74, 77, 95, 102, 112-113, 131, 134-136, 141, 164, 181, 184, 212
MCDM 18-19, 28-29, 33-35, 42, 44
MCDM: TOPSIS and MOORA 33
Mean Error 267, 274
Mean Square Error 9, 267, 271-272, 274-276
micro-EDM 18-19, 31-32, 54
mobility 235, 237, 240-243, 245-246, 249, 251, 268
Monel k-500 137-138, 141, 146, 155
MRR 18-21, 23, 25, 27-29, 33-34, 38-39, 45-46, 48-53, 102, 134, 164, 181, 183-187, 189, 191-192, 212
mutual fund 267-271, 273-275

N

Net Asset Value 267-269, 273, 275

O

Open Ended Fund 267, 269
optimization 1, 4-5, 7, 18, 20-21, 24-25, 27, 29, 31-33, 35, 41-42, 44, 52-54, 73-74, 76-78, 90, 92-95, 98, 105, 109-112, 132-136, 138, 142, 153-160, 162-164, 166, 176, 178-184, 187-188, 190-194, 196-197, 207, 210, 212, 215-217, 220, 229, 232-234, 238, 271, 280-281
organic semiconductor 250, 254
Overcut 18, 20-22, 24, 29, 33-34, 45-46, 48-53, 138, 146

P

part programming 55, 58-61, 64
Pearson correlation coefficient 215, 224, 229
photovoltaic device 250
polygon cycle 61-62, 64, 69-70
Preparatory Function 55, 60
process analysis 160
product quality 47, 195-198, 200
pulse duration 76, 78, 84-85, 89-90, 92, 212
pulse interval 76, 78, 84, 86, 89-90

R

regression 9, 11-14, 20, 29, 34, 51, 95, 106, 118-119, 125, 130, 149, 160, 165-166, 171-172, 187, 197-199, 215-216, 227-228, 238, 243, 247, 270-275, 278-279
Root Mean Square Error 267, 272, 274, 276
RSM 18-19, 21, 34, 77, 96, 105, 114, 118-119, 125, 134, 137, 146, 160, 163-165, 179-180

S

scanning speed 1, 4, 7, 12-14, 146-147, 149-155, 164-165, 172-173, 175
Smart Factory 196, 203, 207, 214
Smart manufacturing 195-196, 201, 207, 214
Spearman's coefficient 33, 41, 43
spherical cycle 61-62, 64, 68
spindle speed function 55, 60
surface roughness 2, 31, 33-34, 38-39, 44, 46, 54, 76-78, 90, 92, 94, 112, 114, 116-118, 124, 126-135, 164, 181, 184, 186
Surface Roughnesss 114
surface temperature rise 1, 4, 13
surface topography 76, 90, 94

T

Teaching-Learning Based Optimization 181, 184, 187
Thermoelastic Force 1, 4, 11-16
thermoplastics 160-161, 163-165, 167, 169, 179-180
Tool Selection Function 60
TOPSIS 33, 35-36, 39-43, 76-78, 84, 87-90, 92, 95
transparent 160-162, 164-165, 169, 179-180, 251, 253-254
trepan drilling 137, 140-142, 144, 146, 155, 157-158
TTLW 160, 163
TWR 18, 20-22, 25, 27-29, 45-46, 48-53
type of power 1, 4, 13

V

vector cycle 61-62, 64-66
voltage 20, 33, 38, 45-46, 48, 50-53, 56, 76, 78, 89-90, 96, 102-103, 105-107, 109-110, 114, 117-118, 121-128, 130-132, 134, 181-182, 184, 186-187, 255-257, 259-260, 262

W

WEDM 32, 34, 44, 73, 76-80, 84, 90, 93-105, 110-120, 126-127, 135
WEDT 114, 117-118, 120-127, 134-135
wireless sensor networks 235, 247-249
WS 160, 176, 178

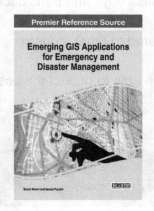

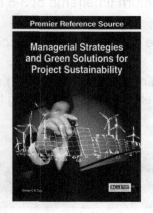

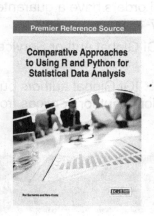

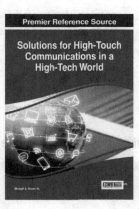

Printed in the United States
by Baker & Taylor Publisher Services